Church of England Record Society

Volume 2

THE SPECULUM OF ARCHBISHOP THOMAS SECKER

The Speculum compiled by Archbishop Thomas Secker (1758–68) is a major source for our understanding of the Church of England in the mid-eighteenth century. It is a parish by parish digest of the returns submitted to the archbishop between 1758 and 1761 for the diocese of Canterbury and the peculiars (parishes under his jurisdiction mainly in London, Middlesex, Surrey, Sussex, Norfolk and Suffolk). It contains very full information on the size and social structure of the parishes; the names and qualifications of the clergy; their wealth; whether they were resident, whether they had a curate, the number of services they performed, their relations with Roman Catholics and Protestant dissenters, the existence of parochial schools and charities, and the numbers recently confirmed. Secker frequently cross-referenced the material to printed sources, as well as adding details when later developments occurred, or as defects in the parishes were put right. Part of the significance of the Speculum is its witness of the pastoral pressure applied by Secker, allowing the historian to assess how far an energetic archbishop was able to improve the standards of pastoral provision in the parishes under his care.

JEREMY GREGORY is Lecturer in History at the University of Northumbria.

Hollingbourne V. All Saints. with the Chapel of Hucking
St Margaret. Abp p. Exempt from Adn. Ks books 7 — 6 — 8 Certified
70li — 16 — 8. So now. Hollingbourn near 6 miles long. Contains three
Streets, a mile distant from each other, & 104 Families: two of Gentlemen. [not named] Hucking 2½ miles from Hollingbourn 2½ miles long. 17 Ho. near 80 Inhabitants. A few Dissenters. One Sunday whole Service at the Church:
the next Service once at each. Between 2 & 3 miles asunder. Prayers at the Church W. Fr. in Lent & all Passion Week. & on certain
Holydays with occasional Sermons. Prayers & Sermon Nov. 5. Jan. 30.
Cat. in the Church in Lent. with printed Exp. repeated to y at his House.
Cat. also at the Chapel. Chn sent: not Servants, unless before a Confirmation., 4 Sacr. at each
80 or 90 Con at each time at the Church: about 25 at the Chapel. La-
dy Nortons Charity, see Tenterden p.73., A Gentleman of the Parish sends
several Boys & Girls to two Schools here. The Singers use light & uncommon Tunes here & elsewhere. Shops are needlessly opend on Sundays.

Of the Vicarage & Chapel see here p 242. much improved in prest Vs time.
Church & Chancel large, handsome & in good Repair. Ho. good & in
good Repair. Stable new by Mr Waterhouse., 6 Bells, Hucking Chapel & Chancel
very mean & shamefully dirty. Ho Ho - 2 Bells, Both put into decent Repair, in 1762.
bourn & 12li to Hucking, pd by Mr Fairfax, 20li a year to Holling

V. collated 1684 Entry B. IV. 427 & 1690 543.

Formerly more Hops, but they suit not the Soil: now 26 Acres; the tithe 10s each
Acre. V. now abt 62li. Hucking 12li clear Stipend, 4 Small tithes. Mr Waterh. Jan. 1763
Mr Duppa, a very worthy & pious Gentleman, lives here. 81. Cieled the Church.

Hops 11li, other small tithe abt 38li, 20li Augmentation from an Estate, bought of Mr Colepepper Rect of the Charterhouse, by Mr Fairfax, but after did land Tax. 16s in all 63s See Mr
Waterhouse Nov & Dec. 1763

Benj. Waterhouse MA V. 21 Sept 1741. Resides in V. Ho.
& hath always done so. 1766 V. of Westwell p.75

Joseph Todd Clerk B. A. V. Decr 20. 1770.

William Hassell Clerk B. A. Oct 11 1773. resides

Edward Hasted A.B. Vicar 1790.

Hucking, wch V. is not obliged to serve, to be served every other Sunday
by Mr March of Bicknor p.205 where see

1758 Hol. 93. Hucking. 3. 1762. 50 Hucking 9. 1766 Holl.
41. Hucking 1

THE SPECULUM OF
ARCHBISHOP THOMAS SECKER

EDITED BY

Jeremy Gregory

Principal Lecturer in History, University of Northumbria at Newcastle

THE BOYDELL PRESS

CHURCH OF ENGLAND RECORD SOCIETY

First published 1995

A Church of England Record Society publication
Published by The Boydell Press
an imprint of Boydell & Brewer Ltd
PO Box 9, Woodbridge, Suffolk IP12 3DF, UK
and of Boydell & Brewer Inc.
PO Box 41026, Rochester, NY 14604–4126, USA

ISBN 0 85115 569 3

ISSN 1351 3987

British Library Cataloguing-in-Publication Data
Secker, Thomas
    Speculum of Archbishop Thomas Secker. –
    (Church of England Record Society Series,
    ISSN 1351-3087; Vol. 2)
    I. Title II. Gregory, Jeremy III. Series
    283.4209033
    ISBN 0–85115–569–3

The paper used in this publication meets the minimum requirements
of American National Standard for Information Sciences –
Permanence of Paper for Printed Library Materials, ANSI Z39.48–1984

Printed in Great Britain by
St Edmundsbury Press Ltd, Bury St Edmunds, Suffolk

For Grace Margaret Bee

CONTENTS

ACKNOWLEDGEMENTS

Editing Secker's Speculum has taken far longer than I ever expected, and I am grateful to the Council of the Church of England Record Society for their forbearance. In particular, I would like to thank Melanie Barber, the deputy librarian and archivist of Lambeth Palace Library, who, over the years, has generously given of her unrivalled knowledge of the collections in her care. Without her co-operation and her readiness to help relate evidence from the Speculum to other material, this edition would have been the poorer. Bill Sheils has been a good-spirited general editor, Grayson Ditchfield has helped me track down some particularly recalcitrant Kentish people, Stuart Handley shared his knowledge of Lancashire, and John Walsh and Toby Barnard advised me on Methodist and Irish matters. I would also like to thank my colleagues in the department of Historical and Critical Studies at the University of Northumbria at Newcastle for granting me a period of sabbatical leave which enabled me to complete this edition. I am grateful to the British Academy for a subvention in aid of publication, and to the archbishop of Canterbury for his most generous donation towards the publication of one of the manuscripts of a worthy predecessor.

INTRODUCTION

ARCHBISHOP THOMAS SECKER'S SPECULUM AND THE STATE OF THE CHURCH IN THE MID EIGHTEENTH CENTURY

The Nature and Scope of the Speculum

It was dissatisfaction with the all too frequently bland and unhelpful answers given by churchwardens in the seventeenth century to the visitation queries described by Dr Fincham in the first volume of this society's proceedings which prompted bishops in the early eighteenth century to direct their questions to the parish clergy, in the hope of eliciting fuller responses.[1] Archbishops of Canterbury were amongst the pioneers here. William Wake, first while bishop of Lincoln in 1706 and then at Canterbury in 1716, has been given the credit for developing the system of ten or twelve questions on printed forms, with sufficient space under each question for reply, which became the norm favoured by diocesans throughout the eighteenth century.[2] The surviving series of visitation queries and returns for the diocese of Canterbury covering the years 1716, 1720, 1724, 1728, 1758, 1786 and 1806 are illuminating documents, and can be seen as attempts by eighteenth-century primates to familiarise themselves with their new diocese. They are testimony to the fact that, although living at Lambeth, eighteenth-century archbishops were concerned to have as detailed a knowledge as possible of the clergy and parishioners under their charge. The Speculum of Archbishop Thomas Secker (LPL, VG 2/5) was principally a digest

---

[1] *Visitation Articles and Injunctions of the Early Stuart Church*, I, ed. K. Fincham, Church of England Record Society, I (1994).

[2] *Speculum Dioeceseos Lincolnienses sub episcopis Gul. Wake et Edm. Gibson, 1705-23*, ed. R.E.G. Cole, Lincoln Record Society, IV (1913); Christ Church Library, Oxford, MS Wake 284. For a more detailed discussion of the development of visitation articles, see *Archbishop Herring's Returns, 1743*, ed. S.L. Ollard and P.C. Walker, Yorkshire Archaeological Society Record Series, LXI (1928), pp. v–viii. The Canterbury diocesan returns survive in Christ Church Library, Oxford, MSS 284-7 (1716-28), Lambeth Palace Library, MS 1134/1-4 (1758), ibid., VG 3/1a-d (1786) and ibid., VG 3/2/a-d (1806). Published returns from other dioceses include *Articles of Enquiry addressed to the clergy of the Diocese of Oxford at the Primary Visitation of Dr Thomas Secker, 1738*, ed. H.A. Lloyd Jukes, Oxford Record Society, 38 (1957); *The Diocese of Exeter in 1821: Bishop Carey's replies to Queries Before Visitation*, ed M. Cook, 2 vols. Torquay (1958-60); *The State of the Bishopric of Worcester, 1782-1808*, ed. M. Ransome, Worcestershire Historical Society, 6 (1968); *Wiltshire Returns to the Bishop's Visitation Queries*, 1783, ed. M. Ransome, Wiltshire Record Society, 27 (1972); M.R. Austin, *The Church in Derbyshire, 1823-4*, Derbyshire Archaeological Society, 5 (1972); *Visitations of the Archdeaconry of Stafford, 1829-41*, ed. D. Robinson, Staffordshire Record Society, 4s 10 (1980); *The Archdeaconry of Richmond in the Eighteenth Century, Bishop Gastrell's 'Notitia'. The Yorkshire Parishes*, ed. L.A.S. Butler, Yorkshire Archaeological Society Record Series, 146 (1990); *The Diocese of Llandaff in 1763*, ed. J.R. Guy, South Wales Record Society, (1991); *Parson and Parish in Eighteenth-Century Surrey: Replies to Bishops' Visitations*, ed. W.R. Ward, Surrey Record Society XXXIV, (1994); *Chichester Diocesan Surveys, 1686 and 1724*, ed. W.K. Ford, Sussex Record Society, 78 (1994).

of the returns submitted to Secker as part of his primary visitation of the diocese and peculiars[3] of Canterbury during the summers of 1758 to 1761.

The Canterbury Speculum is a book measuring 38.5 cm × 24 cm, consisting of 468 pages of good quality paper, paginated by Secker on the recto and written in Secker's characteristically regular and rounded hand. After three unnumbered pages (in this edition marked i–iii), those pages numbered 1 to 424 are taken up with the Speculum. Secker began the entries for each parish on a new page, arranged alphabetically within deaneries, starting with the diocese of Canterbury, and then moving through the peculiars. Information under each parish (which was essentially in note-form and often not in continuous prose) was mainly taken from the replies to his visitation queries and broadly followed the ordering of the questions as set out in the visitation articles.[4] These queries largely structured the kind of information clergy gave, and the way it was formulated and expressed. Secker sometimes referred himself to the fuller descriptions in the original returns for more details than he was able to put in the digest, directing himself to 'See more', or, as at page 152 under 'Boughton Blean' to 'See the Answer to Inquiries'. A separate index, listing benefices, clergy, nobility, gentry and 'popish priests' mentioned in the text, compiled in the late eighteenth century by William Dickes, archbishop's secretary, forms the basis of the index in this edition, and is now kept with the Speculum. There is also an index of the benefices (written into pages 426–36) by S.W. Kershaw, Lambeth Librarian, in 1905 (which has not been reproduced here). The volume has a modern buckram binding.

Secker seems to have had something of a *penchant* for Specula. Besides the one for Canterbury, he produced similar documents for his previous sees of Bristol and Oxford.[5] They should be seen as working note-books: the numerous crossings-out, emendations and interpolations in the Canterbury Speculum indicate that information was often corrected or updated as Secker looked into matters further, as defects were put right, or as developments occurred. Indeed part of the significance of the Speculum for the historian is that we can witness pastoral pressure being applied, allowing us to see how far an energetic archbishop such as Secker was able to improve the standards of pastoral provision in his diocese. The Speculum enabled the archbishop to have ready access to a database concerning patronage to livings, the size and social structure of parishes, the names and qualifications of the clergy, their wealth, whether they were resident, whether they had a curate, the number of services they

---

[3] A peculiar is a parish, church or district exempt from the jurisdiction of the bishop of the diocese and subject to someone else. Many of these had arisen from the privileges of the archbishops to exercise jurisdiction in places where they had property. In his autobiography Secker noted, 'I chose to visit as many, as I could conveniently of my Peculiars, because scarce any memory was left, that any ABp had visited them personally: none indeed, excepting that one man at Bocking said, he remembered ABp Tenisons visitation there. Nor could I find, that any ABp had confirmed in his Peculiars excepting in London & at Croydon': *The Autobiography of Thomas Secker, archbishop of Canterbury*, ed. J.S. Macauley and R.W. Greaves (Lawrence, 1988), pp. 43–4. Visitation returns for the Canterbury peculiars can be found in LPL, MS 1115 (1717); ibid., MS 1134/5–6 (1759); ibid., VH/55/1 (1788); ibid., VH/55/2a–b (1807).

[4] See 'Articles of Enquiry', below, p. xli.

[5] 'Bishop Secker's Diocese Book', ed. E. Ralph, in *A Bristol Miscellany*, Bristol Record Society, XXXVII (1985), pp. 23–69. The Oxford Speculum is now lost: see *The Correspondence of Bishop Secker*, ed. A.P. Jenkins, Oxford Record Society, LVII (1991), p. xiv.

performed, their relations with Roman Catholics and Protestant dissenters, the existence of parochial schools and charities, and the numbers recently confirmed. It also represents the ways in which being archbishop also meant being a bureaucrat and administrator (including mastering the use of shorthand).[6] A letter from Secker in 1766 to Samuel Dugard, the vicar of Bersted, reveals the use of the Speculum as an aide-mémoire:

> . . . I not only entertained an Opinion, but am certain, unless I could totally misunderstand your Words, that you promised at your Institution to reside part of the year your self, & to have a resident Curate when you did not, who should perform the whole Sunday service; which you call double Duty. This I wrote down immediately in my Book.[7]

In some parishes, such as Graveney, we can see Secker reacting to the information as he read through the visitation returns, putting questions in brackets which he would later direct in a letter to the incumbent concerned.[8] These notes to himself, and the follow-up letters (many of which survive in Secker's diocesan correspondence at Lambeth Palace Library)[9] tell us something about Secker's pastoral style. The archbishop was keen to be candid (and encouraged frankness from his clergy, as seen in the final visitation question which asked 'is there any other matter relating to your parish of which it may be proper to give me information?'), and was generous and benevolent when he felt that his clergy were trying their best, revealed, for example, in gifts of money to Philip Warham, the vicar of Kennington.[10] But he could be quite sharp with clergy whom he considered were not fulfilling their pastoral duties. As he told Thomas Bland, the vicar of Sittingbourne, 'whoever doth not perform the Duty of his parish as completely as can be reasonably required, must not look for a better'.[11] Above all, Secker wanted to be kept informed. He wrote to Francis Dodsworth at Minster, 'But you have never thought it worth while to signifie any thing to me in relation to the matter, or to shew, that you considered me as having any Concern in it. I cannot in these Circumstances continue your Leave of Absence'.[12] Some clergy seem to have resented the new archbishop's obsession with detail and his attempt to tighten up pastoral care, seeing this as undue interference. The archbishop rather tartly explained to one clergyman that he hoped

> all my Clergy will come in a little time to understand, that I desire to give only equitable Directions, and those to be equitably interpreted. Your admonition to me against the Temptation of power is very kind. I have need to be admonished against all Temptations, and shall be obliged to those who are under my care for doing that good office as they see occasion: hoping they will permit me in my turn to do them the same. But if I know myself at all I am not desirous of exerting power for the sake of exerting it, but only for the Discharge of the Trust committed to me. I

---

[6] I gratefully acknowledge the help of Ann Payne of the British Library in attempting to decipher the shorthand.

[7] LPL, MS Secker 6, f. 197, Secker to Dugard, 27 February 1766.

[8] Sub Graveney.

[9] LPL, MSS Secker 3 and 6.

[10] Ibid., MS Secker 3, f. 215, Secker to Warham, 23 October 1758.

[11] Ibid., f. 250, Secker to Bland, 8 October 1758.

[12] Ibid., f. 243, Secker to Dodsworth, 17 May 1761.

would please all Men for their good to Edification: but if I sought to please any man by neglecting my own Duty, I should not be the Servant of Christ.[13]

As a source for the state of the Church of England in the mid eighteenth century, it could be objected that much of the information in the Speculum comes from the clergy, who were to some extent justifying their own practice and may in some cases have been over-optimistic. But it might be, that to a new diocesan, clergy would have been keen to highlight the difficulties they encountered, to show how well they were doing their job. Moreover, the archbishop would have been more likely to have recorded irregularities than examples of good practice. In any case, the Canterbury Speculum contains not only information directly culled from the visitation returns, it also shows how Secker was able to draw on the rich body of archival evidence left by his predecessors. Noteworthy events relating to specific parishes (especially when and the manner by which former clergy received the benefice) were abstracted from the Registers and act-books of late medieval and early modern archbishops (which in the late 1750s were being indexed by that indefatigable Lambeth Librarian, A.C. Ducarel).[14] Secker further cross-referenced many parishes to previous surveys of the Church, such as the accounts of the archbishopric in 1643,[15] the surveys of the lands belonging to the archbishop and the dean and chapter of Canterbury made by the Parliamentary regime in the late 1640s,[16] the so-called Sheldon Catalogue of 1663,[17] the survey compiled by John Haynes in 1716,[18] records of the diocese collected by John Lewis, vicar of Margate, in the 1730s,[19] and information garnered by Archdeacon John Head and Archbishop Thomas Herring in their surveys of the diocese in the 1750s.[20] He also added material which he had asked Edward Bentham, canon of Christ Church, Oxford, to root out from the papers deposited there by Archbishop Wake.[21] Such documentation could, as he found, be of use when challenging assertions that such and such a practice had always existed, for instance as at Detling, where Secker used information in Wake's papers to show that divine service used to be performed twice on Sundays, contradicting the incumbent's assertion that single duty had been the custom from 'time immemorial'.[22] Above all, Secker comes across as a stickler for detail. At Murston, he even quibbled with the vicar over the precise size of the parish.[23] Secker also consulted printed sources such as William Somner's

[13] Ibid., f. 202, Secker to Holdsworth, 9 November 1758.
[14] Andrew Coltee Ducarel (1713–85) was Lambeth Librarian from 1757–85. He catalogued the printed books and manuscripts at the Library, and completed a digest of the archiepiscopal registers. He also published a *Repertory of the Endowments of the Vicarages in the Diocese of Canterbury* in 1763 and *The History and Antiquities of the Archiepiscopal Palace at Lambeth* in 1785.
[15] LPL, TF 2, 3 and 4.
[16] Ibid, Comm. XIIa/ 19 (dean and chapter); 22 and 23 (archbishopric).
[17] Ibid., MS 1126.
[18] Ibid., VG 2/1.
[19] Ibid., MS 1125.
[20] Ibid., MS 1134 (Head) and MS 1138 (Herring).
[21] Ibid., MSS 1133 and 1483. The archbishop appears to have also consulted diocesan surveys which are now deposited at Canterbury Cathedral Library: Add MS 19 (Wake's book) and MS Z/3/33: 'Archdeacon Greene's Visitation Book'.
[22] Sub Detling.
[23] Sub Murston.

Antiquities of Canterbury,[24] John Lewis's *History of Faversham*,[25] William Newton's *Antiquities of Maidstone*,[26] Richard Kilburne's *Survey of the County of Kent*,[27] John Harris's *History of Kent*,[28] White Kennett's *Case of Impropriations*,[29] Thomas Tanner's *Monastica*,[30] Thomas Philipot's *Villare Cantianum*,[31] David Wilkins's *Concilia*,[32] and John Ecton's *Thesaurus*[33] (from where he probably copied the values of livings in the 1530s as listed in the *Valor Ecclesiasticus*, commonly known as the 'King's book'). Some details seem to have been given *via* verbal or written communication with one of his intimates. In many of the parishes in the diocese, Secker acknowledged that he received information from the Lambeth librarian A.C Ducarel, or from his trusted archdeacon, John Head, and a similar relationship seems to have developed in the Sussex peculiars with William Clarke, canon of Chichester cathedral, or with bishops of those dioceses where the peculiars lay. Moreover, Secker updated the information during the 1760s, adding material from the Inquiries into the number of Catholics in 1765, 1766 and 1767,[34] and data produced as a result of further visitations (including archidiaconal visitations). As a handbook to the diocese, the Speculum was of use to his successors, for there are entries by Archbishops Cornwallis and Moore, or their secretaries, probably following their own visitations. What is more, apart from this chronological range, the Speculum not only contains material relating to east Kent, but, through the peculiars, enables the historian to have some insight into the functioning of the Church in London, Middlesex, Surrey, Sussex, Essex, Norfolk, Suffolk and Lancashire. What, then, does the Speculum tell us of the state of the Church in the mid-eighteenth century, and how can it be fitted into some of the historiographical debates about the period?

A recent interpretation is that by Jonathan Clark.[35] Implicit in Clark's vision of an Anglican hegemony is a Church whose message reached and was abided by the majority of parishioners. Clark's view, which in part stemmed from a desire to treat the Church of the eighteenth century with respect, provoked some backlash. Peter Virgin, for instance, felt that the epithet 'age of Negligence' was a more satisfactory description of a Church which, in his view, was inefficient, self-satisfied and often unpopular.[36] Further, Virgin's Church was one which

---

[24] [Nicholas Battely], *The Antiquities of Canterbury in Two Parts. I. The Antiquities of Canterbury. . . published by William Somner. . ... II. Cantuaria Sacra* (1703).

[25] John Lewis, *The History and Antiquities of the Abbey and Church of Faversham* (1727).

[26] William Newton, *The History and Antiquities of Maidstone. . .from the Manuscript Collections of William Newton* (1741).

[27] Richard Kilburne, *A Topographie, or Survey of the Counties of Kent* (1659).

[28] John Harris, *A History of Kent* (1719).

[29] White Kennett, *The Case of Impropriations and of the Augmentations of Vicarages and other Insufficient Cures* (1704).

[30] Thomas Tanner, *Notitia Monastica: or an Account of all the Abbies, Priories, Friers, heretofore in England and Wales* (1744).

[31] Thomas Philipot, *Villare Cantianum: or Kent Surveyed and Illustrated* (1659).

[32] David Wilkins, *Concilia Magnae Britanniae et Hiberniae*, 4 vols. (1737).

[33] John Ecton, *Thesaurus Rerum Ecclesiasticarum* (1742).

[34] For a parochial breakdown of these returns, see LPL, MS Secker 3, f. 334.

[35] J.C.D. Clark, *English Society, 1688-1832. Ideology, Social Structure and Political Practice during the Ancien Regime* (Cambridge, 1985).

[36] P. Virgin, *The Church in an Age of Negligence. Ecclesiastical Structure and Problems of Church Reform, 1700-1840* (Cambridge, 1989).

saw deep fissures in the clerical body, divided by wealth, social status and politics: echoing older histories which stressed the ways in which the Church in this period was dominated by secular concerns, hardly living up to the ideals of a homogeneous profession.

Faced with such rival interpretations, the material provided by the Canterbury Speculum suggests that both these approaches need to be more nuanced. Although Clark's schema might be supported by references to parishes such as Faversham where, it was alleged, 'no People show a greater regard to Religion, or who more constantly attend the public worship of God on the Lord's Day',[37] or St John's, Margate, where it was noted that 'the Parishioners [are] remarkable for going to church',[38] in general his work seriously underestimates the problems faced by the Church in the parishes, such as the difficulty in getting the laity to send their children or servants to catechism, or to attend services in church themselves. Time and again, from reading the Speculum, we gain the impression of a clergy who claim they are willing to offer services, and of a laity who are unwilling to attend. Against Clark's clericalist vision of the period, the Speculum sheds some light on what the laity expected and wanted in religious terms, and indicates that their views were not always in accord with those of the clergy. On the other hand, Virgin's picture of an 'Age of Negligence' seriously downplays the many areas of clerical activity and vitality.

Patronage and Clergy

In one striking regard, the data in the Speculum challenges some of the traditional assumptions of this as a period when the Church was under the thumb of the landowning classes. In the diocese of Canterbury, 60% of livings were in the hands of ecclesiastical patrons. 5.2% were Crown livings, 27.3% were in private hands, 3% belonged to peers, and 2.2% belonged to educational institutions. There were also a couple of elective livings, where the parishioners could choose their minister: St Mary's, Dover, and the chapel of Small Hythe, Tenterden. 105 benefices in the diocese (nearly 40%) were in the gift of the archbishop, and he presented to a further 67 benefices out of the 112 peculiars.[39] That archbishops in the eighteenth century had a greater control over ecclesiastical appointments in their diocese than even the most impressive of nineteenth-century 'reformers', such as Samuel Wilberforce, had a crucial impact on those appointed to Canterbury livings, ensuring that at any time a sizeable section of the clergy had been primatial nominees. And the archbishops could also influence the distribution of Crown patronage, as at Minster where Secker was able to persuade the Lord Chancellor to present Thomas Salt.[40]

The geographical mobility of the archbishops and the cathedral clergy was largely responsible for promoting clergy from without the area, and illustrates

---

[37] LPL, MS 1134/2 f. 96.

[38] Sub St John's, Margate.

[39] D. Hirschberg, 'The Government and Church Patronage in England, 1660–1760', *Journal of British Studies*, XX (1980–1), 109–39.

[40] D. McClatchey, *Oxfordshire Clergy, 1777–1869. A Study of the Established Church and the Role of Its Clergy in Local Society* (Oxford, 1960), p. 10. see also M.J.D. Roberts, 'Private Patronage and the Church of England, 1800–1900', *Journal of Ecclesiastical History*, XXXII (1981), 199–223. Sub Minster.

the ways in which the Church in the Canterbury diocese drew on a national patronage network. Although there were a group of local families who provided personnel for the parishes (and the local lay patrons such as the Honywoods at Hinxhill, the Tyldens at Milsted, or the Filmers at Crundale did tend to promote members of their own family), less than 40% of the incumbents mentioned in the diocesan sections of the Speculum whose geographic origins are known were natives of Kent. Nearly 12% came from the London area, reflecting the close connections between the capital and the diocese.[41] A large percentage (50%) came from further afield. John Nairn, the rector of Stourmouth, was born in Bermuda.[42]

What was the social status and educational experience of the parish clergy in the mid-eighteenth century? There was never the wholesale domination by the gentry which was supposed to have made the second half of the eighteenth century the age of the 'fox-hunting parson'. Very few sons of the nobility held a parochial benefice, and less than a third had gentry backgrounds.[43] At the other end of the scale, the sons of plebeians did not disappear. Well over a quarter of those appointed between 1750 and 1780 were of plebeian origins.[44] Nonetheless, those of low social origin were becoming an increasing minority within the diocesan clergy. However, the decrease in the number of clergy from low-born families was a consequence of a move in favour not only of those from gentry backgrounds, but also of those from clerical and professional families. The substantial number whose fathers had also been incumbents (amounting to 38% in the period 1750 to 1780) was instrumental in advancing a sense of 'professionalism' and group identity within the Church, and clerical dynasties, where the same family provided the incumbent of a parish over three generations, such as the Curteis' at Sevenoaks and the Hodsons at Thornham, were not uncommon.[45] The Bagnalls were one family were it became almost traditional to enter the clerical profession. William was rector of Badlesmere from 1662 until his death in 1713. His sons were beneficed in the diocese. Henry, after being curate at Appledore from 1698, was presented to Hawkhurst in 1704. Thomas was presented to Chillenden in 1710. Henry's son, also Henry, was the rector of Shadoxhurst from 1734 to 1761.[46] Likewise George Horne, who as leader of the Hutchinsonian movement and dean of Canterbury from 1781, has attracted a great deal of attention from recent historians, was the son of Samuel, the vicar of Otham (1727–69) who was noted by Secker as being 'Good [and] Resides constantly',[47] and who was followed in the benefice by George's younger brother William. Clerical dynasties such as these might affect the nature of the profession in several ways. They could provide a sense of continuity between the parishioners and the clergy, and to some degree they allowed prospective clergy to gain an insight into the demands of the profession,

---

[41] W.J. Gregory, 'Archbisop, Cathedral and Parish: the diocese of Canterbury, 1660–1805', Oxford University D.Phil thesis (1993), p. 385.

[42] Sub Stourmouth.

[43] Gregory, 'Canterbury', p. 385.

[44] Ibid.

[45] Sub Sevenoaks and Thornham.

[46] Sub Shadoxhurst.

[47] Sub Otham. For the recent interest in Horne see, for example, Clark, *English Society*, pp. 221–6 and R. Hole, *Pulpits, Politics and Public Order in England, 1760–1832* (Cambridge, 1990).

ensuring that many recruits already had direct experience of clerical life as the son of a parish minister.

Educationally, the vast majority (well over 90%) of beneficed incumbents in 1758 were, the Speculum reveals, graduates. Whilst there were enormous divisions in the wealth of the clergy, in the diocese of Canterbury their educational experience was increasingly homogeneous, and those who were not graduates had little chance of promotion to a benefice. The intellectual credentials of the mid-century clergy can also be seen in the numbers who published (about 10%). Indeed Secker was pressured by Robert Neild, the curate of Ivychurch, who '[d]esired me to read some Sermons which he w[oul]d publish: [I] excused myself'.[48]

One way in which archbishops were able to influence the complexion of the diocesan clergy was by their control over the ordination process. There is some evidence that the Church's hierarchy used clerical testimonials as a kind of quality control, using members of the profession to comment on prospective new recruits. In 1759 Secker pointed out to a hopeful ordinand the usefulness of references in the selection of ministers, for 'when a clergyman is shunned by most of his Bretheren, it may very well set him to examine himself strictly whether he hath given them occasion for it'.[49] Secker also relied on examinations as a way of weeding out the unsuitable from the profession. In 1759 Charles Fortescue, who while deacon was curate at Stowting, applied to be ordained priest, but Secker failed him on the grounds that he was 'extremely ignorant of Latin'.[50] The Speculum often noted when an incumbent or curate had been ordained, and shows that Secker himself frequently held ordinations at Lambeth for those to be given a title in his diocese (in the text noting which ceremony in the year, marked by 1. 2. or 3.).[51]

After ordination, valuable professional experience could be gained whilst serving as a curate. In the Speculum Secker was careful to record the names of curates, with their qualifications. He had complained in his *Charge* to the clergy in the diocese in 1758 that many curates in the diocese had not obtained a licence, and were thus not registered with the diocesan management.[52] It was also often difficult for the diocesan hierarchy to know exactly who curates were, since their turnover could be rapid. Appledore, for instance, had 40 curates between 1660 and 1800.[53] This was because curacies were often a step on the ladder to acquiring a benefice, not an office for life: Solomon Pawley at Smarden was rare in having been a curate for 40 years, but even he was described as 'quiet' and 'contented'.[54] Curates were more likely to be younger clergy, who were in the process of gaining pastoral experience, which helped to ensure that the Church in the diocese of Canterbury was not broken into a hierarchy of distinct career patterns. Curates might also be instrumental in

---

[48] Sub Ivychurch.

[49] LPL, MS Secker 3, f. 206, Secker to Burnett, 6 July 1759.

[50] Sub Stowting.

[51] LPL, VG 1/10.

[52] Thomas Secker, *Eight Charges Delivered to the Clergy of the Dioceses of Oxford and Canterbury* (1769), p. 221.

[53] J. Winnifrith, 'Land Ownership in Appledore, 1500–1900', *Archaelogia Cantiana*, XCVII (1981), 1–6.

[54] Sub Smarden.

fostering a link between the Church and the parish. At Warehorne, for example, William Wing Fowle, who had been born in the vicinity, was recognised as being 'liked by the People'.[55] By registering the names of curates in the Speculum, Secker was able to regulate this often hidden rung on the clerical ladder. Charles Prince, the curate of Appledore and Brenzett was described as 'drunken' and 'bad',[56] and was dismissed, although in 1767 he was reinstated because he had apparently 'reformed' himself. At Brookland Secker noted that the curate Coleby 'served things in a Hurry', which he 'forbade' in 1768.[57] William Preston, a curate at Tenterden, 'proved very troublesome',[58] and was removed. Secker was clearly concerned to eliminate what he considered to be bad practice and noted those who disappointed him. John Wearg, the assistant at Queenborough, was 'Brought to Trial for a Forgery, but got off. Hath officiated as a Priest: Drinks with low company. The Corporation petitioned the ABP to ordain him Priest. The ABP hath required Mr Delafaye over and over to dismiss him'.[59] But others were commended (such as Francis Whitfield, noted by Secker as 'good'[60]) and received further promotion.

Since it was difficult to remove clergy from their benefice, the majority stayed within the diocese once they had been presented to a living. Very few clergy were dismissed on account of misconduct, although Secker frowned on beneficed clergy who did not live up to his ideal of clerical behaviour, such as Edward Taylor from Patrixbourne, who was suspected of horse-racing.[61] Only Samuel Bickley, the vicar of Bapchild, was deprived by Secker, this was in 1764 on a charge of attempting to commit sodomy (though the archbishop gave him some money in recompense).[62] Some parishes thus saw a remarkably low turnover of incumbents. There were, for example only three vicars of Appledore during the whole of the eighteenth century, despite the high turnover of curates there.[63] Indeed clergy prided themselves on the length of time they had served in a parish, contrasting this 'stability' with the 'instability' of nonconformist preachers. Edward Harrison, perpetual curate of Leeds, proudly boasted that during his thirty-four year incumbency he had been absent for a total of only five weeks, and lived on vegetables and distributed good books.[64] But the consequences of such longevity (when there was no concept of clerical retirement) were the attendant problems of old-age and illness. Secker excused Edmund Barrell, at the ripe age of eighty-eight, from residing and performing duties at Boughton Malherbe.[65] George Shocklidge, who had been the vicar of Northbourne for fifty years, was noted as being 'old, infirm' and made 'mistakes',[66] and the doddery Peter Innes was 'superannuated' from Kingston

---

[55] Sub Warehorne.
[56] Sub Appledore.
[57] Sub Brookland.
[58] Sub Tenterden.
[59] Sub Queenborough.
[60] Sub Hothfield. Whitfield had served his apprenticeship as curate at Newchurch, before being presented to the vicarage of Godmersham in 1778.
[61] Sub Patrixbourne.
[62] Sub Bapchild. See Secker's *Autobiography*, p. 48.
[63] John Johnson (1696–1725); John Disney (1726–77); Richard Podmore (1777–1806).
[64] Sub Leeds.
[65] Sub Boughton Malherbe.
[66] Sub Northbourne.

and lived at Maidstone with his relatives.[67] At Willesborough the vicar was blind,[68] and at Tenterden the curate suffered from 'mortification in his foot from gout'.[69] It has sometimes been said that the eighteenth century Church was deaf to the new religious impulses of the age. In the diocese of Canterbury this might have been literally so, when we read of the incumbent of Elham who was too deaf to hear responses, and whose voice was too low to be heard.[70] This could have more alarming results such as at Lynsted where the incumbent was too deaf to catechise or to notice that the Catholics were increasing.[71] At Folkestone, William Langhorne's voice was so frail that 'many of the parishioners, unable to hear him go to the [nonconformist] meeting'.[72] Not that such cases were inevitably terminal. The curate of Grain had had a paralytic stroke during divine service in 1761, but, as Secker observed, this had later been cured by lightning.[73]

Whilst some social historians (of a left-wing persuasion) have stressed the alienation of the parishioners from their clergy,[74] it is worth noting the alienation that could be experienced from the clerical side. The loneliness and melancholy suffered by James Bernard at Badlesmere[75] could lead to depression for bachelors like Robert Launce, the incumbent of Slindon, who shot himself in 1764.[76] And at Wadhurst the vicar, Samuel Bush, was unable to go to church because he 'imagine[d] his parishioners to be in Conspiracy against him'.[77] In these situations, clerical friendships could provide some comfort amidst the rural isolation (such as the clerical dining club attended by Joseph Price of Brabourne[78]) and help foster a sense of professional identity. When Theophilus Delangle was unable to officiate at Goodnestone, through illness, neighbouring clergy helped him out,[79] and the vicar of St Peter's, Sandwich revealed that, when he was away, neighbouring clergy did his duty.[80]

Another way in which clerical solidarity can be viewed is through their political affiliation. Linda Colley has argued that the survival of the Tory party into the mid-eighteenth century owed much to the dissatisfaction displayed by the parish clergy to the Whig regime. In her account 'the parson was the backbone of the Tory party', stiffening much of the party's ideology and she highlights the differences between the Whig dignitaries and what she believes to have been the Tory parish clergy.[81] The flaw in Colley's argument is that she

---

[67] Sub Kingston.
[68] Sub Willesborough.
[69] Sub Tenterden.
[70] Sub Elham.
[71] Sub Lynsted.
[72] Sub Folkestone.
[73] Sub Grain.
[74] Inter alia, E.P. Thompson, 'Patrician Society, Plebeian Culture', *Journal of Social History*, VIII (1974), 390; R.W. Malcolmson, *Life and Labour in England, 1700–1800* (1981), p. 85.
[75] Sub Badlesmere.
[76] Sub Slindon.
[77] Sub Wadhurst.
[78] See *A Kentish Parson. Selections from the Private Papers of the Revd Joseph Price Vicar of Brabourne, 1767–1786*, ed. G.M. Ditchfield and Bryan Keith-Lucas (Stroud, 1990), p. 10.
[79] Sub Goodnestone by Wingham.
[80] Sub St Peter's, Sandwich.
[81] L. Colley, *In Defiance of Oligarchy. The Tory Party 1714–1760* (Cambridge, 1982), pp. 107, 131–2. 153–4.

assumes that the Whig government was seen as inimical to Anglican interests and that Anglican attitudes found their natural outlet in Tory politics. She tells us much about Tory Anglicanism, but perhaps the most interesting development of the period after 1714 is not so much this traditional alliance as the creation of Whig Anglicanism. The Church was actually safe in Whig hands. In the election of 1734, Thomas Curteis, the rector of Shoreham wrote to the duke of Dorset, the most influential Whig magnate in the region, that 'if the clergy were only to decide the election we should carry the point'.[82] Archbishops such as Wake and Potter (and Secker himself) can be described as High-Church Whigs who did much to reconcile the Tory clergy to the Whig regime. By the 1754 election the Whig allegiance of the Canterbury clergy was pronounced. Of the 209 Kent clergy whose names can be found, 145 (70%) supported the Whig candidates.[83]

The Church and the Local Economy

The Speculum also informed Secker about the economic situation of his clergy, providing him with details of the values of the livings, which, since they depended on the harvest or the size of the glebe, fluctuated annually (hence the various values given under each parish). Interpretations of the period have often concentrated on tithe disputes, as evidence of conflict and lay resentment. Discussion in the diocese of Canterbury usually centred on the issue of whether hops, which in Kentish legend had come to England at the same time as the Reformation, along with other 'new' and market gardening crops were in fact titheable, and whether such crops belonged to the rector or to the vicar. Secker was told that the income of Milton had been much lessened because hops were no longer grown,[84] and the vicar of Tarring complained that the lay rector took the clover seeds from him, which were small tithes.[85] Certainly there were protracted disputes, such as that at St Paul's, Canterbury, between the vicar, Thomas Lamprey, and Mrs Rooke, the rector, or at Monks Horton between Bryan Fausset who was 'at law' with Mr Robinson,[86] but difficulties such as these were with individuals, not with the whole parish. Incumbents also sometimes grumbled that collecting tithes could be time-consuming. The vicar of Westwell moaned that the income of between £100 and £110, was paid by over 70 individuals and took 3 days to gather.[87]

But it may be that we have exaggerated the economic plight of the clergy. Although there were clear problems over the collection of tithes, such disputes as there were decreased during the eighteenth century, rather than building up steadily into the rural outburst of the Swing riots of the 1830s. Significantly, the greatest number of confrontations between parishioners and clergy which reached the Court of Arches was in the late seventeenth and early eighteenth

---

[82] Kent Archives Office, Maidstone, MS C148, f. 48, Curteis to the duke of Dorset, 29 December 1733.

[83] A.N. Newman, 'Elections in Kent and its Parliamentary Representation, 1715–1754', Oxford University D. Phil. thesis (1957), p. 172.

[84] Sub Milton.

[85] Sub Tarring.

[86] Sub Monks Horton; sub St Paul's, Canterbury.

[87] Sub Westwell.

centuries,[88] suggesting that in many parishes tithe disputes had ended by the mid-century and had reached a state of equilibrium. One explanation for this is that for the much of the eighteenth century, clergy in the south-east of England could take advantage of a fairly stable economic situation. Moreover that section of the parish which had been most obstinate in paying tithes in the seventeenth century – the Quakers – were by the mid-eighteenth century 'paying their dues without compulsion'. At Benenden, for instance, the incumbent revealed that he let the Quakers work off their dues in his garden, and that they were respected by all the parish.[89] And at Deal, the rector let them off paying Easter Offerings.[90] Moreover, especially in the towns, variables such as surplice fees often added to the income. Also, it was not usual for any extra income to be allocated to a clergyman in lieu of a parsonage house, yet few other professional men were likely to have free accommodation. It is true that, by the mid-eighteenth century clerical sensibilities often found the houses too small for incumbents and their families, which encouraged them to live elsewhere, or to indulge in a programme of rebuilding or improvement. An indication of this attitude is found in the description of the 'mean house' at Marden, where the largest room was 14' square. By 1758 the house at Ripple had been new-built of brick, and boasted sash-windows. At Sittingbourne the stable and chaise house had been recently rebuilt, suggestive of what were increasingly seen as necessities in some clerical households.[91]

The zeal with which incumbents collected their tithes has embarrassed ecclesiastical historians, to whom it has often appeared rather unseemly, yet it is possible to argue that the necessity of exacting their just dues was more urgent for the clergy of the eighteenth, than for those of the sixteenth century. Not all, of course, were like Edward Smith at Harrietsham with his nine children, or the vicar of Detling with his six daughters,[92] but income through tithes was often crucial in the clergyman's task of providing for his family, hence the various schemes established to look after and support clergy families (such as the poor vicars' fund set up to help the most needy in the diocese, and the diocesan society founded to help distressed clerical dependants).[93]

Indeed one of the most common justifications of pluralism and the related problem of non-residence was the claim that the maintenance of wives and families made such practices inevitable, although Thomas Kemp's excuse for his non-residence at St Michael's Crooked Lane on the grounds that he was chaplain to his wife, Lady Bamff, was stretching the point a little.[94] But if pluralism and non-residence were frequent, the important question is what were its pastoral effects. One of the reasons why Secker was keen to be so precise about the

---

[88] *Index of Cases in the Records of the Court of Arches, 1660–1913* (British Record Society), ed. J. Houston (1972), pp. 618–9.

[89] LPL, MS 1134/1, f. 61.

[90] Sub Deal.

[91] Sub Marden; sub Ripple; sub Sittingbourne. Other such improvements included the 'handsome garden' recently laid out at the parsonage at Otterden. Note also the £500 which had been lately spent on the parsonage house at Boughton Blean.

[92] Sub Detling.

[93] For the poor vicar's fund established in the diocese, see LPL, MS 1153, and for the diocesan scheme for helping the families of poor clergymen, see *An Account of the rules of the Society for the relief of the Widows and Orphans of Poor Clergymen, Canterbury, 20 August 1751.*

[94] Sub St Michael's, Crooked Lane.

parishes an incumbent served was so that he would be able to keep track on the incidence of pluralism, and monitor its consequences for the parish. The archbishop wanted to sort out the precise mileage involved, so that he could assess the potential pastoral damage. At Betteshanger he noted that the curate lived at Goodnestone, which 'is called 3 and must be 6 miles' away.[95] And Secker was annoyed that Thomas Guise served Stowting 'but once and lives at Petham 8 miles off'. The archbishop was resolved that he 'must not go on so'.[96] Many of the parishes held in plurality, however, involved nearby or even contiguous parishes (this was especially true of the small and poor parishes in the Dover deanery), and was thus less damaging than might be supposed. There was also the difference between technical and real non-residence. John Wentworth resided one and a half miles away from Brenzett, but this was because of a robbery at the vicarage house in 1748.[97] Henry Rand, the incumbent of Bearsted, lived in the next-door parish of Maidstone, but visited his parish almost every day. Moreover the parishioners testified that the vicar's non-residence 'was no material inconvenience to them'.[98] At Latchingdon, the parishioners certified that they were satisfied with a non-resident curate, and, at Kingsnorth, Philip Hawkins went to reside two miles away at Ashford 'with the Consent of the Parishioners'.[99] At Adisham, Francis Walwyn admitted that he lived for the greater part of the year at Canterbury 'from where I go over to my parish on weekdays and on Sundays constantly. . . Residing at Canterbury (6 miles [away]) I can attend ye duties of my parish, and at ye same time reap the benefit of constant exercise, which being conducive to the preservation of my health, I beg leave to continue.'[100] What is more, Walwyn had a resident curate. And, to complicate the picture, the mere fact of residence might not mean that the vicar performed his duty fully, since the resident rector of Tangmere failed to live up to Secker's expectations.[101]

The Value of Livings

Despite the difficulties facing an incumbent in collecting his tithe, the general value of livings rose in the century between the Restoration and the compiling of the Speculum. Moreover, because of augmentations, poorer livings in the diocese rose at a greater rate than richer ones. The most sustained attempt at augmentation was Queen Anne's Bounty: in 1736 94 of the livings in the diocese were valued at under £50, the poverty-line drawn by the Bounty, in 1758 62 were deemed below this level, and by 1809 only 15 were valued at less than £50.[102] Especially significant for the relationship between the Church and the wider community were the contributions made by the laity to the improvement

---

[95] Sub Betteshanger.
[96] Sub Stowting.
[97] Sub Brenzett.
[98] Sub Bearsted.
[99] Sub Latchingdon; sub Kingsnorth.
[100] LPL, MS 1134/1, f. 9.
[101] Sub Tangmere.
[102] Figures from I. Green, 'The First Years of Queen Anne's Bounty', in *Princes and Paupers in the English Church, 1500–1800*, ed. R. O'Day and F. Heal (Leicester, 1981), p. 243; LPL, VG 2/5; ibid., VG 2/7.

of livings. Poor livings in the Canterbury diocese, for example, received augmentations from Sir Philip Boteler's fund. £14,000 was left to Boteler by his aunt in 1763 and, as he lived at Teston in Kent, Secker was able to persuade him to give money to thirty eight parishes (though some parishes such as Goodnestone by Faversham were recommended by Secker but not augmented).[103] In all the value of fifty seven Canterbury livings was improved by gifts from the laity during the eighteenth century.[104] It is indicative of the relations between Church and society in Kent that over two thirds of the diocesan livings receiving augmentation in this period did so to match gifts of money and land given by the laity, as opposed to receiving augmentation by lot. On top of this, incumbents of several of the larger livings, such as St John's, Margate, received subscriptions and extras.[105]

Moreover, the position of the poorer incumbents and curates (who were usually younger men who would 'progress' to their own livings) contrasts favourably with the lot of poor clergy in France and America. The Speculum shows curates often receiving between £40 and £50, apart from which they might also receive free lodging, the use of the garden and surplice fees. Much of the initial support for the French Revolution came from curés battling against the wealthy dignitaries, and in 1789 they supported the sale of Church property to pay off the national debt. In England there was no such full-scale revolt of the lower clergy on class lines, although John Horne (later Horne Tooke), who, as the Speculum shows, sometimes acted as curate of Knockholt in 1759 and 1760 before becoming incumbent of the chapel of ease at Brentwood from 1760 to 1773, took up radical politics, backed John Wilkes in the Middlesex election of 1768, and organised the Society for supporting the Bill of Rights.

Apart from documenting the financial position of the clergy, the Speculum is also testimony to the ways in which the poor might receive money and gifts of food through the auspices of the parish church, for incumbents were often the trustees of local charities and benefactions. Many clergy expressly mentioned the use of the offertory money for the poor and needy. This was often, though not always, reserved for 'poor communicants', an indication of the way in which active Church membership had wider repercussions. Such use of poor relief was a clear attempt to control the lower orders, by obliging them to attend church, by giving charity only to the honest poor, by giving bread and beef rather than money (which might be misspent), and by using it for teaching the poor. It was also suspected at Stisted that the loaves distributed from the Offertory had reconciled some of the dissenters to the Church.[106] Secker was keen to check that these charities were not lost.

A significant feature of the period, indicative of the wider economic relationship between the clergy and their parishioners, was the ability of many incumbents to persuade the laity to give towards the costs of the repair, improvement and building of parish churches. The power of Anglican projects

---

[103] LPL, MS 1120, f. 95, Secker to Boteler, 5 November 1765; sub Goodnestone by Faversham.

[104] Gregory, 'Canterbury', p. 165.

[105] Sub St John's, Margate.

[106] Sub Stisted. In the London, Sussex and Surrey peculiars, special note ought to be made of the numerous charities established by Alderman Henry ('Dog') Smith, who died in 1627. See D. Stroud, *The South Kensington Estate of Henry Smith's Charity. Its History and Development* (1973).

to extract money from the laity is worth remembering as a corrective to the view that the social hold of religion was increasingly marginal.[107] The affection shown by certain sections of the laity for the Church was revealed in donations of church plate and contributions to church repair. Linda Colley has claimed that such donations are a litmus test for discovering Tory gentry, for these were the keenest to sponsor refurbishment programmes.[108] The earl of Thanet, a prominent Tory in the diocese, gave an altar-piece and new pews to Hothfield in the 1720s, thus conforming to Colley's model.[109] But it is equally important to remember that Whigs too could claim to be supporters of the Church, and Whig laymen contributed generously to the up-keep of many parish churches, such as the M.P. Robert Marsham who had Maidstone church neatly refurbished, and Mr Fairfax who beautified Leeds church.[110]

And evidence of more general parochial good-will can be found. Extensive repairs were carried out at St Peter's, Thanet in 1758 (including installing an organ). The vicar, Cornelius Willes, noted that the church was 'uncommonly neat' and that the parishioners had raised well over £600 for repairing and decorating the church: 'They seem to have the honour and credit of the Church much at heart; they behave well to their clergy and there have been no quarrels of any kind between them for the last century'.[111] And at Faversham, Secker was informed that £2000 had lately been laid out on it by parishioners.[112] He himself gave money towards beautifying Marden chancel,[113] and supported the brief for the speedy repair of Sittingbourne which had been damaged by fire.[114]

Lay finance was also necessary for the building of new churches. The eighteenth century is not usually seen as a century of church building and certainly fell far behind its successor. Part of the explanation for a southern diocese like Canterbury, was that there was already a proliferation of churches and so little need to build more. Nevertheless, as the Speculum reveals, certain areas of the diocese saw a marked growth in population which, although it did not compare with the huge up swing after 1800, forced the Church to build new places of worship. In 1673 a chapel of ease was built with governmental backing for the dockyards at Sheerness in the parish of Queenborough.[115] In 1716 Wake consecrated a chapel to serve the parishioners of Lower Deal. Its financing indicates how such a cost could be spread over a range of inhabitants and did not depend on a single donor. In 1707 the parish bought the ground and in 1712 procured an Act to put a duty on all the coals landed at Deal harbour.[116] A similar method was employed in the building of a chapel of ease at Ramsgate in 1791,[117]

---

[107] For instance, W.K. Jordan, 'Social Institutions in Kent, 1480–1660. A Study of the Changing Pattern of Social Aspirations', *Archaeologia Cantiana*, LXXV (1961), 124.

[108] Colley, *Defiance of Oligarchy*, p. 117.

[109] Bodl., MS Eng. Th. c. 24, f. 395: Hasted, *History of Kent* VII, p. 523.

[110] Ibid., IV, p. 317. etc.

[111] Sub St Peter's, Thanet; see LPL, MS 1134/3, f. 195.

[112] Sub Faversham.

[113] Sub Marden.

[114] Sub Sittingbourne. Secker's letter encouraging local clergy to subscribe to the brief was reprinted in *The Gentleman's Magazine* 1763, p. 372.

[115] Hasted, *History of Kent*, VI, p. 233.

[116] Sub Lower Deal. On its funding more generally, see C. W. Chalklin, 'The Funding of Church Building in the Provincial Towns of Eighteenth-Century England', in *The Transformation of English Provincial Towns*, ed. P. Clark, pp. 284–310.

[117] Sub Ramsgate; Hasted, *History of Kent* X, p. 346.

in response to the large increase in the population. More significantly, perhaps, evidence from the peculiars shows that in parishes in the industrialising north, such as Saddleworth in Lancashire, the Church, far from being ineffectual as traditional studies have suggested, was actually doing rather well, furthering Church extension and building chapels of ease to meet the growth in population.[118]

Pastoral Work of the Clergy

The Speculum sheds some light on the pastoral work of the clergy, and especially interesting are Secker's comments on the pastoral abilities of the incumbents. For instance John Clough, the vicar of Ashford, was described as 'Grave, good [and] sensible'.[119] Pastorally, the archbishop placed stress on teaching the catechism (which was carried out in the majority of parishes for at least part of the year, and in some throughout the year) and he also noted the provision for parochial education, particularly through the charity schools. For, as William Marsh, the rector of Bapchild, had observed:

> not one in three in any Parish, that he knows, in this Country, knows who Jesus Christ is, or why he came into the World; & that Servants think the Sacram^t is only for their Superiors. He ascribes it to their not being able to read, nor taught their Catechism, & wd have more Gifts for these Purposes.[120]

In Linda Colley's portrayal of Tory Anglicanism, support for charity schools is used as a sign of Tory political affiliation.[121] But the Whigs were just as aware of the need for such schools in educating the poor. There was plenty of support, for instance, at Queenborough, where government influence at the Royal Dockyard was strong.[122] Clergy were also active in some of the leading grammar schools in the South-East (such as the King's School, Canterbury, and schools at Tenterden, Sevenoaks, Ashford and Croydon), as well as sustaining private schools. William Gilpin, for instance, ran a private school at Cheam, during whose summer holidays he embarked on tours of the Wye, which he would later publish as illustrations of Picturesque Landscape.[123]

The Speculum is also a major source for the range and frequency of services offered by the clergy. What is clear is that there was not the steady decline in the performance of Sunday duty during the eighteenth century which has been claimed by A.J. Russell.[124] Secker saw 'whole service', both morning and evening prayer as the ideal for each parish, chiding incumbents who viewed this as 'double' duty.[125] In the urban parishes 'whole service' was usually put into practice, and is evidence of urban piety (complicating the assumption that the

---

[118] See M. Smith, *Religion in Industrial Society. Oldham and Saddleworth, 1740–1865* (Oxford, 1994).

[119] Sub Ashford.

[120] Sub Bapchild.

[121] Colley, *Defiance*, pp. 110, 117.

[122] Sub Queenborough.

[123] Sub Cheam. See W. Gilpin, *Observations on the River Wye. . . Relative chiefly to Picturesque beauty; made in the Summer of the Year 1770* (1782).

[124] A.J. Russell, *The Clerical Profession* (1980), pp. 54–5.

[125] For example, LPL, MS Secker 6, f. 197, Secker to Dugard, 27 February 1766.

Church was weaker in urban than in rural areas). All of the London parishes had whole service on Sundays and two thirds had week-day services as well.[126] At Newington Butts, for instance, the young Samuel Horsley was exemplary in providing sacrament once a month and at great festivals, service twice on Sundays, and week-day prayers.[127] At St Mary's, Dover, an elective living, the parishioners made the vicar sign a contract that he would reside and provide the requisite Sunday and week-day services (in return, the parishioners gave him a handsome house).[128] The situation in the smaller rural parishes was somewhat different. Here incumbents often acknowledged that they only performed one service on a Sunday, and had abandoned week-day services, because there was no chance of getting a congregation in the afternoon. At Stourmouth, the rector claimed that he had tried to have two Sunday services, but the parishioners did not like it. This did not mean that parishioners were necessarily deprived of the chance to attend twice. Clergy maintained that it was quite possible for inhabitants to attend a neighbouring parish church, since in spread-out parishes, they often lived nearer to another church than their own. At Graveney, for instance, only four houses were described as being 'within Gun-shot' of the church.[129] The two parishes of Ash and Woodnesborough 'ran into each other' and 'the inhabitants mutually resorted to each others churches'.[130] At Burmarsh, service was only performed once because the inhabitants were mainly 'Lookers, servants to the Graziers', who went 'to Dimchurch, a mile off the other part of the Day, and [saw] their Cattle by the way':[131] suggestive of the ways in which agricultural routine interfered with church attendance. William Marsh, the rector of Bapchild, blamed churchwardens for not presenting absenters, and he felt that 'the minister would only raise a Flame by presenting'.[132]

Edward Sedgwick, the curate of St Mary's in the Marsh, echoed the reports of many clergymen when he told Secker of the 'unwillingness of people to attend unless there is a sermon, choosing rather to go to a neighbouring church where there is a sermon preached, than to stay at home and hear prayers only'.[133] The vogue for sermon gadding, which has been seen as a feature of the early Anglican church, continued through the eighteenth century. Thus clergy of neighbouring parishes operated a kind of unofficial rota, ensuring that they preached at different times, thereby enabling parishioners to hear two sermons, and although this led to non-attendance at their own parish, this was a sign not of lay indifference but rather of commitment to Anglican worship. There is also evidence of a drive by Secker to improve the number of services in rural parishes, and the pressure which he put on the clergy ensured that in certain

---

[126] See V. Barrie-Curien, 'The Clergy in the diocese of London in the eighteenth century', in *The Church of England c.1689–c.1833. From Toleration to Tractarianism*, ed. J. Walsh, S. Taylor and C. Haydon (Cambridge, 1993), p. 96. See also id., *Clergé et Pastorale en Angleterre au XVIIIème siècle: Le Diocèse de Londres* (Paris, 1992).

[127] Sub Newington Butts. On Horsley, see F.C. Mather, *High Church Prophet. Bishop Samuel Horsley (1733–1806) and the Caroline Tradition in the Later Georgian Church* (Oxford, 1992), pp. 36–8.

[128] Sub St Mary's, Dover.

[129] Sub Stourmouth; sub Graveney. Six churches were within a mile and half of the parish of Graveney.

[130] Sub Ash.

[131] Sub Burmarsh.

[132] Sub Bapchild.

[133] LPL, MS 1134/3, f. 77.

parishes at least the frequency of services increased.[134] The archbishop told Josias Pomfret, the vicar of Snave, 'I do not apprehend that the duty done in your parish is less than it used to be, but less than it ought to be. And custom is no reason for continuing what is wrong.'[135] The Speculum also reveals the sound and practical pastoral advice which the archbishop offered his clergy. At Boughton Alulph he suggested that the incumbent should read lectures on the catechism to attract parishioners to the afternoon service.[136]

One reason which clergy regularly gave for the non attendance of their parishioners at services was the presence of an alehouse. Their concern with the rival attractions of the alehouse is an indication of the way in which 'Puritan' aims were absorbed into mainstream Anglicanism in the eighteenth century. Clerical attacks on the influence of the alehouse and the evils of Sunday trading were elements within a Protestant sabbatarianism which clergy tried to impose on the parishes. But in the attempt to make Sundays into a day devoted to religion, ministers recognised that they might have to contend with different – and sometimes competing – understandings of the purpose and role of the Sabbath. In a statement reminiscent of the battles between godly pastors of the early seventeenth century and their recalcitrant parishioners, the vicar of Ripple complained in 1758 that 'there are too many who seem to consider the Lord's Day merely as a day of rest, if not festivity, but they are chiefly plough servants – stupid and ignorant'.[137] At Keston, Secker was informed that 'full half the Parish, especially of the Common people, never go to Church in their Lives, owing to their Ignorance & Vice and the Libertinism of the Age. . . Fornication, Drunkeness, Profaness increase every day'.[138] At Northfleet, it was remarked that the 'Chalk-cliff men direct themselves on Sundays like the Colliers in the North', and as an attempt to combat such indifference, the rector of Halstow exhorted parents to bring children to Church, so that they would learn to distinguish Sundays from other days.[139]

Other reasons for absenting from Sunday service included those Londoners who were indulging in the already fashionable week-ends away in the country, or riding their horses for exercise, and the want of clothes amongst the lowest sort.[140] At Graveney one absentee was described as being on ill-terms with his wife: 'they think it not fit to go to Church because they quarrel so much',[141] and at Dover privateering was blamed for 'corrupt[ing] the morals of the People', leading to non-attendance at the parish church.[142] Yet even in the large and more populous parishes it was possible for some incumbents to whittle down the number of non-attenders. The vicar of Folkestone reported in 1758 that 'the meanest are absent. . . bred up in ignorance and brutality', but, he boasted, 'lessened by two thirds since I came by my diligence in visiting the sick and poor and relieving their wants'.[143] The problem of absentees also explains the interest

---

[134] Sub Graveney.
[135] LPL, MS Secker 3, f. 253, Secker to Pomfret, 23 October 1762.
[136] Sub Boughton Blean.
[137] LPL, MS 1134/4, f. 233.
[138] Sub Keston.
[139] Sub Northfleet; sub Halstow.
[140] For a London parish, see sub St Dionis Backchurch; for lack of clothes, see sub Dymchurch.
[141] Sub Graveney; LPL, MS 1134/2, f. 130.
[142] Sub St Mary's, Dover.
[143] LPL, MS 1134/2, f. 100.

in the 'families of note' (which headed each entry), some of whom leased land from the archbishop, as did Sir Brook Bridges at Goodnestone, and Secker used the renewal of the lease to persuade him to give up his claim to the benefice as a donative.[144] Such interest in the parish notables is sometimes seen as evidence of clerical fawning, but it is better explained by the fact that when leading members of the parish attended (such as William Pitt who was 'constant at the sacrament' at Hayes, or the earl of Guilford at Waldershare, or Lord Winchilsea at Eastwell), there was a higher turnout of the parish at services.[145] At Knockholt, James Collins 'the only substantial man in the parish' was described as being 'well disposed & promises to influence the people rightly'.[146]

The clearest division in the pastoral provision between town and country parishes can be seen in the frequency with which the Eucharist was celebrated. Some urban parishes had communion once a month and at great festivals. But at rural Guston, it was reported that, despite the efforts of the incumbent, 'they refuse to have four sacraments'.[147] And no-one turned up for the sacrament on Christmas day 1758 at Grain.[148] Secker was particularly keen to note those parishes which had few communicants, often writing later to the incumbent to inquire why.[149] The reluctance of various sections of the parish to communicate was explained by the archbishop: 'some imagine that the sacrament belongs only to persons of advanced years, or great leisure, or high attainment and it is a very dangerous thing for common people to attend on'.[150] At Folkestone the vicar moaned that 'there are still a great number of men well-advanced in years, who have never received the sacrament. . . they keep away from it out of superstitious awe'.[151] It may have been partly because of this that Robert Jenkins, the rector of Westbere, 'preached a Sermon of his Fathers on the Sacramt 22 Sundays together, as he owned: but others say, 14 months; & went on preaching, notwithstanding the ABP^s Admonition, till the Dean of Canterbury got it from him'.[152] But, with Secker's prodding, there is evidence of improvement in some parishes. The number of Communion services at Reculver, for instance, rose from three to four.[153] A related concern was with the numbers who were sent to be confirmed at the visitations.

The Church and Nonconformity

The Speculum also reveals the relationship between the Church and dissent. There were, even in the mid-eighteenth century, echoes of an earlier period, when Secker was informed of a couple of Muggletonians living at Little Brickhill and of a female Quaker preacher at Cranbrook.[154] Yet the impression is

---

[144] Sub Goodnestone.

[145] Sub Hayes; Waldershare; Eastwell.

[146] Sub Knockholt.

[147] Sub Guston.

[148] Sub Grain.

[149] For example, sub Luddenham, where Secker commented that the number of communicants was '[too few]'.

[150] Secker, *Charges*, p. 60.

[151] LPL, MS 1134/2, f. 103.

[152] Sub Westbere.

[153] Sub Reculver.

[154] Sub Little Brickhill; sub Cranbrook.

that by 1758 Old Dissent had lost its vigour. Numbers had declined, meeting houses had closed (the one at St Clement's, Sandwich had been converted into a beer cellar)[155] and erstwhile dissenters had been baptised into the Church (with the encouragement of archbishops).[156] At Cranbrook, the Tempest family, who had plagued early eighteenth-century clergy, had by now conformed, and at Tenterden it was noted that 'several Creditable Dissenters have joined in Communion with the Church in the last 2 years'.[157] The rector of St Andrew's, Canterbury thought that this decline in the dissenting interest was 'owing to the moderation with which they have been treated'.[158] Dissenting congregations also suffered if their ministers took orders within the church, and Potter and Secker were especially keen to give former dissenters promotion, a fact which is perhaps related to their own dissenting backgrounds.[159] For example, Edward Penry, the vicar of Borden, had been educated at Doddridge's Academy and brought up as a dissenter before conforming, and Liscombe Stretch of Leysdown, Joseph Price of Brabourne, Thomas Gwatkin of Pagham, Henry Dell of Bethersden, James Devis, the curate of Little Chart, John Howlett of Boughton Monchelsea, and Richard Morgan, curate at Northbourne, had all been nonconformists.[160] The fact that many Presbyterians, even in London, also attended the parish church indicates that the Elizabethan practice of semi-separatism continued well into the eighteenth century. At St Vedast's, Foster Lane, it was noted that some of the dissenters 'often come to Church, all subscribe to the Morning Prayers and treat the minister with Respect'.[161] In some cases there is evidence of a gender divide such as at Stisted where 'the boys follow[ed] the father, the girls the Mother'. Here too is evidence of concentric rings of support for the Church and dissent. All dissenters in the parish were reported as attending the church sometimes, except those who communicated at the meeting house, 'and even these send their children in bad weather'.[162]

The few pockets of Catholicism in Kent in the mid century conformed to John Bossy's model of seigneurial leadership,[163] yet the evidence qualifies Colin Haydon's suggestion that there had been a considerable mellowing in clerical attitudes to Catholics.[164] Suspicion still lurked. The Hales family kept a popish priest at Hackington and the vicar complained that because the management of the parish almshouse was in their gift, it had been filled with Catholics.[165] At Doddington the Thornicroft family were deemed to be 'peaceful', although it was noted they had put their papist game-keeper in to 'pervert' the parish.[166] The incidence of recusancy was noticeably higher in Sussex than in other southern

[155] Sub St Clement's, Sandwich.
[156] Gregory, 'Canterbury', pp. 217–18.
[157] Sub Cranbrook; sub Tenterden.
[158] LPL, MS 1134/1, f. 175.
[159] Gregory, 'Canterbury', p. 19. See also S. Taylor, 'Archbishop Potter and the Dissenters', *Yale University Gazette*, LXVII (1993), pp. 118–126.
[160] Sub Borden, Leysdown, Brabourne, Pagham, Bethersden, Little Chart, Boughton Monchelsea, Nortbourne.
[161] Sub St Mary Vedast's, London.
[162] Sub Stisted.
[163] J. Bossy, *The English Catholic Community 1570–1850* (1975), pp. 149–181.
[164] C. Haydon, *Anti-Catholicism in Eighteenth-Century England. A Political and Social Study* (Manchester, 1993), esp. pp. 164–203.
[165] Sub Hackington.
[166] Sub Dodington.

counties. Remarkably, at Slindon, Secker learned that 85 out of the 185 inhabitants were Catholic. He advised the incumbent:

> Having so many Papists in your parish, you ought to be peculiarly careful, & prudent in your Conduct. . . I fear the priests of the Church of Rome ordinarily ← take more pains with their Laity, than we do with ours: which ought not to be so. And as they study every way to make converts, so should we.[167]

Yet even erstwhile Catholic priests might conform and find promotion within the Church, as did James Smith who, having survived the Lisbon earthquake, conformed to the Church of England, being promoted by Secker to Eastbridge in 1765. In his *The Errors of the Church of Rome Detected* (1777), Smith noted that his conversion had been influenced by the services he had attended whilst a child at Bath Abbey, thinking that they were more orderly and reasonable than the Catholic mass he was used to.[168] He became chaplain to Archbishop Cornwallis in 1781.

It is often argued that the emergence of Methodism was a sign of reaction against the Church, and can be taken as evidence of a Church in decline, which had lost its hold on the population. By 1758, Methodists had developed a footing in the coastal region, making particular headway at the garrison at Sheerness. Methodist infiltration was also apparent in Canterbury itself, where the meeting was led by Edward Perronet, the son of the Evangelical vicar of Shoreham.[169] Yet the Speculum complicates our understanding of the emergence of Methodism as a reaction to the deficiencies of Church. Perronet, for example, leased the house where he held his meetings from the archbishop,[170] and the preacher at Teynham had had 'no lasting effect'.[171] In the Weald, traditionally the centre for nonconformity in Kent, the development of Methodism was slow; in the few parishes in the area which contained Methodists, they were reported to attend church, and receive the sacrament regularly. Moreover, parishes such as Bexley, which had an Evangelical minister, did not stop the growth of Methodism.[172] Indeed the Speculum reminds us that in many ways we ought to view Methodism as a movement from within, rather from without the Church. At Shoreham, for instance, it was the rector, Vincent Perronet, later called the 'archbishop of Methodism', who encouraged a Methodist meeting within the parish, headed by his unmarried daughter 'the bold, masculine-minded Damaris',[173] who entertained itinerant preachers, attended their sermons and had preaching in his kitchen every Friday evening. At St Vedast's, Foster Lane, the trustees of the school sometimes encouraged 'Methodist and antinomian preachers',[174] and one of the late-eighteenth century leaders of London Methodism, Erasmus Middleton, was appointed lecturer at St Leonard's Eastcheap in 1775,[175] reminiscent of the ways in which 'puritan' preachers in the

---

[167] LPL, MS Secker 6, f. 226, Secker to Launce, 5 October 1759.
[168] James Smith, *The Errors of the Church of Rome Detected* (1777), pp. 6–7.
[169] Sub Harbledown; LPL, MS 1134/1, f. 191.
[170] Sub St Margaret's, Canterbury.
[171] Sub Teynham.
[172] Sub Bexley.
[173] DNB, sub Perronet, Vincent.
[174] Sub St Vedast's, Foster Lane.
[175] Sub St Leonard's, Eastcheap.

early seventeenth century had acquired posts within the Church.[176] And the religious society which met at St Michael's, Crooked Lane at eight o'clock every evening for prayers and had sacrament every Sunday, sounds Methodist but in fact there were 'no Methodists amongst them'.[177]

What then does the Speculum tell us of religious life in the mid-eighteenth century? Against the models proposed by Clark and Virgin, it might be suggested that the Speculum, with its evidence of a concern to improve the nature of the clerical profession, evidence of clerical tribalism, evidence of lay gifts to the Church, evidence of the problems in demarcating dissent from the establishment, as witnessed by semi-separatism, evidence of suspicion of Catholics, evidence of concern about the youth in the parish, and worries over the temptations of the alehouse, evidence of lay love of sermons and the difficulties in getting parishioners to attend the sacrament, shows distinct similarities to the character of religious life as described for the early seventeenth century by Professor Collinson and Dr Fincham.[178] As far as religious life in the parishes was concerned, the world of George III was not perhaps as far removed from the world of James I as we have been accustomed to believe.

Editorial Conventions

In reproducing the Speculum for publication, and in an effort to capture its spirit as far as possible, the original spelling and capitalisation have been retained. Because Secker recorded his information in note-form, it has sometimes been necessary silently to add punctuation in places where the sense would otherwise have been unclear. Secker noted his material succinctly and often in an abbreviated manner, but his abbreviations are usually self-explanatory and thus have not been expanded within the text. Instead, a list of abbreviations used by Secker and his successors is given below. The first category of abbreviation is the capital letter or letters standing for a frequently used noun (e.g. R = rector, V = vicar, C = curate, P = patron, ABP = archbishop, BP= bishop). The second category of abbreviation is a contraction in which words are shortened (often in superscript) (e.g. wch for which), mainly leaving out two or three internal letters. A third category of abbreviation is the shortening of ends of words (e.g. Improp. for Impropriator, approp. for appropriation, augm. for augmented). The final category of abbreviation is the reference to published sources used by Secker. These have either been identified in the list of abbreviations, or in the footnotes. Secker also sometimes used an adapted form of shorthand known as the Mason System No. 2, originally devised by William

---

[176] See Paul Seaver, *The Puritan Lecturerships: the politics of religious dissent, 1560–1662* (Stanford, 1970). On the London lectureships, see also H.L.E. Garbett, 'Ecclesiastical History, 1666–1907', in VCH *London* I, pp. 357–8.

[177] Sub St Michael's, Crooked Lane.

[178] P. Collinson, *The Religion of Protestants. The Church in English Society, 1559–1625* (Oxford, 1982); K. Fincham, *Prelate as Pastor. The Episcopate of James I* (Oxford, 1990).

Mason in *La Plume Volante* (1707). Unfortunately it has not been possible to decipher these small passages, but they have been marked by three asterisks (***). Erased or deleted matter including illegible entries are indicated by { }. Secker often added or corrected information between the lines in the text, and in this edition such additions have been presented between ⟨ ⟩. Secker's own bracketed interpolations in the text are marked, as in the original, usually by square brackets, thus [ ], occasionally by round brackets ( ). The few footnotes used by Secker are indicated by a superscript number followed by an asterisk. Other superscript numbers indicate editorial notes. These are largely concerned with the basic life, educational and career details of the parish clergy and curates at their first mention in the Speculum. Whilst every effort has been made to list all the livings which a cleric may have served, these are largely reserved for those to which he was formally licensed. As Secker himself complained, arrangements for curates were often informal,[179] and thus it has not always been possible to name all of the parishes a cleric may have attended to. In any case a clergyman may have begun his curacy several years before being formally licensed, and thus there may well be a discrepancy between the date of the licence and the time when he actually served. The Speculum often reveals licences being endorsed in the 1790s, given to clergy who had been serving on an unofficial basis for some years before, testimony to Archbishop Moore's campaign to tighten up procedures. Also, information in the act-books about when a clergyman died is sometimes at slight variance with other sources. This is because of the time-lag before the incumbent was 'noted as dead' by the diocesan officials. The principal sources for the data concerning the clergy are John and J.A. Venn, *Alumni Cantabrigienses*, 8 vols (1922–7 and 1940–54), J. Foster, *Alumni Oxonienses*, 8 vols (1881–2 and 1888), G.D. Butchaell and T.V. Sadleir, *Alumni Dublienses, 1505–1905*, 2 vols (1924), and E.H.W. Dunkin, Claude Jenkins and E.A. Fry, *Index to the Act Books of the Archbishops of Canterbury, 1663–1859*, 2 vols (1929–38). Matriculation dates are also given, although it should be noted that, at Cambridge in particular, students were often admitted a year or more before they matriculated. Elsewhere, the editorial notes seek to identify other individuals and to clarify textual references. Here I have relied in particular on Edward Hasted's *History of Kent*, the first edition of which was published between 1778 and 1799, and was compiled with the help of a number of the clergy mentioned in the Speculum,[180] [G.E.C.], *The Complete Peerage*, *The Complete Baronetage*, Ruvigny's, *The Jacobite Peerage*, Burke's *History of the Commoners*, the *Dictionary of National Biography* and the relevant volumes of *The History of Parliament: the House of Commons*, Owen Manning and William Bray, *The History and Antiquities of the County of Surrey*, 3 vols (1804–14), Thomas Walker Horsfield, *The History, Antiquities and Topography of the County of Sussex*, Thomas Wright, *The History and Topography of the County of Essex*, 2 vols (1835), Alfred Suckling, *The History and Antiquities of the County of Suffolk*, 2 vols (1846), and the *Victoria County History*. Other reference works consulted are A.B. Emden, *A Biographical Register of the University of Oxford to AD 1500*, 3 vols (1957–9). A.B. Beaven, *The Aldermen of the City of London*, 2 vols (1908–13), A.

---

[179] *Charges*, p. 221.
[180] John Boyle, *In Quest of Hasted* (Chichester, 1984).

Bellenger, *English and Welsh Priests, 1558–1800* (1984), W.A. Shaw, *The Knights of England*, 2 vols (1906).

ABBREVIATIONS USED IN THE SPECULUM BY SECKER AND HIS SUCCESSORS

a	aged
Abb Battel	Battle Abbey
ABP, ABp	archbishop
abs	absent
acct	account
Acct in ABP Potter's time	LPL, VG 2/3.
AD^n	archdeacon
AD^n Green's Book	Canterbury Cathedral Archives and Library, MS Z/3/34: 'Archdeacon Greene's Visitation Book'
adv.	advowson
aftwds	afterwards
agreemt	agreement
agst	against
al.	alias
Ald.	alderman
Anab.	anabaptist(s)
ann. regn.	year of reign
apartmt	apartment
App.	appendix
app	apprentice
app[rop]	appropriation, -iated
Augm	augmented
B.A.	bachelor of arts
bapt.	baptised
Bar^t	baronet
bec.	because
betw.	between
Boteler's legacy	legacy of Sir Philip Boteler to augment livings
BP, Bp	bishop
Br. N	Brasenose College, Oxford
C(ur)	curacy, -curate, Cambridge
Cant	Canterbury
Cap(ella)	chapel

Cat	catechism, -catechised
Cert[ified]	value of the living as certified by Queen Anne's bounty
cess	cession
Ch	church
Chap	chapel
Chapl.	chaplain
Chartae Misc.	LPL, Cartae Miscellanae[1]
Ch Ch [X^{st} Ch]	Christ Church (Oxford)
Ch^n	children
Ch of coals	chaldron of Coals
Chr.	Christmas
Ch W^n	churchwarden
cl	cleric
Co.	county
col.	collate
Coll.	college
Comp.	company, -complaint
Com(s).	communicant(s), communion
Comm. Ann	yearly average
Conf.	confirmed
Cong.	congregation
Cont.	continued
D	dean
d	deacon, -deanery, died, pence
da.	daughter
DCh	dean and chapter
D.D.	doctor of divinity
Ded.	deduct-, deductions
destructa	destroyed
Disp.	dispensation (for plurality, non residence)
Diss.	dissenter
dist.	distant, -distance
Dul.	Dulwich College
E	east, -earl
East. Off.	Easter offerings
Eccl(esia) Destructa	church destroyed
Ecton	John Ecton, *Thesaurus Rerum Ecclesiasticarum* (1742).
Ed	edition

---

[1] D.M. Owen, *Catalogue of Lambeth Manuscripts 889–901* (1968).

Entry B	Entry Book (i.e. Act-books of the archbishops, kept at Lambeth)[2]
Esq	esquire
Ev.	evening
Exc.	excused, excommunicated, except
Excl	exclusive
Exempt	those parishes exempt from the jurisdiction of the archdeacon
exp	expounded, -exposition (of catechism)
F	fellow, -feet
Fam.	family, -families
Fri.	Friday
G	guinea
Gent	gentleman
Gibson Papers	LPL, MSS 929–942: Papers of Edmund Gibson
gr.	great
Harris, *History of Kent*	John Harris, *The History of Kent* (1719).
Haynes's Book	LPL, VG 2/1. Survey by John Haynes, 1716.
Head	LPL, MS 1134: Visitation of the diocese of Canterbury (by Archdeacon Head).
Herring	LPL, MS 1138: 'Account of the archdeaconry in ABp Herring's time'.
HHd	hogshead
Ho[s]	house[s]
Hosp	hospital
Ib.	*Ibidem* (in the same place)
Imropr	impropriator, -iated
incorp	incorporated
Indep.	independent(s)
Inhab	inhabitants
Inst	institution, instituted
Int.	interest
Jnr	junior
K	King
[White] Kennet	White Kennett, *The Case of Impropriations and of the Augmentations of Vicarages and other Insufficient cures* (1704).
Kilb(urne)	Richard Kilburne, *A Topographie, or Survey of the counties of Kent* (1659).
K[s] Book	King's book (*Valor Ecclesiasticus*)

---

[2] Secker frequently referred to the act books of his predecessors (calling then Entry Books). These are at Lambeth Palace. For post-Restoration references, see also the *Index to the Act Books of the Archbishops of Canterbury, 1663–1859* ed. E.H.W. Dunkin, C. Jenkins and E.A. Fry, 2 vols (1929–38).

Lambard[e]	William Lambarde, *The Perambulation of Kent* (1574).
Ld	lord
LD	lady day (i.e. 25 March)
Lewis expos.	John Lewis, *The Church Catechism Explained, by way of Question and Answer and Confirmed by Scriptural Proofs* (1700).
Lewis notitia/ book	LPL, MS 1125
lic	licence/licensed
Lit. Dim.	letters dimissory
LLB (BCL)	bachelor of civil law
m	mile(s)
M.A. (A.M.)	master of arts
Magd.	Magdalen
memb.	membrane
mercht	merchant
M. Ho.	meeting house
Mich.	michaelmas, Michael
Mid.	Middlesex
Mids.	midsummer
Min	minister
Mon.	monastery
morn	morning
N	north
Newcourt	Richard Newcourt, *Repertorium Ecclesiasticum Pariochiale Londinense* (2 vols) 1710.
Newton's Antiquities	William Newton, *The History and Antiquities of Maidstone* (1741).
Nom	nomination, -nominated
Nonr	nonresidence-, nonresident
O	Oxford
Off	offering(s)
ord.	ordained, ordinary
Ordination book	LPL, VG 1/10
P.	patron
Par.	parish
Parl^t	parliament
Parochial Survey/ Book..1663	LPL MS 1126: 'Sheldon catalogue'
P.C.	perpetual curate
pd	paid
Pens.	pension (usually paid by lay impropriator)
Ph.	Philip
Philipot	Thomas Philipot, *Villare Cantianum; or Kent surveyed and illustrated* (1659).

p.h.v.	*pro hac vice* (for this turn)
poor vicar	Those clergy supported by the fund established by Tenison (LPL, MS 1153).
Pr	priest/ prayers
pres.	presented,- presentation
Presb(y)	presbyterian
pres^t	present

Pr — priest/ prayers
pres. — presented,- presentation
Presb(y) — presbyterian
pres^t — present
Propr. — proprietor
Qrs — quarters
Qu. — Queen/ Query
Qus bounty — Queen Anne's Bounty
R., Rect — rector,- rectory
Rec. — recommended
rec^d — received
Reg. — Register (i.e. archbishops' registers, kept at Lambeth)
Repr. — representative
Res. — resigned
S — south
Sac(r). — sacrament (i.e. Holy Communion)
sal. — salary
Sat. — Saturday
sd — said (aforesaid)
sen. — senior
sequ. — sequestrator
Serms. — sermons
Servts — servants
sevl — several
six preacher — position at Canterbury cathedral
Smith's charity — benefaction given by Alderman Henry Smith (d. 1627).
Somner — [Nicholas Battely], *The Antiquities of Canterbury in Two Parts. I. The Antiquites of Canterbury. . . published by William Somner. . . II. Cantuaria Sacra* (1703).
Sr — sir
S.S. — South Sea
St$^{(s)}$ — saint(s)
St Austin — St Augustine
ST/B/D/P — Sanctae Theologie Baccalarius/ Doctor/ Professor
Steph — Stephen
Strype's Survey — [John Stow], *A Survey of the cities of London and Westminster, brought down from the year 1633 to the present time. . .by John Strype* (1720).

Subscr.	subscription
Sund.	Sunday
Surpl	surplice (fees)
Suss.	Sussex
Tanner, Book of the diocese	Norfolk Record Office, DN/REG 30–31
Tanner, *Monastica*	Thomas Tanner, *Notitia Monastica: or, an Account of all the Abbies, Priories, Friers, heretofore in England and Wales* (1744).
Tenemts	Tenements
Test.	testimonial
Thanksg.	Thanksgiving
Thu.	Thursday
Tri. Sun.	trinity sunday
Tues.	Tuesday
V[ic].	vicar, – vicarage
val.	value, – valued
Vic. Gen	vicar general
Vis	visitation
W	west
w.	with
Wake	This is probably Canterbury Cathedral Archives and Library: Add MS 19.[3]
Wake's expos.	William Wake, *The Principles of the Christian Religion Explained: in a brief commentary upon the Church-Catechism* (1694).
Wake 1717	LPL, MS 1115 (Visitation of the Peculiars, (1717)
Wake's Papers at Ch. Ch.	Christ Church Library, Oxford, Wake MSS, Arch. Epist. W. Letters 6–10 (Canterbury diocese, 1716–26).
wch	which
W[edn].	Wednesday
Whitg.	Archbishop Whitgift
Whits.	Whitsunday
Wilkins, Conc(ilia)	David Wilkins, *Concilia Magnae Britanniae et Hiberniae* 4 vols. (1737).
yr	year

Throughout the text l has been rendered £

---

[3] It is not absolutely clear which of the various surveys compiled for or by Wake Secker used. They all contain similar information, but likely contenders besides this, are 'The Names of all the Rectories, Vicaridges and Curacies within the Diocese of Canterbury and the present Incumbents and Patrons thereof': Christ Church Library, Oxford, MS Wake Letters 6, ff. 284–330, or, less probably, LPL, VG 2/1a.

ABBREVIATIONS USED IN FOOTNOTES

adm.	admitted
C	Cambridge
CCCC	Corpus Christi College, Cambridge
CCCO	Corpus Christi College, Oxford
DNB	*Dictionary of National Biography*
Essex	Thomas Wright, *The History and Topography of the County of Essex*, 2 vols (1831).
Hasted	Edward Hasted, *The History and Topographical Survey of the County of Kent.* Ist published Canterbury, 1778–99. Here 2nd ed. (12 vols, 1797–1801).
LPL	Lambeth Palace Library
m.	matriculated
O	Oxford
preb	prebendary
Secker's *Autobiography*	*The Autobiography of Thomas Secker, archbishop of Canterbury*, ed. J.S. Macauley and R.W. Greaves (Lawrence, 1988).
Surrey	Owen Manning and William Bray, *The History and Antiquities of the County of Surrey*, 3 vols (1804–14).
Sussex	Thomas Walker Horsfield, *The History, Antiquities and Topography of the County of Sussex*, 2 vols (1835).
TCD	Trinity College, Dublin
Turner's *Diary*	*The Diary of Thomas Turner, 1754–1765*, ed. D. Vaisey (Oxford, 1985).
VCH	*Victoria County History*

Note on the authors of the text

The vast majority of the Speculum was written by Archbishop Secker. But entries dated after August 1768 are by Archbishop Cornwallis, or his secretaries, and after 1783 by Archbishop Moore, or his secretaries.

Note on principal informants

Secker usually acknowledged the source of his information. Apart from the manuscript and printed sources listed in the abbreviations, Secker frequently mentioned information (written and verbal) from the following:

'Dr Ducarel':	Andrew Coltee Ducarel (1713–85), Lambeth librarian, 1757–85.
'AD^n' or 'AD^n Head':	John Head (1702–69), archdeacon of Canterbury, 1748–69.

'Mr Clarke':   William Clarke (1676–1771), R. Buxted, Sussex, 1724–68, V. Salehurst, 1743–71, R. Amport, Hants, 1770–1, preb of Chichester, 1727–21.
'BP Pearce':   Zachary Pearce (1690–1774), bishop of Bangor, 1748–56, bishop of Rochester, 1756–74.

Note on dates

Because before March 1752 England operated on the Julian calendar, eleven days behind the New Style or Gregorian calendar, Secker's information about events before that date are in Old Style, which means that dates in the text between January and March 25 until 1752 are given for the previous year. In the footnotes, however, the year is taken to begin on 1 January.

Note on spelling of parishes

Eighteenth-century spelling was notoriously idiosyncratic. In the text, parishes and places are spelt as Secker intended. In the footnotes, modern spelling has been adopted.

Note on pagination

Secker paginated his MS and frequently cross referenced his material. The cross-references within the text, therefore, and the page numbers given in the Index, refer to these page numbers and not to the pagination of the modern edition.

Visitation Articles issued by Secker in 1758 to clergy in his diocese, and to the peculiars in 1759. (They are similar to the queries issued by Wake in 1716 and by Secker in Oxford in 1738, and were the basis of those issued by archbishops Cornwallis and Moore.)

1. What is the extent of your parish? What villages or hamlets, and what number of houses doth it comprehend? And what families of note are there in it?
2. Are there any Papists in your parish, and how many, and of what rank? Have any persons lately been perverted to Popery and by whom, and by what means? And how many and who are they? Is there any place in your parish in which they assemble for worship, and where is it? Doth any popish-priest reside in your parish, or resort to it?, and by what name doth he go? Is there any popish school kept in your parish? Hath any confirmation or visitation been lately held in your parish by any Popish bishop, and by whom, and when? And how often is this done?
3. Are there in your parish any Presbyterians, Independents, Anabaptists, Methodists or Moravians? And how many of each sect, and of what rank? Have they one or more meeting-houses in your parish, and are they duly licensed? What are the names of their teachers, and are they qualified according to law? Is their number lessened or increased of late years, and by what means?
4. Are there any Quakers in your parish, and how many? Is their number lessened or increased of late years, and by what means? Have they a meeting-house in your parish duly licensed, and how often do they meet there? Do any of them, and how many in proportion, pay your legal dues without compulsion? If not, do you lose such dues? Or how do you recover them? And what facts do you know, which may help set their behaviour towards the clergy, or that of the clergy towards them, in a true light?
5. Are there any persons in your parish who profess to disregard religion, or who commonly absent themselves from all public worship of God on the Lord's Day? And from what motives and principles are they understood so to do? And what is the number of such persons, and is it increased of late? And of what rank are they?
6. Do you reside constantly upon your own cure, and in the house belonging to it? If not, where, and what distance? And how long in each year are you absent? And what is the reason for such absence? And have you a licensed curate residing in the parish? Or at what distance from it? And who is he? And doth he serve any other?, and what cure? And what salary do you allow him? And is he in deacon's, or priest's orders?
7. Is public service duly performed twice every Lord's Day in your church, and one sermon preached? If not, what is the reason? And on what days besides are prayers read there? Is there any chapel in your parish? And at what distance from the church? And how often are there prayers and sermons in it? How often and at what times do you catechize in your church? Do your parishioners duly send their children and servants, who have not learned their catechism, to be instructed by you? And do you either expound it to them yourself or make use of some printed exposition, and what is it? Are there any persons, who frequent public worship and are not baptized? And whence doth this proceed? How often is the sacrament of the Lord's Supper administered? And how many usually receive it each time?

8.   Is there any free-school, hospital, or alms-house in your parish? And for how many, and what sort of persons? and who was the founder, and who are the governours, and what are the revenues of it? And are they carefully preserved, and employed as they ought? And are the statutes and ordinances made concerning it well observed?

9.   Is there any voluntary charity school in your parish? And for how many boys or girls? And how is it supported? And what are they taught? And are they also lodged, fed, or clothed? And how are they disposed of, when they leave the school?

10.   Have any lands, or tenements, or tithes, or pensions, or sums of money to be placed out at interest, been given at any time to your church or poor? And what are they? And for what particular uses were they given? And are they carefully preserved, and applied to those uses, and to no other?

11.   By whom and to what uses, is the money given at the offertory disposed of?

12.   Is there any other matter relating to your parish of which it may be proper to give me information? And what is it?

Thomas Cantuar

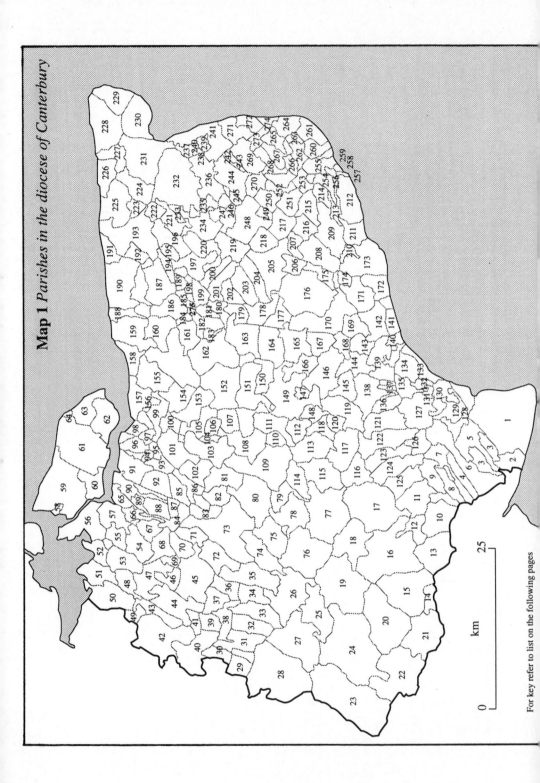

Map 1 *Parishes in the diocese of Canterbury*

For key refer to list on the following pages

km

0   25

Parishes in the Diocese of Canterbury

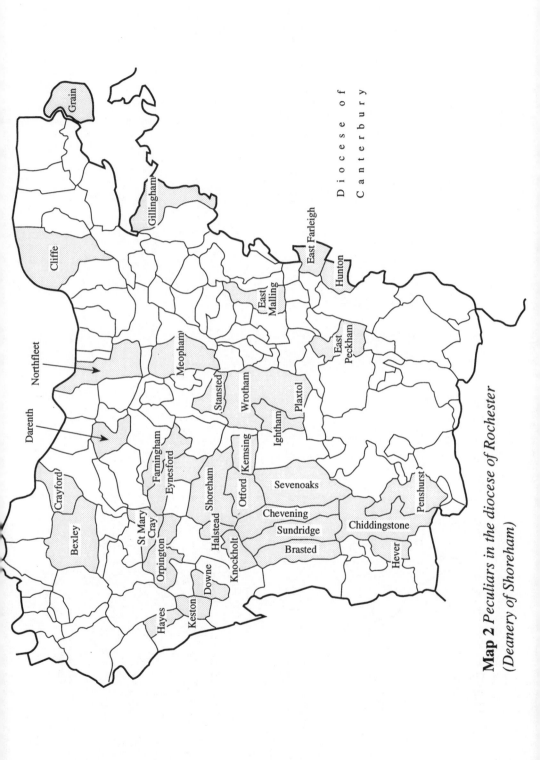

Map 2 *Peculiars in the diocese of Rochester*
(Deanery of Shoreham)

Grain

Gillingham

Cliffe

Diocese of Canterbury

East Farleigh

Hunton

East Malling

Northfleet

Meopham

East Peckham

Darenth

Stansted

Wrotham

Plaxtol

Ightham

Crayford

Farningham

Eynesford

Kemsing

Sevenoaks

Penshurst

Bexley

St Mary Cray

Shoreham

Otford

Chevening

Chiddingstone

Orpington

Halstead

Sundridge

Hayes

Keston

Downe

Knockholt

Brasted

Hever

Map 3 *Peculiars in the diocese of Chichester (West Sussex)*

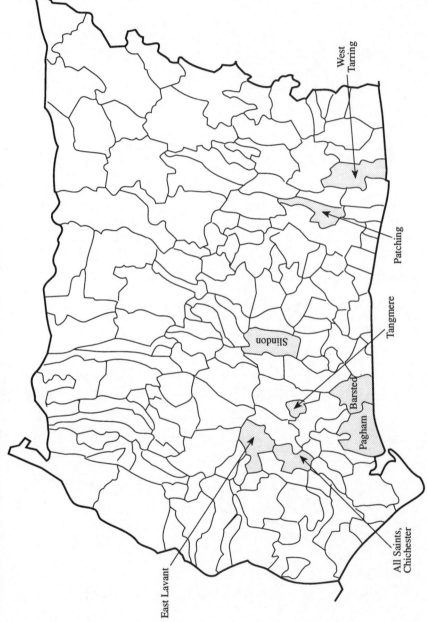

West Tarring

Patching

Tangmere

Slindon

Barsted

Pagham

East Lavant

All Saints, Chichester

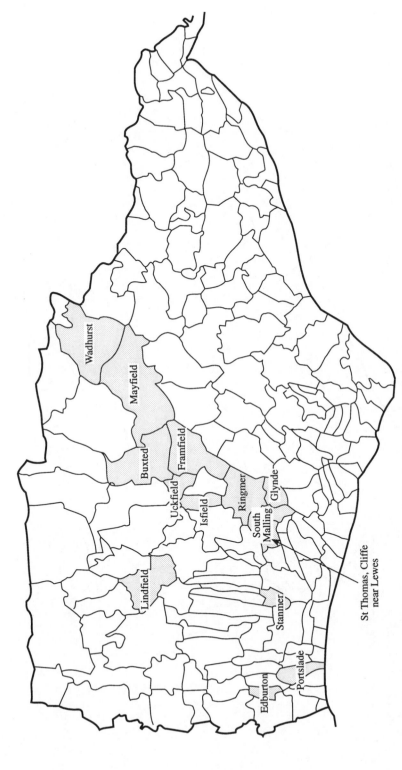

Map 4 *Peculiars in the diocese of Chichester (East Sussex)*

Wadhurst

Mayfield

Buxted

Framfield

Uckfield

Isfield

Ringmer

South
Malling

Glynde

Lindfield

Stanmer

Edburton

Portslade

St Thomas, Cliffe
near Lewes

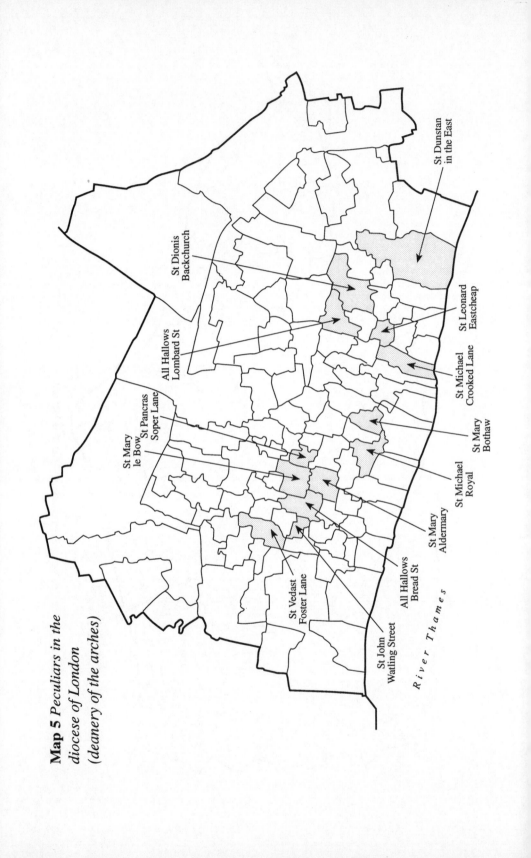

Map 5 *Peculiars in the diocese of London (deanery of the arches)*

St Dunstan in the East

St Dionis Backchurch

St Leonard Eastcheap

All Hallows Lombard St

St Michael Crooked Lane

St Mary le Bow

St Pancras Soper Lane

St Mary Bothaw

St Michael Royal

St Mary Aldermary

St Vedast Foster Lane

All Hallows Bread St

St John Watling Street

River Thames

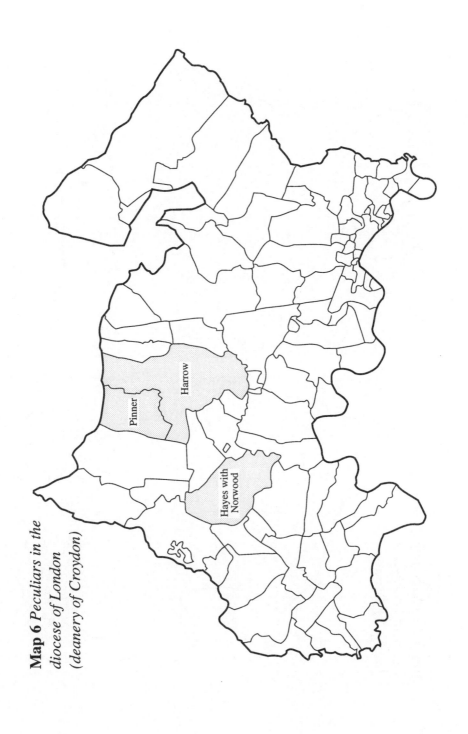

Map 6 *Peculiars in the diocese of London (deanery of Croydon)*

Pinner

Harrow

Hayes with Norwood

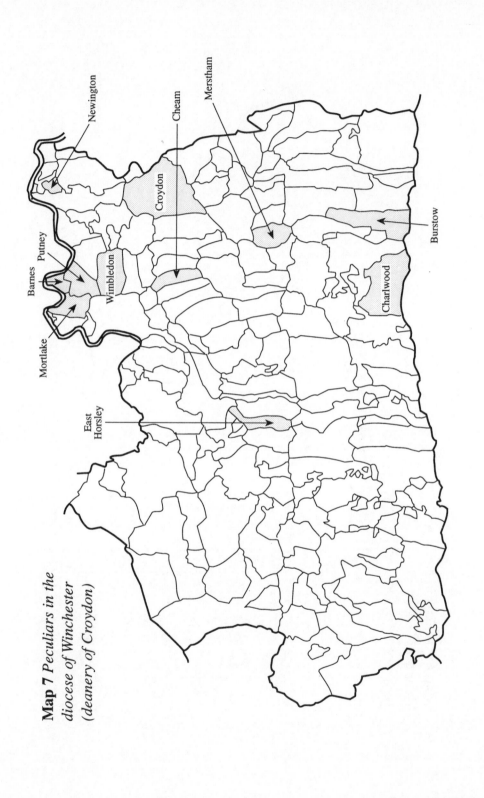

Map 7 *Peculiars in the diocese of Winchester (deanery of Croydon)*

Newington

Merstham

Cheam

Croydon

Burstow

Putney

Barnes

Wimbledon

Charlwood

Mortlake

East
Horsley

ARCHBISHOP SECKER'S SPECULUM

Page i

NB. Livings, the Tenths of which are here mentioned before the Certified value, were certified into the Exchequer, pursuant to Acts in Qu. Annes Time. The rest, of which the certified value is mentioned, were certified by ABP Wake to the Governors of the Queens Bounty, 26 July 1717. See Wakes Reg I. fol 342, 343. He doth not specifie, how the Value arises, though 1 Geo. I. c. 10 in Obedience to which he certified them, directs it.

The State of the Buildings, Quantity of Glebe, number of Bells, & other articles intermixed with these, are taken from Archdeacon Heads Parochial Visitation Book, 1759.

In Grindals Register fol 571 is a List of Benefices in the ABP[s] Gift copied into the Parochial Book 1663 differing in sev[l] particulars from the present List.

1758 Conf. by me & BP Yonge[1] of Bristol (c[d] not go to Cranbrook)   10344
1762 Conf. by BP Green[2] of Lincoln, the Gout preventing me. . .   7848
1766 Conf. by me & BP Keppel[3] of Exeter, at 14 places..   7852

[1] Philip Yonge (1709–1783), of Lisbon, Portugal, m. Trinity C 1728, scholar 1729, BA 1732, MA 1735, DD 1750, fellow, 1734, public orator, 1746–52, master Jesus C, 1752–58, vice-chancellor, 1752–4, V. Barrington, Cambs, 1748, V. Over, R. Loughton, Bucks, 1752, R. Therfield, Herts, 1757–62, preb of Westminster, 1750, preb of St Paul's, 1754–61, bishop of Bristol, 1758–1761, bishop of Norwich, 1761–83.
[2] John Green (1706?–1779), of Beverley, Yorks, m. St John's C 1724, scholar, BA 1728, MA 1731, BD 1739, DD 1749, fellow, 1731–50, regius professor of Divinity, 1748–56, master of CCCC, 1750–63, vice-chancellor, 1758, V. Hinxton, Cambs, 1731–47, R. Borough Green, 1747, R. Somersham, 1749–56, R. Barrow, Suffolk, 1750–62, dean of Lincoln, 1756, bishop of Lincoln, 1761–79, preb of St Paul's, 1771–9, royal chaplain, 1753–6.
[3] Frederick Keppel (1729–77), m. Christ Church 1747, BA 1752, MA 1754, DD 1762, canon of Windsor, 1754, archdeacon and preb of Exeter, 1762, dean and registrar of the order of the garter, 1765, bishop of Exeter, 1762–78, royal chaplain.

Page ii

Church of Canterbury 1758

D[r] John Lynch,[1] Dean, 10 Jan. 1733. died 25 May 1760.
William Freind[2] DD. June 1760.
John Potter[3] DD 19 Dec. 1766.
Brownlow North[4] L.L.D. Oct[r]. 6. 1770.
John Moore[5] prebendaries DD. Sept[r]. 19. 1771.
The Honourable & Reverend James Cornwallis[6] L.L.D. April 28 1775.
D[r] Sam. Holcombe[7] 12 Dec. 1721. Died Apr. 1. 1761.
D[r] Wm Ayerst[8] 28 Oct. 1724. died May 9. 1765.

⟨NB. *These three Prebends were granted by the Crown to the ABP 31 Aug 1 Ed 6. in exchange. See Chart. Misc. vol. 13 N°. 21. Valued in K[s] Books, each at 40[f]⟩.
*1. D[r] Wm Geekie[9], 17 June 1731. died July 22 1767.
D[r] John Griffith[10], 4 March 1737 died Mar. 9. 1765.
*6. D[r] Samuel Stedman[11], 8 Feb. 1738. Dead.
D[r] Francis Walwyn[12], 9 Apr. 1744.

3

D[r] John Potter[13] 25 Sept. 1745.
*4.D[r] Tho Tanner[14] 16 Jan 1745.
Dr Arthur Young[15] 27 June 1746. Dead 1759.
M[r] [now D[r]] William Tatton[16] 14 May 1754.
M[r] [now D[r]] Tho. Curteis[17] 8 May 1755. Richard Lucas[18] MA June 3 1775.
M[r] [now D[r]] John Davies[19] 26 May 1755. Died Jan or Feb. 1766.
D[r] John Head[20] 16 July 1759. died Dec[r.] 1769.
M[r] Geo. Secker[21] 1761. DD 1762. Resigned Apr. 15. 1766.
D[r] Dampier[22], inst. Apr. 4. 1765. Resign'd June 1769. Bennet Storer[23] D.D.
M[r] Richard Sutton[24] inst. June 3 1765. DD in 1766 Inst. July 1. 1769.
Lynford Caryl[25] D.D. March 1. 1766.
Heneage Dering[26] MA Apr. 28. 1766. DD the same year.
David Durell[27] D.D. Jan. 27. 1767. Edward Buckworth[28] Nov[r]. 6: 1775.
*1.John Benson[29] MA July 25. 1767. Ric[d.] Palmer[30] DD. Inst Dec[r]. 20. 1769.
*6.Geo. Berkeley[31] LLD. June 8. 1768 W[m] Barford[32] DD. Inst. June 20. 1770.

Six Preachers

M[r] Mich. Bull[33] 16 Feb. 1701. ord. Pr. Feb. 15. died 26 Aug. 1763.
D[r] Nicholas Carter[34] 20 Aug. 1726. Tho[s]. Pennington[35] DD. 1770.
M[r] Herbert Taylor[36] 17 Nov. 1726. died Sept. 29. 1763.
M[r] Thomas Rymer[37] 30 March 1734. Dead, 1759.
M[r] Edw. Lunn[38] 7 Nov. 1743. Dead July 30. 1764.
M[r] Geo. Sykes[39] 10 Sept. 1755. died June 9. 1766.
Mr John Benson[40] 7 Aug. 1759. Resigned July 1767.
M[r] Thomas Forster[41] 5. Oct 1763. died Sept. 13. 1764.
M[r] Robert Gunsley Ayerst[42], 1 Nov. 1763.
M[r] George Hearne[43] 1764.
M[r] John Derby[44] May 1766.
M[r] John Duncombe[45] July 8. 1766.
M[r] Tho. Thompson[46] Aug. 19. 1767. Osmund Beauvoir[47] M.A. June 16th 1773.

[1] (1692-1760), of Kent, m. St John's C 1714, BA 1718, MA 1721, DD 1728, R. All Hallows, Bread Street, London, 1723-30, R. Sundridge, 1727-33, R. All Hallows the Great, London, 1730-2, R. Ickham, 1731-60, R. Eynesford, 1731-60, R. Bishopsbourne, 1731-60, master of Harbledown Hospital, 1731, master of St Cross Hospital, Winchester, treasurer of Salisbury, 1735-60, preb of Canterbury (stall IV), 1728-34, dean of Canterbury, 1734-60.

[2] (1715-66), of Westminster, m. Christ Church 1731, MA 1738, DD 1748, R. & V. Witney, Oxon, 1739, R. Islip, 1747-8, royal chaplain, canon of Westminster, 1744-56, canon of Christ Church, Oxford, dean of Canterbury, 1760-66.

[3] (1713-70), son of archbishop John Potter, m. Christ Church 1727, BA 1731, MA 1734, BD 1741, DD 1745, V. Blackburn, Lancs, 1738-42, R. West Terring, Sussex, 1738-47, V. Elme cum Emneth (sine cure), 1739, V. Lydd, 1742-70, R. Chiddingstone, 1742-47, R. Wrotham, 1747-70, archdeacon of Oxford, 1741-66, preb of Canterbury (stall XII), 1745-1766, dean of Canterbury, 1766-1770.

[4] (1741-1820), m. Trinity O 1760, BA 1762, MA (All Souls) 1766, DCL 1770, fellow, canon of Christ Church, Oxford, 1768-70, dean of Canterbury, 1770-1, V. Lydd, 1770-75, V. Boxley, 1771-75, bishop of Coventry and Lichfield, 1771-74, bishop of Worcester, 1774-81, bishop of Winchester, 1781-1820.

[5] (1730-1805), of Gloucester, m. Pembroke O 1745, BA 1748, MA 1751, BD and DD 1763, canon of Christ Church, Oxford, 1763, tutor to the son of the duke of Marlborough, 1766, preb of Durham, 1769, dean of Canterbury, 1771-75, bishop of Bangor, 1775-83, archbishop of Canterbury, 1783-1805.

[6] (1742-1824), m. Christ Church 1760, BA 1763, MA (Merton) 1766, DCL 1775, R. Ickham,

1769-71, R. Adisham, 1770-1, V. Wrotham 1770-81, R. Boughton Malherbe, 1773-9, PC. Plaxtol, 1773-81, dean of Canterbury, 1775-81, R. Newington, Oxon, 1781-93, dean of Windsor, 1791, dean of Durham, 1794, bishop of Coventry and Lichfield, 1781-1824, 4th earl Cornwallis, 1823.

[7] (1666-1761), of London, m. Pembroke C 1684, BA 1686, MA 1689, DD 1717, fellow, 1687-93, V. Cherry Hinton, Cambs, royal chaplain, 1716, R. Grafton Flyford, Worcs, V. Severn Stoke, 1724, R. St Benets Gracechurch Street, London, 1728-49, PC. Christ Church, Old Southgate, preb of Canterbury (stall IX), 1721-61.

[8] (?1683-1765), of Kent, m. University 1700, BA 1703, MA 1707, BD 1717, DD (Lambeth) 1728, fellow Queens' C, 1718, chaplain to Lord Raby, R. Much Birch, Worcs, 1716, R. Little Birch, 1718, chaplain to Sir Robert Sutton, R. Gravesend, 1723-6, V. Northfleet, 1723-6, R. Stourmouth, 1726, St George's and St Mary, Canterbury, 1726, R. St Swithin's, London and North Cray, 1728, preb of Canterbury (stall III), 1724-65.

[9] (1690-1767), of London, m. St John's C 1706, BA 1711, MA 1714, BD (Queen's O) 1723, DD (Lambeth) 1729, chaplain to duke of Somerset, archbishop's chaplain, R. Southfleet, 1729-67, R. Chevening, 1730-32, R. Woodchurch, 1729-31, PC. Deal, 1730-53, R. All Hallows, Barking, 1733-67, R. Dursley, Glos, 1738-67, archdeacon of Gloucester, 1738-67, preb of Canterbury (stall I), 1731-67.

[10] (1696-1765), of Shropshire, m. University, 1712, BA (Christs) 1719, MA 1722, DD 1741, R. Eckington, Derby, 1721-65, R. Whiston, Yorks, 1738-49 and 1759-65, R. St Michael Queenhithe, London, 1739, R. Prestwich, Lancs, 1752-65, preb of Canterbury (stall II), 1738-65.

[11] (1701-68), of Bury St Edmunds, m. Caius C 1720, BA 1724, MA 1727, DD 1739, fellow 1725-38, R. Gaywood, Norfolk, 1738-68, R. Denver, 1738-69, chaplain to bishop of Bristol, royal chaplain, 1747-68, archdeacon of Norfolk, 1756-68, preb of Canterbury (stall VI), 1738-68.

[12] (1702-70), of Kent, m. University 1719, BA 1722, MA 1725, BD 1745, DD 1745, R. St Mary Bredin and St Andrew's, Canterbury, 1745-57, R. East Peckham, 1752-6, R. Great Mongeham, 1756-70, R. Adisham, 1757-70, preb of Canterbury (stall VII), 1744-70.

[13] See n. 3.

[14] (?1717-86), of Norwich, m. Christ Church 1734, BA 1737, MA 1744, DD (Lambeth) 1749, R. St Edmund and St Nicholas Acons, London, 1742-, R. Childerstone, 1742, R. Merstham, Surrey, 1742-5, R. Hadleigh and Monks Eleigh, 1745-86, dean of Bocking, 1761-86, preb of Canterbury (stall IV), 1746-86.

[15] (1693-1759), of Suffolk, m. Pembroke Hall C 1711, LLB 1716, LLD 1728, R. Bradfield Combust, Suffolk, 1719-59, R. Bradfield St Clare, 1719-59, V. Exning, 1748-59, chaplain to Arthur Onslow, speaker of house of Commons, preb of Canterbury (stall V), 1746-59.

[16] (1718-82) of Westminster, m. Merton 1735, BA 1738, MA 1741, preb of York, 1765-1782, R. of Rotherfield, Sussex, 1746?, R. West Chiltington, 1746, V. of East Peckham, 1766-75, R. St Dionis Backchurch, London 1775-82, preb of Canterbury (stall IX), 1754-1782.

[17] (1706-75), of Kent, m. Jesus C 1725, BA 1728, MA 1731, DD (Lambeth) 1758, V. Kemsing, 1739-44, V. Rottingdean, 1744-51, R. Sevenoaks, 1747-75, R. St Dionis Backchurch, London, 1756-75, preb of Canterbury (stall XI), 1755-75.

[18] (1725-89), of London, m. Merton 1742, BA 1746, DD (Lambeth) 1777, R. Wakerley, Northants, 1751-83, R. Edith-Weston, Rutland, 1753-86, R. Great Casterton, Northants, 1782-4, V. East Peckham, 1787-89, preb of Canterbury (stall XI), 1775-89.

[19] (1707?-66), of Kent, m. Christ Church 1726, BA 1729, MA 1732, DD (Lambeth) 1758, R. Hamsey, R. East Peckham, preb of Canterbury (stall X), 1755-66.

[20] (1702-69), of Kent m. Christ Church 1719, BA 1723, MA 1726, DD (Lambeth) 1749, R. St George's, Canterbury, 1730-60, V. Woodnesborough, 1730-36, V. Selling 1732, R. Burmarsh, 1737, R. Pluckley, 1735-60, R. Ickham, 1760-69, archdeacon of Canterbury, 1748-69, master of St John's Hospital, Canterbury and St Nicholas Harbledown, 1760-9, preb of Canterbury (stall V), 1759-69.

[21] (1723-68), of Coventry, m. Christ Church 1740, BA 1744, MA 1746, DD (Lambeth) 1762, V. Yardley and Sandon, Herts, 1752, V. St Mildred's Bread Street, London, 1755, R. Eynesford, 1760-63, R. All Hallows the Great and Less, London, 1761, R. Brasted, 1763, canon of St Paul's, 1754-68, preb of Canterbury (stall VIII), 1761-66.

[22] Thomas Dampier (17?-1777), of Blackford, Somerset, m. King's 1732, BA 1736, MA 1741, DD 1755, fellow 1732, preb of Canterbury (stall II), 1765-69, fellow of Eton 1767, canon of Windsor, 1769-74, preb of Durham, 1771-3, master of Sherburn Hospital, Durham, 1773-4, dean of Durham, 1774-7.

23 (1726-1804), of Leicestershire, m. Trinity C 1744, BA 1749, MA 1763, DD (Lambeth) 1775, R. Gunby, Lincs, 1750, R. Harby, 1763, preb of Canterbury (stall II), 1769-1804.

24 (1712-85), of Nottinghamshire, m. Wadham 1730, BA 1733, MA 1736, DD (Lambeth) 1766, R. Averham, Notts, 1740, R. Boothby Graffoe, Lincs, 1740, R. Whitwell, Derbs, 1752, preb of Canterbury (stall III), 1765-85.

25 (1712-85), of Nottinghamshire, m. Jesus C 1724, BA 1728, MA 1732, DD 1751, master 1751-81, vice-chancellor, 1758-9, 1773-4, V. Fordham, Cambs, 1735-5 and 1742-5, V. Comberton 1745, V. All Saints', Cambridge, 1748, V. Barnburgh, Yorks, -1781, preb of Canterbury (stall X), 1766-1781.

26 (1720-1802), of Ripon, m. St John's C 1737, BA 1741, MA 1744, DD (Lambeth) 1766, V. Tadcaster, Yorks, 1744-52, V. Burely-on-the-hill, 1752-61, PC. Wye, 1754, R. Milton Keynes, 1761-1801, chaplain earl of Winchilsea, preb of Canterbury (stall VIII), 1766-1802.

27 (1728-75), of Jersey, m. Pembroke O 1747, BA 1750, MA 1753, DD 1764, principal of Hertford, 1757-75, vice-chancellor, 1765-8, V. Ticehurst, preb of Canterbury (stall XII), 1767-75.

28 [Everard] Buckworth. (17?-92), of Lincolnshire, m. Trinity Hall 1747, adm. Lincoln's Inn 1747, LLD 1768, R. Washingborough, Lincs, R. Harrington, preb of Lincoln, 1773, preb of Canterbury (stall XII), 1775-1802.

29 (1724-1804), of Gloucester?, m. Trinity C, DD (Lambeth) 1770, V. Sibbertswold, 1759-61, R. Ruckinge, 1761-64, R. Great Chart, 1762-80, R. St Michael Royal, London, 1780-90, V. Boxley, 1784-1804, V. Littlebourne, 1789-93, six-preacher, 1759-67, preb of Canterbury (stall I), 1767-1804.

30 (1744-1805), of Lincolnshire, m. Jesus C 1732, BA 1736, MA 1766, DD (Lambeth) 1770, R. Scott Willoughby, Lincs, 1740, R. St Swithin's, London, 1776-1805, chaplain to house of Commons, preb of Canterbury (stall V), 1769-81.

31 (1733-1795), of London, m. Christ Church 1752, BA 1756, MA 1759, DCL 1763, R. Bray, Berks, 1759-95, chancellor of Brecon, 1762, R. Acton, 1764, V. Cookham, Berks, 1775, V. East Peckham, 1775-87, R. St Clement Dane, London, 1786-, preb of Canterbury (stall VI), 1786-95, V. Ticehurst, Sussex, 1792-5.

32 (17?-1792), of Chalbury, Dorset, m. King's C 1738, BA 1743, MA 1746, DD 1771, fellow 1741, taxor 1748-57, fellow Eton, 1784, proctor 1761-2, public orator, 1762-8, V. Milton, Cambs, 1751, V. Fordingbridge, Hants, 1768-73, R. Kimpton, Herts, 1773, R. All Hallows, Lombard Street, London, 1778-92, preb of Canterbury (stall VII), 1770-92, chaplain to the speaker of the house of Commons.

33 (1675-1763), of Westminster, m. CCCC 1692, BA 1696, MA 1699, fellow 1699-1702, V. Hougham, 1702-8, R. St James', Dover, 1702-8, R. Brasted, 1708-63, six-preacher, 1702-63.

34 (16?-1774), of Buckinghamshire, m. Emmanuel 1707, BA 1711, MA 1717, DD 1728, C. Sutton, 1716-55, V. Tilmanstone, 1716-55, V. Herne, PC. St George's Deal, 1718-57, R. Ham 1734-74, R. Woodchurch, 1755-74, six-preacher, 1726-1770.

35 (?-1802), of Canterbury, m. Exeter 1747, BA (Christ Church) 1751, MA 1754, B & DD 1770, six-preacher 1754-1802, R. Kingsdown, 1754-1802, C. Sutton, 1755-66, R. Tunstall, 1766-86, C. Eastry, 1790-1802.

36 (1698-1763), of Patrixbourne, Kent, m. St John's C 1714, BA 1718, MA 1721, fellow, 1720-7, C. St Margaret's, Canterbury, 1726, R. St Alphege, 1726-53, R. Hunton, 1728-63, V. Patrixbourne, 1753-63, six-preacher, 1726-63.

37 (1708-59), of Middlesex, m. Queens' C 1728, BA 1730, MA 1733, V. Barton, Cambs, 1733, V. Sibbertswold, 1752-59, six-preacher, 1734-59.

38 (1678-1764), of Kent, m. CCCC 1697, BA 1701, MA 1704, C. Nonington, 1705-64, R. Denton, 1705-64, six-preacher, 1743-64.

39 (1689?-1766), of London, m. Trinity C 1708, BA 1711, MA 1715, C. Eastchurch, 1713, V. Selling, 1714-16, V. Preston near Faversham, 1715-66, R. Hawkswell, Essex, 1731-57, R. Rayleigh, Essex, 1757-66, chaplain to bishop Hoadly, 1736, six-preacher, 1755-66.

40 See n. 29.

41 (1712-64), of Newcastle upon Tyne, m. Exeter 1728, BA 1731, MA 1734, C. Bicester, Oxon, 1734, C. Cuddesdon, R. Chartham, 1759-64, R. St George's and St Mary, Canterbury, 1760-64, six-preacher, 1763-4.

42 (1723-1816), of Shorne, Kent, m. University 1738, BA 1742, MA 1744, V. Holy Cross, 1747-83, V. Speldhurst, 1777, six-preacher, 1763-84.

[43] (1723–1806), m. Trinity Hall 1743, no degree recorded, R, St Alphage, 1761–1806, six-preacher, 1764–1806.

[44] (?1724–78), of Cowley, Middlesex, m. New College, 1741, BA 1745, R. Norton, 1765–67, six-preacher, 1766–78.

[45] (1729–1786), of London, m. CCCC 1745, MA 1752, C. Sundridge, 1753, V. West Thurrock, Essex, 1763– preacher St Anne's Soho, R. St Andrew's, Canterbury, 1757–86, V. Herne, 1773–86, master of Harbledown and St John's Hospital, 1786, six-preacher, 1766–86, chaplain to bishop Squire of St David's.

[46] (1708–73), of Gilling, Yorkshire, m. Christs 1728, BA 1749, MA 1735, fellow 1738–46, preacher Bunting, Walkhampton and Knapwell, Cambs, 1742, C. Fen Drayton, 1744, S.P.G. missionary to New Jersey, 1745–50 and to West Africa, 1751–6, V. Reculver, 1757–61, V. Elham, 1761–73, six-preacher, 1767–73.

[47] (1720–89), of Essex, m. St John's C 1738, BA 1743, MA 1746, DD (Lambeth) 1782, fellow 1746–51, V. of Calne, Wilts, 1749–53, V. Littlebourne, 1753–1789, V. Milton, 1764–89, PC. Iwade, 1766–, head-master, King's School, Canterbury, 1750–82, six-preacher, 1773–89), FSA 1784, FRS 1785.

Page iii

Archdeacon

M[r]. [now D[r]] William Backhouse[1] collated Dec[r]. 13. 1769.

[1] (1730–88), of Sebergham, Cumberland, m. Christs 1748, scholar 1748, BA 1752, MA 1755, DD 1771, fellow 1752, V. Meldreth, Cambs., 1764–67, R. St Mary le Bow, London, 1769–71, R. Ickham, 1771–88, V. Deal 1775–88, V. Coldred, 1775–88, master Eastbridge Hospital, 1777–88, archbishop's chaplain, archdeacon of Canterbury, 1769–88.

[Deanery of Bridge]

Page 1
D. Bridge
Adisham let by D[r] Regis[1] for 138[£] Staple for 120.

Adisham, R. Holy Innocents, cum Cap. Staple S[t] James. Exempt from AD[n]. ABP Patron. Kings Books 28-3-1½. Pres[t] value 200[£], if not 280[£]. Adisham hath 40 Houses: Staple 54. Here is Groves, belonging to D[r] Lynch[2], Dean of Canterbury. A Request for pulling down the Vicarage House of Staples, see in ABP Wakes Papers at Christ Church vol. 2. Service once at Church, once at Chapel, 3 miles off. Catechism expounded at each from Trinity Sunday all the Summer. 4 Sacramts. 20 Communicants at the Church: 30 or 40 at the Chapel. Prayers on good Friday & Christmass Day. Church & Chancel handsome & in good Order. Near 300[£] laid out on Ho. by D[r] Walwyn & much more wanted. Outho. in good Order. Glebe 8 Acres. 4 Bells. Staple Chapel & Chancel pretty good. Ho. a Cottage in good Repair. No outho. Glebe ½ Acre. 4 Bells.

Francis Walwyn[3] DD. R. Inst 19 Jan 1757. Resides chiefly at Canterbury: but almost constantly here on Sundays. R. also of Little Mongeham p. 189.
James Cornwallis[4] M.A. Inst. 1st Sept[r]. 1770.
John Lynch[5] DD. Col. March 30. 1771.

John Lucas[6], Cur. Resides. Salary 45$^£$. Gone to Ireland. Returns 1766.
Henry Shove[7] C. 1762 from Harrietsham. Lives betw. Ch & Chap. at Brooke near Wingham. 1765 Oct. obliged to remove to Betshanger, 4 miles off. Will quit the Curacy. See above.

1758 Confirmed, from Adisham 49: from Staple 48. 1762 Staple 17. Adisham 17. 1766. Adisham 23. Staple 21.

John Palmer[8] A.B. Rector 1781. resides.

[1] Balthazar Regis (169?-1757), of Ireland, m. TCD, BD (Cambridge) 1717, DD 1721, R. Adisham, 1717-57, R. Little Mongeham, 1719-57, chaplain to archbishop Wake, 1719, royal chaplain, 1725-57, canon of Windsor, 1751-7.
[2] See p. ii, n. 1.   [3] Ibid., n. 12.   [4] Ibid., n. 6.
[5] (1735-1803), of Kent, son of Dean Lynch, m. Christ Church 1753, BA 1757, MA 1760, DCL 1765, R. All Hallows, London 1761-71, R. Adisham, 1771-82, R. St Dionis Backchurch, London, 1782-1803, preb of Canterbury, 1781-1803, archdeacon of Canterbury, 1788-1803, master St John's & Harbledown hospitals, 1788-1803.
[6] Perhaps (1691-), of London, m. New Inn Hall O 1715, BA (Exeter) 1719, C. Bredhurst, 1726.
[7] (1731?-1773), of Canterbury, m. Wadham 1748, BA 1751, fellow, MA 1757, C. Rainham, 1758, Harriestham, Bredhurst, Betteshanger, Barfreston, PC. Sutton, 1766-1772, V. Lynsted, 1766-67, R. Little Mongeham, 1770-72, sequestrator of Newnham, 1770, V. Doddington, 1772-3.
[8] (17?-1818), of Lincolnshire, son of Prebendary Palmer (see p. ii, n. 30), m. St John's C 1774, scholar 1774, BA 1778, MA 1783, R. Adisham, 1781-1818.

Page 2
D. Bridge
Ash C. St Nicolas. belonged to the Coll. of Wengham. ABP P. 〈Adv. granted by Qu. Mary. Wilkins 4. 178〉. Exempt from AD^n. Certified 70$^£$: worth 80$^£$: of which 10$^£$ is reserved 〈by Juxon〉 in the ABP^s Lease of St Gregorys Priory 〈& 10$^£$ in that of Overland〉.[1]* 14 Villages, 310 families. Service once every Sunday [1759 twice 〈so 1764〉]. Prayers on Holydays & Wedn. Fr. in Lent, when Cat. is exp. 8 Sacram^{ts}: 100 Communicants. The Vicarage House doth not belong to the Minister, but is let out upon Lease. A school for 25 boys & 25 Girls, endowed by Gervase Cartwright[1] Esq & his 2 Sisters with a Farm of 35$^£$ a Year. Minister and Ch. W^{ns} & 3 others, Trustees.[2]*
[1]* & 50$^£$ in that of Ash to the Curate or Curates of Ash, Overland and Richborough. Of this 50$^£$, 33-6-8 was added by Juxon. Kennet, p. 256. 16-13-4 was pd by ABP in 1643. This last is called in the Book 1663 the old stipend. Lic. to Alex. Milles[2] to serve the Cure 1679 Entry B. 1V. 95. Another VI, 110, 381.

Benjamin Longley[3] Cur. 〈Lic〉 23 Aug. 1753. V. also of Tong p. 228. V. of Eynsford p. 356. & Cur of Woodnesborough p. 203. [1759 hath quitted Woodnesborough]. Resides in a hired House, near the Church.

Richard Laurence[4] 1783 – The Crown presented Archbishoprick vacant.
Robert Phillips[5] A.M. 1783.
Nehemiah Nisbett[6] 1784. does his own duty.

1758 Conf. 130. 1762. 64 1766. 117

[2)]* Church in pretty good Repair, & great Chancel. North Chancel much out of Order. Directed to be repaired. No Ho. or OutHo. 5 Bells. N. Chancel ⟨a fine Building with handsome monumts, wch adds both to the Strength and Beauty of the Church⟩ belongs to a Farm lately bought by Mr Allen[7] a Brewer & Dealer in Hops at Canterbury, called Moland Farm. The owner will resign his Title by Deed. ⟨Mr Milles[8] advises against this⟩. The Chw[n] is repairing it. A new window put in W. End of the Church. The Floor of the porch paved, & other necessary Repairs made. 1764 Mr Allen will repair Moland Chancel handsomely. Hath done it 1766.

[1] In 1720 and 1721. The two sisters were Eleanor and Anne: Hasted IX, p. 220.
[2] (16?-1714), PC. Ash, 1679-1714, V. St Clement's, Sandwich, 1680-1714.
[3] (17??-83), of Kent, m. Trinity Hall 1732, LLB 1738, R. Fenstanton, Hunts, 1739-50, V. Tonge, 1750-83, V. Eynesford, 1750-83, PC. Ash, 1753-83.
[4] (1709-72), of Wrockwardine, Shropshire, m. Pembroke O 1727, BA 1731, MA (Queens' C) 1739, V. Bredgar, 1745-72, V. Lenham, 1763-72, PC. Ash, 1783.
[5] (1722-1798), of Oxford, m. Wadham 1738, BA 1742, MA 1746, PC. Walmer, 1771-98, R. Ringwould, 1777-84, PC. Ash, 1783-4, V. Bekesbourne, 1784-98.
[6] Glasgow Coll, MA 1770, C. Eastry, 1777, PC. Ash, 1784-1802, V. Tilmanstone, 1788-1802, R. Tunstall, 1802-1812, C. Newington by Sittingbourne, 1810-12.
[7] William Allen bought Moland Farm in 1753 from Mrs Frances Rooke: Hasted IX, p. 200.
[8] Probably Richard Milles (c.1735-1820), MP for Canterbury, 1761-80. He leased Reculver and Herne parsonages from the archbishop: Hasted IX, p. 24.

Page 3

Beaksbourn ⟨called Livingsbourn by Somner p. 62. & often in the Lambeth Registers⟩ V. S[t] Peter. belonged to the Priory of S[t] Gregory. ABP P. Certified 69-12-8. Kings Books 6[£]. Now not 80[£]: of which 10[£] & 4 Quarters of Wheat & 18 Qrs of Barley are reserved in the ABPs Lease of S[t] Gregorys Priory. 41 Houses. Sir Tho. Hales[1] of Howletts. good. 2000[£] a year. ⟨Died Oct 6. 1762. His Son Sir Tho. Pym Hales[2]⟩. Here are Remains of ABP[s] Palace, a neat Dwelling. Usually the whole Service on Sundays: & morning Prayers on Holydays & Fridays. Cat on Sund. W. Fr. in Lent & several Sundays in the Summer. Lewis's Exp[3]. given to the Children. 8 Sacram[ts]: from 20 to 40 Com. Vicarage House very good: chiefly new built by Mr Bedford. Church & Chancel neat & in good Order. Large Garden. 2 Bells.

Will. Bedford[4] MA. V. 3 Aug 1726. R. of Smarden p. 72. Resides here. Serves no other Cure.
Robert Phillips[5] A.M. 1784. does his own duty.

1758 Conf 27. 1762. 21. 1766. 16

[1] (c.1694-1762), 3rd Bt, of Bekesbourne. MP for Minehead, 1722-27, MP for Camelford, 1727-34, MP for Grampound, 1734-41, MP for Hythe, 1744-61, MP for East Grinstead, 1761-2.
[2] (c.1726-73), MP for Downton, 1762-68, MP for Dover, 1770-3.
[3] John Lewis (1675-1747), of Worcester, m. Exeter 1694, BA 1697, MA (CCCC) 1712, R. Acrise 1699-1706, V. St John's Margate, 1706-47, R. Eastbridge, 1706-47, R. Saltwood, 1706-9, V. Minster 1709-47, master Eastbridge Hospital, 1719-47. His *The Church Catechism Explained. By way of Question and Answer and Confirmed by Scriptural Proofs* (1700) was a much used pastoral aid. By 1753 it had gone through 24 editions.

[4] (1701–83), of London, m. Clare 1719, BA 1723, MA 1726, V. Bekesbourne, 1726–83, R. Smarden, 1728–83.
[5] See p. 2, n. 5.

Page 4
D. Bridge

Bishopsbourn ⟨R. St Mary⟩ with Barham ⟨R.⟩. St John Baptist. ABP P. K^s books 39-19-2. In ABP Wakes Papers vol. 2. Bishopsbourn is said to be let at 90$^£$, Barham at 170$^£$. Now called 300$^£$ ⟨AD^n. 320$^£$⟩. Bishopsbourn 41 Houses. Stephen Beckingham[1] Esqr, married to a Daughter of Mr Sawbridge[2]. A Charity School, supported by the present Rector. Barham several villages, 125 Houses. Sir Edw. Deering[3] hath one in Right of his Lady: seldom there. M^r ⟨Henry⟩ Oxenden[4], son to Sir George[5], hath one, called Broom: usually there. ⟨A Charity School here also, as above⟩. At Bishopsbourn a Family of Quakers, pay all Dues without Compulsion. The whole Service is performed there on Sundays, & Prayers read on Holydays, when a Congregation can be got. Children catechized. 4 Sacram^{ts}. Usually above 20 Com. At Barham whole Service on Sundays Prayers on all Holydays, & then children Catechized, & W. Fr. in Lent. 8 Sacraments: 60 Com. often more. Pens. Prior. St Gregory 4$^£$ Ecton. Church & chapel & chancels handsome & in good Repair. Parsonage Ho. large & old & in good Repair: as also Out Ho. No Ho. at Barham, a very handsome Barn. Glebe of Church 2 Acres, of Chapel one. Each 4 Bells. See an acct of the place in J. Frosts Letter Aug 19 1760[6]. 1765 B^{ps}bourn besides Land adjoining to the House 107-15-0 Ded Land & Window Tax 13-6-6. Barham 226-10-0. Ded Land Tax 20$^£$. 1767 R will buy 2 Acres joining to the Glebe & designs to give it to the Rectory: hath laid out 1000$^£$.

John Lynch[7] DD. R. May 1. 1731. R. of Ickham p. 15. R. of Eynsford sine Cure p. 355. Dean of Canterbury, where he usually resides. Died May 25. 1760.
John Frost[8] MA ⟨R.⟩ 20 June 1760. R. also of Pluckley p. 69. Died Apr. 28 1765.
John Fowell[9] DD July 3. 1765 holds with it Chartham p. 7.

Cur. at Bishopsbourne, John Tucker[10], ⟨V. of Sheldwich p. 175⟩ 2^d Master of Canterbury School, where he resides [above 5 miles off. Occasional Duty done by Barret[11], Cur. at Kingston p. 16 wch adjoyns.]. Salary 40$^£$. Now, 1760, Cur. at Barham. Quits it Mich 1762. Mr Freeman[12] to come. See below.
Wm Taswell[13] min. Can. of Cant & V. of Brookland.

Cur. at Barham, Samuel Fremoult[14] R. of Wootton p. 109 which adjoyns. Salary 40$^£$. But Mr Tucker reads afternoon Prayers here also: & hath 10 Guineas from Mr Fremoult. Mr Fr. hath now, 1760 quitted this. Resides in the parish 1762. 1763 Doth occ. Duty for Mr Freeman, min. Can. of Cant. who resides there, but is Cur. here. 40$^£$. Afternoon prayers at 2 in Winter & 4½ in Summer. See p. 92.

Mr Davis[15]. Curate in 1786.

1758 Conf. from B^{ps}bourn 13, from Barham 73. 1762 B^{ps}bourn 8. Barham 17. Mr Tucker cd get no more. 1766 Bishopsbourn 15 Barham 65.

[1] Lived at Bourne Place from 1756 and married Mary Sawbridge: Hasted IX, p. 333.

[2] John Sawbridge (c.1732–95). Descended from an ancient and wealthy Kentish family settled at Olantigh in Wye. Supporter of John Wilkes. Founder member of society of Supporters of the Bill of Rights. Lord mayor of London, 1775.

[3] [Dering], (1706–62), 5th Bt. MP for Kent, 1733–54, and leader of the east Kent Tories.

[4] (1721–1803), 6th Bt.   [5] (1694–1775), 5th Bt. MP for Sandwich, 1720–54.

[6] Frost was Secker's nephew. See n. 8.   [7] See, p. ii, n. 1.

[8] (1719–65), of Nottingham, m. Exeter 1740, BA 1744, MA 1748, V. Sibbertoft and R. Lillingstone Lovell, Northants, 1754–60?, R. Bishopsbourne, 1760–65, R. Pluckley, 1760–65.

[9] (1725–1803), of Hilperton, Wiltshire, m. Exeter 1741, BA 1745, MA 1747, BD 1759, DD 1762, fellow 1745–64, proctor 1756, professor of moral philosophy, 1757–61, R. Bishopsbourne, 1765–1803, R. Chartham, 1764–1803, R. Old Romney, 1763–63, R. Hunton, 1763–65, R. Eynesford, 1763–1803.

[10] (1724–1776), of Kent, m. Trinity C 1739, BA 1744, MA 1751, R. Charlton, 1755–8, R. Ringwould, 1755–8, 1770–6, R. Sheldwich, 1757–76, PC. Thanington, 1764–76, R. Milton, 1764–70, 2nd master King's School, Canterbury, 1753–76.

[11] William, (1724–), of Canterbury, Kent, m. St John's C 1742, BA 1746.

[12] Thomas Freeman, (1726–1808), of Oxford, m. Christ Church 1744, BA (New College) 1751, MA 1752, R. Old Romney 1763–88, R. St Paul and St Martin's, Canterbury, 1788–1808, minor canon of Canterbury, 1762–1808.

[13] (1709–?), of Newington, Surrey, m. Christ Church, 1727, BA 1731, MA 1734, C. Hawkhurst, 1737–39, R. Almondsbury, Glos, 1755–64, V. Wotton-sub-Edge, Glos, 1755?–, V. Brookland, 1764–71, minor canon of Canterbury, 1764.

[14] Of Kent, m. CCCC 1727, BA 1731, C. St John's Thanet, 1736, R. Wootton, 1739–79.

[15] Henry Montague Davis (1755–1807), of Westminster, m. Christ Church 1770, BA 1774, MA 1779, C. Bishopsbourne, 1789, V. Westwell, 1790–1803, V. Eynesford, 1791–1807, R. Bishopsbourne, 1803–7, chaplain to Viscount Sackville.

Page 5

Boughton alias Bocton Aluph V. All S[ts]. Moyle Breton[1] Esqr P. belonged to the College of Wye. Kings books 6–5–0. Certified 58–6–10. Now called 60[f] ⟨AD[n] 70[f]⟩. 50 Houses. Service once on Sundays, bec. the People chuse to hear ✓ Sermons in Afternoons. [1759 Service twice : but V. saith they will not come. Told him, he shd read Lectures on the Catechism]. Pr. on Ash W. Pr. & Sermon on good Fr. & Whitsun – Tuesday. The last called a Charity Sermon. ⟨1[f] given for it⟩. Qu abt. Chr. Day. Cat. in Lent. 4 Sacram[ts]: 40 Com. 6 Alms Houses, built either by the Moyles or the Finches: long repaired by the Parish. 50[s] a year pd to the poor out of some Lands by the Vicar, parish officers & chief Inhabitants. Ch. & Chancel neat & in good order. Ho. very neat & pretty. Out Ho. in good Repair. Glebe 21 Acres. 5 Bells.

Rob[t] Breton[2] LL.B V. 1752. R. of Kenardington p. 126 ⟨where see⟩. Cur. of Ruckinge p. 139. Lives near. His House repairing. [1759 Resides]. March 1760 serves Bilsington p. 112. 10 miles off. I allow it for a time. Sept. 1760 H. Friend[3], Cur. of Bilsington. May 1761, Mr Br officiates twice, & 1764. 1768 hath resigned Kenardington where see. Serves this only once, & Eastwell ⟨p. 60⟩ once for 17[f]. L[d] Winchelsea[4] objects. To serve Brook p. 6.

1758 Conf 20. 1762. 33. 1766. 14

[1] According to W. Berry, *Kent Genealogy* (1830), Moyle Breton died in 1735.

[2] (1726–1808), of Kennington, Kent, son of Moyle, m. St John's C 1745, LLB 1751, fellow All Souls, V. Boughton Aluph, 1752–1808, R. Kenardington, 1753–68, C. Upchurch, 1758, C. Ruckinge.

3 Henry (1737–1805), of Birchington, Kent, m. St John's C 1755, scholar, BA 1759, MA 1764, R. Frittenden, 1761–1805, C. Burmarsh, C. Bilsington, C. Aldington.
4 Daniel Finch (?–1769), 8th earl of Winchilsea and 3rd earl of Nottingham. He was the patron of Eastwell.

Page 6
D. Bridge
Bridge See p. 30

Brook R. St Mary. Ch. of Canterbury P. ⟨Tenths 14–8½⟩. Certified 30^f. Augm with 400^f ⟨See below⟩. 1724 Purchase made, ⟨1736⟩ which brings in 16^f. ⟨56 AD^n⟩. 20 Houses. Service once. Children said to be too small for cat. See my Letters upon this. 3 Sacram^{ts} [1759. 4]. 20 Com. Dean Godolphin^1 gave 100^f DCh of Canterbury 100^f: the Queens bounty 200^f. A purchase made 1736. Church & Chancel very indifferent. Ho. mean, in pretty good Repair. Glebe 9 Acres. 3 Bells.

John Gostling^2 MA. R. ⟨18 July 1751⟩. Cur. of Nackington p. 43. lives with his Father^3 at Canterbury.

Ph. Warham^4 Cur. V. of Kennington p. 67 3 miles off. Salary 20^f & Surplice Fees. Resigns it Mich 1767, Mr Apsley^5 to serve it with Smeeth p. 110. Jan. 1768 Going to Ruckinge. LD Mr Breton^6 of Boughton p. 5 to serve it. Robert Breton Cur Sal £21.

1758 None conf. 1762. 20. 1766. 17.

1 Henry Godolphin (1648–1733), of Godolphin, Cornwall, m. Wadham 1664, BA 1668, MA 1672, B & DD 1685, fellow All Souls, 1668, fellow Eton, 1677, provost, 1675, preb of St Pauls, 1683–1733, dean of St Paul's, 1707–26.
2 (1725–1804), of Canterbury, Kent, m. Pembroke C 1743, BA (CCCC) 1748, MA 1751, R. Brook, 1751–1804, R. Milton, 1770–1804, V. Alkham, 1784–6, R. St Peter's, Canterbury, 1786–1804.
3 William Gostling (1696–1777), of Canterbury, Kent, m. St John's C 1712, BA 1716, MA 1719, C. Littlebourne, 1720, R. Brook, 1722–33, V. Littlebourne, 1733–53, V. Stone-in-Oxney, 1753–77, minor canon of Canterbury, 1727–77.
4 Philip, of Kent, m. Jesus C 1721, BA 1724, C. Crundale, 1726, V. Kennington, 1730–77.
5 Probably William Apsley (1741–?), of Ashford, Kent, m. Merton 1757, BA 1761, C. Luddenham, 1763–66, C. Rainham, 1765 to Deal chapel.
6 See p. 5, n. 2.

Page 7
Chartham St Mary, with Chapel of Horton, demolished ⟨now private property⟩ R. ABP P. Kings Books 41–5–10. Now 210^f [1749. 250^f]. 4 miles long. Two Boroughs, Raddington & Shelmsford. 104 Houses. Sir Will. Fagg^1 Bar^t. I think 7 or 800^f a year. 2 Families of Quakers. No Difficulty in getting their Tithes. Whole Service on Sundays. Morning Prayers every Holyday & W. Fr. in Lent. Cat. Exp. on Sundays in Lent. 4 Sacramts: 60 Com. Very bad House, large. Church & Chancel large & handsome. Glebe 31 Acres. 6 Bells. Mr Kingsford^2, married a prostitute. A Ho. called the Vicarage, ruinous, of no Use.

Geo. Fawler Tilsley[3] LLB. R. 14 Dec. 1724. Suspended & sequestred, lives at Chipping Norton. [1759 Died there in June.

Tho. Forster[4] MA. F. of Univ. Coll R. 13 June 1759. Goes to reside next Spring. Apr. 1763 M[r] Gregory[5] doth week day Duty & preaches 13 Serms. 20[f]. died Sept. 13 1764.

John Fowell[6] DD R. Oct 6 1764. R. of Hunton p. 364. V. of Eynesford p. 355.

Geo. Lynch[7] Cur. Son to D[r] Lynch[8] the Physician, good. Resides. Salary 40[f] March 1760. Gone to Charing. Returned. Gone to Lympne.

James Smith[9], was a popish priest. R. of Eastbridge.

M[r] Stock[10]. Curate.

1758. Conf. 38. 1762. 42. 1766. 61.

[1] (c.1726–91), 5th Bt.

[2] William Kingsford who, until 1768, owned a large house in the parish: Hasted VII, p. 298.

[3] (1695–1759), of London, m. New College 1713, BCL 1717, R. Chartham, 1724–59.

[4] See p. ii, n. 41.

[5] Presumably Francis Gregory (1721–1801), of Wotton-sub-Edge, Glos, m. Christ Church 1739, BA 1742, R. Brook, 1746–51, V. Milton 1751–64, R. St George and St Mary, Canterbury, 1764–1777, C. Thannington, 1777–1801, V. Stone, 1777–1801, minor canon of Canterbury.

[6] See p. 4, n. 9.

[7] (–1789), of Canterbury, Kent, m. CCCC 1750, BA 1754, MA 1757, fellow, 1758–65, C. Charing and Chartham, 1760, C. Dymchurch, V. Lympne, 1765–89, R. Cheriton w. Newington, 1770–89.

[8] Of Staple, Kent m. St John's C 1717, MB 1722, MD 1727.

[9] (17?–84), of Lisbon, received into C of E 1765, MA (Lambeth) 1781), R. Eastbridge, 1765–84, V. Alkham, 1772–84, poor vicar, 1772, V. St Cosmus Blean, 1781–84, archbishop's chaplain, 1781.

[10] John Agge Stock (1725–92), of Didcot, Oxon, m. Oriel 1741, BA (All Souls) 1744, MA (Exeter) 1747, C. Chartham, 1758, C. Charing, 1763, V. Postling, 1767–92, six-preacher, 1789–92.

Page 8

D. Bridge

Chilham ⟨S[t] Mary⟩ with Molash, S[t] Peter. V. belonged to the Abbey of Syon. M[r] ⟨Rob[t]⟩ Colebrook[1] P. Lives here in Chilham Castle. Kings books 13-6-8. Now 150[f] ⟨AD[n] 170[f]⟩. Chilham, 128 Houses, 130 Families. Molash, 50 Houses, 62 Families. One Sunday, whole Service at Chilham: the next, Prayers & Sermon once there & at Molash. They are united Parishes. The Churches 3 miles distant. Prayers, Sermon, Sacramt at Chilham on good Friday. Prayers on Holy days, W. & Fr. in Lent, when the Catechism is expounded, & every day in Passion Week. Two Sacramts there every quarter, 80 or 90 Com. One at Molash, 30 or 40 Com. The Vicarage House built by M[r] Colebrook, the inside not finished. M[r] Colebrooks Estate is charged with 20[f] a year for the poor, by the Will of Sir Dudley Diggs[2]: & he hath not paid it these 4 Years. AD[n] Head sent to him abt it. See AD[n]s Letter Aug. 24. 1759 & Aug 29. Church & Chancel large & handsome. Ho. new built, handsome, not finished. Out ho. very bad. Repaired 1760. Glebe 23 Acres. 6 Bells ⟨one cracked. See Mr Colebrookes Letter. All new cast⟩. Chapel & its chancel mean & indifferent. No Ho. 3 Bells. Aug 1761 M[r] Colebrooke is sd to have sold the Advowson for 1000[f] in favour of M[r] Kenrick[3] of Bennet Col. The next Turn only is sold. See M[r] Kenricks Letter 26 Feb. 1762[4].

Seq. of it granted 20 Sept. 1737 Entry B. VIII. 87.

Wadham Knatchbull[5] D.D or LLD. V. 2 March 1738. Prebendary of Durham. Resides there. See Letters. Pleads Sickness. Died on or before Dec. 30 ⟨27⟩ 1760.

Philip Francis[6] MA V. 15 June 1761. Will reside, but keep Curate. Void by Cession on or before Feb. 1. 1762.

Jarvis Kenrick[7], presented by John Skey[8] of Aldenham Co. Hertf. Esqr patron for this turn, V. July I 1762. 1764 Resides, & behaves well.

Ant. Lukyn[9] Cur. was of Christ Church. Behaves regularly AD^n May 1759. Vicar resides.

1758 Conf. Chilham 55 Molash 20. 1762. Chil. 30 Mol. 4. 1766 Chilham 45 Molash 18.

[1] The family had owned Chilham Castle from 1724. Robert died in 1784: Hasted VII, p. 275.
[2] [Digges], (1583–1639), diplomatist and judge.
[3] Jarvis Kenrick (1737–1808), of London, m. CCCC 1755, BA 1759, scholar 1761, MA 1763, C. Histon, Cambs, 1762, V. Chilham, 1762–1808.
[4] This particular letter has not survived. But see LPL, MS Secker 3, ff. 145–6, Matthew Kenrick (Jarvis' father) to Secker, 26 April 1762, and Secker's reply, f. 147, 28 April. Secker delayed Jarvis's institution on the grounds of ignorance of the Bible.
[5] (1708–60), of Mersham, Kent, m. Trinity Hall C 1725, LLB 1730, LLD 1741, fellow 1731–9, V. Chilham, 1739–1760, preb of Durham, 1738–60, chancellor diocese of Durham.
[6] (1706–73), of Dublin, m. TCD 1724, BA 1728, R. Skeyton, Norfolk, 1744–73, V. Chilham, 1761–2, chaplain Chelsea Hospital, 1764–8, R. Barrow, Suffolk, 1762–73.
[7] See n. 3.
[8] Hasted calls him John Key: VII, p. 292.
[9] (1727–78), of Canterbury, Kent, m. Christ Church 1744, BA 1748, MA (Kings C) 1773, C. Chilham, V. Reculver, 1762–79, R. St Mildred's, Canterbury, 1772–78.

Page 9

Chillenden, al. Challenden, al. Cholmden ⟨al Chelmden al. Chelynden⟩. All Sts V. Pens. Prior. de Ledes 8^s. Ecton. King, P. ⟨Tenths 10^s⟩. Certified 26$^£$. Now 40$^£$ ⟨See below⟩. 18 Houses. Service once a fortnight, as usual, on Sundays. Directed to be every Sunday. See Letters[1]. Will be so, AD^n May 1759. Land Tax 5$^£$. Other Deductions considerable. The House very mean, fit only for a Labourer. No Offertory: 4 Sacramts: 15 Com. Church & Chancel bad & dirty. Ho. mean, in tolerable Repair. Out Ho. Repair wanting. Glebe 2 Acres. 1 Bell. 1767 augm with 400$^£$ by Sir Ph. Boteler & Qu^s bounty.

Josias Pomfret[2] MA. R. 20 Nov. 1725. R. of Snave p. 144. Cur. of Ickham p. 15. where he resides. Hath 200$^£$ a year estate. 1765 hath lost his Voice by a paralytick stroke.

Robert Pitman[3] Clerk, Rector Janry 4; 1776. resides.

Fra. D'Aeth[4] Cur. R. of Knowlton p. 187. just by, where he resides. Cur. also of Beauxfield, p. 77. Mr Del'Angle Junr[5], Cur of Walmer p. 201, Serves this also. Oct. 1759 Hath quitted it to his Father[6], who serves it (with Goodneston p. 13) 20$^£$. May 1761. M^r D'Aeth serves this with Knowlton p. 187. So 1764. Wm Windle[7] P. Cur. here & at Knowlton p. 187 where see.

1758 Conf. 4. 1762. 4 1766. 10.

[1] LPL, MS Secker 3, f. 253, Secker to Pomfret, 24 November 1758.

[2] (1697-1776), of Biddenden, Kent, m. CCC0, BA 1719, MA 1722, R. Chillenden, 1725-76, R. Snave, 1753-76, C. Ickham.

[3] (17?-1807), 'literate', C. Appledore, 1771, R. Chillenden, 1776-1807, V. Westcliffe, 1784-1807, poor vicar, 1804.

[4] (1725-84), of Knowlton, Kent, m. Wadham, 1743, C. Whitfield, 1753-84, R. Knowlton, 1753-84, V. Godmersham, 1767-71.

[5] John Maximilian De L'Angle (1727-83), of Tenterden, Kent, m. Christ Church 1744, BA 1748, MA 1752, PC. Walmer, 1757-70, C. Goodneston, C. Betteshanger, C. Barfreston, R. Danbury and R. Woodham Ferrers, Essex, 1770-83.

[6] Theophilus De L'Angle, (1695-1763), of Newnham, Kent, m. Christ Church 1712, BA 1716, MA 1719, V. Tenterden, 1723-63, V. Snargate, 1756-63.

[7] Univ of Aberdeen, ordained priest in 1767.

Page 10

D. Bridge

Crundall R. S[t] Mary. Pens. Prior. de Ledes 35[s] Ecton. S[r] Edw. Filmer[1] Bart P. K. Books 11-10-10. Now 100[£]. 25 Houses. Service once on Sundays [1759 twice]. Prayers, Chr. Day, good Fr. Easter Tuesday, Ascension. 4 Sacramts, 15 Com. Cat. in Summer, not exp. A Gift of 4[£] a year for teaching Cat. A good Parochial Library, given by M[r] Forster[2], formerly Rector; who gave the former and other Charities, which see. Church & Chancel very neat. Ho. of Brick, new, very handsome built by M[r] Forster. Out Ho. in good Repair. Glebe 9 Acres: 6 more given by M[r] Forster. 3 Bells. Very small congregation, wn there is no Sermon. M[r] Forsters will bears date 15 Nov. 1728. See it. He gives in it to ⟨the Filmer family for⟩ his Successors 3 Acres of Land, a Rent charge of 4[£] & another of 2[£].

Edm. Filmer[3] R. 27 June 1751. Resides, good. Preached Vis. Serm. 1758. 13 Dec 1759 R. of Hinxhill p. 122.

1758 Conf. 16 1762. 14 1766. 17.

[1] (1683-1755), 3rd Bt.

[2] Richard Forster (1651-1728), of Chester, m. Brasenose 1666, BA 1669, MA 1673, usher of Free School Tonbridge and schoolmaster Town Sutton, R. Beckley, Sussex, 1682-99, C. Ulcombe, R. Crundale, 1698-1729, V. Eastchurch, 1699-1729.

[3] (1727-1810), 6th Bt, of East Sutton, Kent, m. CCCO 1745, BA 1749, MA 1752, R. Crundale 1751-1806, R. Hinxhill, 1759-70, chaplain to Lady Mary Raymond.

Page 11

Elmston R. Henry Partridge[1] Esq[r] P. ⟨of Kings Lynn, Norfolk⟩. Kings Books 6-7-8½. Certified 69-2-2. Now called 70[£]. 7 Houses. No Rector hath resided for 70 years past. The Parsonage House is unfit. Service once. [1759 twice]. Two other churches within a mile. Cat. exp. in Lent. 4 Sacram[ts]: 12 or 14 Com. Church & chancel clean and handsome. Ho. & Out Ho. pretty good, in good Repair. Glebe 10 Acres. 2 Bells.

David Turner[2] MA, ⟨pres. by King, on Lapse⟩ R. 13 Apr. 1745. Resides at Fordwich, 6 miles off. I blamed him for this, & the half Service, at the Visitation: & then, having heard, that he had been suspended for having a

Bastard, & thinking by mistake, that it was lately, I exhorted him, in general words, to behave properly. He said, he always had. I intimated a Doubt of it. But being instantly told by a note from D[r] Potter[3], that probably I had been misinformed, I said openly in Court, that I apprehended I had. And learning afterwards, that he was believed innocent, & he not coming to Dinner, I begged his pardon the next Day by a Letter. He only said to the Servant, that it required no Answer. Died some time before Oct 16. 1765.

Tho. Hutchesson[4] AB Nov. 4. 1765. Cur of S[t]. Nicolas, Lynn. Will reside at Mich. 1767 Lives at Preston near Wingham, close by.
Robert Stedman[5] A.M. 1789 dead.
John Gregory[6] A.M. 1792.

M[r] Stedman, Cur. Sal £20.

1758 Conf. 9. 1762. None. 1766. 4.

[1] Recorder of Kings Lynn, who died in 1793: Hasted IX, p. 133.
[2] (1704–65), of Margate, Kent, m. St John's C 1720, BA 1725, MA 1728, C. Hunton, 1729, R. Elmstone 1745–65.
[3] See p. ii, n. 3.
[4] (1726–89), of Wisbech, Cambs, m. Magdalene C 1743, BA 1748, R. Crostwick, Norfolk, 1756–89, R. Elmstone, 1765–89, V. Northbourne, 1772–89.
[5] (1743–92), of Kent, m. Peterhouse 1763, BA 1766, MA, 1773, V. Preston by Wingham, 1767–92, V. Willesborough, 1773–89, R. Elmstone, 1789–92.
[6] (1767–1839), of Canterbury, Kent, m. Lincoln, 1784, BA 1787, MA 1791, C. Walmer and East Sutton, 1789, C. Patrixbourne, 1790, V. Preston by Wingham, 1792–1828, R. Elmstone, 1792–1839.

Page 12
D. Bridge
Godmersham V. S[t] Laurence, with Challock Cap. S[t] Cosmus and Damian. Exempt from AD[n]. ABP P. Appr. to Ch. of Canterbury. K[s] books 9–3–9. Now 70[f] ⟨60 AD[n]. Betw. 90 & 100[f] see M[r] Knights[1] Letter⟩. Augm. with 10[f] from DCh. Cant. Doth that make part of the 70[f]? The Chapel hath an Augm. of 10[f] from the gr. Tithes, wch belong to Sir Rich. Lloyd[2] ⟨as Lessee to ABP. reserved by his Lease from Juxon's time⟩. Is that part of the 70[f]? Godmersham hath 52 Houses. Tho. Knight Esq[r]. Changed his Name from Brodnax, to May, thence to Knight, for Estates, ***. Challock 44 Ho. Service once at church, once at Chap. & on the chief Holydays at Church. 4 Sacramts at each: 50 or 60 Com. at Church: 20 or more at Chapel. Cat. on Sundays in Lent. V. will expound. Benefactions to the poor, which see. Church & chancel handsome. Ho. new built of Brick, very neat. Stable in good Order. 5 Bells. Challock Church & chancel very dirty ⟨not repaired May 1765, 1766⟩. No Ho or Out Ho. 4 Bells. Chancel belongs to the Son of the late Sir Rich[d] Lloyd. He lives in Town: perhaps in Qu[s] square, as his Father did. See p. 67. Lic. to take down S. Isle of Church &c Entry B VII. 342

Aden Ley[3] BA V. 13 Feb. 1752. Resides 10 or 11 months in a year. 1766 Disorderd in his Head. December 8. 1766. dead.

Lewis Pugh[4]. BA V. 18 March 1767. Was C. to D[r] Burton[5]. To reside before Mich. Void by Cession abt May 20 1767.

Francis D'Aeth[6] 7 July 1767 holds it with Knowlton & Whitfield. To reside here. Coming Mich 1767.

Pierce Dod[7] V. 19 June 1772.

Francis Whitfeld[8] Clerk, Vicar, June 3: 1778. resides.

1758. Conf. 77. 1762. 23. Challock 17 1766. Godm. 26. Challock 14.

[1] Thomas Knight (?1701–71), MP for Canterbury, 1734–41. Changed name by private act of parliament, in 1727 from Brodnax to May, and in 1738 to Knight. On that occasion one MP is alleged to have proposed 'a general bill to enable that gentleman to take what name he pleases.'

[2] (c.1696–1761), of Hintlesham Hall, Suffolk. MP for Mitchell, 1745–7, MP for Maldon, 1747–54, MP for Totnes, 1754–59. In 1745 the widow of the 3rd earl of Winchelsea died, leaving Lloyd the whole of her estate.

[3] (1726?–66), of Staffordshire, m. Emmanuel 1745, BA 1749, V. Godmersham, 1753–66.

[4] (1722–17?), of Dolgelly, Merioneth, m. Magdalene C 1740, BA 1744, V. Godmersham 1767–7.

[5] Probably John Burton, (1696–1771), of Devon, m. CCCO 1713, MA 1720, DD 1752, V. Mapledurham, Oxon, 1734–66, R. Worplesdon, Surrey, 1766–71.

[6] See p. 9, n. 4.

[7] [Dodd], (1736–), of London, m. University 1753, BA (All Souls) 1756, V. Godmersham, 1772–8.

[8] (1743–1810), of Ashford, Kent, m. University 1753, BCL 1804, C. Newchurch, 1766, V. Godmersham, 1778–1804, R. Westbere, 1804–10.

Page 13

Goodneston by Sandwich ⟨Wingham⟩ Cur. Holy Cross. Not certified. Appr. to Ch. of Cant. ABP. of Cant. P. But Ecton saith, Sir Brooke Bridges Bart[1)*]. 33[£]. 58 Ho. Sir Brooke Bridges[1], young, a large Estate. Service once on Sundays. No mention of Holydays. Cat. in Lent. 4 Sacramts. 30 Com. No Offertory. An Hospital for 4 Persons, who have each 5 Guineas yearly: vested in Trustees by Gabriel Richards[2] Esq[r]. Cur. (see below) in his Answers to Inquiries abt Tenterden calls this, his Donative: & saith, his Patron calls it, Royal Peculiar. Church & chancel in good Repair. No Ho or out Ho. 4 Bells.

[1)*] Godneston, the Advowson of it granted to the See of Canterbury by Qu. Mary. Wilkins Conc. vol 4. p. 178. There is another near Feversham

NB. Sir Brooke Bridges forbids the minister to take a License or attend Visitations. He holds Chislett Park of the ABP by a Lease for Lives. W[n] he comes to renew, it will be proper to settle the matter of Goodneston with him. 1766 he gives up his Claim.

Lewis, in his MS Notitia, saith, p. 114. that a yearly pension of is pd to the Cur. out of the Exchequer: & that Gabr. Richards of Roling in this parish Gent who died Sept. 17 1672 gave to the Use of the Minister a Ho. & Orchard value 6–10–0 a Year; & to 4 single men & women an Alms Ho. with Lands of 20[£] a year, his Relations to have the Preference.

Theoph. De L'Angle[3] Cur. V. of Tenterden p. 73. R. of Snargate p. 143. Resides here, good. Cur also, Oct. 1759 of Chillenden p. 9. May 1761, unable to officiate: neighbouring Clergy do it. Dead.

John Maximilian Del'Angle[4], son to the above. May 1765 serves it & Walmer p. 201 once.

Mr Thomas[5] assis[t]. Cur.

1758 Conf.32. 1762. 14. 1766. 26.

[1] (1732–91), of Goodnestone Park. 3rd Bt. MP for Kent, 1763–74.
[2] His will of 1671 said that only people born in Kent should live there: Hasted IX, p. 247.
[3] See p. 9, n. 6   [4] Ibid., n. 5.
[5] William Thomas (17?–1803), of Kent, m. CCCC 1766, BA 1771, C. Eastry, 1772, V. St Mary, Sandwich, 1775–1803, PC. Goodnestone near Wingham, 1793–1803, poor vicar.

Page 14
D. Bridge
Hardres great or upper, R. S[t] Peter & Paul: with Stelling Cap. S[t] Mary. Sir Will. Hardres Bart[1] P. Ks. Books 19–13–1½. Now 110[£]. Hardres hath 40 Ho. Sir Will. Hardres, Bart ⟨1000[£]⟩. *** Stelling 50 Ho. A small Anabaptist meeting. No settled Teacher. A few Families of them. Service once a Sunday. 4 Sacramts, 20 or 30 Com. at each. Two miles asunder. Catechizing on Week Days. Prayers then, not on others. [But I suppose on the chief Holidays]. Church & chancel indifferent. Ho & Out Ho. neat & in good order, by Mr Cobb. Glebe 33½ Acres. 3 Bells. Chapel & its chancel in good Repair. No Ho. Glebe 8 Acres. 3 Bells.

Tho. Cobb[2] BA, R. 21 Sept 1750. Good. Resides. Cur. of Fairfield p. 121. R. of Hope p. 123.
John Charles Beckingham[3] L.L.B. 1794.

Mr Benson[4] Cur. Sal £50.

1758 Conf. Hardres 22 Stelling 15. 1762 Hard. 16. Stell. 17. 1766 Hardr. 12. Stelling 17.

[1] (1718–64), 5th Bt.
[2] (1703–1794), of New Romney, Kent, m. Oriel 1720, BA 1724, C. Fairfield, 1734, C. Lydd, 1734, R. Upper Hardres, 1750–94, R. Hope, 1759–94, chaplain to Lord Bellenden.
[3] (17?–1807), of Kent, m. Trinity Hall 1782, LLB 1788, C. Lympne and Burmarsh, 1784, C. Upper Hardres and Stelling, 1790, R. and patron Upper Hardres, 1794–1807.
[4] Probably Martin Benson, (1761–1833), of Canterbury, Kent m. Jesus C, 1779, BA 1782, MA 1785, C. St Michael Royal, London, 1783, V. King Charles the Martyr, Tunbridge Wells, 1786–1829, R. Orgarswick, 1788–91, R. St Dunstan's in the East, London, 1790–91, R. Merstham, Surrey, 1791–1833.

Page 15
Ickham ⟨al. Ilkham⟩ R. S[t] John, with Weld ⟨al. Well⟩ Chap. [{I believe} demolished] Exempt from AD[n]. ABP P. K[s] Books 29–13–4. Now 240[£] [AD[n] Head saith, 320[£] ⟨335⟩.] 70 Ho. A village, called Brambling of the Street. Mrs Barret[1], [was ⟨Miss⟩ Pudner,] & her son a minor ⟨His Tutor, Mr Delap⟩ [will have 3000[£] a year. ⟨21 Feb. 26. 1765 well disposed⟩. Revd Mr Birch[2] married his Sister]. Charles Knowler[3] Esq[r] Capt. of a Man of War. Whole Service on Sundays [only every 2[d] Sunday in ABP Wakes time]. Prayers on Holidays &

during Lent. Cat. then & at other times. 4 Sacr. 40 Com. Seldom fewer. A Charity School, voluntarily supported by the Rector & Mrs Barret. Church & chancel very handsome. Ho. & outho. pretty good. 3^f to the poor, 1^f to the minister for a Sermon. Glebe 20 Acres. 4 Bells.

John Lynch[4] DD. R. 5 May 1731. See Bishopsbourn p. 4.
John Head[5] DD AD[n] of Canterbury. 17 June 1760.
James Cornwallis[6] M.A. Dec[r]. 9. 1769.
William Backhouse[7] DD. June 27. 1771.
Houstonne Radcliffe[8] D.D. 1788.
Josias Pomfret[9]. Cur. See Chillenden p. 9. Salary 40^f with the Parsonage House. Resides. 1765 hath lost his voice by a paralytick stroke.
Wheler Bunce[10] to come at LD 1765. Came. Gone. Vic. of S[t] Clements, Sandwich p. 103.
Hopkins Fox[11] see p. 16 to be Cur at Mich 1766. Ord. Pr. Tr. S. 1767. V. of Lynsted.
J. White[12] see p. 50. 42^f, surplice fees & use of parsonage Ho. from Mids.

1758 Conf. 25. 1762. 28. 1766. 45.

[1] Katherine Barrett (1717–85), the 4th wife of Thomas Barrett. He died in 1757: Hasted IX, p. 114.
[2] William Dejovas Birch (1731–92), of Goudhurst, Kent, m. Peterhouse, scholar 1747, BA (Sidney Sussex) 1751, MA 1754, fellow 1753–4, taxor 1755, moderator 1755.
[3] Later admiral Knowler. He died in 1788: Hasted IX, p. 177.
[4] See p. ii, n. 1.   [5] Ibid., n. 20.
[6] Ibid., n. 6.   [7] See p. iii, n. 1.
[8] (1739–1822), of Liverpool, m. Brasenose 1758, BA 1761, MA 1764, B & DD 1784, fellow, V. Gillingham and Upberry, 1780–1822, R. Mersham, 1786–89, R. Ickham, 1789–1822, preb of Ely, 1787, preb of Canterbury, 1795–1822, archdeacon of Canterbury, 1803–1822, master St John's Northgate and Harbledown Hosps, 1803–22, sub-dean of Bath and Wells, 1812–1822, archbishop's chaplain.
[9] See p. 9, n. 2.
[10] (1737–1809), of Hackington, Kent, m. St John's C 1755, BA 1759, MA 1762, fellow, 1761–7, C. Hauxton, Cambs, 1759, C. Barfreston, C. Ickham, V. St Clement's, Sandwich, 1766–1809, R. Ham, 1774–1809.
[11] (1742?–93), of Nackington, Kent, m. Trinity C 1759, BA 1763, MA 1768, BD 1786, fellow 1765, C. Kingston 1764, C. Queenborough, V. Lynsted, 1767–93, R. Ruckinge, 1780–93, chaplain to Lord Sondes.
[12] John White (1738–89), of White Roding, Essex, m. Trinity C 1759, scholar 1763, BA 1764, MA 1767, fellow 1765, C. Sternfield, Suffolk, 1764, R. Little Mongeham, 1772–89, PC. Sutton, 1772–89.

Page 16
D. Bridge
Kingston R. S[t] Giles. Tho. Barret[1] Esq[r] P. Ecton. But Mrs Eliz. Peters[2], ABP Herrings Book ⟨see below⟩. K[s] book 16^f Certified 77–33–0. Now 100^f. 48 Ho. Lady Grey[3], [mother to Sir James Grey[4]:] Thomas Payler[5], Esq[r] [changed his name from Turner:] John Winchester[6] Esq[r], [was a Surgeon, an Estate left him by Mr Marsh]. Whole Service on Sundays. Prayers W. & Fr. in Lent. Ch[n] not duly sent to be catechised. 4 Sacr. 25 Com. 7^f a year given by the Will of Tho. Turner[7] of Ileden in this Parish, Esq[r] for Bread for the Poor of it every Sunday. Given. Rev[d] Mr Birch[8], Patron, AD[n]. Church & chancel in pretty good Repair.

Ho & out Ho. greatly out of Repair. ⟨Repaired 1766. Bad still⟩. Glebe 16 Acres. 3 Bells.

Peter Innes[9] R. 23 Dec. 1718. Superannuated. Lives at Maidstone with his Relations. Hath Burham V. Dioc. Roch. called 58$^£$.
John Nairn[10] A.M. 1769. resides.

Will. Barrett[11], Priest, Cur. Resides. 35$^£$ a year. [1759 serves also Ewell p. 83. & doth whole Duty here. AD^n]. Drunken. Sent away 1763. Dead.
Markham[12] Cur. Chr. 1763.
Taswell[13] May 1764 was minor Can. of St Pauls. Gone.
Fox, Hopkins[14] ⟨different from Fox of Boughton and Egerton⟩ BA Cur. bapt. Mar. 11. 1741/2 ord. Deacon 23 Sept. 1764. 2. 40$^£$. Gone.
Taswell again. C. minor Can. of Cant. will reside 3 months & be often there. See AD^n Dec. 17. 1765.

1758 Conf. 11. 1762. 9. 1766. 17.

[1] See p. 15, n. 1.
[2] The owner of Kingston manor. The daughter of Peter Peters MD of Canterbury, she was the second wife of Thomas Barrett (see n. 1): Hasted IX, p. 342.
[3] Lady Hester Gray, bought Dennehill in 1725. Her husband, Sir James Gray, had been created a Scottish baronet in 1707: Hasted IX, p. 346.
[4] Died in 1775: ibid.
[5] The owner of Ileden. He died in 1771: Hasted IX, p. 344.
[6] John Winchester, who died in 1781, was left Nethersole House by John Marsh, a barrister of the Inner Temple, in 1752: Hasted IX, p. 264.
[7] Hasted says William Turner, in 1746: IX, p. 348.
[8] See p. 15, n. 2.
[9] (?1692–1769), of Margate, Kent, m. University 1709, BA 1713, MA 1716, R. Kingston, 1718–69, V. Burnham, 1740–69, chaplain to the earl of Aylesford.
[10] (1729–1806), of Bermuda, m. Peterhouse, 1747, scholar, BA 1751, MA 1764, C. Great Mongeham 1755-7, PC. Wingham, 1756–71, 'deputy' at Stodmarsh, until 1761, R. Stourmouth, 1761–1806, R. Kingston, 1769–1800, chaplain to Viscount Torrington.
[11] See, p. 4, n. 11
[12] Samuel Markham, (1723–97), of London, m. Christ Church 1741, BCL 1748, bar-at-law, Inner Temple 1748, V. Bearsted 1765-7, V. Leatherhead, Surrey, 1767, evening preacher, St Dunstan's in the West, London, minor canon of Rochester.
[13] William Taswell (1709–1800), of Newington, Surrey, m. Christ Church 1727, BA 1731, MA 1734, C. Hawkhurst, 1737-9, V. Almondsbury, Glos, 1755–65, V. Wotton-sub-Edge, 1755, V. Brookland, 1764–71, V. Tenterden, 1771–77, minor canon of Canterbury.
[14] See p. 15, n. 11.

Page 17
Littlebourn V. St Vincent. Belonged to the mon. of St Austin. Ch. of Canterbury P. K^s books 8$^£$. Now 80. 76 Ho. Mr Henry Denne[1] Sen. ABP^s Tenant for the Court Lodge. Mrs Holness[2], Lessee of DCh. One Kingsfoot, a miller, Anabaptist Teacher at Wingham. Service once on Sundays [1759 usually twice. See below]. Sermons the other part at Ickham, & Wickham, near. Prayers on some of the chief Holidays, if a Congregation. Cat. in Summer months: few Ch^n, no Serv^{ts}. 4 Sacr. 40 or 50 Com. Some small charities, which see. One is, ½ Acre yearly of the ABP^s Wood, called Pine Wood, wch is not assessed. Only

½ service for 60 years past: exc. w[n] Mr Gostling[3] tried the whole, & then only 5 or 6 came. Church & chancel clean & in good Order. Ho & out Ho. small, in good Repair. 5 Bells. 1765 part of the Church fallen down. May be repaired for 180[f]. Given 50[f], augmented with 50[f] a year by DCh of Cant. D[r] Ducarel.

Osmond Beauvoir[4] MA. V. July 3. 1753. Master of Cant. School. Resides there. Officiates here every Sunday afternoon: bound by Statutes to attend the Scholars to Cath. in morning [& afternoon:] & both Masters bound. Will officiate twice, w[n] not engaged to preach for a Prebendary. Doth so ⟨1766⟩. Mr Pomfret doth occ. Duty from Ickham, or clerk brings the vicar word. *** Dec. 17. 1764. V. also of Milton near Sittingbourn p. 217.
John Benson[5] D.D. 1789. resigned.
Joseph Price[6] B.D. 1794.

M[r] Hasted[7] Cur. Sal £30.

1758 Conf. 35. 1762. 44. 1766. 36.

[1] The Denne family had been lessees since the Restoration: Hasted IX, p. 150.
[2] The family had long rented the lands on a beneficial lease: ibid., p. 156.
[3] William Gostling, see p. 6, n. 3.
[4] See p. ii, n. 47.   [5] Ibid., n. 29.
[6] (1736–1807), of ? East Anglia, m. Peterhouse '10 year man' 1765, BD 1775, C. Rumburgh and South Elmham, Norfolk, C. Lowestoft, PC. Tunstall, Norfolk, 1765–82, R. Hellington, 1766–1808, V. Brabourne, 1767–86, C. Monks Horton, 1767–76, R. Monks Horton, 1776–86, V. Herne, 1786–94, V. Littlebourne 1794–1807. Price had been a dissenter. See *A Kentish Parson. Selections from the Private Papers of the Revd Joseph Price Vicar of Brabourne*, 1767–1786, ed. G.M. Ditchfield and Bryan Keith Lucas (Stroud, 1991).
[7] Edward Hasted (1760–1855), of Sutton, Kent, son of the historian, m. Oriel 1778, BA 1781, C. East Farleigh, 1784, C. Littlebourne, V. Hollingbourne 1790–1855, JP Kent.

Page 18
D. Bridge
Nonington C S[t] Mary with Womenswold or Wymenswold Chap. S[t] Marg. Belonged to the College of Wengham. Exempt from AD[n] ⟨adv. granted by Qu. Mary⟩. ABP P. Certified 71-6-8. Now 53[f] ⟨20[f] of it reserved in the ABPs Lease and 13-6-8 besides by ABP. The 20[f] reserved by Juxon. 75 or 80[f]⟩. Nonington hath 5 small Hamlets, 70 Ho: John Plumptre[1], W[m] Hammond[2], Esq[rs], good. Service once 2 Sundays in 3. Wymenswold hath 2 Hamlets, 25 Ho. Mr Winchesters[3] Ho. see p. 16 partly in Wymenswold. Service every 3[d] Sunday once. 4 Sacr. at each. 50 or 60 Com. at Church. 20 at Chap. Cat. 6 or 8 Sundays at each. In 1596 Edw. Boys of Fredville in this Parish Esq[r] gave all the small Tithes of the Parish, exc. those of 120[f] a year, that had been sold away, & the Tithes of his Woodlands, & of all Lands that He or his Heirs shd ever occupy, to the Curate. Mrs Boys hath the great Tithes. An Almshouse for 2 Families, of which see. Church & Chancel pretty good. But a Chancel in the South Isle shamefully dirty. ⟨Repaired & cleaned by M[r] Plumptre⟩. Ho. small, in good Order. No outho. Glebe 1 Acre. 3 Bells. Wymenswold Church & Chancel indifferent. Ho. a mean Cottage. A small Barn by Mr Lunn. Glebe 2½ Acres. 1 Bell.

Lic. to Wm Lunn[4] to serve the Cure 1695 Entry B. IV. 536 Father of prest Incumb.

Edw. Lunn[5] Cur. Lic. 15 March 1704. ⟨Died before July 30 27 1764⟩. R. of Denton p. 98. where he resides: 5 or 6 miles off. Serves this also. [Qu. occ. Duty.]. To have a Curate see p. 109. 1763 Ld Guilford[6] asks it for Mr Greenall. Robt Greenall[7] BA. C. 14 Aug. 1764. R. of Blackmanston p. 113. V. of Waldershare p. 200. Serves both.
Blaydon Downing[8] M.A. C. Feb^{ry} 1. 1771.

Wheler Bunce[9], Cur. 25$^£$. Cur. also of Barfreston, p. 179. Nov. 1761, 1764, Gone.

1758 Conf. Nonington 39. Wymenswold 7. 1762. Non. 2 + 35 Wymenswold 4. 1766 Nonington 33 Wymenswold 8

[1] (1710–91), MP for Penryn, 1758–61, MP for Nottingham, 1761–74. Owner of the manors of Fredville and Sole.

[2] Owner of St Albans manor and lessee of the rectory of Wimlingswold: Hasted IX, p. 256.

[3] See p. 16, n. 6. Hasted notes that Edward Boys also left 40s to the poor in 1596, and that Sir Edward Boys left £6 in 1634 to be used for 'setting the poor to work': ibid., p. 259.

[4] (16?–1705), of Kent, m. CCCC 1653, BA 1657, MA 1660, PC. Swingfield, 1675, C. Nonington, 1695–1705, R. Denton, –1705.

[5] See p. ii, n. 38.

[6] Francis (1704–90), Ist earl of Guilford, 3rd baron Guilford.

[7] (17?–71), m. Merton 1747, BA 1751, V. Blackmanstone, 1755–71, V. Waldershare, 1755–71. C. Tilmanstone, PC. Nonington, 1764–1771.

[8] (1744–1819), of Ilford, Essex, m. Trinity O 1761, BA 1765, BCL 1773, V. Waldershare, 1771–99, R. Blackmanstone, 1771–7, PC. Nonington, 1771–1817, R. Ivychurch, 1777–89, C. Denton.

[9] See p. 15, n. 10.

Page 19
Patricksbourn See p. 20.

Petham V. All S^{ts} with Waltham V. St Barth. The first belonged to the mon. of St Osythe, Essex: the 2d to St Gregorys Priory, Cant. The Honywoods[1] were P. of Petham, the ABP of Waltham: now alternatively of both ⟨See below⟩. Petham Ks books 8–0–2½. Waltham 7–15–5 ⟨See below⟩. Both now 130$^£$. AD^n 160$^£$. Petham had a few Years ago 77 Families & 366 Inhabitants. Tho. Thomson of Kenfield Esqr [600$^£$ a Year]. Waltham 74 Families, 297 Inhabitants. Sermons once a Sunday at each, & 4 Sacr. & abt 30 Com. Cat. in Afternoons in Lent. Churches 2 miles distant. Some small charities, wch see. In the ABP^s Lease of St Gregorys Priory 20$^£$ a year is reserved to the Vicar of Waltham. Petham church & chancel clean and neat. Ho. handsome and in good Repair. A good Stable. Glebe 2{½} Acre. 4 Bells. Waltham church ⟨neat,⟩ much improved: Chancel indifferent, in good Repair. Ho. mean. Glebe 1½ Acre. 3 Bells.
Disp. to hold Petham with Waltham 1669. Entry B. II. 186. Again 1691 IV. 464. United by ABP with Consent of Patron 4 July 1698 quantum in nobis est & de jure possumus. See Instrumnt at length p. 582 &c wch saith both were not worth 80$^£$ a year, appoints the Clerk to be presented to Waltham [I suppose with

Petham annexed] the Pres. to be alternate, the usual service to be continued, both V. Houses to be kept up, and all Fees to be pd for each as before.

Tho. Randolph[2] DD. V. 14 Sept. 1737. The union was made [qu.how] ⟨see above⟩ in his Predecessors time: & he ⟨Randolph⟩ was collated by the ABP: so that the Honeywoods have the next Turn. He is R. of Saltwood with Hythe p. 107 & President of CCC, where he usually resides.

Thomas Randolph[3] A.M. 1783.

Bryan Fausset[4] Priest, Cur. 42$^£$. Hath a Living in ⟨Shropshire, Dioc.⟩ Herefordshire ⟨of 100$^£$ a year. All Souls, patron.⟩ : wd change for one in Kent. See his Letter. Resides in the Vicarage Ho. Brought in F. of All Souls in ABP Potters time by an Appeal. Coll. objected agst his morals. Now 1765 lives in a House of his own, near, & serves Petham only. Mr Guise[5] lives in the Vicarage & serves Waltham & Stouting: but must not go on so. He served Petham & Waltham: but died Oct. 15. 1765. Widow & 2 ch^n. Poor.

Tho. Randolph[6], son to Dr Randolph to be C. D. will be P. Tr. S. 1766. Wm Tournay[7] Cur. Sal. £60.

1758 Conf. Petham 40. Waltham 45. 1762. Pet 20 Walth 12. 1766 Petham 25 Waltham 39.

---

[1] Family long resident at Evington in Elmsted. Sir John Honywood (1710–81), 3rd Bt. Thomas Thompson of Kenfield died in 1762, leaving four sons and three daughters: Hasted IX, p. 312.

[2] (1701–83), of Canterbury, Kent, m. CCCO 1715, BA 1719, MA 1723, BD 1730, DD 1735, president of Corpus, 1748–83, vice-chancellor, 1756–9, Lady Margaret professor of Divinity, 1768–83, V. Petham and Waltham, 1737–83, R. Saltwood w. Hythe, 1746–770, archdeacon of Oxford, 1767–83, preb of Worcester, 1768.

[3] (1741?–1808), of Islip, Oxfordshire, m. Christ Church 1759, BA 1763, MA 1760, R. Saltwood w. Hythe, 1770–1808, V. Petham w. Waltham, 1783–1808, chaplain to bishop of St David's.

[4] (1720–76), of Nackington, Kent, m. University 1738, BA 1742, MA (All Souls) 1745, FSA 1763, R. Monks Horton, 1765–76, C. Nackington, 1767–76, V. Albury, Shropshire.

[5] Perhaps Samuel (?1729–65), of Chipping Wycombe, Bucks, m. Christ Church 1745.

[6] See n. 3.

[7] (1762–1827), of Hythe, Kent, m. Oriel 1780, BA 1784, MA 1789, C. Saltwood w. Hythe, 1785, R. Eastbridge, 1790–1827, R. Denton, 1792–1827, R. Hope 1795–1827, C. Swingfield, 1822–27.

Page 20
D. Bridge

Patricksbourn V. St Mary. Pens. 6$^£$ Ecton. with Bregge or Bridge Chap. St Peter: whence the Deanery takes its Name. Belonged to the Priory of Merton in Surrey. Mr Herbert Taylor[1] P. Ecton: but Lady Breams[2], ABP Herrings book ⟨See below⟩. Ks books 5–7–3½. Now (See below). Patricksbourne 25 Families: Bridge 59. One Papist. Prayers twice once a Sunday at each: Sermon at each every other Sunday. Cat. where no Sermon [1759 Cat. expounded]. Morning Prayers on Holy-days: & on W. Fr. from LD to Mich. Morn. & Ev. Prayers on Fast days. 5 Sacr. at each: betw. 30 or 40 Com. A Private Boys School & Girls School. The Library of John Bowtell[3] D.D. Vicar of this Parish, given to the succeeding vicars by his widow, who died Oct 1757 [A Catalogue of it put in ABP^s Registry 1759]. [The Income is 80$^£$ a year, besides the Tithe of a few

Acres of Hops, & of some Wood, wn felled. The present vicar hath also the great Tithes & Patronage. The whole was never united before, & probably may not again. See his Letter 1759]. Ch. & Chancel very neat & in good Repair: as also Ho. & out Ho. Glebe 42 Acres. 3 Bells. Chapel & its chancel in good Repair. No Ho. 3 Bells. Lic. to take down the spire of Bridge VI. 75.

Herbert Taylor[4] MA V. 22 Jan. 1753. R. of Hunton p. 364. Resides at his Family Seat in the Parish, called Bifrons. The Vicarage Ho. in good Order. Died. Sep. 29. 1763.
Edw. Taylor[5] MA V. 1 Nov. 1763. Ordained priest by me March 11. 1759. Presented by his elder brother. To live at Bifrons with his mother. *** A Horse-racer 1765. It was pretended to be his Brothers Horse.

Henry Pix Heyman[6] Cur. Sal. £45.
John Gregory[7] Cur. Sal. £40 & surplice fees lic by Archdeacon.

1758 Conf. 37. 1762. 15 Bridge 18. 1766 Patr. 13 Bridge 17.

[1] See p. ii, n. 36. He held the patronage from 1731: Hasted IX, p. 281.
[2] The widow of Walter Br[ae]ms: Hasted IX, p. 279.
[3] (1668–1753), of Thaxted, Essex, m. St John's C 1686, BA 1690, MA 1693, BD 1781, DD 1718, fellow, 1694–1722, V. Patrixbourne, 1698–1753, R. Staplehurst, 1719–53.
[4] See n. 1.
[5] (1735–98), of Kent, m. St John's C 1751, BA 1755, MA 1758, V. Patrixbourne, 1763–98, R. Ruckinge, 1794–8, succeeded to the Bifrons property in 1767. He was the son of Herbert Taylor, the previous incumbent. His elder brother, also Herbert, died in 1767.
[6] (–1808), of Kent, m. Emmanuel 1780, scholar 1782, BA 1784, MA 1787, BD 1794, C. Patrixbourne, 1785, C. Burmarsh and Lympne, 1788, PC. Whitfield, 1792–99, V. Fressingfield, Suffolk, 1797–1808, succeeded as 5th baronet in 1790.
[7] See p. 11, n. 6.

Page 21
Petham See p. 19.

Preston by Wingham V. S[t] Mildred. Belonged to S[t] Austins Mon. Church of Cant. P. Tenths 0-19-6. Certified 28[f]. Now 100[f] ⟨80[f]⟩. One M[r] Wybourn[1] having left 50[f] ⟨AD[n] saith 40[f]⟩ a year or more, on Condition, that V. reside & perform the whole Service. 58 Ho. Service once [1759 ⟨1764⟩ twice]. Most of the Parishioners live as near Stourmouth or Elmston Churches as their own, & have gone to them these 40 Years. 4 Sacr. 40 Com. Two Tenemts & Lands, worth 10[f] a year, given to repair & beautifie the Church. So applied. Church & Chancel clean & in good Repair. Ho. & out Ho. very good & in Repair. A small Library. Glebe 2 Acres: Mr Wyburns Gift 32 Acres. 5 Bells.

Pet. Vallavine[2] LLB V. 18 July 1743. R. of Monkton p. 266. Divides his time between them. [1759 Resides here. See above]. Officiates but once, May 1761. Saith, 1766, that he doth the whole Duty. Dead 11 Jan. 1767.
Robt Stedman[3] BA V. 5 Aug. 1767 collated on a Lapse. Will reside in the Parish immediately, & in the House as soon as it can be put in order.
John Gregory[4] A.M. 1792.

1758 Conf. 25. 1762. 12. 1766. 11.

[1] Robert Wyborn[e in his will of 1711 left his house and 32 acres of lands to the vicar and his successors, on the condition that they reside in it, the vicarage having burnt down: Hasted IX, p. 138. He also left a charity for the poor.
[2] (1698–1767), of Cambridgeshire, m. Peterhouse 1723, LLB 1728, R. Reculver, 1726–9, R. Monkton w. Birchington, 1729–1767, V. Preston, 1743–67.
[3] See p. 11, n. 5.   [4] Ibid., n. 6.

Page 22
D. Bridge
Stodmarsh Cur. S[t] Mary. Belonged to the Hospital of poor Priests ⟨of wch see Somner p. 71 &c⟩. AD[n] of Cant. Patron. Certified 30[f]. Now 40[f] ⟨See below⟩. 20 Ho. Service once: was only every other Sunday, till the present Incumbents time. Cat. the Summer half year: will be exp. 4 Sacr. 20 Com. Church & Chancel small, in pretty good Repair. Ho & out Ho. very much want Repair. Glebe 4 Acres. 2 Bells. What follows is extracted from the Register Book. Possession of this Benefice is given by the immediate Collation of the AD[n] of Cant. no Licence being at all necessary from the ABP as the present ABP told me when I applied to him for one, Will. Newton[1]*[1]. 1721. ⟨See next Line⟩. Church & Chancel small, in pretty good Repair. Ho & out Ho very much want Repair. Glebe 4 Acres. 2 Bells. M[r] Bunce saith, he was presented ⟨or nominated⟩ by AD[n] Lisle[2], & licenced by the ABP.
[1]* Mr Lewis saith Newton was presented in 1719 and died in 1744
1767 augm. with 400[f] by S[r] Ph. Boteler & Qus. bounty.

John Bunce[3] Cur. 26 July 1744. V. of Hackington p. 36. Resides there. ***
Allen Fielding[4] A.B. 1787.

John Nairn[5] Deputy. Priest. 20[f]. Very good. Cur. also of Wingham p. 25. 3 miles off. Vacant Dec. 2 1761.
Fra. Gregory[6], min. Can. of Cant. C. See p. 35. C. also of S[t] Margarets p. 39. R. of S[t] Georges p. 35. May 1765 M[r] Twyman[7] p. 44. M[r] Taswell[8] will come. 1766 M[r] Gostling[9] Jun[r] serves it with Nackington.

Thomas Lamprey[10] A.M. Cur Sal. £20. Lic by Archdeacon.

1758 Conf. 4. 1762. 4. 1766. 6.

[1] (16?–1744), of Maidstone, Kent, m. Magdalene C 1672, BA 1763, MA 1676, C. Adisham, 1719, V. West-Hythe, 1720–32, PC. Stodmarsh and Wingham, 1720–44, C. Guston, 1736–44, minor canon. See his *The History and Antiquities of Maidstone* (1741).
[2] See p. 27, n. 3.
[3] (1708–1786), of Brenzett, Kent, m. Trinity Hall 1724, V. Hackington, 1734–86, PC. Stodmarsh, 1744–86, poor vicar.
[4] (1754–1823), son of Henry, of Covent Garden, London, m. Christ Church 1770, BA 1774, MA 1800, V. Sibbertswold, 1782–87, V. Hackington, 1787–1823, PC. Stodmarsh, 1787–1823, V. St Cosmus Blean, Canterbury, 1803–16, master Eastbridge Hosp., 1803–23, six-preacher, 1815–23.
[5] See p. 16, n. 10.   [6] See p. 7, n. 7.
[7] Wheler Twyman (1725–79), of London, m. Christs 1742, BA 1745, MA 1756, C. Sheldwich, 1749, R. Luddenham 1755–79, V. Sturry, 1757–79, C. Chislet, chaplain to Viscount Erwin.
[8] See p. 16, n. 13.   [9]. ee p. 6, n. 2.

[10] (1734–1800), m. All Souls 1752, BA (New College) 1756, MA 1758, V. Halstow, 1759–1800, C. Stodmarsh and Stourmarsh, 1790–1800, V. Stalisfield, 1796–1800.

Page 23

Stourmouth R. All S[ts]. Pension to the Chamberer of Rochester. 10[s] Pens. 40[s] Ecton ⟨See below⟩. BP of Rochester P. K[s] books 19[£]. Now 140[£]. 28 Ho. Not one Alehouse. Regular people. Service once, as it hath been immemorially by the V. of Preston, exc. one Year, w[n] the parishioners desired to have it so again. The Churches a little more than a mile distant [See below]. Poor ch[n] taught Cat. at Rectors Expence: & say it publickly, when able. 4 Sacr. 30 Com. Lands worth 5–15–0 a year given for the Use of the Church: & 40[s] for bread for the poor. So applied. The Rector pays the above Pension of 40[s] to the ABP. Church & chancel pretty, in good Repair. Ho. & out Ho. tolerable, in pretty good Repair. Glebe 12 Acres. 3 Bells.

Philip Bearcroft[1] DD. R. 18 July 1743. V. of Elham p. 99 and Master of the Charterhouse, where he resides. Died 17. Oct. 1761.
John Nairn[2] AB R. Dec. 2. 1761. Cur. of Wingham ⟨p. 25⟩, where he resides, but is to have the full Service here. Hath it 1764 only ½ till Chr. See Oct. 2. 1764. Will officiate at each place once, & have a Curate to serve this once, March 1765. Mr Rogers[3] p. 260 assists him. 1766 Doth the whole.

Pet. Vallavine[4] Cur. See p. 21. 27[£] & Surplice Fees [R. promises to get a resident Cur. & give 40[£] & Surplice Fees. Not done May 1759.] Mr John Gill[5] officiates alternately here and at Monkton p. 266. May 1761 M[r] Vallavine serves this with & from Preston p. 21. See above.
M[r] Lamprey[6]. Cur Sal. £25. lic. by Archdeacon.

1758 Conf. 12. 1762. 15. 1766. 11.

[1] (1697–1761), of Worcester, m. Magdalen Hall 1712, BA (1716), fellow Merton, 1717, MA 1719, B & DD 1730, V. Elham, 1719–61, R. Stourmouth, 1743–61, master Charterhouse 1753–61, secretary to the Society for the Propagation of the Gospel, 1739, preb of Wells, 1755, chaplain to George II, 1738.
[2] See p. 10, n. 5.
[3] William Rogers (1722–73), of Langhane, co. Carmarthen, m. Jesus O 1738, BA 1741, V. Herne, 1756–73.
[4] See p. 21, n. 2.   [5] (1726–71), of Canterbury, Kent, m. St John's C 1745.   [6] See p. 22, n. 10.

Page 24

D. Bridge
Wickhambreux al. Wickham R. S[t] Andrew. The Heirs of – Hay Esqr P. Ecton: ⟨In Err. corrected, Herb Palmer of Wye Esqr⟩ but S[r] Tho. Palmer[1] Bart ABP Herrings book. K[s] book 29–12–6. Now 220[£]. 56 Ho. of wch the Hamlet of Grove contains 22. Whole Service. Prayers on the Holydays of the great Festivals & W. Fr. in Lent: not till the present Rectors time. Cat. exp. & will be every Sunday. 4 Sacr. never less than 50 Com. 4[£] a year for the poor of Wickham & Littlebourn. So applied. Church & chancel handsome, in good Repair. Ho. excellent, built by Mr Young[2]. OutHo. the same. Glebe 20 Acres. 6

Bells. Lic. to Mr Young to pull down the old Ho. & rebuild it 1714. Entry B. VI. 153.

Tho. Hey[3] M.A. R. 9 Apr. 1755. Good. V. of East-Church p. 209. Resides here. Pres. by Tho. Kynaston of Lincolns Inn Gent. Patron for this time.

Rector resides. M[r] Lamprey[4] Curate occasionally.

1758. Conf 16. 1762. 20 1766. 24.

[1] Sir Thomas Palmer (1682–1723), MP for Kent, 1708–10, MP for Rochester, 1715–23. Left his estate to Herbert Palmer, his illegitimate son. Sir Thomas's 3rd wife afterwards married Thomas Hey, whom she also survived: Hasted IX, p. 235.

[2] Alexander Young (1669–1755), of St Lawrence Jewry, Middlesex, m. Christs 1686, BA 1689, MA 1692, BD 1703, R. Caldecote, Northamptonshire, 1705, R. Clipston, 1707–15, R. Wickhambreux, 1713–55, V. Eastchurch, 1729–55.

[3] (1727–1807), of London, m. CCCC 1746, BA 1750, MA 1753, DD (Lambeth) 1797, R. Wickhambreux, 1755–1807, V. Eastchurch, 1755–1807, preb of Rochester, 1788–1807, chaplain to the earl of Lincoln. Thomas Kynaston, who presented him, was born in 1733 at Panfield, Essex, and was admitted to Lincoln's Inn in 1750.

[4] See p. 22, n. 10.

Page 25

Wingham C. S[t] Mary. Formerly a College. Exempt from AD[n]. P. as Wickhambreux p. 24. 148 Ho. S[r] Geo. Oxenden[1], [at Dean Lady Palmer[2], [mother of M[r] Hey of Wickham Mrs Masters[3], ⟨dead Sept 1759⟩ [widow, hath 1000[£] a year, wch comes to S[r] G. Oxenden.]. Certified 46–10–0. Now 50[£]. 12 Anabaptists. A meeting Ho. Licenced. Teacher John Kingsford, not qualified. Service once. Prayers on the Holydays of the great Festivals & W. Fr. in Lent. Cat. then: will exp. 4 Sacr. 120 Com. A Place called Brook. Some small Charities. Rightly applied. Church very handsome. 3 chancels: belong to Lady Palmer, Sir Geo. Oxenden, Mrs Masters: all in good Repair, want whitewashing. No Ho. or out Ho. 16[£] a year for a School of 20 Boys, AD[n]. 8 Bells. Lic. to Cur. 1719 Entry B VI. 325. VIII. 272 IX. 248.

John Nairn[4] BA Cur. 21 Apr. 1756 Cur. of Stodmarsh p. 22. *** Resides here. No House. Dec. 2. 1761 R. of Stourmouth p. 23. Serves this once every Sunday. John Loftie[5] Cur. Licens'd April 5 1771. does his own duty. William Thomas[6].

Brook Henry Bridges[7] Sal[y]. all the Profits. lic. 1793.

1758 Conf. 92. 1762. 70. 1766. 58.

[1] See p. 4, n. 5.   [2] See p. 24, n. 1.

[3] Probably Elizabeth Masters, who in 1728 donated a large silver flaggon to the church: Hasted IX, p. 237.

[4] See p. 16, n. 10.

[5] (1735–1800), of Sittingbourne, Kent, m. Christ Church, 1752, BA 1756, C. Sellinge and Stowting, 1758–9, C. Luddenham, 1759, R. St Dunstan's, Canterbury, 1767–1800, PC. Wingham, 1771–1800.

[6] See p. 13, n. 5.

[7] (1770–1855), of Middlesex, m. Christ Church 1788, BA 1792, MA 1794, C. Goodnestone next Wingham, 1793, R. Danbury and R. Woodham Ferrers, Essex, 1795–1855.

Page 26
D. Bridge

Wye C. S[t] Martin & S[t] Gregory. Belonged to the Abbey of Battel, Sussex. ABP P. ⟨so in 1663⟩ Ecton. ⟨Corrected in Err⟩. And he leases the Rectory to M[r] Sawbridge[1], but excepts not the Advowson of V. wch perhaps was not granted with R. 12 July 3 Eliz. & wch ABPs Books say Ld Winchilsea hath. Certified 55–10–3. Now called 50[£]. It is divided into 5 Boroughs. Ab[t] 140 Ho. John Sawbridge ⟨of Ollantigh⟩ Esqr ***. ⟨Jacob & J. Elias, his brothers⟩. One family of Nonjurors: 7 of Anabaptists, lessening. Whole Service. Only half, till lately on the Increase of the School, wch induced the Incumbent & Master to quit a Curacy ⟨See below⟩. Prayers on Feasts & Fasts, & W. Fr. in Lent. Then Cat. exp. Ch[n] come regularly. L[d] Winchilsea[2] Patron of the Free School[1)*] The minister sent a Copy of the Benefaction Tables in the Church [{not} recd ⟨see it⟩]. [No answer abt Sacr. ABP Herrings Book saith, there is one almost every month.]. Ch & chancel large & handsome. No Ho. 8 Bells.

[1)*] Lady Joanna Thornhill[3] gave Benefactions to the Minister & the poor, & the Residue of her Estate for the Education of poor children. In ABP Wake's Papers, left to Christ-Church vol. 2 is a Petition from the minister, that he wd get her will put in Execution for a School. The Sum left by her 2300[£]. Sir Geo. Wheeler[4] gave the College of Wye to the Schoolmasters.

Curacy & Chapel of Wye resigned by John Wilkinson[5] 17 Aug 1743 Entry B VIII 242. W[m] Whitmell[6] nom Cur 7 Feb 1743 on resign. of Wilkinson VIII. 256. Heneage Dering[7], nom. to chapel of Wye, void by Death of last Incumb. & belonging to the Donation of L[d] Winchilsea, lic. to preach in the said chapel Apr. 15. 1754. Resigned it 17 Oct. 1754. Johnson Towers lic. by the same Form as Dering Oct 22. 1754.

Johnson Towers[8] Cur. 22 Oct. 1754. Resides in the College adjoining to the Ch. Yard, & belonging to him as School-master. Absent only 4 Sundays, ab[t] his Scholars. 1760 Cur. of Eastwell p. 60 by L[d] Winchilseas Desire. Will have whole Service here again, as soon as his Usher, now 19, is of age for Deacons Orders. 1761 Chosen master of Tunbridge School. May 1761. To quit. L[d] W. hath got a Cur. always takes a Bond of Residence.

Parsons[9] Philip subscribed 1761. Cur. of Eastwell. He attends the visitation. Hath a subscr. of 17[£] a year (Mr Sawbridge 5 G[s]) & serves it twice.

1758 Conf. 96. 1762. 70. 1766 May 31, Conf. here 250. Of Wye 74.

[1] See p. 4, n. 1.   [2] See p. 5, n. 4.
[3] In her will of 1708: Hasted VII, p. 362.
[4] [Wheler] (1650–1723). Traveller and cleric. Knighted in 1682, took holy orders in 1683, preb of Durham, 1684, R. Houghton le Spring, Durham, 1709–23. In 1692 he purchased the ancient archiepiscopal palace at Charing.
[5] (1703–43), of Cumberland, m. Queen's O 1720, BA 1724, MA (King's) 1727, R. Eastwell, 1730–4, PC. Wye, 1730–43.
[6] (?–1754), of East Haddon, Northants, m. Christs 1732, scholar 1730, BA 1735, MA 1738, fellow, 1740–5, taxor, 1742, PC. Wye, 1744–54.

[7] See p. ii, n. 26.

[8] (1724–?), of Kendal, Westmoreland, m. Queen's O 1740, BA 1744, MA 1747, PC. Wye, 1754–61, master Tunbridge school, 1761–5, R. Pett, Sussex, 1765–.

[9] (1729–1812), of Dedham, Essex, m. Sidney Sussex 1748, BA 1752, MA 1776, PC. Wye, 1761–1812, R. Eastwell, 1766–1812, R. Snave, 1776–1812, master Oakham School, 1761, chaplain to Lord Sondes.

[Deanery of Canterbury]

Page 27
D. Cant.
Archdeacons. See Ant. of Cant. pt. 1. p. 150 &c & Cant. Sacr. part. 4. After the AD[ns] there mentioned, followed

Tho. Green[1] D.D.
Tho. Bowers[2] DD 6 Nov. 1721.
Sam. Lisle[3] DD 1 Sept 1724 See patent Entry B VII. 64.
John Head[4] MA 9 April 1748. Now D.D.
William Backhouse[5] M.A. Dec[r]. 13. 1769.
John Lynch[6] L.L.D. 1788.

[1] (1658–1738), of Norwich, m. CCCC 1675, BA 1679, MA 1682, BD 1690, DD (Lambeth) 1695, felllow, 1680–95, master Corpus, 1698–1716, vice-chancellor, 1699 and 1713, V. St Benets, Cambs, c. 1682, V. Minster, 1695–1708, R. Adisham, 1708–17, V. St Martins-in -the-Fields, 1717–23, preb of Canterbury, 1701–21, archdeacon of Canterbury, 1708–21, royal chaplain, bishop of Norwich, 1721–3, bishop of Ely, 1728–38.

[2] (1660–1724), of Shrewsbury, m. St John's C, 1677, BA 1681, MA 1684, DD (Lambeth) 1716, chaplain of Morden College, Blackheath, 1705–7, preb of Canterbury, 1715–24, archdeacon of Canterbury, 1721–24, bishop of Chichester, 1722–24.

[3] (1683–1749), of Blandford, Dorset, m. Wadham 1700, scholar, 1701, BA 1703, MA 1706, fellow 1707, DD (Lambeth) 1721, BD and DD 1739, warden, 1739–44, chaplain to Levant Company in Smyrna and Alpeppo, 1710–16, R. Leven, Yorks, 1718, R. Holwell, Beds, 1720, R. Tooting Graveney, Surrey, 1721–8, R. St Mary-le-Bow, London, R. Fetcham, Surrey, 1726, V. Great Bookham, Surrey, 1728, V. Northolt, 1729–49, sinecure R. of Corwen, Co. Merioneth, 1745–8, chaplain to Wake, 1721, preb of Canterbury, 1728–44, archdeacon of Canterbury, 1724–48, bishop of St Asaph, 1744–8, bishop of Norwich, 1748–9.

[4] See p. ii, n. 20.   [5] See p. iii, n. 1.

[6] (1735–1803), of Lambeth, Surrey, son of Dean Lynch (see p. ii, n. 1), m. Christ Church, 1753, BA 1757, MA 1760, DCL 1765, R. All Hallows, Bread St, London, 1761, R. Adisham, 1771–81, R. St Dionis Backchurch, 1782, master St John's and Harbledown, 1786, preb of Canterbury, 1781–1803, archdeacon of Canterbury, 1788–1803.

Page 28
D. Cant.
All Saints R. with S[t] Mildreds R & S[t] Marys in the Castle R. united. ⟨Not united in 1663⟩. The King, P. Only the Chancel of S[t] Mary Castle standing 4[f] a year being left for the Repair of it. Somner p. 166 who saith a particular Incumbent was then lately inducted into it. Wake, I think, speaks of the three as united, Sept. 19. 1684. K[s] books 17-7-11. Wake, 30[f]. Now 80[f] ⟨AD[n] 109[f]⟩. All S[ts] 70 Ho. S[t] Mildreds 150. Mr Sandys[1]. All S[ts] hath two Jewish Families, & one

Dissenting meeting House, disused of late. A school & Hosp. within it, but not belonging to it. ABP P. In St Mildreds is Maynards Spital, with 10 Dwellings, left by John Maynard to the Mayor and some of the Aldermen of Cant. [But Somner p. 74 saith, it was founded by one Mayner[2] in H. the 2ds time. He speaks of a Chapel belonging to it &c.]. Five Almshouses, given by Tho. Harris[3] late of Cant. Gent. His Trustees are reduced to two: who are thought to abuse the Trust. Not known, who can call them to Account. Gifts to the amount of 14–12–0 a year to the Church & of 15–10–0 to the Poor. Tables of them in the Church. ChW^ns account for them yearly. Prayers & sermon in each Church every Sunday. Prayers on some week Days tried. No Congregation. Cat. on Sunday Evenings tried: reduced to Lent. A Set of Cat. Sermons. 6 Sacr. in each Church. Numerous Com. All Sts Church & Chancel very mean, though much hath been done to them. 3 Bells. Ho. very mean, but well repaired. St Mildreds Ch. & Chancel handsome. 5 Bells. Ho. pretty good & in good Repair.

Lease of messuages in All S^{ts} conf 1674 Entry B. 111. 248.

Inst. to St Mildred, no mention of the others 26 Aug 1684. IV. 426.

Inst. to St Mildred, All S^{ts} & St Mary de Castro V. 288

1765. A papist in each parish. See Letter.

Theodore Delafaye[4] R. 16 Jan 1745. Neither parish hath a proper Parsonage Ho. Resides in the next. Chaplain of the Garrison at Sheerness p. 218 & Cur. of Queenborough p. 222.

Anthony Lukyn[5] M.A. R. Octr. 27 1772.

W^m. $Theoph^s$. Mountjoy Webster[6] A.B. Rector, Decr. 29. 1778.

Edwd. Wm Whitaker[7] A.B. Rector 1783 resides.

1758 Conf. ⟨at Cant. in 3 Days 1789⟩. All S^{ts} 10, St Mildreds 28. 1762. All S^{ts} 25. St Mildreds 39. Conf. at Cant. in all 1511 ⟨on 4 days⟩. Precincts of Cath were 36, Workhouse: 6. 1766 Conf. at Cant. in 4 Days at Cath. 1667. All S^{ts} 20. St Mildred 24. Workhouse 24. ⟨1766 Ch. Ch. 19⟩.

John Francis[8] Curate Sal. £40 & surplice fees lic by the Archdeacon.

[1] Richard Sandys, who died in 1763: Hasted XI, p. 249. He was the grandson of Sir Richard Sandys Bt.

[2] Hasted agrees with Somner: ibid., p. 190.

[3] These were built in 1726. Harris was a hop-merchant: ibid., p. 198.

[4] (1704–1772), of Utrecht, m. Merton 1724, BA 1726, MA 1727, C. Queenborough, 1743–72, R. All Saints and St Mildred's, Canterbury, 1746–72, chaplain of garrison at Sheerness.

[5] See p. 8, n. 11.

[6] Of Southwell, Notts, m. St John's C 1756, BA 1760, R. All Saints and St Mildred's, 1778–1783, R. St John's, Clerkenwell.

[7] (1752–1818), of London, m. Christ Church 1773, BA 1771, R. All Saints and St Mildred's, 1783–1818.

[8] (1749–1828), of Soham, Cambridge, m. Pembroke C 1767, BA 1771, MA 1774, C. Soham, 1771, PC Stuntney, 1777, R. Cowden 1778–84, R. Westley Waterless, 1784–9, V. Willesborough 1789–92, C. All Saints and St Mildred's, 1790–1818, R. Orgarswick, 1792–1828, R. All Saints and St Mildred's, 1818–28, six-preacher, 1802–28, poor vicar, 1798, 2nd master King's School.

Page 29

S[t] Alphage R. Exempt from AD[n]. United to S[t] Mary Northgate V. which belonged to S[t] Gregorys Priory. ABP P. K[s] Books S[t] Alph. 8–13-4. S[t] Mary 11– 19–4½. Both now 100[£] ⟨AD[n] 80[£]⟩.[1]* S[t] Alph 163 Ho. 2 Papists of low Rank[2]*. 2 Presbyterians, meeting Ho. Teacher, – Sheldon. 8 Anabaptists, a meeting Ho. Teachers, Benge & Huggot. 6 Methodists. All of low Rank. S[t] Mary, 148 Ho. One Papist, 3 Methodists, of low Rank. S[t] Johns Hospital. ABP. P. Jesus Hosp. founded by S[r] Johns Boys[1] in hath { } a Warden, 8 poor men & 4 women with a nurse: income 130[£]. A Subscription Charity School for 28 Boys, clothed & taught. 5–16–0 yearly in Bread to the Poor. Prayers & Sermon in each Ch. every Sunday. Prayers W. Fr. at S[t] Alphage. Cat. in Lent. 6 Sacr. in each: abt 80 Com. S[t] Marys Church & Chancel, neat & in good Repair: 4 Bells. No Ho. S[t] Alphage, Church, Chancel, Ho. in good Order. No. outho. 3 Bells. Churches large.

[1]* 100[£] including 10[£] for the Ho. But great Deductions & Duty, & people poor. AD[n].

[2]* 1765 ⟨In S[t] Alph⟩ A poor Irishman, always a Papist. A man of bad character, perverted from the Dissenters 10 years ago, & his wife. In S[t] Mary, a profligate Irishman, once a marine.

John Airson[2], MA R & V. 31 Jan. 1753. R. of Orgarswick p. 134. Resides in his Minor Canons house. *** Qu Parsonage Ho. Vacant Jan. 28. 1761 by his Inst. to S[t] Martin & S[t] Paul p. 40.
Geo. Hearne[3] R & V. 28 Apr. 1761. See p. 30 resides.

1758. Conf. S[t] Alph 25. S[t] Mary 43. 1762. S[t] Alph. 51. S[t] Marys North. 65. 1766 S[t] Alph. 92. S[t] Mary Northg. 72.

[1] (c.1535–1612), MP for Sandwich, 1572, MP for Midhurst, 1593, MP for Canterbury, 1597–1604. He served five archbishops as steward of the liberties, and rented several estates from the see. The hospital was founded in 1595, although Hasted says 1612: XI, p. 195.
[2] (1724–1788), of Bicester, Oxon, m. New College, 1741, BA 1744, MA 1747, R. Orgarswick, 1750–88, R. St Alphage, 1753–61, V. St Martin's and St Paul, 1761–88, minor canon of Canterbury.
[3] See p. ii, n. 43.

Page 30

D. Cant.

S[t] Andrews R. with S[t] Mary Breadman R. so called because near the Bread-market Somner p. 164. Pens. Prior. Christ-Church 6–8. Ecton. ABP P. two turns: Ch. of Cant. one. K[s] books 22–6–8. Now 120[£] ⟨or 140[£] or 150[£]⟩. S[t] Andrew 76 Ho. One Papists, in Trade[1]*. 3 Families of Presb. 5 Anab. & 3 Methodists. Number lessend by Moderation. 3 Families of Quakers. One fourth of the Rent of Lands in Stodmarsh, which fourth amounts to 6[£] clear, given by M[rs] Cadell[1], abt 50 Years ago, to the Rector for a Sermon & Sacr. on good Friday. S[t] Mary, 75 Ho. One Presb. Family, one Anab. A Methodist Preacher, abt 18 years old. Prayers & Sermon in each every Sunday, & every other Friday evening: on which in Lent, Cat. but no Exp. 6 Sacr. at each, besides 3 great Festivals. Com. from 100 to 40. Offertory distributed by Ch. W[n]s. Churches &

chancels indifferent, but in good Repair. Parsonage of S[t] Andrews mean, but in pretty good Repair: of S[t] Mary Br. very mean. 5 Bells.
Collation to S[t] Andrews R 23 June 1673 Entry B. 111 198. to both ⟨as one⟩ V. 9, 342.
[1]* In 1765, 7. See particulars. One perverted, he knows not by whom: the others came papists.

John Duncombe[2] MA ⟨R⟩ 20 Jan 1757 the first of ABP[s] two turns. Assistant Preacher to D[r] Squire[3] at S[t] Anns Westm. to be more useful, & live with his Father[4], & because his Eyes being bad, he cannot read Prayers. *** Coming to reside at Mids 1761. 1763 holds a Living in Essex, w[ch] he calls small, for a minor of 18. It is West Thurrock V. 80[f] a year.
William Gregory[5]. Rector 1786 resides.

Geo. Hearne[6] Priest, Cur. Good. 40[f], wch R. hath at St Anns. Gone. See p. 29.

1758 Conf. S[t] Andr. 28 S[t] Marys 13. 1762 S[t] Andr. 32. S[t] M. 23. 1766 S[t] Andrew 41. S[t] M. 17.

[1] Hasted notes that Arthur Kay, rector of St Andrew's, 1673-1701, paid £4 for divine service for the Corporation every Burghmote day: XII, p. 652.
[2] See p. ii, n. 45.
[3] Edward Squire (1713-60), of Warminster, Wilts, m. St John's C 1730, BA 1734, MA 1737, DD 1749, fellow, 1735-44, V. Minting, Lincs, 1741, R. Toppesfield, Essex, 1749-50, R. St Anne's Westminster, 1750-66, V. Greenwich, 1751-66, preb of Wells, 1743-61, archdeacon of Bath, 1743-61, dean of Bristol, 1760, bishop of St David's, 1761-66.
[4] William Duncombe (1690-1769), writer and friend of archbishop Herring.
[5] (1761-1803), of Aberdeen, m. Balliol 1776, BA 1780, MA 1783, R. St Andrew's, 1786-1803, V. St Cosmus Blean, 1792-1803, master Eastbridge Hosp, 1789-1803, six-preacher, 1786-91.
[6] See p. ii, n. 43.

Page 31
S[t] Cosmus Blean, al S[t] Cosmus & Damian V. Hospital of Eastbridge Propr. & Patron. K[s] books 10[f]. Certified 73-14-6. Now called 70[f] ⟨or 80[f]⟩. See the Endowment A.D. 1375 in App. to Battelys Somner N° 18. 44 Ho. straggling, poor, most above ½ mile from the Church. Service once a Sunday, as the last 80 Years. Cat. in summer. 4 Sacr. 40 Com. Church & chancel in good Repair. House indifferent, but in repair, & lately improved. 2 Acres of Glebe. Endowed with gr. Tithes. 1 Bell.

Rich. Leightonhouse[1] A.M. V. 21 Oct 1728. Good. Resides in his Minor Canons House, a mile from the Parish, 2 miles from the Church. Cur. of Fordwich p. 34.
Robert Neild[2] Clerk V. March. 27. 1771.
James Smith[3] A.M. 1781.
W[m] Thomas[4] A.M. 1784. quitted.
William Gregory[5] A.M. 1792.

M[r]. Howdell[6], Cur.

1758 Conf. 9. 1762. 16. 1766. 17

[1] (1690-1770), of Washingborough, Lincolnshire, m. King's, 1711, BA 1715, MA 1718, C. Minster, 1718, V. St Cosmus Blean, 1728-70, minor canon of Canterbury.

[2] (1718-80), of Lea, Cheshire, m. St John's C 1743, BA 1747, MA 1758, C. Snave and Ivychurch, c. 1755, V. St Cosmus Blean, 1771-80.

[3] See p. 7, n. 9.

[4] (1757-1803), of Cambridge, m. Christs 1774, scholar 1775, BA 1779, MA 1782, fellow, 1779-85, V. St Cosmus Blean, 1784-92. Probably C. Fobbing, Essex, 1789-1803.

[5] See p. 30, n. 5

[6] William Howdell (1728-1804), of Staple, Kent, m. St John's C 1745, BA 1749, V. West Hythe, 1733-1804, second master King's school, Canterbury, 1777-9, C. St Cosmus, Blean, 1790, C. Harbledown, 1796.

Page 32

D. Cant.

S[t] Cross ⟨Westgate⟩ V. belonged to S[t] Gregorys Priory. ABP P. united to S[t] Peters R. Ch. of Cant. P. Alternate. K[s] books S[t] Cross 13-2-0½ S[t] Peters 3-10-10. Both now 80[£] clear. S[t] Cross 182 Ho. 2 or 3 Papists of low Rank: 2 Anab. 3 or 4 Methodists. 27[s] & 6-8 for Bread for the Poor. S[t] Peter 108 Ho. 3 Presb. 2 Anab. An Hospital for 6 Clergymens widows, founded by Mr Coggan[1], & endowed with 3[£] a year: ½ of wch the Chamberlain of the City keeps for Repairs. D[r] Agar[2] gave 10[£] a year for each of them. Mrs Lovejoy[3] 4[£] a year amongst them &c [who appoints them? ⟨See below⟩]. 1-16-0 a year to the poor. Prayers twice, Sermon once, on Sundays, & Cat. exp. 4 Sacr. at each Church. Com. from 50 to 80. Church good, Chancel tolerable. House very mean, let out in Tenem[ts] to poor persons. Glebe ¾ of an Acre. 5 Bells. The City Jayl is in this Parish. AD[n] Head.

D[r] ⟨John⟩ Aucher[4] Preb. of Cant. ⟨who died March 12. 1701⟩ left an Estate of ab[t] 90[£] a Year for 6 poor widows of Clergymen of this Diocese. Each hath constantly 10 Guineas a year, & commonly 2 Gs more, & sometimes a Ch. of Coals. Each hath also 2 Gs yearly from the ⟨Canterbury⟩ Society for Orphans & Widows of Clergy. ⟨They dwell in a House called Cogans Hospital, because⟩ given by Mr Cogan, who gave also an Estate, w[ch] is lost: but the Mayor & Ald. who are his Trustees, let D[r] Auchers Widows live in the Ho. His Trustees are D[r] Geekie[5], Walwyn[6], Randolph[7] Pr. of Corpus; M[r] Taylor[8] of Bifrons, & AD[n] Head[9], who agree to nominate by Turns. This from the AD[ns] Letter Sept. 25. 1760. His Grant was made Dec. 8. 1696 & is in a Box in the Audit House, Cant. See an abstract of it.

Inst. to S[t] Peters on pres. by the K. patron thereof 1672 Entry B. III. 163.
Collation to Westgate holy Cross V. 1679 IV. 78 & on the next vacancy 87.

Robt Gunsley Ayerst[10] MA V & R. ⟨Pres. by DCh.⟩ 14 Jan. 1746. Resides near S[t] Peters, but not in a House belonging to R or V. 1768 wants to change it for a Country Living for his Health. I promised my consent to an equitable Exchange. John Gostling[11] V & R 1786 does his own duty.

William Adams[12] A.M. Curate. Licensed Sept[r]. 21: 1773. Salary £40 p an.

1758 Conf S[t] Cross 19 S[t] Peter 20. 1762 S[t] Pet. 23. S[t] Cross. 28. 1766 S[t] Pet. 28 S[t] Cross 31.

[1] John Cogan founded the hospital in 1657. He was in charge of the sequestration of royalist and ecclesiastical estates in Kent, and endowed the hospital with lands which, in 1660, were returned to the original owners, leaving the hospital on a precarious financial footing. A public subscription in 1772 raised £343–13s: Hasted XI, p. 184.

[2] Benjamin Agar.   [3] Elizabeth Lovejoy. In 1694.

[4] (1619–1701), of Bishopsbourne, Kent, m. CCCC 1635, BA 1638, MA (Peterhouse) 1641, DD (Lit. Reg) 1660, fellow of Peterhouse, 1640–4, 1660–1, R. All Hallows, Lombard Street, 1663–85, R. Westbere, 1661–81, preb of Canterbury, 1660–1701.

[5] See p. ii, n. 9.   [6] Ibid., n. 12.   [7] See p. 19, n. 2.

[8] Herbert Taylor, see p. ii, n. 36.

[9] Ibid., n. 20.   [10] Ibid., n. 43.   [11] See p. 6, n. 3.

[12] Of Kent, m. Emmanuel 1768, BA 1772, MA 1775, C. Great Hardres 1773, C. Holy Cross, 1778.

Page 33

St Dunstans V. belonged to St Gregorys Priory. ABP P. Between 80 & 100 Ho. Tho. Knowler[1] Esqr Capt in the Royal Navy, worthy man. Tenths 10^s. Certified yearly value $18^£$. Augm. in 1714 with $400^£$ ⟨$200^£$ by ABP Tenison⟩. Now $70^£$ ⟨AD^n $40^£$ See below⟩. A few Presb. & Anab. Some Parishioners go to the Methodist Meeting, but regularly to Church also. No V. House. Prayers & Sermon once: & Cat. exp. after Evening Prayers. 4 Sacr. Com. from 40 to 80. A reading & writing School adjoyning to the Church: a good Master. V. pays for $sev^£$ poor Ch^n there. An Estate of 13 or $14^£$ a year, in Feoffees, for poor not receiving Alms. Ch. W^ns distribute the Offertory. Church & Chancel very handsome. 1¼ Acre Glebe. 5 Bells.

Crown presented on Lapse 1709 Entry B. V. 344.

1765 A Steward of Sr Edw. Hales[2], lately come, & his Family, & a woman married out of Sir Edws family, & a young woman, whose Father lives in his Family, Papists. Reports of attempts to make Converts, groundless. Mr Johnson. 1767 Value 46–15–0 reckoning the $400^£$ to produce only 2 percent. & some poor Houses not to pay. See Mr Saunders's[3] Letter. Taxed to King & poor. No Curacy to be had with it just now.

Isaac Johnson[4] MA V. 8 Nov. 1743. Learned. R. of Wormshill p. 257. Cur. of little Hardress p. 38. Resides. Died March 13 1767.
John Loftie[5] BA V. 17 June 1767. To reside at Mich. C. of Harbledown p. 37.

Joshua Dix[6] Cur. lic endorsed by the Archdeacon.

1758 Conf. 21. 1762. 19. 1766. 24.

[1] A descendant of Thomas Knowler, alderman of Canterbury: Hasted XI, p. 514.

[2] (c.1730–1802), 5th Bt, the great-grandson of Sir Edward Hales who was created a Jacobite peer in 1692, having accompanied James II in 1688 on his flight to France.

[3] John Saunders (1731–1807), of Maneddwy, Pembs, m. Merton, BA 1754, MA (Jesus C) 1779, chaplain Christ Church, Oxford, V. Newington, 1760, V. Farningham, 1768, chaplain to viscount Falkland.

[4] (1715–67), of Hertfordshire, m. Jesus C 1735, BA (St John's) 1738, MA 1741, R. Wormshill, 1741–67, V. St Dunstan's, 1743–67.

[5] See p. 25, n. 5.

[6] (1744–1810), of Epwell, Oxon, m. New College 1761, BA 1765, MA 1767, clerk Magdalen chapel, 1768–1802, chaplain, 1802–9, V. Brookland, 1772–88, PC. Nackington, 1776–1810, R. Old Romney, 1783–1810, C. St Dunstans, 1790, V. River, 1807–1810, C. Harbledown, 1808–10, C. Fordwich, minor canon of Canterbury.

Page 34

D. Cant.

Fordwich R. S[t] Mary. Earl Cowper[1] P. Tenths 0–11–6½. Clear certified value 42[£]. Now 100[l] ⟨AD[n] 60⟩. 34 Ho. John Graydon[2] Esq[r], batchelor, 50 resides here. *** sober, charitable. Younger brother with him, who is constant at Church & Sacr. Service once a Sunday. Sturrey Church within ½ mile. They go thither. Thus it hath been above 60 years. Younger Ch[n] cat in Summer every Sunday. Elder & servts will not come. 4 Sacr. 30 Com. Some small Charities, which see. Church & Chancel in good Repair, want whitewashing. House indifferent, but in good Repair. 12[£] a year in Land by Mr Bigg[3], & 50[s] in Bread by Col. Short[4], to the poor. AD[n]. Glebe 3½ Acres. 4 Bells.

Spencer Cowper[5] MA, now DD. R. 5 Apr. 1742. Dean of Durham. Preaches w[n] at his brothers in the Neighbourhood.
James Deason[6] R. June 24 1774.
William Stephenson[7] A.M. 1787.

Rich[d] Leightonhouse[8], Cur. See p. 31. 30[£]. Lives within two miles. M[r]. Dix[9]. Cur. Sal. £30.

1758 Conf. 7. 1762. 14. 1766. 6.

[1] William (1709–64), 2nd earl.   [2] Died in 1774: Hasted IX, p. 65.
[3] Stephen Bigg, by will of 1646: ibid. Also, Thomas Bigges, by will of 1669 gave 50s to distribute bread to the poor.
[4] Died in 1716: Hasted IX, p. 61.
[5] (1713–74), of Hertingfordbury, Herts, m. Exeter 1729, BA 1732, MA 1734, B & DD 1746, R. Fordwich, 1742, preb of Canterbury, 1742–6, dean of Durham, 1746–74.
[6] R. Fordwich, 1774–87.
[7] (1733–99), of Yardley Park, Northants, m. University 1750, BA 1754, MA 1756, R. Fordwich, 1787–99, C. Herne, 1790.
[8] See p. 31, n. 1.   [9] Joshua Dix. See p. 33, n. 6.

Page 35

S[t] George R. DCh. Cant P. Rent to Ch W[ns] 3–4 Pens. Mon. Christ-Church 5sEcton. with S[t] Mary Magd. ⟨al. Burgate⟩ R. red. Prior S. Gregory 2–8. To the Hospital of S[t] James 4[s] Ecton ⟨Not united in 1663⟩. S[t] George K[s] books 7–17–11, S[t] M. Magd. 4–10–0. Now 100[£] [AD[n] Head saith], 140[£] ⟨but in his Vis. Book 100[£]⟩ & S[t] Mary 40[£]. S[t] George 120 Ho. 7 or 8 Gentlemens Families. 2 Papists, 2 families of Presb. One Anabaptist, one Quaker. A Quaker Meeting Ho. They submit quietly to distraining for their Tithes. A Charity School for 20 Girls, who are clothed, taught to read & work, not put out. Two Tenemt[s] of 3–10–0 yearly for repair of the Church. So applied. Two more of 4–10–0 given to the Parish, but now in Dispute. S[t] Mary Magd. 70 Ho. 3 or 4 Gentlemens Families, 4 of Anab. one of Presb. One Parsonage Ho. to both Parishes. Prayers twice & sermon once in one or other Church. Prayers in S[t] Geo. W. Fr. & Holydays. Cat. W. Fr. in Lent, with Lewis's Exp. 6 Sacr. at each besides the great Festivals. Com. from 70 to 120. Church & chancel in good Repair. House & Outhouses very good. Lic. to rebuild part of Ho 1730 Entry B VII. 285. Glebe, a Ho. & Garden, let for 4[£] a Year. 4 Bells. S[t] M. Magds Church & chancel in good Repair. No Ho. 3 Bells.

Inst. to both as one 1684. Entry B. IV. 424. See 489.
1765. 2 Papists, one De Reck & his wife. He is a Prussian, teaches musick & languages: 7 years at Cant.

John Head[1] MA, now DD. R. 3 Jan 1729. AD[n] [& 1759 Preb. of Cant. & R. of Pluckley p. 69. Resides 4 months there, 4 here, & 4 at Court, as Dep. Clerk of Closet. Void by Cession 17 June 1760.
Tho. Forster[2], MA of Univ Coll R. 1760. R of Chartham p. 7. died 13 Sept. 1764.
Francis Gregory[3], see below, R. Dec. 4. 1764. resigned, & was succeeded by James Ford[4], below.

Fr. Gregory Cur. minor Can. of Cant. & V. of Milton near Sittingbourn p. 217. Resides in his Min. Can. Ho. Gone.
James Ford A.B. Instit[d]. Aug[t]. 21: 1777. resides.

1758 Conf. S[t] Geo. 30 S[t] M. Magd. 24. 1762 S[t] Geo. 36 S[t] M. Magd. 44. 1766 S[t] Geo. 37. S[t] M. Magd. 39.

[1] See p. ii, n. 20.   [2] See p. ii, n. 41.   [3] See p. 7, n. 5.
[4] (1752–1824), of Uley, Glos, m. Magdalen O 1770, BA 1774, minor canon of Durham, 1775-7, minor canon of Canterbury, 1777-1824, R. St George's, Canterbury, 1777-1824.

Page 36
D. Cant.
John Whitgift, archbishop of Canterbury, 1593–1604.
Hackington al. St Stephens V. Pens. Prior. S. Gregor. 13–4 Ecton. AD[n] of Cant. Prop. & Patr. K[s] books 5-2-3½. Now 80[f 2)*]. 30 Ho. W[m] Deedes[1] Esqr ⟨son of Preb[2]. 1000[f] a year⟩ & Mrs Randolph[3], ⟨clergymans⟩ widow, both constant at Church & Sacramt. 40 Papists, besides Ch[n]. The Chief, S[r] Edw. Hales[4] Bar[t] & his Lady, 2 Mrs Darells[5] of the Family of Cale-Hill, Peter Holford Esqr & his Lady, & Mr Wright her son by a former Husband, Persons of large Fortunes. A Chapel in S[r] Edw[s] Ho. Mr Brown & Mr Booth, Priests, quiet. A Popish BP preached & confirmed in the Chapel June 18. 1758.[3)*] Whole Service every Sunday. Sermon, by Custom, in the Afternoon. Cat. in Lent & most of the Summer. 4 Sacr. 40 or more Com. Almshouses founded by S[r] Roger Manwood[6] K[t], a Protestant, for 6 aged, poor, honest persons. Old pews in the Church for them. But S[r] Edw. Hales, who appoints them, as Possessor of the chief mansion Ho. hath put in 4 Papists. Sir Roger made the Mayor & Aldermen of Cant. Visitors, & they visit yearly the I[st] Wedn. in December yearly. Income betw. 4 & 5[f] a year to each of the 6. Some small Gifts to Church & poor, which see. 13 Dec 1588 an Agreemt was made, signed & sealed by the ABP, AD[n], Sir Roger Manwood his Lessee, & the Vicar, that future V[s] shd have the Tithes of Corn & Hay, paying 10[f] a year to AD[n], & shall always reside, & have no other Cure of Souls, no minor Canonry, or preferm[t] w[t] ever, under the Penalty of 5[f] a month payable to AD[n], & shall pay the Procurations, repair the chancel, & bear all Burthens, ord. & extraord. & shall swear at his Institution to do these things. Whitgifts Reg. pt 1. fol 480. The Conditions have been long nelected. See AD[n]

Heads Letter, Sept. 8 1759[1]*. Church, Chancel, House, very good. A large Garden. 6 Bells.

Bunce[7], John, LLB V. 11 May 1734. Minister of Stodmarsh p. 22. Resides in V. Ho. here. Good. One of the 10 poor vicars. AD^n Head {thinks} ⟨saith⟩ he is Ordinary of the County Jayl with a salary of $10^£$ a year out ⟨of⟩ the County Stock by order of the Justices, & $5^£$ charged on marsh Land. ***
Allen Fielding[8] A.M. V. 1787.

1758 Conf. 16. 1762. 15. 1766. 10.
[1]* In Consequence of Whitgifts Injunction of Residence by this Instrument, Simon Hughes[9] on his Institution 24 Nov. 1719 promises & declares, that he will constantly reside. Wake Reg. 1. fol. 307. Entry Book. VI. 310.
[2]* ABP Whitgift obtained & confirmed an Augm. of it, Dec. 1588. Le Neves[10] BP^s p. 55.
[3]* 1765 No increase of Papists. See Particulars. Mr Power, Sir Edws. priest. Mr Brown, Mrs Darells. Tho. Hawkins Esqr, Mrs Fuller, papists. No mention of Mr Holford or Mr Wright.

[1] (1733–93), chairman of the quarter session for east Kent.
[2] Julius Deedes (1693–1752), of Canterbury, m. CCCC 1710, scholar 1711, BA 1714, MA 1717, C. Great Mongeham, 1717, R. Dymchurch, 1719–52, R. Great Mongeham, 1730–52, preb of Canterbury, 1739–52.
[3] Catherine, widow of Herbert Randolph (1694–1755), of Canterbury, m. Christ Church 1711, BA 1715, MA (All Souls) 1716, R. Deal, 1726–55, R. Woodchurch, 1730–55, six-preacher 1728–55.
[4] See p. 33, n. 2.
[5] The Darells had lived at Calehill in Little Chart from the reign of Henry IV. The junior branch of the family lived at Scotney: Hasted VII, p. 458.
[6] (1523–92), judge and steward of the liberties to archbishop Parker. Besides the seven almshouses, he gave the church a new peal of bells and a new trancept. He also founded a grammar school at Sandwich.
[7] See p. 22, n. 3.   [8] Ibid., n. 6.
[9] (c.1676–1728), of Kent, m. CCCC 1695, BA 1698, MA 1702, V. Bethersden, 1704–11, R. Smarden, 1710–28, V. Hackington, 1719–28, preb of Chichester, 1725–8.
[10] John Le Neve, *The Lives and Characters of all the Protestant Bishops of the Church of England since. . .1559* (1720).

Page 37
Harbeldown R. St Michael Pens. Prior. S. Greg. 13–4–Ecton. ABP P. K^s books 9–2–6. Certified 63–14–3. Now $130^£$ ⟨AD^n $140^£$. See below⟩. Formerly here were two Parishes. The Church of the other was St Nicolas, now the Chapel of the Hospital: & the Tithes of it are approp. to Eastbridge ⟨p. 46⟩ Hosp. ⟨[See Somner p. 44]⟩. A place called the Mint, containing 9 or 10 Cottages, deemed extraparochial, was probably part of it, being the $Endowm^t$ of a Chantry, founded by ABP Wittlesee[1] in St Nicolas's Church. St Michael hath between 50 & 60 Ho. Mostly labourers, very poor. Papists, a man formerly servt to Mrs Darell[2], & a Farmers Wife, lately perverted by the same Family. A Family of Anab. & 3 persons Methodists, who go to Mr Perronets[3] Meeting House in the Palace. A few of the distant poor, & some in the *Mint* neglect Church. Whole Service on Sundays. Prayers & Sermon on Chr. Day. Prayers Ash W. Good Fr. Cat. W. in Lent & in Summer with Exp. Ch^n sent. 4 Sacr. 20 Com. Parsonage

Ho. small & inconvenient: much improved lately. Church & chancel neat & in good Repair. 8 Acres of Glebe. 3 Bells.

Inst to R. of S[t] Nicolas Harbledown 1670 Entry B. III. 43. It is exempt from the AD[n] Battely App. to Somner p. 57: therefore probably subject to the Commissary & probably also the Master of Eastbridge Hosp. May be obliged to nominate a Curate to the ABP.

In 1758, 1759, 1760 abt 108[£], besides above 20[£] for Land tax, poors rate, tenths & Tithe Dinner.

Henry Hall[4] MA. R. 26 March 1750. V. of E. Peckham p. 354 [was Librarian to ABP Herring]. Resides in Parish. Mr Gostling[5] min. Can. was Cur. 35[£], & now officiates in his Absence. R. also of Orpington Sine Cure p. 371. Died Nov. 1. 1763.

John Benson[6] MA. R. 25 Jan. 1764. R. also of Great Chart p. 56. Serves this from Canterbury, a mile & ½ off. ⟨1767⟩ Mr Loftie[7] of S[t] Dunstans to assist him on Sunday afternoon & week Days. 20[£] & surpl. fees.

W[m] Nance[8] LLB. Rector 1780.

1758 Conf 55. 1762. 17. & from the Hospital 16 1766. 14

M[r] Howdell[9]. Cur. Sal. £25 & surplice fees, lic by Archdeacon.

[1] William Whittlesey, archbishop, 1369–74.   [2] See p. 36, n. 5.
[3] Edward Perronet (1721–92), one of Wesley's itinerant preachers; after c. 1770 he joined the Countess of Huntingdon's connexion.
[4] (1717–63), of London, m. Kings 1736, fellow 1739, BA 1741, MA 1744, R. Harbledown, 1750–63, V. Herne, 1752–6, R. Orpington, 1755–63, V. East Peckham, 1756–63, treasurer of Wells 1762–5, Lambeth Librarian, 1748–51, chaplain to Herring.
[5] See p. 6, n. 3.   [6] See p. ii, n. 29.   [7] See p. 25, n. 5.
[8] (1746–1814), of St Creed, Cornwall, m. Exeter 1768, LLB (Peterhouse) 1779, V. Boxley, 1775–80, R. Harbledown, 1780–1814, R. Great Chart, 1780–1814.
[9] See p. 31, n. 6.

Page 38
D. Cant.
Holy Cross see S[t] Cross p. 32

Little al. Nether Hardres. ⟨al Netherheards⟩. R. S[t] Mary. Pens. Prior. Merton 13–4 Ecton. The King P. K[s] books 7–19–6½. Certified value 58–19–0. Now 70[£] ⟨AD[n] 100[£]⟩. 23 Ho. ⟨AD[n] 50⟩. Service once. Cat. wn Service is in Afternoon. 4 Sacr. 20 Com. R. lends 2 Rooms of the Parsonage to a woman, who teaches ch[n] to read & work: & he & Cur. pay for some poor ch[n]. Ch. W[n] distributes Offertory Money. Church & Chancel small & dirty. House & out houses mean, in tolerable Repair. 11 or 12 Acres of Glebe. 1 Bell.

John Minet[1] MA R. 5 Jan 1743. R. of Eythorn p. 185. Resides there
Henry Thompson[2] R. 23. ⟨Novr⟩ 1771. does his own duty.

Isaac Johnson[3] MA Cur. vicar of S[t] Dunstans p. 33. Resides at Cant. { } mile off. Salary here 26[£]. Gone Dec. 1765.

Bryan Fausset[4] R. of Horton p. 102. Lives near.

1758 Conf 22. 1762. 11. 1766. 10

[1] (1694–1771), of Dover, Kent m. St Catherine's C 1714, BA 1718, MA 1721, C. Bekesbourne, 1722–26, C. St. Alphage, Canterbury, 1722, R. Eythorne, 1723–71, R. Lower Hardres, 1744–71, chaplain to the earl of Essex.
[2] (1736–1805), of Kent, m. St John's C 1755, BA 1759, C. Sheldwich, V. Sellinge 1763–84, V. Lower Hardres, 1771–1805, R. Badlesmere, 1784–1805.
[3] See p. 33, n. 4.   [4] See p. 19, n. 4.

Page 39

S[t] Margarets R. belonged to the College of poor priests See Somner ⟨p. 71⟩. AD[n] of Cant. P. Certified 63-10-0. Now called 50[f]. AD[n] 70[f]. 100 Ho. Several noted Families. See their Names. Papists, Philip Darel[1] Esqr ⟨gone before 1765⟩, his brother James, a Priest, with him, one Burden a Currier lately perverted ⟨Dead⟩. Many of the lower Sort, few others, resort to the Methodist *Meeting Ho, in the Palace,* ⟨[*which is licenced. AD[n]*]⟩ *Teacher Perronet*[2]. No House for the Incumbent. Whole Service, exc. 3[d] Sunday of the Month, when the Minister officiates at S[t] Mary Bredin, of wch he is Sequestrator. [Always whole Service in ABP Wakes Book]. Prayers every W. & all Passion Week. Cat. exp. in Lent. 4 Sacr. betw. 50 & 60 Com. What was Hosp. for poor Priests is now by Act of Parl[t] City Workhouse. [See the Grant by Qu. Eliz. in Somner App. p. 19 N° 25a. Church & Chancel in good Repair. 3 Bells.
K. pres. on Lapse 1727 Entry B VII. 181.
1765 Papists, Newton a Taylor, wife & 2 Ch[n]. Came Papists into the Parish.

Tho. Leigh[3] MA R. 11 Oct 1737. Resides in the Palace. Seq. of S[t] Mary Bredin p. 41. Cur. of Iwade p. 213. R. of Murston p. 220. May 1765 Mr Leigh officiates.
Gilman Wall[4] Master of Arts R. June 25 1774. does his own duty.

Fra. Gregory[5] min. Can. C. Also C. of Stodmarsh p. 22. R of S[t] Georges p. 35. Hopkins Fox[6] ord Pr. May 25. 1766. See p. 16. Gone to Ickham p. 15.

1758 Conf. 24. 1762. 40. Visitation held here 1758, 1762, 1766. 1766 Conf. 48.

[1] For the Darells, see p. 36, n. 5. Philip rebuilt Calehill house in the mid-eighteenth century: Hasted VII, p. 459.
[2] See p. 37, n. 3.
[3] (1707–74), of Rostherne, Cheshire, m. University 1725, BA 1728, MA 1731, V. Hackington, 1731–3, R. and P. Murston, 1733–37, R. St Margaret's, Canterbury, 1737–74.
[4] (1747–1803), of Cambridge, m. Christs 1764, scholar 1765, BA 1769, MA 1772, C. Deptford, Kent, 1769–74, R. St Margaret's, Canterbury, 1774–1803.
[5] See p. 7, n. 5.   [6] See p. 15, n. 11.

Page 40
D. Cant.

St Martin R. Exempt from AD^n. ABP P. united with St Paul V. ⟨Not united in 1663⟩. Ch. of Cant. Propr. & Patr. Alternate. St Martins K^s books 6–5–2½, St Pauls 9–18–9. Both now, $100^£$ [1)*]. St Martins abt. 30 Ho. chiefly Labourers in Hop Grounds. The Mote, a decayed Seat of Earl Cowper[1], where he sometimes resides a few Days. Some poor neglect Church notw. Admonitions. Lady Mabella Finch[2] left $100^£$, now in the Funds, Interest partly for sick poor, partly for teaching, & apprenticing children. So applied. She left also $10^£$ a year charged on Lands to the Rectory: wch is paid, Land Tax deducted. St Paul 180 Ho. Inhabitants, as above. Mrs Rooke[3]: hath been but once at this Church of 10 Years. One Papist, was Servt to Sir Edw. Hales[4]: keeps a publick Ho. 3 or 4 Presb. One Anab. 2 or 3 poor Quakers, who pay nothing. An Almshouse founded in 1656 by John Smith[5] of Highgate Esqr for 4 poor men & 4 poor women. His widow Ann augmented the Income to abt $8^£$ a year for each. She gave also $20^£$ a year for an Afternoon Sermon in St Pauls Church by an able & orthodox minister to be named by her Trustees. ⟨Licenced as Entry B. VIII 235⟩. [Do they always name the Vicar?]. Lands settled for these purposes. Residue, for apprenticng poor ch^n. A few other small Charities. Morning Pr. at St Martins, exc. once in 6 weeks, wn R. reads at Cath. as min. Can. Serm. at St Pauls in afternoon: & Cat. exp. on Sundays, & Pr. W. Fr. both in Lent only. 4 Sacr. at each. Com. St Martins, 20 or 30: St Pauls from 60 to 90. Off. distr. by Ch. W^ns. St Pauls Church in good Repair & handsome, & so the Chancel. Ho. mean, but in pretty good Repair. DCh pay $10^£$, Land Tax deducted. 3 Bells. St Martins Church & Chancel in bad Condition: probably built in the 3^d Cent. [in the time of the Romans. See Somner]. Ho & outho. very mean. Glebe near an Acre. 3 Bells. 1764 Given Leave by Letter to take down a poor old House.

[1)*] $140^£$, besides the $20^£$ Lecture, wch the Incumbent may refuse to let another preach. AD^n Head from Mr Lamprey & others. Mrs Rooke at Law with Trustees. No Lecturer app. since Lamprey. AD^n May 1765. Nov. 1766. St Pauls mentioned without St Martins Entry B IV 477 & v.v. 493.

Tho. Lamprey[6] MA R & V. 14 June 1743 coll. by ABP. Master of St Johns, Master & Reader of Harbledown Hosp. Resides in his min. Can. Ho. Died Sept 2. 1760. Left a son, & 4 Das & an Estate worth 4 or $5000^£$.
Airson[7] John R. 27 Jan 1761. See p. 29 Is he licenced as above.

Thomas Freeman[8] A.M. Rector Jan. 15. 1788.

1758 Conf. St Martins 5 St Pauls 34. 1762 St Mart. 9 St Paul 40. 1766. St Martin 13 St Paul 58

---

[1] See p. 34, n. 1   [2] Wife of John Finch. She died in 1669.
[3] Frances Rooke, the daughter in law of Sir George Rooke (1650–1709) who captured Gibraltar. Her husband, also George, died in 1739.
[4] See p. 33, n. 2.
[5] Ann augmented them in 1662: Hasted XII, p. 650.
[6] (1694?–1760), of Marston, Warwicks, m. Lincoln 1708, BA (Christ Church) 1712, MA 1715, V. St Mary Magdalen, Canterbury, 1720–43, V. St Paul and Martin, Canterbury, 1743–60, reader St Nicholas Hosp. Harbledown, 1746, R. Stonar, 1752–58, minor canon of Canterbury, 1743–60.

7 See p. 29, n. 2.
8 See p. 4, n. 12.

Page 41

St Mary Bredin al. Bredne V. Mon. St Sepulchri Propr. Ecton. Henry Lee Warner[1] Esqr. P. K^s book 4-1-5½. Certified value 18-18-0. Now called 18$^£$ ⟨augm 1767 with 400$^£$⟩. 57 Ho. Mrs Pudner [widow of Capt.], Mr Morrice, Mrs Donne, [sister to BP Thomas[2] of Sarum]. One family of Presb. Mr Kingsford. Service every third Sunday Morning. At other times they go to St Margarets, where Ch^n are cat. 4 Sacr. 40 Com. Church & Chancel very neat. House indifferent: in pretty good Repair. 3 Bells.

The Rectory of St Mary Bredney was given by the ABP to the Crown 31 Aug 1 Ed 6. See Chart. Misc. vol 13. N° 21.

1765. Papists, Mrs Porter ⟨Sister to Prebendary Sutton[3]⟩, son, 3 daughters, 3 men servts, 4 maid servts. One Rogers & wife, wife of one Whale. All came Papists into the Parish.

Curteis Wightwick[4] was V. here, inst. 24 Nov. 1742. Now Mr Leigh[5], see here p. 39 is Sequestrator & serves it.

Gilman Wall[6], Sequestrator 1775. does his own duty.

1758 Conf 9. 1762. 7. NB. 1766. 12. NB.

1 Of Walsingham Abbey, Norfolk: Hasted XI, p. 240.
2 John Thomas (1696-1781), of Westminster, m. Christ Church 1713, BA 1716, MA 1719, BD 1727, DD 1731, fellow All Souls 1720, preb of St Paul's, 1731, R. St Benet's and St Peter's Warf, 1733-7, canon of St Paul's, 1742-8, royal chaplain, 1742, bishop of Peterborough, 1747-57, bishop of Salisbury, 1757-61, bishop of Winchester, 1761-81.
3 See p. ii, n. 24.
4 (1704-53), of Ashford, m. Pembroke, O, 1722, BA 1725, MA 1730, R. Bonnington, 1742-53, V. St Mary Bredin, 1742-53, R. Bircholt, 1744-53, R. Kenardington, 1746-53, chaplain to Lord Bellenden.
5 See p. 39, n. 3.   6 Ibid., n. 4.

Page 42

D. Cant.

St Mary Bredman. See St Andrews p. 30
St Mary Castle. See All Saints p. 28
St Mary Magd. See St George p. 35
St Mary Northgate. See St Alphage p. 29
St Mildreds. See All Saints p. 28

Milton next Cant. R. St Nicolas. Will Rebow[1] Esqr P. Ecton. Rich. Honeywood ⟨of Co. Essex⟩ Esqr ⟨presented Broderip⟩ ABP Herrings book. ABP Wake puts both. Tenths 5¼^d. Certified 20$^£$. ABP Wake puts 30$^£$ & 22$^£$. Augmented with 200$^£$ Mich. 1757. ⟨AD^n 25$^£$⟩. Only one Ho. Prayers & Sermon the first Sunday in the month. So for 100 years. They go to Thanington Church, ½ a mile off, & receive the Sacramt there. No person hath been baptized in 21 years.

Church very small, is repairing well. Chancel very mean. No Parsonage Ho. 1 Bell. It is imagined that a promise of not raising the Tithes will be expected from the next R.

Will. Broderip[2] MA R. 11 Nov. 1737. Min. Can. of Cant. where he resides. C. of Thanington p. 45. V. of Brookland p. 117. Chaplain of S[t] Johns Hosp p. 48. Died Apr. 18. 1764.
John Tucker[3] R June 1764. C. of Thanington p. 45. V. 0f Sheldwich p. 175.
John Gostling[4] M.A. R. July 3. 1770. does his own duty.

1766 Conf. 7.

[1] Hasted IX, p. 31, explains the patronage. Robert Honywood, of Charing and Markshall, Essex, inherited the patronage subject to his wife's life on whom it was settled at her marriage. On his death, she remarried Sir Isaac Rebow of Colchester, on her death, it became the property of Robert Honywood, who died in 1735, bequeathing it to his son Richard, an infant who died in 1758, when his uncle Philip Honywood, inherited it. He died in 1785.
[2] (1707–64), of Wells, Somerset, m. Balliol 1725, BA (New College) 1730, MA 1732, R. Milton, 1737–64, C. Thanington, 1737–64, reader St John's Hosp, 1737–64, V. Brookland, 1744–64, minor canon, 1744–64.
[3] See p. 4, n. 10.
[4] See p. 6, n. 3.

Page 43
Nackington al. Natyndon C. S[t] Mary. Belonged to the Priory of S[t] Gregory. ABP P. Certified 62–18–10. Now called 40[£], wch Sum is paid by the ABP[s] Lessee of S[t] Gregorys ⟨Church Dues in 1663 10[£]⟩. 13 Ho. Widows of Christ. Mills[1], ⟨***⟩ & Bryant Fausset[2] Esq[rs] ⟨Latter dead⟩. Service once on Sundays. Cat. exp. in afternoon. 4 Sacr. 20 Com. Church small & mean. Chancel in good Repair No Ho. 1 Bell. Licence to serve it Entry B. II. 175 1V. 51.

Cha. Norris[3] ⟨LLB⟩ Cur. 11 Aug. 1733. V. of Brabourn p. 97. Cur. of Goodneston p. 160. & of Horton p. 102. His Deputy here, John Gostling[4], R. of Brooke p. 6. Resides with his Father[5] at Cant. 2 miles off. Salary 20[£] & Surplice Fees. [I think he serves nothing else.] Died Jan 19. 1767.
Bryan Faussett[6], M.A. Cur. lic. 12 Feb. 1767. Rector of Horton p. 102. Resides here.
Joshua Dix[7] Clerk. Cur Lic March 6: 1776. does his own duty.

Mr Gostling[8] Jun[r] serves this with Stodmarsh 1766.

1758 Conf. 19. 1762. 16. 1766. 17

[1] Mary, the wife of Christopher Mill[e]s who had purchased Nackington House and died in 1752. She died in 1781: Hasted IX, pp. 296–7.
[2] Mary, the wife of Bryan Fausset. He rebuilt Heppington manor, and died in 1750: ibid., p. 295.
[3] (1707–67), of London, m. All Souls 1726, BA 1730, BCL (St Edmund Hall) 1733, R. Goodnestone, 1731–1767, V. Brabourne, 1733–67, C. Nackington, 1733–67.
[4] See, p. 6, n. 3.   [5] Ibid., n. 4.

[6] See, p. 19, n. 4.   [7] See, p. 34, n. 9.
[8] Same as n. 3.

Page 44
D. Cant.
St Paul. See St Martin p. 40.
St Peter. See St Cross p. 32.
St Stephen. See Hackington p. 36.

Sturrey V. St. Nicolas. Belonged to Mon. of St Austins. ABP P. K^s books 13-1-8. Now 60^f. ⟨70 AD^n⟩. 109 Ho. Prayers & Sermon once a Sunday. Fordwich Church within ½ mile [1759 twice Prayers]. Prayers & Cat. on Fridays in Lent. 4 Sacr. 40 Com. [V. will endeavour to increase the Number.]. Steph. Bygge[1] of Fordwich Gent. gave by Will, in 1646 to 6 poor Housekeepers of Sturrey & 6 of Fordwich 20^s each yearly, to be pd out of Lands, & 40^s for putting Ch^n apprentices. So applied. Church & Chancel large & in very good Order. 5 Bells. Ho. pretty good, much improved by Mr Twyman. Outhouses very little. Commandmt^s to be made new. 2 Acres of Glebe. 5 Bells.

Wheler Twyman[2] AM V. Aug 27. 1757. Resides at his own Ho. of Rushborne, within a few yards of the Parish. R. of Luddenham p. 167 where see.

Wm Chafy[3] A.M. Vicar 1780. does his own duty.

1758 Conf. 38. 1762. 38. 1766. 33

[1] [Bigg]. See p. 34, n. 3.   [2] See p. 22, n. 7.
[3] (1746–1826), of Purse-Caundle, Dorset, m. St John's C 1762, BA 1766, MA (Sidney Sussex) 1769, fellow 1769, minor canon, 1777–1826, V. Faversham, 1778–80, V. Sturry, 1780–1826, R. Swalecliffe, 1791–1826, chaplain to earl Cowper.

Page 45
Thanington C. St Nicolas. Belonged to the Priory of St Gregory. ABP, P. Certified 40^f, wch Sum is pd by ABP^s Lessee of St Gregorys ⟨Surplice Dues reckoned 10^f in 1663⟩. ⟨Augm. 1767 with 400^f by S^r Ph. Boteler & Qu^s bounty⟩. 32 Ho. Whole Service generally. [See below]. Ch^n cat. when sent, to wch Parents are admonished. 4 Sacr. 25 Com. Church in good Repair. Chancel cieled & well repaired 1759. No Ho. 3 Bells. A Curate licenced under the greater Seal, durante Beneplacito 1663 Entry B. I. 4. III. 87, 224. IV. 189.

Will. Broderip[1] MA C. 12 Nov. 1737. See Milton p. 42. He serves that once a month, & attends at Cath. as min. Can. one Sunday in 6: & so cannot always perform the whole Service here. Thanington is ½ a mile from Cant. Dead Apr. 20. 1764 ⟨Died Apr. 18⟩.
Tucker[2], John. C. Lic. June 13. 1764. R. of Milton p. 42. V. of Sheldwich p. 175.
Francis Gregory[3] Clerk A.M. Curate. Licensed May 21: 1777. does his own duty.

1758 Conf. 9. 1762. 11. 1766. 18

Westgate. See S[t] Cross p. 32.

[1] See p. 42, n. 2.   [2] See p. 4, n. 10.   [3] See p. 7, n. 5.

Page 46
D. Cant   Hospitals
Auchers, al. Cogans, al. Clergymens widows See p. 32

East-bridge al. Kings-bridge Hosp. founded by S[t] Tho. Becket, & bearing his
Name. See Somner p. 60. ABP. Stratford[1] new founded it & gave Rules to it,
wch see ib Ap. p. 13. whence some have deemed him the original Founder. ABP
P. Henry Heaton[2] BD Master ⟨coll.⟩ 24 Juy 1753. Worth to him 30[£] a year, as
Mr Lamprey[3] saith: others say 40 or 50[£]. There is a Rectory of East-bridge p.
120 in the Deanery of Lympne.
The Church of S[t] Nicolas Harbledown was appropriated to this Hospital by ABP
Stratford abt 1340. See a Paper from D[r] Ducarel.
Collation to this 1664 Entry B. I. 94.
Lease of the manor of West Blean &c & the Tithes of the Manor of Westgate
Court &c for 3 lives, Rent 39–3–4 of wch 13–8–0 for the maintenance of out
brothers & sisters, & 4[£] being an Increase, for ⟨such of⟩ the In-brothers as the
Master shall think poorest, confirmed by the ABP, the Instrumnt of Conf.
bearing Date the 11th of Sept. last but sealed 11 Feb. 1670 Entry B. III. 56. A
Lease of the same to persons & for lives in part different for 43–3–4 [no
appropriation mentioned & of woods excepted in the former Lease for 4–16–0
conf. March 6. 1670 p. 62. A Lease of 6 Acres of Land in Herbaldowne for 21
years, conf 10 Apr. 1671 p. 91. One of 11 Acres Rent 3[£] for D° 1672 p. 154.
⟨again 1V. 210⟩. The above Lease for 43–3–4 conf 1679 IV. 72. One of 6
Tenemts for 3[£], at length, granted 5 Aug 1678 conf 11 Nov. 1679 p. 91, 92. One
of 40 Acres 3 Apr. 1682 conf. 22 Apr. ⟨again 55⟩. One of a Tenmt 1682. 213.
D[r] John Batteley[4] AD[n] of Cant & Master of this Hosp. grant Lease of 11 Acres.
479.
In a Bag in the MS Library intitled Rotuli incerti aevi N° 43[5] is an Account of the
Estates of Eastbridge Hospital given to ABP Islip[6] by the Master on his quitting
it. D[r] Ducarel.

Henry Heaton.
W[m] Backhouse[7] D.D. Collated to the Office or place of Master of Eastbridge
Hospital Aug. 7: 1777.

[1] John Stratford, (12??–1348), archbishop, 1333–48.
[2] (?–1777), of Doncaster, m. CCCC 1730, BA 1734, MA 1737, BD 1745, fellow, 1735–54, taxor,
    1738, V. Boughton Blean, 1752–77, V. Hernehill, 1752–4, R. Ivychurch, 1754–77, master of
    Eastbridge Hosp, 1753–77, preb of Ely, 1759–77, chaplain to archbishop Herring.
[3] See p. 40, n. 6.
[4] (1646–1708), of Bury St Edmunds, Suffolk, m. Trinity C 1662, scholar, 1664, BA 1666, MA
    1669, DD 1684, fellow 1668, tutor, R. Hunton, 1683–1708, R. Adisham, 1684–1708, archdeacon
    of Suffolk, 1687–8, archdeacon of Canterbury, 1688–1708, master of Eastbridge, 1684, preb of
    Canterbury, 1688–1708, archbishop's chaplain (Sancroft and Tillotson).

[5] LPL, Estate Documents 296.   [6] Simon Islip (12??–1366), archbishop, 1349–66.
[7] See p. iii, n. 1.

Page 47

Hospitals

Harbledown al. Herbaldown. S[t] Nicolas. [Founded by ABP Lanfranc[1] for leprous persons. See Somner p. 42–47.]. ABP Patron. Tho. Lamprey[2] MA, Master. ⟨died Sept. 2. 1760⟩. See here p. 40. [Hath no Allowance, as Master: but 8[£] a year from the Stipends of the Poor for reading Prayers, on Wednesdays, at the Chapel, of which see here p. 37.].
John Head[3] D.D. Master Sept 1760. AD[n] & Preb. of Cant.

Tho. Lamprey consti & app. Reader in room of James Henstridge[4] 4 Jan 1745 Entry B VIII. 299.

[Jesus Hospital. See here p. 29]

[1] (?1005–89), archbishop, 1070–89.   [2] See p. 40, n. 6.   [3] See p. ii, n. 20.
[4] (1675–1745), of Rochester, Kent m. St John's C 1693, BA 1697, MA 1703, organist Dulwich College, 1698–1703, C. Lenham, 1699, V. Seasalter, 1700–1710, R. All Saints and St Mildred's, 1710–45, R. Brook, 1734–45, master Harbledown, minor canon of Canterbury, chaplain to earl Ferrars.

Page 48

D. Cant.   Hospitals
S[t] Johns Cant. ABP Patron. Tho. Lamprey[1] MA ⟨died Sept. 2 1760⟩, Master see p. 47. Hath no Allowance as such. Will. Broderip[2] MA See here p. 42. Chaplain. He reads Prayers in the Chapel W. Fr. Salary, 8[£] from the Stipends of the poor.
John Head[3] DD Master, Sept. 1760. AD[n] & Preb. of Cant.
Licence to John Stockar[4] to be Chaplain 1680 Entry B. IV. 142. See VI. 180. VIII. 90.

[1] See p. 40, n. 6.   [2] See p. 42, n. 2.   [3] See p. ii, n. 20.
[4] (1616–1709), of Chilcompton, Somerset, ('by nation a Frenchman', Act Book) m. Lincoln 1633, BA 1636, student Lincoln's Inn 1640, V. St Mary's Northgate, Canterbury and R. St Alphage, 1663–1709, reader St John's hospital, 1680.

Page 49

Hospitals

S[t] Laurences Hospital. Dissolved & held by M[rs] Rooke[1]. See Somner p. 38, 39, 40.

Hospital of poor Priests. See here p. 39.

[1] See p. 40, n. 3.

[Deanery of Charing]

Page 50

D. Charing

Ashford V. St Mary [i.e. Ford over the Esh] belonged to the Coll. of S[t] Stephen Westm. Ch. of Rochester P. K[s] books 18-4-2. Now 100[£] ⟨80 AD[n] see below⟩. 314 Ho. Market on Saturdays. D[r] Isaac Rutton[1], [800[£] a year, doth not practice]. Geo. Hooper[2], Tho. Hussey[3], Esqrs. A Hamlet, called Beaver. 20 Families of Presb. A Meeting Ho. Tho. Gellibrand, Teacher. 24 of Anab. ⟨A meeting Ho.⟩ Geo. Green. Teacher, Tho. Wanstall, Breeches-maker, Assistant. Whether qualified, unknown. Increased by fresh Families coming. 4 or 5 of Quakers. A Meeting Ho. At Whitsuntide a general Meeting. Pay their Dues pretty regularly. Whole Service. Prayers W. Fr. Holydays. Cat. exp. W. Fr. in Lent. Ch[n] & Servts not duly sent. Sacr. monthly, & 3 at Chr. Easter & 2 at Whits. From 80 to above 100 Com. A free School for Townsmens Sons, founded by Sir Norton Knatchbull[4]: V. & 3 neighbouring Clergymen, & the Proprietors of Mersham Hatch, Governors or Visitors. Income 30[£], no House. Much raised by the present Master, Mr ⟨Steph⟩ Barrett ⟨nom. by S[r] W Knatchbulls[5] Guardians Lic Jan 4, 1749 see below⟩: different from Cur. of Kingston p. 16. A workhouse, 40 persons in it. D[r] Turner[6] Pres. of CCC gave Lands for teaching & putting out 6 poor Boys. Lands worth 49[£] a year given for Repairs of the Church & worth 10[£] ⟨22 AD[n]⟩ to the poor ⟨by Sir J. Fagg[7] & Fam. AD[n]⟩. So applied. The widow of Mr Copley[8] R. of Pluckley & deprived in the great Rebellion, gave 20[s] for a yearly Sermon June 3, & 10[s] to 10 poor persons, issuing out of Lands. So applied. Church very noble. Chancel handsome: roof wants Repair. Ho. large, old, in good Order ⟨Faculty granted to lessen it 1765⟩. Glebe 17 Acres. 6 Bells. M[r] Barrett[9] resigned the School. Rev[d] W[m] Hodgson[10] MA made master by Sir Edw. Knatchbull[11] Aug. 1764. M[r] Barrett coming again 1766. Small tithes 30[£] Glebe 30[£] Easter book & Casualties 20[£] 1663.

John Clough[12] V. 19 Aug. 1721. R. of Horton p. ⟨102⟩. Grave, good, sensible. Resides in V. Ho. constantly. Cannot officiate 1762. Died before Nov. 20th 1764.
Charles Coldcall[13] MA V. 20 Apr. 1765. holds Ashburnham Co. Suss. with it & is preb. of Rochester. Resigned Oct. 10 1765.
James Andrew[14] MA. V. 10 Dec. 1765. Preb. of Rochester, will reside in Spring. Doth. DD. 1766.
James Bond[15] V August 9 1774.

Polhill[16] W[m] C. 1762 was C at Rainham p. 224. Good voice. R. of Bircholt, p. 96.
John White[17] was C. at S[t] Andrew Undershaft. March 1764. 40[£] a year &c Liked. ⟨Gone⟩.
Mr Hyde[18] Jan 1766. Mr Gerard[19] F. of Wadham to be Cur till Easter.
Luis Hoffman[20] C. AM of Jesus Oxf. P. See his testimonial. P. by BP Lowth[21] 1767.

1758 Conf. ⟨here 1434, of this parish⟩ 92. 1762. Conf. here 899. Of this parish 118. 1766 Conf here May 30. 564. Of this parish 95.

D[r] Andrews[22] Cur.

1 'A physician of long and extensive practice in these parts', who died in 1792: Hasted, VII, p. 534.
2 Died in 1759, leaving £500 to new pew Tunbridge church: Hasted V, p. 250.
3 Died in 1779; Hasted VII, p. 340.
4 (1602–85), Ist Bt, MP for Kent, 1640, MP New Romney, 1640–8 and 1660–77.
5 Sir Wyndam Knatchbull (1737–63), 3d Bt, MP for Kent, 1760–3.
6 Thomas Turner (1645–1714), of Bristol, m. Hart Hall 1662, CCCO 1663, BA 1666, MA 1669, BD 1677, DD 1683, fellow 1672, president 1688, V. Milton near Sittingbourne, 1672–95, R. Thorley, Herts, 1680–9, archdeacon of Essex, 1680, canon of Ely, 1686, canon of St Paul's, 1682.
7 (1627–1701), Ist Bt, MP for Rye, 1645–53, MP for Sussex, 1654–9 and 1681–5, MP for Steyning, 1660–81 and 1685–1701.
8 John Copley, R. Pluckley, 1616–43, restored in 1660.
9 Stephen Barret, (1720–1801), of Sutton, Yorkhire, m. University 1738, BA 1741, R. Purton and Ickleford, Herts, 1744, R. Hotham, Herts, 1743, master Ashford free School, 1749–78, R. Hothfield, 1773–1801.
10 Possibly (1728–?), of Penrith, Cumberland, m. Queen's O 1746, BA 1750.
11 (1704–89), 7th Bt, MP for Armagh, 1727–60.
12 (1689–1764), of Whittering, Northamptonshire, m. St John's C 1706, BA 1710, MA 1713, V. Stockbury, 1716–21, V. Ashford, 1721–64, R. Monks Horton, 1728–64, chaplain to Rt Hon Eliz. Hatton, minor canon of Rochester, 1713–21.
13 (1722–93), of Epsom, Surrey, m. Christ Church 1741, Kings, 1742, BA 1747, MA 1750, fellow 1745, R. Catsfield, R. Ashburnham, Sussex, 1750–93, V. Ashford, 1765, V. Aylesford, 1771–93, R. Kingsdown, 1782–93, preb of Rochester, 1760–93, preb of Chichester, 1754, chaplain to earl of Ashburnham.
14 Andrew(s), (1718–91), of Probus, Cornwall, m. Exeter 1738, BA 1741, MA 1745, B & DD 1766, V. Ashford, 1765–74, R. Eynesford, 1784–91.
15 (1750–), of Probus, Cornwall, m. Exeter 1770, C. Shadoxhurst, 1772, C. Bircholt, V. Ashford, 1774–1826, PC. Bilsington, 1786–1826.
16 (1736–1822), of Maidstone, Kent, m. University 1754, BA 1758, C. Ashford, 1762, R. Bircholt, 1762–74, master Ashford School, 1764–78, R. Orlestone, 1764–80, C. Rainham, C. Linton, 1765, V. Linton, 1773–79, V. Detling, 1779–1822.
17 See p. 15, n. 2.
18 Perhaps William Hyde, (1727–?), of Wantage, Berks, m. Magdalen O 1744, chorister 1734–44, clerk, 1744–9, BA 1748.
19 James Gerrard, (1741–83), of Monks Risborough, Bucks, m. Wadham 1757, BA 1761, MA 1765, B & DD 1777, warden, 1777–83, R. Monks Risborough, 1783–89.
20 (1742–?), of London, m. Jesus O 1760, scholar 1763–70, BA 1764, MA 1767.
21 Robert Lowth (1710–1787), of Hampshire, m. St John's O 1729, fellow New College, BA 1733, MA 1737, DD 1754, professor of poetry, 1741–51, archdeacon of Winchester, 1750, preb of Durham 1755, bishop of St David's, 1766, bishop of Oxford, 1766–77, bishop of London, 1777–87. Author of *De Sacra Poesi Hebraeorum* (1753).
22 See n. 14.

Page 51

Benenden V. S[t] George. Mon. Combwell Propr. Ecton. Norris Esq[r] ⟨Dame Eliz. Norris[1]⟩ P. Tenths 2–15–3. Certified 40[£]. So called now. ⟨45[£] AD[n] 50[£] Mr Dunn. See his Letter Sept. 1. 1762⟩. ABP Wakes papers at Ch. Ch. vol. 2 say, that there is no Glebe, nor Tithe, 2[d] an Acre on Land, 1½[d] for the fall of a Calf: in all 33[£] a Year. 140 Ho. 150 Families. Lady Norris. ⟨Now John Norris[2] Esq[r] at Hempsted⟩. Her Ho. 50 Years ago belonged to a Papist. Sev[£] then: now only John Jenks, a large Farmer, who hath been at no place of Worship lately. A Priest occasionally at his Ho. one night, 9 years ago. 3 Families of Presb. 2 of Anab. Tho. Love, the master of one, a Teacher. Three old Quakers: their Descendents baptized. Whole service in Summer, once in Winter. V. serves also a Church in Sussex. Prayers on Holydays, W. Fr. in Lent, every day in Passion Week. Ch[n] & Serv[ts] cat. in Lent. Expositions & other good Books given by V. 8 Sacr. sometimes above 100 Com. A free School, founded by Edm. Gibbon of Benenden Esqr with a House & Land worth 61–10–0 a year. In 1695 Major Gibbon[3] of Hole Esqr added an Exchequer Annuity of 14[£] a year to the master: but if he was Parson, Vicar, Curate, or Reader, to poor Girls. ⟨V. is not Master⟩. To the poor 12–10–0 yearly from Lands. One Mitchel & one Briant, Methodist Teachers, preached each once here in 1758. Acct of Kent[4] 4° saith, the Steeple here is separate from the Church, at some Distance: the Foundation, Stone; the rest, a very high Spire of exceeding large Timber, curiously compacted. p. 1137, 1138. Church & chancel very clean & handsome. Ho. & out Ho. in good Order. An Orchard. 6 Bells. Of the School & annuity see M[r] Norris 2 Sept 1761. The Master hath abt 33[£] & a House worth 3[£]: the Usher 20[£]. Pres. by Univ. Oxon 1699 Entry B. IV. 619.

John Williams[5] LLB ⟨of St Mary Hall⟩ V. 19 Apr. 1744. Hath constantly resided in V. Ho. One of the 10 poor vicars. Inst. to Blodwell, Dioc. S[t] Asaph, [but I find it not in Ecton Apr. 27. 1761. I have promised not to take Advantage of a Lapse.
Joseph Dunn[6] of Magd. Coll. Cambr. BA ord Pr. by BP Mawson[7] 14 Dec ⟨Sept⟩ 1760. V. 3 Dec. 1761. To be Schoolmaster also. Mr Norris desires that he may be one of the 10 poor vicars. Done Sept. 1762.

Vicar resides.

James Dunn[8] A.B. Cur. Sal. £40 lic. 1791.

1758 Conf. 14. 1762. 146. 1766. 39

[1] Wife of Sir John Norris (1670–1749), MP for Rye, 1708–22 and 1734–49, MP for Portsmouth, 1722–34, admiral of the fleet.
[2] (1702–67), MP for Rye, 1727–32.   [3] John Gibbon
[4] *A Compleat History of Kent* [1730].
[5] (1719–?), of Llanfwrog, Denbigh, m. St Mary's Hall 1739, BCL 1751, V. Benenden, 1744–61.
[6] (1737–99), of Middleton, Durham, m. Magdalene C 1755, BA 1759, MA 1762, C. Chatteris, Cambs, 1759, C. Stretham, Cambs, 1760, V. Benenden, 1761–99.
[7] Matthias Mawson, (1688–1770), of London, m. CCCC 1702, scholar, BA 1705, MA 1708, BD 1716, DD 1725, fellow, 1707–24, moderator, 1708, taxor, 1709, master CCCC, 1724–44, vice-chancellor, 1730–2, R. Connington, Cambs, 1731–2, R. Hadstock, Essex, bishop of Llandaff, 1738–40, bishop of Chichester, 1740–54, bishop of Ely, 1754–70.
[8] (?–1829), of Durham, m. Emmanuel 1787, BA 1791, MA 1794, BD 1801, C. Benenden, 1791, R. Preston, Suffolk, 1810–29, V. Little Melton, Norfolk, 1810–29.

Page 52
D. Charing
Bethersden al. Betrisden V. S[t] Beatrice. Belonged to the Priory of S[t] Gregory. ABP P. K[s] Books 12[£]. Now hath 100[2)*], of which 30[£] is reserved in ABP[s] Lease of S[t] Gregorys Priory. 80 Ho[1)*]. 2 Families & 4 Persons Anab. Whole Service. Prayers on principal Holydays, & W. Fr. in Lent. Sermons on State Holydays, Ash W. & Good Fri. Cat. May – Sept. Shall be exp. 4 Sacr. 60 Com. each time.

Lands worth 13^f a year given to the Church. So applied. Church & chancel clean & handsome. Ho. Brick, in very good Order. Out Ho good. Glebe 1½ Acre. 5 Bells. Very dirty in Winter: only pond-water. Ho. ¼ mile from church: a good foot-way at all times.
1)* 110 Ho. 124 Families
2)* Income 109^f Taxes 14^f, 1760. See Letter[1].

Henry Dell[2] V. 26 March 1747 ⟨died Oct. 17. 1763⟩. Was a Dissenting Minister. Good. Resides constantly in V. Ho. May 1760. declining, unable to officiate: helped by his neighbours: will get a Curate, wn he can. 2 Daughters, above 30.
William Jones[3] BA V. 9 Dec. 1763. Will go to reside before Mids. Void by Cession June 28 1765.
Henry Kent[4] MA. V. 21 Nov. 1765. Will reside next year ⟨early in Autumn⟩ & have a resident C. Now. Going thither Nov 1766. Come back Dec. 1766.
David Martin[5] Vicar 1781.
Liscombe Maulby Stretch[6] Vicar 1786.
Daniel Wilcox[7] Vicar 1787.
Evans[8], James, BA of St Johns Camb. C. ord. Deacon Sept. 21. 1760. 2. 40^f. Going Jan 1762. Gone. Mr Dell doth part of Duty & hopes to have a Curate by LD. May 1763 Mr Jones[9] serves this with Wood Church & Kenardington.
Apsley[10] Will. BA of Merton C. bapt Feb. 25. 1740/1. Ord. D. Sept. 25. 1763. 2. 40^f. Gone.
Geo. Jeffreyes[11] P. D. June 1766. Was of Ch. Ch. Gone Dec. 1766.
Evans[12] P. C. See Mr Kents Letter Jan. 10. To reside immediately. Behaves well 1768.

1758 Conf. 30. 1762. 23. 1766. 39

[1] LPL, MS Secker 3, f. 10, Dell to Secker, 11 August 1760.
[2] (?–1763), V. Bethersden, 1747–63. In the 1720s he had been a minister to a dissenting congregation in Canterbury.
[3] (1726–1800), of Lowick, Northants, m. University 1745, BA 1749, MA (Sidney Sussex), FRS, 1775, C. Finedon, Northants, c. 1750, C. Wadenhoe, 1754, V. Bethersden, 1763–5, R. Pluckley, 1765–77, PC. Nayland, Suffolk, 1777, R. Paston, Northants, 1777–1800, chaplain to bishop of Norwich, 1790, R. Hollingbourne, 1798–1800.
[4] (1719–?), of Potterne, Wiltshire, m. Merton 1737, BA 1741, MA 1745, BD & DD 1769, V. Bethersden, 1765–81.
[5] (17?–1821), Glasgow Coll, C. Leysdown and Minster in Sheppey, 1766, V. Bethersden, 1781–86, V. Leysdown, 1786–1821, C. Eastchurch, 1790.
[6] (17?–1813), A dissenter, V. Leysdown, 1762–86, V. Bethersden, 1786–7.
[7] (17?–1806), of Corby, Lancs, m. Clare Hall 1767, BA 1771, MA 1774, R. High Halden, 1780–1806, V. Bethersden, 1787–1806, chaplain to Rt Hon Joh Charles Villiers.
[8] Of Kent, m. St John's C 1756, scholar 1757, BA 1760, MA 1763. Perhaps V. of Lazonby, Cumberland, 1763–71.
[9] Richard Jones. See p. 115, n. 6.
[10] (1741–), of Ashford, Kent, m. Merton, 1757, BA 1761, C. Luddenham, 1763–66, C. Rainham, 1765–66, to Deal chapel.
[11] (1737–?), of Castle Morton, Worcs, m. Christ Church 1756, BA 1761.
[12] See n. 7.

Page 53

Biddenden R. All Saints ABP P. K^s books 35$^£$. Now 180$^£$ ⟨See below above 200$^£$⟩. 30 Ho. in a Street, 130 more: 750 Inhabitants. 2 Papists: 2 Presb. 28 Anab. A meeting Ho. Teacher lately dead: no Successor: many have lately conformed. 2 Quakers, poor. Whole Service. 2 Sermons for some years. R. is willing to cat. instead of one [1759 doth both]. Prayers on Holy-days. 4 Sacr. { } Com. A free School for Latin, founded by Sir John Mayney[1] abt 1522, endowed with Lands of 20$^£$ a year, in the Hands of 21 Feoffees, who fill the vacancies of the Trust. Well managed. Lands of 20$^£$ a year, given, as is said for Bread & Cheese for the poor on Easter Day, not known by whom. A small part so given: the rest to the poor in other ways. Also 5 or more Acres of Woodland given for the poor: from the Timber of it, 8$^£$ a year purchased at Bredgar. Church & chancel handsome. Ho & outHo. in good Order. Glebe 17 Acres. 6 Bells.

200$^£$ formerly, now 160$^£$: of wch the Glebe is 20$^£$. 1663.

John Mather[2] MA. R. 5 March 1746. Resides now.
Wm Philip Warburton[3] M.A. Rector 1794.

1758. Conf. 47. 1762. 53. 1766. 40.

[1] Owner of Biddenden Place. Probably died in 1566.
[2] (1717-1794), of Oxford, m. CCCO 1734, BA (New College) 1739, MA 1743, C. Lewknor, Oxon, 1749, R. Biddenden, 1747-94.
[3] (1762-1821), of Elmstead, Essex, m. Jesus C 1778, scholar, 1780, BA 1782, MA 1785, fellow 1785, C. Harleston, Norfolk, 1783, R. Ruckinge, 1793-4, R. Biddenden, 1794-7, V. Lydd, 1797-1821, archbishop's chaplain.

Page 54

D. Charing

Boughton al Bocton Malherb. St Nicolas. R. Galfridus Mann[1] Esqr P. K^s books 13-15-0. Now 130. R. saith ab^t 110$^£$. Ab^t 35 Ho. {James} ⟨Tho.⟩ Best[2] Esqr [at Chilson, 4 or 5000$^£$ a year, married sister of Mr Scot[3] of Scots Hall p. { }]. His Park &c chiefly in Lenham. Mr Mann hath the chief Property, but does not reside here. 7 Anab. Families: some have conformed. Prayers & Sermon once a Sunday, morning & Evening alternately. The other part at Egerton p. { }]. But that, though the nearest Church is two miles off. [See the Letters. Promised to serve this twice, & Egerton once. Doth so 1759 when he can get Hearers]. Boughton Church is at one End of the Parish ⟨but one Ho. near it⟩: & other Churches as near some Parishioners. Cat. exp. on Sundays in Lent. 4 Sacr. 40 or 50 Com. 500$^£$ lately expended on the Parsonage Ho. Church in pretty good, Chancel in good Repair: Ho. in very good, much improved by Mr Foot. Out Ho. in good Order. Glebe 4 Acres. 4 Bells.

Abt a Colony of Fr. Protestants settled here in 1681 See Entry B V. 180[4].

Francis Hender Foote[5] R 5 Dec. 1750. V. ⟨of Linton p. 247⟩. Cur. also of Egerton p. 61. Resides. Hath some Estate of his own: 3000$^£$ with his Wife. Large Family. Obliged May 1764 to be much absent for a yr: hath M^r ⟨Wm⟩ Bearcroft[6], Deacon, for Cur. 50$^£$, residence Egerton. ord. Pr. June 2 1765. 2.

Mr Fox[7] see p. 61. different from Hopkins Fox p. 16. Sept. 1766 Mr Foote resides & will reside, chiefly here.
Honble James Cornwallis[8] M.A. R. May 19 1773.
Edward Beckingham Benson[9] A.B. Rector, Septr. 29: 1779.
Robert Foote[10] A.M. Rector 1782. resides.

1758 Conf. 47. 1762. 19. 1766. 25

[1] Army clothier from London. Bought the manor and advowson in 1750. According to Hasted (V, p. 405) he died in 1756 and was succeeded by his son Horatio, MP for Maidstone, 1774–84 and Sandwich, 1790–1807.
[2] Thomas Best, died 1795.
[3] Caroline, the sister of Edward Scott. Scot Hall is in Smeeth: Hasted VIII, p. 7.
[4] See also Bodl., MS Tanner 36, f. 239, Sancroft to Stanhope, 27 February 1682.
[5] (1725–73), of Bloomsbury Square, London, m. St Edmund Hall 1749, LLB, R. Boughton Malherbe, 1750–773, C. Egerton, 1756–73, V. Linton, 1751–73, chaplain to Lord Chesterfield. He inherited Charlton Place, Canterbury.
[6] (1740–), m. Peterhouse 1757, BA 1767, MA 1775, founder's day preacher Charterhouse, 1779.
[7] Perhaps John Fox (1732–), of Kingswinford, Staffs, m. Pembroke O 1750, BA 1753.
[8] See p. ii, n. 6
[9] (1775–95), of Cambridge, m. Hertford, 1773, BA 1777, MA 1780, V. Linton, 1779–82, R. Boughton Malherbe, 1779–82, V. Deal and Coldred, 1788–95, six-preacher, 1784.
[10] Son of Francis. (1758–1805), of Boughton Malherbe, m. Merton 1772, BA (University) 1779, MA 1782, V. Linton, 1782–99, R. Boughton Malherbe, 1782–1804, V. Shorne, 1799–1804, preb of Rochester.

Page 55

Charing V. St Peter & St Paul. Exempt from AD^n. St Pauls Ch. Propr. & Patr. K^s books 13$^£$. Was a Sine Cure in 1534, & then rated at 47-5-4 Ecton. Certified 72$^£$. Now 118$^£$. 130 Ho. Geo. Sayer[1] [of Pete] Esqr [1000$^£$ a year: wife a great Fortune]. 4 Families of Anab. Whole Service. Prayers W. Fr. Cat. on Sund. W. Fr. in Lent. Sacr. monthly & on great Fest. Com. from 30 to 50. Subscription proposed for teaching poor Ch^n to read. 1$^£$ a year, the Interest of 100$^£$ secured by Land, [here must be some mistake ⟨It is only 20$^£$⟩] lately given by Mr Roger Payne[2] of Otterden, for as many Poor Persons, frequenting Church & not receiving Parish Alms, as V. & ChW^{n}s please. Church & Chancel large & in pretty good Order. Ho. neat & in good Order: much improved by Mr Pinckney. Out ho. wants some Repair. Glebe 3½ Acres. 1 Bell.
The Manor of Charing, & Advowson of the Rectory & Vicarage were given by the ABP to the Crown in Exchange 31 Aug 1 Ed. 6. See Chart Misc. vol. 13. N° 21.
A procuration of 1-6-8 was p^d for the Rectory in ABP Warhams time: but the Barrell[3] family, who are now Lessees of the Rectory, denied to ABP^s Potter & Herring, that they had ever paid it, & supposed it might be due from their Landlords the DCh of St Pauls. On this ABP Herring applied to me, as Dean. I found no proof that DCh had ever p^d it.

Will Pinckney[4] V. 13 Oct. 1755 of the K^s Chapel & min. Can. of St Pauls. Resides here 4 months in the year.
Edm. Marshall[5] V. 1 Feb. 1766 will reside. R. of Fakenham Dioc. Roch. Hath a Lecture in London. Promised to quit it at LD. Desires to keep it. Refused March 27. Resides here with his family May 1768.

Best[6], Demy of Magd. Coll. Ox. Cur. Resides 40^f. Gone.

Geo. Lynch[7], LD 1760. See Chartham. Gone back thither. No Cur Chr. 1760.

John Harbin[8] BA of Wadh. Coll. ord. Deacon June 1760 by BP Lavington[9], Cur. Feb. 1761. Married, hires Ho, near Church. {To be ord. Pr. Tr. S. Mich} ord. Pr. by me 7 March, 1762. 40^f.

John Stock[10] Cur. 1763 Good. Rec. for prefermt by Dr Bentham[11]. V. of Stanway Co. Gloc. a very small Income, & cannot do the Duty there bec. lame by a fall. Gone May 1765.

Abra^m. Purshouse[12] AB. Licensed July 7: 1778, with a Salary of £30 p.ann. Mr Jones[13] Cur. of Egerton Sal £20.

John Barwick[14] A.B. Cur. Sal £50 lic. by Archdeacon.

1758 Conf. 92. 1762 35. 1766. 51.

[1] He died in 1778. His rich wife was Mary Greenhill of Maidstone: Hasted VII, p. 436.
[2] By his will of 1701: Hasted V, p. 546.
[3] The Barrells were of Rochester, and had the lease for many years: Hasted VII, p. 447. Edmund Marshall (see n. 5) was their relation.
[4] (1714–?), of Oxford, m. Christ Church, 1732, BA, 1736, MA, 1747, V. Charing, 1755–66, minor canon of St Paul's, and of King's chapel.
[5] (1734–97), of London, m. St John's C 1749, BA 1753, MA 1756, R. Fawkham, Kent, 1758–97, V. Charing, 1766–97, PC. Egerton, 1773–97.
[6] Probably Henry (?–1782), of Lincoln, m. Magdalene C 1748, BA 1752, MA 1755, DD 1767, fellow 1752, V. Edlington, Lincs, 1755, R. Mavis Enderby, Lincs, 1769–.
[7] See p. 7, n. 7.
[8] (1735–?), of Wareham, Dorset, m. Wadham 1754, BA 1758, R. Hampreston, Dorset.
[9] George Lavington (1686–1762), of Midenhall, Wilts, m. New College 1706, BCL 1713, DCL 1732, R. Heyford Warren, Oxon, 1717–30, R. St Michael Bassihaw, 1730, R. St Mary Aldermary, London, 1742, preb of Worcester, 1719, preb of St Paul's, 1731, R. Shobrooke, Devon, 1742–62, archdeacon of Exeter, 1747–8, bishop of Exeter, 1748–62.
[10] See p. 7, n. 10.
[11] Edward Bentham, (1707–76), of Ely, Cambs, m. CCCO 1724, Oriel, BA 1729, fellow Oriel 1731–52, MA 1732, tutor, 1732–52, BD 1744, DD 1749, vice-principal, Magdalen Hall, 1730, canon of Christ Church, 1754, regius professor of Divinity, 1763–76. See his correspondence with Secker, LPL, MS 1133.
[12] (1754–1831), of Southwark, Surrey, m. Pembroke C 1773, BA 1777, MA 1780, C. Charing, 1778–86, V. Brabourne w. Monks Horton, 1786–1831, R. Frinsted, 1822–31.
[13] Probably Henry Jones (1735–?), of Glanyrafondda, Carmathen, m. Christ Church 1756, BA 1760.
[14] (1767–1834), of Kent, m. CCCC 1785, BA 1789, MA 1805, C. Charing and Egerton, 1790, V. Charing, 1799–1834, PC. Egerton, 1816–34, R. Boughton Malherbe, 1804–34.

Page 56

D. Charing

Chart great. R. St Mary. ABP P. K^s books 25–6–0½. Now 180^f or more 〈200 AD^n. 210^f Dr Wray〉. 61 Ho. Widow of Nicolas Toke[1] of Goddington Esqr, who hath 2 Sons. 2 Families of Anab. Whole Service Prayers generally on Fasts & Feasts. Cat. in Lent: to be exp. 4 Sacr. 40 Com at least. Fr. Toke[2] of this Parish Esqr left by will in 1583 Tenemts & Lands 〈worth 8^f〉 for 2^s a week for 2 poor Widows, to be appointed by the Tokes of Goddington. So applied. 2–15–0 for the Poor, 6–16–4 for repairing the Church. So applied. Church & Chancel large & decent. Ho. & Out Ho. good. 5 Bells. Glebe 12 Acres. 5 Bells.

Tho. Wray[3] MA R. 25 Nov. 1757. Chapl. to ABP Hutton[4]. Resided after his Death. In June 1759 came to Lambeth. R. also of Ruckinge p. 139. but now of Wittrisham May 2. 1761 p. 149. Void by Cession Apr. 10 1762. See p. 414. John Benson[5] MA R. May 3. 1762. R. of Ruckinge p. 139. Will reside. Gone. William Nance[6] L.L.B. Rector 1780. resides.

Nath. Bristed[7] of Emman. Coll. Deacon, Cur. till {Chr.} ⟨Mich⟩ 1759. Will. Holcombe[8] BA of Christs Coll. Camb. ord. Deacon 23 Sept 1759. 1. 40$^£$. To reside. Ord. Pr. 1 June 1760. Gone.
Eaton[9] To come for Pr. orders at Chr. 1761. Gone.
Laughton[10] minister of Stamford & Lyddington, but obliged to quit them for Debt: otherwise good. BP of Lincoln[11] consents, Jan. 26. 1762. 2.
Allen[12] W^m BA of Chr. Col. Camb bapt 10 Nov 1738. Ord. D. 28 March 1762 ⟨Gone to Ruckinge⟩.
Markham Sam[13]. C. Chr. 1763 40$^£$ & the Use of the House. Gone Oct. 1765.
Herbert Randolph[14] P. Oct. 1765.
Thos. Scott[15] Curate, Licensed Decr. 21: 1773. Salary £40 p. ann.
Robert Monkhouse[16] Cur. Sal. 42$^£$ & Surplice fees lic by the Archdeacon.

1758 Conf. 43. 1762. 23. 1766. 29

[1] Katherine, 2nd wife of Nicholas Toke. Their two sons were John and Thomas: Hasted VII, p. 508.
[2] Ibid., p. 509. Hasted notes that the land produced £11-2s-6d.
[3] (1723-78), of Bentham, Yorkshire, m. Christs 1740, scholar 1742, BA 1744, MA 1747, DD 1762, fellow, 1746-58, senior Greek Lecturer and Mildmay preacher, 1756-8, R. Croxton, Norfolk, 1755, V. Bourn, Cambs, 1755-8, R. Great Chart, 1757-62, R. Ruckinge, 1760-61, R. Wittersham, 1761-2, V. Rochdale, Lancs, 1762-78, chaplain to archbishop Hutton.
[4] Matthew Hutton (1693-1758), archbishop, 1757-8.
[5] See p. ii, n. 40.   [6] See p. 37, n. 8.
[7] (1733-1810), of Lewes, Sussex, m. Emmanuel 1754, BA 1758, MA 1762, master Free School, Shaftesbury, Dorset, 1761, C. Great Chart, 1759, R. South Heighton w. Tarring Neville, Sussex, 1765-74, head-master Sherborne School, 1766-90, V. Bishop's Caundle, Dorset, 1780-1810, V. Sherborne, Dorset, 1781-1810.
[8] (1736-96), of Pembrokeshire, m. Christs 1754, scholar, BA 1758, MA 1761, fellow 1761-2, R. Cosheston Pembs, 1761?, V. LLangadock, Carm., 1780, V. Mathrey, Glam., 1780, R. Manerdivy, Pemb, 1788, V. Penbryn, Card, 1789, preb of St David's, 1780-96.
[9] Perhaps Stephen Eaton, (1738-?), m. Merton 1757, BA 1760, MA 1763, R. St George, Middlesex, R. Thorley, Herts, V. Northall, Middlesex, R. St Anne's, Westminster, archdeacon of Middlesex.
[10] Perhaps Siddall Laughton, (1746-?), of Altrincham, Cheshire, m. Trinty C 1743, scholar 1744, BA 1747.
[11] John Green. See p. i, n. 2.
[12] (?-1811), of Cresselly, Pembs, m. Christs 1758, scholar 1759, BA 1762, C. Great Chart, 1762-3, C. Ruckinge, 1763-8, R. Little Chart, 1768-1811, chaplain dowager countess of Ferrers, 1764.
[13] See p. 16, n. 12.
[14] (1748-1819), m. CCCO 1762, BA 1765, MA (Magdalen) 1768, BD 1777, PC. Wimbledon, 1777-1819.
[15] (1756-91), of Smeeth, Kent, m. Merton 1775, LLB (Peterhouse), C. Great Chart, 1778, V. Bredgar, 1780-81, V. Lenham, 1781-91, R. Denton, 1785-91.
[16] Perhaps (1757-98), of Braithwaite, Cumbria, m. Queen's O 1758, C. Appledore, 1782, C. Great Chart, 1790, R, Mottram, Lancs.

Page 57

Chart Little R. S[t] Mary ABP P. K[s] books 13–10–10 ⟨Now 105[£] at least. But see below⟩. 28 Ho. Philip Darell[1], Esq[r], Papist. 12 Papists in all. AD[n] saith many Converts have been made. Cur. saith, none in his time. Mr Darells brother, James, a Priest, here sometimes. Whole Service. No weekly Duty. [Qu. great Festivals]. Cat. exp. in Lent. 3 Sacr. [must be 4]. 25 Com. 10[s] a year left by Mr Fotherby[2], once R. for a Charity Sermon, & 30[s] for industrious poor. Church clean & neat, & chancel. Ho. & out Ho. old, in tolerable Repair. Glebe 28 Acres. 5 Bells. R. saith, See Letter Oct. 9. 1762, that after Curate is pd & the Repairs of a ruinous old Ho. made, part of which he rebuilt, he receives but 35[£] a year Com. Ann. 1767 Barn & Oast burnt. Glebe 20[£]: tithe 64.
1765. 31 Papists. See the acct.

Edw. Watkinson[3] MD. R. Low spirited. Resides at Ackworth in Yorkshire. Was robbed here & frighted away. Died 19 Oct. 1767.
W[m] Allen[4] BA R. Jan 30. 1768 was Cur. of Ruckinge. Will reside after LD. does his own duty.

James Sawkins[5] Deacon, Cur. [Ord. Pr. Sept. 24. 1758. 2]. 40[£]. Resides. [Had a very good character: but suspected of Incest, 1759, with his brothers Widow, with whom he went off suddenly]. Till a Cur. can be got, M[r] Howdell[6], Cur of Pluckley, p. 69, a mile off, Serves it once a Sunday.
Archibald Brakenridge[7], F. of S[t] Johns Oxford, Cur. 40[£] ord. Pr. 1 June 1760. 2. Going Aug 1760 to S[t] Bennets Grace-Church.
Devis, James. Cur. to reside at Mich 1760. 40[£] Surp. Fees, Parsonage Ho. was a Dissenting minister, ord. by Lit. Dim. from ABP Herring. D[n] by BP Hayter[8] & Pr. by BP Ellis[9] 1754. May 1761, resides, behaves well. Going July 1761.
James Allen Gorsse[10] coming hither from Ruckinge ⟨42[£]⟩. Serves it from Ashford 6 miles off.
John Tattersall[11] Cur. lic by the Archdeacon.

1758 Conf. 20. 1762. 16. 1766. 13.

[1] See p. 39, n. 1.
[2] John Fotherby (15?–1619), of Grimby, Lincs, m. Queens' C 1577, BA 1581, MA (Trinity) 1584, V. Headcorn, 1584–1602, R. Smarden, 1586–1619, R. Little Chart, 1602–19.
[3] MD, R. Little Chart, 1744–67.   [4] See p. 56, n. 12.
[5] (17?–99), of Canterbury, m. St John's C 1752, LLB 1758, V. Frampton, Dorset, 1776–99, R. Bettiscombe, Dorset, 1784–99.
[6] John Howdell (1727–62), of Staple, Kent, m. St John's C 1743, BA 1747, usher King's School, Canterbury, 1749, R. Bircholt, 1750–62.
[7] (1736–?), of St Anne's Westminster, m. St John's O 1754, BCL 1761.
[8] Thomas Hayter (1702–62), bishop of Norwich, 1749–62, bishop of London, 1761–2.
[9] Anthony Ellys (1690–1761), bishop of St David's, 1752–61.
[10] A teacher of French in Ashford, he also acted as curate at Mersham for John Chapman.
[11] (1751–1801), of Charing, Kent, m. CCCO 1767, BA 1771, MA 1775, C. Ulcombe, 1778, PC. Bredhurst, 1783, C. Little Chart, 1790, V. Harewood, Yorks, 1792–1801, royal chaplain.

Page 58

D. Charing

Cranbrook V. St Dunstan. ABP Propr [qu] & Patr. ⟨Mr Lawson[1] V. of Throughley p. 178 is Impropriator⟩. Kings books 19-19-4½ ⟨Called 90$^£$ w^n Mr Johnson[2] was coll 21 Apr 1707. 60[1] tithes 1663⟩. Now 100$^£$ ⟨90 AD^n: 40 of it from Houses⟩. 200 Ho. in the Town, & 280 in the Hamlets. The chief are Milkhouse (where are the Ruines of a Chapel, not used since the Reformation: w^n the Lands ⟨[worth 84$^£$ a year]⟩ were granted to Sr John Baker[3] of Sissingherst in this Parish) upper & lower Wilsley, Goldford, Hartley, Haseldens Wood, Glassenbury, Colliers Green, Plushinghurst. Wm Tempest[4] Esqr, Geo. Tempest[5] his younger son, John Cooke[6] Esqr, Messrs Plummer[7], Weston[8], Holden[9]. D^s of St Albans[10], Heiress to Sr Walt Roberts[11], hath a furnished Ho. at Glassenbury, but lives not there. Formerly many Presb. & Anab. Much declined. One Family, & 3 others, Quakers. All have Meeting Houses. The Quaker doth not refuse paying Tithe, but is dilatory. Seldom any Speaker. The Presb. Teacher, Robt Nois, inoffensive. The Anab. Dan. Dobel, Farmer & Salesman of Cloaths. Mr Tempest is a man of Learning & FRS & was an active Justice, & went to Church, till being exc. [for what?] in the late Vicars Time, he turned Anab. & then Sabbatarian: but now acquiesces in his Ch^{ns} going to Church. He is infirm, lives chiefly in London, & seldom goes to any publick Worship. Some careless Absenters of all Ranks. Not increased. Glebe scarce an Acre.

Two Sermons on Sundays: one on good Fr. Ascension Day, Nov. 5 [Chr.] Jan 30. Prayers on Holydays, W. Fr. Cat. Sund. W. Fr. in Lent. Sacr. monthly, Chr. good Fr. Easter. Asc. Whits. Tr. S. 120 Com. on a common Sunday. At Easter & Chr. 40 or 50 more.

A Grammar School for all Ch^n born in the Parish, founded abt 1570 by Simon Lynch, endowed with 46$^£$ a year. Qu. Eliz. incorporated it by her own name. made the V. & 12 Freeholders of the Parish, Governors, who fill up Vacancies. She gave nothing to it. Now it is at a low Ebb, though Mr Samuel Venner[12], chosen 2 or 3 years ago, is very capable of teaching. Governors must fill up wn reduced to 6. No Statutes. Also a Writing School, founded by Alex. Dence[13] in 1573 endowed with the Interest of 160$^£$.

D^s of St Albans pays 2^s a week for teaching 12 poor Ch^n, & something is paid out of the Offertory for others. A Farm of 14$^£$ a year & the Interest of 100$^£$, given to poor who have no Parochial Relief. 18$^£$ a year for putting out poor Boys Apprentices. Only two of four Trustees left: the last to chuse new ones.

V. demanded of Mr Tho. Warren 1^s for an Easter Offering. He refused, which no one had done before. The Cranbrook Justices decided agst the Vicar. He appealed to the Quarter Sessions, in Summer 1758. Qu. the Event.

The Houses on the Glebe are out of Repair. V. desires that matter may be examined. Church & chancel very noble: 6 Bells. Ho. & Out Ho. old, in good Repair.

Richd Ellsworth Esqr gave in 1714 40^s a year to V. to be laid out in Books. This became due in 1724. Nothing pd till 1759: & then only 49$^£$ to Mich 1753. Mr Disney proposed putting out 40$^£$ to Interest. See his Letter 22 Dec. 1759. I advised distributing the whole in Books immediately. Done, May 1761, & much money laid out on the Houses. See p. 111.

A Lease by V. 1663 of 6 Tenemts & 11 Days Work of Land, for 21 years at

2-12-8 (before but 14ˢ-4ᵈ) conf. by ABP Entry Book 1. 3. A Lease of one Tenemt & 3½ days work Conf. ib. p. 45. Rent 10ˢ 6 years, then 20ˢ.

1 Johnson Lawson (1719–78), of Canterbury, m. St John's C 1738, BA 1742, MA 1777, V. Throwley, 1758–9, dean of Battle, Sussex, 1776–8.
2 John Johnson (1671–1725), of Frindsbury, Kent, m. Magdalene C, 1678, BA 1682, MA (CCCC) 1685, C. Lower Hardres, 1683, V. Boughton Blean, 1687–97, C. Hernehill, 1687–98, V. St John's, Margate, 1697–1703, V. Appledore, 1697–1725, V. Cranbrook, 1707–1725. Author of *The Clergyman's Vade Mecum; or, an Account of the Ancient and Present Church of England: the Duties and Rights of the Clergy, and of their Privileges and Hardships* (1706).
3 It was sold to Sir John in c.1549: Hasted VII, p. 104. He died in 1558.
4 (1682–1761), m. Kings 1700, FRS 1702, protonotary of the court of Common Pleas.
5 He was Tempest's 2nd son. He died in 1785: Hasted VII, p. 98.
6 Owner of Great Swifts house. He died in 1782: ibid.
7 Samuel Plummer, the owner of Plushinghurst, his family were formerly clothiers: ibid., p. 97.
8 John Weston, descended from a family of clothiers: ibid., p. 94.
9 Robert Holden. Owned estates of Holden and Hockredge: ibid. p. 99.
10 Jane (17?–78), wife of George, 3rd duke of St Albans (1730–86).
11 Sir Walter Roberts (1691–1745) 6th Bt, of Glassenbury Park, Kent. After his death the baronetcy became extinct.
12 (1723–), of Ireland, m. Christ Church 1742, BA 1746, V. Sutton Valence, 1747–64.
13 Hasted says that the school was founded by Samuel Dence and that Alexander Dence left lands for the poor: VII, p. 108.

Page 59
Cranbrook continued.
Joseph Disney[1] MA V. Dec. 21. 1725. V. of Appledore p. 111. Resides here in V. House. Had a Curate at 40ᶠ a year: but in Summer 1758 had had none from Chr. before.
Richard Podmore[2] LLB. Vicar, Novʳ. 19: 1777. resides.

Tho. Greenall[3]. Cur. lic. Feb. 4. 1768 50ᶠ P. resides

1758 Conf. 27. 1762 Conf. here 1413. Of this Parish 385. 1766 Conf. here 597. Of this Parish 162.

1 (1695–1777), of Buckinghamshire, m. Christ Church 1714, MA Kings 1724, C. Lambeth, 1722–5, V. Cranbrook, 1725–77, V. Appledore, 1726–77.
2 (1744–1807), of Condover, Salop, m. Christs 1763, LLB 1769, C. Rochdale, 1766–71, C. Saddleworth, 1771–6, V. Sittingbourne, 1776–8, V. Cranbrook, 1777–1807, V. Appledore, 1777–1807.
3 (1742–1815), of Middleton, Westmoreland, m. St John's C 1765, C. Cranbrook, 1768, master Cranbrook school, 1805, V. Bethersden, 1808–15.

Page 60
D. Charing
Eastwell R. Sᵗ Mary. Pens. Collegio Wye 8ˢ Ecton. E. of Winchilsea[1] P. Tenths 19ˢ 8ᵈ. Certified 42ᶠ. Now 60 or 70ᶠ 〈Let for 45ᶠ ADⁿ〉. 14 Ho. Ld Winchilsea resides in his ancient Mansion Ho. sevᶠ months each year. Service once. They go to Boughton Aluph, a mile & ¼. Cat. in Lent. Mʳ Dering[2], Ld Winchilseas Chaplain reads wn his LP is here daily Prayers in the House. 4 Sacr. Com. usually 18: but 30 or more wn his LP is there, who is always one. The Rent of a

small Ho. & Garden given & applied to repair the Church. Church in pretty good Order. Chancel wants whitewashing. Ho. new built of Brick by Ld Winchilsea. Out Ho. in good Order. Glebe 18 Acres & 3 Yards of Woodland, mentioned in AD[n] Greens Book: but the present Tenant of the Tithe knows nothing of it. 3 Bells.

John Adcock[3] BA R. 15 July 1747. Hath been extravagant. Said to serve a Cure & been Tutor in a Family in Rutlandshire. Dead.
Philip Parsons[4] R. Apr. 2. 1766. Cur. of Wye p. 26.

John Norcross[5], Cur. for 8 years past. 20^f R. of Hoathfield p. 66 & V. of Willesborough ⟨p. 148⟩, where he lives, 4 measured miles off. Seems good. Gone.
Johnson Towers[6] Cur. of Wye p. 26.
Parsons[7] Philip R. {June 1763 qu} ⟨Apr. 2. 1766⟩. Cur. of Wye p. 26. See above.
Rob. Breton[8] V. of Boughton Aluph C. here Feb. 1768 for 17^f a year. See Wye p. 26. L[d] Winchilsea objects agst. him. M[r] Gorsse[9] to serve it from Ashford with Smeeth p. 112.
Mr. Norwood[10] Cur. Sal £20
John Doncaster[11] AB. Cur Sal. £25 lic. 1794.

1758 Conf. 7. 1762. 9. 1766. 4

[1] See p. 5, n. 4.   [2] Heneage Dering. See p. ii, n. 26.
[3] (?-1766), of Oakham, m. Emmanuel, 1739, BA 1744, R. Eastwell, 1747-66.
[4] See p. 26, n. 9.
[5] (1693-?), of Barton, Lancaster, m. Brasenose 1709, BA 1713, MA 1716, R. Hothfield, 1721-73, V. Willesborough, 1729-73, C. Eastwell, c. 1750-60.
[6] See p. 26, n. 8.   [7] See n. 4.
[8] See p. 5, n. 2.   [9] See p. 57, n. 11.
[10] Edward Norwood, (1746-1831), of Ashford, Kent, m. CCCO 1764, BA 1767, MA (Oriel) 1770, R. & P. Sevington, 1777-1831, C. Willesborough, 1790-1831, R. Milsted, 1821-31.
[11] (1773-1846), of Doncaster, Notts, m. Trinity C 1790, Christs, 1791, BA 1794, MA 1797, DD 1816, fellow, 1796-1815, C. Eastwell, 1794, C. and lecturer Great St Andrew's Cambridge, 1798-1804, lecturer in Hebrew, 1799-1801, C. Fen Drayton, 1802-8, R. Navenby, Lincs, 1814-38, head-master Oakham School, 1808-46.

Page 61
Egerton Cur. S[t] James. Exempt from AD[n]. ⟨Dn &⟩ Ch. of S[t] Pauls Propr & Patr. 70 Ho. dispersed. Mr Mann[1] hath the chief Property. 5 Families of Anab. Lessening. Service once on Sunday, Chr. good Fr. & other Solemn Days. The other part at Boughton Malherb p. { }. Cat. exp. after 2d Lesson on Sundays. 4 Sacr. 70 Com. No House or Glebe. 30^f a year from the gr. Tithes. Surplice Fees small, & often remitted in part or the whole. Houses of 8 or 10^f a year in Trustees. ChW[n]s are Trustees, the minister not, & so can give no Account. The Inhabitants have of late years more than once added 10^f a year for a resident minister & the whole Service. Church large & handsome. Chancel in good Order. 6 Bells.

Francis Hender Foote[2] LLB ⟨Camb⟩. Cur. ⟨lic. May 20 1756 on nom of DCh St Pauls⟩. R of Boughton Malherb p. 54, 2 miles distant, where he resides: & of Linton p. 247.
Edmund Marshall[3] M.A. Cur. Licens'd May 22 1773.
Wm Bearcroft[4], Deputy. See p. 54. Gone.
Fox[5] 1765. 50$^£$. Apartmt at Egerton. Going at Chr. 1765. Stays.

1758 Conf. 65. 1762. 41. 1766. 56

[1] See p. 54, n. 1.
[2] Ibid., n. 5.
[3] See p. 55, n. 5.
[4] See p. 54, n. 6.
[5] Probably John Fox, ibid., n. 7.

Page 62
D. Charing

Frittenden R. St Mary. Mr Henry Bagnall[1] P. ⟨Now, May 1761, his two Daughters⟩. K^s books 15–18–9. Now 120$^£$ ⟨100 AD^n. Some say 130 or 140$^£$⟩. 68 Ho. 2 Families of Presb. 6 of Anab. Whole Service on Sundays. Generally Prayers on Holydays, & cat. Sunday afternoon all Summer. 4 Sacr. 90 Com. An Acre of Land for Repair of the Church: & 2 Tenem^{ts} worth 22–10–0 a year for poor not receiving monthly pay. Church & chancel clean & in good Order. Ho. new & handsome. Out Ho. in good Repair. Glebe 12 Acres. 6 Bells.

Henry Bagnall[2] Junr, MA, R. 11 June 1737. Resides here in the Parsonage Ho. R. of Shadockshurst p. 142. Dead ⟨before⟩ Apr. 3 1761.
Henry Friend[3] BA R. 1 Oct. 1761. Ord. pr. by me Sept 1760. Resides there March 1762.

1758 Conf. 36. 1762. 40. 1766. 36

[1] (1700–61), of Falconhurst Kent, m. Jesus C 1724, BA 1727, MA 1732, R. Shadoxhurst, 1734–61, R. Frittenden, 1737–61.
[2] Ibid. His father was also Henry, (1673–1748), of Badlesmere, Kent, m. All Souls 1691, V. Lympne, 1728–48, R. Frittenden, 1726–37.
[3] See p. 5, n. 3.

Page 63
Halden al. High Halden R. St Mary. ABP P. Kings books 19–4–7. Now 100$^£$. 62 Ho. 1 Family Presb. 2 Anab. Two Sermons on Sundays: prayers W. Fr. in Lent, Advent, & Week before Sacr. every Day in Passion Week & every Holyday. Cat. exp. Sunday afternoon, May–Sept. 10 Sacr. Com. 30–80. A Free School for writing & Arithm. founded by James Tilden[1] of this Par. & endowed with 13–10–0 a year, for 14 Ch^n. 11 Feofees. Well managed. Land, called Poors Field, 1–16–0 a Year so applied. Church & Chancell clean & handsome. Ho. & out Ho. in good order. 5 Bells, & a St^s Bell.

Tho. Payne[2] R. 5 Oct. 1713. Hath been Chaplain at Constantinople 40 years. [Died June 18. 1759]. AD^n of Brecknock.

Benj. Burridge[3] BA. collated 23 Oct. 1759. See below.
Daniel Wilcox[4] A.M. 1780. resides.

Benj. Burridge[5] Cur. near 30 Years. 40^f & Surpl. Fees. Resides in Parsonage Ho. Good.

1758 Conf. 32. 1762. 19. 1766. 30.

[1] Probably in the late seventeenth century. By Hasted's time it educated 50 scholars, of whom 15 were boarders: Hasted VII, p. 225.

[2] (1689-1759), of Whitechapel, London, m. Magdalene C 1706, BA 1710, MA 1713, C. Maidstone, 1712, R. High Halden, 1713-59, chaplain at Constantinople, archdeacon of Brecon, 1736.

[3] (?-1780), of Holborn, London, m. Magdalen Hall O 1717, BA 1721, C. Stone, 1723, R. High Halden, 1759-80.

[4] See p. 52, n. 7.   [5] See n. 3.

Page 64
D. Charing
Hawkhurst, Cur. ⟨formerly V. 1663⟩ St Laurence. Pens. Abb. Battel 5^s-10^d Ecton. Christ-Church, Oxford P. Was a Rectory in {1134} ⟨1534⟩ & rated at 36-13-4. Now certified at 27-2-6 Ecton, where also it is first called V. Kings books 12-10-0. Called in Wakes book 20^f ⟨pd by College⟩. Afterwards augm. in 1720 with 400^f by Queens Bounty & Sir Tho. Dunk[1]. Purchase made of 17^f a year. Called at present 40^f ⟨with Surpl. Fees 50^f AD^n. Others say 70^f. See below⟩. 210 Ho. Sam. Boys[2] Esqr, of an old & considerable Family [4 or 500^f a year]. 4 Presb. 8 Anab. Declining. 2 Sermons on Sunday. Prayers W. Fr. in Lent, every Day in Passion Week, Mond. Tuesd. in East. & Whits. week, & all Holydays. Cat. exp. W. Fr. in Lent. 8 Sacr. abt 100 Com. each time. A Free School to teach 20 Boys reading, writing & Accounts: & 6 Houses for 6 decayed House keepers, who have each abt 8^f a year, & a Coat or Gown once in 2 years: both by Sir Tho. Dunk. Cur. Chw^{n}s, & 12 others, Trustees: Ld Halifax[3] Visitor. Tho. Eddenden[4] left 24^f a year to Ch W^{n}s & 4 others, for charitable Uses. All well managed. A very handsome Church, large & neat. Chancel in good Order. 6 Bells.
Lic. ⟨on nom.⟩ from Ch. Ch. during their pleasure Entry B VIII. 92, 131. See 382.
DCh of Christ Church cannot augment this with Dr Stratfords[5] Legacy, the only Fund they have for that purpose till they have augmented their Livings in 5 other Counties. Augm. 1767 with 200^f Sir Ph. Botelers money & 200^f Qus Bounty.

John Chawner[6] MA Cur. ⟨lic⟩ 29 July 1751 ⟨on Resign of his predecessor⟩. Resides constantly, except a month in 2 years, but not in the Ho. belonging to the Cur. Is not Schoolmaster.

1758. Conf. 7. 1762. 188. 1766. 78

[1] Died in 1718.

[2] Lived at Elfords, the family home, and died in 1772: Hasted VII, p. 147.

[3] George Montagu, 2nd earl of Halifax (1716-71), head of board of trade, 1757-61, lord lieutenant of Ireland, 1761-3, secretary of state, 1762-5, lord privy seal 1770, secretary of state, 1770-1. In

1741, he married Anne, daughter of William Richards, who had inherited in 1718 the property of Sir Thomas Dunk (see n. 1). She brought her husband £110, 000. The marriage was delayed for some time because she had inherited the money on condition of marrying someone engaged in commercial life. This obligation Halifax is said to have fulfilled by becoming a member of one of the trading companies in London.

4 [I]ddenden, by will of 1556, 'the produce of which is given away at Christmas, yearly, in gifts of money': Hasted VII, p. 152.

5 William Stratford (1672–1729), of Manchester, m. Christ Church 1688, BA 1692, MA 1695, BD 1703, DD 1705, canon of Christ Church, 1703, chaplain to the house of Commons, archdeacon of Richmond, 1703–29. Left money to augment livings.

6 (1727–97), of Sudbury, Derbyshire, m. Christ Church 1745, BA 1748, MA 1751, C. Hawkhurst, 1751–97.

Page 65

Hedcorn al. Headcron V. St Peter & St Paul ⟨Belonged to the K^{ts} Templars⟩ ABP P. St Johns Coll. Cambr. Impr. Tenths 1–11–4. Certified 45$^£$. ⟨See below⟩. Above 130 Ho. A Ho. called Muttonden, formerly a Friary, pays 6–8 for the Tithe of a large Estate. Some Anab. & a small Meeting Ho. Meriam a Farmer, & Boreman a Wheeler, Teachers. M^r ⟨[Samuel]⟩ Whiston[1], a former Vicar ⟨[inst. Apr. 12. 1673]⟩, gave a Ho. worth 5$^£$ a year to his Successors. V. is said in ABP Wakes papers at Ch. Ch. vol. 2 to be worth 80$^£$ a year, including Mr Whistons Augm. of a Ho. & 6$^£$ a year & a new planted Orchard. ⟨70$^£$ AD^n. 80 or 90$^£$ Sir Tho. Rider[2]. 1767⟩. 2 Sermons on Sundays. Prayers twice a week. Cat. exp. in Lent, & often on Sundays. 2 Sacr. at each great Festival & one at Mich. 50 or 60 or more Com. Offertory given to put poor Ch^n to School. 2 Tenemts of 5$^£$ a year for poor Housekeepers. Many Complaints, which see, of William Pec{ke}he, who farms the great Tithes, worth above 300$^£$ a Year, of the above Coll. They have been mentioned to the Master, 1758. Church large & clean. Chancel neat. Ho. & out Ho. in good Repair. 1$^£$ for 2 Sermons. 5$^£$ from Parsonage. 6 Bells. Feb. 1762 Mr Hardy, V. saith the House is in very bad Repair, & the Outhouses & Fences abt the Garden and Orchard almost in intire Ruine. He will repair them as soon as he is able. Hath laid out 30$^£$ in 1762 & will lay out 30 more in 1763. People poor, & so tithes lost. Sept. 1767 Ho. in tolerable Repair: a Barn bad, but useless: wd build a Stable & Wood house instead of it, by verbal Leave.

Peter Hay ⟨Heyman⟩[3] BA V. 10 Aug. 1728. Hath always resided. Seems odd, zealous, diligent. Wants money to print ags^t the Anab. See his Answers to Inquiries. One of the 10 poor Vicars. Died Jan 1762.
Joseph Hardy[4] V. Feb. 1762. See 254. Schoolmaster at Sutton Valence, 2,1cÅ miles off. Resides there: is to have a resident Cur. here. Chosen one of the poor Vicars July 16. 1767.
David Evans[5]. Vicar 1786.

M^r. Todd[6] Cur of Stapleherst p. 253 hath officiated once a day for Mr Hardy, who hath been there twice a week himself. David Evans coming March 1763. 40$^£$ & V. Ho. Resides.

Mr Evans[7] Cur. Sal £46.

1758 Conf. 55. 1762. 2 + 24. 1766. 36

[1] (1642–1716), of Northampton, m. Merton 1661, V. Headcorn, 1673–1716.

[2] Descended from the Riders of Low Layton in Essex. Sir Thomas inherited in 1728 and died in 1786; Hasted V, p. 340.

[3] (1696–1762), of Whitechapel, m. Merton 1714, BA 1723, C. Boughton Malherbe, 1724, V. Headcorn, 1728–62, poor vicar.

[4] (1723–86), of Tunstall, Lancashire, m. Christs 1745, LLB 1755, head-master Sutton Valence School, 1746–86, V. Headcorn, 1762–86, PC. Bilsington, 1769, V. Monkton and Birchington, 1772–86, poor vicar.

[5] Possibly (1759–), of Dihewyd, co Cardigan, m. Jesus O, 1781, BA 1785, MA 1788, C. Bethersden, 1784, V. Headcorn, 1786–1801.

[6] Joseph Todd (1732–73), of Newbiggin, Cumberland, m. St John's C 1751, BA 1757, V. Hollingbourne, 1770–73.

[7] See n. 5.

Page 66
D. Charing

Hothfield R. of S[t] Mary. Pens. Colleg. Wye 10[s] Ecton. Earl of Thanet[1] P. Kings books 17–5–0. Now 112[£] ⟨80 AD[n]⟩. 58 Ho. In 1751, 332 Inhabitants, of which 29 were under 5 Years of Age. Earl of Thanet. Whole Service. Prayers on the Holydays of Chr. East. Whits. & W. Fr. in Lent. Cat. Exp. in Lent. Prayers every morning in L[d] Thanets Chapel when the Family is there. 4 Sacr. Com. from 30 to 60. A School, founded by Thomas, Earl of Thanet[2], 40 years ago, & endowed with an Estate of 20[£] a year for a Master & Mistress to teach 12 poor Boys to read & write, & 12 poor Girls spinning & needle-work. Lands worth 20–16–0 yearly, given at different times to the poor. So applied. A neat Church. South Chancel wants white washing. Ho. & out Ho. old, in pretty good Repair. Glebe 16 Acres. 4 Bells.

John Norcross[3] R. 16 Aug. 1721. Cur. of Eastwell p. 60 & V. of Willesborough p. 148. where he resides. Ab[t] 5 miles from hence.
Stephen Barrett[4] Clerk M.A. R. Oct: 14 1773. resides.

James Menteath[5] Priest, Cur. 40[£]. Chaplain to L[d] Thanet, lives in his Ho. [Gone, July 1759.].
Nicolas Brown[6], see p. 112, quits Bilsington ⟨& Sellinge⟩ to serve this. 40[£]. Going at Mich ⟨1760⟩ to be Min. Can. at Rochester.
{Steph. Barrett[7] of Ashford. Whole Duty.} shd. not be erased.
{Steph. Greenhill[8] C. 1761. R. of Sevington p. 141 4 miles asunder.} A person to be ord. Tr. S. 1761 to reside. Josh. Newby[9] of Br. N. born 11 Apr. 1738. 40[£]. Ord. Deacon 17 May 1761. 1. Gone. Going to Harrietsham Mich 1764.
John Loftie[10] C. See p. 167 comes May 1763. 40[£] to reside at Ashford. Gone.
Edm. Mapleloft[11] BA of Chr. Coll Camb. Cur. 40[£] bapt. May 6. 1742, ord. D. Dec. 1764, to serve from Ashford. Ord pr. May 25. 1766. Gone LD 1767.
Fra. Whitfield[12] from Newchurch 133 qu if now March 1768. Yes. Commended.

1758 Conf. 33. 1762. 28. 1766. 22.

[1] Sackville Tufton, 8th earl of Thanet (1733–86).
[2] Thomas Tufton, 6th earl of Thanet (1644–1729). MP for Appleby, 1668–78.
[3] See p. 60, n. 5. [4] See p. 50, n. 9.

5 (1718–1802), of Burrowin, Perthshire, m. Balliol 1736, BA 1739, MA 1742, R. Barrowby, Lincs.

6 (1736–1810), of Northumberland, m. Christs; 1754, BA 1759, MA 1762, DD 1787, fellow, 1762–71, minor canon Rochester, 1760–5, preacher Bunting, Walkhampton and Knapwell, Cambs, 1764, V. Sutton Valence, 1765–1803, R. Ingoldsby, Lincs, 1770–1810.

7 See n. 4.

8 (17?–77), m. Jesus C 1724, BA 1729, C. Egerton, 1731–37, C. Eastwell, 1731–7, R. Sevington, 1731–77.

9 (1738–1811), of Kildwick, Yorks, m. Brasenose 1757, BA 1760, MA 1763, fellow, R. Great Rollright, Oxon.

10 See p. 25, n. 5.

11 (1741–1805), of Stanningfield, Suffolk, m. Christs 1760, scholar 1762, BA 1764, MA 1767, fellow, 1769–85, R. Croxton, Cambs, 1781–5, R. Anstey, Herts, 1784–1805.

12 See p. 12, n. 8.

Page 67

Kennington al. Kenyngton V. S[t] Mary belonged to the Mon. of S[t] Austin. Ecton. ⟨See below⟩. ABP P. ⟨Adv. granted by Qu. Mary⟩. Tenths 1-4-0. Certified 30[f]. Now 35[f] ⟨See below⟩. 60 Ho. S[t] John Charlton[1], a Shropshire Gentleman. One Quaker. Service once on Sundays. Prayers, Ash. W. Good Friday. Cat. exp. from Ash W. to Whits. 4 Sacr. near 50 Com. Gifts of 5–11–0 yearly to the Poor: 10[s] yearly for the Repair of the Church: 40[s] a year to V. out of the Parsonage, ⟨1 Qr wheat, & 1 Qr Barley See below⟩ for which the ABP[s] Lessee is Sir] Rich. Lloyd[2], whose Tenant threatens to take the Vicars Hay Tares [qu into his Corn Tithe. The Roof of the Chancel presented as ruinous. Lessee to repair it, Timber being allowed him. ⟨See p. 12 & below⟩. The Parsonage is very small. Church dirty & out of Order. Ho. small, in good Repair. Out ho. tolerable. Glebe 5 Acres. 5 Bells. The above Wheat & Barley are reserved to V. in the ABP[s] Lease, but not in that of the Lessee to his undertenant, nor are they pd. The 40[s] are not reserved to him in the ABP[s] Lease, but are pd. Both are mentioned as due to him from ABP in a Terrier of 1630, wch see. Before I knew that the Lessee pd the 40[s], I sent to V. 10[f] for the 5 years I had been ABP, & afterwds made him a present of it: but am not obliged to continue it. I had given him 5 Guineas before. In the Accounts of the See for 1643 this pension of 2[f] is mentioned. 1765 It is said the Chancel will be repaired this Summer. I promised to get the Wheat & Barley pd him on the [1)*]. Augmented Dec. 1765 wth 200[f] Qu[s] Bounty & 200[f] Sir Ph. Botelers money.

[1)*] Renewal of the Lease Dec. 1764 but forgot it. For this I gave him 10 Guineas Apr. 1766, though the Difference betw. the 32[s] w[ch] he rec[d] clear out of the 40[s] & the Corn w[ch] he shd have rec[d] in the 7 yrs come not to much above 8 G[s]. He is now to receive the corn. I gave him also 8 G[s] for the other 40[s] a year.

Philip Warham[3] BA ⟨V⟩ 25 Feb. 1729. Cur. of Brooke p. 6. Resides here in the Vicarage House. Complains of the Poorness of the Vicarage. He hath the 5[f] a year of the poor vicars. Sept. 4 1766 M[r] Majendie[4] desires this, wn vacant, for M[r] Gorse[5] of Ashford. I did not promise him. Resigns Brook Mich 1767. Moyle Breton[6] Vicar. Nov.8: 1777. resides.

1758 Conf. 13. 1762. 28. 1766. 21

1 Owner of Apley, Shropshire. He had rich mining interests and died in 1776: VCH *Shropshire* XI, p. 217.

[2] See p. 12, 2.   [3] See p. 6, n. 5.
[4] JP.   [5] See p. 57, n. 11.
[6] (1744–1821), of Kennington, Kent, m. University 1761, DCL, C. Newchurch, 1767, C. Hinxhill, V. Kenardington, 1768–1821, V. Kennington, 1777–1821, patron Boughton Aluph, 1808–21.

Page 68
D. Charing

Newenden al Newynden R. S[t] Peter. ABP. P. K[s] books 7–13–4. Now 70[£] ⟨90 AD[n]⟩. 12 Ho. 2 of them uninhabited. Parsonage Ho. cannot hold any Family. No minister hath resided within memory. Service once on Sundays. A Church not two miles off. Prayers on sev[£] other Days. A Sermon also on the Accession Day. Ch[n] too young to be catechized 4 Sacr. 10 Com. Church & chancel very mean. Ho. a Cottage 1–10–0 to the church. Glebe 2 Acres. 1 Bell.

Rich. Morton[1] MA. R. 28 July 1743. Resides at Wittresham p. 149 [4 miles off]. Cur. there, & comes hither once or twice a week. Serves it himself in Summer: but M[r] Chadsley[2] V. of Rolvenden p. 70 in Winter. May 1761 always once himself AD[n]. *** 1767.
Thomas Morphett[3] M.A. R. Oct[br]: 31 1772.

Tho. Greenall[4], ord. Deacon March 3, 1765 proposed to serve this with Bodiham Co. Sussex. Lives 2¾ miles from Newenden Church. 21[£] here. Feb. 1768 Gone to be Curate at Cranbrook.
M[r] Greenhall[5]. Cur. Sal. 21.

1758 Conf. 3. 1762. 8. 1766. 1.

[1] (1701–1772), of Tunbridge Wells, m. St John's C 1716, BA 1720, MA 1724, C. Staplehurst, 1725, R. Newenden, 1743–72.
[2] Daniel Chadsley (1710–69), m. CCCO 1727, BCL (Merton) 1737, V. Rolvenden, 1737–69.
[3] (1741–1812), m. of Tenterden, Kent, m. Trinity C 1758, BA 1762, fellow 1763, MA 1765, V. Rolvenden, 1769–1812, R. Newenden, 1772–1812.
[4] See p. 59, n. 3.   [5] Ibid.

Page 69
Pluckley R. St Mich: Pension to St Gregorys Priory 1–6–8 Ecton. ABP P. K[s] books 20–1–5,1cÅ besides 5–13–4 for Pevington R. St Mary: the church demolished & the Parish united to this. ib. Now 180[£] [AD[n] Head saith, 210 or 215 ⟨in his Vis. book 200[£]⟩]. One Village, 3 Hamlets, 22 Farm Ho. 50 Cottages, 93 Families, 411 Inhabitants. Sir Edward Dering[1], Bart, [at Surenden, 4 or 5000[£] a year, two Sons by his first Wife, sev[£] Ch[n] by the last. 4 Anabaptists. Whole Service. Prayers on Holydays, W. Fr. in Lent, & all Passion Week. Cat. exp. W. Fr. Lent. 8 Sacr. 50 Com. School to teach 12 boys reading, writing & Arith. & 8 Girls knitting & sewing also, supported by Sir Edw. & R. The Boys work, w[n] ever their Parents want them. Lands of 7[£] a year given to the poor, & of 1[£] to the Church. The money so applied. Church large & in good Repair, & chancel ⟨bought by D[r] Head & improved, at 1200[£] expence⟩. The Ho. exceeding good: Outho. new built & very handsome. Glebe 33 Acres. 5 Bells. See J. Frosts[2] Acct of the place Aug. 30. 1760.

1765 240^f Ded. Land Tax & quit rent 11–14–6¾.
Papist, Wm Mitchel, a Journeyman Taylor.

John Head[3] DD. ⟨R.⟩ 29 Dec. 1735. See St George p. 35. Void by Cession, 17 June 1760 on his Collation to Ickham.
John Frost[4] MA. R. 26 June 1760. R. of Bishopsbourn p. 4. Died Apr. 28. 1765.
Will. Jones[5] BA R 28 June 1765 was V. of Bethersden p. 52. Will reside immediately.
Willm Disney[6] B.D. Rector July 24: 1777. resides.

John Howdell[7] BA. Cur. R. of Brickholt p. 96. Resides here. 40^f with Surp. Fees & East. Offerings, worth 7 or 8^f more. ⟨Sept⟩ 1762, Sick for last 10 months. Service only once. Died Oct. 1762.
Johnson Lawson[8] C. V. of Throughley p. 178.
Saml Parlby[9] Clerk B.A. Curate, Licensed May 26: 1777, with a Salary of 40^f p ann.

1758 Conf. 48. 1762, none. Curate sick. gave notice in Ch. directed the young people to come to him for Instruction. None came. 1766. 30

[1] (1705–62), 5th Bt, of Surrenden, MP for Canterbury, 1733–54. Leader of east Kent Tories.
[2] See p. 4, n. 6. [3] See p. ii, n. 20.
[4] See p. 4, n. 6. [5] See p. 52, n. 3.
[6] (1731–1807), of Cranbrook, Kent, m. Trinity C 1749, BA 1753, fellow, 1754, MA 1756, DD 1789, professor of Hebrew, 1757–77, R. Paston, Northants, 1771–7, R. Pluckley, 1777–1807.
[7] See p. 57, n. 6.
[8] (1719–78), of Canterbury, Kent, m. St Johns C 1738, BA 1742, MA 1777, V. Throwley, 1758–78, dean of Battle, Sussex, 1776–8.
[9] (1755–1803), of Coningsby, Lincs, m. Lincoln 1727, BA 1776, C. Pluckley, 1777, R. Market Weston, Suffolk, 1789, C. Stoke Nayland, ?–1803.

Page 70
D. Charing
Rolvenden al. Rownden V. St Mary. belonged to the College of Cobham. Ecton. DCh. of Rochester P. Tenths 1^f. Certified 44^f. Now 80^f ⟨V. saith but 60^f⟩. 70 Ho. & Families. Phillipps Gybbon[1] [of Hole] Esqr. 10 Presb. in 3 Families: 10 Anab. in 2 Families. Teacher of these, Tho. Avery, a Farmer: they meet at a private Ho. licenced. 20 Methodists, chiefly Serv^{ts}, meet once a fortnight at a private Ho. not licenced. A strolling Teacher. They go constantly to Church. Dissenters much lessend. Generally whole Service [See Newenden p. 68]. Sermons 30 Jan. Good Fr. Nov. 5 Prayers on all Holy Days. Cat. in Lent. 4 Sacr. 80 Com. 312^f a year in long Exch. Annuities given to charitable Uses, after the Death of Phillipps Gybbon & 5–10–0 likewise at present. Church & Chancel large & handsome. Ho. very good. Outho. in good Repair. 10^f of the Income from the Church of Rochester. Glebe 6 Acres. 5 Bells & a Sts Bell. Methodists suppressed here & in the Neighbourhood: Mr Moneypenny[2] of this place enforced the Conventicle Act agt them: they have appealed to the Ks Bench: Mr Preston[3] of Tenterdens Letter, Feb. 3. 1761. Perhaps the last not true.

Dan. Chadsley[4] LLB V. 27 July 1737. Resides in V. Ho. See Newenden p. 68. Serves Small Hythe 3 miles distant. And I hope, though I do not require, that he will usually serve Rolvenden twice notwithstanding.
May 1761 Serves it once.
Thomas Morphett[5] V. Jan^{ry} 26th 1769. resides.

1758 Conf. 36. 1762. 65. 1766. 41.

[1] (1678–1762), MP for Rye, 1707–62. Hole was a substantial property in Rolvenden.
[2] The ecclesiastical *cause célèbre* of 1761. The judgement was reversed by the King's bench.
[3] William Preston (1713–), of Oxford, m. Merton 1728, BA 1733, MA 1736.
[4] See p. 68, n. 2.   [5] Ibid, n. 3.

Page 71

Sandhurst R. St Mich. ABP P. K^s books 20^f. Now 200^f ⟨said to be worth 300^f⟩. 87 Ho. 14 Families of Anab. A Meeting Ho. John Burch, & Will. Coppen, Teachers. One Mitchel, a Methodist, preached once or twice lately without Encouragemt. Whole Service. 2 Sermons in Summer. Prayers Mond. Tuesd. in East & Whits. Week, 30 Jan. Ash W. Good Fr. Asc. Day. 5 Nov. Cat. on Sunday afternoon from East to Whits. 6 Sacr. 40 Com. A small Alms Ho. given by Sir John Fowle[1] in 1632 & an Acre of Land by the same. Church good. Chancel in good Order. Ho. very handsome. Outho. pretty good. Glebe 10 Acres. 5 Bells.

Henry Hodson[2] R. 15 Nov. 1753. Resides. Succeeded his Father[3] without a Disp. Serves Bodiham, Dioc. Chich. twice with it. Forbidden Dec. 1765. Good. See AD^n Dec. 11 1765. Hath with it Thornham V. 20 miles off.

William Hussey[4] A.M. Rector 1781. resides

1758 Conf. 13. 1762. 69. 1766. 22

[1] The owner of the manor of Sandhurst. The money raised was distributed in clothes to the poor women of the parish: Hasted VII, p. 160.
[2] (1719–81), of Headcorn, Kent, m. St John's C 1737, BA 1741, MA 1744, R. Sandhurst, 1753–81, V. Thornham, 1768–81, chaplain to duke of Bolton.
[3] Also Henry, (1684–1771), of Titchwell, Norfolk, m. Christs 1700, BA 1704, R. Conisholme, Lincolnshire, 1711, V. Headcorn, 1716–23, R. Sandhurst, 1723–53.
[4] (–1831), of Sussex, m. CCCC 1772, BA 1775, MA 1778, fellow, 1776–81, C. Wimbledon, 1775, R. Sandhurst, 1781–1831.

Page 72

D. Charing
Smarden R. St Michael. ABP P. ⟨Adv. granted by Qu. Mary⟩. K^s books 24–3–6. Now 180^f ⟨220^f AD^n⟩. 132 Ho. Cha. Ott{a}way[1] ⟨Esqr⟩ [son of Genl] preparing the Family seat at Romden for his Reception. 27 Families of general Anab. Teachers Matth. Vane & Dan. Husmar. 16 of particular: Teachers, Tho. & John Birch. The former bury mostly in ch. yard: the latter in Ground belonging to the Meeting Ho. Lessend by 4 or 5 Families in the last 20 Years. Two Sermons on Sundays. Prayers on ⟨all⟩ Holydays & W. Fr. in Lent. Cat. in

Lent. 8 Sacr. betw. 30 & 40 Com. at each. A Free School, in wch all the Boys of Smarden, & 6 from Bethersden are taught Reading, Writing, & Arith. endowed by Steph. Dodson[2] in 1720 with 18^f a year in Land, & the Interest of 180^f. A good Ho. & School Room. 4 Trustees. Well managed. Jac. Turner[3] of London mercht gave in 1686 Lands worth 11-15-0 for wheat & coals for the poor. Minister & 5 others Trustees. Abt 80 Years ago James Tilden[4] left Lands & Houses worth 30^f a year for a School for the Ch^n of the particular Anab. their Teacher to be their Master. And he enjoys a House & Lands worth 10^f a year: but there is no School yet. A good Church, large, clean. Chancel in good Order. Ho. & Outho. old & in good Repair. 5 Bells. A Field for the Repair of Bells & Bell-ropes.

Wm Bedford[5] MA R. 9 Sept. 1728. V. of Beaksbourn p. 3. where he resides. Spends a week here 3 or 4 times a year.
John Porter[6] A.M. 1784. quitted.
Wm Mackenzie[7] A.M. 1793.

Solomon Pawley[8] Cur. 40^f & Surpl. Fees. Resides. was of Westm. School & Tr. Coll. hath been a Cur. in Kent 40 years: hath nothing: a quiet contented man. A Living given him by DCh. Cant. Continues here 1766, 1768.
Mr Kirkbank[9] Cur.

1758 Conf. 39. 1762. 29. 1766. 32.

[1] Charles-James Otway, an officer in the army, died in 1767. His father had been lieutenant of Minorca, and died in 1721: Hasted VII, p. 481.
[2] Hasted noted that 40 boys and girls were taught there: ibid., p. 482.
[3] He also gave in his life-time £100, for the repair of the church: ibid., p. 482.
[4] Probably the same as p. 63, n. 1.   [5] See p. 3, n. 4.
[6] (1751–1819), of Morthen, Cheshire, m. Trinity C 1768, BA 1773, MA 1776, DD (Lit Reg) 1792, fellow, 1774, regius professor of Hebrew, 1790–5, R. Smarden, 1784–93, R. Tansor, Northants, 1792–4, R. South Collingham, Notts, 1794, bishop of Killala, 1795–8, bishop of Clogher, 1798–1819.
[7] R. Smarden, 1793–1821.
[8] (17?–77), of Wateringbury, Kent, m. Trinity C 1721, scholar 1722, BA 1725, MA 1728, C. Penshurst, 1728, C. Biddenden, C. Smarden, 1758–77, V. Aylsham, Norfolk, 1765–77.
[9] Thomas Kirkbank (1721–1829), C. High Halden, 1781, V. Appledore, 1814–1829.

Page 73

Tenterden V. St Mildred. belonged to the Mon. of St Austin. DCh. Cant P. with the Chapel of Small Hythe, of which see p. 74. K^s books 33–12–11. [Now 120 AD^n Head ⟨Ms Vis book 140^f. 130 Disp. 1756⟩]. 5 Boroughs, 260 Ho. 6 Anab. 300 Presb. who have a meeting Ho. Teacher, Hancock. Lessened. 6 Quakers. They pay their Tithes without Compulsion. 2 Sermons on Sundays Prayers on W. Fr. & Holydays. Cat. W. Fr. in Lent. Sacr. first Sund. of each Month: 100 Com. & on great Festivals near 200. A Grammar School: a Ho. & 20^f a Year for the Master. Corporation, Trustees, Lady Norton[1] gave 50^f a year ½ to this, ½ to Hollingbourn Parish, 1^f to the minister of each for Sermons Jan. 1 Nov. 1. the rest for ⟨poor⟩ Widows & putting out Apprentices. See the particulars. Lady Mainard[2] gave 24^f a year for poor Widows. Mrs Sheldon[3] 8^f a year for putting children Apprentices. Church noble & handsome, cieled finely with Irish Oak. Chancel very handsome. Ho. & OutHo. good & in good Repair. Glebe 3 Acres. 6 Bells. Tho. Blackmore[4] Esqr, Dissenter: hath 1500^f a year in Tenterden, & as much from an Uncle of the same name lately dead in Hertfordshire: single. His uncle was of the Ch. of England. Mr Huson of Tenterden, who died in 1738, left to the Dissenters a Farm in Romney Marsh, wch lets for 40^f a year: & former Legacies to them in money produce abt 30^f a year more for their minister. Sev^t creditable Dissenters have joined in Communion with the Church in the last two years. July 1763.

Theoph. De L'Angle[5] MA V. 8 July 1723. R. of Snargate p. 143. Cur. of Goodneston by Sandwich p. 13. Resides there. Was 16 years here, then forced to go for his Health. Died June 30. 1763.
Matthew Wallace[6] MA V. Dec. 9 1763.
Joseph Matthew[7] V. June 1772.

John Holland[8] BA Cur. Priest. 40^f with other Perquisites. Lives in V. Ho. March 1760. Mortification in his Foot from Gout. Assisted by Neighbours. Dead.
Wm Preston[9], formerly of Merton Cur. AD^n 1761, on the same Terms with Mr Holland. Proved very troublesome: almost mad.
Wallace[10] Matthew, MA of Edinb. ord. pr. be me. 1761.
Mr Morphet[11] ord. Pr. by me assists Mr Wallace, who is going to Edinburgh 1765
Mr Price[12]. Cur. Sal. £50.

1758 Conf. 131. 1762. 98+6. 1766 Conf. here June 5. 429. Of Tenterden 206.

[1] Dame Frances Norton, by deed in 1719. The charity was settled by a commission of charitable uses in 1748: Hasted VII, p. 214.
[2] Lady Jane Maynard, in her will of 1660: ibid.   [3] Anne Shelton, in 1674: ibid.
[4] The owner of Westwell House, died 1789: ibid., p. 204.
[5] See p. 9, n. 6.
[6] (17?-72), of Edinburgh, MA Edinburgh College 1755, V. Tenterden, 1763-72.
[7] Perhaps (1734-72), of Kildare, m. TCD 1751, BA 1756, MA?, V. Tenterden, 1772-96.
[8] Perhaps John (1710-), of Eglwysfach, co Denbigh, m. Jesus O 1728, BA 1732.
[9] See p. 70, n. 3.   [10] See n. 7.
[11] See p. 68, n. 3.   [12] Probably David Price.

Page 74
D. Charing
Tenterden continued

Chapel of Small Hythe. St John Baptist. Certified 45^f. An Estate belongs to it, let for 48-15-0, in the Hands of Feoffees, Gentlemen of Tenterden parish, who fill up vacancies. Jer. Curteis[1] Esqr, now Treasurer. Walt Scott 1759, 4-11-0¼. A Ho. for the Chaplain. 20 Ho. AD^n in 1759 found the Chapel scandalously dirty & ruinous: no Communion Table: the Seats broken: a Crack through the East Wall. The Treasurer saith, the Repair will take two Years Profits: but that the Crack was probably soon after the building, & hath not grown worse in mans memory. He promises to rectifie all, & show the Feoffmt & Accounts. The Inhabitants chuse, the Feoffees approve, the Vicar presents, the ABP licences, the minister. ABP Wake 11 Dec. 1715 collated Humphrey Hammond[2], as patron in full Right. Reg. Wake 1, f.298. Service used to be once a fortnight: now, 1760, once a week. Chaplain imagines he hath no Cure of Souls. Go on.

ABP Warham 5 May 1509. (See his Reg. f. 338, 339.) on the Complaint of the Inhabitants of Small Hythe, that Distance, Roads, Waters, Weakness, Sickness, kept them from duly attending the Church & receiving the proper Sacramts & Rites, & their Request that he wd licence them a Chaplain to officiate in the Chapel there built, the former to be maintained & the latter repaired by them & other X^n people; appoints that they present a fit person to the Vicar, who shall with his Approbation officiate in the Chapel: & if the Vicar admits him not in 6 Days, the Ordinary shall, on his taking an Oath of Obedience to the Vicar. He may administer Penance & the Eucharist to the Aged & Infirm, & church weakly women, & bury in the Chapel Yard the Dead of contagious Diseases or cast on the Shore of the Town, provided neither the Rector, Vicar, nor Inhabitants of Tenterden suffer Detriment. But others shall be buried, & all baptized & married, at the Parish Church: where the Chaplain shall go to High Mass on the principal Feats after the Chapel mass; & all Inhabitants of Small Hythe, who are able, on all Feast Days. And, they shall make their Offerings & pay their Rates as before. Lic. to serve this Chap. Entry B. II. 117. VI. 231.

The Chaplain hath each years balance, wch for 23 years ending 1758 hath been 34–10–0. See papers relative to this chapel. See Entry B. VIII. 52.

$Rich^d$ Thoresby[3], Chaplain, 28 Apr. 1736, then a Curate in the neighbourhood, now R. of {a} Church ⟨St Catharine Coleman⟩ in Fenchurch Street. He ⟨served it himself 10 years or more then⟩ gave his Deputy a Guinea every other Sunday, & never knew it served oftener: but will allow him half the Income, & even 20^f a Year, to serve it every Sunday: & at present will give up the Remainder for Repairs. Resigned 1766.

Tho. Morphett[4]. AM. lic. Aug. 7. 1766.

Richd Moor[5] cur. of Stone p. 145 & Deputy at Fairfield p. 121. served here. But now 1760 Dan. Chadsley[6] V. of Rolvenden p. 70 serves this once a Sunday. So 1765.

[1] A gentleman from Rye: Hasted VII, p. 149.
[2] (1678–1736), of Waldron, Sussex, m. All Souls 1697, BA 1701, MA (CCCC) 1711, R. East Guildford, Sussex, 1706, C. Small Hythe, 1716–36.
[3] (1704–74), of Leeds, m. St Catherine Hall C 1722, BA 1726, C. Wittersham, 1728, C. Small Hythe, 1736–66, R. St Catherine, Coleman Street, London, 1745–74.
[4] See p. 68, n. 3.
[5] Possibly of Somerset, m. St John's C 1731, BA 1736. Perhaps in-brother at Holy Trinity hospital, Croydon, 1786–1804.
[6] See p. 68, n. 2.

Page 75

Westwell V. St Mary. Exempt from AD^n. ABP Propr. & Patr. Kings books 13^f. Certified 67–14–0. Now 80^f ⟨was 85 or 90^f See below. AD^n 100^f See below⟩. 83 Ho. & Cottages, of which 12 in a Village near the Church, the rest scattered. Whole Service on Sundays. Prayers on no other Day. [Qu. Good Fr. Ch. & State

Holidays]. Cat. from LD to Harvest. 4 Sacr. abt. 40 Com. each time. A ⟨voluntary⟩ Charity School for boys & Girls, number not limited: taught only to read. Lady Gore[1] pays the mistress. Two small pieces of Land for the Poor. 30^f clear reserved to V. out of ABP^s Lease, by Juxon, ⟨& pd clear⟩. Church large & out of Order. Chancel wants whitewashing. Ho. & Out Ho. neat & in good Order. Glebe 2 Acres. 4 Bells. By V^s account, wch see, it is at least 110^f a year. 1766. House mean, but in repair: income between 100 & 110^f a year, pd by 70 Persons, 3 days in collecting. A Dinner given each Day, expence near 5^f. Curate pays the Vicar 50^f a year clear, & pays for Repairs & all other Deductions, & hath the rest of the Income.

Fra. Fred. Giraud[2] V. 23 May 1757 ⟨pres. by K. P. in full Right Entry B.⟩. Had then the Care of the Free School of Faversham, during the Masters Absence [Returns Mids 1759 to reside here. Serves it twice one Sunday, once the next: & then goes to Davington p. 155 or Owre p. 172, 12 or 14 miles off. Dec. 1762 Gone I think to be Cur. at Ospring. Void by Cession June 25. 1766.
Benj. Waterhouse[3] MA V July 26. 1766 V. of Hollingbourn p. 243. Resides there.
Henry Monatagu Davis[4] A.M. Vicar 1790.

R. Foster[5]. F. of St Johns Camb. Deacon, Cur. 40^f Surpl. Fees, Use of V. Ho. & Garden. Gone. 1761 May, Mr Giraud serves it.
John Adey[6] C. 1763 See p. 248. Desires time for quitting. See his Letter. Hath a Living in Essex, as good as Westwell. Hath the Income, repairs, & pays V. 50^f a year.
Mr Gorsse[7] Cur.

1758 Conf. 37. 1762. 27. 1766. 35

[1] She has not been traced.
[2] (1726–1811), of Pinache, Germany, m. All Souls 1744, BA 1748, dep. master Faversham Grammar School 1752, head-master 1762, C. Oare, 1755, V. Westwell, 1757–66, V. Preston by Faversham, 1766, V. Marden, –1811.
[3] (1718–90), of Langley, Kent, m. University 1735, BA 1738, MA 1741, V. Hollingbourne, 1741–70, V. Westwell, 1766–90.
[4] (1755–1807), of Westminster, m. Christ Church 1770, BA 1774, MA 1779, C. Bishopsbourne, 1789, V. Westwell 1790–1803, V. Eynesford, 1791–1807, R. Bishopsbourne, 1803–7.
[5] Probably Ralph Foster (1731–1804), of Newton-by-the-sea, Northumberland, m. St John's C 1750, BA 1754, MA 1757, BD 1765, fellow, 1754–74, proctor, 1763–4, C. Horningsea, Cambs, 1766–73, R. Great Warley, Essex, 1772–1804.
[6] Probably (1723–), of Dursley, Glos, m. Oriel, 1741, BA 1745, 7. Goudhurst, 1757–59.
[7] See p. 57, n. 11.

[Deanery of Dover]

Page 76
D. Dover

Alkham V. S[t] Anthony with Cap. Le Ferne S[t] Mary. Abbey of S[t] Radegund was Propr. Pens, 13-4 Ecton. Now ABP Propr. & Patr. K[s] books 11[£]. Certified 53-9-6 〈See below〉. Called now 50[£]. 〈Alkham〉 60 Ho. 4 Hamlets. Service once on Sundays. Cat. now. 4 Sacr. 30 Com. Cap. le Ferne, 30 Ho. one Hamlet. Service once a Fortnight. 4 Sacr. From 15 to 20 Coms. The ABP pays a Pension of 4[£] a year to this Vicarage. And V. pays the above Pension of 13-4 to the ABP. He saith, his small Tithes & Glebe are let for 31-17-0 and that his accidental Advantages from Wood have been on an average 12[£] a year, & from Seeds but once above 5[£], in the 10 Years, that he hath been V. See 〈below &〉 his Letters abt Burmarsh. Church large very dirty. Chancel the same. V. Ho. a mean Cottage out of Repair. Glebe 2 Acres. 4 Bells. Chapel & its chancel dirty. No Ho. 1 Bell. Alkham 40[£] Caple Le Fern 20[£], AD[n].

Rich. Smith[1] V. 17 Dec. 1747. R. of Burmarsh p. 118. Cur. of Hythe p. 107. ever since 1745 & Schoolmaster there, where he resides. No school there before.
James Smith[2] V. 26 June 1772.
John Gostling[3] A.M. Vicar 1784.
Alex[r]. James Smith[4] Vicar 1786.

Tho. Tournay[5] Cur. Also Cur. of Hawking p. 87. Had been Deacon 7 Years. Ord. Pr. 24 Sept. 1758. 1. Resides here 〈see below 30[£]〉. Surpl. Fees. Seq. also of Ewel see p. 83. Not now 1759. Married: no convenient Ho. nearer than Dover, 4 miles off. Going hither with my Consent, Feb. 1760. Quits this on having S[t] James's Dover & Hougham Aug. 31. 1762.
John Kemeys[6] Cur. March 25. 1763 also of Hawking p. 87. Gone to Postling.
Holbrook[7] M[r] 1764. Gone Apr. 1765. Talks of turning Methodist. Queteville[8] officiates. Gone.
W[m] Williams[9] May 29. 1765 P. with Hawkinge p. 87.

1758 Conf. Alkham 69. Cap. le Fern. 28. 1762. Alkham 8 Capel 16, 1766 Alkh. 22. Cap. 4.

[1] (1712-72), of Higham, Kent, m. Jesus C 1730, BA 1734, MA 1737, C. Hythe (Saltwood) 1745, V. Alkham 1747-72, R. Burmarsh 1754-72.
[2] See p. 7, n. 9.   [3] See p. 6, n. 2.
[4] 'a literate person', C. Alkham and Ewell, 1781, V. Alkham, 1786-1835.
[5] (1730-95), of Ashford, Kent, m. Hertford 1747, BA (Lincoln) 1751, C. St James's, Dover and V. Hougham, 1762-95, R. Yate, Glos., 1765-95.
[6] (1711-), of Lamblivion, c. Glamorgan, m. Jesus O 1730.
[7] Perhaps William Holbrook (1728-), of Holborn, London, m. Trinity O 1745, demy Magdalen O 1750, BA 1749.
[8] John Queteville (1728-88), of Jersey, m. Pembroke O 1744, BA 1748, PC. West Langdon, 1772-88, PC. Guston, 1772-88, R. East Langdon, 1772-88.
[9] Ordained in 1758. Perhaps C. Monkton, 1792.

Page 77

Beauxfield al. Bewfield al. Whitfield ⟨Said in Parochial Book 1663 to come from S[r] John Gage[1] K[t]⟩ V. [But no Institution taken of late]. ABP Impr. & Patr. Tenths 14[s] Certified ⟨See below⟩ 26[£], of which, 20[£] is reserved in ABP[s] Lease ⟨by Juxon⟩. 26 Ho. 2 Families of Anab. Service once every other Sunday, as usual: & at no other time. Ch[n] instructed in Cat. just after Whits ⟨for 6 Sundays⟩. 4 Sacr. 16 or 18 Com. each time. No Offertory. Church small, in good Repair. Chancel the same. No Ho. 1 Bell. The small Tithes are 14[£] a year. It is 33[£] clear. 1767 augm with 400[£] by S[r] Ph. B. & Qu[s] bounty.
Lic. to serve the Curacy of Whitfield Entry B. III. 269. IV. 559.

Fra. D'Aeth[2] Cur. ⟨lic.⟩ 20 June 1753. Cur. also of Chillenden p. 9. & R. of Knowlton p. 187. where he resides, 5 miles from hence. See more there. I believe Mr {De l'Angle Jun[r]} ⟨Lernoult⟩[3] serves this in his Absence in Berks. Mr D'Aeth promised AD[n] to serve this every Sunday. See his Letter May 22. 1759. Doth so. But see here p. 187. V. of Godmersham p. 12.
Thomas Delannoy[4] lic cur. 1784 does his own duty.
W[m] Tournay[5] A.B. lic - 1788. resigned.
Sir Henry Pix Heyman[6] lic 1792.

James[7], Cur. 20[£] serves it once every Sunday. Cur. also of Charlton p. 79. AD[n] May 27. 1760 Quits it Sept 1762. Mr Greenall[8] till 1764.
Queteville[9] to serve this once, with Guston p. 86 & Langdon p. 183. No complaints 1768.
Tho[s]. Denward[10] Curate Licensed July 10: 1778. Salary 20[£] p ann.

1758 Conf. 16. 1762. 20. 1766. 19

[1] (1642–99), 4th Bt.   [2] See p. 9, n. 4.
[3] Probably Philip Lernoult, C. Stourmouth, 1727.
[4] [De Lannoy (1755–1830), of Canterbury, Kent, m. Jesus C 1775, BA (Sidney Sussex) 1778, MA 1783, PC. Whitfield, 1784–88, PC. West Langdon, 1788–1830, R. East Langdon, 1788–1830, PC. Guston, 1788–1830, V. Westcliffe, 1807–30, C. Charlton by Dover, 1814.
[5] (1762–1833), of Dover, Kent, m. Wadham 1780, scholar 1781–9, BA 1784, MA 1799, BD 1802, DD 1806, fellow 1789–99, warden, 1806–31, PC. Whitfield, 1788–91, R. St James's Dover and V. Hougham, 1795–1818, preb of Lincoln, 1800–12, preb of Peterborough, 1817, preb of St Paul's, 1818–33.
[6] (17?–1808), of Kent, m. Emmanuel 1780, scholar 1782, BA 1784, MA 1787, BD 1794, fellow 1786, C. Patrixbourne 1788–, C. Burmarsh, 1788, PC. Whitfield 1792–99, V. Fressingfield, Suffolk, 1797–1808, 5th Bt.
[7] Alexander James (17?–1813), of Rochester, m. Clare 1742, BA 1747, MA (Christs) 1750, fellow 1749–75, V. Fen Drayton, Cambs, 1763–72, V. St Margaret's at Cliffe, 1773–1813, PC. Buckland, 1773–1813.
[8] Probably Thomas Greenall, see p. 59, n. 3. Might be Robert Greenall, V. Waldershare and PC. Nonington, 1755–71.
[9] See p. 76, n. 8.   [10] C. Stelling 1772, C. Whitfield and Charlton, 1778.

Page 78

D. Dover

Buckland C. St Andrew. Belonged to the Priory of Dover. Now ABP. Impr. & P. Exempt from AD^n. [There is also Buckland R. p. { } in Ospring D]. 26 Ho. Mr Bryan,[1] belonging to the Ordinance. Certified 20$^£$ ⟨into the Exchequer⟩. Called ⟨in BP Wakes book 32$^£$⟩ now but 18$^£$ ⟨AD^n 25$^£$⟩, of which, 12$^£$ ⟨{shd be} are free of Land Tax⟩ is reserved in ABP^s Lease ⟨by Juxon. See below⟩. Two Anab. Service once a Fortnight. Cat. ⟨exp.⟩ on Sundays in Lent: & w^n ever Ch^n and Servants come. 4 Sacr. 20 Com. each time. No Ho. 3 Bells.

Wm Barney coll to V. of Buckland[2] near Dover 20 March 1673 Entry Book III. 220 not said how vacant. Rich Marsh[3] held the C. of Buckland near Dover with St Marg. at Cliff V. Aug 13 1700 IV. 619.

1767 Augm with 200$^£$ S^r Ph. B^s money 200$^£$ Qu^s Bounty.

John Marsh[4] BA Cur. Lic. 19 Feb. 1732. V. of Westcliffe p. 94 & Cur. of St Margarets at Cliffe p. 90. Lives at Dover, a mile off.

Alexander James Clerk[5] M.A. Cur. Licens'd 13th Oct^r: 1773.

1758 Conf. 25 1762 Omitted to set down. 1766 8

[1] He has not been traced.
[2] V. Buckland, 1674–84.
[3] (1671–1733), of Waltham, m. St John's C 1688, BA 1692, MA 1695, fellow 1696–1701, V. St Margaret's at Cliffe, 1700–33, C. Buckland, 1706–33, V. Westcliffe, 1706–33.
[4] (1705–73), of St Margaret's at Cliffe, Kent, m. St John's C 1722, BA 1726, MA 1733, C. Buckland, 1733–73, V. St Margaret's at Cliffe, 1733–73, V. Westcliffe, 1733–73.
[5] See p. 77, n. 7.

Page 79

Charlton R. St Peter. Rich. Monins[1] Cl. P. Certified 32$^£$. Now called 30$^£$. ⟨AD^n 40$^£$ See below⟩. 25 Ho. Service once a fortnight in Summer, once in 3 weeks in Winter, as usual. Cat. in Lent. 3 Sacr. 4 or 5 Com. [NB. No Dissenters. R. hath promised to preach on Sacr. And there must be 4.]. No Parsonage Ho. Church & chancel small, in pretty good Order. Glebe ¾ Acre. 1 Bell. Service once a fortnight, till a Curate can be provided. Mr Monins saith, it is let for 36$^£$, clear 32–14–0. See AD^{n}s Letter, May 27. 1760.

The King claimed to be Patron pleno Jure in 1665 Entry Book I. 183. But the Clerk of Mr Monins was inst. p. 189.

Rich. Monins[2] R. Feb. 21 1758. R. also of Ringwold p. 191. where he resides, & where see more. Good. Prayed, as Patron, to be admitted.

Thomas Gurney[3] R. June 28. 1771.

Thomas Johnson[4] B.A. R. July 5 1774.

A. James[5], Cur. 20$^£$ ⟨Pr. F. of Christs Coll. Resides at Dover⟩. To serve it every Sunday. Cur. also of Beauxfield. p. 77. AD^n May 27. 1760 Sept. 1762. Seq. of Lydden p. 89. Quits Whitfield.

Thos. Denward[6] Curate, Licensed July 10: 1778. Salary £12 p ann.

Thos. Delannoy[7]. Curate Sal. £15.

1758 Conf. 5. 1762. 5 NB. 1766. 10

[1] (1733-70), of Ringwould, Kent, m. St John's C 1751, BA 1755, MA 1758, fellow, 1755-60, R. Charlton, 1758-70, R. Ringwould, 1758-70.
[2] Ibid.
[3] (17?-74), of Kent, m. CCCC 1758, BA 1760, MA 1765, V. Bapchild, 1764-5, C. Whitstable 1765-74, V. Seasalter, 1765-74, R. Charlton, 1770-74.
[4] (1747-1802), of Canterbury, Kent, m. St John's C 1767, BA 1772, C. Great Chart, 1771, R. Charlton, 1774-1802, PC. Whitstable, 1774-1802, V. Seasalter, 1774-1802, poor vicar, 1789.
[5] See p. 77, n. 7.   [6] Ibid., n. 10.   [7] See p. 77, n. 4.

Page 80
D. Dover
Cheriton R. St Martin. Pens Prior: Folkestone 20^s. {W^m} ⟨James⟩ Brockman[1] Esqr P. K^s books 16-12-6. Now 100^f. 110 AD^n. 44 Ho. Service once here & at Newington. Churches ½ mile distant. Same Congregation. Cat. on Sunday afternoon at each in Summer. A Course of Cat. Sermons. 4 Sacr. 20 Com. No Offertory. Church neat. Chancel in good Order. Ho. new & handsome by Mr Bilton[2]. Glebe 15 Acres. 4 Bells.

Edm. Parker[3] R. 19 May 1743. V. of Newington p. 91 Resides there.
George Lynch[4] MA. May 22. 1770.
John Barnes Backhouse[5] A.B. 1790
Julius Drake Brockman[6] A.B. 1793.

Thomas Gates[7] Clerk Cur Lic Sept. 23: 1776, with a Salary of £50 p ann.
Mr Hussey[8] Cur.

1758 Conf. 43. 1762. 26. 1766. 23.

[1] William Brockman (1658-1741), MP for Hythe, 1690-95, had three sons, William, James and John, all of whom died unmarried.
[2] Henry Bilton (16?-1743), m. TCD, MA 1694, R. Cheriton, 1719-43.
[3] (-1770), of London, m. CCCC 1720, V. Newington, 1739-70, R. Cheriton, 1743-70.
[4] (1789), of Kent, m. CCCC 1751, BA 1754, MA 1757, fellow 1758, V. Lympne 1765-89, R. Cheriton, 1770-89, V. Newington, 1770-89 (petitioned for union of Cheriton and Newington, 1770).
[5] (1766-1838), of Caldbeck, Cumberland m. Trinity C 1785, scholar 1787, BA 1789, MA 1792, C. Ickham, 1789, R. Cheriton w. V. Newington, 1790-93, R. Edburton, Sussex, 1792-6, R. Deal, 1795-1838, R. Little Chart, 1811-38, rural dean, JP Kent and Cinque Ports.
[6] (1769-1849), of Newington, Kent, m. Oriel 1787, BA 1790, R. Cheriton w. V. Newington, 1793-1849.
[7] (1751-), of Beeding, Sussex, m. Oriel 1768, C. Cheriton, 1776.
[8] Perhaps John Hussey (1751-), of Ashford, Kent, m. Hertford 1778.

Page 81
Dover, St James's. C. ⟨R. Ecton. Right. See below⟩. ABP P. Exempt from AD^n. Tenths 9^s-9^d. Certified 24^f. Augm. 1714 with 400^f by Queens Bounty & ABP Tenison. Now scarce 40^f ⟨1767 Augm. with 400^f⟩. 50 Families. Mr Russell[1], ***. One Presb. 3 Anab. 4 Methodists. One Quaker, a meeting Ho. No Speaker. Service once 3 Sundays in the Month. Prayers W. Fr. in Lent. Cat. then, & when else there is Occasion. 4 Sacr. above 20 Com. Interest of 50^f for Bread for the Poor. An Arbitration betw. R. of St James, Dover & the Master &

brethren of the Maison Dieu there concerning Tithes, See in Warhams Reg. fol 338. Church & Chancel handsome & in good Repair. Ho. small, in good Repair. No outHo. 6 Bells.

22 Nov. 1606 ABP as Patron pleno jure collated John Graye[2] BD to this Rectory vac. by resign. of Wm Wattes[3] Reg. Bancr. f. 227a. And 22 Apr. 1608 he collated Walter Richards[4] MA on the Resign. of John Graye ib. f. 283b. These are the two last Collations. Nov. 28 1664 on a representation, that this hath been held time out of mind with Hougham & been accounted as it were annexed, & a petition to hold this with Hougham by Sequestration, a fiat granted directed to the Commissary Entry B. I. 101. The like 1674 III. 251. V. 21, 304.

Edw. Hobbs[5] Cur. ⟨licenced⟩ 4 May 1712 ⟨See Entry Book⟩. V. of Hougham p. 88. Cur. of Lydden p. 89. Resides here. In ABP Wakes Time served this every other Sunday, & Hougham every Sunday. A good Schoolmaster wanting. Dr Ducarel. Died July 31. 1762.

Tho. Tournay[6] BA. Cur. licenced 31 Aug. 1762. V. of Hougham p. 88. R. of Yate Co. Gloucester, worth 176$^£$ a yr & perhaps 120$^£$ more. See his paper. Wants to change it for a Living in Kent.

William Tournay[7] A.M. collated 1795.

1758 Conf. 39. 1762 omitted to set down 1766. 52.

Dover Castle hath a Chaplain, with a Salary of abt 36$^£$ a year, & doth not reside. So the ministers of Dover do the Duty. He is old 1759

[1] Michael Russell: Hasted IX, p. 581.
[2] (15?-1621), of London, m. Queens' C 1580, BA 1584, MA (Emmanuel) 1587, BD 1594, fellow 1587, R. Snave, 1600-21, V. Teynham, 1600, V. Alkham, 1600-7, V. St James's, Dover, 1606-8, V. St Mary's, Dover, 1608-16, R. Deal, 1617-21.
[3] V. St James's, Dover until 1606.
[4] (15?-1642), m. Emmanuel 1589, BA 1593, MA 1596, V. St Mary's, Dover, 1601, V. Brookland, 1602-16, V. St James', Dover, 1608.
[5] (1684-1762), of Summerton, Somerset, m. Pembroke O 1702, V. Hougham, 1712-62, C. St James's Dover, 1712-62, C. Lydden.
[6] See p. 76, n. 5.
[7] See p. 77, n. 5.

Page 82

D. Dover

Dover St Marys C. The Rectory was granted in K. Johns time to the Hospital of St Mary, or Maison Dieu at Dover. See Warhams Register fol. 138. This Hospital was dissolved by H.8. Ecton saith the King is P. But in fact the Parishioners chuse their minister, whom the ABP licences, whence perhaps Wake saith the ABP is P. See below. Nov. 23 1756 the Parishioners assembled, after due notice, chose Thomas Edwards[1] to be minister of the Parish in the Room of Wm Byrch[2] dec^d, on condition, that he shd constantly reside in the House purchased by the Parishioners for the minister, & read the Liturgy & preach twice every Sunday, & administer the Communion the 1st Sunday in every month, & read prayers W. Fr. in the forenoon, & observe all Feasts & Holydays enjoyned by the Church & usual, & do all other Duties, which a

Clergyman ought. And they order, that the Ch W^{n}s shall pay him, in Consideration of this 20$^£$ a quarter, out of the Rate for repairing the Church & maintaining the Minister, so long as he resides in the Parish, & doth his Duty as Minister, & no longer: the 1st Paymnt to be made LD 1757 ⟨[This 80$^£$ a year is said to have been pd ever since 1660]⟩: & that he shall receive all Fees & Perquisites belonging to the minister, wch have been usually taken by his Predecessors. And Mr Edwards came to this Vestry & agreed with them to be their minister on these Terms. And He & 32 of them signed this Agreem^t, a Copy of which was attested by the Ch W^{n}s, & sent by Mr Edwards to the ABP, who intended to grant a Licence upon it, but did not. ⟨Licenced by the commissary Jan 27. 1757. To reside there or in Diocese wth ABPs consent⟩. Exempt from AD^n. No certified value ⟨ABP Wake saith there is a Stipend of 15$^£$ a year⟩. [Besides the above 80$^£$, Surpl. Fees 40$^£$. Inconveniences appeared at last Election. AD^n]. Ab^t 1000 Ho. Presb meeting Ho. Teacher, Holt. Not many Anab. Teacher, Mr Prall, in the Sack-Cloth Trade. Both much lessend & lessening. Half a dozen Methodists lately, an Itinerant Teacher sometimes. Books from Mr Wesley[3]. Likely to drop. 6 or 7 Families of Quakers. They all pay to the above Rate. Privateering corrupts the morals of the People. Service as above. Cat. in Lent. Com. usually 100: but many more at great Festivals. A little Bread to the poor 1st Sund. in Month. ChW^{n}s give the Offertory partly to the poor at the Ch. Door, partly for schooling of poor Ch^n. Church & chancel noble & in good Repair. Handsome Ho. lately settled by the Parishioners on the minister. Out Ho. none. 8 Bells. Oct. 16. 1663 a Curate licenced by ABP the last C. having written word that he had left it. No. nom. mentioned Entry B. I. 12. 10 March 1698/9 John Macqueen[4] admitted to C. void by death of John Lodowick[5]. No nom. mentioned IV. 599. 12 Jan 1731 Wm Byrch elected Lecturer & Curate sic on Resign of Wm Nairn[6] VII. 346.
Tho. Edwards Cur. as above. R. of Ore, near Hastings, 50$^£$.
John Lyon[7] does his own duty.

1758 Conf. ⟨here 796. Of this parish⟩ 361. 1762. Conf. here 446. Of this parish 288. 1766 Conf here June 2. 607. Of this parish 335.

Dover, St Peters, R. Eccl. destructa. The King P. Kings Books ⟨Tenths 8^s Certified⟩ 24$^£$ Ecton. ⟨qu.⟩ Once there were 7 Churches ib.

---

[1] Perhaps (1726–?), of LLanrhaedr, co Denbigh, m. Jesus O 1745, BA 1748, MA (Magdalene C) 1753.

[2] (1703–56), of Kent, m. Christs, 1721, BA 1725, PC. St Mary's, Dover, 1732–56, R. Great Mongeham, 1752–56.

[3] John Wesley (1703–91), founder of Methodism.

[4] PC. St Mary's, Dover, 1699–. [5] 'a Fleming', PC. St Mary's, Dover, 1661–99.

[6] Of Kent, m. Queens' C 1714, BA 1717, MA 1731, C. Great Chart, 1719, C. Adisham, 1720, V. St. Mary's, Dover, 1729–32.

[7] (1725–), of Warrington, Lancs, m. Queen's O 1743, C. Acrise, 1771, PC. St Mary's, Dover, 1772–1817.

Page 83

Ewel V. St Marys & St Peter. al. Temple Ewel ⟨Kings Books 6–13–4. Value 1663 20$^£$ at most⟩. Belonged to the Commandery[1] of Swynfield. Ecton. { } Angel[2] Esqr P. Ecton. ABP Wake. Heirs of Mr Chandler P. ABP Herrings book. Jo. Dawling[3] was V in ABP Wakes Time. Afterwards Mr Pike[4] officiated. Then Mr Monins[5] was Cur. by Sequestration. Certified 13–10–8. In ABP Wakes book it is called 30$^£$, the Figure 3 altered from 2, & 12$^£$. Mr Tournay[6], Cur. of Alkham p. 76 had had in 1758 the Sequestration from the AD^n near 7 Years, & saith the utmost Value he believes, doth not exceed 25$^£$ ⟨Augm. 1766 with 400$^£$⟩. 22 Ho. Service once a Fortnight: in ABP Wakes time once in 3 weeks. 4 Sacr. 20 Com. Cat. not mentioned. No House for the Minister. Steeple much out of Repair. Church in pretty good Order. Chancel wants whitewashing. 3 Bells. Tithe of Wood & all other vicarial Tithes, usually pd: only Mr Angel will not pay, bec. there is no Vicar, & he lets the Ch. Yard. His Estate there is abt 200$^£$ a year. AD^{ns} Letter May 12. 1761. Caveat ⟨10 Jan 1725–6⟩ from John Angell Esqr patron on death of Dawling Entry B. VII. 110.

Tho. Tournay, Sequestrator, as above. Lives at Alkham, two miles off. For the last 3 Years he hath exchanged Duty with Mr Hobbes[7] of Lydden p. 89. for Mr Hobbes's Convenience, who is near 80. [1759. Mr Barrett[8], Cur. of Kingston, p. 16 serves it. Hath given it up, 1761.

Harvey[9] Cur.of Sibbertswold p. 196 will serve it once a fortnight. The AD^n hath given him the Sequestration. He will have 15$^£$ a yr besides wt Mr Angel shd pay. 1765 Mr Angel hath of late paid his Dues.

M^r ⟨Wm⟩ Williams[10] Curate of Alkham, Capel & Hawkinge (the two first served each once a week, the last once a fortnight,) will serve this also: & AD^n knows not how to do better. Sept. 1766 Hath ½ a Guinea every other Sunday John Gostling[11] Sequestrator.

Alexander James Smith[12] – Cur sal. £50 with Alkham.

1758 Conf. 11. 1762. If any, not set down. 1766. 9.

[1] i.e. belonged to the Knights Templar.
[2] John Angell.
[3] Of Kent, m. Emmanuel 1688, BA 1691, MA 1695, V. Alkham, 1695–26, V. Ewell, 1695–1726.
[4] Richard Pike (–1751), V. Ewel, 1747–51.
[5] Of Dover, Kent, m. St Johns' C 1711, fellow, V. Ewell, 1726–47, V. Alkham 1725–47, R. Ringwould, 1727–47, master King's School, Canterbury, 1734–47, R. Rattlesden, Suffolk, 1747–50, preb of Bristol, 1746–50.
[6] See p. 76, n. 5.   [7] See p. 81, n. 5.   [8] See p. 4, n. 11.
[9] (1735–1821), of Kent, m. CCCC 1754, scholar, BA 1758, MA 1761, V. St Lawrence, Ramsgate, 1766–93, V. Eastry, 1772–1821, minister new chapel of ease, Ramsgate, 1789–1821, six-preacher, 1796.
[10] See p. 76, n. 9.   [11] See p. 6, n. 2.   [12] See p. 76, n. 4.

Page 84

D. Dover

Folkestone C. St Mary & St Eanswith. Belonged to the Priory of Folkestone. Now ABP. Improp. & P. ⟨adv. granted bu Qu. Mary⟩. K^s books 10–0–2½. Now ⟨called⟩ 80$^£$: ⟨but⟩ 70$^£$ {of it} ⟨is⟩ reserved by ABP^s Lease ⟨& 20$^£$ more paid by himself. The 70^f was reserved by Juxon⟩. In the Town & 3 Hamlets 550 Ho. 20 Families of Anabaptists, 2 Meeting Ho. Morris, a Farmer, Teacher of the General: Wanston, a Glover, of the Particular. They come to Church, wn they have no Teacher of their own. Somewhat lessened. 24 Families of Quakers: lessened by Intermarriages with those of the Church. Not industrious to make Proselytes. Meet on Sund. & Thursd. The Lessees Tenant distrains for their Tithes: both small & great belong to him. Absenters lessend 2/3 in the last 5 years by the Ministers Diligence & Charity. Little Lewdness: for they marry very young. 2 Sermons now, without any Consideration for it. One before, & Prayers but once every other Sunday. Cat. in Lent. Ch^n & servts sent: neglected before. Cat. Sermons. Sacr. once in 6 weeks. 100 Com. Prayers on W. (not before) Fr. & Holydays. A Free School for teaching 20 boys, founded by Sir Eliab Harvey[1], endowed with a Farm of 30^f a year. The Master hath 10^f two years, & 30^f the third. The Overplus was given for buying Boats for poor Fishermen. The famous Harvey[2], born here, contributed 200^f to these Purposes, & for a House & Copper to tan their Nets. Mayor & Jurats, Governors: some neighbouring Gentlemen, Feofees. Ld Folkestone[3], to w^m most of the Land in the Parish belongs, voluntarily cloaths 30 poor Ch^n every Christmass. 24^f in Land given by several Persons for Bread & Cloaths for the poor, & putting out poor children. Mr Hammond left 25^f to the poor: his brother to manage it, then the Ch W^{ns} to have it. By his managemt it was sunk: but his Heirs, Mr Andrews of Hythe & his Daughters are able to make it good. ABP desired to assist in procuring it. [But did he leave Assets?].

Cur. had a general permission from ABP^s to baptize Adults. Desires a Continuance of it. Hath bapt. 7 most of them Housekeepers.

No House for the Minister. The last bought a good Ho. & Garden, which his Widow wd sell for 200^f. Church & Chancel, noble & in good Repair. 6 Bells Admission to C. 1671 Entry Book III p. 127. 1699 IV. 599. Licence to shorten the Church V. 220.

[1] Founded in 1674: Hasted VIII, p. 183. He was the brother of William (see n. 2).
[2] William Harvey (1578–1657), physician and discoverer of the circulation of blood.
[3] Jacob des Bouverie (c.1694–1761), Lord Folkestone, MP for Salisbury, 1741–47, president of the society of Arts, 1755–61.

Page 85
Folkestone continued.

Will. Langhorne[1] AM. Cur. 14 Feb. 1753. {Cur also} ⟨Rector⟩ of Hawkinge p. 87. Resides constantly here. Doth more Duty than his predecessors. See last p. See also Hawkinge. Many of the Parishioners, unable to hear him, go to the Meeting House. AD^n from Mr Lunn[2]: but thinks on Inquiry, that he speaks as loud as most clergymen. Mr Foster[3] hears the contrary.

John Tims[4] C. 29 April 1772. does his own duty.

1758. Conf. 186. 1762. 6+116 1766. 182.

[1] (1721–72), of Kirkby Stephen, Westmoreland, MA (Lambeth) 1756, PC. Folkestone, 1753–72, R. Hawkinge, 1754–72.

[2] See p. ii, n. 36.

[3] Probably Samuel Foster (1722–), of Plymouth, Devon, m. Magdalen O 1738, clerk 1738–41, BA 1742, R. Eastbridge, 1757–65.

[4] (1747–1813), of Dorchester, Dorset, m. St John's C 1765, BCL 1781, C. Orlastone & Shadoxhurst, 1769–1772, PC. Folkestone, 1772–1813, R. Hawkinge, 1772–1813.

Page 86

D. Dover

Guston al. Gulston. C. S[t] Martin. Belonged to the Priory of Dover. Now ABP Impr. & P. Certified 14[£]: 10[£] of it reserved ⟨by Juxon⟩ in ABP[s] Lease. 22 Ho. ⟨13-6-8-old stipend 1663⟩. Service once a month. 3 Sacr. Number of Com. not named, nor Cat. Exempt from AD[n]. They refuse to have 4 Sacr. Abt 10 or 12 Com.

An Appropriation of the Church of Guchsistone to the Priory of Dover, reserving 8 marks payable yearly to the Vicar: Lieger book of the Priory, fol. 121 where it is called also Gostone.

Church & Chancel mean, but in good Repair. No Ho. 1 Bell.

Licences to Serve the Cure of W. Langdon & Guston 6 July 1674 Entry B. III. 230.

1765. 17 or 18[£] a year. Mr Ratray 1767 Augmented by Lot & with Sir Ph Botelers Benefaction 400[£].

John Ratray[1] Cur. ⟨lic.⟩ 24 July 1744. Cur. of River p. 92 ⟨quitted⟩ of and E. & W. Langdon p. 183, 202. Resides at E. Langdon, a mile off. [Will serve this once a Fortnight in Summer]. M.A. of Aberdeen, ord. pr. by BP Gibson[2] 20 Dec. 1719. 1764 can do nothing. Mr Queteville officiates for him. See here p. 77, 183.

John Queteville[3] Cur Licens'd November 20 1772.

Thomas Delanney[4] lic. 1788.

1758 Conf. 13. 1762. 3. 1766. 22

[1] MA Aberdeen, C. East Langdon, 1719, C. West Langdon, 1738, C. Guston, 1744, R. East Langdon, 1763–72.

[2] Edmund Gibson (1669–1748), bishop of Lincoln, 1716–20, bishop of London, 1720–48.

[3] See p. 76, n. 8.　　　　　　　　　　[4] See p. 77, n. 4.

Page 87

Hawkinge R. S[t] Michael. ABP P. Tenths 14[s]-9½. Certified 30[£]. Now {called} ⟨let for⟩ 40[£] ⟨See next line⟩. 19 Ho. Service once a Fortnight: will be once a Week, when the Glebe Houses are repaired, & a Person can be found to officiate. It was augm. 1718 with 400[£] by the Queens Bounty & ABP {Wake} ⟨Tenisons will. See below⟩. And Land is purchased with it. And the Glebe & Tithes were once let for 50[£]. It is 3 miles from Folkestone. No Cat. but for Confirmation. 4 Sacr. 20 Com. Offertory money distributed by Ch W[n]s. Church & Chancel small, in tolerable Repair. Ho. indifferent, in good Repair. A good Barn. 1 Bell Sept. 1762. Service hath been but once a fortnight.

1767 Augm with 200[£] S[r] Ph. B[s] money & 200[£] Qu[s] Bounty.

Will. Langhorn[1] MA R. 14 Feb. 1753. Cur. of Folkestone p. 85 where he resides. His Predecessor served this also. But he hath a Curate. It was served but once a fortnight till Apr. 1767 w^n Mr Langhorne began to serve it the other Sunday at 9 & Folkestone at 11.
John Tims[2] R. 29 April 1772. does his own duty.

Tho. Tournay[3] Cur. see Alkham p. 76. 13^f. Gone 31 Aug. 1762. Gives but 10^f.
John Kemeys[4] Cur March 25 1763 also Cur of Alkham p. 76. Gone.
Wm Williams[5] P. with Alkham p. 76 1766.

1758 Conf. 3. 1762 1 + 2.

[1] See p. 85, n. 1.
[3] See p. 76, n. 5.
[5] See p. 76, n. 9.

[2] Ibid., n. 4.
[4] See p. 76, n. 6.

Page 88
D. Dover
Hougham al. Huffham V. St Laurence. Belonged to the Priory of Dover. ABP Impr. & P. Tenths 13^s-4^d. Certified 46^f. Now called 40^f see below. 25^f reserved by Juxon in ABP^s Lease of Farthingloe & Huffham. 20 Ho. Service once 3 Sundays in a month. [In ABP Wake & Herrings time once every Sunday ⟨But see p. 87⟩. And the former calls it 55^f ⟨See below⟩]. The 4th they go to Cap. le Fern, half a mile off. Cat. when there is Occasion. 4 Sacr. 16 Com. Church & Chancel clean & in good Repair. No Ho. Glebe 2½ Acres. 3 Bells.
The Book of 1663 saith the Vicarage was accounted 50^f a year before the Augmentation.

Ed. Hobbes[1] V. 14 May 1712. Cur. of St James's Dover p. 81. & Cur. by Seq. of Lydden p. 89. Lives at Dover, above 2 miles off. Dead.
Tho. Tournay[2] V. inst 31 Aug 1762. C. of St James's Dover p. 81. To serve each once a Sunday & quit Lydden. Feb. 1765 Inst. to the Rectory of Yate (see p. 81) in Gloucestershire. The BP gives him Leave of Absence. I have told him that I shall not at present declare Hougham void. He designs to lay up money from it to buy a House, I think, for St James's Dover.

William Tournay[3] A.M. 1795.

1758 Conf. 15. 1762 None set down. 1766 17

[1] See p. 81, n. 5.   [2] See p. 76, n. 5.   [3] See p. 77, n. 5.

Page 89
Lydden al. Leden V. St Mary. Belonged to the Abbey of Langdon. ABP. Impr. & P. Tenths 12^s-7^d ¼. Certified 32^f. 18^f of it is reserved ⟨by Juxon⟩ in ABP^s Lease. Augm. 1718 with 400^f by the Queens Bounty & ABP {Wake} ⟨Tenisons will⟩. Yet said to be under 30^f now. 12 Ho. Service once a fortnight. Cat. when

needful. 4 Sacr. 8 Com. No V. Ho. Roof of the Church very bad. Chancel bad. Glebe 40 Perches. 1 Bell. 1762 Service to be once every Sunday.

Collation to V. March 3. 1669. Not said how vacant Entry B. II. 232. Another ⟨of Andrew Pearne[1]⟩ on the death of that V. Nov. 3 1673 III. 207. Another 1675 on the Death of Pearne to Tho Griffin[2]:. 260. On Griffins Death to Arth. Tucker[3] 1705 V. 131.

Ed. Hobbs[4] Cur. by Sequestration. See p. 88. Lives at Dover, 4 miles off. Exchanges with M[r] Tournay. See p. 83. Dead.

Tho. Tournay[5] Cur. by Sequestration {July} ⟨Aug⟩ 1762. Quits it on having S[t] James's Dover & Hougham, wch see.

A. James[6] Cur. of Charlton p. 79. Quits Whitfield p. 77.

Richard Harvey[7], Sequestrator 1775.

M[r] Freeman[8] Cur Sequestrator 1794.

1758 Conf. 4. 1762. 35. 1766. 11

[1] Andrew Perne (1644–75), of West Wratting, Cambs, m. St John's C 1662, BA 1666, V. Lydden, 1673-5.

[2] Perhaps (16?–1704), m. Trinity C 1636, BA 1639, V. Lydden, 1675-1704.

[3] Of Suffolk, m. CCCC 1671, BA 1675, V. Lydden, 1705.

[4] See p. 81, n. 5.   [5] See p. 76, n. 5.

[6] See p. 77, n. 7.   [7] See p. 83, n. 10.

[8] Thomas Freeman, see p. 4, n. 12.

Page 90

D. Dover

S[t] Margarets at Cliff V. Belonged to the Priory of Dover. ABP Impr. & P. Tenths 13[s]. Certified 46[£]. 26[£] of it ⟨1762 clear of Land Tax⟩ reserved in ABP[s] Lease ⟨by Juxon⟩. Now called 40[£]. But in ABP Wakes Book 66[£] ⟨See below⟩. Exempt from AD[n]. 65 Ho. & 2 Light Houses. Service once 3 Sundays: the 4th at Westcliff, a small half mile distant, as in the time of the last Incumbent. Cat. exp. on Sundays in Lent, & at other times. 4 Sacr. 40 Com. at each. Church & Chancel large & handsome. No Ho. 1 Bell. The Lessee of the Great Tithes saith, that the small Tithes & Glebe are worth 30[£] a year, & pay, at 4[s], 1[£] to the Land-tax, wch is the proportion through the parish.

John Marsh[1] BA V. 19 Feb. 1732. Resides at Dover, 3 miles off, as his Father[2] the late V. did. Cur. of Buckland p. 78 & V. of Westcliff p. 94. where see. Alexander James[3] Clerk M.A. V. Oct: 13 1773. resides.

1758 Conf. 35. 1762. 28. 1766. 44

[1] See p. 78, n. 4.   [2] Richard Marsh, ibid., n. 3.   [3] See p. 77, n. 7.

Page 91

Newington near Hythe V. St Nicolas. Belonged to the College of Wye. James Brockman Esqr P. K^s books 7–12–6. Certified value 48–17–3. Now 53$^£$ ⟨See below⟩. 53 Ho. James Brockman[1] of Beachborough Esqr Batchelor, 600$^£$ a year. Service once, & ⟨Cat.⟩ as at Cheriton p. 80 which see. 4 Sacr. 30 Com. Land of 2–5–0 for poor not receiving Parochial Relief. Church & Chancel neat & in good Order. Ho. indifferent, but in good Order. Glebe 2 Acres. 5 Bells. The Vicar saith June 13. 1767 he believes the Income is a confirmed modus, under 44$^£$ a Year, & that the Surplices Fees do not raise it to 47$^£$. Mr Brockman is dead, & succeeded in his Estate by Mr Drake[2], who was Curate of Dimchurch p. 119 & will probably live here.

Edm. Parker[3] V. 29 Oct. 1739 Resides here. R. of Cheriton p. 80.
Ralph Drake Brockman[4] B.D. May 19th 1770.

1758 Conf. 58. 1762. 36. 1766. 23.

[1] (1696–1767). He died unmarried.
[2] Ralph Drake (1724–81), of London, m. St John's O 1742, BA 1746, MA 1750, BD 1755, V. Newington, 1770–81. Assumed name Brockman, on inheriting the estates of his first cousin once removed.
[3] See p. 80, n. 3.   [4] See n. 2.

Page 92

D. Dover

River V. St Peter & St Paul. al. Ryver. Belonged to the Abbey of St Radegund. ABP P. Tenths 14–1¼. Certified 8$^£$. K. John 26 July ann. regn. 17. gave the Rectory to the Abbey: wch Gift ABP Steph. Langton[1] confirmed, reserving 5$^£$ to the Vicarage Reg. Warham fol. 131 b. But 25 Sept. 1511 the ABP admitted a vicar, presented by the Abbey, to the vicarage & a Pension of 4 marks, payable to him by it. ib. fol. 343 a. This 2–13–4 is mentioned in the Lease of River ⟨& in the accts. of the AB^{rick} in 1643 & in the parlt survey⟩, as due to V. from ABP. He hath also some Glebe & Tithes, worth abt 7–15–0. See his Letter Oct. 30. 1759 and the Vicarage was augmented by Lot with 200$^£$ in 1739 & with 200$^£$ in 1757 ⟨& with 400 in 1766⟩. 2½ miles long, 1½ broad. Abt 24 Ho. Service once a month on Sundays. [will be once a fortnight in Summer]. Cat. at any time, wn the Ch^n & Servts are capable of Instruction. 3 Sacr. No V. Ho. They refuse to have 4 Sacr. Abt 10 or 12 Com. Church & Chancel small & clean Glebe ¾ acre. ⟨Mr Ratray saith 3 or 4⟩. 1 Bell. Sequ. of River V. 10$^£$ to R. of Buckland 1666 Entry B. 11. 14.

John Ratray[2] Sequestrator. Cur. of Guston p. 86 & of W. Langdon p. 202 & of E. Langdon p. 183 where he resides, 3 miles off. He quits it on taking the Rectory of E. Langdon.
Mr Freeman[3], Cur. of Barham p. 4 where see, will serve this once in 3 weeks. AD^n Feb. 10. 1763. I have desired it may be oftener. Mr Harvey[4] of Sibbertswold will do the occ. Duty from Barfreston. Mr. Fr. will do as much as he can. Serves it once a fortnight 1766.

Mr Delannoy[5] Cur. Sal £15.

Thomas Edwards[6] Cur. Sal. £14 & surplice fees lic. by Archdeacon.

1758 Conf. 15. 1762 Conf. 9. 1766. 15.

[1] Archbishop of Canterbury, 1207–28. [2] See p. 86, n. 1.
[3] See p. 4, n. 12. [4] See p. 77, n. 4.
[5] See p. 79, n. 6. [6] Perhaps C. Whitfield and River, 1790.

Page 93

Swinfield C. S[t] Peter. Belonged to the Commandery[1] of Swynfield. Sir Tho. Palmer[2] P. ⟨1761 Lady Palmer. Dead. John Cosnan[3] of Wingham Esq[r] 1767⟩. Certified 20[£]. 50 Ho. One Family of Quakers. One, notoriously wicked. Service once. Cat. in Lent. 4 Sacr. 25 or 30 Com. I am told, that no Admission to it is mentioned in the Register Books. Church & Chancel in pretty good Order. No Ho. 3 Bells. Sheperheath V. joined to this in 1663.

Tho. Rymer[4] DD. Cur. R. of Acrise p. 95.
Resides there. R. of Wittresham p. 149. Died March 23. 1761.
William Swanne[5] A.M. 1783.
Philip Papillon[6] A.M. 1785.

John Hardy Francklyn[7], Priest, Deputy here, & Cur. ⟨R.⟩ of Acrise p. 95. 40[£] for both. Lives at Elham, p 99 [4 miles from hence]. He may be Curate of Swinfield, but doubts abt taking it, yet serves it 1761. Hath taken it 1764. lic. March 24. 1767.
M[r]. Webster[8] Cur. Sal. £28.
Cha[s]. Eaton Plater[9] A.B. Sal £25 lic. by Archdeacon.

1758 Conf. 10. 1762. 25. 1766. 19.

[1] i.e. belonged to the Knights Templar.
[2] See p. 24, n. 1.   [3] He died in 1778: Hasted IX, p. 236.
[4] (1679–1761), of London, m. Queens' C 1697, BA 1701, MA 1704, DD 1726, R. Acrise, 1706–61, PC. Swingfield, 1708–61, R. Wittersham, 1723–61.
[5] (1730–85), of London, m. Christ Church 1748, BA 1751, MA 1757, C. Boughton Monchelsea, 1775, R. Acrise, 1782–5, PC. Swingfield, 1783–85.
[6] (1760–1809), of Acrise, Kent, m. Oriel 1777, BA 1781, MA 1784, R. Eythorne, 1784, PC. Swingfield, 1785, R. Bonnington, 1785–1803, V. Tunbridge, 1803–09.
[7] (1727–82), of Weymouth, Dorset, m. Balliol 1746, BA 1750, R. Acrise, 1761–82, C. Swingfield, 1767–82.
[8] Probably William Theophilus Mountjoy Webster, see p. 28, n. 6.
[9] (1767–1843), of Kent, m. Emmanuel 1787, BA 1790, C. Acrise and Swingfield, 1790, PC. Whitstable, 1803–43, V. Seasalter, 1803–43, V. River, 1810–35, poor vicar, 1807.

Page 94

D. Dover

Westcliff V. S[t] Peter. DCh. Cant. Prop. & P. ⟨1663 9[£] old stipend: 24[£] augm. Do not DCh. pay old stip⟩. Certified 24[£]. So called now. But ABP Wake 31[£] augm. 3 Ho. No Ho. for V. Service once a month, as in the last V[s] time. Cat.

when needful. 4 Sacr. 5 Com. each time. Church & chancel in good Order. 1 Bell.

John Marsh[1] BA. V. ⟨7 July 1733⟩. Resides at Dover 2½ miles off, as he always hath done. Cur. of Buckland p. 78 & V. of S[t] Margarets p. 90. [At these 3 places he officiates 6 times in a month. Might he not officiate every Sunday at S[t] Marg. wch is at least 40[£], & twice in a month at each of the others?]. Promises that he will 1766.
John Bearblock[2] V December 7 1773.
Robert Pitman[3] V. 1784 does his own duty.

1758 Conf. 2 1762 None set down. 1766. 4.

[1] See p. 78, n. 4.
[2] (17?–84), C. Ringwould, 1770, V. Westcliffe, 1773–84, R. Blackmanstone, 1778–84.
[3] (17?–1807), 'literate', C. Appledore, 1770, R. Chillenden, 1776–1807, V. Westcliffe, 1784–1807, poor vicar, 1804.

[Deanery of Elham]

Page 95
D. Elham
Acris al. Awkeridge R. ⟨Acrisse. Wake⟩. S[t] Martin. The King P. K[s] books 7[£] Now 70[£]. ABP Wake 80[£]. See below 23 Ho. David Papillon[1] Esq[r], 1500[£] a Year, old. Was Com. of Excise ***. Service once. No Prayers, but on Sunday. [qu. good Fr. Chr. day]. Cat exp. in Lent. 4 Sacr. 20 Com. No Offertory. Church & chancel small, in good Repair. Ho. & out Ho. neat & in good Order. 1[£] to the Church. Glebe 37 Acres. 1 Bell.
1767 R. saith this & Swinfield, after Land Tax & poor Sess ⟨pd⟩ are but 95[£] a year. This before Swinfield was augmented. He laid out near 130[£] on the buildings.

Tho. Rymer[2] DD. R. 26 June 1706. Was a considerable man, excellent preacher. Resides. Died March 23. 1761.
John Hardy Francklyn[3] BA of Ball. ord D. by me June IV. 1750 Pr by BP. Thomas[4] of Pet. 17 June 1753. See below. R. Apr. 6 1761 married ⟨young⟩ Mr Papillons sister. Hath sisters dependent on him. See his Letter, Apr. 13. 1767.
W[m] Swanne[5] A.M. Rector 1782.
Giles Powell[6] – Rector 1785.

John Hardy Francklyn Priest. Cur. See Swinfield. Lives at Elham, a mile & half from this Parish. 40[£] for both. See above.

W[m] Webster[7] Cur.

Charles Eaton Plater[8] A.B. Sal £21 lic. by Archdeacon.

1758 Conf. 13. 1762. 15 1766. 17.

1 (1691–1762), MP for New Romney, 1722–34, MP for Dover, 1734–41, commissioner of the excise, 1742–54.
2 See p. 93, n. 4.   3 Ibid., n. 7.
4 See p. 41, n. 2.
5 See p. 93, n. 5.
6 (1741–1826), of co. Limerick, m. Trinity College Dublin 1757, BA 1761, R. Acrise, 1785, C. Postling, 1815.
7 See p. 28, n. 6.   8 See p. 93, n. 9.

Page 96

D. Elham
Bircholt R. St Marg. Charles Hayes[1] [of Bloomsbury, ABP Wake] P. K^s books 2–10–0. Wake, 10$^£$ Now called 20$^£$. No Church [Nor any Remains of one. Wake]. 4 Ho. [5 Wake ⟨1767⟩]. No answer to Inquiries.. They go to Hinxhill Church p. 122.

John Howdell[2] BA R. ⟨pr. by K. on lapse⟩ 24 Sept. 1750. Cur. of Pluckley p. 69 where he resides. Died abt 20 Oct. 1762.
Wm Polhill[3] BA R. 11 Nov. 1762 pres. by John Cale[4] of Barming Co. Kent Esqr, nephew to the above Mr Hayes. Cur. of Ashford p. 50 {Gone} R. of Orleston p. 135 Master of Maidstone School p. 250.
John Thomas Jordan[5] B.A. R. February 19 1774.

Jude Holdesworth[6] R. of Hinxhill, p. 122 which is very near, doth the occasional Duty. Dead.

1758 Conf. none. 1762 none

1 Hasted VIII, p. 12.   2 See p. 57, n. 6.   3 See p. 50, n. 16.
4 Cale was a barrister at law and died in 1777: Hasted VIII, p. 12.
5 (1750–1820), of Kent, m. Queens' C 1768, scholar 1772, BA 1772, MA 1775, BD 1784, fellow, 1774, C. Hunton, 1772–5, R. Bircholt, 1774–1820, R. St Botolph's, Cambs, 1775–8, V. Oakington, Cambs, 1778–91, R. Little Eversden, 1791–7, R. Hickling, Notts, 1797–1820.
6 (16?–1759), of Reed, Herts, m. Christs 1713, BA 1719, MA 1723, C. Smarden, 1721, R. Hinxhill, 1722–59, V. Tonge, 1723–50, R. Rucking, 1750–59, archbishop's chaplain, 1750.

Page 97

Brabourn al. Bradborne V. St Mary. Belonged to the Monastery of Horton. Now ABP Impr. & P. K^s books 11–12–6. Now 80$^£$. 16$^£$ of it, with a Q^r of wheat & a Q^r of Barley reserved in ABP^s Lease ⟨by Juxon⟩. Tithes let for 70$^£$ a year Divided into E. & W. 53 Ho. 2 Families of Anab. come lately. Service once a Sunday here, once at Horton p. 102, the Churches a mile & half asunder. Parents, though exhorted publickly & privately, will not send their Ch^n to be catechized, but before a Confirmation ⟨He saith the same of Horton⟩. 4 Sacr. 20 Com. ⟨very few⟩. A young Man from Elham teaches writing & reading in the Chancel. Legacies of 3–15–10 to the poor not receiving parochial Relief. A good Ho. & out-Houses for the Vicar. Church indifferent. Chancel the same. Mr Scots[1] chancel very dirty. Ho. & out Ho. neat & in good Order. 5 Bells.

John Richards[2] coll to Bradbourn R. void by the Death of W[m] Johnson[3], as also to Bradbourn V. 3 March 1675 Entry B. II. 282.

Cha. Norris[4] LLB. V. 11 Aug. 1733. Resides. Hath laid out money on the V. Ho. See Nackington p. 43 & here above Cur. also of Horton p. 102. Died Jan. 19. 1767.
Joseph Price[5] V. March 2. 1767. Resides May 11.
Ditto V. Febry 27: 1776.
Abraham Purshouse[6] Vicar 1786.

Consolidated wth Monks Horton Pa. 102 Sept. 22nd 1777.
M[r] Macock[7] Cur of Horton Sal £25.

1758. Conf. 41. 1762. 16+11. 1766. 30.

[1] Edward Scott, who died in 1765; Hasted VII, p. 7.
[2] m. Jesus O 1666, BA 1670, MA 1673, C. Monks Horton, 1676, R. Brabourne, 1676.
[3] 1676), V. Brabourne, 1664–1676, R. Monks Horton, 1668–76.
[4] See p. 43, n. 3.   [5] See p. 17, n. 6.
[6] (1754–1831), of Southwark, Surrey, Pembroke Hall C 1773, BA 1777, MA 1780, C. Charing, 1778–86, V. Brabourne w. Monks Horton, 1786–1831, R. Frinsted, 1822–31.
[7] Henry Macock (1743–1816), of Oxford, m. Lincoln 1758, BA 1763, MA 1764, V. Harwell, Berks, C. Sellinge, 1790, V. Sellinge, 1803–16, C. Lympne, 1814–16.

Page 98
D. Elham
Denton R. S[t] Mary Magd. Tho. Whorwood[1] Esq[r] was P. He died abt 12 years ago & gave the Rectory to Univ. Coll. See below. K[s] books 5-19-4½. Certified 59-3-0. Now 60[£]. 24 Ho. M[r] Whorwoods uninhabited since his Death. Service once on Sundays. Prayers on the principal Holy days. Cat. in Lent, & then some good Book given. 4 Sacr. 30 Com. each time. 25[£] given for 6 two penny Loaves for poor persons every Sunday from Chr. to Mich. The Gift of this Rectory to University College was declared null & void by the Court of Chancery. Miss Scot[2] P. Church & Chancel & Parsonage Ho. small & but in indifferent Order. Glebe 7 Acres. 3 Bells. Exch. of part of Ch. yard by Licence 1729 Entry B VII. 252.

Edw. Lunn[3] R. 1705. Resides constantly in the Parsonage Ho. Cur. of Nonington p. 18 which he serves with this. Died July 27. 1764.
W[m] Robinson[4] R. Nov. 15. 1764. Resides & serves it once, & no other place. Hath a rich wife. 1756 will serve it twice. 1767 Doth. 1768 hath Burghfield in Berks: desires to hold this with it & stay here: so doth the patroness.
Thomas Scott[5] LLB. Rector 1785.
William Tournay[6] A.M. 1792.

M[r]. Downing[7] Cur.

1758 Conf. 13. 1762. 22. 1766. 12.

[1] Died in 1745.

[2] Whorwood bequeathed the patronage to his wife, and afterwards to his relation Cecilia Scott: Hasted IX, p. 360.

[3] See p. ii, n. 38.

[4] (1729–1803), of Cambs., m. St John's C 1748, BA 1751, fellow, 1752–60, MA 1754, R. Denton, 1764–85, R. Burghfield, Berks, 1767–1800, succeeded to family estates on death of Lord Rokeby. The poet Thomas Gray visited him at Denton Court in 1766: the church yard at nearby Thanington was supposedly his 'Country Churchyard': DNB.

[5] See p. 56, n. 15.

[6] (1762–1827), of Hythe, Kent, m. Oriel 1780, BA 1784, MA 1789, C. Saltwood, 1785, R. Eastbridge, 1790, R. Hope, All Saints, 1795, R. Denton, 1792–1827, C. Swingfield, 1822.

[7] See p. 18, n. 8.

Page 99

Elham V. S[t] Mary. ABP nominates, Merton Coll. presents. K[s] books 20[£] Certified 59-15-2. Now 120[£]. 12 Hamlets, 200 Ho. One Quaker, pays Tithes & Church Rates without Trouble. Whole Service. Prayers W. Fr. Holydays. Cat. exp. in Lent. 8 Sacr. 150 Com. A free School, endowed by the Will of Sir John Williams[1] K[t] 7 Apr. 1723, with Ho. & Lands worth 18[£] a year. Master to have Ho. & 6[£] a year; for teaching 6 Boys reading, writing, Catechism. The Remainder to cloath them once in 2 years, & put them out. Trustees, Vicar, Ch W[ns], Overseers. V. pays the Master for teaching 6 Girls reading & Cat. Revd. D[r] Warley[2], deceased, gave 50[£]: Interest to be given 6 poor widows every Sunday in the Church. Done. Church & Chancel large & in good Order. Ho. pretty good by D[r] Bearcroft. Glebe 7 Acres. 3 Bells.

ABP Boniface[3] granted the Rectory of Elham to Merton Coll. in 1268 reserving to himself & Successors the power of appointing a vicarage & nominating a vicar to the College, wm they shall present in 40 Days, else ABP shall collate. See Reg. Warham. f.128b. No provision there, that the vicar shall be of Merton Coll. The last 4, at least, were of it. 12 Oct. 1691 John Lipps[4] AM [of Merton inst Entry B. IV. 471 on the Death of Hen. Hannington[5]. 21 March 1691 W[m] Hunt[6] of Merton inst on Res. of Lipps 477. 5 Sept 1707 Robt Harrison[7] of Merton on Cession of Hunt V. 226. 9 Nov. 1711 John Hill[8] ⟨of Merton⟩ on Cession of Harrison VI. 60. {1 March 1730} 10 Apr. 1731 Ph. Bearcroft of Merton on death of Hill.

Phil. Bearcroft[9] DD. V. 10 Apr. 1731. V. of Stourmouth p. 23 & master of the Charterhouse, where he resides. Died Oct. 17. 1761.

Tho. Thompson[10] nominated Nov. 20 1761 inst. Nov. 24. One of the poor vicars 1767. Declines it. Made one of the 6 Preachers Aug. 19. 1767.

Edward Fulham[11] Master of Arts V. December 8 1773.

William Cornwallis[12] A.M. Vicar Mar. 3: 1778.

Pet. Murthwaite[13] F. of S[t] Johns Camb. Priest. Cur 40[£] & Surp. Fees. Lives in V. Ho. Gone.

Robt Ingram[14] Cur. Perpetual Cur. of Bredherst p. 236. Resides here. V. of Orston Co. Nottingham, Oct 1759. Saith, Nov. 24. that he hath Leave to stay at Elham 2 or 3 Years. Too deaf to hear the Responses; & his Voice too low to be heard. AD[n]. Going at Mich 1760 to a Living in Essex.

Hen. Thompson[15] C. 40[£] See p. 224. ord. pr. Dec. 21. 1760. 2. Resides, May 1761. Gone.

Edward Young[16] Clerk A.M. Cur. Lic. Sept[m]. 18: 1774. Salary £50 p. ann.

Mr Williamson[17]. Cur. Sal. 45 Guineas.

William Filmer[18] cur. sal. £45 House, Garden & Surplice Fees lic. by Archdeacon.

1758 Conf. 83. 1762. Conf. here 170. Of this Parish 69 1766. 44 at Cant.

[1] (1653–1723) 2nd Bt, MP for Hereford, 1700–5.
[2] Jonas Warley (16?–1722), of Kent, m. Clare 1665, BA 1669, MA 1672, DD 1710, fellow, R. Loughton, Essex, 1673, V. Witham, 1680, archdeacon of Colchester, 1704–22.
[3] Archbishop, 1243–70.
[4] (1664–?), of Faversham, Kent, m. Merton 1682, BA 1685, MA 1688, V. Elham, 1691–2.
[5] (1617–91), of Hougham, Kent, m. Caius 1639, C. St James's, Dover and Buckland, 1639, V. Elham–91.
[6] (1668–1727), of London, m. Merton 1684, BA 1691, V. Elham, 1692–1707, R. Alderton, Suffolk, 1707–27.
[7] (1682–), of Oxford, m. Merton 1697, BA 1701, MA 1704, V. Elham, 1707–11.
[8] (1686–1731), of Mere, Wilts, m. Merton 1705, BA 1708, V. Elham, 1711–31.
[9] See p. 23, n. 1.   [10] See p. ii, n. 46.
[11] (1749–1832), of Compton, Surrey, m. CCCO 1765, BA 1769, MA (Merton) 1772, V. Elham, 1773–78, preb of Chichester, 1773, R. St Nicholas, Guildford, 1777–1832 and of Penton Mewsey, 1790–1832.
[12] (1751–1828), of Ipswich, m. Merton 1767, BA 1771, MA 1774, V. Elham, 1778–1828, R. Wittersham, 1778–1828.
[13] (1721–1800), of Cumberland, m. St John's C 1742, BA 1746, MA 1749, BD 1757, fellow, 1748–68, V. North Stoke, Oxon, 1767–1800.
[14] (1727–1804), of Beverley, Yorks, m. CCCC 1746, BA 1750, MA 1753, fellow, 1754–60, PC. Bredhurst, 1758–62, C. Hernehill, C. Boughton Blean, V. Orston, Notts, 1759–60, V. Wormingford, Essex, 1760–1803, V. Boxted, 1768–83.
[15] See p. 38, n. 2.
[16] (1751–?), of Ashford, Kent m. University 1768, BA 1771, MA 1774, C. Elham, 1774.
[17] Perhaps William Williamson (17?–1804), R. Westbere, 1799–1804.
[18] (1762–1830), of Crundale, Kent, m. CCCO 1779, BA 1783, MA 1787, BD 1795, C. Elham, 1790, V. Borden, 1794–7, R. Heyford Purcell, Oxon, 1797–1830.

Page 100
D. Elham
Elmsted V. St James. Belonged to the Priory of St Gregory. Pens. to Prior. 1–6–8 Ecton. Now ABP Impr & P. Tenths 13–4. Certified 45$^£$ ⟨94$^£$ AD^n⟩. Now 80$^£$ ⟨20$^£$ of it reserved in ABP^s Lease⟩. Said in ABP Wakes Papers at Ch. Ch. vol. 2 to be worth 100$^£$. 75 Ho. Sir John Honeywood[1], exemplary in Piety, Sobriety, Charity. [3 or 4000$^£$ a year. ***]. Lady Filmer[2], Relict of Sr Edw[3]. of a most amiable Character, with her Family. One Anab. Several have come into the Parish, & been bapt. by V. Service once here by V. & once at his other Parish, Hastingleigh p. 101. A mile distant. The people go to both. Prayers at both on Chr. day Ash W. good Fr. &c. Cat. exp. at each alternately in Summer. 6 Sacr. here. Com. usually 50 or 60. Church indifferent & dirty. Chancel in good Order. Ho & Out Ho. small in good Repair. Glebe 1 Acre. 6 Bells.

John Conant[4] MA V. 15 May 1736. R. of Hastingleigh p. 101. Resides there. Serves both.
Nicholas Simons[5] A.B. Vicar, June 25: 1779. does his own duty.
William Welfitt[6] D.D. Vicar 1795.

1758 Conf. 49. 1762. 3 NB + 19. 1766. 30

[1] See p. 19, n. 1.   [2] Mary Filmer (1699–1761). She had 20 children.   [3] See p. 10, n. 1.
[4] (1707–79), of London, m. Pembroke O 1723, BA 1727, MA 1730, R. Hastingleigh, 1734–79, R. Elmsted, 1736–79, preb of Bangor, 1735, chaplain to viscount Garnock.
[5] (1754–1839), of Chislet, Kent, m. Christ's 1772, BA 1776, MA (Clare) 1779, V. Elmsted, 1779–95, R. Hastingleigh, 1779–95, V. Welton, Yorks, 1795–1807, R. St Margaret's, Canterbury, 1806–22, V. Minster, 1807–39, R. Ickham, 1822–39, JP in Leicestershire.
[6] (1745–1833), of Hull, m. University 1764, BA 1768, MA 1772, BD & DD 1785, R. Bliborough, Leics, 1773, V. Welton, Yorks, 1779, R. St Benet, Gracechurch St, London, 1791, R. Hastingleigh, 1795–1833, R. Elmsted, 1795–1833, V. Ticehurst, Sussex, 1795–1833, V. Minster, 1807–33, preb of Canterbury, 1785–1833, vice-dean, 1799.

Page 101

Hastingleigh R. S[t] Mary. ABP P. K[s] books 10–5–0. Certified 68–19–0. Now 80[f]. Said in ABP Wakes Papers at Ch. Ch. vol. 2 to be at least worth 100[f]. 25 Ho. Service, See Elmsted p. 100. 4 Sacr. here. 25 or 30 Coms. Church & Chancel indifferent. Ho. very handsome, greatly improved by M[r] Conant. OutHo. in good Order. Glebe 15 Acres. 1 Bell.
The Advowson was granted by the Crown to the ABP in exchange 31 Aug 1 Ed. 6. See Chart. Misc. vol. 13 N°. 21.

John Conant[1] MA R. 14 Dec. 1734 V. of Elmsted p. 100. Resides here. Serves both.
Nicolas Simons[2] A.B. Rector, June 25: 1779, resides.
William Welfitt[3] D.D. Rector 1795.

1758 Conf. 6. 1762. 6. + 3. 1766. 9

[1] See p.100, n. 4.   [2] Ibid, n. 2.   [3] Ibid, n. 3.

Page 102

D. Elham
Horton al. Monks Horton R. S[t] Peters. Pens. Mon. Horton 5[s] Ecton. ABP P. ⟨Paroch book 1663 saith it was given to the ABP in the 3[d] Exchange⟩. Tenths 15[s] 1[d]. Certified 40[f]. Now called 80. But R. saith 60, and fears it will be less ⟨AD[n] 50[f]⟩. 21 Ho. Matthew Robinson Morris[1] Esq[r], Repr. for Canterbury ***. Service once, See Brabourn p. 97. The same Complaint as there ab[t] Cat. R. hath promised to inquire & endeavour. 4 Sacr. 20 Com. Church & Chancel bad & dirty. Ho. mean, let to 2 poor Tenants. Out Ho. out of Repair. 50[s] to the poor, AD[n]. Glebe 14 Acres. 4 Bells. All the Land in Grass: but 18[f] clear. 1765 See AD[n] Jan. 11.1767 Now 50[f] a year. The Rector at Law with M[r] Robinson.

John Clough[2] MA R. 10 Feb. 1727. V. of Ashford p. 50. Resides there. Died before Nov. 20 1764.
Bryan Faussett[3] M.A R. May 8. 1765. Cure. of Nackington p. 43.
Joseph Price[4] Clerk B.D. Rector Febry 26: 1776.

Consolidated with Brabourne Pa. 97.
Cha Norris[5] Cur. 20[f]. See Brabourn p. 97. Still 1765 ⟨dead⟩.
Joseph Price C March 1767 V. of Brabourn p. 97.

1758 Conf. 3. 1762. 4. 1766. 2

[1] Matthew Robinson (afterwards Robinson Morris) (1713–1800), MP for Canterbury, 1747–61, created 2nd baron Rokesby in 1794. He succeeded to his mother's Kentish estates in 1746 and took the additional name of Morris.

[2] See p. 50, n. 12.   [3] See p. 19, n. 4.

[4] See p. 17, n. 6.   [5] See p. 43, n. 3.

Page 103

Lyminge al. Lymege R. S[t]. Mary & S[t] Edburg, with Stanford Cap. All S[ts] & Paddlesworth, S[t] Oswalds. Exempt from AD[n]. Arabella Taylor[1] ⟨widow⟩ P. ⟨Grindals List copied in Par Book of 1663 gives the Advowson to the ABP⟩. K[s] books 21-10-0. Now called 300[£]. See here below. Many Houses & Cottages [104 ABP Wake]. Service once at the Church, once at one of the Chapels alternately, every Sunday, in ABP Wakes time, till 1720: then only once a month at Paddlesworth: & now in the Winter only every 3[d] Sunday at Standford. And this is called the usual Duty for Time immemorial. No Cat. for many Years past. Now Cur hath 40 Scholars, whom he catechizes, & will soon in the Church. 4 Sacr. at Church, 3 at the Chapels. Not said how many Com. Capt. Bedingfield[2] left 15[£] a Year to educate a Boy for Univ. or Trade. Parish Officers to give a Copy of the Will. {No Offertory.}. The Ch[n] are to be chosen out of Dimchurch, Smeeth, or Lyminge. See Answers from Dimchurch ⟨p.119⟩. No Offertory. Glebe 29 Acres.

Lyndon[3], the last Incumbent, is supposed to have conveyed the great Tithes to M[rs] Taylor the Patroness by Deed: & the present to have at least promised her them upon Honour. She is dead. He was her brother in Law & now enjoys the whole Income of R &V.

Inst. to R 23 Feb. 1670 Entry B III. 59. Rich. Halford[4] V [see next p] inst. 14 Jan. 1714 { } to R void by Death of Abiel Borset[5] & lapsed to R.VI. 171. Quintus Naylor[6] inst. to R. 4 July 1726 on death of Halford [see next p here] VII. 124. John Lyndon to R & V separately 3 Feb 1734/5 on death of Naylor, R. with chapels VIII. 27

Ralph Price[7] R. 27 Jan. 1757 ⟨on death of Lyndon⟩ See V. p.104.
Ralph Price[8] Clerk A.M. Rector, December 17:1776.

[1] Annabella Taylor: Hasted VIII, p. 90.

[2] Timothy Bedingfield in his will of 1693 left lands in Woodchurch and Lyminge towards the education of those poor male children from Dymchurch, Lyminge or Smeeth, whose parents did not receive alms and who belonged to the Church of England, to be sent to university or established in trade: Hasted VIII, p. 267.

[3] John Lyndon (c.1699–1756), of Dublin, m. TCD 1717, R. Lyminge, 1735–56.

[4] (1679–1726), of London, m. Queens' C 1697, BA 1701, MA 1704, V. Lyminge, 1713, R. Lyminge, 1715–26.

[5] (1633–1714?), of Leics, Christs 1649, BA 1653, MA 1656, minister at New Brentford, 1657–61, V. Lyminge, 1671–1714, minister of Richmond, Surrey, 1660–96.

[6] R. Lyminge, 1726–34.

[7] (1715–76), of Wantage, Berkshire, m. Trinity O 1733, BA 1737, C. Farnborough, Berks, R. & V. Lyminge, 1757–76.

[8] (1746–1811), of Farnborough, Berkshire, m. Trinity O 1763, BA 1767, MA?, R. & V. Lyminge, 1776–1811.

Page 104

D. Elham

Lyminge al. Lymege V. &c as in p.103. Exempt from AD^n. K^s books 10-18-9. Now { }. Nothing in the Books concerning the Separation of it from the Rectory. It is first mentioned Reg. Winchelsey fol. 50a. when that ABP collated to it in 1310. R & V. have commonly been different Persons. See Instances in a separate Paper. The Chapels are usually mentioned in the Institutions to each. Of the Extent & Service of the Parish, see under the Rectory, p. 103. V. Ho. 2 Rooms on a Floor unfit for a Family. Church & Chancel in pretty good Order. 2 Ho. one called the Vicarage: both pretty good. Out Ho. intolerable Order. 5 Bells. Paddlesworth Chapel extremely bad & dirty. No Ho. 1 Bell. Standford clean & in pretty good Order: chancel wants whitewashing. No Ho. Glebe 8 Acres: 2 Bells.

Alex. Pollock[1] pres. by Wm Taylor[2] to V. inst 27 Oct. 1693. Non constat from the Registers, that ABP ever <u>presented</u> to it. Entry B IV. 495 Wm Forster[3] pres. by John Taylor voided by death of Pollock inst. 18 July 1712. Note in marg. that Paddlesworth & Stanford were in former pres. not in this. VI. 82. Rich. Halford[4] pres by same with the 2 Chapels on death of Forster 26 Dec 1713 p. 133. Quintus Naylor[5] pr. by Arabella Taylor 6 June 26 on death of Halford VII. 123 with the Chapels: but p. 124 saith Registers before Restor. shew they belong to R. not V. John Lyndon[6] R. & V. separately 3 Feb. 1734/5 on death of Naylor. V. without Chapels VIII. 27.

Ralph Price[7] V. 27 Jan. 1757 Inst. to R. the same Day ***. Cur. of Farnborough, Berks. Resides there bec. he hath bad Health, & can get the Parish served from Oxford, w^n needful. 1759 Resides here. 1760 Differences abt small Tithes. 1761 Agreed. Differd again. Trial. See AD^n July 27. 1761

Ralph Price[8] Clerk A.M. Vicar December 17:1776 resides.

David Price[9] Pr. Cur. 40^f. Resides in the Parish in a hired Ho. Teaches School. See p. 103. 1760 Gone to be Chaplain at Sheerness.

1758 Conf 93. 1762. 22. 1766. 8.

[1] V. Lyminge, 1693-1712.   [2] For the patronage see Hasted VIII, p. 84.
[3] (1686-17?), of Doxford, Northumberland, m. Sidney Sussex 1704, BA 1710, V. Lyminge, 1712-13.
[4] See p. 103, n. 4.   [5] Ibid., n. 6.
[6] Ibid., n. 3.   [7] Ibid., n. 7.
[8] Ibid., n. 8.   [9] Also chaplain of Sheerness, 1760.

Page 105

Postling V. St Mary. Canon S. Radegund Propr Ecton. Now ABP Impr. & P. K^s books 6-8-1½. Now 110^f ⟨120^f AD^n⟩. The Rectory being leased out by the ABP at 6^f a Year, ABP Sancroft in 1688 granted a Lease of it to the Vicar for 10^f a year clear of all Taxes & paymts for 21 years, if he sh^d so long continue Vicar; & therein declared his Intention to be, that in pursuance of the Act 17 Car. 2. the Profits of the Rectory, subject to the 10^f a year sh^d be a perpetual Augmentation of the Vicarage, & that the ABP sh^d make a new Lease to each new Vicar, without any Fine & deliver it to him with his Letters of Collation; which he trusts his Successors will the rather do, as the additional 4^f a year will be of more value to them, than the Fines usually taken. And the Lease continues to be granted in this manner. In 1643 the ABP pd the vicar a pension of 1–6–8 yearly.

21 Ho. Whole service, till of late, the Rector being 67 & 1/4 of a mile from Church, in a wet Situation, officiates only once in the severest part of the Winter. Prayers. Jan 30, Good Fri. Easter Tuesday, & Asc. Day. Sermons on all occasional Fasts. Cat. from the first or 2d Sunday after Easter, as long as needful. 4 Sacr. 17 or 18 Com. each time. A small Alms House. V. sends 4 poor Ch[n] to School & excites the Parishioners to send theirs. Some small Benefactions. Church & Chancel small & clean. Ho. very neat. Out Ho. in good Order. Glebe 16 Acres. 3 Bells.

Silas Drayton[1] MA 21 Jan. 1750. Resides constantly. Good. Hath Leave of Non-Residence Apr. 30. 1763 on acct of his Health. Dead.
John Agge Stock[2] MA V. 5 March 1767 See below resides.
Rich[d.] Blackett Dechair[3] L.L.B. 1792.

Kemeys John[4] Cur. Apr. 1764. Gone March 1765. Unfit.
John Stock Cur see p.55. 40[f].

Thomas Downe[5] Cur. Sal. £25 lic. 1794.

1758 Conf. 41. 1762: 12. 1766. 23.

[1] (169?–1767), of Kent, m. CCCC 1710, BA 1714, MA 1720, R. Crundale, 1729–51, V. Postling, 1751–67.
[2] See p. 7, n. 10.
[3] [de Chair] (1764–1814), of Westminster, m. St Mary's Hall O 1783, BCL 1790, R. East Horsley, Surrey, 1788–92, V. Postling, 1792–1814, V. Sibbertswold, 1792–1814.
[4] See p. 76, n. 6.
[5] (17?–1838), of Kent, m. CCCC 1787, scholar 1789, BA 1791, C. Stowting and Postling, 1794, V. Lydden, 1814, C. Barfreston, 1815–38.

Page 106
D. Elham
Saltwood R. S[t] Peter & S[t] Paul, with the Chapel of Hythe S[t] Leonard. Exempt from AD[n]. ABP. K[s] books 34[f] Now 200[f].
Saltwood hath 40 straggling Ho. Service once. Cat exp. in Summer every other Sunday. 4 Sacr. 30 or 40 Com. 5 Guineas a year from Lands by Revd. Mr Geo. Barnesly[1] for religious Education of poor Ch[n]: pd by R. to a Schoolmistress. Land, called Church-Land, of 10[f] a year. R. knows not yet by whom: of w[ch], 5[s] is given to the poors Rate, the rest to the Church Rate. 10[s] a year to the poors Rate by one White[2] out of Oxenden Farm. Hythe hath 120 Ho. M[rs] Deedes[3]. 7 Families of Anab. A meeting Ho. No settled Teacher. Lessening. One Quaker. Service once. Prayers on Holydays, & W. Fr. in Lent. Then Cat. exp. 5 Sacr. 90 or 100 Com. S[t] Bartholomews Hosp. founded by Hamo[4] BP of Rochester, Revenues betw. 60 & 70[f] a year for 5 poor men & 5 poor women, natives of Hythe. 3 Governors, chosen by the Corporation. S[t] Johns Hosp. ancient, Founder unknown, Revenue betw. 30 & 40[f] a Year, managed by Trustees, who when reduced to two, add others. Both well conducted. A voluntary Charity School for 33 Boys or Girls, who are only taught Reading, Writing & Accounts: under the Care of M[r] Smith[5], who hath also opened a Grammar School, See

Alkham, p. 76. To this Charity School D[r] Tenison[6], BP of Ossory, gave Land worth 27[s] a Year. Several small Gifts to the Poor, which see.

Both Churches & Chancels handsome & in good Order. Saltwood very good Ho. Hythe none. Glebe 70 Acres. Saltwood 5 Bells: Hythe 6. Lic. to remove the Ruines of an Old Granary & lay out wt shd rebuild it on the parsonage Ho. Entry B. VI. 48.

[1] (1645–?), of Hallam, Yorks, m. Magdalene C 1661, BA 1665, MA 1668, R. Markshall, Essex, 1670–4, R. Sedlescombe, Sussex, 1674, R. Northiam, 1677.
[2] Hasted noted that the farm now belonged to William Evelyn: Hasted VIII, p. 227.
[3] Margaret Deedes. The Deedes family had resided at Hythe for 200 years: ibid., p. 238.
[4] Haymo de Hythe, bishop of Rochester, 1319–52. The hospital was founded in 1336: Hasted VIII, p. 247.
[5] Richard Smith, see p. 76, n. 1.   [6] Edward Tenison (1673–1735), bishop of Ossory, 1731–5.

Page 107
Saltwood & Hythe continued
Tho. Randolph[1] DD. R. 8 March 1745. See Petham p. 19.
Tho. Randolph[2] M.A. R. Jan[y] 3[d]. 1770.

Rich. Smith[3] Cur. See Alkham p. 76. 45[£] Resides here. His School brings him in, by his own acct, 40[£] a year. And he hath also the Care of the Charity School. And his Salary from thence pays an assistant at his own School.
William Tournay[4]. Cur. Sal. £50.

1758 Conf. ⟨here {796} 599. Of⟩ Saltwood 33. Hythe 97. 1762 Conf here 309. Of Saltwood 23, Hythe 57. 1766 Conf. at Hythe 383. Of Saltwood 15, Hythe 54.

[1] See p. 19, n. 2.   [2] Ibid., n. 3.
[3] See p. 76, n. 1.   [4] See p. 19, n. 7.

Page 108
D. Elham
Stouting R. S[t] Mary. M[r] John Collier[1] P. ⟨Mr Cranston the R. saith he is Patron⟩. K[s] books 7–17–11. Now called 100[£]. R. saith not 90[£]. 30 Ho. Service once a Sunday. [1759 twice]. Cat. every other Sund. afternoon from LD to Mich. 4 Sacr. 20 Com. 6 Acres of Land left for repairing the Church. So applied. It is small & indifferent. Chancel dirty. Ho. indifferent. {Chancel} Out Ho. in good Order. 3 Bells. Glebe 8 Acres.
James Cranston[2] MA. R. 28 Feb. 1725. Resides at Bexhill near Hastings, Sussex: where he was Cur. till confined to his Ho. by Lameness. Hath a temporal Estate.
George Holgate[3] LLB. R. May 25. 1771.

John Loftie[4] of Ch. Ch. Deacon Cur. 26[£] Also Cur. of Sellinge p. { }. 2½ miles off ⟨or more. Lives at Ashford 6 miles from each⟩. Ord. Pr. Chr. 1758 to serve this twice. Salary 40[£] ⟨& surpl. Fees⟩. [Going away Mids. 1759. Cha. Fortescue[5] BA Deacon, to come at Mids. & apply for Pr. Orders at Chr. Did apply: extremely ignorant of Latin: not ordained. Gone, May 1760. Tho. Guise[6] BA ord. Deacon by me May 25. 1755. Pr. by BP Thomas[7] of Sarum 23 Oct

1757. Lives at Lyminge 3 miles off, & keeps a Horse: hath a Wife ⟨Dead⟩ & no Income but this Curacy. 1765 serves it but once & lives at Petham 8 miles off: must not go on so.

Ralph Sergeant[8] C. P. Nov. 1765 See p. 277. Did not come. Come Feb. 1766. Going.

stet {W^m Warren[9] from New Church p. 133. coming Jan 1766} Is here 1768. Mr Stock[10] Cur. Sal. 25 Guineas.

Thomas Downe[11] A.B. Cur. Sal. £25. lic. 1794.

1758 Conf. 18. 1762. 9. 1766. 13

[1] Hasted noted that Collier owned the patronage in George I's reign. He presented Cranston, and then Cranston owned it: Hasted VIII, p. 51.

[2] (169?–1771), of Sussex, m. Jesus C 1709, BA 1712, MA 1715, R. Stowting, 1726–71.

[3] (1740–1803), of Middlesex, m. St John's C 1759, LLB 1765, C. Carleton St Peter, Norfolk, 1765, R. Stowting, 1771–1803, PC. Theydon Bois, Essex, 1791.

[4] See p. 25, n. 5.   [5] (1735–1806), m. Exeter 1754, BA 1758.

[6] (1731–?), of High Wycombe, Bucks, m. Hertford 1750, BA (Merton) 1754.

[7] John Thomas (1696–1781), bishop of Peterborough, 1747–57, bishop of Salisbury, 1757–61, bishop of Winchester, 1761–81.

[8] Ralph Sergeant, see also p. 277.   [9] C. Swalecliffe, 1764.

[10] See p. 7, n. 10.   [11] See p. 105, n. 5.

Page 109

Wotton. St Martin. R. John Brydges[1] Esqr. P. Kings books 8–10–2½. Now 80$^£$ ⟨70$^£$ AD^n⟩. 21. Ho. John & Edw. Brydges[2] Esq^{rs}, live at Wotton Court. Latter married Dr Egertons[3] Da. Good. [800$^£$ a Year betw. them ***]. Parsonage Ho. rebuilt by the present R. Service once. Cat. exp. on Sundays. 4 Sacr. 20 Com. each time. Church & Chancel neat & in good Order. Ho. almost new by Mr Fremoult. Out Ho. in good Repair. Glebe 13½ Acres 1 Bell. 1762 Whole Service from Mich.

Sam. Fremoult[4] R. 28 Dec. 1739. Resides. Cur. of Barham p. 4 where see. Not now, 1760. Doth he serve any other place? Married: rich: going to live 15 miles off. Church served, first by Mr Barret[5] of Kingston, then by himself from that Distance. Now to have a ⟨resident⟩ Curate here, to assist Mr Lunn[6] also at Denton wch is near, or Nonington p. 18 wch is 5 or 6 miles off. March 1762 coming to live at his own House at Barham, wch is near. Will serve it twice 1766. 1767. Resides here, & serves it twice. Edward Tymewell Bridges[7] A.M. Rector 1780 resides.

1758 Conf. 19. 1762. 7. 1766. 15.

[1] Barrister, owned patronage from 1704 until his death in 1722.

[2] His two sons, who both died in 1780: Hasted IX, p. 368.

[3] Jemima, daughter of William Egerton, who was a prebendary of Canterbury, 1724–38.

[4] See p. 4, n. 14.   [5] Ibid., n. 11.   [6] See p. ii, n. 38.

[7] (17?–1808), of Wootton, Kent, m. Queens' C 1767, scholar 1770, BA 1771, MA 1774, fellow, 1772, R. Otterden, 1780–1808, R. Wootton, 1780–1808.

[Deanery of Lympne]

Page 110

D. Lympne

Aldington ⟨called Allington Entry B. V. 228⟩. R. St Martin with Smeeth St Mary, a Parish united to it. ⟨Exempt from AD^n⟩. ABP P. K^s books 38-6-8. Now 250$^£$ ⟨AD^n 200$^£$⟩. Aldington hath 65 Ho. Smeeth 50. ⟨2 or 3 miles asunder⟩. In the latter Edw. Scott[1] of Scotts Hall Esqr [ab^t 300$^£$ a Year now: will have 300$^£$ more at his Mothers Death. Large Family]. One Family of Anab. lately come. Service once at each Church on Sundays, & Thanksgiving or Fast Days, with a Sermon. Prayers Ash. W. good Fr. & Chr. Day. Cat. Sundays in Lent. Cur. doth not. exp. but R. supplies that Default another Way. 4 Sacr. in each. abt. 70 Com. each time. R. pays for teaching 2 or 3 Ch^n of each Parish to read. 10$^£$ a Year to the poor by BP White[2] of Peterborough, lost above 40 Years, R. knows not how. A Portion of Rents given for breeding of a Boy of Smeeth to Divinity, Law or Physick: not so applied within Memory. ⟨See Lyminge p. 103⟩. Other small Gifts, which see. Erasmus[3] was R. here. Kent[4] p. 1182. In this Parish, Mr Lewis, in a fol. Ms of the Churches of the Diocese, which AD^n Head hath, places the Chapel at Street al. Courthop Street, or the Chapel of our Lady of Court at Street, which see in his map. Church & Chancel large & in pretty good Order. Ho. & out Ho. good & in good Repair. Glebe 15 Acres. 5 Bells. Smeeth Chapel & Chancel neat & in good Order. No Ho. Glebe 8 Acres. 3 Bells.

John Chapman[5] MA [now DD.] R. 23 Aug. 1739. R. of Mersham p. 131. contiguous to this. Resides there, where see more.

David Ball[6] L.L.B. Rector 1785. does his own duty.

John Dawson[7] Pr. Cur. 45$^£$ with all common Surplice Fees. Resides. [Hath been there abt 12 Years, rec. to me by Mr Scott, as very good. Gone to be V. of Sellinge by Hythe p. 140 but serves this once: & Mr Tournay[8] of Bonnington p. 114 once. Mr Tournay lives at Mersham just by, & doth the Sunday Duty of Aldington. Salary 23$^£$ & the Fees & the occasional Duty of Smeeth, Salary 1 G. Mr Hodgson[9], who takes Ashford School from Mids 1764 is to do the Sunday Duty there. Cur. also at Hinxhill p. 122. 1767 Mr Whitefield[10] to serve Smeeth: {but see Newchurch 133}. Mich 1767 Mr Apsley[11] to serve this & Brook ⟨p.6⟩ from Ashford. Jan. 1768 going to Ruckinge. LD Mr Gorsse[12] to serve it from Ashford, with Eastwell.

1758 Conf. Aldington 25, Smeeth 11. 1762. Ald 14. Smeeth 11. 1766 Aldington 17 Smeeth 20.

[1] Edward Scott died in 1765. He had twelve children: Hasted VIII, p. 7.

[2] Thomas White (1628-98), bishop of Peterborough, 1685-90. He was deprived for non-juring.

[3] Desiderius Erasmus (c.1469-1536). Humanist. V. Aldington, 1511.

[4] [Anon], *A Compleat History of Kent* (1730), p. 1182.

[5] (1704-84), of Hampshire, m. Kings 1724, BA 1728, MA 1731, DD (Oxford) 1741, fellow 1727, R. Aldington, 1739-84, archdeacon of Sudbury, 1741, R. Saltwood, 1741-44, R. Mersham, 1744-84, treasurer of Chichester, 1750, presented himself to the precentorship of Lincoln, but was ejected 1760, archbishop's chaplain, 1741.

[6] (1740-1823), of Royston, Yorkshire, m. St John's C 1759, BA 1763, LLB 1773, C. Thurcaston, Leics, C. Anstey, V. Chislet, 1777-85, V, St Nicholas in Thanet, 1777-85, R. Aldington, 1785-1823, V. St Mary, Sandwich, 1809-23.

[7] (1720–72), of Rochdale, Lancashire, m. St John's C 1738, BA 1742, C. Aldington, V. Sellinge, 1761–72.

[8] Robert Tournay (1731–85), of Ashford, Kent, m. Hertford 1749, BA 1753, MA (Christs) 1765, R. Bonnington, 1757–85, R. Newchurch, 1765–85.

[9] See p. 50, n. 10.   [10] See p. 12, n. 8.

[11] See p. 6, n. 6.   [12] See p. 57, n. 11.

Page 111

Appledore V. St Peter & St Paul. with Chap. of Ebeney ⟨3 miles off⟩, St Mary, in the Isle of Oxney. belonged to the Priory of St Martin, Dover. Now ABP Impr. & P. Kings Books 21$^£$. Now 120$^£$ or more ⟨sd to be 200 AD^n. Called 120$^£$ 1707 Entry B. V. 247. 140$^£$ in 1663⟩. Bad air. Appledore 47 Ho: Ebony 15. Service once a Sunday at each. Prayers at Appledore on Holydays, & on W. Fr. in Lent, when Ch^n are cat. 4 Sacr. 20 Com. At Ebony no Prayers on Holydays: nor would the People come, the Chapel being a mile from any House. Only one Child, abt 7 years old, capable of being catechized. [Why?]. 4 Sacr. there. 12 Com. Church & Chancel large, want whitewashing. Ho. in good Repair. Stable in Repair. Glebe 11½ Acres. 6 Bells. Chapel small, wants whitewashing. No chancel, or Ho. Glebe 6 Acres. 1 Bell. 1760 Trees ⟨in⟩ ch. yd sold for above 40$^£$, wch & a considerable sum besides hath been laid out on the Houses. Was not this at Cranbrook? Yes. Disp. to V. for nonr. bec. unhealthy Entry B. II. 113. Repeated III. 185.

Jos. Disney[1] MA. 4 Apr. 1726. V. of Cranbrook p.59. Resides there. Comes hither sometimes: not so often, because not so able, as formerly.
Richard Podmore[2] LLB. Vicar, Novr. 24: 1777.

Peter Collet[3] BA of St Johns Oxford, Cur. Priest. 40$^£$ & Surplice Fees. Resides. Going, March 1760 to be Schoolmaster & Cur. at Rye.
Sam. Vickers[4] BA ⟨F⟩ of St Johns Coll Ox. Resides in V. Ho. ord. Deacon by BP Hume[5] Tr. S. 1760. Pr. by me Sept. 20. 1761. 1. Going May 1762. Mr Disneys son[6] officiates. Mr Moor[7] of Stone doth the weekly Duty, Oct 1762. Charles Prince[8] Cur. ⟨a drunken bad man⟩ May 1763. Gone May 1764. Mr Morphet[9] for a while.
Wm Colby[10]. Gone. Prince (see above) serves it with Brenzett & Snargate 1766. Directed another to be got.
Evans[11] June 1767. Gone July. Mr Prince again. Said to be reformed. No complaints 1768.
Tho: Edward Podmore[12] A.B. Curate. Licensed Mar. 2: 1779, Salary £50 p ann.
Thomas Jefferson[13] Cur. Sal. £50.

1758 Conf Appledore 33. Ebony 5. 1762. Appledore 22 Ebony 7. 1766 Appledore 19 Ebony 7.

John Rice[14] Cur. Sal £50 & Surplice fees lic. by Archdeacon.

[1] See p. 59, n. 1. [2] See p. 58, n. 20. [3] (1745–?), of London, m. St John's O 1751, BA 1756.

[4] (1736–?), of London, m. St John's O 1754, BA 1758, MA 1763, fellow, 1754–68, BD 1768, proctor 1767.

[5] John Hume, bishop of Bristol, 1758, bishop of Oxford, 1758–65, bishop of Salisbury, 1765–82.

[6] William (1731–1807), of Cranbrook, Kent, m. Trinity C 1748, BA 1753, MA 1756, DD 1789, fellow, professor of Hebrew 1757–71, R. Pluckley, 1777–1807.

[7] See p. 74, n. 6.   [8] (1739–?), of Wallingford, Berks, m. Trinity O 1757, BA 1760.
[9] See p. 68, n. 3.   [10] William Coleby.   [11] David Evans.
[12] (1764–?), of Condover, Salop, m. Christ Church 1772, BA 1777, C. Appldore, 1779.
[13] C. Appledore, 1784.
[14] (1755–1805), probably of Pembroke, m. Merton 1774, C. Appledore, 1790, R. Warden, 1783–1805. Possibly.

Page 112
D. Lymne

Bilsington C. S[t] Peter & S[t] Paul. Formerly a Priory. Sir Tho. Rider[1] Bart. P. Ecton. Wake. ABP. Herring. No Admissions to it mentioned of late Years. Certified 30[£]. So called now. Sir Tho. Riders Tenant inhabits the old Priory. 5 or 6 Farm Ho. & a few Cottages. The Curate calls it a Donative: & saith his Stipend of 30[£] a year is paid out of the Priory Estate: that the Place is unhealthy, and the Water bad: that he never heard of any ministers Residence, nor is there any Provision made for it. Service once a Sunday. 4 Sacr. No mention of other Days, nor of the Number of Communicants. Cat. was exp. in Lent, when he served it personally: but the officiating Curate can best answer sev[l] Questions now. [Therefore he shd have sent to him for Information. Church neat & in good Order. Chancel wants whitewashing No Ho. 3 Bells.

Richard Husband[2] Cur. chosen min Can. of Rochester ⟨above⟩ 20 Years ago, & hath resided there ever since. Vicar of Wateringbury.
Joseph Hardy[3] Cur. Licens'd June13[th] 1769.
James Bond[4] Curate Lic. 1786.

Jude Holdsworth[5] R. of Hinxhill p. 122. where see, serves this Place from thence. Above 5 miles off. 18[£] [June 10. 1759 ord. Nicolas Brown[6], bapt. Apr. 4. 1736, Deacon to serve this Parish, Salary 20[£] & Sellinge p. 140. 3 or 4 miles off from Bilsington, wch is yet more from Ashford, where he resides. Proposes to leave Bilsington at Chr. 1759 ⟨for Hothfield p. 66⟩. Mr Husband desires it may be served with Ruckinge p. 139. March 1760 Mr Breton[7] serves it from Boughton Aluph p. 5 at least 10 miles off.
Friend[8] Hen. B.A 20[£] Cur. also of {Bilsington} Burmarsh p. 118 ord. Deacon June 1. 1760. 2. Pr. Sept 21. 1760. Leaving Burmarsh for Newchurch ⟨p. 133⟩ July 1761.
W[m] Allen[9] See Ruckinge p. 139.

1758 Conf. 10. 1762. 9. 1766. 13.

[1] Of Boughton Monchelsea. One of the grand jury of the County of Kent, he was knighted in 1744.
[2] (1697–1769), of Exton, Shropshire, m. St Mary's Hall O 1714, BA (Christ Church) 1718, MA (Christs) 1724, R. Ruddington, Salop, 1722, PC. Strood, Kent, 1738–47, V. Newington, 1738–9, V. Stockbury, 1747–50, V. Wateringbury, 1750–69, PC. Bilsington, –69.
[3] (1723–86), of Tunstall, Lancashire, m. Christs 1746, LLB 1755, head-master Sutton Valence School, 1746–86, V. Headcorn, 1762, PC. Bilsington, 1769–86, V. Monkton, 1772–86, poor vicar.
[4] See p. 50, n. 15.   [5] See p. 96, n. 6.
[6] (1737–1803), of Ewart Northumberland, m. Christs 1754, BA 1759, DD 1787, fellow, 1762–71, C. Bilsington, 1759, minor canon of Rochester, 1760–5, preacher Bunting, Walkhampton and Knapwell, Cambs. 1764, V. Sutton Valence, 1765–1803, R. Ingoldsby, Lincs. 1770–1810, (probably chaplain of Chatham Dockyard, 1770–1801).
[7] See p. 5, n. 2.

[8] (1737–1805), of Birchington, Kent, m. St John's C 1755, BA 1759, MA 1764, C. Bilsington, Burmarch, Aldington, R. Frittenden, 1761–1805.
[9] See p. 56, n. 12.

Page 113

Blackmanston R. K[s] books $4^£$ ⟨$40^£$ 1663⟩. ABPP. Now $20^£$ or $25^£$. No Church, nor House, nor Answer to Inquiries.

A Petition of Henry Hurt[1], R. of S[t] Mary in Romney Marsh to ABP Tenison, setting forth that ABP Sancroft permitted Sam. Warren[2], Vicar of Ashford, to enjoy the profits of Blackmanstone, abt $16^£$ a year, on condition of paying to Hurt 20^s a year, as had been done time out of mind, wch Warren did from 1682 to 1691: but there being at LD 1695, 3½ years due, he refuses to pay, there being no Inhabitants in Blackmanston: but Hurt desires the Pension may be continued, as there may be more Inhabitants hereafter. Gibson Papers vol. 13. N°. 90.

Rob[t] Greenall[3] BA R. 26 Apr. 1755. V of Waldershare p. 200. Cur. of Tilmanstone p. 199. where he lives.
Bladon Downing[4] M.A. R. Feb. 1. 1771.
John Bearblock[5] Clerk. Rector. Mar. 31. 1778.
Henry Dimock[6] A.M. Rector 1784.

[1] (1643–1700), of Coventry, Warwickshire, m. St John's O 1662, BA (Catherine Hall C) 1666, C. Burmarsh, 1666, R. Burmarsh, 1675, C. St Mary in Marsh 1668, R. St Mary in the Marsh, 1679–1700.
[2] V. Ashford, 1673–1721, R. Blackmanstone –1721.
[3] See p. 18, n. 7.   [4] Ibid., n. 8.   [5] See p. 94, n. 2.
[6] (1730–1810), of Gloucester, m. Pembroke O 1745, V. Chipping Norton, Oxon, R. Blackmanstone, 1784–1810, R. St Edmund the King, London, 1784–1810.

Page 114

D. Lymne

Bonnington R. S[t] Rumwald: to which ABP Whitgift in 1583 united Fawkenherst R. S[t] Leonard. ⟨See here p. 124⟩. See Strype I. 3. c. 4. p. 133. John Turner[1] Esqr P. But Ecton saith, that Sir John Shelley[2] K[t] is P. of Fawkenherst. In 1742 John Turner presented. In July 1753 Hannah Turner, Widow. In Oct 1753 W[m] Mapletoft Gent. In 1757 Hannah Turner Widow. All as Patrons in full Right. In K[s] books Bonnington is 10-12-8½. Fawkenherst 4-18-4. Lewis's Map, near Bonnington hath Hurst, marked as demolished. 18 Ho. chiefly Cottages. One Quaker. Income now $60^£$ ⟨$70^£$⟩. AD[n]. Service once a Sunday. Other Churches near. Service on Chr. Day & good Fr. Cat. in Summer. 4 Sacr. 10 or 12 Com. No Offertory. Church small & clean. Ho & outHo. in good Repair. Glebe 26 Acres. 1 Bell.

Rob. Tournay[3] R. 11 Aug. 1757. Resides at Aldington, p. 110 within a mile, to avoid the marsh air. ⟨Cur at Sellinge near Ashford 1760. p. 140⟩. {Cur. of Burmarsh p. 118} Rector also of Newchurch p. 133.
Philip Papillon[4] A.M. Rector 1785.

M[r] Kirkbank[5] Cur.

John Waller[6] A.M. Cur. Sal. £25. lic. 1790.

1758 Conf. 12. 1762. 2. NB. 1766. 1. NB.

[1] Died in 1748: Hasted VIII, p. 333.
[2] (1692–1771), 4th Bt, of Michelgrove, Sussex. MP for Arundel, 1727–41, MP for Lewes, 1743–47.
[3] See p. 110, n. 8.
[4] Of Acrise, Kent, m. Oriel 1777, BA 1781, MA 1784, R. Eythorne, 1784, PC. Shinfield, 1785, R. Bonnington, 1785–1803, V. Tunbridge, 1803–09.
[5] Thomas Kirkbank, C. High Haldon, 1781, C. Newchurch, C. (& V) Appledore, 1814–1829.
[6] (1721–1822), of Kirkby Stephen, Westmoreland, m. Queen's O 1738, BA 1786, MA 1790, C. Newchurch and Bonnington, 1790, head-master Appleby Free Grammar School, R. Sulhamstead-Abbots, Berks, 1808–22.

Page 115

Brenzett al. Brentset V. S[t] Eans with. Belonged to the Coll. of Wye. Will. Brockman[1] Esqr P. K[s] books 7-18-11½. Cert. 71-6-0½. Now called 70[f].19 Ho. Service once a Sunday. No weekly Duty. Qu. Cat. in Lent. 4 Sacr. 20 Com. at each. Mr De l'Angle[2], R. of Snargate p. { } saith, see his Letter, that the Parishioners of Brenzett go to Snargate the other Part of the Sunday as conveniently as they could to their own Church. Church & chancel clean & in good Order. Ho: small, in good Order. Glebe 2 Acres. 3 Bells.

John Wentworth[3] V. 18 Feb. 1737. Cur. of Brookland p. 117 where he resides, 1½ mile off, with ABP Herrings Leave, because of a Robbery at the Vicarage Ho. in 1748. Serves Brenzett from thence. R. of Snargate p. 143. To get a Curate for this & that, 50[f] Sal. & serve Brookland. Mr Crook of Cranbrook, 15 miles off, proposed & rejected Sept. 1765. 1768 Apr. Serves this & Snargate each once.
Ric[d] Jones[4] V. July 26. 1770.
Anthony Egerton Hammond[5] A.M. 1792 resigned.
John Wood[6]. 1794.

Charles Prince[7] C. See above & p. 111. A drunken man, must not stay.
Daniel Joanes[8] Cur. of Brookland £52 10[s] 0[d].

1758 Conf. 16. 1762. 1766. 7.

[1] (1658–1741), MP for Hythe, 1690–95.
[2] Theophilus De L'Angle (1695–1763), of Newnham, Kent, m. Christ Church 1712, BA 1716, MA 1719, V. Tenterden, 1723–63, R. Snargate, 1756–63.
[3] (1798–70), of Salisbury, Wilts, m. Magdalen Hall 1725, BCL 1733, chorister Magdalen O 1729–31, V. Brenzett, 1738–70, R. Snargate, 1763–70.
[4] (1740–92), of Cranmore, Somerset, m. Oriel 1758, V. Brenzett, 1770–92, poor vicar, 1789.
[5] (1760–1801), of Nonington, Kent, m. Christ Church 1777, BA 1782, MA 1787, C. Patrixbourne, 1782, R. Knowlton, 1784–92, R. Ivychurch, 1789–1801, V. Brenzett, 1792–94, V. Lympne, 1794–1801, chaplain to Earl Thanet.
[6] (1755–1831), of Cumberland, m. Emmanuel 1794, BD (ten yearman) 1797, C. Linton, 1790–4, V. Lympne, 1793–4, V. Brenzett, 1794–1831, V. Herne, 1794–1831.
[7] See p. 111, n. 8.
[8] (1750–1822), of Llandewi Brefi, Cardigan, m. St Edmund Hall 1779, C. Brookland and Brenzett, 1782, C. Ivychurch, 1797, R. Ruckinge, 1799–1822.

Page 116
D. Lymne
Bromhill Cur. not certified. Ecc. Destructa. It stood in Sussex. Ecton. Bromhill
R. stands marked for a desolate church, at the bottom of Lewis's map, in
Romney Marsh.

Page 117
Brookland V. St Austin. Belonged to St Austins Mon. at Cant. DCh Cant. P. K^s
books 17-12-8½. Now near 90^f. 44 Ho. Service once [1759 twice] on Sundays.
No weekly Duty {Qu.} ⟨Chr. Day Good Fr. occ. Holydays⟩. Cat. in Lent. 4
Sacr. 30 Com. Within a mile of Brenzett. A voluntary Charity School, supported
by these two Parishes & Fairfield: 10^f Salary for teaching 10 Ch^n to read &
write. Church & Chancel large & handsome. Ho. small, in ⟨pretty⟩ good
Repair. 2^f to the Church. Glebe 1 Acre. 5 Bells & a Sts Bell.

Will. Broderip[1] MA V. 5 Oct. 1742. See Milton p. 42. Resides at Canterbury.
Dead Apr. 20. 1764.
Wm Taswell[2] BA V. Aug. 9. 1764. Cur of Kingston p. 16.
Joshua Dix[3] V. 13 May. 1772.
Richard Sharpe[4] A.B. 1788.

John Wentworth[5] Cur. 30^f. See Brenzett p. 115. Resides here.
Coleby[6] C. of Old Romney serves it in a Hurry at 1½[7]. Deacon. Forbid 1768.
Geo. Jenkins[8] C. Apr. 1768. 50^f See letter to Dr Potter[9] in {Brookland} Old
Romney.

1758 Conf. 18. 1762. 13. 1766. 27.

[1] See p. 42, n. 2.   [2] See p. 4, n. 11.   [3] See p. 33, n. 6.
[4] (1753–1809), of London, m. Clare 1773, BA 1776, C. Runham, Norfolk, 1777, C. New Romney,
    1786, V. Brookland, 1788–1809, poor vicar 1789.
[5] See p. 115, n. 3.   [6] William Coleby, see p. 111, n. 10.
[7] i.e. the service was at 1.30 p.m.   [8] George Jenkins.
[9] See p. ii, n. 3.

Page 118
D. Lymne
Burmarsh R. All Saints. The King P. K^s books 20-10-10. Now 100^f ⟨90 AD^n⟩.
1698 Acres of Land, almost all Pasture. 10 Ho. inhabited by Lookers, servants
to the Graziers. Service once a Sunday. They go to Dimchurch, a mile [or two]
off the other part of the Day, & see their Cattle by the way. The Income here is
5^f Glebe, 4^s an Acre for a little ploughed Ground, & a modus of 1^s from the 1698
Acres above. See the Letters in 1758 about the Service. AD^n Head thought it shd
not be increased, & it is not. Cat. Sunday afternoons in Summer. 4 Sacr. 15
Com. No Offertory. Church small & clean. Chancel in good Order. Ho. small,
in good Repair. A good Stable. Glebe 2 Acres. 3 Bells.

Rich. Smith[1] R. See Alkham p. 76 & Hythe p. 107. Lives at Hythe.
William Wing Fowle[2] M.A. R December 17 1772.

Rob[t] Tournay[3] Cur. R. of Bonnington p. 114. 24$^£$ and Surplice Fees. Lives at Aldington p. 110, 4 miles off. {at Sellinge}

Henry Friend[4] BA 24$^£$. Cur. also of Bilsington p. 112. where see. Going, July 1761.

Edward Sedgwick[5], 30$^£$. Cur. also of S[t] Marys p. 130.

{Geo. Lynch C. Vicar of Lymne}

John Cha[s]. Beckingham[6]. Cur. Sal £25.

1758 Conf. 3. 1762. 6. 1766. 9.

[1] See p. 76, n. 1.
[2] (1738–1809), of Dymchurch, Kent, m. St John's C 1752, scholar, BA 1756, MA 1772, C. Warehorne, 1758 (1766? also officiates at Snargate and New Romney), R. Snargate, 1770–1802, R. Burmarsh,1772–1809, C. Old Romney, 1790, R. Ivychurch, 1802–09.
[3] See p. 110, n. 8.   [4] See p. 5, n. 3.
[5] (1726–?), of Langley, Kent, m. St John's C 1745, BA 1749, C. West Peckham, 1750, C. Snave, 1758, C. St Mary's in the Marsh.
[6] (17?–1807), m. Trinity Hall 1782, LLB 1788, C. Lympne and Burmarsh 1784, C. Upper Hardres and Stelling, 1790, R. Upper Hardres, 1794–1807 (also Patron).

Page 119

Dimchurch R. S[t] Peter & S[t] Paul. The King P. K[s] books 7-2-8½. Wake 60$^£$. Now called 80$^£$. 70 AD[n]. 33 Ho. chiefly Graziers, their Lookers, & Labourers at the Wall along the Shore. 3 Families of Absenters, plead want of Cloaths & promise. Another, that of Joseph Macket, supposed to have 3 Ch[n] by Eliz. Goldfinch, his late Wifes Daughter. Saith, she hath not sworn them to him 〈See AD[ns] Letter. Sept. 22. 1759 & Oct. 27〉. Service once a Sunday. [See Burmarsh] p. 118. Cat. every Sunday & prayer Day in Lent: & every Sunday Afternoon in Summer. Will be exp. 4 Sacr. between 40 & 50 Com. Of Capt. Bedingfields[1] Benefaction, See Lyminge p. 103 & the Answers here. In ABP Wakes vol. of Charities, Hospitals &c at Ch. Ch. p or N°. 205 is an Acct of this Charity. The Estate is there said to be 70$^£$ a year. See the Extract from that Account. Church & chancel small & neat: only Chancel wall cracked & bulged. Ho. & OutHo. small & good. Glebe 9 Acres. 3 Bells.

Claudius {Drake} Clare[2] LLB. R. 8 June 1752.V. of Lymne p. 129. Went Chaplain to a Man of War about Chr. 1757. Not returned 1759. Gone to the E. Indies 1761. Returned. Officiates Oct. 1762. 1764 Livings sequestred for Debt. Died before Chr. 1764. May 1765 sd to be promised.

John Raisbeck[3] R. 31 July 1765. Lives in Hampshire.

William Webster[4] A.B. 1787. resides.

Ralph Drake[5] BD. F. of S[t] Johns Oxford Cur. of both the above parishes, which are 4 miles asunder. Resides at Hythe, as M[r] Clare did, at least 5 miles from Dimchurch & 3 or 4 from Lymne. Hath the Care of M[rs] Deeds's[6] Affairs, & cannot serve them otherwise. 40$^£$ & Surp. Fees.

Geo. Lynch[7] C. Vicar of Lymne.

1758 Conf. 16. 1762. 14. 1766. 9.

[1] See p. 103, n. 2.
[2] (17?–64), of Kent, m. CCCC 1736, LLB 1742, V. Lympne, 1748–64, R. Dymchurch, 1752–64.

[3] (1726–87), of Appleby, Westmoreland, m. Queen's O 1756, R.Dymchurch, 1765–87.

[4] (17?–1835), of Yorks, m. St John's C 1775, BA 1780, R. Dymchurch, 1787–1835, C. St Mary in the Marsh, 1810–35, R. Blackmanstone, 1810–35.

[5] See p. 91, n. 2.   [6] The wife of Prebendary Deedes. He died in 1752, see p. 36, n. 2.

[7] See p. 7, n. 6.

Page 120
D. Lymne

Eastbridge R. The Church demolished. ABP P. K[s] books 5–6–8. Now 30[f]. Some say 24. 3 Ho. 2–2–0 given, qu. to whom, for doing occasional Duty. M[r] Foster made from 18[f] to 20[f] clear. 30[f] or a little more 1663.

The Advowson was granted by the Crown to the ABP 31 Aug 1 Ed. 6. See Chart Misc. vol 13. N° 21.

Tithe all in Pasture at 6[d] an Acre: great part of the Land Tithe free. 1663.

{Joseph} ⟨Sam. in Entry Book, & pres. by King P. in full Right on death of last Incumbent⟩ Foster[1],R. 23 May 1757. Cur. to M[r] Tindal[2] at Colchester. Hath not read Prayers or Articles.

All these things from M[r] Blackwell, at the Grasshopper in Lombard Street, who procured him this Rectory. No Inquiries, I believe, sent to him. Died abt March 1765.

James Smith[3]. R. 13 Aug 1765 formerly a Popish Priest.

William Gunsley Ayerst[4] A.M. 1784.

William Tournay[5] A.M. 1790.

[1] Perhaps Samuel (1722–?), of Plymouth, m. Magdalen O 1738, BA 1742, R. Eastbridge, 1757–65.

[2] Perhaps John Tindal (c.1713–74), m. Sidney Sussex 1731, LLB, R. Chelmsford, Essex, 1739–74, R. Alphamstone, 1756.

[3] See p. 7, n. 9.

[4] (1758–90), m. Trinity C 1776, BA 1780, MA 1783, R. Eastbridge, 1784–90.

[5] See p. 19, n. 7.

Page 121
Eastinghanger. See Ostinghanger p. 136.

Fairfield C. S[t] Tho. Becket. DCh Cant. Impr. & P. whose Lessee is Lady Guilford[1]. Certified 50[f], which she pays. 6 Ho. None for the minister. 4 Persons, Presbyterians. Service once a Fortnight in Summer: once a month in Winter. Ch[n] chiefly abroad: not cat. till lately. 4 Sacr. 9 Com. [Service once every Sunday orderd at Vis. 1758. Curate desired time: tells L[d] Guilford[2] May 1759, that he is endeavouring to find the means of doing it. Exempt from AD[n]. Church & chancel small pretty clean. 3 Bells. Lic. to W[m] Stockwell [3] Entry B VI. 396 another VII. 197.

Tho. Cobb[4] BA Cur. 15 June 1734. R. of Great Hardres, p. 14, where he resides, 20 miles off from hence. [R. of Hope 1759, p. 123. wishes to have his pension from Lady Guilford, Tenant to Ch. of Cant. p[d] quarterly or half yearly. Richard Kilsha[5] A.M. 1795.

Rich. Moore[6] Pr. Deputy here. Cur. of Stone p. 145 where he resides, & of Small Hythe p. 74. Salary 10[f]. Stone is two miles from Fairfield. See AD[ns] Letter May 24. 1762.

M[r] Jackson[7] Cur. Sal. £25.

1758. I believe none Conf. 1762. 11. 1766. 6

[1] Katherine, Countess dowager of Rockingham, died 1766. She was the daughter and co-heir of Sir Robert Furnese Bt of Waldershare Park.
[2] Frederick, 2nd earl of Guilford. Died in 1790.
[3] Act Book says William Stockwood (c.1684–1784), of Peterborough, m. Clare 1709, BA 1712, MA 1716, DD (Lambeth?), fellow 1718, PC. Fairfield, 1723–34, R. East Langdon, 1725–38, R. Ockley, Surrey, 1725–84, R. Henley upon Thames, 1737–84, preb of Worcester, preb of Westminster, 1768–84.
[4] See p. 14, n. 2.
[5] (1749–1829?), of London, m. Oriel 1766, BA 1769, MA 1772, PC. Fairfield, 1795–1832, R. Barkston, Lincs, 1801–29.
[6] See p. 74, n. 5.
[7] William Jackson, C. Appledore, 1780, PC. Fairfield, and C. Stone 1790, perhaps V. Christchurch, Hants, 1795–.

Page 122
D. Lymne
Fawkenhurst see Hurst p. 124

Hinxhill R. S[t] Mary. Heir of Sir Geo. Choute[1] Bart P. Tenths 15–8. Certified 34[£] Now 80[£] ⟨70 AD[n]. Called 80[£] in Mr Holdsworth Disp⟩. Service once every Sunday. Cat. in Lent. 3 Sacr. [must be 4]. Generally not less than 30 Com. 40[s] a year given to the poor: distributed by the minister. Church, Chancel Ho. outHo. in pretty good Order. Glebe 12 Acres. 3 Bells.

Jude Holdesworth[2] R. 18 Aug. 1722. Resides in the Parsonage Ho. R. of Ruckinge p. 139. Cur. of Harty p. 162. Cur. of Bilsington p. 112. [Not now, 1759]. Died Oct 1759.
Edm. Filmer[3] MA R 13 Dec. 1759. R. of Crundall p. 10. Resides there.
John Honywood[4] clerk B. A. Nov[r]. 8. 1770.

Steph. Barrett[5], master of Ashford School, C. 20[£]. {Gone Mich 1760} ⟨Gone to a Living in Essex⟩.
John Norcross[6] See p. 148 ⟨generally officiates⟩. {or Mr Menzies from Ashford} ⟨Not 1764⟩.
W[m] Hodgson[7] Cur. master of Ashford School p. 50. Serves also Smeeth p. 110.
M[r] Barret[9] from Ashford once 1768.
M[r] Breton[9]. Cur. Sal. £25.

1758 Conf. 14. 1762. 15. 1766. 18

[1] [Chute], (1665–1721), MP for Winchilsea, 1696–98.   [2] See p. 96, n. 6.   [3] See p. 10, n. 3.
[4] (youngest son of Sir John Honywood, patron) (1766–1801), of Elmsted, Kent, m. Brasenose 1764, BA 1767, MA (All Souls) 1771, R. Hinxhill, 1770–1801.
[5] See p. 50, n. 9.
[6] (1693–1773), of Barton, Lancs, m. BNC 1709, BA 1713, MA 1716, R. Hothfield, 1721–73, V. Willesborough, 1729–73.
[7] See p. 50, n. 10.   [8] See p. 50, n. 9.   [9] See p. 67, n. 6

Page 123

Herst see Hurst p. 124.

Hope R. All Saints. Now no Church ⟨See below⟩. The King P. K^s books 10–1–0½. Now 80 or 90^f. 2 Ho. Service once a Month in ABP Wakes time. The Roof of the Church fell in, 20 Years ago. Old & New Romney & Ivychurch are near. No Answers to Inquiries.

Rob. Kelway[1] R. 14 July, 1709 ⟨R. of St Marys in the Marsh p. 130⟩. died Apr. 1759.
Tho. Cobb[2]. R 24 Apr. 1759 R. of Gr. Hardress p. 14 where he resides, Cur of Fairfield p. 121.
William Tournay[3] A. M. R. 1795.

Mr Sharpe[4] Cur.

1958 Conf. 4. 1762. none

[1] (1680–1759) of Huntingdon, m. Gonville and Caius 1697, scholar 1697–1703, BA 1701, MA 1705, V. Northbourne w Shoulden, 1705–23, R. Hope, 1709–59, R. St Mary in Marsh, 1723–59, chaplain to lord Sunderland.
[2] See p. 14, n. 2.   [3] See p. 19, n. 7.
[4] Richard Sharpe (1753–1809), of London, m. Clare 1772, BA 1776, C. Rainham, Norfolk, C. New Romney, 1786, V. Brookland, 1788–1809.

Page 124

D. Lymne
Hurst al. Herst al. Fawkenherst. R. St Leonard. Sir John Shelley[1] {Kt} ⟨of Mitchel Grove Bart⟩ P. No Church. K^s books 4–18–4. Now 40^f ⟨30 AD^n⟩. One House. Of the Union of this with Bonnington, see p. 114. And qu. how it came to be dissolved. No Answers to Inquiries.
Inst. to it 1683 Entry B. IV. 318. Pres. to it by Qu. on Lapse 1704 V. 145.

John Myonnet[2] R. 16 Feb. 1756.
George Carter[3] A.M. Rector 1779.

1758 None conf. 1762. None.

[1] See p. 114, n. 2.   [2] R. Fawkenhurst, 1756–79.
[3] (1755–1818), of Wye, Kent, m. Oriel 1772, BA 1775, MA 1778, R. Fawkenhurst, 1779–1818, R. Orlestone, 1780–1.

Page 125

Ivechurch al Iviechurch R St George. Exempt from AD^n. ABP. K^s Books 44–16–8. Now 300^f ⟨AD^n 210^f: Mr Neild 225^f See below⟩. 6 miles long. 18 Ho. 54 Inhabitants above 16 years old. Service once every Sunday. None on Holydays [qu. Good Fr. Ch. Day.]. Cat. exp. in Lent. Seldom above 3. 4 Sacr. from 8 to 16 Com. No Offertory. Chiefly Graziers, & their Lookers: often kept in the Field from Morning to 12 or even 3 O'clock. Hence the Winter Congregation is from 3 or 4 to 8 or 10 grown Persons: & in Summer from 15 to 30 such. Never more unless from other Parishes. Scarce any, when only

Prayers. They go for a Sermon to Brenzett, a mile off. From one End of the Parish they go to to Brookland Church, as nearer than their own, except on Sacram^t Days. [From Mich 1758 Service twice.]. Church & Chancel large & dirty. Ho. & OutHo. in pretty good Order. Glebe 8½ Acres. 5 Bells. Lic. for taking away an useless Granary granted to Dr Sydal[1] who was abt to improve the Ho. Entry B.VI. 125.

Henry Heaton[2] MA. R. 12 Nov. 1754. R. of Boughton Blean p. 152. Resides there 1759.
Bladen Downing[3] LLB. Rector, Nov^r.24: 1777.
Anthony Egerton Hammond[4] A.M. 1789.

Robt Neild[5] Pr. Cur. of this only, from mids to Chr. 1747. Salary here 40$^£$: then Cur. of Snave also, Salary 24$^£$ there & 35$^£$ here. Qu. what salary, now Service is twice again. 45$^£$, & abt 4$^£$ for gathering the Tithe. 1762. Desired me to read some Sermons, wch he w^d publish: excused myself. 1763 asked for Snargate. M^r. Jones[6], Cur. Sal. £45.

1758 Conf. 15. 1762. 6. 1766. 14

---

[1] Elias Sydall (16?-1733), of Norwich, m. CCCC 1688, BA 1692, MA 1695, DD 1705, fellow, 1696-1703, taxor 1698, PC. St Benet's, Cambridge, 1699-1702, R. Biddenden, 1702-4, R. Ivychurch, 1705-31, R. Great Mongeham, 1707-30, preb of Canterbury, 1707-28, dean of Canterbury, 1728-33, bishop of St David's, 1731, bishop of Gloucester, 1731-3.
[2] See p. 46, n. 2.   [3] See p. 18, n. 8.   [4] See p. 115, n. 6.
[5] See p. 31, n. 2.
[6] Daniel Jo(a)nes. See p. 115, n. 9.

Page 126
D. Lymne
Kenardington al. Kenerton R. St Mary. Moyle Breton[1] Esqr P. K^s books 12-1-0½. Now 120$^£$ ⟨90 AD^n True⟩. 22 Ho. 3 Anab. Service once on Sundays, & on no other Day [qu. Chr. good Fr.]. Cat. in Lent. 3 Sacr. between 20 & 30 Com. Church, Chancel, Ho. outHo. in pretty good Repair Glebe 7 Acres. 1 Bell.

Rob. Breton[2] LLB. R. 27 Feb. 1753 *** V. of Boughton Aluph. p. 5. Resides there. [was] Cur. of Ruckinge p. 139. [Not now 1759]. Resigned abt Dec. 17. 1767.
Moyle Breton[3] BA R. Jan. 26. 1768 presented by { } Breton & desired in the same Instrument to be admitted they being joint Patrons. Serves it, I fear from Ashford. Good young man will get Service twice if he can. The above Moyle Breton, having vacated this Rectory by Cession, was reinstituted to it Decr. 12: 1777.
No. Cur. at Visitation 1758. Geo. Burnett[4], ord. Deacon 24 Sept 1758 & Pr. March 11. 1759 to reside here, & serve this & Snargate, p. 143, 20$^£$ or 21$^£$ each, provided Mr Breton served Boughton, being the larger parish, tho' of less Income, twice. Mr Burnett went away Aug 1759: & Mr Breton is to serve them, & Mr Holdsworth[5] to serve Boughton once, till a Cur. can be got for the two former. March 1760 Mr Jones[6] serves it ⟨once⟩, with Woodchurch twice. So 1764, 1765.

Hassell[7] W[m] BA of S[t] Johns Camb. ord. Deacon ⟨Feb. 15. 1761⟩. Cur. of this & Snargate p. 143. 24[£] for each. To be ord Pr. Tr. S. 1761. 2. Going to Warehorn at Mich.
M[r] Davis[8]. Cur. Sal £21.

1758 Conf. 17. 1762. 13. 1766. 5

[1] See p. 5, n. 1.   [2] Ibid., n. 2.   [3] See p. 67, n. 6.
[4] Nb, LPL, MS Secker 3, f. 206, Secker to Burnett, 6 July 1759.
[5] Jude Holdsworth. See p. 96, n. 6.   [6] Perhaps Richard Jones. See p. 115, n. 5.
[7] (1737–89), of Sturry, Kent, m. St John's C 1757, BA 1761, V. Hollingbourne, 1773–89, poor vicar, 1777.
[8] Benjamin Davi(e)s, (1827), C. Kenardington, 1790, V. Stalisfield, 1800–1827, C. Warehorne, 1811, R. & V. Newchurch, 1812–27.

Page 127
Kingsnoth R. S[t] Michael. Sir Nathanael Powell[1] Bar[t] P. K[s] books 11-9-9½ ⟨Now 120[£]. AD[n] 140⟩. 34 Ho. Whole Service on Sundays, Ashw. & good Fr. [{probably} on Chr. day also]. Cat. exp. every Year. 4 Sacr usually betw. 40 & 50 Com. 40[s] a Year given to the Church. So applied. Church in good Order. Great Chancel, the same: North chancel very bad. Ho. very good. Outho. in good Repair Glebe 18 Acres. 5 Bells.

Philip Hawkins[2] MA R. 21 Aug. 1749 ⟨pres. by Committee of the Estate of Dame Frances Powell[3], a Lunatick⟩. Good. Resides constantly in the Parsonage Ho. 1762 Going to reside at Ashford, 2 miles off, with the Consent of the Parishioners. Rector resides.

1758 Conf. 32. 1762. 20. 1766. 18.

[1] (c.1688–1708), 3rd Bt, of Wyerton Place in Boughton Monchelsea.
[2] (1725–98), of London, m. Pembroke O 1740, BA 1744, MA 1747, R. Kingsnorth, 1749–98.
[3] Frances, wife of Sir Christopher Powell (1690–1742), 4th Bt, MP for Kent, 1735–41.

Page 128
D. Lymne
Lydd V. All Saints ⟨K[s] books 55-12-1. Now 420[£]. Let for 450, AD[n]⟩. Belonged to the Abbey of Tinterne Com. Monm[1]. ABP now Propr. & P ⟨Adv. granted by Qu. Mary⟩ & leases the Rectory to the present V. Exempt from AD[n]. 6 miles long, 4 broad. 120 Ho. A Limb of the Cinque Ports, governed by a Bayliff & Jurats. Whole Service. 2 Sermons from May day to Mich. Only in the afternoon the rest of the year. Cat. exp. W. Fr. in Lent. 8 Sacr. [NB] betw. 20 & 30 Com. V. gives 10[£] a Year for teaching 12 Ch[n] Reading, Writing & Accounts: 6 more are taught out of the Offertory money. The rest given to poor Families. Harts Farm, 34[£] a Year, ⅓ given to the Corporation, ⅓ for beautifying or repairing the Church, at the choice of the Corporation. ⅓ for poor Housekeepers not receiving Parochial Relief. An annuity of 40[s] a year ½ for Cloth for the Poor, ¼ money for them, ¼ for a Sermon. Church & chancel large & handsome. Ho & OutHo. neat & in good Repair. 5 Bells.
Disp. from Residence, being unhealthy 1670 Entry B. III. 13. VI. 85 The Form.

John Potter[2] DD. V. 29 June 1742. Had verbal Leave of Non-residence from ABP Potter at his Institution. Designs to be more here. Preb. of Cant. R & V. of Wrotham p. 380. AD^n of Oxford, R of Enmeth Dioc. Ely [called in Ecton, Elme with Emneth R. a sine Cure].
Honble Brownlow North[3] LLD. V. Oct. Feb. 1770.
John Huddesford[4] Master of Arts V. May 18 1775.

Goodwin[5] Cur. Good. 50$^£$ & Surplice Fees, & use of V. Ho. & Gardens, clear of all Deductions.

1758 Conf. 97. 1762. 2 at Hythe 18 at Ashford. 1766. 67.

[1] i.e. Tintern Abbey in the County of Monmouth.
[2] See p. ii, n. 3.   [3] Ibid., n. 4.
[4] (1746-97), of Oxford, m. Trinity O 1761, BA 1764, MA 1767, V. Lydd, 1775-97.
[5] Possibly Richard Goodwin (1717-?), of Gilsborough, Northants, m. Wadham 1734, BA 1738.

Page 129

Lymme al. Lympne V. St Stephen. AD^n Propr & P. Tenths 18^s-1½^d. Certified 25$^£$. Now 80$^£$ ⟨augm. 1767 with 400$^£$ by S^r Ph. B & Qu^s Bounty⟩. 30 Ho. chiefly Graziers & their Lookers. 2 Families of Anab. Service as at Dimchurch p. 119. Com. at Easter & Whits. last abt 50. Sev^l small Benefactions to the poor, which see in the Answers to Inquiries, & 20^s yearly for a Sermon. Church, Chancel, in good Repair, want whitewashing. Ho. {indifferent: it &} ⟨small in bad Order⟩. Out Ho. in tolerable Repair. Glebe ½ Acre. 5 Bells.

Claudius Clare[1] LLB V. 6 Dec. 1748. V. of Dimchurch p. 119 where See. Died before Chr. 1764.
Geo. Lynch[2] MA. V. 15 Jan. 1765. intends to reside & serve {Bromley} Dimchurch.
Stephen Tucker[3] A.M. 1789.
John Wood[4] 1793 resigned.
Anth^y. Egerton Hammond[5] A.M. 1794.

Ralph Drake[6] BD Cur here & at Dimchurch p. 119. Gone {where see.}
John Charles Beckingham[7] Cur. Sal. £25.

1758. Conf. 47. 1762. None set down. 1766. 54

[1] See p. 119, n. 2.   [2] See p. 7, n. 7.
[3] (1765-1838), of Canterbury, m. Trinity C 1781, BA 1785, MA 1788, C. Tunstall and Kingsdown, 1787, V. Lympne, 1789-93, V. Lynsted, 1793-1800, V. Borden, 1797-1838, R. Markshall, Essex, 1800-38, poor vicar, 1792-97, chaplain to Lord Teynham.
[4] -1831), C. Linton, V. Lympne 1793-4, V. Brenzett, 1794-1831, V. Herne, 1794-1831.
[5] Ibid., n. 6.   [6] See p. 91, n. 2.   [7] See p. 118, n. 6.

Page 130

D. Lymne
St Marys in the Marsh R. ABP. P. K^s books 23-3-9. Now 90$^£$ ⟨AD^n 95. Above 80 not 90, clear, except Cur. Mr Marsh⟩. Chiefly labouring People. Service once on Sundays for the People will go to Sermons. On no other Day [qu. Cat. in

Lent. 4 Sacr. 12 or 13 Com. 4 Acres of Land in Newchurch Parish, given to this Church. So applied. No Offertory. Church clean in good Order: so Chancel. Ho. very mean, in tolerable Repair. Out Ho out of Repair. Glebe 4 Acres. 3 Bells. See Blackmanstone p. 113.

Rob. Kelway[1] MA R 30 March 1723. R. of Hope p. 123. died Apr 1759. William Marsh[2] BA inst. 7 Apr. 1759. R. of Bicknor p. (205). V. of Bapchild p. 204. But he resigned the last 7 Apr. 1759. Resides between the two latter.

Edw. Sedgwick[3] Priest, Cur. Also Cur of {Newchurch} Snave p. {133} 144. Schoolmaster at New Romney, where he lives, abt 2½ miles from S[t] Marys, which is abt half way to {Newchurch} Snave. Salary 25$^£$ {at each} here, 24$^£$ there. Nov. 1761 is to hold this with Burmarsh p. 118.
M[r] Raisbeck[4] Cur. Sal £50.

1758 Conf. 7. 1762. 1.+ 1. 1766. 2.

[1] See p. 123, n. 1.
[2] (1718–1814), of Dover, Kent, m. St John's C 1738, BA 1742, R. Bicknor, 1743–1814, V. Bapchild, 1751–59, R. St Mary in Marsh, 1759–1802, C. Tonge, 1759, 1767, 1790, R. Murston, 1802–14.
[3] See p. 112, n. 5.   [4] See p. 119, n. 3.

Page 131
Medley see Midley

Mersham al. Marsham R. of S[t] John Bapt. ⟨180$^£$ of old: 120$^£$ now 1663⟩. ABP P. K[s] books 26–16–10½. Now 200$^£$ ⟨Perhaps 250$^£$⟩. 90 Ho. 560 Inhabitants. S[r] Wyndham Knatchbull Wyndam[1], of Hatch, Bar[t]: on his Travels. 4000$^£$ a year. 10 Quakers, including Ch[n]. One pays his Tithes like his Neighbours. The other lets his great Tithes be taken in kind: his small Tithes are got by Application to the Justices. Some Absenters, decreasing. Whole Service, except sometimes in the Rectors Absence. Prayers on all Holy days & W. Fr. in Lent, & every Day in Passion Week. Cat. exp. every Sunday in Lent. 4 Sacr. 75 Com. Mrs Jane Knatchbull[2] in 1698 left an Estate for paying 10$^£$ a year for teaching poor Ch[n] reading writing & accounts, & the Residue to other poor Persons. This is done by the Family. 20^s by Rich. Brett[3] to the poor. Church, Chancel, large, pretty good. Ho. new ⟨Lic. 1728 Entry B. VII. 238⟩ by D[r] Archer[4], & handsome. Outho. large, in good Order. Glebe 40 Acres. 5 Bells.

John Chapman[5] DD R. 25 June 1744. Resides for the most part, & pays amply for serving the Cure in his Absence. R. of Aldington with Smeeth p. 110. Treasurer of Chichester, & AD[n] of Sudbury.
Thomas Drake[6] D.D. Rector 1784.
Houstonne Radcliffe[7] D.D. Rector –1786.
William Cole[8] D.D. Rector 1789.

M[r] Stoddart[9] Cur.

1758 Conf. 26. 1762. 22. 1766. 28

[1] See p. 50, n. 5.

[2] (c.1640–99), wife of Sir John Knatchbull (1636–96). 2nd Bt, MP for New Romney, 1660–, MP for Kent, 1685–95.

[3] In 1711: Hasted VII, p. 599.

[4] Henry Archer (1688–1744), of Greenwich, m. Clare 1704, BA 1708, MA 1711, DD 1724, fellow, 1710–24, V. Faversham, 1724–44, V. Herne, 1724–26, R. Mersham, 1726–44.

[5] See p. 110, n. 5.

[6] (1745–1820), of Yorks. m. St John's C 1764, scholar, BA 1768, MA 1771, DD 1784, fellow, 1769, R. Endellion, Cornwall, 1774–7, R. Mersham, 1784–6, R. Hadleigh, Suffolk, 1786–90, R. Little Hormead, Herts, dean of Bocking, 1787, V. Rochdale, 1790–1820.

[7] See p. 15, n. 8.

[8] (1753–1806), of Mersham, Kent, m. King's 1774, BA 1778, MA 1781, fellow, 1776–81, DD (Lambeth) 1795, assistant master Eton, 1778–9, R. Waddesdon, Bucks, 1781–9, R. Mersham, 1789–1806, V. Shoreham, 1796–1806, preb of Westminster, 1792–1806.

[9] Charles Stoddart (1740–1812) of Chollerton, Northumberland, m. Christs 1758, scholar, BA 1763, MA 1766, master Ashford school, 1778–1812, R. & V. Newchurch, 1785–1812.

Page 132

D. Lymne

Midley al. Medley R. No Church. Charles E{w}ve[1] of Rotherhith mercht P. K^s books 30$^£$. Now 120$^£$. 3 Ho. No Answer to Inquiries. See Old Romney p. 138. The patronage of this Rectory was given by the ABP to the Crown in Exchange 31 Aug. 1 Ed. 6. See Chart Misc. vol. 13. N°. 21.

Matthias Unwin[2] R. 8 Aug. 1754. R. also of Buckland p. 154. No Church there neither. The same patron.
William Lupton[3] Clerk A.M. Rector, May 14: 1776.
John Jenner[4] D.D. Rector 1782.

[1] Patron from 1753: Hasted VI, p. 399.

[2] (1711–75), of London, adm. Queens' C 1740, 'ten year man', V. Long Claxton, Leics, 1739–53, R. Bonnington, 1753–3, R. Buckland, 1754–75, R. Midley, 1754–75.

[3] (1733–82), of Leeds, m. St John's C 1750, BA 1754, MA 1757, R. Blagdon, Somerset, 1761–6, V. Long Claxton, Leics, 1766–76, V. Headingley, Leeds, 1769–82, R. Buckland, 1776–82, R. Midley, 1776–82.

[4] (1746–1828), of Essex, m. Jesus C 1764, BA 1767, MA 1770, DD 1782, fellow, V. All Saints, Cambridge, 1775–83, R. Buckland, 1782–1828, R. Midley, 1782–1828.

Page 133

Newchurch R & V. St Peter & St Paul. ABP P ⟨See below⟩. Exempt from AD^n. K^s Books R. 8-4-2 V 19-16-0½. Both now 130$^£$ ⟨110 ADn⟩. [qu. when separated & reunited.]. 2910 Acres, besides 9 of Glebe. 13 Ho. most of them Cottages. Service once on Sundays, & only then. [qu. Chr. Day, good Fr.]. Cat. w^n Ch^n are sent, which is not often. 4 Sacr. 12 Com. [Service to be twice when a Cur. can be got.]. Church in pretty good Repair. Chancel wants paving. Ho. mean, in tolerable Repair. No Out Ho. Glebe 8 Acres. 5 Bells.
Disp. from Residence for unhealthiness VI. 89. None but natives able to reside VII. 294.
R. 10$^£$ V. 100$^£$ 1663.

Arth. Kight[1] collated 13 July 1738 first to the V. by ABP Patron for this Turn, then by another Instrum^t to the K. by the ABP Patron pleno jure: the Rector, when there is one, being Patron of the V. & the ABP ⟨So Entry B VI. 78⟩, when there is no Rector. ⟨So 1664 R. resigns V & presents to it 1664⟩. Cur. of Old Romney p. 138. Resides at New Romney p. 137. Hath taken great pains without Success to get a Curate for Newchurch. Serves it once a Sunday himself. Nov. 1763. Unable. ⟨Died abt March 20. 1765⟩.

Rob[t] Tournay[2], coll. 17. Sept. 1765. R. of Bonnington p. 114. holds this by Disp. with R & V here, which I fear shd not have been allowed.
Charles Stoddart[3] A.M. 1785.

Henry Friend[4] Cur of Bilsington p. 112 to serve this twice, 40[f] & that once, living at Aldington, 2 miles from Bilsington. Goes away Dec. 20 1761. Will recommend an acquaintance. 1764 ill served by M[r] Sedgwick[5], who hath S[t] Marys & Burmarsh & is gouty.
Wm Warren[6] C. 1765 from Swacliffe, p. 271 to have 40[f] from R & 10[f] from me ord. pr. March 3. 1765. {Going June. 1766}
Fran. Whitfield[7], of Univ. Coll. 5 yrs standing. Ord. D. Mar. 31. 1766. 1. 24 before Chr. Pr Dec 21 1766 but see p. 110
Moyle Breton[8] of Univ. Coll. 6 yrs. ord D. June 14. 1767 24 before Chr. 42[f]. 2. Pr. Dec 20. 1767.
M[r] Kirkbank[9] Cur. Sal. £25.

1758 Conf. 18. 1762. 9. 1766. 14.

[1] (1704–1765), of Kidlington, Oxon, m. Oriel 1719, BA 1724, MA 1727, R. & V. Newchurch, 1738–65.
[2] See p. 110, n. 8.   [3] See p. 131, n. 9.
[4] See p. 5, n. 3.   [5] See p. 118, n. 5.
[6] See p. 108, n. 9.   [7] See p. 12, n. 8.
[8] See p. 67, n. 6.
[9] Thomas Kirkbank (17?–1814), C. High Halden, 1781, V. Appledore, 1814–29.

Page 134

D. Lymne
Orgarswick ⟨Orgarwick Entry B IV. 157⟩ R. No Church. DCh Cant P. K[s] books 3[f]. One Ho. No Answer to Inquiries. AD[n] 20[f] a year.

John A{ye}irson[1] MA R. 5 Jan. 1750. Min. Can of Cant & R of S[t] Alphage p. 29.
Martin Benson[2] A.M. 1788.
Henry John Todd[3] A.M. 1791.
John Francis[4] A.M. 1792.

M[r] Raisbeck[5] Cur.

[1] See p. 29, n. 2.
[2] (1761–1833), of Canterbury, Kent, m. Jesus C 1779, BA 1782, MA 1785, C. St Michael Royal, London, 1783, V. king Charles the Martyr, Tunbridge Wells, 1786–1829, R. Orgarswick, 1788–91, R. St Dunstan's in the East, London, 1789–91, R. Merstham, Surrey, 1791–1833.
[3] (1763–1845), of Salisbury, m. Magdalen O 1779, chorister 1771–9, clerk 1779–84, BA 1784, fellow Hertford, MA 1786, PC. St John and St Bridget, Beckermet, Cumberland, 1787–1803, R. Orgarswick, 1791–92, V. Milton next Sittingbourne, 1792–1801, R. All Hallows the Great, Lombard Street, London, 1801–10, V. Ivinghoe, Bucks, 1803, R. Woolwich, 1803–5, V. Edlesborough, Bucks, 1805, R. Cullesden, Surrey, 1807–20, V. Addington, Surrey, 1812–20, minor canon of Canterbury, six preacher, 1818–32, Lambeth Librarian, chaplain to king, 1812, preb of York, 1830, archdeacon of Cleveland, 1832.
[4] See p. 28, n. 8.   [5] See p. 119, n. 3.

Page 135

Orlaston al. Orleston R. St Mary. Sr Philip Boteler[1] P. Tenths 9–1. Certified 40$^£$. ⟨AD^n 50 clear {R saith 38$^£$} See below⟩. So called now. 17 Ho. Service once on Sundays. Prayers on Chr. Day. Cat. exp. every Sunday during Summer. 4 Sacr. 15 Com each time. 40^s a year given to the Church. So applied. No Parsonage Ho. Church, chancel, neat & in good Order. Glebe 17 Acres. 3 Bells. R saith it is near 50$^£$, and by S^r Ph. Botelers allowance of Wood to him, above 50$^£$. Augm. 1767 with 400$^£$ by Sir Ph. B & Qu^s bounty.

Blemell Pollard[2] R. ⟨Sept. 24. 1751⟩. Cur. of Shadoxhurst p. 142. Resides there. Dead before June 16. 1764.
W^m ⟨{or Robt}⟩ Polhill[3] R. Sept. 3. 1764 R. of Bircholt p. 96. Master of Maidstone School p. 250.
Geo. Carter[4] A.M. Rector 1780.
Wm Philip Menzies[5] A.B. Rector 1781.

Yate[6] Cur here & at Shadoxhurst, where see p. 142. Went away Jan 1768. No service.
Henry Jones[7] [V. of Bearsted] serves them May 1768. Scandalous. Gone, the same month.
Tho. Morgan[8] BA of Ch. Ch. D^n 23 Aug 1767 by BP Moss[9] serves them June 1768.
Mich. O'Clare[10] June 1769 see p. 142.
Mr Monkhouse[11] Cur. Sal. £25.
Mr Smith[12] cur. lic. 1791 Sal. £25.

1758 Conf. 9. 1762. 2. 1766. 2.

[1] (?–72), 4th Bt. He lived at Teston in Kent.
[2] (17?–64), of Huntingdonshire, m. Jesus C 1729, BA 1734, C. Shadoxhurst, 1736, R. Orlestone, 1751–64, R. Shadoxhurst, 1761–64.
[3] See p. 50, n. 16.   [4] See p. 124, n. 3.
[5] (1757–1819), of Ashford, Kent, m. University 1774, BA 1778, MA 1788, R. Orlestone, 1781–1819, PC. Minster, 1788–1819, V. Frindsbury, V. Sutton Valence, 1803–19, minor canon of Rochester, royal chaplain.
[6] Possibly William Yate (1725–?), of Dorsington, Glos, m. Balliol 1746, BA 1751.
[7] (1735–), of Glanyrafondda, co Carmathen, m. Christ Church 1756, BA 1760, C. Queenborough, 1763, V. Bearsted, 1767–73, V. Chart Sutton, 1773–83.
[8] (1744–?), of Llanbardarn, co Cardigan, m. Christ Church 1763, BA 1767, C. Staplehurst, 1810.
[9] Charles Moss (1711–1802), bishop of St David's, 1766–74, bishop of Bath and Wells, 1774–1802.
[10] C. Orlestone and Shadoxhurst, 1769.
[11] See p. 56, n. 16.
[12] John Smith, C. Shadoxhurst and Orlestone, 1791, C. Kingsnorth, 1805.

Page 136
D. Lymne
Ostinghanger al. Eastinghanger R. St Tho. Becket. No Church. The King P. K^s books 7–12–6. Only the name in ABP Wakes book. Not that in ABP Herrings. Lies between Saltwood & Sellinge. Qu abt Houses, & who pays the First Fruits &c. AD^n Head saith, that he believes there are several Ho. in Ostinhanger, & that the People go to Sellinge Church, & hath been told, that no Tithes have been paid to any one for many years past.

There are in the Register Books Admissions to the Rectory of Ostringhanger or Westinghangre, from 1282 to 1523 which is the Date of the last Institution. No mention of it afterwards. The Crioll[1] or Kyriel Family were Patrons, till 1478: after that, the Ponynges[2] Family.

M[r] Lewis in a fol. Ms of the Churches of the Diocese, w[ch] AD[n] Head hath, saith, that the Church is long since demolished & the Tithes a Lay Fee: that it is now reputed to belong to the parish of Stan{d}ford just by, [p. 104] to which Chapel the few Inhabitants of this Parish resort, & there is paid to it out of this Rectory 10[s] a year, but qu. how long.

[1] Sir John de Criol founded a chantry in Westenhanger 19 Edward III. According to Hasted, the family had the patronage until 'about the start of Henry VIII's reign', and then alienated to Sir Edward Poynings, a favourite of the king: Hasted VIII, pp. 70-2.

[2] On the death of Sir Edward Poynings in c.1523, the church went to the Crown: ibid., p. 76.

Page 137

Romney new V. S[t] Nicolas [with the Chapels of S[t] Martin & S[t] Laurence in Oadens-town destructa. Ecton]. All Souls Coll. Propr. & P. Exempt from AD[n]. K[s] books 6-16-3. Wake, 60[f]. Now called 130[f] part of which is a Coll. Lease worth 10[f] ⟨Called in Mr Jacobs[1] Disp. 100[f]⟩. Abt 2000 Acres of Land. 109 Ho. Whole Service on Sundays. Prayers W. Fr. & on the other Days the Rubrick directs. Ch[n]. Cat in Lent. Lewis's Exp. used. Abt 7 Sacr. abt. 70 Com. John Southland[2] of New Romney Gent. left in 1610 3 Farms, let now at 35[f] a Year, for a Schoolmaster, who is to pay 5[f] a Year to two poor Couples in an Hospital, wch M[r] S. founded for them, & 5[f] to the Parish Church, & to repair the School House & Hospital, & to teach 2 Boys, appointed by the Mayor, Reading, Writing & Arithmetick, till they are 14. M[r] Sedgwick[3], Cur of S[t] Marys in the Marsh p. 130, from whose Answers there this Account is taken, {is} ⟨hath been⟩ the Master 3 years, & laid out more than the Income on Repairs, & therefore desires not to be licenced yet. A Charity School founded on Subscription, & first established by M[r] Deffray[4] formerly R of Old Romney [died in 1738]. The Trustees put what number of Children they will to learn Reading, Writing, Arithmetick. An Annuity of 5[f] a Year & 2[f] a Year in Land left by Tho. Baker[5] Gent. to the Persons in the above Hospital. Church & chancel very large & handsome. Ho. a mean cottage in good repair. No outHo. 8 Bells.

Rich. Jacob[6] MA ⟨V.⟩ 2 Aug. 1749. V. of East-Malling p. 353. Saith he resides there. qu. 27 miles from hence. {Dead, Oct} ⟨Died Sept⟩ 1762.
John White[7] DD V. Jan 1. 1763. To reside in abt a year. Not come June 1764. See his Letter, & the Answer. Saith Oct 4. Service is twice & he cannot get a House.
Salisbury Price[8] D.D. V. December 7 1774.
William Rugge[9] Clerk A.M. Vicar July 28: 1775.
Edm[d]. Isham[10] Clerk A.M. Vicar Feb[y] 3: 1777.
Peter Rashleigh[11] A.M. Vicar 1785.
Seymer Love[12] A.M. Vicar 1788.
Willoughby Bertie[13] A.M. V. 1793.

John Edward Wilson[14], Cur. Priest. Resides. 40[f]. V. of Sellinge p. 140. A native, & {I think} member of the Corporation here, & inhabits a Ho. of his own. Mayor, 1759. Died May 11. 1761.

W. Fowle[15], coming June 1761 from Warehorn p. 146 see next p.

Richard Relhan[16] Clerk A.B. Curate, Licensed May 26: 1777, with a Salary of £50 p ann.

Richard Sharpe[17] Cur. Sal. £50.

1758 Conf. ⟨here 323. Of this Parish⟩ 65. 1762. 23. 1766 Conf. here June 4. 224. Of this Parish 49.

---

[1] (1715–62), of Canterbury, Kent, m. Balliol 1732, BA 1736, MA (All Souls) 1740, V. New Romney, 1749–62, V. Upchurch, 1749–52, V. East Malling, 1757–62.

[2] The schoolmaster was to be 'a scholar of Oxford or Cambridge, sufficient to teach the Latin tongue as well as the English': Hasted VIII, p. 459.

[3] See p. 112, n. 5.   [4] John Deffray, of Huguenot origin, R. Old Romney, 1690–1738.

[5] In 1728: Hasted VIII, p. 459.   [6] See n. 1.

[7] (1717–?), of Rendcomb, Glos, m. Oriel 1732, demy Magdalen 1740, BA 1736, MA 1739, BD (All Souls) 1748, DD 1753, V. New Romney, 1763–74, R. Brimpsfield and Minchinhampton Common, Glos, 1774–.

[8] (1725–76), of Westbury, Bucks, m. Trinity O 1744, BA 1748, MA (All Souls) 1752, BD 1759, DD 1763, V. New Romney, 1774–75, V, Little Marlow, Bucks, 1775–6, R. Buckland, Surrey, 1775–6.

[9] (1741–86), of St George's, Hanover Square, London. m. Brasenose 1759, BA 1763, MA (All Souls) 1766, V. New Romney, 1775–7, R. Buckland, Surrey, 1776–86.

[10] Edmund Isham (1745–1817), of Oxford, m. Lincoln, 1761, BA 1764, MA (All Souls) 1768, BD 1777, DD 1783, warden, 1793–1817, vice-chancellor, 1796–8, V. New Romney, 1777–81, R. Elmley, 1782–88, R. Harpsden, Oxon, 1788–1817.

[11] (1745–1836), of Wykeham, Herts, m. University 1765, fellow All Souls, BA 1772, MA 1775, bar-at-law Middle Temple, 1772, V. New Romney, 1781–81, R. Woldingham 1781, V. Barking, Essex, 1781, R. Southfleet, 1787–1836.

[12] (1748–93), of Londonderry, Ireland, m. Christ Church 1765, BA (All Souls) 1770, MA 1774, V. New Romney, 1781–93.

[13] (1761–?), of Kenn, Devon, m. Trinity O 1774, BA 1778, MA (All Souls) 1782, BD 1794, V. New Romney, 1793–

[14] (1729–?), of Romney, Kent, m. Balliol 1747, BA 1751, V. Sellinge, 1754–61.

[15] See p. 118, n. 2.

[16] (1754–1823), of Dublin, m. Trinity C 1772, BA 1776, MA 1779, fellow and chaplain of King's 1781, FRS 1787, founder fellow of Linnean society, 1788, C. New Romney, 1777, R. Hemingsby, Lincs, 1791–1823.

[17] See p. 117, n. 4.

Page 138

D. Lymne

Romney old R. S[t] Clement. ABP P. K[s] books 15–19–2. Wake 120. Present R. 154[£]. 1728 Acres, besides Agney 667 Acres, which pays Tithes to R. of Medley p. 132 who pays R. of Old Romney 4[£] a year by Composition, & besides near 30 Acres of Glebe. 18 Ho. No Parsonage House. Whole Service on Sundays. Prayers only then. [qu. Chr. Day, good Fr. Ch[n] Cat. when sent. 4 Sacr. Com. from 8 to 17. Church clean in good Order. Chancel handsome. Glebe 26 Acres. 3 Bells.

See Letter to D[r] Potter[1] Sept {17} 15 1767.

John Peters[2] MA R. 6 Feb. 1738. Morning Preacher at Spring Garden Chapel, Lecturer at S[t] Clement Danes. Resides at Isleworth Middlesex. Is here abt 6

weeks in a Year. Had Leave of Absence from ABP Potter. {Died March 29. 1762. Mistake.} Died March 5. 1763.
John Fowell[3] D.D. 29 July 1763. Void by Cession Oct. 14. 1763.
Tho. Freeman[4] MA. R. 7 Dec. 1763 minor Can. of Cant. & Seq. of River
Joshua Dix[5] A.M. 1783.

Arthur Kight[6] Cur. 40^f V. of Newchurch p. 133. Resides at New Romney p. 137 2 miles off. Nov. 1763. Unable to officiate any more. Died 1765.
Mr Fowle[7] serves this with New Romney 1764. Not now 1766
James Smith[8]. Gone.
Colby[9]. C. D. Doth Whole Service. Shd be P. Gone Apr. 1767. Mr Fowle see p. 137 serves this with Brookland Apr. 1768. To take Priests orders or quit. Ord Pr. Tr S 1768.
Mr Fowle Cur. Sal. £30. & Surplice fees lic by Archdeacon.

158 Conf. 18. 1762. 3 NB 1766. 18

---

[1] See p. ii, n. 3.
[2] (1692–?), of London, m. Christ Church 1709, BA 1712, MA (Hart Hall) 1715, R. Old Romney, 1739–1763.
[3] See p. 4, n. 9.
[4] Ibid., n. 12.
[5] See p. 33, n. 6.
[6] See p. 133, n. 1.
[7] See p. 118, n. 2.
[8] See p. 7, n. 9.
[9] See p. 117, n. 6.

Page 139

Ruckinge al. Roking R St M. Magd. ABP P. Kings books 14–13–4. Wake 100^f. Now 140^f ⟨See below⟩. 40 Ho. Publick service never more than once a Sunday in the present Rectors memory. No further Answer abt Service. 20^s a year from an Estate in Romney Marsh, for the poor. 1759 Whole Service. Church dirty. Chancel pretty {neat} well. Ho. indifferent, in bad Repair. Out Ho. in good Repair. Glebe 36 Acres. 5 Bells. Let for 150^f. Taxes low. Mr Wray. 80^f, besides 50 to the Curate & all other Deductions. Dr Porteus[1] 1767

Jude Holdesworth[2] ⟨R.⟩ 13 Nov. 1750. R. of Hinxhill p. 122. where he resides, 7 miles from hence. Saith he was allowed by ABP Herring to serve them together. Died Oct. 24. 1759.
Tho. Wray[3] MA R 3 Apr. 1760. R. of Great Chart p. 56. Void by Cession May 2. 1761. See p. 149.
John Benson[4] MA 12 Sept. 1761. V. of Sibbertswold p. 196 ⟨Now 1762 R. of Great Chart p. 56⟩. Void by Cession Jan 25. 1764.
Beilby Porteus[5] MA R. 13 March 1764. R. of Wittresham p. 149 void by Cession Aug. 19 1767.
John Jenkinson[6] MA R 14 Oct. 1767. V. of Gillingham p. 358.
James Allen Gorsse[7], ord. Deacon, March 11. 1759. Cur. 40^f. Resides at Ashford, abt 4 miles off, where he assists in the School. Mr Hawkins[8] of Kingsnoth p. 127 promises to do the occasional Duty. Qu. if Mr Gorsse doth not also serve Bilsington p. 112. Not now, 1760. Going Jan 1762.
Wm Allen[9] D. ⟨1762⟩ from Gr. Chart p. 56 to serve this twice & Bilsington p. 112 once, ord. Pr. 19 Dec. 1762, 2 or 3. 50^f. July 1763 going to reside there. R. of Little Chart 1768.

Apsley[10] from Brook & Smeeth Jan. 1768.

Hopkins Fox[11] A.M. Rector 1780.
William Philip Warburton[12] A.M. 1793.
Edward Taylor[13] A.M. 1794.

M[r] Bond[14] Cur.

1758 Conf. 11. 1762. 12. 1766. 24.

[1] Beilby Porteus (1731–1809), of York, m. Christs 1748, BA 1752, MA 1755, DD 1767, R. Wittersham, 1762–5, R. Ruckinge, 1764–67, preb of Peterborough, 1764–76, R. Hunton, 1765, R. Lambeth, 1767–77, archbishop's chaplain, 1762, bishop of Chester, 1777–87, master St Cross Hosp., Winchester, 1767–77, bishop of London, 1787–1809.
[2] See p. 96, n. 6.   [3] See p. 56, n. 3.
[4] See p. ii, n. 40.   [5] See n. 1.
[6] (1718–80), of Wickenby, Lincs, m. Merton 1737, BA (Brasenose) 1740, MA 1743, V. Gillingham, 1753–80, R. Ruckinge, 1767–80.
[7] See p. 57, n. 11.   [8] See p. 127, n. 2.
[9] See p. 56, n. 12.   [10] See p. 6, n. 5.
[11] See p. 15, n. 11.   [12] See p. 53, n. 3.
[13] See p. 20, n. 5.   [14] See p. 50, n. 15.

Page 140
D. Lymne
Sellinge al. Selindge ⟨by Hythe. Direct near Ashford⟩ V. S[t] Mary. Belonged to Dover Hosp. or S[t] Austins Mon. Cant. The King P. at least the {two} ⟨four⟩ last Turns[1)]*. ⟨Exempt from AD[n]⟩. There is a Selling p. 174. in the D. of Ospring. Tenths 13[s] 11[d]. Certified 36[£]. Now 40[£] ⟨AD[n] 80[£]. Augm. 1767, with 400[£] by S[r] Ph. B. & Qus bounty⟩. Near 3 miles long & 2 broad, exclusive of 114 Acres of Pasture in Romney Marsh belonging to V. 49 Ho. A Family of Anab. Service once on Sundays, & on all extraordinary Festivals. Cat. with Lewis's Exp. every other Sunday. 4 Sacr. 30 Com. M[r] Godfrey[1], who hath an Estate in the Parish supports a School for some poor Ch[n]. Donations of abt 17[£] for the Poor. So applied. Church & chancel large, in good Repair. Ho. indifferent, wants Repair: Out ho. in good Oder. 13 Acres called Poor Land. Glebe 14 Acres. 4 Bells.
[1)]* The Advowson of Sellinge (qu. which) was given to the See of Cant. by Qu. Mary. Pres to Sellinge by Crown 1705 V. 186.

John Edward Wilson[2] V. in July 1754. Cur. of New Romney, p. 137 abt 10 miles off. See there. Died May 11, 1761.
John Dawson[3] R. June 30. 1761. See p. 110. Resides here. Bad Health, cannot attend Visitation.
Charles Moore[4] M. A. V. Aug[t] 20 1772.
John Conant[5] A. M. Vicar. April 30: 1778.

John Loftie[6], Cur. 22[£] & Ho. Promised to reside, but serves it from Ashford. Gone.
Nicolas Brown[7]. Deacon, Cur. See Bilsington p. 112. Salary 22[£]. Mr Dawson of Smeeth, p. 110 a mile or two off. promises to do the occasional Duty
Stephen Barrett[8], master of Ashford School, 7 miles off. Gone.
Robt Tournay[9] C. & R. of Bonnington p. 114. Gone.
M[r] Macock[10]. Cur. Sal. £25.

1758 Conf. 35. 1762. 22. 1766. 33.

[1] Died 1769. A great benefactor to the parish: Hasted VIII, p. 312.
[2] See p. 137, n. 14.   [3] See p. 110, n. 7.
[4] (1743–1811), of London, m. Trinity C 1760, BA 1764, MA 1767, fellow 1765–71, R. Cuxton, 1770–1811, V. Sellinge, 1772–78, V. Boughton Blean, 1778–1803, V. St Nicholas, Rochester, 1803–11, six-preacher, 1792–1811, C. Hernehill, 1790.?
[5] (1735–1811), of Farthingstone, Northants, m. Lincoln 1753, BA 1757, MA 1775, R. St Peter's Sandwich, 1766–1811, V. Sellinge, 1778–1811, V. Teynham, 1803–11.
[6] See p. 25, n. 5.   [7] See p. 112, p. 6.
[8] See p. 50, n. 9.   [9] See p. 110, n. 8.
[10] Henry Macock (1743–1816), of Oxford, m. 1758, BA 1763, MA 1764, V. Harwell, Berks. C. Sellinge, 1790, V. Sellinge, 1803, C. Lympne, 1814–6.

Page 141
Sevington R. S[t] Mary. Edw. Boys[1] Gent P. Tenths 17^s–$4\frac{3}{4}^d$. Certified $35^£$ Wake, 40. Now betw. 60 & 70. AD[n] $50^£$. 12 Ho. 6 of them inhabited by Labourers. A man & his wife Quakers. He pays his Tithes as regularly as others. Service once on Sundays ⟨see below⟩. Willesborough Ch is very near. Prayers only on such others Days, as are appointed on particular Occasions. [qu. Chr. Day, good Fr. Cat in Lent. 4 Sacr. abt 16 Com. Wrote to desire whole Service on Sundays, as R. hath only this. He will do it, when his Neighbours want him not, as they often do, to help them. The Parsonage Ho. small. Part of Brick: much improved by Mr. Greenhill. Church & Chancel clean & in good Repair. Glebe 10 Acres. 4 Bells.

Steph. Greenhill[2] BA R. 10 Apr. 1731. Resides at Ashford 2 miles off. {1761 Serves Hothfield p. 66}. 1765 Serves Willesborough p. 148.
Edward Norwood[3] A. M. Instituted Aug[t] 13: 1777, on the presentation of Edward Norwood[4] Gent.
Rector does his own duty.

1758 Conf. 5. 1762. 7. 1766. 2.

[1] Edward Boys, the owner of Boys Hall in the parish of Willesborough: Hasted VII, p. 568.
[2] See p. 66, n. 8.
[3] (1746–1831), of Ashford, Kent, m. CCCO 1764, BA 1767, MA (Oriel) 1770, R. Sevington, 1777–1831, C. Willesborough, 1790–1831, R. Milsted, 1821–31.
[4] From Ashford. He purchased the advowson in 1776: Hasted VIII, p. 582.

Page 142
D. Lymne
Shadoxhurst al. Shadocksherste R. S[t] Peter & S[t] Paul. The King P. Tenths 15–$3\frac{1}{2}$ Certified $38^£$. Now called $40^£$ ⟨called $80^£$, 1764. See below⟩. 20 Ho. Service once on Sundays. Prayers on Chr. Day. Cat. exp. on Sundays during Summer. 5 Sacr. 25 Com. 40^s a Year to the poor. Church & Chancel mean, want whitewashing. Ho. & out Ho. indifferent. in good Repair. Glebe 8 Acres. 3 Bells.
1767 Augm. with $400^£$ by S[r] Ph. Boteler & Qus bounty.

Henry Bagnall[1] MA R. 4 Feb. 1733. R. of Frittenden p. 62 where he resides, abt 15 miles off. Dead before Apr. 3. 1761.

Blemel Pollard[2] R. Aug. 24. 1761 See below. Dead before June 16 1764.
Robt. Polhill[3] R. July 2. 1764. V. of Goudhurst, p. 240.

Blemell Pollard Cur. Salary { }. R. of Orleston p. 135. Resides here in the Parsonage Ho. Writes Jan. 17. 1764 from Ashford
Yate[4] Pr. Cur. here & at Orleston, p. 135 ⟨where see⟩. 50^f, Surpl. Fees. Pars. Ho.
Tho. Morgan[5] see p. 135.
Mich. O'Clare[6] June 21st. 1769.
Mr Monkhouse[7] Cur. Sal. £25.
Mr Smith[9] Cur. lic. 1791. Sal £25.

1758 Conf. 10. 1762. 12. 1766. 9

[1] See p. 62, n. 1. [2] See p. 135, n. 2.
[3] (1734–1801), of Maidstone, m. University 1751, BA 1754, MA 1757, V. Goudhurst, 1759–1801, R. Shadoxhurst, 1766–1801.
[4] See p. 135, n. 6. [5] Ibid., n. 8.
[6] Ibid., n. 10. [7] Ibid., n. 11.
[8] Ibid., n.12.

Page 143
Snargate R. St Dunstan. ABP P. K^s books 17–6–8. Wake 60^f. Now 100^f ⟨See below⟩. 1484 Acres. 9 Ho. Service once on Sundays. Ch^n, when any, Cat. in Lent. 4 Sacr. Few Com. R. saith it was reckoned but 90^f in his Predecessors time, & is but 80^f, & that all the People go to Brenzett p. 115 [a mile or two off] the other part of the Day. Church in pretty good, Chancel in good Repair. Ho. very mean, but in Repair. No outho. Glebe 2½ Acres. 3 Bells.

Theop. De l'Angle[1] MA. R 2 Apr. 1758. V. of Tenterden p. 73. Cur. of Goodneston near Sandwich p. 13. where he resides. Died June 30. 1763.
John Wentworth[2]LLB R. {17} ⟨16⟩ Nov. 1763. R. of Brenzett p. 115 where see. Serves each once.
Wm Wing. Fowle[3] Augs^t 10. 1770. does his own duty.

Cur. See Kenardington p. 126 March 1760 Mr Fowle Cur. of Warehorn ⟨p. 146.⟩ officiates here, without lessening the Service there.
Wm Hassell[4] BA of St Johns Camb. ord. Deacon Feb. 15. 1761. Cur of this & Kenardington p. 126. 21^f each. Pr. May 17. 1761. Going to Warehorn at Mich. Married.
Charles Prince[5] Cur. 1761 See p. 111.

1758 Conf. 11 1762. 13. 1766. 11

[1] See p. 13, n. 3. [2] See p. 115, n. 3.
[3] See p. 118, n. 2. [4] See p. 126, n. 7.
[5] See p. 111, n. 8.

Page 144

D. Lymne

Snave R. S[t] Augustin. ABP P. K[s] books 19–17–11. Wake 90[f] ⟨so AD[n]⟩. Now 100. 11 Ho. 37 Inhabitants above 16. 4 Absenters, from what motives R. knows not. [He or Cur. should know]. Service once on Sundays. R saith, it was but 90[f] in his predecessors Time, & now less, & when Cur. Taxes &c are paid, is but 40[f] clear: that the House is too mean to live in, & the Air & water bad; & the Congregation in Winter sometimes but 4 or 5. See the Letters. No Prayers on Holydays [qu. Chr. day, good Fr.]. Cat exp. in Lent, if any come on notice: seldom above 3. 4 Sacr. from 7 to 15 Com. No Offertory. Church & Chancel small, pretty clean. Ho. & OutHo. indifferent, in tolerable good order. Glebe 11 Acres. 3 Bells.

Lic. to Edw. Bushnell[1] to rebuild parsonage Ho. 1723 Entry B. VII. 27.

The manor of Snave was granted by the Crown to the ABP in Exchange 31. Aug. 1 Ed. 6. See Chart. Misc vol. 13. N° 21

Josias Pomfret[2] R. 29 Sept. 1753. V. of Chillenden p. 9. & Cur. of Ickham p. 15 where he resides.

Philip Parsons[3] Clerk Rector Febry 7: 1776.

Rob[t] Neild[4] Cur. Also Cur. of Ivechurch p. 125. Now 1759 at the last place only. Both 1764.

Edw. Sedgwick[5] Cur. from Mich 1758. 24[f]. Cur. also of S[t] Marys in the Marsh p. 130. where see. Resides at New Romney. Nov. 1761 Leaving this for Burmarsh, at Chr. Mr Neild of Ivychurch to serve it for a while. Still 1766. Must not go on. Doth, 1767.

Theoph[s]. Jones[6] Cur. Sal. £24. lic. by Archdeacon.

1758 Conf. 5. 1762. 2. 1766. 4.

[1] (16?–1724), of Kent, m. Jesus C, BA 1681, C. Ivychurch, 1681, R. Snave, 1683–1724.
[2] See p. 9, n. 2. [3] See p. 26, n. 9.
[4] See p. 31, n. 2. [5] See p. 118, n. 5.
[6] (1752–1835), of Cardiganshire, m. Pembroke O 1773, BA 1777, C. Snave, 1790, R. St Mary's in the Marsh, 1802–35.

Page 145

Stone in Oxney ⟨See Tenham p. 177⟩ V. S[t] Mary. Belonged to S[t] Austins Mon. Cant. DCh. Cant. P. Kings books 8–14–4½. Wake 100. Now 140. 42 Ho. Service once two Sundays, twice the 3[d] [1750 Always twice ⟨see below⟩]. Qu. Holydays. Cat. in Lent. Crossmans Exp[l]. 4 Sacr. 50 Com. Land rented at 13–4 for the poor. Church pretty clean. Chancel wants whitewashing. Ho. small, in good Repair. Stable in Repair. 3 Loads of Hay & 2 of Straw from the Parsonage. Glebe 3½ Acres. 5 Bells.

W[m] Gostling[2] MA V. 23 July 1753. Minor Can. of Cant. where he resides: but visits his Parish sometimes.

Francis Gregory[3] M.A. Vic July 3. 1777.

Rich[d] Moore[4] Priest, Cur. Resides in V. Ho. 40[f] & Surpl. Fees. Cur. also of Fairfield p. 121. Qu. how he serves it with this. And of Small Hythe p. 74. The

Parishioners of Stone are content to be without Prayers every other Sunday, provided they have two Sermons. See AD[ns] Letter May 24. 1762 by wch Mr M. is to do whole Duty at Stone & ½ at Fairfield. 1765 Doth so, w[n] well. M[r]. Jackson[5] Cur. Sal. £40. House &c w. Surplice fees lic. by Archdeacon.

1758 Conf. 18. 1762. 10. 1766. 24

[1] Henry Crossman, *An Introduction to the Knowledge of the Christian Religion* (Colchester, 1754).
[2] See p. 6, n. 3.   [3] See p. 7, n. 5.
[4] See p. 74, n. 5.   [5] See p. 121, n. 7.

Page 146
D. Lymne
Warehorn R. S[t] Matthew. Pension of 10[s] to the Priory of Horton. Ecton. The King P. K[s] books 19[f]. Wake 100[f]. R. saith, now above 100[f] ⟨AD[n] 145. 135 M[r] Pearsall[1], house discomprehended⟩. 40 Ho. Tho. Hodges[2] Esq[r] [a Grazier, worth 1000[f] a Year]. Whole Service. Prayers on Holy days. Cat. in Lent. 4 Sacr. 30 Com. 7[f] a Year given for poor not receiving Parish Allowance. So applied. The air pretty good. Church & chancel large & handsome. Ho. & OutHo. pretty good, orderd to be repaired. 8 Acres & Int. of 10[f] to poor: 2-5-0, and 4-10-0 to church. AD[n]. Glebe 40 Acres. 5 Bells. The Rector Jan 13 1762 saith there are but 2 benefactions: one of 4-10-0 ⟨a year⟩ of wch 2[f] is for the poor, & 5[s] for the Church; another of 4[f] a year for the poor, & that there is nothing to shew for either, nor any Terrier. Curate has asked & believes neither is properly applied, Feb. 26. 1762.

John Bate[3] BA R. 13 Apr. 1737. Resides in London, his wife & this place being unhealthy. Will go thither himself sometimes in the Summer. See the Letters. She is dead Apr. 1760 and he Oct. 1761.
John Pearsall[4] MA of Pemb. Coll. Ox. R. Dec. 16. 1761. Master of the Free School, Guilford, where he resides, but hath no Scholars.
John Fleming Stanley[5] Clerk R. 24 Sept[r]. 1771.
Donald Maclean[6] A.M. Rector 1783. Charles Williams[7] Rect. 1796.

Will. Wing Fowle[8] Cur. ord. Pr. 11 March 1759. Lives in the Parsonage Ho. 40[f]. Born in the Marsh. Hath near 100[f] a year of his own. Liked by the People. March 1760 officiates also at Snargate p. 143. June 1761 going to New Romney p. 137.
W[m] Hassell[9] to come ⟨Mich 1761⟩ from Snargate p. 143 & Kenardington p. 126. Will want to keep Snargate with this. May 1762 going to Chislet.
Tho. Watson[10], abt 30, coming, Dec. 5. 1762. In the mean time, Mr Cotton[11]. He serves this only, 1764. Things are settled between him & R. Fresh Disputes. Going at Mich 1766.
Matthias Rutton[12] Clerk. Cur. Licensed June 4: 1776, with a Salary of £50 p ann.
M[r] Davis[13] Cur. Sal £50.

1758 Conf. 22. 1762. 20. 1766. 17

[1] (1718-?), m. Pembroke O 1736, BA 1739, MA 1745, R. Warehorne, 1761-71.

2 Owners of Parkers manor: Hasted VIII, p. 372.
3 (1710-61), of Boughton Malherbe, Kent, m. St John's C 1727, BA 1731, MA 1742, R. Warehorne, 1737-61.
4 See n. 1.
5 (1746-83), of Westminster, m. Hertford 1765, R. Warehorne, 1771-83.
6 R. Warehorne, 1783-96.
7 Perhaps (1754-1807), of Ashurst, Sussex, m. Jesus O 1763, demy Magdalen O 1766-75, BA 1768, MA 1770, fellow 1775-83, BD 1782, R. Warehorne, 1796-1807.
8 See p. 118, n. 2.   9 See p. 126, n. 7.
10 Probably (1731-), of Bamborough, Northumberland, m. Pembroke C 1751.
11 Probably Charles Cotton (1737-?), of Newton Purcell, Oxon, m. New College 1754, BA 1757, MA 1761.
12 (1748-1818), of Ashford, Kent, m. St Alban Hall O 1775, C. Warehorne, 1777, V. Sheldwich, 1781-1818, C. Throwley, 1790, R.Cowling, 1783-18-5, V. Selling, 1805-14, six-preacher, 1806-18, R. Badlesmere, 1814-18.
13 See p. 126, n. 8.

Page 147
Wellesborough See Willesborough

West Hythe V. St Mary. AD^n of Cant. Propr. & P. K^s books 8-14-4½. Now 27$^£$ ⟨clear⟩. Only the walls of the Church standing. Half the Parish is Sea Beach. 11 Ho. Inhabitants Graziers or their Lookers. Two Families of Anab. A small V. Ho. They go to Lymne, which is near, & where all occasional Offices have been performed for them above 100 Years ⟨2$^£$ allowed for it⟩. They find the Bread & Wine at Sacr there once in 3 times.

Will. Howdell[1] BA. V. 12 Apr. 1753. Chapl. of a Man of War in the Mediterranean, afterwds in N. America. 1761 came to ask my Leave to go with the Expedition.

Mr Beckenham[2] Cur.

1758 I suppose Conf. with the parishioners of Lymne. 1762. 2.

1 (1728-1804) of Staple Kent, m. St John's C 1745, BA 1749, V. West Hythe, 1753-1804, second master Kings school Canterbury, 1777-9.
2 [John Charles Beckingham], see p. 118, n. 6.

Page 148
D. Lymne
Willesborough V. St Mary. Belonged to St Austins Mon. Cant. DCh. Cant P. K^s books 18-16-8. Wake 55. Now 80$^£$ clear ⟨AD^n 70$^£$⟩. 1200 Acres, besides a Common of 100. 59 Ho. of which 34 are Cottages. Mr Boys[1], a Minor. 2 Families of Anab. Sometimes come to Church. There was a wealthy Quaker, now dead. His Ch^n were baptized with his Consent. Service once on Sundays. So immemorially. Sevington within ¾ of a mile. V. performed Service twice for above 6 months. Few would come. Prayers on Ash W. Sermon also on good Fr. & on Days appointed by the Governm^t. Cat. exp. from the beginning of Lent to Whits. 4 Sacr. 38 or 40 Com. A small Almshouse founded by Joan Master[2] in Q. Elizs time. Church & chancel in good order Ho. very good & handsome. No out Ho. 3-10-0 to the poor. AD^n. Glebe 4 Acres. 5 Bells.

John Norcross[3] MA V. 17 Sept. 1729. Resides constantly in V. Ho. R. of Hothfield p. 66. Cur. of Eastwell p. 60. Not now 1760 see Hinxhill p. 122. 1765 He is unable through Age ⟨blind 1766⟩. Mr Greenhill[4] of Sevington p. 141 serves it.

Robert Stedman[5] M.A. V. Oc^{tr}: 1773 does his own duty.

John Francis[6] A.M. V. 1789. resigned it & again instituted 1792.

Edward Norwood[7] A.M. Cur. Sal. £25. Lic. by Archdeacon.

1758 Conf. 27. 1762. 25. 1766. 23.

[1] See p. 141, n. 1.
[2] In 1574. The Master famiy owned Streetend: Hasted VII, p. 572.
[3] See p. 60, n. 5.   [4] See p. 66, n. 8.
[5] See p. 11, n. 5.   [6] See p. 28, n. 8.
[7] See p. 141, n. 3.

Page 149

Wittresham R. St John Baptist ABP P. ⟨Direct near Tenterden⟩. Exempt from AD^n. K^s books 15-8-6½. Wake 180^f. Now 218^f ⟨220^f Dr Wray. 140 clear of Cur &c Dr Stinton⟩. 64 Ho. One Family of Presb. 2 of Anab. 3 partly Anab. Lessening. 11 Absenters, growing better. Two Sermons every Sunday. A Sermon on Chr. day, Ash W. good Fr. Asc. day, & all State Festivals & Fasts. Prayers W. Fr. in Lent. Offerd through the Year: but the Parishioners said they could not attend. Cat. exp in the Church in Lent, & in the School once a Week. 4 Sacr. 40 Com. each time. A Charity School, supported by R. Cur. & Inhabitants, for teaching 12 Boys & Girls. The Offertory money is applied to this, & an Acct given of it. Church large, very dirty, & out of Repair. Chancel dirty. Ho. & out Ho. good & in good Repair. Glebe 12 Acres. 5 Bells. A Sts Bell. Unhealthy. Let for 204^f, including the Ho. & Glebe for 16^f, pd by 53 Persons at old Mich & old LD, the Rector giving them Beef & Pudding. The Commissioners of the Level pay 19-10-10 ⟨of this⟩ for the Tithe of Lands, which they use for better carrying the Waters to Rye. Taxed to the King at 90^f, but not to Poor or High-Ways. No Easter Offerings. No burial fees, but for Strangers: 5^s for a Marriage, 6^d a Churching. Christenings not named. This from Mr Morton, Curate. Disp. to R. for nonr. because unhealthy Entry B. II. II3.

Tho. Rymer[1] DD R. 10 July {23} 1723. R. of Acris p. 95 where he resides. Cur. of Swinfield p. 93. Died March 23, 1761.
Tho. Wray[2] MA R. May 2. 1761. R. of Gr. Chart p. 56. Void by Cession Apr. 10. 1762 See p. 414.
Beilby Porteus[3] MA of Christs Coll R. Aug. 23. 1762. ⟨Void by Cession Aug 19. 1765⟩. R of Ruckinge p. 139 ⟨1764 & of Hunton p. 364⟩.
George Stinton[4] DD. R. Aug. 21. 1765. Void by Cession Sept. 17. 1767.
Tho. Wintle[5] MA of Pembroke Coll. R. Sept. 22. 1767.
Stanhope Ellison[6] Master of Arts R. April 16 1774. See below.
Richd Morton[7] Cur. R. of Newenden p. 68. 48^f & Use of Ch. Yard & Surpl. Fees, worth 2^f more. A good Preacher in Debt, said to have appointed a Ch W^n agt the R^s will. See a Petition of the Inhabitants, to the Rector, that he might live

in the Parsonage Ho. It is said, that he may have one near the Church for 5^f a Year.

William Cornwallis[8] A.M. Rector, Mar 9: 1778. resides.

1758 Conf. 29. 1762. 2+2. 1766. 34.

[1] See p. 93, n. 4.   [2] See p. 56, n. 3.   [3] See p. 139, n. 1.
[4] (1730–83), of Ilfracombe, Devon, m. Queen's O 1748, fellow Exeter, 1750–67, BA 1754, MA 1755, B & DD 1765. R. Wittersham, 1765–67, chancellor of Lincoln cathedral, 1766, V. All Hallows, Barking, London, 1767–83, R. Halstead, 1770–1, R. Newington, Oxon, 1771–81, R. & V. Wrotham, 1781–83, FRS, FSA.
[5] (1738–1814). of Gloucester, m. Pembroke O 1753, BA 1756, MA 1759, BD 1768, R. St Peter's Wallingford, Berks, 1767–74, R. Wittersham, 1767–74, R. Brightwell, Berks, 1774–1814.
[6] (1718–78), of Wigan, Lancs, m. Brasenose 1739, BA 1745, MA (St John's C) 1761, R. St Benedict, London, 1757–74, V. Thorpe, Surrey, 1765–74, R. Wittersham, 1774–78, V. Boughton Blean, 1777–8.
[7] See p. 68, n. 1.   [8] See p. 99, n. 12.

Page 150
D. Lymne
Woodchurch R. All Saints. ABP P. Exempt from AD^n. K^s books 26–13–4. Wake 150^f. Now 220^f. 91 Ho. 3 Families Presb. Whole Service. Morning Prayers on all Holydays. Cat. all. Summer ⟨will be exp⟩. 7 Sacr. 60 Com. each time: at Mich. Sometimes above 80. 3–8–0 charged on Houses, for the Poor. So applied. R. pays for teaching 6 poor Ch^n. Church & Chancel large & handsome. Ho. large, of Timber, in good Repair. Out Ho. the same. Glebe 18 Acres. 6 Bells.

Nic. Carter[1] DD. R. 13 Sept. 1755. R. of Ham, p. 166. One of the 6 Preachers at Cant. Cath. & Cur of St Georges Chapel, Deal where he resides.
John Courtail[2] R. March 31 1775.

Rich. Jones[3] Cur. Priest. 40^f besides living Rent-free in the Parsonage Ho. & other Advantages. Good. ***Served this a while with Kenardington p. 126. Desired July 1761 to do it constantly. Refused *** 1762 Serves Fairfield once a month ***.
Nicholas Todd[4] Cur. Sal. £45 House &c lic by Archdeacon.

1758 Conf. 66. 1762. 39. 1766. 45

[1] See p. ii, n. 34.
[2] (1806), of Exeter, of French refugee parents, m. Clare Hall, BA 1736, MA 1739, fellow 1736–56, senior proctor 1753, R. Great Gransden, Herts, 1747–59, V. Little Gransden, 1751–9, V. Burwash, Sussex, 1759, V. Ninfield, Sussex, 1768–, R. Woodchurch, 1775–1806, R. Felpham, Sussex, 1778, preb of Chichester, 1761, archdeacon of Lewes, 1770.
[3] See p. 126, n. 6.   [4] C. Woodchurch, 1790–.

[Deanery of Ospringe]

Page 151
D. Ospring
Badlesmere R. St Leonard. Ld Rockingham ⟨Geo. Monson Watson[1] Esqr⟩ P.
Tenths 10–2½. Certified 46. Now 80^f ⟨100^f⟩. 16 Ho. Mr Franklyn[2], M^r
Chapman[3]. Service once on Sundays. Cat. exp. 4 Sacr. 18 Com. All the Houses
but one near other Churches. ABP Potter settled the present Service. A little
above 40^f remains, after Cur. & every thing is paid. Church & Chancel small &
clean. Ho. small, in bad Condition. Out Ho. in good repair. Glebe 8 Acres. 1
Bell.
Lic. for taking down an old chancel ⟨on S. Side⟩ on petition of Mr Watson Entry
B. VI. 132 for selling 2 of 3 Bells for Repairs of Church p. 165.

James Bernard[4] MA R 27 Aug. 1726. Resides here, but is melancholy. R. also of
Leveland p. ⟨164⟩. Hath some Fortune, which he hath vowed to give the
Society for Propagating the Gospel. Dead before Feb. 14. 1763.
Will. Gurney[5] MA R 2 May 1763. R. also of Leveland p. 164 was V. of Selling
p. 174 will reside here. Doth, 1764, 1765, ⟨1767⟩ & serves both his Livings. A
Horseracer 1765. AD^n saith it was not he, but a Farmer of his name.
Henry Thompson[6] A.B. Rector 1784.

Jo. Arnald[7] Cur. 20^f V. of Selling, adjacent Parish, where he lives [3 miles off]
p. 174 & R. of East Langdon p. 183. See his Letters. Gone. Oct 1762.
Sawbridge[8] Wanley C. Oct. 1762. See p. 162. C. of Throughley p. 178 just by.
Richard Halke[9]. Curate Sal. £50. lic. endorsed by Archdeacon.

Consolidated with Leveland pa. 164, March 16 1773.

1758 Conf. 28 1762. 11. 1766. 1.

[1] Presumably Lewis Monson Watson (1728–95), who was created baron Sondes in 1760. Thomas
Watson (1715–46), earl of Rockingham, bequeathed his estates to Lewis Monson, the 2nd son of
John, baron Monson. Lewis took the additional name of Watson.
[2] Arthur Franklyn, owner of Woodscourt manor from 1743. He died in 1764: Hasted VI, p. 479.
[3] James Chapman, who had estates in Frinsted, Bredgar and Eastchurch. He died in 1797: ibid., p.
570.
[4] (1692–1763), of Ospringe, Kent, m. St John's C 1708, BA 1712, MA 1715, V. Selling, 1716–27,
R. Badlesmere, 1726–63, R. Leaveland, 1726–63: 'insane and sequestered for many years': Venn.
[5] (17?–84), of Kent, m. CCCC 1751, BA 1755, MA 1761, V. Selling, 1763–63, R. Leaveland,
1763–72, R. Badlesmere, 1763–84, V. Bredgar, 1772–80, R. Luddenham, 1780–84.
[6] See p. 38, n. 2.
[7] John Arnald (17?–1800), m. Emmanuel 1722, BA 1725, BCL 1770, C. Fairfield, 1728–34, V.
Waldershare, 1729–38, V. Selling, 1735–63, R. East Langdon, 1738–63.
[8] Wanley Sawbridge (1732–96) of Wye, Kent, m. Emmanuel BA 1757, MA 1760, PC. Harty,
1760–96, V. Stalisfield, 1779–96.
[9] (17?–1814), of Kent, m. CCCC 1762, BA 1766, MA 1769, fellow (Clare) 1771, C. Ospringe,
1770, V. Urchfont, Wilts, 1775–80, V. Faversham, 1780–184, V. Selling, 1784–1805, C.
Badlesmere, 1790, R. Badlesmere, 1805–14.

Page 152

D. Ospring

Boughton Blean al under Bleane V. S[t] Peter & S[t] Paul. Belonged to the Monastery of Feversham. ABP Propr. & Patr. Exempt from AD[n]. K[s] books 9-4-9½. Wake 60[f] ⟨130 in Disp IX. 94⟩. Now 130[f] ⟨AD[n] 90[f]⟩. Sev[l] Hamlets. Boughton Street, South-Street, Norlane, Oversland, Wyeborough, Fairbrook, Nash, Brenley, Colkins: of which see the Answer to Inquiries. {Tho} Abt 160 Ho. in all. Tho. Hawkins[1] of Nash Esq[r], a Papist, above 87. His eldest son[2] with a wife & Ch[n] are in France. Abt 6 Papists more besides Ch[n]. See the Particulars ⟨1765. 11 Papists⟩. Place of Worship in a Garret at M[r] Hawkins's. L[d] Teynhams[3] Priest, Colgrave[4], & Sir Edw. Hales's[5], Pool[6], come occasionally. The other principal Family is that of Mrs Marsh[7], widow ***. Service once on Sundays ⟨1759 Whole Service⟩ Chr. day & good Fr. & on the other part of the Day at Hernhill. Boughton Street is in the middle betw. both Churches. Prayers on Holy days w[n] a Congregation can be got: & W. Fr. in Lent, w[n] Cat. is exp. Then also Cat. Sermons. Some poor persons Absenters. Cur. hath talked to them. In afternoons sometimes 3 or 400 at Church. 4 Sacr. 50 or 60 Com.

A Workhouse for this Parish, Ospring & Selling. The Rules the same with those of Feversham. Cur. endeavours to make it effectual, & gives them Books. A Master & 2 Mistresses teach School: 13 taught by a voluntary Subscription, which Cur. got revived. Arthur Whatman[8] left 15[s] a year to the Minister for a Sermon Nov. 5 & 5[s] for the Clerk, & 20[s] for a Collation for the Minister & parish officers, & 3[f] for the poor on that Day. Many Gifts to the poor, which see. Church & Chancel large & handsome. Ho. & out Ho good. 39[f] a year to the poor. A large Garden. 6 Bells.

V. having been long void. A seq. granted to Robt Skeyne[9] V. of Hernhill June 6. 1671 Entry B. III. 81 & on his death John Gamlin[10] was collated to Hernehill, & admitted to serve the Cure of Bocton Bleane 9 Aug 1676 p. 295.

[1] (c.1674-1766). His family had lived at Nash for several centuries. Hasted recounts how during the Jacobite rebellion of 1715, the house was plundered by the neighbourhood: VII, p. 10.

[2] John Hawkins, who marrried Susan, the daughter of Robert Constantine of Dorset: ibid., p. 11.

[3] Henry Roper (c.1708-81), lord Teynham.   [4] Andrew Colegrave, S.J. (1717-68), of France.

[5] See p. 33, n. 2.   [6] Perhaps Francis Pole (1711-67), of Lancashire.

[7] Roberta-Catherine Marsh, the wife of Terry Marsh who owned the manor of Scarbuts. He died in 1757: Hasted VII, p. 13.

[8] In 1674: ibid., p. 14.

[9] Skean (?-1676), MA, V. Hernehill, 1660-76, C. Boughton Blean, 1666 (granted sequestration 1671).

[10] (16?-1715), of Middlesex, Queens' C 1665, BA 1669, MA 1672, C. Wooton, C. Boughton Blean, 1676-, V. Hernehill, 1676-81, V. Faversham, 1682-1715, V. Preston, 1684-1715.

Page 153

Boughton Blean continued

Henry Heaton[1] DD. 17 Nov. 1752. R. of Ivechurch p. 125. Lived with ABP Herring, then chiefly with his Friends in Yorkshire. Now, 1759, Resides. here. Stanhope Ellison[2] A.M. Vicar. July 21: 1777. Charles Moore[3] A.M. Vicar, Feb[ry] 4: 1778. resides.

Robt Ingram[4] Cur. V. of {Selling} Bredherst p. 236. Resided here. {where now?}

Salary 20^f, Surpl. Fees, Use of House. Cur. also of Hernhill p. 163 where see. Seems diligent & serious. Perpetual Cur. of Bredherst, p. 236. Gone to Elham p. 99.

1758 Conf. 69. 1762. 50 1766. 84.

[1] See p. 46, n. 2.	[2] See p. 149, n. 6.
[3] See p. 140, n. 4.	[4] See p. 99, n. 14.

Page 154
D. Ospring
Buckland R. There hath been no Church these 30 years. Not marked in Lewis's map, as demolished. A good Bell, & a Font laid by. Communion Plate &c in the hands of a neighbour. Cha. Eve[1] Esqr P. Tenths 11–4. Certified 44–5–0. Now 50^f. 3 Ho. A substantial Farmer, Mr John Marshall. They go to Church at Teynham, which is near. Glebe 3 Acres.

Matthias Unwin[2] R. 8 Aug. 1754. Inst. the same day to Midley, where See. Resides at Buckland near Faversham.
William Lupton[3] Clerk A.M. Rector May 14: 1776.
John Jenner[4] D.D. Rector 1782.

James Allett[5] Cur. Salary 1–1–0 & desires no more. {R} V. of Teynham p. 177. & V. of Rodmersham p. 225.

1758 I believe none Conf. 1762. 1

[1] Patron from 1753: Hasted VI, p. 399.   [2] See p. 132, n. 1.
[3] (1733–82), of Leeds, Yorks. m. St John's C 1750, MA 1757, R. Blagdon, Somerset, 1761–6, V. Long Claxton, Leics. 1766–76, R. Buckland, 1776–82, R. Midley, 1776–82, V. Headingley, Leeds, 1769–82.
[4] (1746–1828), of Essex, m. Jesus C 1764, BA 1767, MA 1770, DD 1782, fellow and tutor, V. All Saints, Cambridge, 1775–83, R. Buckland, 1782–1833, R. Midley, 1782–1828.
[5] Of Oxon, m. Emmanuel 1736, BA 1740, MA 1743, V. Rodmersham, 1751–76, V. Teynham, 1753–76, C. Eastchurch.

Page 155
Davington al. Daunton R. St Mary Magd. Here was the Nunnery of Davington, granted 38 H. 8 to Sir Tho. Cheney[1]. Tanner Not. Mon. p. 215. 27 Feb. 1713 Institution to this Rectory was granted to Tho. Lees[2] MA of St Edm Hall Oxon, presented by Wm Day of Feversham Patr. pro hac vice, it being vacant by the Death of John Sherwin[3] Cl ⟨Entry B. VI. 138⟩. 23 Sept. 1728 A Caution was entred agt granting Inst. to the Rectory without the knowledge of DCh. of Cant ⟨& 1728 of Wm Sherwin[4] Entry B. VII. 216 as well as the former⟩. In ABP Wakes Parochial Book, They & Mr Sherwyn are called Patrons. It is there said to contain 12 Families, to be distant ¼ of a mile from Feversham, & to be worth 20^f a year: which last the ABP certified. See below. AD^n Head in a Letter 22 Sept. 1759 saith, that a Ch W^n from Davington appeared from the earliest Visitations till 1643: that from 1660 to 1688 the Books are full of Ch W^{ns} of Davington sworn, sometimes more than one at a Visitation; that they exhibited Bills, & Inquiry was made abt Repairs &c: that abt 1693, though the minister

appeared, no Ch. W^n came, & there hath been none for many Years: that one Mr Sherwin hath got Possession of the great Tithes, by means of a Mortgage of them, which he had: that he appoints the Curate, buys the Books, Surplice &c & denies all Eccl. Jurisdiction here: that in ABP Herrings time, he, the AD^n, by Dr Simpsons[5] Advice, directed the then Curate to appoint a Ch. W^n: on which Mr Sherwin shut up the Church for 3 months; & that this being laid before the ABP, he declined doing any thing upon it: that M^r Fr. Frederick Giraud[6] serves it now by Mr Sherwins appointmt, once a fortnight & receives $12^£$ a year from him: & that Mr Sherwin hath the Character of an obstinate, Purse-proud man. May 1760 He wants some one to serve it for $6^£$ a Year, wch no body will. So there is no Curate. AD^n. None 1765.
1767 augm. with $400^£$ by Sr Ph. Boteler & Qu^s bounty, if Mr Sherwin will comply.

John Sayer[7] C. Jan 1761 See Luddenham p. 167.
In 1663 it is marked vacant: heirs of Jo. Edwards[8] Esqr, Patron
A Nunnery founded here by K. Steph in 1153 or H. 2 in 1156. Grants confirmed to them by H.3 in 1255. Complain of Poverty to Ed. 3 in 1343. Grant of Monasteries under $200^£$ a year to H.8 1535. The name or value of this Nunnery is not read in the Register of the gen^l Suppression of religious Houses, as Lambart[9] saith, who had heard that is escheated to the King before, or forfeited for not maintaining the due Number of Nuns. Adjoining to the Nunnery & almost under the same Roof, is a little Church or Chapel, wch now serves the Parish, as probably it did then, for prayers & $Sacram^{ts}$. The dissolved Nunnery was, as hath been said, given to the King & the Estate made a Lay Fee. Particularly the Church or impropriate Parsonage, with the Scite & other Estate of the Nunnery there. H.8 is s^d to have granted in his 38th year (1547) to Sir Thomas Cheyney. Lewis Hist. of Faversham p. 77–80.
Oct. 1766 Mr Halke[10] of Luddenham wd serveit, & hath written to Mr Sherwin. No Answer. May 1767 AD^n saith he gives $10^£$ a yr & it is served once a month. Mr Giraud. does his own duty.

[1] Died in 1559.
[2] (1687-), of Faversham, Kent, m. All Souls 1703, BA 1707, MA (St Edmund Hall) 1710, V. Davington, 1713-, R. Goodnestone by Faversham, 1720-.
[3] (1640-1714), m. Magdalen Hall O 1656, BA 1660, MA 1662, R. Luddenham, 1674-1714.
[4] William Sherwin of Deptford: Hasted VI, p. 376. His grandson was the patron in 1758, and died in 1786.
[5] (c.1699-1764), Sir Edward Simpson of Fishlake, Yorks, m. Trinity C 1718, LLB 1724, LLD 1728, master Trinity Hall, 1735-64, advocate Doctors' Commons, 1736, chancellor diocese Bath and Wells, 1738, of London, 1747-58, MP for Dover, 1759-64, Consistorial Commissionary general, diocese of Canterbury, 1755-9, Principal, Court of Arches, 1758-64, Commissiary of deaneries of Arches, Shoreham, Croydon, Newington and Risborough, 1758-64.
[6] See p. 75, n. 2.
[7] (1716-?), of Westminster, m. Pembroke O 1734, BA (Balliol) 1738, MA 1741, C. Upper Worton, Oxon, 1741-.
[8] The owner of Davington manor. He died in 1631: Hasted VI, p. 376.
[9] William Lambarde (1536-1601), historian of Kent. Author of *Perambulation of Kent* (1574).
[10] See p. 151, n. 9.

Page 156

D. Ospring

Doddington V. St John Baptist ⟨See Tenham p. 177⟩. AD^n of Cant. Propr. & Patr. Tenths 13–4. Certified 15$^£$. And so augmented by Lot in 1752. But AD^n Parker[1], who was such from 1670 to 1687 reserved to it from his Lease of the Great Tithes ⟨dated 2 Aug. 27 Car. 2. by ABP {Sancrofts influence} Sheldons influence⟩ 40$^£$ or 42$^£$ a year. See Kennet of Impropriations p. 306 & the Vicarial Tithes are worth 30$^£$ a Year. 50 Ho. Mrs Thornicroft[2] of Sharsted, [a maiden Lady, of good Fortune]. 3 Families of Gentry besides. Repeated attempts by Ld Teynhams[3] Family at Linsted to make Converts here to Popery, without success. He hath settled his Gamekeeper & wife here, perverted before. V. hath precautioned his People publickly & privately, & given Books. Service once on Sundays, & the other part of the Day at Newnham p. 168. the adjoyning Parish. Prayers on all Festivals & Fasts, W & Fr. in Lent, & all Passion Week. Cat. exp. in Lent & religious Tracts given away. 4 Sacr. from 40 to 60 Com. Dr Lisle[4], AD^n of Cant. gave by Deed an Exchequer Order for 14$^£$ a Year ⟨for 99 years⟩ for teaching poor Ch^n in Doddington & Newnham. AD^n for the time Visitor of the Trust, who hath a Copy of the Deed. 40^s a Year to the Church, out of 20 Acres of Mrs Thornicrofts Land, which Acres pay no Tithes. Annuities of 3–10–0 to the poor. All properly applied. AD^n Lisle also established in the V. Ho. a small parochial Library, a Catalogue of which AD^n Head hath. Church & Chancel extremely neat & handsome. Ho. & Out Ho. very good, chiefly by Mr Shove. Glebe ½ Acre. 6 Bells. These two Gifts of AD^n Lisle were out of the Estate of Mr Dan. Somerscales[5]. V. here for 43 years ending 1737, who built the Vicarage Ho. & made the AD^n his Trustee for charitable Uses. See his Epitaph[6] & an acct of this matter. In 1669 V. Ho. was irreparably gone to ruine Entry B. II. 183.

Henry Shove[7] MA V. 7 Sept. 1737. V. of Rainham p. 224. Resides chiefly here, sometimes there. Seq. also of Newnham p. 168 {Cur of Bredhurst p. 236}. Hath a Curate from London for this Winter Nov. 1767.

Henry Shove[8] M.A. V. Oct^r: 30 1772.

Francis Dodsworth[9] Master of Arts V. December 10 1773. resides.

Dodsworth Fra. Cur. V. of Minster p. 264. Resides 1764, 1765. Serves this & Newnham p. 168.

1758 Conf. 62. 1762. 14. 1766. 29.

---

[1] Samuel Parker (1640–88), of Northampton, m. Wadham 1657, BA 1660, MA (Trinity) 1663, DD (Lit Reg) 1671, president Magdalen O, 1687–8, R. Chartham, 1667, R. Ickham, 1672, archdeacon of Canterbury, 1670–88, master of Eastbridge hosp, 1673, preb of Canterbury, 1672–85, bishop of Oxford, 1686–8.

[2] Ann Thornicroft (1701–90): Hasted VI, p. 310.

[3] See p. 152, n. 3.   [4] See p. 27, n. 3.

[5] (1651–1737), of Croxton, Lincs, m. Jesus C 1673, BA 1677, MA 1780, V. Hinxton, Cambs, 1682–94, V. Doddington, 1694–1737, V. Newnham, 1694–1737.

[6] LPL, MS Secker 3, f. 153.

[7] (16?–1771), of Gatton, Surrey, m. Jesus C 1713, BA 1717, MA 1720, V. Rainham, 1723–72, R. St Margaret's, Canterbury, 1727–37, V. Doddington, 1737–71.

[8] See p. 1, n. 7.

[9] (1731–1806), of Thornton Watlass, Yorks, m. St John's C 1748, BA 1752, MA 1755, V. Silkstone, Yorks, 1756–7, R. Hollingbourne, 1757–73, V. Minster in Thanet, 1757–73, V. Doddington, 1773–1806, treasureship of Salisbury, 1760–1806.

Page 157
Eastling ⟨al. Easling⟩ R. S[t] Mary. Earl of Winchelsea[1] P. K[s] books 16[£]. Wake, first 200, then 120[£]. Now called 200 ⟨AD[n] 160⟩. A village of 10 Ho. 20 more dispersed. Farmers &c. An Absenter, who will use no Prayer, but the Lords Prayer, & confines his Religion to repeating that often, & reading the Bible in his Chamber. Whole Service on Sundays. Prayers Ash W. good Fr. Chr. Day. R. could not get a Congregation on other Holydays. Cat. exp. in Lent. 4 Sacr. Com. from 15 to 36. Produce of 20[£] laid out in Land. given to the Poor. Church & Chancel very decent & handsome. Ho. very good. Outho. in very good Order. A handsome Garden. Glebe 29 Acres. 6 Bells.

Maurice Gleyre[2] R 2 May 1752. Resides constantly in the Parsonage Ho.
Anthony Shepherd[3] D.D. Rector 1782. resigned it & was again instituted 1792.

M[r.] Tattersall[4] Cur. Sal. £50.

1758 Conf. 44. 1762. 18. 1766. 14.

[1] See p. 5, n. 4. [2] R. Eastling, 1752–82.
[3] (1721–96), of Kendal, m. St John's C 1740, BA 1744, MA (Christs) 1747, BD 1761, DD 1766, fellow of Christs 1746–83, Plumian professor of Astronomy, 1760–96, V. Croxton, Norfolk, 1756–8, V. Bourn, Cambs, 1758–63, R. Barton Mills, Suffolk, 1763–82, R. Eastling, 1782–96, R. Hartley Wespall, Hants, 1792–6, master of mechanics to George III, 1768–96, canon of Windsor, 1777–96.
[4] John Tattersall. See p. 57, n. 12.

Page 158
D. Ospring
Faversham al. Feversham V. S[t] Marys. Belonged to S[t] Austins Mon at Cant. DCh. Cant P. Tenths 2-13-9. Certified 38-18-3. ⟨140[£] in 1724⟩. Now called 120[£] ⟨See below⟩. Comprehends the N. side of the Village of Ospring. In all, abt 400 Ho. Three Quakers. The Parishioners constant at Church. Whole Service on Sundays. Prayers W. Fr. all Holydays & Passion Week. Cat. W. Fr. in Lent. Ch[n]. sent. Sacr. 3 great Festivals. Com. 130 or 140 & first Sunday of every Month. Com. abt 60. Qu. Eliz. founded a free-school, endowed it with Lands, now rented at 82[£] a Year, & put it under the Care of the Corporation ⟨See below⟩. Tho. Menfield[1] gave the Corporation 1000[£] for 6 Almshouses for 6 poor Widows each to have 4[£] a Year. Tho. Napleton[2] Esq[r] gave them Lands, now rented at 60[£] a Year, for an Hospital for 6 poor old men, to have each 5[£] a Year & a new Coat every 2[d] Year. Two Charity Schools for 10 Boys & 10 Girls. The Boys learn Reading, Writing, Arithmetick: the Girls Reading, Sewing, Knitting: both cloathed. Supported by Subscriptions, Benefactions, & 6[£] of the Offertory Money. Other Charities to Church & Poor, see in Lewis's Antiquities of Faversham. Since it was published, M[rs] Frances Pysing[3] gave a large Benefaction for painting the Altar piece, & providing a Communion Table. M[r] Stephen Smith[4] left 200 to purchase an Annuity: out of which 20[s] to the Vicar for Prayers at 6 on Christmass Eve, 20[s] to the Clerk, Organist, Sexton & Bellringers, & 5[s] for Candles: the rest to the poor. John Marsh[5] Esq[r] gave the Interest of 2000[£] to the free Drudgers of this Town [Fishers with Oyster Nets]. See other Benefactions to the Poor & Charity schools. A Paper in ABP Wakes 2[d] vol. at Ch. Ch. saith, the V. of Faversham is in a Way of being worth 300[£] a year

from Hops only. The Town is rich: chiefly from the Corn Trade, partly by Oysters. School-master, Mr Hill[6] ⟨salary 60^f, no Boys. AD^n. All Souls Coll P⟩: absent for some time at Yalding, Dioc. Rochester, which he held for a minor: & then Mr Giraud[7] Junr supplied his place. Church very noble: 2000^f lately laid out upon it by the Parishioners. Chancel the same. Ho. very good. Mr Marsh[8] hath laid out 400^f upon it, & built a new Stable. Glebe 1½ Acre. 8 Bells. I think Mr Giraud[9] of Westwell is come to be Schoolmaster here. 100^f heretofore: now scarce 40^f.

17{56} 65 Wm Ragan, Journeyman Taylor, – Barnes Journeyman Shoemaker, James Rumley who hath lately taken the Ship Inn, papists.

[1] [Mendfield], mayor of Faversham, in his will of 1614. In 1760 the corporation spent £100 on repairs: Hasted VI, p. 359.
[2] By his will of 1721: ibid., p. 360.
[3] When the church was rebuilt in 1754. The rebuilding cost £2, 300, on top of which £400 was spent on a new organ, £100 on ornaments and £90 on the great chancel 'so that the whole of it is now made equal to, if not the most elegant and spacious of any parish church in this county, and is extensive and spacious enough to afford convenient room for all the parishioners of it.': ibid., p. 363.
[4] Will of 1729: ibid., p. 361.   [5] Will of 1751: ibid.
[6] Daniel Hill (1713–1805), of Dinnington, Somerset, m. All Souls 1731, BA 1735, MA (Trinity C) 1769, C. Ospringe, 1735, V. East Malling, 1762–1805, R. Addington, 1768–1805.
[7] See p. 75, n. 2.
[8] (1709–78), of St Margarets at Cliffe, Kent, m. St John's C 1727, CCCC, 1728, BA 1732, MA 1756, V. Faversham, 1744–78, minor canon of Canterbury.
[9] See n. 7.

Page 159
Faversham continued.

Richard Marsh[1] BA 4 July 1744. Resides constantly in V. Ho. [Good, esteemed].
William Chafy[2] A.M. Vicar. Decr 8: 1778.
Richard Halke[3] A.M. Vicar 1780 resides.

1758 Conf. ⟨here 843. Of this Parish 267⟩. 1762. Conf here 461. Of this Parish 165. 1766 Conf. here May 22. 510. Of this Parish, 164.

George Naylor[4] A.B. Cur. Sal 50 Guineas lic. 1792.

[1] See p. 158, n. 8.   [2] See p. 44, n. 3.   [3] See p. 151, n. 9.
[4] (17?–1854), of Middlesex, m. St John's C 1786, BA 1790, C. Faversham, 1792, V. Bramfield, Suffolk, 1795–1854, R. Byton, Heref., 1806–54, R. Rougham, Suffolk, 1853–4.

Page 160
D. Ospring
Goodneston by Faversham R. St Bartholomew. Mr Pixley & Mr White[1] P. by Turns Ecton ⟨vid. Reginald Pole, archbishop of Canterbury, 1556–8. f. 82⟩. Mary Pixley presented last[1)]*. Tenths 10–3. Certified 30^f. Now 40^f)*. 8 Ho. besides the Parsonage. Service once every other Sunday. Cat. only before a Confirmation. No exp. 4 Sacr. 6 or 7 Com. [At the Visitation 1758 Service once

every Sunday was directed. See Letters afterwards[2]. Sept. 1759 Still only once a fortnight: AD[n] Heads Letter Sept. 22. 1759. He adds, that Mr Norris lets it for 16[£] a year, besides the Curates Salary ⟨see below⟩, Repairs &c, & can scarce maintain his Family. Church & Chancel small & in good Repair. Ho. shamefully bad ⟨presented 1764⟩. A pretty good Barn. Glebe 3 Acres. 1 Bell.

[1)]* M[r] Ladd[3], son to Mr Ladd, once a Silversmith at Canterbury, who now lives at Boughton. Mr Ladd saith Mr Norris gave a Lease, of 40 years, of the Tithes, at a Rent presented to him & that he expects the next Rector to do the same, w[ch] one Clergyman hath refused. D[r] Potter.

Recommended to S[r] Ph. Boteler, but not augmented by him.

Cha. Norris[4] BA R 10 Feb. 1730. See p. 43. Resides at his V. of Brabourn 20 miles off. Died 19 Jan. 1767.

Athelstan Stephens[5] see p. 163 Apr. 29. 1767 pres. by Michael Lade of Faversham Esq[r] Patr. for this turn. He hath one turn in three. Required service every Sunday.

Rector does his own duty.

W[m] Henry Giraud[6], who is the elder, Cur. 14–14–0 & Surpl. Fees. V. of Graveney ⟨p. 161⟩, a mile off, where he lives.

1758 Conf 9. 1762. 3

[1] Thomas Pixley and Daniel White: Hasted VI, p. 554.
[2] LPL, MS Secker 3, ff. 176–7, Secker to Norris, 24 August 1758.
[3] Two turns were sold with the manor to Michael Lade in about 1748. He died in 1778: Hasted VI, p. 553.
[4] See p. 43, n. 1.
[5] (1736–1805), of Berthdee, co. Montgomery, m. Oriel, BA 1758, R. Goodnestone, 1767–1805, V. Graveney, 1769–1805.
[6] (169?–1769), son of a Waldensian minister of Torre Pelice, m. Gonville and Caius 1713, BA 1717, master of Faversham school, V. Graveney, 1727–69. His son, Francis Frederick, see p. 75, n. 2.

Page 161

Graveney V All S[ts]. Belonged to the Mon. of S[t] Mary Overy in Surrey. Now ABP Propr. & P. ⟨Adv. granted by Qu. Mary⟩. Tenths 1–4–0. Certified 50[£]. So called now. 23 straggling Ho. 25 Families. The Lord of the Manour, a Yeoman. His Ho. nearest the Church: 3 more within Gun shot. The V. Ho. further. An Absenter, who pleads, that he & his wife are always quarrelling. A Farmer & his Wife have not been at Church these 12 Years, reason unknown, [hath not V. asked?] yet send their Ch[n] & Servants. Service once. Prayers on Chr. Day & Easter Monday. [Shd be on good Fr. also]. When V. catechizes [doth he not every year?] it is in Summer for 4, 5 or 6 Sundays, in the Chancel after Service, for he doth not hear well. 4 Sacr. Not above 8 Com. [Doth V. exhort them?]. ⟨No Offertory⟩. 3 Acres of Land, let for 2–7–0 given, unknown by whom, or whether to church or poor, added to the Church Sess. Church in pretty good, chancel in good order. Ho. neat. Barn in good Order. Glebe 1¾ Acre. 3 Bells. V. hath ⅓ of the Corn Tithes, which he lets for 16[£] a year: but they are worth 18[£] or 20[£]. See Letters 1763.

W[m] Henry Giraud[1] BA V. 26 June 1727. Lives here in V. Ho. Cur. of Goodneston p. 160. One of the 10 poor vicars.

Athelstan Stevens[2] V. May 25th 1769. does his own duty.

1758. Conf. 22. 1762. 13. 1766. 18

[1] See p. 160, n. 6.   [2] Ibid., n. 5.

Page 162
D. Ospring
Harty R [now C.] ⟨S[t] Thomas the Apostle⟩. Julio de Newham[1] gave to the Nuns of Davington Ecclesiam de Herteia by the Consent & Advice of ABP Todvild Reg. Warham f. 158 b. Probably Todvild stands for Theobald[2] who there confirms the Grant, as he was made ABP in 1138. No Admissions to Harty are found in the Register books. Rich[d] Thornhill[3] Esq[r] is called Patron in Wake. Now John Sawbridge[4] Esq[r]. K[s] books 20–60½. Certified 20[f]: which Mr Sawbridge pays, deducting of the full Land Tax: but saith the Stipend due is only 20 Marks ⟨see below⟩. 11 Ho. of which 5 are uninhabited, & 5 rented by out-dwellers. Service once a month. Cat. exp. betw. Easter & Whits. Seldom more than 2 or 3. 1 Sacr. 6 or 7 Com. [Cur. promises, that there shall be Service once a Fortnight, when he can provide for it. In ABP Wakes time were 3 Sacr. & in ABP Herrings.]. Church & Chancel very small dirty & bad. No Ho. 1 Bell. Augmented by Lot with 200[f] Dec. 1765 & with 400[f] by Sir Ph. Boteler & Qu[s] Bounty 1767.

Jude Holdsworth[5] Cur. R. of Hinxhill p. 122 & of Ruckinge p. 139. Died Oct 1759.
Wanley Sawbridge[6] licenced 1760. See 151, 178. Worth 10000[f], Oct. 1762. Good.

Jos. Murthwaite served it. 10–6 each Sunday. Cur. of Minster in Shepey p. 218, 219 & of Leysdown p. 215. Dead.
James Allanson[7] serves it. Cur. of East-Church p. 209 where see. Mr Sawbridge gives him the whole Income, & he is to serve it once a fortnight. He doth so, May 1760. M[r]. Martin[8] Cur. Sal £20

1758 Conf. 8.

[1] Hasted notes Fulke de Newnham in 1153: VI, p. 373.
[2] Archbishop of Canterbury, 1138–61.
[3] He sold the manor of Harty together with the advowson to Jacob Sawbridge in 1704: Hasted VI, p. 282.
[4] See p. 4, n. 2.   [5] See p. 96, n. 6.   [6] See p. 151, n. 8.
[7] [Allenson] (1717–?), of Aldenham, Herts, m. University 1741.
[8] Probably David Martin, See p. 52, n. 5.

Page 163
Hernhill V. St Michael. Belonged to the Monastery of Feversham. Now ABP Prop. & P. ⟨Adv. granted by Qu. Mary⟩. Exempt from AD[n]. K[s] Books 15[f], Certified 58[f]. Wake 50[f]. Now 130[f] ⟨AD[n] 100[f]. ABP pays 13–4, reserved in his Lease. 130[f] in Disp. IX. 94⟩. 60 Ho. dispersed. The chief Collections of them are, Staple Street, Downs Forestall, & Dargate. Mr Steph. Riou, Lieut. in Horse Guards, excused from Service. Mr Kingsland Venner, married M[rs] Rious Sister,

hath a decent Fortune, lives at Bosinden, an extra parochial Place, the only Dissenter here, & sometimes comes to Church: Mr Squires[1], Tenant to Dr Salmon of Tavistock, Lessee of the great Tithes. Service here as at Boughton Blean p. 152, which see. Only as the Children of Hernhill go to school in Boughton Parish, they are catechized there in Lent, with the same Convenience as if at Hernhill. Com. here abt. 30. This & Boughton had gone together for Ages, till Mr Heaton[2] resigned this for Ivechurch. Several small Benefactions to the Poor, which see. [1759 Service twice]. Church & Chancel neat & handsome. Ho. & out Ho. new by Mr Heaton. Glebe 12 Acres. 3 Bells.
Held by Disp with Boughton Blean p. 152. Residence as usual there 1704 V. 171.

Charles Hall[3] DD V. 1 Feb. 1758. Domestick Chaplain to the ABP & Fellow of CCC Oxon. Vacant by Cession 23 Apr. 1760.
Tho. Hebbes[4] MA V. 26 Apr. 1760. Lecturer of Kensington, where he resides by my Leave. Rec. by Princess Amelia[5].
Henry Poole[6] Clerk A.M. Vicar. Febry 1: 1777.

Robt Ingram[7] Cur. 20^£ & Surpl. Fees. Now 40^£ Cur. of Boughton Blean p. 152, 153. Perp. Cur. of Bredherst p. 236. Gone.
Athelstan Stephens[8] BA of Oriel Coll. ord. pr. Dec. 21. 1760. 1. Apr. 1767 required full Service
Henry Phillips[9] Clerk A.B. Curate, Licensed May 26: 1777 with a Salary of £40 p ann.
Mr Moore[10]. Cur. Sal. £30. Lic by Archdeacon.

1758 Conf. 28 1762. 28. 1766. 20

[1] Thomas Squire, built Bessborough house: Hasted VII, p. 19.
[2] Henry Heaton. See p. 46, n. 2.
[3] (1718–74), of Basingstoke, m. CCCO 1733, BA 1737, MA 1741, BD 1749, DD 1757, V. Hernehill, 1758–60, R. All Hallows, Bread Street, 1760–2, R. and dean Bocking, 1761–74, R. Southchurch, Essex, 1764–74.
[4] (1733–1776), of London, m. Trinity C 1753, BA 1756, MA 1759, chaplain Trinity, 1758–60, V. Hernehill, 1760–76).
[5] (1711–86), the daughter of George II.
[6] (1744–1810), of Llanyhangell, co Merioneth, m. Jesus O 1760, BA 1763, MA 1775, R. Whitchurch, Edgware, Middlesex, 1776–1810, V. Hernehill, 1777–1810, chaplain to prince of Wales.
[7] See p. 99, n. 14.   [8] See p. 160, n. 5.
[9] (1754–), of Carmathen, m. Jesus O 1773, BA 1777, C. Hernehill,1777.
[10] Charles Moore. See p. 140, n. 4.

Page 164
D. Ospring
Leveland R. St Laurence. Geo. Monson Watson[1] Esqr P. Tenths 8^s. Certified 30^£. Now 60^£ ⟨AD^n 20^£⟩. 8 Ho. Service once on Sundays & on Chr. day & good Friday. Cat. exp. to 2 Ch^n. 4 Sacr. 10 Com. Church small, & in tolerable Repair, & chancel. Ho. a mean Cottage in tolerable Repair. Glebe 4 Acres. 1 Bell.

James Barnard[2] MA R. 21 Sept. 1726. R. of Badlesmere p. 151. where he resides. Non compos. The Living sequestred. Dead before Feb. 14. 1763.

Will. Gurney[3] MA R. May 2 1763. R also of Badlesmere p. 151 ⟨See there⟩. Was V. of Selling p. 174. Serves both his Livings.

Benj. Dawney[4] Cur. V. of Stalesfield p. 176. betw. 3 & 4 miles off. Salary not mentioned. Told the last ABP, that he wd lay it out on V. Ho. there.

Consolidated with Badlesmere pa. 151.

1758 Conf. 5. 1762. 4. 1766. 4

[1] See p. 151, n. 1.   [2] Ibid., n. 4.
[3] Ibid., n. 5.   [4] (?–1779), V. Stalisfield, 1748–79.

Page 165

Linsted V. St Peter & St Paul. AD^n of Cant. Propr. & P. ⟨See Tenham p. 177⟩. K^s books 8–3–11½. Certified 70–12–4. Now called 70$^£$ ⟨90$^£$ AD^n. 100$^£$ Mr Shove[1]⟩ of which 10$^£$ is a Pension reserved by AD^n Parker[2]. See Doddington p. 156. A Hamlet called Greenstreet. 80 Ho. Ld Teynham[3]. All his Family, except 2 or 3 Servants, Papists. & 2 or 3 whole Families besides. Mr Best[4] saith 12 have been perverted within this Year. & that V. is deaf & knows it not. But on writing to him to inquire, he persists, that none have for a great while past, but a Servt boy of L^d T^s two Years before, & a dying poor man, to whom V. had given the Sacram^t. Threatened on this, they are cautious. In L^d T^s Ho. a Chapel, & Priest called Colgrove. A Popish BP lately there for a Fortnight. Sir Cha. Molloy[5] hath a Ho. & Estate here, & resides 3 or 4 months in the Summer. He is a Justice of Peace, & the Papists in Awe of him. Some absenters. Hopes of their Amendmt. Service once on Sundays: the other part at Kingsdown, the next Parish, Churches scarce two miles asunder, as immemorially. Prayers on all State Holydays, every Day in Passion Week, & on Easter Monday. V. cannot cat. much because deaf: but will contrive, that it shall be done more. 5 Sacr. From 30 to near 60 Com. V. Ho. not good, but in good Repair. V. the only one who hath resided for a Century past. 20^s a Year used to be paid out of a Farm in the Parish. The Landlord now refuses it: & the Parish cannot prove their Right. Church & 3 chancels, very handsome. One belongs to Ld Teynham, one to Mr Huguesson[6]. Ho. good, but wants some Repair. No outho. Glebe, an Orchard & Field, 2 Acres. 5 Bells.
1766 Ld Teynham & his Family gone. Still 40 Papists left. So the Vicar. I am told, that there are many more, & that Ld T. is returning. At least his priest continues there. Feb. 18. 1767 Ld Teynham & Family abt 16, Mr Roper[7] and Family abt 6. Other Adults chiefly poor 23. Their ⟨young⟩ Children 14. Turn over

[1] Henry Shove, see p. 156, n. 7.   [2] Samuel Parker, ibid., n. 1.
[3] See p. 152, n. 3.   [4] Probably Thomas Best of Chilston. See p. 54, n. 2.
[5] Knighted in 1743.   [6] William Western Hugessen (1735–64).
[7] Philip Roper, uncle to Lord Teynham.

Page 166
D. Ospring
Linsted continued

John Irons[1] MA V. 28 July 1726. Resides constantly, very near his V. Ho. which is not convenient for his Family, & uses a great Part of it. Cur. of Kingsdown p. 214 〈resigned 1765〉. Good. One of the 10 poor Vicars. Infirm & unfit for Duty: must have a Curate. Promises to have one before Mich 1766 Dead Nov. 1766.
Henry Shove[2] MA V. 11 Nov. 1766. Will put the House in order & be resident in it by the End of next Summer: & then will quit Sutton by Dover. In the mean time will have a resident Curate here. M[r] Penry[3] hath served it with Bapchild & Tong: & comes to reside here at LD. 1767. Accepted his Resignation Oct. 13. 1767.
Hopkins Fox[4] MA. V. 14 Oct. 1767. Desires Jan. 1768 to serve Teynham with it. Allowed. Hath laid out much, & will more, on V. Ho. Vicar resides part of the year & does duty himself. M[r] Mackenzie[5] Cur. for the other part.
Stephen Tucker[6] A.M. Vicar 1793.

1758 Conf. 75. 1762. 34. 1766. 27

[1] (1689-1766), of Gosworth, Oxon, m. Wadham 1704, scholar 1704, BA 1707, MA 1710, fellow, 1711-31, BD 1729, V. Lynsted, 1726-66.
[2] See p. 1, n. 7.
[3] Edward Penry. Was a dissenting minister, who had been educated at Doddridge's academy in Northampton. V. Bapchild, 1765-98, poor vicar, 1789, C. Rodmersham, 1790.
[4] See p. 15, n. 11.
[5] Probably William Mackenzie, C. Eastling, 1784, R. Smarden, 1793-1821.
[6] See p. 129, n. 3.

Page 167
Luddenham R. S[t] Mary. The King P. Kings books, 12-8-4. Pension to the Abbey of Feversham 3-6-8 Ecton. Wake 80[f]. ABP Herrings book 90[f]. AD[n] Head thinks 100[f] or more. 14 Ho. Service once on Sundays. [Said in ABP Wakes & ABP Herrings books to be twice. R. complied very readily to have it so now.]. No Prayers on Holydays [Qu. Chr. Good Fr. Ch[n] & Servts not duly sent to be cat. 4 Sacr. 6 Com. [Too few]. Church & chancel small, pretty clean. Ho. mean, wants Repair. Barn in pretty good Order. Glebe 1½ Acre. 1 Bell.

Wheler Twyman[1] R. 20 May 1755 V. of Sturrey, p. 44 near which he resides, abt 15 miles from hence.
William Gurney[2] A.M. Rector 1780.
John Tucker[3] A.M. Rector 1784.

Will Gurney[4] Cur. Deacon. ord. Pr. Sept 24. 1758. 3. 20[f] & Surpl. Fees. Cur. of Sheldwich p. 175. 4 miles off, where he resides. Gone from serving Luddenham.
John Loftie[5] Cur. See Stouting p. 108. Came at Mids. 〈1759〉 to do whole Duty. Qu. Salary. 35[f]. Gone to Germany Sept. 1760, Mr Hill[6] 〈curate〉 of Ospring to officiate till Mich. then another Curate to come.
John Sayer[7] ord pr. by me 1742. 35[f] & Surpl. Fees. Serves also Davington p. 155. Lives at Faversham. Will officiate here twice every 〈other〉 Sunday.

March 1762 Gone or going see AD[ns] Letter March 17. 1762. Gone. M[r] Sawbridge[8] hath served it. He is going.

Mr Row[9], Cur. here & at Norton p. 169. Dismissed.

Frederick Dodsworth[10] at both May 1764. See p. 236. M[r] Bedford[11].

Apsley[12] C. from Oct. 14. 1764. 40[f]. To live at Faversham 2 miles off. Going Apr. 1765.

Fr. Fr. Giraud[13] with Owre 1766.

Mr Halke[14] coming hither. To serve Davington with it. See AD[n] Sept 1766. bapt. July 1. 1744. ord. Deacon 21 Sept. 1766. Gone to Ospring p. 170. Feb. 1767. Oct. 6. 1767 allowed M[r] Penry[15] to serve it with Bapchild for a short time. A person to come for Orders on this Title Tr. S. 1768. AD[n] Vis.

James Coulton[16] BA of Tr Col. C. born Sept 21, bapt Oct 10. 1744, ord D. Tr. S. 1768, ordained priest 18th Dec[r]. 1768. Sal. £40.

1758. Conf. 11. 1762. 10. 1766. 6.

M[r]. Wilson[17] Cur. Sal. £25.

[1] See p. 22, n. 7.   [2] See p. 151, n. 5.
[3] (1758-1811), of Canterbury, Kent, m. Trinity C 1775, scholar, BA 1779, MA 1782, second master King's school Canterbury, 1779–82, headmaster 1782-5, C. Luddenham, 1780, R. Gravesend, 1784–1811, R. Luddenham, 1784–11, PC. Wingham, 1800–11.
[4] See n. 2.   [5] See p. 25, n. 5.   [6] See p. 158, n. 6.
[7] See p. 155, n. 8.   [8] See p. 151, n. 8.   [9] Jacob Row.
[10] (1739–1821), of Thornton Watlass, Yorks, m. Christs 1756, scholar 1756, BA 1760, MA 1764, DD 1784, C. Cleasby Chapel, Yorks, 1766, PC. Bredhurst, 1763–82, C. Calne, Wilts, 1767–82 V. Figelden, Wilts, 1768–, V. Spennithorne, Yorks, 1778–1821, canon of Windsor, 1782, chaplain to earl Shelburne.
[11] See p. 3, n. 4.   [12] See p. 6, n. 5.   [13] See p. 75, n. 2.
[14] See p. 151, n. 9.   [15] See p. 166, n. 3.
[16] (1744–?), of Colchester, m. Trinity C 1764, BA 1769, MA 1772.
[17] Probably Joseph Wilson, C. Ospringe, 1780.

Page 168
D. Ospring

Newnham V. S[t] Peter & S[t] Paul. Belonged to the Priory of Lesnes ⟨See below⟩. Wake sets down M[r] Hulse & Widow Lovelace[1] as Patrons. ABP Herrings book leaves a Blank. Ecton saith, D[r] Ward. Sept. 5. 1623 Richard Ames[2] MA was inst. to it, being vacant by the Resignation of Tho. Mill[3] the last Incumbent, on the Presentation of John Hulkes[4] of Newnham Gent. Reg. Abbot part 2. fol 333 a. And 19 Feb. 1627 Nathanael Chambers[5] MA was inst to it, being vacant by the Resignation or Dimissionem of Richard Amyes, Patron the same ib. p. 354b. And these are said, on search, to be the two last Institutions. It was held by Sequestration in ABP Wakes time, & is now. Tenths 11–3. Certified 15[f] ⟨See below⟩. Now called 20[f]. AD[n] 18[f]. Mr Dawney[6] saith from Mr Lowther[7] V. of Otterden, that it is worth 50 or 60[f]. See below.

33 Ho. Service once on Sundays. Prayers on Fast Days, & in Easter Week on the Day of chusing Parish Officers. Cat. in Lent: & religious books, particularly agst Popery, given away. Of AD[n] Lisles[8] Charity see Doddington p. 156. 9[s], the Rent of an Acre of Land in Westwell, given to the Poor. In Warhams Register fol 158 b. is a Grant, without Date, of the Rectory of Newham to the Nuns of

Davington, made by Julian of Newham. Newnham hath been held by Sequestration with Doddington ever since the Restoration at least. AD[n] Head. Church & Chancel small & decent. Ho. & outHo. small & indifferent but in good Repair. Glebe 1¾ Acre. 4 Bells.
Augmented by Lot & with Sir Ph. Botelers Benefaction 1767.

Henry Shove[9] Sequestrator. V. of Doddington p. 156. within a mile, where he resides & serves both. V. of Rainham p. 224. See p. 156.
Sampson Steel[10] V. 19. Dec[r]. 1771. does his own duty.

1758 Conf. 45. 1762. 1. NB + 10. 1766. 18.

[1] From the early seventeenth century, the Hulse and Lovelace families had had alternate presentations: Hasted VI, p. 420.
[2] Of London, m. Queens' C 1611, BA 1615, MA 1617, V. Newnham, 1623-7.
[3] V. Newnham, 1615-23.   [4] [Hulse]. Died in 1651: Hasted VI, p. 420.
[5] Of Kent, m. Queens' C 1611, BA 1615, V. Doddington, 1619, V. Newnham, 1627.
[6] Presumably Benjamin Dawney, V. Stalesfield, 1748-79.
[7] John Lowther (1714-79), of Isel (Irbey?), Cumberland, m. Queens' C 1731, BA 1737, R. Otterden, 1748-79.
[8] See p. 27, n. 3.   [9] See p. 1, n. 7.
[10] (1744-1803), of Caverswall, Staffs, m. Christs 1767, LLB 1775, C. Newnham and Bredgar, 1770, V. Newnham, 1771-1803, poor vicar, 1774-1803, C. Bredgar (endorsed) 1790, V. Tonge, 1801-1803.

Page 169
Norton R. S[t] Mary. BP of Rochester P. Kings books 10-18-4. Pens. to the Priory of Davington 6-8, of Rochester 10[s] Ecton. Now 120[f] ⟨160 BP Pearce[1]⟩. One Gentlemans Ho. [Huguesson ⟨essen⟩[2] ⟨of Provender Esq[r]⟩, Young, good, was of Wadham]. 5 of Farmers, 5 of Labourers. Service once on Sundays: was twice, but few would come. [R. complied willingly to officiate twice again.]. Prayers on Holy days W. Fr. in Lent, & all Passion Week. No mention of Cat. 4 Sacr. 20 Com. or more. The Parsonage Ho. a very good one. Church & Chancel small, very clean & neat. Ho. in good Order, much improved by Mr Robinson. Out ho. in pretty good Repair. Glebe 28 Acres. 1 Bell. The parish aguish.

Tho. Robinson[3] LLB R. 17 March 1734. ***Resides constantly in the Parsonage Ho. Dead, May 24. 1761.
Tho. Taylor[4] BA Cur. of S[t] Martins in the Fields, ord Pr. by BP Gibson[5] in 1725, inst. May 30. 1761. Hath had a bad Ague, desires to appoint a resident Curate, will be here wn his Health permits. Died Feb. 2. 1765.
John Derby[6] BA R 8 Apr. 1765 will reside. Resides Aug. 1765. Void by cession Aug 1767.
W[m] Strong[7] A.M. R 26 Aug. 1767. Will reside. Resides May 1768.

Mr ⟨Jacob⟩ Row[8] Cur here & at Luddenham June 1762. Not serve both. Was to have here 40[f] a year & Ho. Was pupil to BP Yonge[9]. Drunken & mad. Dismissed 1764.
Dodsworth[10], Fred. serves them May 1764. See p. 236. M[r] Bedford[11] in his Absence.
Charles Allen[12], ord. Pr. by BP Keene[13] 1765.

1758 Conf. 27. 1762. 2 + 14. 1766. 11.

[1] Zachary Pearce (1690–1774), bishop of Bangor, 1748–56, bishop of Rochester, 1756–74.

[2] See p. 165, n. 6.

[3] (1698–1761), of Lastingham, Yorks, m. St John's C 1716, LLB 1722, R. Norton, 1735–61.

[4] Probably (1699–1765), of Coventry, m. Balliol 1718, BA 1722, R. Norton, 1761–65.

[5] Edmund Gibson (1669–1748), bishop of Lincoln, 1716–20, bishop of London, 1720–48.

[6] See p. ii, n. 44.

[7] (1740–1815), m. Trinity C 1758, scholar 1759, BA 1762, MA 1765, fellow 1763–8, R. Norton, 1767–1815, six-preacher, 1778–1815, chaplain to bishop of Rochester.

[8] See p. 167, n. 9.   [9] Philip Yonge. See p. i, n. 1.

[10] See p. 167, n. 10.   [11] See p. 3, n. 4.

[12] (1730–95), of Dorking, Surrey, m. Magdalen O 1746, BA 1766, MA 1766, R. St Nicholas, Rochester, R. Westbere, 1779–95.

[13] Edmund Keene (1714–81), bishop of Chester, 1752–71, bishop of Ely, 1771–81.

Page 170

D. Ospring

Ospring V. St Peter & St Paul. Belonged to the Hospital of Ospring. Now St Johns Coll. Camb. Propr. & P. K^s books 10$^£$ ⟨See below⟩. {Part} ⟨One side⟩ of Ospringe-Street is in Feversham Parish. 76 Ho. & cottages: 12 in the Town of Feversham, 19 in the Street, & adjoyning Water Lane: the rest dispersed. Service once on Sundays [1759 twice]. Prayers W. Fr. in Lent & all Passion Week [& doubtless on Chr. Day]. Ch^n Cat in Lent. 4 Sacr. From 40 to 60 Com. 12–10–0 a year left by different persons to the poor. So applied. Present value 100$^£$ a year. Church very clean & handsome. No steeple. Chancel in good order. Ho. indifferent, wants some Repairs. Stable in good Repair. 10^s Gift to the minister, Glebe 28 Acres. 1 Bell.

Edw. Barnard[1] DD V. 2 Apr. 1756. Master of Eton School: resides there. Gives away most of the Income.
Jeremiah Jackson[2] Clerk A.M. Vicar, May 21: 1777.

Fr. Frederick Giraud[3] Cur. Lives at Faversham p. 158 where see. Cur. of Davington p. 155 & of Owre p. 172. Gone.
Daniel Hill[4], Schoolmaster of Faversham p. 158. 50$^£$. He saith, 40$^£$ & Surpl. fees. Going to be V. of E. Malling p. 353.
Fr. Fr. Giraud[5] above, I think, returned hither Dec. 1762. School master at Feversham.
Robt. Gegg[6]. ⟨Pr.⟩ Cur. of Pembroke Coll. Sept. 1765.
Richd Halke[7] D. from Luddenham p. 167 where see Feb. 22. 1767. Ordained priest 18th Decr. 1768. Sal £40.

Richard Halke Licenced July 11 1770.
Richard Wilson[8] A.B. Curate, Licensed May 31: 1779, Salary £45 p ann.
Joseph Wilson[9] Curate. Sal £45.

1758 Conf. 75. 1762. 38. 1766. 26

[1] (1716–81), of Harpenden, m. St John's C 1735, BA 1739, MA 1742, BD 1750, DD 1756, fellow, 1744–56, headmaster of Eton, 1754–64, R. St Pauls Cray, 1752, V. Ospringe, 1756–77, provost of Eton, 1764, canon of Windsor, 1760, chaplain to king, 1760.

[2] (1750–1828), of Ireland, m. St John's C 1767, BA 1771, MA 1774, R. Manton, Rutland, 1774–1828, headmaster Uppingham school, 1777–93, V. Ospringe, 1777–1814, R. Offord Darcy, Hunts, 1814–28.

3 See p. 75, n. 2.   4 Ibid., n. 6.   5 See n. 3.
6 (1738–?), of Gloucester, m. Pembroke O 1755, BA 1759, MA 1762.
7 See p. 151, n. 9.
8 (1755–1784), of Fulbourn, Cambs, m. St John's C 1772, scholar 1775, BA 1776, MA 1780, C.
   Ospringe, 1779–80, C. Fulbourn, Cambs, 1780. He died in 1784 at his lodgings at Charing Cross
   when he was described as 'chaplain of the *Sampson*, guard-ship'.
9 See p. 167, n. 17.

Page 171

Otterden al. Ottrinden R. S[t] Laurence. Granville Wheler[1], Clerk, P. Kings books 6–14–2. Certified 62–17–10. Now 80[f]. 22 Ho. scatterd. Granville Wheler, Clerk, Otterden. Francis Barrell of Hall Place Esq[r] ***, Tenant to Capt. Chr. Cresswell Payne[2]. One female Absenter, because of a vow made in Passion several years ago, obstinate. Whole service. Prayers on Holydays, W. Fr. when M[r] Wheler is there. Cat. 20 Sundays in the Year: will be exp. 4 Sacr. & when Mr Wheler is there, the first Sunday in each Month. Between 20 & 30 Com. each time. 10[f] every 10th year for the Repair of the chancel: but Taxes deducted. 40[s] a year to the Poor. Church & Chancel new built, very neat, by Lady B. Hastings[3]. Ho. & outho. very good, Handsome Garden, by Mr Lowther[4]. Glebe 17 Acres. 3 Bells. Lic. to exch. part of Ch. yd 1729 Entry B VII. 254.

John Lowther R. 9 Nov. 1748. Resides constantly in the Parsonage Ho. Edward Tymewell Bridges[5] A.M. 1780.

M[r] ⟨Geo⟩ Jones[6], Curate Sal £30. & Surplice fees lic. by Archdeacon

1758 Conf. 23. 1762. 13. 1766. 9

1 (c.1700–71), of London, m. Christs 1717, scholar 1718, BA 1721, MA 1724, fellow 1722, FRS
   1728, R. Leake, Notts, 1737–70, prebendary of Southwell, 1753–70. He purchased Otterden Place
   in 1748, where he carried out experiments in electricity. Patron from 1748.
2 Charles Payne, the owner of Hall-Place died unmarried in 1741. He left his estate to Christopher
   Cresswell, a youth in the family who was later an officer in the army and took on the name Payne,
   dying unmarried in 1764: Hasted V, p. 543.
3 Lady Elizabeth Hastings, the sister of George, earl of Huntingdon and the half-sister of the wife of
   the Rev. Granville Wheler (see n. 1). She left £400 for rebuilding the church in 1739, which, with
   another £500 donated by Wheler, was spent on rebuilding the church in 1753: Hasted V, p. 543.
4 See p. 168, n. 8.   5 See p. 109, n. 7.
6 Possibly George Jones (1760–1803), of St Mary's Pembroke, m. Jesus O 1781, C. Otterden, 1790,
   V. Teynham, 1797–1803, poor vicar, 1797–1803.

Page 172

D. Ospring

Owre al Oare, C. S[t] Peter. ABP P. Certified 7[f]. But rec[d] then 15[f] from the Lease of S[t] Gregorys Priory, to which it belonged: and was augmented by Lot in 1746 with 200[f] ⟨again with 200[f] Dec. 2. 1762. See below⟩. 24 Ho. One Farmer. He the principal Inhabitant. ⟨Income, only 1[f] Easter Off. & Surpl. Dues besides w[t] is above⟩. Service once a Fortnight on Sundays: & for the last two Years on Ch. day & good Fr. Cat on Sundays in Summer. Exp. given to such as can read. 4 Sacr. From 8 to 12 Com. No Offertory. Church & Chancel small, in pretty good Repair. No Ho. 1 Bell. Lic. to serve it, being void by Cession Entry B. II. 132. Again, not sd how void III. 241. Land in Ospringe purchased with 260[f] Apr.

1764. And it is again augmented with above 60$^£$ of ABP Wakes money, & above 130$^£$ of mine, if I live 12 months, making 200$^£$ to wch the Governors will add 200$^£$: & then it must have service every Sunday. Again augm. with 400$^£$ by S^r Ph. Boteler & Qu^s bounty 1767.

Francis Fred. Giraud[1] Cur. ⟨licenced⟩ 27 May 1755. He served Ospring p. 170 & Davington p. 155 with it till Mids 1759 when he went to reside at his Vicarage of Westwell p. 75. where see how he serves this still. 1766 Service every Sunday. By whom? Mr Giraud with Luddenham. See p. 173.

1758 Conf. 5. 1762. 13. 1766. 3

[1] See p. 75, n. 2.

Page 173
Preston by Faversham. V. St Catharine. Belonged to the Mon. of Faversham. ABP P. ⟨not proprietor of gr. Tithes⟩. K^s books 8-12-6. Certified 77-17-11. Now 100$^£$ ⟨AD^n 110$^£$⟩. 17 Ho. One Family of Absenters from Idleness. Service once on Sundays. [1759 twice, with Exp. of Cat.]. Parishioners do not send their Ch^n as they ought, & have not Power to send servants. 4 Sacr. Com. from 12 to 18. Interest of 30$^£$ for teaching poor Ch^n to read. An Acre of Land belongs to the Parish, for what Use unknown: let in 1697 for 99 years at 15^s a Year. Church & Chancel handsome & very clean. Ho. very good, a new Stable, by Mr Sykes[1]. Glebe a Garden & Orchard. 3 Bells.

Geo. Sykes[2] MA V. 13 Oct. 1715. Resides in V. Ho. R. of Rayleigh, Essex, worth 150$^£$ a year. See Mr Girauds Petition. Died June 9. 1766.
Fra. Fred. Giraud[3] BA V. 25 June 1766. To reside here & serve Owre once, if it can be done conveniently: if not, to have a Curate there.

1758 Conf. 41. 1762. 12. 1766. 18

[1] See p. ii, n. 39.   [2] Ibid.   [3] See p. 75, n. 2.

Page 174
D. Ospring
Selling V. St Mary. Belonged to the Mon. of St Austin Cant. Lewis Monson Watson Esqr ⟨now Lord Sondes[1]⟩ P. Tenths 13-4. Certified 37$^£$. Now 50$^£$ ⟨AD^n 60. Ld Sondes 70$^£$⟩. 60 Ho. The Families of Greenstreet & Chambers, the most considerable. Service once on Sundays: twice, as long as there was a Congregation. Ch^n duly cat. 4 Sacr. Abt 60 Com. 100 at Easter. Church & Chancel handsome. Ho. very well, outho. small: both in good Repair. Glebe 5 Acres. 4 Bells. There is a Sellinge D. Lymne p. 140. 1763 May. R. saith, House is bad & in bad repair. AD^n thinks otherwise. 1766 V. lives in it.

John Arnald[2] V. 17 Dec. 1735. Resides constantly in V. Ho. R. of East Langdon p. 183. Cur. of Badlesmere p. 151. Void by Cession, Oct. 1762.
Gurney[3] Will MA V. Jan 25. 1763. C. of Sheldwich just by p. 175 will reside here, & serve Sheldwich with it. Void by Cession May 2. 1763.

Henry Thompson[4] V. May 24. 1763. hath 400^f a yr Estate. Single. Serves Sheldwich p. 175. May 1765.
Richard Halke[5] A.M. Vicar 1784.

Mr Thompson[6] Cur.

1758 Conf. 76. 1762. 24. 1766. 30.

[1] See p. 151, n. 1.	[2] Ibid., n. 7.	[3] Ibid., n. 5.
[4] See p. 38, n. 2.	[5] See p. 151, n. 9.	[6] See n. 4.

Page 175

Sheldwich al. Shelwich. V. St James. Belonged to S^{t}Austins Mon. DCh Cant P. Tenths 13–8. Certified 40^f. Now 50^f. AD^n 40. 65 Ho. Honble Lewis Watson[1] at Lees Court. Service once on Sundays. No Prayers on other Days. [qu Chr. good Fr]. Cat. every other Sunday in Summer. 4 Sacr. abt 30 Com. Lady Visc. Sondes[2] left 100^f, Interest ½ to the poor of Sheldwich, the other half to the Poor of Throwley. Lewis E. of Rockingham[3] gave for that 100^f an Annuity of 4^f a Year, out of a Farm in Throwley called Bellhorn, wch is so applied. Church & chancel in good Order. No Rails. Ho. small, in good Repair, let out to a poor Family. 7^f a Year for 14 Boys schooling, AD^n. 4 Bells.

Jo. Tucker[4] V. 5. Nov. 1757. 2^d Master of Cant. School, 10 miles off. Cur. of Bishopsbourne p. 4 ⟨then at Barham⟩. Quits the Cur at Mich 1762. 1764 R. of Milton p. 42. Cur of Thanington p. 45.
Benjn. Symonds[5] Clerk, Vicar, April 30: 1777.
Matt^h Rutton[6] Clerk ⟨A.M.⟩ Vicar 1781 does his own duty

Will Gurney[7] Cur. 20^f Surpl. Fees. Resides in the Parish. See Luddenham p. 167. Cur of Throwley p. 178.
H. Thompson[8] Cur. V. of Sellling p. 174. May 1765. So 1766, 1767.

1758 Conf. 40. 1762. 23. 1766. 18.

[1] See p. 151, n. 1.
[2] Catherine (c.1658–96), wife of Lewis, 1st earl of Rockingham.
[3] Lewis (1655–1724), MP for Canterbury 1681, MP for Higham Ferrers, 1689, lord lieutenant of Kent, 1705–24, earl of Rockingham, 1714.
[4] See p. 4, n. 10.
[5] (17?–81), 'ten year man' Trinity C 1772, V. Sheldwich, 1771–81.
[6] See p. 146, n. 12.   [7] See p. 151, n. 5.   [8] See p. 38, n. 2.

Page 176

D. Ospring
Stalesfield V. St Marys. Belonged to St Gregorys Priory. ABP Propr. & P. K^s books 5-6-8. Certified 53-18-3. Now 60^f ⟨AD^n 80^f See below⟩. 48 straggling Ho. Joseph Cussans, desperately wicked: an Informer agst Smugglers: will swear any thing. Service once on Sundays, Chr. Day & good Fr. Never more in memory. V. Ho. ½ mile from Church. Yet V. would have read daily Prayers: but could have no Congregation on Week-days. Cat. through whole year or great Part. The Complete Catechist[1] used. 2 Sacr. each Quarter. Com 38 or 40 each

Quarter. Interest of 20^f given by Roger Payne[2] of Otterden Esqr for the Poor. So applied. The Parishioners go the other part of the Day to Otterden ½ mile off. Church in pretty good Repair. Chancel repaired 1759. Ho. made good & a Stable built, by Mr Dawney. Glebe 3 Acres. 1 Bell. The V. demands a Pension of 16–8 from the ABP^s Lease of St Gregorys Priory. I paid for Mr Wilbrahams[3] Opinion which is, that it cannot be recovered. Abt 75^f of late.

Benj. Dawney[4] V. 4 July 1748. Resides constantly in V. Ho. Serves Leveland p. 164. 3 or 4 miles off. Is continually repairing his V. Ho. here with the Salary of that Curacy. 1760 saith he had laid out above 66^f this Year upon it. 1763 Had laid out in 1762 185^f besides 45^f recd for Dilapidations. Not now Cur. of Leveland, but of Throwley p. 178 ⟨Not now 1766⟩. House almost finished 1765 ⟨Finished 1766⟩. Single man. Serves Wichling 1766.

Wanley Sawbridge[5] A.M. Vicar, Mar 23: 1779. resides.

1758 Conf. 32. 1762. 15. 1766. 19.

---

[1] [Anon], *The art of Catechising; or the Compleat Catechist. In four parts. Fitted for the meanest capacities, the weakest memories, the plainest teachers, and the most uninstructed learners* (1691).

[2] By will in 1701. The father of Charles Payne at Otterden, p. 171, n. 2.

[3] Randle Wilbraham (1694–1770), bencher of Lincoln's Inn, 1743, and deputy steward of Oxford University. MP for Newcastle-under-Lyme, 1740–47, MP for Appleby, 1747–54, and MP for Newton, 1754–68. He was highly sought after in ecclesiastical disputes.

[4] See p. 164, n. 4.   [5] See p. 151, n. 8.

Page 177

Tenham V. St Mary. AD^n of Cant Propr. & P. Ks books 10^f. Certified 63–3–4. Now 70^f ⟨AD^n 90^f See below⟩. 2 Hamlets: 60 Ho. A Methodist Teacher, name unknown, was here a while ago: but without any lasting effect. Service once on Sundays. Prayers on good Fr. [qu. Chr. Day]. It is said there was a Chapel, near the Church. Cat. exp. in Lent. 4 Sacr. abt 60 Com. 10^f a Year pd to V. out of the Parsonage. 40^s a Year given to the poor by Mr Marshall[1] of Buckland. There hath been no Offertory: but V. intends, that there shall. The Air unwholesome. Church & chancel large & handsome. Ho. pretty good, in good Repair. No outho. 6 Bells. Very unhealthy. AD^n

Mr Lewis in his folio ⟨Ms⟩ Parochial Book in the Lambeth Library, saith, the Church of Tenham with the Chapels of Doddington, Lynsted, Stone & Iwade, was appropriated to the AD^{nry} A.D. 1227 by ABP Langton[2]. Doddington & Lynsted are now Vicarages. Stone cannot mean Stone in Oxney which is far distant. Lewis in Stone p. 173 saith, it was granted to DCh of Ch. Ch. {Oxford} Cant. by H.8 by the mistaken name of Stone juxta Faversham. But probably there was a Stone near Faversham, as none of the other places granted by Langton is far from it. It is within a mile of Faversham: a small part of the walls of the chapel remain. The AD^n leases the great & small tithes of it for 4^f a year & 50^f Fine in 7 years. See his Letter July 26. 1766.

James Allet[3] V. 30 Nov. 1753 V. of Rodmersham p. 225. Doth occasional Duty at Buckland p. 154. Lives at the Rectory of Murston p. 220. for the sake of better Air, at a moderate Distance from these places. 1767 Gone to Sandwich on Acct of his Health. David Martin[4] Cur. Gone Aug.

Wm Lewis[5] from {Queenborough} ⟨Murston⟩ serves this & Rodmersham ⟨p. 225⟩ Sept. 1767. Mr H. Fox[6]. desires to serve it with Linsted March 1768 25^f. William Grainger[7] Clerk A.M. Vicar Nov^r· 13: 1776.
John Cautley[8] A.M. Vicar. Septr. 22: 1778.

M^r. Fox Cur.

1758 Conf. 110. 1762. 22. 1766. 18

[1] See p. 154, n. 2. But Hasted notes that the 40s was given by Thomas Brooke in 1669: VI, p. 262.
[2] Stephen Langton, archbishop of Canterbury, 1207–28.
[3] See p. 154, n. 6.   [4] See p. 52, n. 5.
[5] William Lewis. Perhaps later the chaplain to the East India Company in Bengal.
[6] See p. 15, n. 11.
[7] (1732–78), of Cumberland, m. Christs 1751 BA 1755, MA 1777, R. Salcott Virley, Essex, 1761, V. Teynham, 1776–78, chaplain to lord Cathcart.
[8] (17?–98), of Penrith, Cumberland, m. Pembroke Hall C 1750, BA 1755, MA 1758, R. St Rumbold, Colchester, R. Hollingbourne, 1774–98, V. Teynham, 1778–98.

Page 178
D. Ospring
Throughleigh al. Throwley V. St Mary. Preb. of Rougemer in St Pauls Cath, London, P. K^s books 7-11-8. 45 Ho. & near 70 Families. {Now} ⟨Wake⟩ 50^f, ⟨Now⟩ perhaps 80^f. ⟨AD^n 70^f. See below⟩. Service once on Sundays only, except on extraordinary Occasions. [1759 twice during the Summer, with Exp. of Cat. in Afternoon, & lately in the Form of a Sermon, to bring people: for they are backward ⟨See below⟩. Churches of Eastling & Leveland are near]. Prayers on Festivals & Fasts when a Congregation can be got. 4 Sacr. 70 Com. Offertory was given to poor receiving Parochial Relief, now to poor Com. who receive none. A free School for 12 Ch^n, an Alms Ho. for 5 old Persons, both founded by Sir Tho. Sondes[1]. Governor now, Honble Lewis Watson[2] Esqr. The Master hath a Ho. & 12^f a Year: each of the Poor an Apartmt & 20^s. The Lecture in Form of a Sermon begins to have good Effects. Church & Chancel in good Repair. Ho & outho. pretty good, much improved by Mr Lawson. Glebe 20 Acres. 4 Bells. Income abt 59^f besides 6-6-0 for the House & Orchard. See Mr Lawsons Letters, & Mr Dawneys.

James Lawson[3] BA V. Feb. 19. 1757. died July 1758.
Johnson Lawson[4] V. Aug 8. 1758 brother to the former. Resides here in the Summer, Curate at Finchley in the Winter. Apr. 1760 Hath been very ill: going to {Tunbridge} the sun. Oct. Better: going to Canterbury. Apr. 1761 able to officiate a little here. Resides, 1766. Oct. 1766 Given him Leave to reside in the neighbourhood, to repair his House, for 2 yrs, if he cannot do it sooner. Abt to repair May 1768.
Walter Williams[5] A.M. Vicar Mar 10: 1779.

Will. Gurney[6] Cur. 20^f & Surpl. Fees. Resides at Sheldwich p. 175. Direct near Faversham. Gone. V. of Sellinge.
Sawbridge[7], Wanley C. See p. 162. C of Badlesmere p. 151, just by. Gone.
Benj. Dawney[8] Cur. 1763, 4. V of Stalesfield p. 176, 20^f, now 25^f. Gone.
M^r. Rutton[9]. Cur. Sal. £30 lic. by Archdeacon.

1758 Conf. 70. 1762. 3. NB + 18 1766. 28

[1] Died in 1592.   [2] See p. 151, n. 1.   [3] V. Throwley, 1757–8.
[4] (1719–78), of Canterbury, m. St John's C 1738, BA 1742, MA 1777, V. Throwley, 1758–78, dean of Battle, Sussex, 1776–8.
[5] Probably (1740–1811), of Lampter, co. Pembroke, m. Jesus O 1753, BA 1757, C. Pinner, Middx, 1764, V. Harrow on the Hill, 1776–1811, V. Throwley, 1779–1811.
[6] See p. 151, n. 5.   [7] See p. 151, n. 8.
[8] See p. 164, n. 4.   [9] See p. 146, n. 12.

[Deanery of Sandwich]

Page 179
D. Sandwich
Barfreston al Berfreyston al. Barston R. ⟨S[t] Mary⟩. S[t] Johns Coll. Oxon P. Tenths 15–5. Certified 30[f]. Augm. with 400[f] in 1728. {Qu. if since}. See below. Now called 50[f]. Allowed to be 40[f] clear. 8 Ho. One Family of Anab. Church old. Service once a fortnight. It is near Eythorn, 2 miles from Sibbertswold. Was every Sunday in ABP Wakes time. R. promises it shall now. [{not} done {Sept} Oct. 1759.]. No Ch[n] to Cat. 4 Sacr. 8 or 9 Com. Mr Humphrey Duncalf[1] of London mercht paid 200[f]: & the Queens Bounty 200[f]. This one Augmentation is in Ecton multiplied into four. Church & Chancel small & very old. Chancel wants whitewashing. 2 Bells. Ho. new, but very dirty, & let out to a poor Family. Barn in good Repair. Glebe 9 Acres. 2 Bells.
Proposal for rebuilding Ho. 1703. Entry B. V. 77.

John Chalmers[2] D.D. R. 19 May 1758.
Henry Peach[3] B.D. 1780.
Tho[s]. Luntley[4] LLD. 1780.

Tho. Rymer[5] Cur. V. of Sibbertswold. Dead.
John Max. del' Angle[6] Cur. 20[f]. Cur. also of Walmer p. 201.
Wheler Bunce[7], 20[f]. ⟨Nov. 1761⟩. Cur. also of Nonington p. 18. Good character. Going.
Henry Carter[8] to serve this with Ham p. 186 each every Sunday. Apr. 1765. Doth so 1766. Going.
Mr Shove[9] Jn[r], with Sutton by Dover, p. 198 Mich 1766. Going Mich 1767.
Mr Foote[10] will serve it, May 1768.
M[r] Freeman[11]. Cur.
M[r] Lade[12] Cur 1794.

1758 None. Conf. 1762. 6. 1766. 4

[1] Hasted notes that the president and fellows of St John's contributed: X, p. 77.
[2] (1727–79), of Burstow, Surrey, m. St John's O 1745, BA 1749, MA 1753, BD 1758, DD 1766, R. Barfreston, 1758–79.
[3] (1741–1813), of Whitchurch, Oxon, St John's O 1757, BA 1761, MA 1765, BD 1770, V. Compton St Nicholas, Berks, 1767–80, R. Barfreston, 1780–80, R. West Cheam, Surrey, 1780–1813.

4 (1740–1800), of Hereford, m. St John's O 1759, BCL 1764, DCL 1769, R. Brampton Bryan, R. Barfreston, 1780–1800, preb of Hereford.

5 See p. ii, n. 37.   6 See p. 9, n. 5.   7 See p. 15, n. 10.

8 (17?–1818?), of Kent, m. CCCC 1756, scholar, BA 1760, MA 1763. Perhaps R. Little Wittenham, Berks, 1764–1818.

9 Henry Shove. See p. 1, n. 7.   10 Francis Hender Foote. See p. 54, n. 5.

11 See p. 4, n. 12.

12 (1762–1842), of Boughton, Kent, m. Jesus C 1779, BA 1783, MA (Clare) 1786, fellow Clare 1786, C. Grantchester, Cambs, 1784–5, C. St Martins & St Pauls, Canterbury, 1785–92, R. Knowlton, 1792–1834, R. Ringwould, 1802–8, V. Graveney w. R Goodneston, 1806–7, R. Wickhambreux, 1807–42.

Page 180

D. Sandwich

Bettishanger al. Betshanger R. St Mary. Wm Morrice[1] Esqr P. Tenths 12–5¼. Certified 40$^£$. ABP Herrings book 45$^£$. But R. saith, it is only 40$^£$, out of which Land Tax &c will take 7$^£$ ⟨See below⟩. 3 Ho. No Parsonage Ho. or Convenience for Residence. R. saith, Service used to be but once a month, now once a Fortnight. [1759 once every Sunday.] No Ch^n to be cat. 4 Sacr. 6 Com. Offertory distributed by Ch. W^n. Church & Chancel small, clean & in good Repair. No Parsonage Ho. 3 Bells. 1763 R. saith he lets the tithes of Great Betteshanger for 40$^£$ a yr, & they are rated to the Land Tax at 29$^£$. The Tithes of little Betteshanger & Finglesham are leased by the ABP. The Lessee values them at 70$^£$: they are rated to Land Tax at 42$^£$. No Glebe. 1765 The R. hath been offerd 60$^£$ for the Parsonage: but will not take it out of the Hands of his patrons Tenant.

John James[2] BA R. 22 Dec. 1743. R. of Deal p. 181. where he resides. Serves it from Deal once a fortnight & omits Service there. Cannot get a Curate here till Ripple is filled.

John Kenrick[3] Clerk A.M. Rector April 3^d: 1776. does his own duty.

James Morrice[4] A.M. Rector 1793.

John Maximilian De l'Angle[5] Cur. Also Cur. of Walmer p. 201. Resides at Goodneston near Sandwich p. 13 [I suppose with his Father. But it is called 3 & must be near 6 miles from Bettishanger, & 9 from Walmer. Salary was 10$^£$ for serving here once a fortnight.

Will Rogers[6] C. R. of Ripple p. 192. 1764. Serves each once. Dead.

Henry Shove[7] Junr C. also C. of Sutton p. 198. Lives here serves both cannot get a Ho. Leaves both.

Montagu Pennington[8] A.M. Cur. Sal. £25. lic. by Archdeacon

1758 Conf. 2. 1762 None set down. 1766 3

1 The advowson was alienated to Salmon Morrice in 1730. He died in 1740 and was succeeded by his son William, who died in 1758, to be followed by his son William, who died in 1787: Hasted X, p. 46.

2 (1718–76), of Rochester, Kent, m. Oriel 1735, BA 1739, R. Betteshanger, 1743–76, PC Wingham, 1744–56, R. Deal, 1755–76.

3 (1731–93), of Llangernew, co. Denbigh, m. Brasenose 1750, BA 1754, MA 1761, R. Ripple, 1770–93. R. Betteshanger, 1776–93. In 1787 he became patron of Betteshanger.

4 (1740–1815), of Betteshanger, Kent, m. Christ Church 1758, BA 1762, MA 1767, V. Flower, Northants, 1777–1815, R. Betteshanger, 1793–1815.

[5] See p. 179, n. 6.   [6] R. Ripple, 1764–67.   [7] See p. 256. n. 8.
[8] (1763–1849), of Mongeham, Kent, m. Trinity O 1777, BA 1781, MA 1784, C. Tunstall and
    Kingsdown, 1785, PC. Walmer, 1786, PC. Sutton, 1789–1835, C. Tilmanstone and Betteshanger,
    1790, V. Westwell, 1803–6, V. Northbourne, 1806, PC. St George's chapel, Deal, 1814–49.

Page 181
Colerede See Sibbertswold

Deal R. St Leonard. ABP P. Exempt from AD^n. Kings book 19-10-0. Now 150^f. Parish divided into upper, middle & lower Deal. 700 Ho. A Presb. Meeting Ho. 35 Families attend there. Teacher, John Say. Anab. meeting Ho. 8 Families. No constant Teacher. Both much diminished. Quakers Meeting Ho. 2 Families. Only Easter Offerings due from them: which R. connives at their not paying. Whole Service. Prayers on Holydays. Cat. once a week in Lent. Sacr. 1st & 3^d Sunday in every month, & on the great Festivals. Abt 80 Com. John Hockley[1] Surgeon left 20^f, the Interest to Cur. of Deal chapel for a Sermon & Sacr. on good Fr. Sev^l small Gifts by him & others, for the Poor. See Deal Chapel p. 182. Church & Chancel in good Repair. Ho & outho. very good. 5 Bells.
1765. When Mr James first had it, he let the Tithes, as he found them, at 80^f a year: the other Profits made 70^f more: the deductions were abt. 20^f. Now he hath taken the tithes himself, & finds them worth 140^f a year: & the Parsonage worth at least 160^f clear. 1767 worth 250^f a year, clear of the Charge of taking the Tithe in kind. AD^n Head Sept. 9.

John James[2] MA R. 18 Sept. 1755. Resides in the Parsonage Ho. & serves the Cure. R. of Bettishanger p. 180, where see.
William Backhouse[3] D.D. Rector Jan: 13: 1776, resides.
Edwd Beckingham Benson[4] A.M. 1788.
John Barnes Backhouse[5] A.M. 1795.

1758 Conf. 67. 1762. Conf here 235. Of this Parish 117 NB. 1766. 158

[1] In 1735: Hasted X, p. 20.   [2] See p. 180, n. 2.   [3] See p. iii, n. 1.
[4] See p. 54, n. 9.   [5] See p. 80, n. 5.

Page 182
D. Sandwich
Deal Chapel St George. Consecrated by ABP Wake, 1715. By the Act of Consecration the Ch W^{ns} to allow 100^f a year to the Chaplain, to be nominated by the ABP. Dr Ducarel.
Wm Squire[1] AM lic. to serve the Cure of St Georges Chapel, annexed to the Parish of Deal 20 Aug. 1716. Entry B. VI. 223. Nic Carter[2] March 26. 1718 on the Cession of Squire p. 264. He saith it is in the ABP^s Patronage. 1765 Dr Carter preaches perhaps once a month. Otherwise Mr Pennington[3] Cur of Sutton p. 198 preaches here twice one Sunday, & V. performs but ½ Service the next, when he officiates once at Sutton. July 1766 Dr Carter to have Mr Apsley[4] see p. 224 & allow him 40^f a year. 1767 Going at Mich. Mr Atkyns[6] Cur Sept 1767. Mr Philips[6].
Thomas England[7] Clerk A.B. Licensed Novr. 11: 1774.

Lockart Leith[8] 1783.
Philip Brandon[9] L.L.B. 1786.

[1] Probably (1654–1738), of Oxford, m. St Edmund Hall 1669, BA (New Inn Hall) 1672, MA 1675, V. Great Misserden, Bucks, 1676, C. St George's chapel, Deal, 1716–18, R. Reculver, 1717–26, V. Herne, 1726–38.
[2] See p. ii, n. 34.
[3] See p. ii, n. 35.
[4] William, m. Merton, C. Rainham, 1765.
[5] Perhaps Francis Atkyns (1720–96), of Renwick, Cumberland, m. Queen's O 1738, BA 1742, MA (Emmanuel) 1770, V. Horsham, Sussex, 1769–96, V. Stymping, 1772–86, R. Poynings, 1786–96.
[6] Probably Robert Phillips, see p. 2, n. 5.
[7] (1719–83), of Haselborough, Somerset, m. Balliol 1738, BA 1741, PC St George's chapel, 1774–1783.
[8] (1759–86), of Deal, Kent, m. Christ Church 1778, BA 1782, PC St George's chapel, 1783–6.
[9] (1733–1814), of Canterbury, Kent, m. Magdalen hall 1773, BCL 1779, PC. St George's chapel, 1786–1814.

Page 183

East Langdon R. S[t] Austin. Countess of Guilford[1] P. Tenths 14[s]. Certified 46[£]. R. saith this is the value now. ABP Herrings book 60 or 70 ⟨See below⟩. 25 Ho. Service once on Sundays. Prayers on Holydays, Cat. in Lent. 4 Sacr. 30 Com. each time R. hath half the great Tithes: L[d] Bolingbroke[2] the other half. Only 3 Sacr. They refuse to have more. Abt 16 or 20 Com. Ch. & Chancel indifferent, want whitening. Ho bad, in tolerable Repair. Barn & Stable want repairing. Glebe 3 Acres. 4 Bells.

John Arnald[3] R. 4 May 1738 V. of Selling p. 174. where see. Void by Cession Oct 1762.
John Ratray[4] R. see p. 86. 25. Jan. 1763 pres. by L[d] Dartmouth[5] & L[d] Bolingbroke Trustees & Lady Guilford.
John Ratray Cur. 26[£]. Resides in the Parsonage Ho. Cur. of Guston p. 86 of River p. 92 & of West Langdon p. 202.
Queteville[6] C. for this once a Sunday & Guston ⟨p. 86⟩ every other Sunday. 26[£] for Whitfield ⟨p. 77⟩ once a Sunday 26th Apr. 1765. See AD[ns] Letters.
John Queteville R. November 20 1772.
Tho[s]. Delannoy[7] Rector 1788.

1758 Conf. See West Langdon p. 202 1762. 18. 1766. 21.

[1] See p. 121, n. 1.   [2] Frederick St John (1734–87), 2nd viscount Bolingbroke.
[3] See p. 151, n. 7.   [4] See p. 86, n. 1.
[5] William Legge (1731–1801), 2nd earl of Dartmouth. First lord of Trade, 1765–6 and 1772–5, secretary for the colonies 1772–5, lord Privy Seal, 1775–82.
[6] See p. 76, n. 8.   [7] See p. 77, n. 4.

Page 184

D. Sandwich

Eastry V. S[t] Marys ⟨with Chapel of Worth al. Word. S[t] Peter & S[t] Paul⟩. ABP P. Exempt from AD[n]. K[s] books 19-12-1. Wake, 80 ⟨with Worth 164[£]. AD[n]⟩. Now called 120[£]. {The Parish} Eastry comprehends 6 Villages: Harenden, Selson, Statenborough, Hay-Lane, Up-down, Venson. 113 Ho. 2 Families of Note, not named. Worth comprehends 3 Villages: Hacklinge-Borough, Hambridge Stone Cross, Fenderland-Borough: & 50 Ho. Service at each once a Sunday: 2 miles asunder. Prayers at the Church on Holydays & W. Fr. in Lent, when Ch[n] are cat. Servants not sent. 4 Sacr. at each. 40 Com. at Church, 20 at Chapel, each time. A Ho. given to the Schoolmaster, for which he teaches 4 boys to read.

Worth-mennis in the Parish of Worth is held by Lease from ABP. It is said in Parl. Survey to be Tithe free excepting 6-8 to the Proprietors of the Parsonage Tithes of Eastry.

Eastry church & chancel handsome & in good Repair. Ho. & outho. almost new, by Mr Harvey. 5 Bells. Word Chapel & Chancel in good Repair, & Ho. 2 Bells.

Rich[d] Harvey[1] V. 9 July 1757 by Exchange with Mr Sam. Herring[2]. Resides in V. Ho. Going to Ramsgate.

Rich[d]. Harvey[3] V. 25 March 1772.

Nehemiah Nisbett[4] Cur Licensed Dec[r]. 22: 1777, with a Salary of £50 p. ann D[r]. Pennington[5] Cur. Sal. £50. lic. by Archdeacon.

1758 Conf. Eastry 77. Worth 33. 1762 Eastry 47. Worth 18. 1766 Eastry 50. Worth 27

[1] (1729-72), of Eythorne, Kent, m. Hertford 1747, BA 1751, V. Eastry, 1757-72.
[2] Of Norfolk, m. Queens' C 1743, BA 1747, MA 1750, fellow, 1748, V. Eastry, 1753-7.
[3] See p. 83, n. 10.   [4] See p. 2, n. 6.   [5] See p. ii, n. 35.

Page 185

Eythorn R. S[t] Peter & S[t] Paul, with Sutton Chapel. Ecton. No Chapel now. Belonged to the College of Maidstone. Ecton. Sir Rob Furnese[1] & Mr Turner[2] of Cant. Patrons alternately. Wake. M[r] Boys[3] P. Ecton. K[s] books 15-12-0. Wake, 120. Now called 140[£]. The Parish consists of 2 Villages, 44 Ho. A few Families of Anab. & a meeting Ho. Teacher, John Knott, in the Neighbourhood. Decreased. Whole Service, & two Sermons, every Sunday. A Sermon on Chr. Day & good Fr. prayers & Cat. in Lent. 4 Sacr. 20 Com. A Master here, who teaches the Ch[n] of this & the neighbouring Parishes, Reading, Writing & their Catechism. Ch. & Chancel in good Repair. 3 Bells. A good Ho. Outhouses in good Repair. Glebe 6½ Acres.

John Minet[4] R. 3 Jan. 1722. Resides constantly in the Parsonage Ho. R. of Little Hardres p. 38.
Francis D'Aeth[5] R. 14 Dec[r]. 1771.
Philip Papillon[6] A.M. Rector. 1784. resides.

1758 Conf. 26. 1762. 16. 1766. 18

[1] (1687–1733?), 2nd Bt, MP for Truro 1708–10, MP for New Romney, 1710–27, MP for Kent, 1727–33.
[2] William Turner owned the manor of Eythorne from 1729.
[3] According to Hasted, the Boys' had sold the advowson in the 1660s: X, p. 68.
[4] See p. 38, n. 1.   [5] See p. 9, n. 4.   [6] See p. 93, n. 6.

Page 186
D. Sandwich

Ham ⟨al. Hamme⟩ R. S[t] George. The King P. K[s] books 5-6-5½. Pens. to the Prior of Ledes 20[s] Ecton. Now 60[£] ⟨See below⟩. 4 Ho. One is Sir Geo. Oxendens[1]: only a single Person in it, except when he comes for a Day or two, twice or thrice in a Year. Another is a Cottage in which lives an Absenter. Service I[st] Sunday in every Month. No Tradition of its being oftener: sometimes seldomer. [Now 1759 every Sunday.]. 4 Sacr. Seldom more than 3 Com. besides R & the Clerk who lives in another Parish. R. saith, the Income is sometimes less, but usually more than 50[£]. Ch & Chancel small & indifferent. No parsonage Ho. Glebe 10 Acres. 1 Bell.

Nic Carter[2] DD. R. 23 Sept. 1734. See Woodchurch p. 150. Resides at Deal, & serves Ham from thence, 4 miles off.
Wheler Bunce[3] R. November 8 1774. does his own duty.

Hen. Carter[4] BA C. ord. Deacon 19 Dec. 1762. 3. Pr. Dec. 18. 1763 {Gone. 1764}. Apr. 1765 to serve this with Barfreston p. 179 each once every Sunday. Going.
Wheler Bunce V. of S[t] Clement Sandwich p. 193.

1758 Conf. 4. 1762 None 1766. 2.

[1] See p. 4, n. 5.   [2] See p. ii, n. 34.
[3] See p. 15, n. 10.   [4] See p. 179, n. 8.

Page 187
Knowlton R. S[t] Clement. Sir Narborough D'Aeth[1] P. K[s] books 6-5-2½. Certified 56-15-11¼. Now 80 ⟨see below⟩. 3 Ho. Sir Narborough D'Aeth, [good, 1200[£] a year]. Service once on Sundays & Chr. Day. Prayers on good Fr. Cat. just after Whits. 4 Sacr. 12 or 14 Com. each time. No Offertory. An Acre of Land in Chillenden, left to the Rector. Ch. & Chancel made very neat by Sir N. D'Aeth. Ho. & outhouses very good. Glebe 8 Acres. 1 Bell. The Tithes let for 55[£], the Glebe & woodland for 7[£]. Ded. Land tax 8[£]. Tenths & other paymts 2[£]. Clear 52[£], 1764.

Francis D'Aeth[2] R 22 Sept. 1753. {V} C. of Chillenden p. 9. Cur. of Beauxfield p. 77. He is also R. of Wittenham Co. Berks & resides 8 months here, & 4 there: when he sends M[r] Lernoult[3], his Curate there, hither. I refused to promise, that I would not declare this void.
July 20. 1761 Going to Berks for 3 months, Mr Bunce[4] son of Mr Bunce[5] of S[t] Steph. Cant. to be here. Good. AD[n]. Hath quitted Wittenham 1764. Saith this & Whitfield, wch see, are but 65[£] clear. Desires to serve Kingston twice & this once. Refused, but promised to give him 10 Guineas a year. So he serves this &

Chillenden p. 9 each once. Oct. 6. 1767 allowed Mr Longley[6] to serve it with Ash, till a better Provision can be made. See below.
Anthony Egerton Hammond[7] A.B. R. 1783 does his own duty.
William Lade[8] A.M. 1792.

W[m] Windle[9] A.M. of Aberdeen P. Cur. Nov. 8. 1767 & at Chillenden p. 9. 25[£] each.

1758 Conf. 7. 1762. 4. 1766. 6

[1] (1705–73), 2nd Bt.
[2] See p. 9, n. 4. He was half-brother to Sir Narborough D'aeth.
[3] See p. 77, n. 3.   [4] Wheler Bunce. See p. 15, n. 10.   [5] See p. 22, n. 3.
[6] See p. 2, n. 2.   [7] See p. 115, n. 6.   [8] See p. 179, n. 12.
[9] See p. 9, n. 7.

Page 188
D. Sandwich
Mongeham great. R. S[t] Martin. ABP P. Kings books 18–5–0. Wake 130[£]. Now 150[£]. 33 Ho. Service once on Sundays so in ABP Wakes time. Will be twice. Cat. in Lent. 4 Sacr. 26 Com. 20[s] a year given by one Samson[1] to buy Coals for the Poor. R is laying out 300[£] on the Parsonage. Church & chancel in pretty good order. Chancel wants paving. Ho. excellent by Mr Herring. Outhouse, will be repaired. 3 Bells. 1765. Anonymous Complaint abt Church. AD[n] saith that as to the main Building it is strong, & in good Condition: that he hath orderd the Bells to be repaired: & he & R. have recommended cieling the Ch. They have lately had Vestry Disputes abt it, & cannot be obliged to it.

John Herring[2] MA R. 18 Jan. 1757. To reside when his House is repaired. [1759 Resides.

John Apsley[3], Cur. whilst R was absent. R. of Ripple p. 192. a mile off. 40[£] & Surpl. Fees. Dead.

1758 Conf. 14. 1762. 16. 1766. 15.

[1] John Sampson, in his will of 1659: Hasted IX, p. 576.
[2] (17?–1802), of London, m. CCCC 1748, BA 1752, MA 1755, fellow, 1754–8, R. Great Mongeham, 1757–1802. Nephew of archbishop Herring.
[3] (1710–64), of Ashford, Kent, m. Oriel 1727, BA 1730, MA 1733, C. Egerton, 1737–43, R. Ripple, 1741–64.

Page 189
Mongeham little R. ABP P. Tenths 11–6. Certified 35[£]. Now 50[£] ⟨augm. 1767 by S[r] Ph. Boteler & Qu[s] bounty⟩. A Hamlet called Stoddel. 12 Ho. 2 Families of Anabaptists. No Church ⟨none in 1663⟩. The Parishioners go to Sutton [a mile off] as to their Parish church. See there p. 198. No Ho. 8 Acres of Glebe.
Tho. Mander[1] inst. 29 Nov. 1714. ABP consents to his reading articles &c in Tilmanston Ch. Entry B. VI. 166.
The Advowson granted by the Crown to the ABP 31 Aug 1 Ed 6. See Chart Misc. vol. 13. N° 21.

Francis Walwyn[2] DD R 18 Jan. 1757. R. of Adisham P. Resides at Canterbury: & allows the Minister of Sutton 5$^£$ a year.
Henry Shove[3] clerck R. June 15. 1770.
John White[4] Clerk R. Octr. 30 1772.
John Lloyd[5] L.L.B. Rector 1789.
Griffith Griffith[6] A.M. Rector 1792.

1758 Conf 10. 1762. 9. 1766. 1.

[1] (1658-1716), of Chipping Warden, Northants, m. Merton 1673, clerk Magdalen 1677-81, BA 1677, MA 1680, chaplain 1681-90, V. Tilmanstone, 1697-1716, R. Little Mongeham, 1714-16.
[2] See p. ii, n. 12.　　　　　　[3] See p. 1, n. 7.　　　　　　[4] See p. 15, n. 12.
[5] (1748-98), of Montgomery, m. Magdalene C 1767, LLB 1786, R. Little Mongeham, 1789-92, R. St Dunstan's in the East, London, 1791-98.
[6] (1757-96), of Dines, co. Merioneth, m. Hertford 1777, BA 1780, MA 1783, R. Edburton, Sussex, 1784-92, R. Isfield, Sussex, 1792, R. Little Mongeham, 1792-96, R. St Mary le Bow, London, 1792-96, archbishop's chaplain.

Page 190
D. Sandwich
Northbourn V. St Austin, with the Chap. of Shoulden St Nicolas. Belonged to the Mon. of St Austin Cant. ABP Prop. & P. K^s books 12-11-8. Now 60$^£$ ⟨AD^n 80$^£$. Mr Plumptre[1] saith above 100$^£$⟩. The Parish is 6 miles long & 3 broad. 5 Hamlets: Finglesham, Ashley, Minneker, Napchester, Tickenhurst: wch last is 4 miles apart from the rest of the Parish. 91 Ho. 3 Men, 1 woman, 6 Ch^n Anab. Service & Sermon once at Church, once at Chapel, 2 miles off. Prayers on Ash W. & every Friday in Lent, when Ch^n are cat. 4 Sacr. abt 35 Com each time. 4 Alms Ho. for 4 Families by one of the Sandys Family. Tower & N side of the Church want Repair. Chancel in good Repair. V. Ho. very good by Mr. Shocklidge. Glebe 11 Acres. 5 Bells. Chapel & its Chancel in good Order. No Ho. 3 Bells.
The Advowson was granted by the Crown to the ABP in Exchange 31 Aug. 1 Ed. 6 See Chart Misc. vol. 13. N° 21.

Geo. Shocklidge[2] MA V. 6 Apr. 1723. Resides in V. Ho. [Holds an Estate under ABP]. Old. asked for Mr Pennington[3]. Infirm, mistakes, promises to get a Curate May 1767. Hath none Sept. Mr James[4] serves Shoulden.
Thos. Hutcheson[5] V. 19 June 1772. resides.
Edward Birkett[6] vicar 1789.

Richd Morgan[7] C. Ord D. Tr. S. 1768 was a Diss. Minister. See his Papers. 45$^£$ & Surpl. Fees 5$^£$. bapt. 30 Oct 1740.

1758 Conf. Northbourn 57 Shoulden 14. 1762. Northb. 33. Shoulden 1. 1766 Northb. 31. Shoulden 19

[1] See p. 18, n. 1.
[2] (1695-1772), of Ash, Kent, m. Jesus C 1714, BA 1718, MA 1721, C. New Romney, 1719, R. Northbourne, 1723-72.
[3] See p. ii, n. 35.　　　　　　[4] Probably John James. See p. 180, n. 2.
[5] See p. 11, n. 4.　　　　　　[6] (17?-1806), V. Northbourne, 1789-1806.
[7] Probably (1745-1804), of Llanfihangel, co Cardigan, m. Jesus O 1767, BA & MA 1786, V. Reculver, 1782-1804.

Page 191

Ringwould R. ⟨al Ringoule al Kingswold⟩. S[t] Nicolas. Rich[d] Monins[1], Clerk P. K[s] books 13-12-6. Wake 100[f]. Now called 200[f]. Ringwold hath abt 35 Ho. Kingsdown 20 ⟨There is a parish of Kingsdown p. 214⟩. 3 families of Anab. Whole Service [in ABP Wakes time: now] every other Sunday in Summer. 2 out of 3 in Winter. The other part of the Sundays R. officiates at Charlton p. 79. [Must do the whole Duty here ⟨Doth so⟩, & provide a Cur. for Charlton. Saith, Aug. 1759. that he cannot yet find one ⟨Hath one⟩.]. Cat. frequently in Afternoons. Will be exp. 4 Sacr. Generally near 30 Com. each time. Interest of 10[f] for the Poor Widows of Kingsdown. Ch & Chancel in pretty good Order. Ho. & outHouses large & good. Glebe 10 Acres. 5 Bells.

Rich. Monins[2] R. Prayed, as Patron, to be admitted, which was granted 21 Feb. 1758. Resides for the most part here: sometimes at Dover. 5 miles from Ringwold & ½ mile from his other parish of Charlton p. 79.
John Tucker[3] clerk 19. March 1770.
Robert Phillips[4] Clerk A.M. Rector Feby 15: 1777.
George Gipps[5] A.B. Rector 1784 resides.

1758 Conf. 33. 1762. 8. NB 1766. 14.

[1] See p. 79, n. 1.   [2] Ibid.
[3] See p. 4, n. 10.   [4] See p. 2, n. 5.
[5] (1760-1802), of Saltwood, Kent m. Christ Church 1778, BA 1782, C. Detling, 1782, R. Ringwould, 1784-1802.

Page 192

D. Sandwich

Ripple R. al. Ripley. S[t] Mary. Hugh Lloyd[1] Clerk, P. ⟨R. of Llanginhafel Co. Denb.⟩. K[s] books 5-19-4½. Certified 45[f]-3-0¾. Now 65[f]. R. saith 60[f]. 15 Ho. The major Part of the Parish pays no great Tithes, as it belonged to the Chamberlain of S[t] Austins Abbey. It is now called Chamberlains Fee. Service once on Sundays. 6 Churches in a mile & halfs Distance. Prayers on good Fr. Ch[n] Cat. 3 months in Summer, & Questions put to make them understand it. 4 Sacr. From 30 to 38 Com. [Mr Palmer[2], son of Lady Palmer[3] of Wingham p. 25 lives here: hath 600, will have 1200[f] a year.]. Ch. & Chancel good. Ho. new built by Mr Lloyd, improved by Mr Apsley. Outhouses in good Repair. Glebe 9 Acres. 2 Bells. The House is of Brick, sashed, convenient. The Situation in the healthiest & pleasantest part of E. Kent. Edw. Lloyd[4] pres. on death of Henry Yorke[5] by Nordash Rand[6] Esq[r] Patr. pleno jure inst. 10 Dec.1712 Entry B VI. 99.

John Apsley[7] MA 14 Sept. 1741. Good. Resides constantly in the Parsonage Ho. Was Cur. at Gr. Mongeham p. 188. Dead Oct 20 1760 ⟨before Oct 18⟩ 1760. Ho. neglected by the Sequestrator. Wrote word to AD[n] Oct. 21 1761. Care taken. AD[n].
Will. Rogers[8] BA 30 Apr. 1764. C. of Bettishanger p. 180 resides at Northbourn in the mid-way betw. the 2 parishes, 2 miles from each. Hath let his Parsonage Ho. to one, who hath laid out 60[f] in improving it. See his paper. 1766. Died {abt middle of} 9th May 1767. Mich 1767 Mr Leigh[9] Jun[r] serves it.

Henry Lloyd[10] BA Dec. 28 1767 hath a Living in St Asaph Dioc wch the BP permits him to keep. Mr Atkins[11] of Deal chapel or Mr James[12] of Deal to serve it till Mids. then Mr Shove[13] to come & live here & serve it with Sutton.
John Kenrick[14] M.A. Novr 13. 1770. resides.
Charles Philpot[15] A.M. 1793.

1758 Conf. 18. 1762. 19. 1766. 16.

[1] m. Christ Church, BA 1712, MA 1716, V. Mold, Flints, 1718–49, R. Llanganhavel, Denb., 1729–49, canon of St Asaph's, 1725–49.
[2] Charles Fyshe Palmer: Hasted IX, p. 572.   [3] See p. 24, n. 2.
[4] (1680–1741), of Llanvair, co Denbigh, Magdalen Hall 1699, BA (Christ Church) 1703, MA (CCCC) 1716, C. Great Mongeham, 1706–12, R. Ripple, 1712–41, R. Betteshanger, 1716, PC.Walmer, 1724,
[5] (1644–1712), of Kent, m. Queens' C 1659, BA 1662, MA (Magdalen Hall) 1664, C. Hucking, 1679, R. Ripple, 1681–1712.
[6] Nordash Rand sold the advowson to John Paramour for Edward Lloyd: Hasted IX, p. 572.
[7] See p. 188, n. 3.   [8] See p. 180. n. 6.
[9] Egerton Leigh (1734–88), of Murston, Kent, m. Emmanuel 1753, scholar 1754, PC. Minster in Sheppey, 1759, V. St Mary, Sandwich, 1763–75, V. Tilmanstone, 1764–88, R. Murston, 1774–88.
[10] Probably (1728–?), of Llansilin, co Denbigh, m. Jesus O 1746, BA 1749, R. Ripple, 1767–70.
[11] See p. 182, n. 5.   [12] See p. 180, n. 2.
[13] See p. 1, n. 7.   [14] See p. 180, n. 3.
[15] (1760–1823), of Leicestershire, m. Emmanuel 1775, BA 1780, MA 1787, R. Ripple, 1793–1823, C. St Margaret's at Cliffe, 1808, V. St Margaret's at Cliffe, 1813–23.

Page 193
Sandwich St Clements. V. AD^n of Cant. P. K^s books 13–16–10½. Certified 77–10–4. Now called 80$^£$. 450 Acres of Land & 170 Ho. within the Walls. Very few Dissenters. Their meeting Ho. lately converted into a Beer Cellar. Service, see St Peters. St Bartholomews Hospital, extraparochial, adjoyning: founded by Sir Henry Sandwich[1], [Kilburne, Survey of Kent, saith, by Sir Simon of Sandwich] for 12 Sisters & 4 Brothers. The Estate is let at 220$^£$ a year. They receive abt 17$^£$ in money [they cannot receive 17$^£$ each out of that Estate] & have a Ho. & Garden. In the middle of the Square is a Chapel, where an annual Sermon is preached gratis by one of the Ministers of Sandwich. The Mayor & Jurats are Patrons, Governors & Visitors. The Mayor nominates persons free of the Corporation, usually Jurats widows preferably. A Charity School for 10 Boys of each of the 3 Parishes, supported by 12 Subscribers, & a small Collection after a quarterly Charity Sermon. They are taught Reading, Writing, Arithmetick &c 4 years & have a Bible & Whole Duty of Man[2] given them, when the Fund will permit. St Georges Field, of 4 Acres appropriated & applied to the Uses of the Church. The minister takes ⅓ of the Offertory money, the ChW^{ns} the rest: & he believes they in general dispose of it well. No convenient Ho. for the Minister. Church & Chancel in good Repair. Ho. very mean. Let out to a poor Family. A good Barn in good repair. A large Garden. 5 Bells.

Will. Bunce[3] LLB. V. 26 May 1742. R. of St Peters. Resides there. Serves both.
One of the ⟨10⟩ poor Vicars. Dead June 1766.
Wheler Bunce[4] V. 3 July 1766. To serve Ham with it p. 186.
D° V. November 9 1774 resides.

1758 Conf. ⟨here 901. Of this Parish⟩ 57. 1762. 44. Conf. here in all 403. 1766 Conf. here May 27. 811. Of this Parish {& S[t] Peters} 57. 25.

[1] Sir Henry died about 1230. The hospital was founded in 1217.
[2] [Richard Allestree], *The Whole Duty of Man* (1658).
[3] (1714–66), of Brenzett, Kent, m. Trinity C 1730, C. New Romney, 1735, V. St Clement's, Sandwich, 1742–66, R. St Peter's, Sandwich, 1745–66.
[4] See p. 15, n. 10.

Page 194
D. Sandwich
Sandwich S[t] Marys. V. AD[n] of Cant. Propr. & P. Tenths 16–1¼. Certified 40[£]. Now called 50[£] ⟨augm 1767 with 400[£]⟩. 80 Acres without the Walls, abt 160 Ho. within: almost all, small & poor. Very few Presb. Indep. or Anab. Prayers & Sermon once on Sunday. See S[t] Peters. 5 or 6 Sacr. 40 or 50 Com. usually each time. A Free School, founded by Sir Roger Manwood[1] ⟨born here⟩ L[d] Ch. Baron in Qu. Eliz[s] Reign. Mr Conant[2], nominated by Linc. Coll. come lately to be Master. 11[£] a year by Solomon Hougham[3] Esq[r] for Bread for the poor: 4[s] every Sunday, & 12[s] on Chr. Day. The present V. hath built a V. Ho. Qu. Catechizing. Ch. large, handsome & in good Repair. Chancel handsome: Commandmts new, & neat Rails. Ho. partly built new by Mr Rutton, who promises to complete it. 1 Bell.
Licence to teach S[r] R. Manwoods School V. 246.
20 July 1661 John Lodwicke[4] V. 15 Jan 1689. John Thomas[5] V. on resign. of last V.

John Rutton[6] V. 19 July 1706 ⟨on the Death of John Thomas, above⟩. Hath resided constantly several years ***. Doth the whole Service 1761, but in a slovenly indecent manner. AD[n]. Died July 29. 1763.
Egerton Leigh[7] LLD. V. 24 Aug. 1763. Cur. of Minster in Shepey p. 218. Will reside here. Void by Cession. Jan. 26. 1764. Inst. again Feb. 4. V. of Tilmanstone p. 199. Bad.
William Thomas[8] B.A. V March 29 1775.

John Conant[9] BA of Linc. Coll. ord. Deacon 24 Sept. 1758 for Cur. here. 1. 20[£]. Schoolmaster also. [1759 Cur. of Woodnesborough p. 203.

1758 Conf. 58. 1762 S[t] Marys 44. 1766. 37

[1] See p. 36, n. 6.   [2] See p. 140, n. 5.
[3] Died 1697: Hasted X, p. 196.   [4] See p. 82, n. 5.
[5] (1659–1706), of Ovington, Essex, m. St John's C 1674, BA 1678, MA 1692, R. St Peter's Sandwich, 1689–1706, V. St Mary's Sandwich, 1689–1706.
[6] (1681–1763), of London, m. Pembroke O 1697, BA 1701, MA 1704, V. St Mary's, Sandwich, 1706–63, master Free School Sandwich, 1707, C. Elmstone, 1717.
[7] See p. 192, n. 8.   [8] See p. 13, n. 5.
[9] See n. 2.

Page 195

Sandwich S[t] Peters R. The King & the Town P. by Turns. Tenths 16[s]. Certified 28[f]. Now called 40[f] ⟨AD[n] 30[f] See below⟩. 230 Ho. & abt 10 Acres of Land within the Walls. One Papist, a Native of Brussels, likely to return home. 14 Families of Presbyterians: a meeting Ho. Mr Gellibrand Teacher. A few Anab. A meeting Ho. No settled Teacher: sometimes the miller of Barfreston, 7 miles off, p. 179. Prayers & Sermon here on Sunday mornings, this Church being in the middle of the Town: at S[t] Clements & S[t] Marys both, in afternoon; they being at the opposite ends. Prayers here W. Fr. & all Holydays. Cat. W. in Lent here, & Th. at S[t] Clements. Sacr. at one Church at the 3 gr. Festivals, at the other the Sunday after: & so, 1st & 2[d] Sundays in Lent, in Aug. & after Mich. Com. at S[t] Clements from 70 to 120: at S[t] Peters, from 100 to 140. S[t] Peters, from 100 to 140. S[t] Thomas's Hosp. founded by Tho. Ellis[1] & Marg. his wife under Rich. 2 See the Names of the Feoffees. 8 brothers, 4 sisters: abt 10[f] a year each. Corporation, Patrons, Governors & Visitors. Charity School, See S[t] Clements. Offertory, as at S[t] Clements. Ch. handsome: it & Chancel in good Repair. Ho. in good Order, improved by Mr Bunce. 18–5–0 towds repairing the Church, AD[n]. 6 Bells.
Augm. 1767 with 400[f] by Sir Ph Boteler & Qu[s] Bounty.

W[m] Bunce[2] LLB R. 15 Feb. 1744. Resides in Parsonage Ho. Dead, 1766.
John Conant[3] AB R. 1 July 1766. Curate of Woodnesborough p. {195}. ⟨203⟩.

1758 Conf 95. 1762.60. 1766 {See S[t] Clements} 57.

[1] A wealthy draper and MP for Sandwich in the 1370s. He died in 1391 and the hospital was founded about 1392: Hasted X, p. 183.
[2] See p. 193, n. 3.   [3] See p. 140, n. 5.

Page 196

D. Sandwich
Sibbertswold al. Sheperdswell V. S[t] Andrew, with Colerede al. Coldred V. S[t] Pancrace ⟨Colrede belonged to Priory of Dover⟩. [United by ABP Whitgift]. ⟨Sibbersoft⟩ Belonged to the Abbey of S[t] Radegund. ABP Propr. of both & P. The Rectories are let by two different Leases: the Advowson of the Vicarage is not reserved in either. K[s] books Colrede 6–2–6, Sibbertswold 6[f]. Colrede certified 35[f]–7–6, Sibbertswold 43–19–8. Now abt 90[f]: of which 20[f] is reserved ⟨by Juxon⟩ in each Lease from ABP, & shd be clear of Land Tax, and besides this 40[f] pd by the Lessee, the ABP pays 2–6–8.
Sibbertswold hath 35 scattered Ho. James Herbert[1] Esq[r] [a merchant. The Estate belongs to Awnsham Churchill[2].]. Colred 18 Ho. The Churches not ½ mile asunder. Service once at each. At Sibbertswold Prayers on Holydays. Cat. exp. from Lent to Mich. 4 Sacr. between 20 & 30 Com. At Coldred, Prayers on good Fri. & some Holydays. Cat. when any Ch[n] or Servts have not learnt. 4 Sacr. Generally not 20 Com.
Sibbertswold Church & Chancel indifferent, in good Repair but Chancel dirty. Ho. & outhouses good, & in very good Repair, & improved by Mr Rymer. Glebe 5½ Acres. 1 Bell. Colerede Ch & Chancel small, in good Repair: as is the Ho. wch lets for 3[f] a Year. A small good Barn. Glebe 4½ Acres. 1 Bell.

Alex. Innes[3] coll to Sibertswold R [no mention of Colrede] void by death of Jonas Owen[4] 21 Apr 1680 Entry B. IV. 104. Mentioned in the next Coll. on {Death} ⟨cession⟩ of Innes, p. 413.

Tho. Rymer[5] MA V. 11 June 1752. Resides. Dead.
John Benson[6] MA. 7 Aug. 1759. R. of Ruckinge p. 139 ⟨This void by Cession May 3. 1762⟩.
Tho. Hollingbery[7] MA: V. 13 May 1762. Usher at the Charterhouse.
Roger Pettiward[8] D.D. V. June 10. 1771.
Durand Rhudde[9] M.A. V. Oct[r]. 17. 1774.
Allen Fielding[10] A.B. Vicar 1782. John Henry Clapham[11] A.M. V. 1790.
John Rose[12] A.M. Vicar 1787. Rich. Blackett Dechair[13] LLB. V. 1792.

Harvey[14] Cur. was at Lambeth. To live with his Father[15] at Barfreston p. 179. 2 miles off. See Ewel p. 83. Going 1766. Mr Carter[16] desires it. Mr W[m] Lewis[17] to come from Teynham at LD 1768. 42[£] & Surplice Fees. To allow for Ho. & Garden w[t] Mr Carter did. Settled here May 1768.

1759[18] Conf. Sibbertswold 41. Coldred 25. 1762 Sib. 9. Col. 1. NB 1766 Sib. 17. Col. 17

[1] Died in 1760: Hasted IX, p. 382.
[2] Of Henbury, Dorset. Died in 1773: Hasted IX, p. 379.
[3] Aberdeen Univ, C. Barnes, 1671, C. Rotherfield, 1672, V. Reculver, 1679–80, R. Sibbertswold, 1680–84, R. St Michael Royal, London, 1684.
[4] (1600–80), of London, m. St John's O 1618, BCL 1625, R. Ruskington, Lincs, 1630, V. Sibbertswold, 1662–80, R. Wootton, 1663–80.
[5] See p. ii, n. 37.
[6] Ibid., n. 40.
[7] (1732–71), of Dover, Kent, m. Worcester 1751, BA 1755, MA 1758, B & DD 1760, V. Sibbertswold, 1762–71.
[8] (17?–1774), V. Sibbertswold, 1771–4.
[9] (17?–c.1822), m. Kings 1752, BA 1756, MA 1759, DD 1789, V. Sibberstwold, 1774–82, lecturer St Dionis Backchurch, R. Brantham, Suffolk, 1782–1819, R. Great Wenham, –1819.
[10] See p. 22, n. 6.
[11] (1759–1835), of Maryland, m. Clare 1779, BA 1783, MA 1786, fellow, 1783–91, V. Sibbertswold, 1790–92, R. Isfield, Sussex, 1792–1835. Died in Trinidad.
[12] (1755–?), of Lambeth, m. St John's O 1772, BA 1776, MA 1785, B & DD 1808, under master Merchant Taylors' school 1779, V. Sibberstwold, 1787–90, V. Milton, 1790–92, R. St Martin's, Outwich, 1795.
[13] See p. 105, n. 3.   [14] See p. 83, n. 10.   [15] See p. 184, n. 1.
[16] Probably Henry Carter, see p. 179, n. 8. Perhaps Arnold (1734–?), of Guildford, Surrey, m. Magdalen Hall 1750, BA (CCCO) 1753, MA 1757, V. Chart Sutton, 1770–73, V. Bearsted, 1773–83.
[17] See p. 177, n. 5.   [18] This should be 1758.

Page 197
Stonar al. Estanore ⟨al. Stonard⟩ R. S[t] Austin. Henry Crispe[1] Esq[r] P. in 1663. Mr Rooke[2] P. 1719. The King by Lapse 1752. K[s] books 3-6-8. No Church. Ecton. Mr Lamprey[3], minor canon of Canterbury took Institution to it 30 June 1752, had a Trial with Mrs Rook[4] abt Tithes at Canterbury before Ld Ch. Justice Willis[5], was cast, & resigned it 14 July 1758. It is sometimes placed in D. Westbere. The written Evidence, Briefs and Proceedings in this Cause were deposited at Lambeth Nov. 13. 1759[6].

A Caveat agst Admission, on behalf of Ann Crispe[7] 3 March 1665 Entry B. I. 186.

[1] He died in 1663. He was usually called 'Bonjour Crispe': 'as having, when carried away to France, and kept prisoner there, spoken no other words than those in the French language': Hasted X, p. 420.

[2] See p. 40, n. 3.   [3] Ibid., n. 6.

[4] Ibid., n. 3. In 1756 a verdict was found for Lamprey. A new trial of 1757 before Judge Willis found for Mrs Rooke 'at which the chief justice expressed much satisfaction, more than the jury thought decent, as coming from a judge who ought to have behaved more impartially on that occasion.': Hasted X, p. 423.

[5] John Will[e]s (1685–1761), attorney general, 1734, chief justice, 1737, MP for Launceston, 1722–6, MP for Weymouth, 1726, MP for West Loo, 1727–37.

[6] LPL, MS Secker 3, ff. 261–2.   [7] Anne Crispe died in 1707.

Page 198

D. Sandwich

Sutton by Dover C. called in ABPs Lease of the Rectory, East Sutton. There is another East Sutton, Chapel to Sutton Valence p. { }. ABP P. 24$^£$ a year reserved to it ⟨by Juxon⟩ in his Lease, which shd be paid clear of the Land Tax. ⟨It is now 1763 reserved so. Augm with 400$^£$ in 1767⟩. 19 Ho. One obstinate Absenter. Service twice a month. Cat. from LD to Mich. 4 Sacr. 14 Com. John Foch[1] in 1611 left 20^s a Year to the Poor & 20^s a Year to the Church. Marsh Land in Shoulden worth 30^s a Year belongs to the Poor. No Ho. for the Minister. Ch. & Chancel very dirty. Former wants almost every thing: latter wants Repairs in pavemt, Walls & Windows ⟨1765 said to be pretty well repaired⟩. 2 Bells.

C. licenced 1702. Entry B. V. 58.

Tho. Pennington[2] MA C. 7 Oct. 1755. Serves it from Deal 3½ miles off. Cur. at the Chapel there p. 182. R. of Kingsdown p. 214. Serves Sutton only once a fortnight, & then serves Deal Chapel but once. Hath 5$^£$ from little Mongeham. See p. 189.

Henry Shove[3] Junr will serve it once every Sunday from Bettishanger near, & take something to serve with it. Oct. 7. 1766 Licenced. Serves it with Barfreston p. 179. Nov. 1766 V. of Linsted p. 165. Next Summer quits this & goes thither. 1767 Quits Linsted. Serves this & Betshanger ⟨p. 180⟩.

Philips[4] Serves it with Deal chapel. AD^n finds no better way June 68.

John White[5] Clerk Cure: Oct^b. 30 1772.

Montagu Pennington[6] A.M. Cure 1789.

Thomas Tims[7] A.B. Cur sal. £24 lic by Archdeacon.

1758 Conf. 16. 1762. 1 NB + 18. 1766. 6.

[1] Hasted says Thomas Foach left 40s for poor and church: IX, p. 562.

[2] See p. ii, n. 35.   [3] See p. 1, n. 7.

[4] See p. 2, n. 5.   [5] See p. 15, n. 12.

[6] See p. 180, n. 8.

[7] (1753–1811), of Dorchester, Dorset, m. Wadham 1774, BA 1778, C. Sutton, 1790–1811, R. Walmer, 1798–1811.

Page 199

Tilmanstone V. S[t] Andrew. Belonged to the Priory of S[t] John of Jerusalem. ABP Propr. & P. ⟨Adv. granted by Qu. Mary⟩. Tenths 15-3. Certified 45[f]. Now called 60[f] ⟨True⟩. 39 Ho. Mr Harvey[1], 1000[f] a year. *** Service once on Sundays, as immemorially. No weekly Prayers. [qu. Chr. Day. good Fr]. Cat. in Lent. 4 Sacr. Generally between 20 & 30 Com. Church in good Repair: Chancel not. House good, by D[r] Carter[2], ⟨See Lic. Entry B. VI. 302⟩: outhouses the same. 1 Bell. Endowed with ½ the Tithes.

John Jacob[3] MA V. 23 Oct 1755. V. of Margate p. 261 where he resides. Died Dec. 21. 1763.
Egerton Leigh[4] V. Jan 26. 1764. Serves it from Sandwich p. 194.
Nehemiah Nisbett[5] V. 1788.

Rob[t] Greenall[6]. Cur. 20[f] a Surpl. Fees. Resides here. V. of Waldershare p. 200. where see more. See above.
Thomas Pennington[7]. Cur. Sal. £25.

1758 Conf. 5. 1762. 15. 1766. 23

[1] Major Richard Harvey bought the manor of Dane-Court in 1724. His grandson alienated it in 1763 to Gervase Hayward: Hasted X, p. 82.
[2] Nicholas Carter. See p. ii, n. 34.
[3] (1724-64), of Marshall, Glos, m. University 1741, V. St John's Thanet, 1749, V. Tilmanstone, 1755-64.
[4] See p. 192, n. 8.   [5] See p. 2, n. 6.   [6] See p. 18, n. 7.
[7] (1762-1853), of Deal, Kent, m. Trinity C 1777, scholar, BA 1780, MA (Clare Hall) 1783, fellow, C. Tilmanstone, 1784, R. Kingsdown, 1786-1853, PC. Knockholt, 1791-1853, R. Thorley, Herts, 1798-1853, chaplain to the countess of Bath, and lord chief justice Ellenborough.

Page 200

D. Sandwich

Waldershare V. All Saints. Belonged to the Priory of Langdon in Kent. ABP Propr. & P. Tenths 10-9¼. Certified 25[f]. Now called 30[f], of which 20[f] is reserved ⟨by Juxon⟩ in ABPs Lease ⟨augm. with 400[f] in 1766⟩. A mile square, besides a Farm ½ mile round, 4 miles distant from the rest of the Parish. 7 Ho. Earl of Guilford[1]: resides abt 4 months. Service once a Fortnight. So immemorially. [V. assisted at Eythorn p. 185 every other Sunday: but from Chr. 1758 hath officiated every Sunday here]. Cat. in Lent. 4 Sacr. 10 or 12 Com. & when Ld Guilford is here, twice as many. No V. Ho. Ch. & Chancel very neat and pretty. Glebe 1 Acre. 1 Bell.

Robt Greenall[2] BA V. 26 Apr. 1755. R. of Blackmanston p. 113. & Cur. of Tilmanstone p. 199 where he resides, two miles off. 1764 C. of Nonington p. 18. Serves this & that. Bladon Downing[3] M.A. V. Feb. 1. 1771. does his own duty.

1758 Conf. 7. 1762. 2. 1766. 11.

[1] See p. 18, n. 6.   [2] Ibid., n. 7.   [3] Ibid., n. 8.

Page 201

Walmer C. S' Mary. Belonged to the Monastery of Langdon, Kent. ABP Propr. & P. Certified 32$^£$. Called in ABP Wakes book 50$^£$. But Cur. saith, it consists of 20$^£$ a Year [reserved ⟨by Juxon⟩ in the ABPs Lease] out of which 4$^£$ is paid for Land Tax ⟨should not be paid. Reserved clear, 1762⟩, the Small Tithes, which for the last 15 years have been 12$^£$ on an Average, & the Collection of which costs 20^s, & the Glebe & Ch. Yard 1-1-0: & that out of this he pays 2-2-0 yearly to a neighbouring Clergyman for doing any sudden occasional Duty. Remains 25-19-0 ⟨augm. 1766 with 400$^£$⟩. 30 Ho. D. of Dorset[1] sometimes spends a few Weeks at the Castle. One Quaker, who regularly sends his Dues without Compulsion. Service once a Fortnight, as hath ever been usual. Other Churches very near. [Ripple is.]. Will be once a week. ⟨Is so⟩. See Letters]. Cat in Lent. 4 Sacr. betw. 20 & 30 Com. each time. Interest of 24$^£$ a Year given to the Poor. Church small, in good Repair. Chancel very bad & dirty. Glebe ½ Acre. 2 Bells. Lic. to serve the Cure of Walmer & W. Langdon 1680 Entry B. IV 135. of Walmer. V. 4, VIII. 225.

John Maximilian Del' Angle[2], or Jun[3]. C. May 1757. Cur. of Bettishanger, p. 180. but saith he is to return it to Mr Apsley[4] of Ripple p. 192, when Mr Herring[5] comes to reside at Mongeham p. 188 which he doth. He lives at Goodneston near Sandwich p. 13. 9 miles from hence. Serves also Chillenden p. 9. Hath quitted it, & serves Barfreston p. 179. May 1765 serves this once & Goodneston ⟨p. 13⟩ once.
Robert Philips[6] M.A. licens'd Jan^{ry} 2.1771.

Montagu Pennington[7] Cur. Sal. £25.
John Gregory[8] Cur. Sal. £25. lic. 1789.

1758 Conf. 29. 1762. 11. 1766. 17

[1] Lionel Cranfield (1688-1765), created duke of Dorset in 1720, lord warden of the Cinque Ports 1708-12, 1714-17, 1728-65, vice-admiral of Kent 1725, lord lieutenant of Ireland 1730-37 and 1751-55, lord lieutenant of Kent 1746-65.
[2] See p. 9, n. 5.   [3] He was the younger.   [4] See p. 188, n. 3.
[5] Ibid., n. 2.   [6] See p. 2, n. 5.   [7] See p. 180, n. 8.
[8] See p. 11, n. 6.

Page 202

D. Sandwich
West-Langdon C. S' Mary. Belonged to the Priory of Langdon. ABP P. [Hath no Estate here]. Certified 16$^£$. Now called 12$^£$. [qu. by whom payable.]. Abt 16 Ho. Only one Farmer. No Ho. for the Minister. No Church, only some old Walls. They go to Church at East-Langdon, the next Parish, p. 183.
Licences to serve the Cure of W. Langdon & Guston 6 July 1674 Entry B.III. 230, of W. Langdon & Walmer 1580 IV. 135.

John Ratray[1] Cur. ⟨lic⟩ 5 Apr. 1738. Resides at E. Langdon p. 183 where see.
John Queteville[2] Cur. Licenc'd November 20 1772.
Thos Delannoy[3] Cur. 1788.

1758 Conf. 35. This must be for East-Langdon also p. 183. 1762. 6 1766 see p. 183

[1] See p. 86, n. 1.   [2] See p. 76, n. 8.   [3] See p. 77, n. 4.

Page 203

Woodnesborough ⟨al. Wynesborough⟩ V. St Mary. DCh of Rochester P. K^s books 10-0-7½. Wake 40$^£$. Herring 90$^£$ ⟨AD^n 95$^£$⟩. 99 Ho. Chiefly straggling. William Docksey[1] Esqr, Lessee to the Ch. of Rochester for the Parsonage. 3 Absenters. V. will discourse with them. Service once here, & once at Ash ⟨Whole Service 1759⟩. Cat. exp. on Litany Days in Lent. 4 Sacr. 50 or 60 Com. A voluntary Charity School for teaching 15 Ch^n to read & write: the parish Clerk master of it. Names of parts of the Parish: Cold-Friday, Marsh-borough, Comb-borough, Hamel-borough. Ch. & Chancel in good Repair. Ho. very mean, & let out to poor people: chancel very mean & out of Repair. Glebe 6½ Acres, besides Garden & Orchard. 5 Bells.

Jonathan Soane[2] MA V. 19 Aug. 1747. V. of Thornham p. 255. ⟨Was⟩ Master of the Kings School at Rochester, where he lives: but hath generally spent the months Vacation at Whitsuntide here. Dead Jan 1768.
John Clarke[3] D.D. prov. of Oriel V. June 30. 1768. Will continue whole Service.
James Williamson[4] A.M. V. June 26: 1776.
John Smith[5] Vicar 1785.
Benj. Longley[6] Cur. ⟨25$^£$⟩. Also Cur. of Ash p. 2. [but hath quitted this, to do the whole service at Ash.
John Conant[7] BA Cur 1759. 30$^£$. Schoolmaster at Sandwich, adjoyning. Ord. Pr. June 10. 1759. 1.

1758 Conf. 55. 1762. 52. 1766. 44

[1] Of Shellston, Derbyshire: Hasted X, p. 143.
[2] (1690–1768), of Odiham, Hants, m. CCCO 1707, BA 1711, MA (Pembroke) 1714, R. Inkpen, Berks, 1720, V. Thornham, 1721–68, V. Woodnesborough, 1747–68.
[3] (1733–81), of Colvel, Cambs, m. Pembroke O 1749, BA 1752, MA (Oriel) 1756, B & DD 1768, provost, 1768–81, V. Woodnesborough, 1768–76.
[4] (1736–1810), of Kendal, Westmoreland, m. Queen's O 1752, BA 1755, MA 1759, BD 1784, Bampton lecturer 1793, V. Woodnesborough, 1776–85, V. Chart Sutton, 1784–85, R. Winwick, Northants, R. Thorpe Mandeville, 1792, V. Biggleswade, Beds, 1796, preb of Lincoln, 17901–1810.
[5] (1765–1833), of Bedfordshire, m. St John's C 1773, scholar 1773, BA 1777, MA 1780, V. Ellington, Hunts, 1781, C. Horningsea, Cambs, 1783, V. Woodnesborough, 1785–1833, V. Chart Sutton, 1785–1833, C. Betteshanger, 1814.
[6] See p. 2, n. 3.   [7] See p. 140, n. 5.

[Deanery of Sittingbourne]

Page 204

D. Sittingbourn

Bapchild 〈al. Babchild al. Bacchild Ecton. Bakchild Reg. Morton 153 a〉.V. S[t] Laurence. DCh. of Chichester P. & Propr. Tenths 16[s] Certified 27[£]. Now called 25[£] 〈30[£] AD[n]. 50[£] Mr Allen 1765. See below〉. 40 scatterd Ho. One Family of Papists. L[d] Teynhams[1] Priest, Mr Colgrave comes to them. 5 or 6 of low Rank, Absenters. Service once on Sundays. Prayers on good Fr. 〈qu. Chr. Day〉. Ch[n] cat. in Lent. Servants not sent. Cat. explained every Sunday after the 2[d] Lesson out of BP Williams's Exposition[2]. 4 Sacr. ⅓ of the Householders Com. & 10 or 12 other Persons: not many Servants. Number of Com. much increased. No Offertory: will be introduced when opportunity offers. V. saith, that not one in three in any Parish, that he knows, in this Country, knows who Jesus Christ is, or why he came into the World: & that Servants think the Sacram[t] is only for their Superiors. He ascribes it to their not being able to read, nor taught their Catechism: & wd have more Gifts for these Purposes. ChW[ns] will not present Persons for neglecting to send their Ch[n] or servants to Church, or to come themselves: And the Minister would only raise a Flame by presenting. V. Ho. is a Cottage, & very bad. No outho. Church & Chancel tolerable. Glebe 1 Acre. 1 Bell & 1 cracked.

Augmented Dec. 1765 with 400[f]: 200[f] of it Sir Ph. Botelers money. Estate bought at Finham.

Will. Marsh[3] BA V. 27 June 1751. V. also of Bicknor p. 205. 4 or 5 miles asunder. Lives at Bredgar, p. 208. between them, by ABP Herrings Leave. Resigned this Apr. 7. 1759. Holds it by Sequestration, & serves it as before. R. also of S[t] Mary in the Marsh p. 130.

Sir Sam. Bickley[4] inst. Oct. 1759. Cur. of Murston p. 220 where see. Deprived 〈by me at Canterbury〉 26 Jan. 1764 on a presentm[t] of the Ch.W[n] that he had been convicted at the preceding Assizes for Kent of an Attempt to commit Sodomy, which conviction he confessed on this presentmt in the AD[ns] court[5].

Tho. Gurney[6] V. March 6. 1764. C. at Murston p. 220. Resigned Jan 14. 1765.

Charles Allen[7] V. (Cur. of Norton p. 169) 23 Apr. 1765. May be Cur. of Tong p. 225 {abt to be} instituted Sept. 1765 to a Living in Rochester, S[t] Nicolas V. by wch this is void.

Edw. Penry[8] V. Oct 30. 1765. See p. 207. To stay at Chartham a year, if necessary. Oct. 7. 1766 serves this with Tong p. 228 boards at Sittingbourn. Goes to Linsted at LD. Dec. 1767 serves Luddenham.

1758 Conf. 23. 1762. 24. 1766. 11.

---

[1] See p. 152, n. 3. For Colegrave, see n. 4.

[2] John Williams, *A Familiar Exposition of the Church Catechism* (1689). This went through several editions, including ones in 1707 and 1731.

[3] See p. 130, n. 2.

[4] (1719–73), of Offham, Kent m. Sidney 1738, V. Bapchild, 1759–64. Assumed baronetcy in 1754. Died at the King's Head Inn, Enfield.

[5] See account in Secker's *Autobiography*, p. 48.

[6] See p. 79, n. 3.   [7] See p. 169, n. 12.   [8] See p. 166, n. 3.

Page 205

Bicknor ⟨al Bignore⟩ R. The King P. Tenths 11^s. Certified 32$^£$. R saith, 25$^£$ AD^n 37$^£$. 5 Ho. One or two Absenters. Service once on Sundays. Prayers on good Fr. [qu. Chr. Day]. Cat. exp. every Sunday after 2^d Lesson, from BP Williams[1]. No Servants cat. Parents are unwilling to send Ch^n. Monthly Sacr. Most of the Householders Com. each time: few or no serv^{ts}. The same Observations abt the Ignorance of the People &c as in Bapchild p. 204. Church & chancel very mean & dirty: Ho. a mean Cottage, much out of Repair. Barn wants Repair. Glebe 19 Acres. 1 Bell. Allowed Dec. 17. 1763 to be served only every other Sunday, that Huckinge p. 243 for wch no other Provision cd be then made, may be also served every other Sunday. So May 1765.

Will. Marsh[2] BA ⟨Called R above⟩ V. 1 March 1742. See Bapchild p. 204. Cur. of Tong p. 228 ⟨Gone⟩. R. of St Mary in the Marsh p. 130. C. of Wormshill p. 257. Gone. C. of Tong again May 1767.

1758 Conf. 2. 1762. 1

[1] See p. 204, n. 2.   [2] See p. 130, n. 2.

Page 206

D. Sittingbourn.

Bobbing V. St Bartholomew. Belonged to the Monastery of Sexburgh. Wm Tyndal[1], Clerk P. Certified 30–16–0. ABP Wakes book calls it 30$^£$ & mentions an Augmentation of 3–6–8. It is now 40$^£$ ⟨See below. 45 AD^n⟩. 30 Ho. { } Sole[2] of Bobbing Place Esqr. Service once on Sundays. Prayers on Fridays in Lent. Cat. on Sunday in Lent. Frequently explained to them in set Discourses: & in Sermons occasionally. 4 Sacr. 20 Com. No Ho. for the Minister, Church & Chancel handsome & in good order. Glebe 1¼ Acre. 5 Bells.

Titus Otes[3] BA. inst. V. 5 March. 1672. Disp. for nonr. 14 Sept. 1674. Air unhealthy.

1767 Augm with 400$^£$ by Sr Ph. Boteler & Qu Annes bounty.

Joseph Parry[4] V. 15 Oct. 1757. Serves a Cure at Gloucester. This place agrees not with his Health. See Letters.

Robt Wells[5] Cur. ⟨20$^£$⟩. Also Cur. of Upchurch p. 230. Gone.

Arthur Clark[6], Cur. of both, 25$^£$ & Surpl. Fees at each. Lives at Newington, between them. Deacon. To apply for Pr. Ord. At Chr 1759 ordained. 2. Gone to Rainham p. 224, Mich 1760.

John Smith[7] V. of Borden p. 207 serves this too. 25$^£$.

M^r. Evans[8] Cur Sal. £25. & surplice fees. lic by Archdeacon.

1758 Conf. 83. 1762. 19. 1766. 15

[1] Probably (1726–63), of Charfield, Glos, m. Oriel 1742, BA 1746, R. Charfield, 1749–63.

[2] John Sole, son of the recorder at Queenborough. Left Bobbing in 1766 to reside near Faversham: Hasted VI, p. 200.

[3] (1649–1705), of Oakham, Rutland, m. Caius 1667, St John's C (no degree), V. Bobbing, 1673–4, C. All Saints, Hastings, 1674, claimed to be DD of Salamanca. Invented Popish plot in 1678. Joined Wapping Baptists in 1701, and was expelled for hypocrisy.

4 (1721–98), of Abingdon, Berks, m. Pembroke O 1740, BA 1744, MA 1747, V. Bobbing, 1757–98.
5 (1734–1807), of Willingham, Lincs, m. Lincoln 1752, BA 1756, MA 1774, B & DD 1774, V. Market Rasen, Lincs, R. Springthorpe, 1775, R. Willingham, Lincs, 1781–1807.
6 (1736–67), of Painswick, Glos, m. Pembroke O 1754, BA 1757, R. Witchling, 1763–67.
7 (1711–68), of Bonby, Lincs, m. Christs 1729, scholar 1729, BA 1733, MA 1736, C. Worlaby, R. Skirbeck, Leics, 1736, V. Borden, 1760–68.
8 Samuel Evans (1736–99), of Carmarthen, m. Queen's O 1754, V. Sittingbourne, 1778–99, C. Bobbing, 1790, poor vicar, 1789.

Page 207

Borden V. S[t] Peter & S[t] Paul. Belonged to the Monastery of Leeds. Sir Benj. Tichbourne[1] P. A Caution 25 Dec. 1758 by Mrs Seagar[2].[1]* K[s] Books 8–10–0. Above 83$^£$ on a medium of 7 years: or 68$^£$, deducting Taxes. 50 Ho. Service once every Sunday. No Prayers on Week-Days: not usual: none would attend. [qu. good Fr. Chr. Day]. Ch[n] not sent to be cat. 4 Sacr. abt 30 Com. each time. Mr William Barrow[3], who died in 1684, left Estates, valued then at 533$^£$ a Year, but now sunk to abt 465$^£$, to 4 Trustees, who were to fill up Vacancies, for persons of this Parish, immediately above those that are intitled to Parochial Relief. His Will was confirmed & settled by a Decree in Chancery. The present Trustees are, Richd Tylden[4] of Milsted Esq[r], Tho. Bland[5] vicar of Sittingbourne, Hugh Aldersey[6] of Bredgar Gent. Daniel May[7] of Milsted Gent. Sev[l] small charities to the Poor, which see. Church handsome, in good Repair. East-end of Chancel seems to shoot forward. Promise to take Care of it. Ho. in Order. A good Stable. Glebe 4 Acres. 6 Bells.
[1]* Another by Joseph Musgrave: but withdrawn by Letter to my Secretary March 6 1760, bec. the Right of Presentation to the present Advoidance is not in him. The Case with Mr Wilbrahams[8] opinion upon it is in the Registry.
1766 one poor widow, Papist.

Ralf Milway[9] V. 6 May 1710. V. of Halstow p. 211. They have been sequesterd above 20 Years for Debt. He is said to live in the Isle of Scilly. The Sequestrator died in 1758. His Executor is Mr Herbert, a Printseller on London Bridge: Mr Milway died 29 Oct. 1759.
John Smith[10] MA of Christs Coll. Apr. 9. 1760. Will reside at Mich. Serves this May 1761 with Bobbing p. 206.
Thomas Frank[11] Nov[r]. 23^d 1768. resides.
Tho. Bland[12] V. of Sittingbourn, p. 226. Was Cur. & gave the above Account. Salary £22.
Edw. Penry[13], educated at D[r] Doddridges[14] Academy, ord. Deacon June 10 & Pr. Sept. 23. 1759 to serve this & Halstow p. 211. Salary for this, 22$^£$. Lives in V. Ho. Gone to Chatham June 1760.
William Filmer[15] A.M. Vicar 1794.

1758 Conf. 46. 25. 1766. 23

1 Created baronet in 1670.
2 Mary Seagar, died 1765: Hasted VI, p. 78.
3 By the late eighteenth century, they were worth £609–17s–6d: Hasted VI, p. 76.
4 Owner of Milsted manor, he died in 1763: ibid., p. 109.
5 (1717–76), of Tiverton, Devon, m. Sidney Sussex 1732, BA 1737, MA 1740, fellow 1738, R. Tunstall, 1740, V. Sittingbourne, 1742–66, R. Little Warley, Essex, 1745–76.

[6] Owner of Swanton court in Bredgar. He died in 1762: Hasted VI, p. 101.
[7] The May family owned lands in Bapchild: ibid., p. 122.
[8] See p. 176, n. 3.
[9] (1682–1759), of Upchurch, Kent, m. All Souls 1699, BA (Magdalen O) 1702, MA 1705, V. Halstow, 1707–59, V. Borden, 1710–59.
[10] See p. 206, n. 7.
[11] (1730–94), of Darenth, Kent, m. St John's C 1748, LLB 1754, V.Darenth, 1759–66, V. Stockbury, 1766–94, V. Borden, 1768–94, minor canon of Rochester, 1759.
[12] See n. 5.   [13] See p. 166, n. 3.
[14] Philip Doddridge (1702–51) nonconformist divine. Founded academy at Northampton to train dissenting clergy.
[15] See p. 99, n. 18.

Page 208
D. Sittingbourne
Bredgar V. St John Bapt. Belonged to St Johns Hospital, without the Walls of Cant. John Tappenden[1] {Esq^r} ⟨of St Leonard Foster Lane Ironmonger⟩ P.[1]* Tenths 18^s. Certified 36$^£$. Now called 40$^£$ ⟨50 AD^n⟩. 50 Ho. One Justice of Peace: not named. Service once on Sundays. Prayers on all Holydays, & all Passion Week. Cat. W. Fr. in Lent. Exp. the Sunday following. 4 Sacr. Generally betw. 40 & 50 Com. Mr Wm Thatcher[2] of London, gave 100$^£$, since vested in Lands, to pay 5$^£$ a year to a Master or Mistress, to be chosen by V. & Ch W^{ns} to teach 8 poor Ch^n, whom V. names, Reading & the Cat. Benefactions of 4-10-0 ⟨a year⟩ to the Poor, & of 1-14-6 a year for the Repair of the Church. So applied. Church & chancel very clean & decent. Ho. neat & in good Order by Mr Laurence. A new Stable built by him. Endowed with Hay Tithes: Augm. 3-6-8. AD^n. Glebe 2 Acres. 5 Bells.
[1]* Adv. granted to ABP by Qu. Mary. Wilk. vol. 4. p. 178. Pres. from Crown ⟨1699⟩ on Lapse Entry B. IV. 605.

Richd Laurence[3] MA V. 23 March 1744. Resides constantly in V. Ho. Cur. of Tunstal p. 229. Serves both. One of the 10 poor vicars. V. also of Lenham p. 246.
W^m. Gurney[4]. Vicar 1772.
Tho$^{s.}$ Scott[5]. Vicar 1780.
John Lloyd[6]. Vicar 1781.
Charles Cage[7] A.B. Vicar 1794.
James Downes[8] Vicar 1795.

James Thurston[9] BA Cur. ord D. 2 June 1765.1. bapt. 1740/1. 22$^£$ Cur. also of Tunstall, p. 229. Ord. Pr. Sept. 21. 1766 to serve Stockbury inst. of Tunstall. Sampson Steele[10] Cur.

1758 Conf. 40. 1762. 20. 1766. 18

[1] Tappenden had bought the advowson 'about the beginning of George II's reign': Hasted VI, p. 105.
[2] In 1718: ibid., p. 104.   [3] See p. 2, n. 4.
[4] See p. 151, n. 5.   [5] See p. 56, n. 15.
[6] See p. 189, n. 5.
[7] (1770–1849), of Kent, m. Emmanuel 1787, scholar 1788, BA 1791, MA 1802, C. Bearsted, 1792, V. Bredgar, 1794–5, PC. Leeds, 1794–5, V. Bearsted, 1794–1802, R. Leybourne, 1802–49.

8 V. Bredgar, 1795–1802.

9 (17?–1802), of Kent, m. Queens' C 1761, BA 1765, MA 1768, fellow, 1766, V. Ryarsh, 1768–1802.

10 See p. 168, n. 11.

Page 209

Eastchurch V. [R. & V. Ecton] All Saints. Sir Henry Palmer[1] P. ⟨Tho. Kynaston of Lincolns Inn Gent. Patron for the last Turn⟩. K^s books 13-6-8. Now 200$^£$ ⟨Called 170$^£$ in Disp⟩. Endowed with all the Tithes. 60 Ho. No Ho. for the Minister, but a small cottage, built upon the Churchyard, & inhabited by the Curate. Whole Service, & 2 Sermons. [Qu. See below]. Prayers on Saints Days, & in Lent, when Cat. is exp. 4 Sacr. Usually 30 Com. Seldom any money collected at the Offertory. A messuage given by Richd Foster[2] DD vicar of Eastchurch, for teaching poor children, decayed. Sev^l small Gifts to the poor, which see.

This Rectory had been appropriated long to the Abbey de Dunes in Flanders: & was by consent appropriated to the Abbey of Boxley 12 Cal. Aug. 1314. by ABP Walter Raynolds[3] Reg. Warham fol 135, 136. The Abbey was granted 32 H. 8 to Sr Thomas Wyat[4]. Of the Re-endowment See Harris History of Kent p. 108. Ecton. Tho. White[5] inst. to V. & licenced to serve the Cure of the Church 1666 Entry B. II. 46.

Church & Chancel noble & in good Order. Ho. small, in good Order, improved by Mr Hey. No outHo. 5 Bells.

Tho. Hey[6] MA ⟨D.D⟩ V. 28 May 1755. R. of Wickhambreux p. 24. where he resides.

James Allanson[7] Cur. Hath been so near 20 years. Resides. Always doth whole Service, & officiates at Harty p. 162 & Warden p. 231. each once a month. 50$^£$ Surpl. Fees, Use of Ch. Yard & Ho. in it. See above.
Mr Martin[8] Cur. Sal £50.

1758 Conf. 56. 1762. 17 + 4. Cur saith, the Inhabitants are much diminished. 1766. 40.

1 Died in 1706: Hasted VI, p. 257. 2 See p. 10, n. 2.

3 Walter Reynolds, archbishop, 1313–27.

4 Sir Thomas Wyatt (1503–42), poet and intimate of Henry VIII. Given Boxley in 1541.

5 (1628–98), of Aldington, Kent, m. St John's C 1642, BA 1647, DD 1683, R. All Hallows the Great, London, 1666–79, R. St Mary at Hill, London, 1647 and 1661, V. Newark on Trent, 1660–6, V. Eastchurch, 1667, R. Stepney, 1681, archdeacon of Nottingham, 1683, bishop of Peterborough, 1685–90, one of the six bishops who, with Archbishop Sancroft, petitioned against James II's declaration of Indulgence in 1688, and refused the oaths to William and Mary.

6 See p. 24, n. 3. 7 See p. 162, n. 8. 8 David Martin. See p. 52, n. 5.

Page 210

D. Sittingbourne
Elmley R. All Souls Coll. P. Kings books 5$^£$. Now 40$^£$. No Church. Few Houses. The minister of Murston p. 220. takes care of the occasional Duty. No Answer to Inquiries.

Church in a ruinous state: no one remembers Service in it, but w^n Incumbents qualifie. No Remains or Remembrance of a parsonage Ho. nor any Land, owned to be Glebe. The Parish an Island, distinct from Shepey. Intirely Pasture, of sheep & black Cattle. Two Houses: in each a Servt & his Family. They go to a neighbouring Church, & pay the officiating minister an usual Fee for any occasional Duty. The Land belongs to Sir Edw. Hales[1]: two brothers, called Blaxland[2], are his Tenants for the whole. The Rent believed to be above 1000$^£$ a year: the Land Tax said to be above 200$^£$. The paymt to the Rector 40$^£$, hath been so forsev^l years: not known w^n the Composition was made. D^r St Lo[3] Sept. 2. 1765. Mr Lewis's Book saith it was valued at 70$^£$ in 1640.

Tho. Bathurst[4] MA R. 7 June 1751 Void by Cession 1765.
Tho. S^t Lo[5]. LLD. R. 2 Aug 1765 Dead.
John Long[6] BD R 30 Sept. 1766.
Edm$^{d.}$ Isham[7] B.D. Rector 1782.
John Montagu[8] B.D. Rector 1788.

1758 None conf. 1762. none. 1766. none

[1] See p. 33, n 2.
[2] From Graveney Court. They held the lease for many years: Hasted VI, p. 272.
[3] Thomas St Lo (1728–66), of Pulham, Dorset, m. Balliol 1747, BCL (All Souls) 1754, DCL 1759, R. Elmley, 1765-6.
[4] (1715–?), of Goudhurst, Kent, m. Trinity O 1731, BA (All Souls) and fellow 1735, MA 1740, R. Welwyn, Herts, R. Elmley, 1751–65, FAS.
[5] See n. 2.
[6] (1731–97), of Rood Ashton, Wilts, m. Magdalen O 1748, BA 1752, fellow All Souls, 1752, MA 1756, BD 1764, DD 1768, proctor 1763, R. Freshford, Somerset, 1756–81, R. Elmley, 1766–82, V. Whaddon, Wilts, 1770–81, R. Chelsfield, 1781–97.
[7] See p. 137, n. 10.
[8] (1750–1818), of Widley, Hants, m. University 1767, BA 1771, fellow All Souls, 1771–1818, MA 1775, BD 1782, DD 1800, R. Elmley, 1788–98, and 1801–18.

Page 211

Halstow V. St Margaret. DCh. of Cant. Propr. & P. Tenths 16–2¼. Certified 40$^£$ ⟨AD^n 45$^£$ V. saith not 40, 1767⟩. On a medium of 7 years, 36$^£$ a year, or 30$^£$ clear of Taxes. {No Answer to Inquiries}. In 1752, 20 Families. Service once on Sundays. No Cat. 3 Sacr. But this seems transcribed from ABP Wakes Book. Now 20 Families. Prayers & Sermon once on Sundays. Cur. will cat & exp. in Lent, if encouraged. 4 Sacr. 10 Com. [Too few]. Church & Chancel small, in good Repair, want whitewashing. No Ho. 2$^£$& 2 bushels of wheat to the poor. Glebe ⅛ Acre. 3 Bells.

Ralph Milway[1] V. March. 1706. V. of Borden p. 207, where see more. Died 29 Oct. 1759.
Tho. Lamprey[2], Jun. M.A. Dec. 19. 1759. C. of Iwade p. 213 & of Milton p. 217.

Edw. Penry[3] Cur. Salary here 18$^£$. Cur. of Borden p. 207 where see more. Mr Lamprey gives him 20$^£$ here. Gone.
John Saunders[4] Cur. Dec. 1760. See 221.
Henry Friend[5]. Cur. Sal. £50 for this & Newington.

1758 Conf. 13. 1762. 14. 1766. 9

[1] See p. 207, n. 9. [2] See p. 22, n. 10.
[3] See p. 204, n. 8. [4] See p. 33, n. 3.
[5] (1758–1811), of Birchington, Kent, m. All Souls 1775, BA 1779, MA (Queen's) 1761, C. Halstow and Newington, 1782, V. East Farleigh, 1795–1811.

Page 212
D. Sittingbourne
Hartlip V. S[t] Michael. DCh of Rochester Propr. & P. K[s] books 9-10-10. Certified 62–18–8. Now abt 70[£] & above 60[£] clear. 36 Ho. Service once on Sundays. 3 Churches within little more than a mile. Cat. in Lent. 4 Sacr. 15 Com. [very few]. Mary Gibbon[1] widow gave in 1678 a small Tenem[t] & 6 Acres of Land, for the Paym[t] of 20[s] yearly to the Vicar, & for teaching poor ch[n] to read. He & ChW[n]s Trustees. So applied ⟨see next Line⟩. Church & Chancel pretty clean. Ho. mean, in tolerable Repair. Barn in good Order. 6[£] for Schooling, 1[£] to the minister, 3 Sacks of Barley, 1½ of Wheat, 1-6-8 to the poor. AD[n]. Glebe ½ Acre. 5 Bells.

Pierce Dixon[2] V. March. 11 1756. Master of Rochester School, 7 miles off, where he resides. Resigned Aug. 14. 1759.
John Prat[3] BA V. Sept. 3. 1759. 2[d] master. To send me word how he serves his Parish ⟨personally, from LD 1760. Gone to Cliff, 1764⟩. See below. A brother[4] in Orders, confined, maintained by him hath put V. house in repair. Serves it himself June 1767. Desires a Curacy June 1768. To have Bredhurst.
Rich[d]. Hodgson[5], Vicar 1787.
James Jones[6] A.M. 1792. quitted it & was again instituted 1794.
Tho. Gregory Warren Walker[7] A.M. Vicar 1795.

Casar Curtis[8] Cur. V. of Stockbury p. 227. Min. Can. of Rochester, lives there. 20[£]. Dead.
John Heathfield[9] MA of Clare Hall, ord. Deacon, Sept. 23. 1759. 21[£], a small piece of Glebe, & V. Ho. where he is to reside. Feb. 1760 Going to Farningham p. 357.
Shenton[10], Cur. here & at Bredherst ⟨Pr⟩. See July 1764. 24[£] & Surpl Fees. Dismissed by the Vicar for Incontinency March 1765. Dead Apr. 1765.
W[m] Jones[11] of Ch. Ch. to serve this & Bredherst p. 236 where see. 24[£], Surpl Fees, apartmnt in the House. Ord. Pr. June 21 1765. Going to Maidstone June 1766.
Dormer[12], who hath a Living in Suffolk, to serve this & Bredherst June 1766. Going June 1767.

1758 Conf. 15. 1762. 9. 1766. 13

[1] The daughter of Robert Osborne of Hartlip, her third husband was Thomas Gibbon. She also left £50 for educating poor children in Bobbing: Hasted VI, p. 200.
[2] (17?–66), of Kent, m. Queens' C 1731, BA 1735, MA 1738, BD 1747, fellow 1735, taxor 1739, master mathematical school Rochester, V. Hartlip, 1756-9, V. Stockbury, 1759-66.
[3] (1727-1809), of Chatham, Kent, m. Pembroke O 1746, m. St John's C 1747, BA 1750, MA (Clare) 1754, fellow 1753-5, V. Halling, 1754-9, V. Hartlip, 1759-87, V. Monkton, 1786-1809, poor vicar, 1774-1809.
[4] Samuel Pratt (1727-), of Boughton, Kent, m. Oriel 1745, BA 1750.

[5] (17?–92), V. Hartlip, 1787–92.

[6] Probably (1746–1801), of Colva, co. Radnor, m. Magdalen Hall 1784, BA 1788, MA 1791, V. Hartlip, 1792–4, and 94–4, V. Stockbury, 1795–1801.

[7] V. Hartlip, 1795–1810.

[8] (1713–59), of Stroud, Kent, m. St John's C 1732, BA 1736, minor canon of Rochester, 1736–59, V. Hartlip, 1747–50, V. Stockbury, 1750–9.

[9] (1735–1810), of Croydon, Surrey, m. Clare Hall 1752, BA 1756, MA 1759, adm. Middle Temple 1755, R. Stanmer, 1770–1, V. South Mimms and Northaw, Herts, 1773–90.

[10] Perhaps Paul Shenton, of Ewell, Surrey, m. Trinity C 1745, BA 1751.

[11] (1742–?), of Talley, co. Carmathen, m. Christ Church 1762.

[12] William Dormer (1719–1788), of Rochester, Kent, m. University 1735, BA 1739, R. Witchling, 1767–88.

Page 213

Iwade C All Saints. AD^n of Cant. Propr. & P. ⟨Mr Rigden[1] of Feversham his Tenant⟩. Certified 8^f. Augmented since with 200^f by Lot 1730 ⟨& with 400^f in 1766⟩. 2 Farms, & 17 Cottages. Service once a Month, as usual. [1759 once in 3 weeks]. Cat. in Lent. 4 Sacr. 8 Com. No Offertory. No Ho. for the Minister. Now Oct. 3. 1759 to be served once a fortnight, at 3 in the afternoon, except Sacr. Days, when Morning Prayer is omitted at the Curates other parish. Church & Chancell small & dirty. 2^f to the poor. 2 Bells. 1766 shd have Service once every Sunday See above. The chief Farmers are s^d to be nearer to Bobbing Church, than their own: & the rest to go to Milton or Sittingbourn. No body can be got 1766 to serve it once a week.

Iwade was a chapel to Teynham see p. 177.

Tho. Leigh[2] Cur. R. of Murston p. { }. R. of St Margaret, Cant. p. 39. Seq. of St Mary Bredin p. 41. Lives in the Palace at Cant. Hath given up Iwade Oct. 3. 1759.

Fra. Gregory[3] Cur. Oct. 3. 1759. See p. 217 & below here.

Osmund Beauvoir[4] see p. 217.

John Lough[5] cur. lic. 1790.

Egerton Leigh[6], son to Tho[7]. Serves this, & Murston p. 220. & Tong p. 228. Salary here, after the Rate of 20^f a year. [1759 Gone to Minster in Shepey. Lamprey[8], Pr. 8^f. Cur. of Milton by Sittingbourn p. 217. To serve it once a fortnight & have the whole Income.

Mr Lough[9] Cur Sal. £60 for this & Milton.

1758 Conf. 13. 1762. 6. NB

[1] George Rigden: Hasted VI, p. 574.   [2] See p. 39, n. 3.
[3] See p. 7, n. 5.   [4] See p. ii, n. 47.
[5] PC Iwade, 1790, C. Milton next Sittingbourne, 1807, V. Sittingbourne, 1817–26.
[6] See p. 192, n. 8.   [7] See n. 3.
[8] See p. 22, n. 10.   [9] See n. 5.

Page 214

D. Sittingbourn

Kingsdown R. St Catharine. ⟨There is a Kingsdown in the parish of Ringwold p. 191⟩. Eliz. Umfrey[1], widow P. [But Ecton saith, the Chapter of Rochester.]. Tenths 10–11. Certified 45^f. Now called 40^f ⟨Let for 45^f. 60^f 35^f clear of

Curate &c⟩. 7 Ho. A Farmer & his Family, Papists. Service once on Sundays. No Ch[n] fit to be cat. 4 Sacr. 6 Com. No Offertory. A Payment of 5–4 to the Cur. of Bapchild. Ecton. Church small, clean, in good Repair: south side lately rebuilt. Chancel in good Repair. No Ho. Glebe 20 Acres. 2 Bells.

Tho. Pennington[2] MA. R. 16 July 1754. C. of Sutton near Dover p. 198. Assistant at Deal Chapel p. 182. Lives at Deal 30 miles off. 1766 R. of Tunstall p. 229.
Thomas Pennington[3] A.M. 1786.

John Irons[4] MA Cur. 20[f]. V. of Linsted p. 165, 166, the next parish, where he resides. Resigned 1765 on acct of Age & Infirmities.
John Carver[5] C. See p. 239. 20[f] Serves this & Milsted p. 246. Goes Mich. 1766.
Pierrepoint Cromp[6], who hath a Living in Gloucestershire, coming to serve this {& Linsted} ⟨only Aug. 1766⟩. Lives at {Milsted} Frinsted.
M[r]. Tucker[7] Cur. Sal £50 for this & Tunstall.
Edw. Porten Benezet[8] A.B. Curate £21. Lic.1790.

1758 Conf. 6 . 1762. 8. 1766. 5

[1] Wife of Finch Umfrey, of Dartford. She died in 1781: Hasted VI, p. 114.
[2] See p. ii, n. 35.   [3] See p. 199, n. 7.   [4] See p. 166, n. 1.
[5] (1741–?), of Westminster, m. Oriel 1759.
[6] [or Crumpe] (1732–97), of Holme Pierrepoint, Notts, m. Jesus C 1750, BA 1754, MA 1757, R. Cotgrave, Notts, 1756–97, R. Holme Pierrepoint, Notts, 1770–97. His father was V. Newnham, Glos.
[7] Stephen Tucker, see p. 129, n. 3.
[8] (17?–1834), m. CCCC 1786, scholar, BA 1789, MA (St John's) 1792, C. Tunstall and Kingsdown, 1790, V. Newton-by-Castle Acre, Norfolk, 1798–1834, V. Bungay, Suffolk, 1803–34.

Page 215
Leysdown al. Leesdown V. S[t] Clement. Belonged to the Mon. of S[t] Radegund. ABP. Propr. & P. Tenths 1–1–0. Certified 48[f]. Called in ABP Herrings Book 70[f]. The Vicar saith, not 55[f]. 13 Ho. of which 5 are Farm Ho. the rest Cottages, 3 uninhabited. Service once on Sundays. Cat. exp. in Lent. 4 Sacr. 10 Com. One half, worth 50[s] a Year, of a House & Land, given to the Poor. Church & chancel new built & handsome. The walls & Roof of the Ho. very good: inside scarce habitable. Barn extremely out of Repair. Glebe 7 Acres. 1 Bell.
Lic. to V. to reside at East church. V. Ho. being out of Repair & uninhabitable, & the air very unhealthy 1668 Entry B. 137. Leysdown held by Disp with Warden R 1674 III. 240. Without Disp V. 50 VII. 360.
200 or 300 Acres of Ground laid down to Grass lately, on wch the Rectory is sunk 20[f] a year, & the Vicarage must rise nearly, if not quite as much, Mr Leigh 1763.
A Faculty granted to take down the Barn Oct. 14. 1763 Entry book 10 p. 82. Of the value, see Mr Leighs Letter Jan 12. 1765.

Jo. Taylor Lamb[1], V. Feb. 13. 1757. Master of Croydon School. Resides there. Vacant by Cession Nov. 21. 1761.
Liscombe Mautlbe Stretch[2] V. Apr. 20. 1762. See ordination Book Apr. 18 1762[3]. Gone May 1762 to be C. at Warlingham Surrey, till he & I can rebuild the

V. Ho. here. Dec. 1767 Sequesterd for a Debt of 480 to Mr Champion, Mercht at Bristol.
David Martin[4] Vicar 1786 resides.

Jo. Murthwaite[5] Cur. Also Cur. of Minster in Shepey p. 218. Salary here 21^f. 5 miles asunder. Dead.
Egerton Leigh[6], Cur. of both. 30^f & Surpl. Fees. Lives at Minster, where he is Curate p. 218. Gone to Sandwich.
Lewis Lewis[7] Cur. of both Dec. 1763. Lives at Minster. Said May 1764 to keep low Company & drink. Hath 30^f from each. A better to be got. None yet May 1765. Gone 1767.
David Martin[8] D. here & at Minster. 30^f at each. Ord Pr. Sept 21. 1767.

1758 Conf. 9. 1762. None. 1766. 1.

[1] (1727-74), of Ditchling, Suffolk, m. St John's C 1749, BA 1750, master Whitgift's School, Croydon, 1751-74, V. Leysdown, 1757-62, R. Keston, 1761-74, chaplain to Croydon hospital.
[2] See p. 52, n. 6.   [3] LPL, VG 1/10, p. 151.
[4] See p. 52, n. 5.   [5] Also C. Minster.
[6] See p. 192, n. 8.
[7] (1736-?), of London, m. Christ Church 1753, BA 1757.
[8] See n. 4.

Page 216
D. Sittingbourne
Milsted al. Milksted R. St Mary & St Cross. Richd Tylden[1] Esqr P. Tenths 17-6. Certified 44^f. Now called 70^f ⟨80 clearAD^n⟩. 31 straggling Ho. [Richd Tylden Esqr]. One farmer a Papist. Service once on Sundays [1759 twice because R. serves no other Cure] & on Chr. Day. Prayers 5 Nov. Dec. 26. Jan 30. AshW. good F. & Monday in Easter Week. Cat. on Sundays in Lent, & good Fr. Not exp. 4 Sacr. 10 or 12 Com. [very few]. Offertory distributed by Mr Tylden above, the Rectors Father. But he will alter this. Land worth 2-5-0 given for teaching Ch^n to read. Church clean & neat. Chancel wants some Repair. Ho. very neat & in good Repair, by Mr Tylden. Outho. in good Order. Glebe 3 Acres. 3 Bells. 1765. 1 Man, 1 woman, Papists.

Richd Osborn Tylden[2] R. 28 March 1748. Resides constantly in the Parsonage Ho. Good, rich. died Nov. 30.1767.
Ed. Smith[3] BA R. {Feb. 24} ⟨March 3⟩ 1767. was Cur. of Murston p. 220 where see. Gone.
Richard Cook Tylden[4] A.M. Rector 1787.

John Carver[5] C. p. 239. Mr Tylden infirm. 20^f Serves it with Kingsdown p. 214. Goes Mich 1766.

1758 Conf. 28. 1762. 11. 1766. 11.

[1] The Tylden family had been patrons since the reign of Edward I: Hasted VI, p. 111.
[2] Secker is mistaken: he died in 1766. (1723-66), of Milsted, Kent, m. St John's C 1741, BA 1745, MA 1750, R. Milsted, 1748-66.
[3] (17?-87), Edward Smith, of Skirpenbeck, Lancs, m. Christs 1761, scholar 1762, BA 1765, MA 1768, C. Murston, 1766, R. Milsted, 1767-87, R. Frinsted, 1779-87, chaplain to the earl Powys.

4 (17?–1819), of Milsted, Kent, m. Jesus C 1778, BA 1782, MA 1787, RR. Milsted and Frinsted, 1787–1819, chaplain to Betty Maria, dowager baroness of Teynham, 1787. 'A most amiable person and an excellent scholar, suffered a family living to devolve on his brother, in preference to an acceptance of anti-Christian confessions of faith as the condition of tenure': Venn.
5 See p. 214, n. 5.

Page 217

Milton by Sittingbourn V. Holy Trinity. Belonged to St Austins Mon. at Cant. DCh. of Cant P. K^s books 13-2-6. Wake 80$^£$ ⟨AD^n 140$^£$ see below⟩. The Town hath 150 Ho. There are abt 10 Farms, & 20 Cottages besides. One Popish Family of low Rank. Whole Service. Prayers on Holydays & W. Fr. from AshW. to Mich. The Church at a great Distance from the Town. The late Cur. neglected catechizing. Care shall be taken. 4 Sacr. Generally 70 or 80 Com. [But few]. Several Benefactions to the Poor, which see. Out of them the Clerk hath 9$^£$ a year for teaching 10 Poor Boys writing, Reading, & Accounts. One Worsley officiated here, as being in Orders, & was not. See the Book of Cautions[1]. A very aguish Place. Church noble & very neat. Chancel the same. Ho. good & in good order. Stable in good Order. Glebe ½ Acre. 5 Bells. V. saith Milton is much diminished by displanting of Hops: & that this & the Minor Canonry make but 90$^£$ clear.

Francis Gregory[2] V. 18 July 1751. Min Can. of Cant. Cur. of St Geo. & M. Magd. there p. 35. Resides there. Cur. of Iwade p. 213. Void by Cesion Dec. 4. 1764.
Osmund Beavoir[3], MA , V. Dec. 17. 1764. V. of Littlebourn p. 17 holds both.
John Rose[4] A.M. 1790.
Henry John Todd[5], A.M. 1792.

Lamprey[6] Cur. 50$^£$ ⟨& Rooms in V. Ho⟩. Resides. Serves also Iwade p. 213. M^r. Lough[7] Cur. of Iwade.

1758. Conf. 148. 1762. 67. 1766. 75

1 LPL, Caution Book, 1758–85, pp. 1–2. George Worsley *alias* Hughes is there described as 'Son to a Dissenting Schoolmaster at Hertford, & not long since a Broker in Exchange Alley, & between 30 & 40 Years of age. . .falsely pretending to have been ordained by the Bishop of Salisbury'.
2 See p. 7, n. 5.   3 See ii, n. 47.
4 See 196, n. 12.   5 See 134, n. 3.
6 See p. 22, n. 10.   7 See p. 213, n. 5.

Page 218

D. Sittingbourne
Minster in Shepey C. St Mary & St Sexburgh. Belonged to the Priory of Sexburgh. Will Gore[1] of Boxley Esqr P. In ABP Tenisons Visitation book 1712[2], he hath set down with his own Hand Mr Goodyer[3], as Curate, Salary 40$^£$. In ABP Wakes Book of Entries VI p. 298 it appears, that Ric. Tysoe[4] was nominated Cur. by John Gore[5] Esqr, with a Salary of 40$^£$ & Surplice Fees: on which he was licenced. Lately the Salary was but 20$^£$. Mr William Gore saith it was but 30$^£$ before Mr Goodyers time; & that he knows not when it was reduced to 20$^£$, but found it so. He willingly nominated Mr Leigh[6] with 40$^£$: but mention of the Surplice Fees ⟨which are worth 30 or 40$^£$ a year,⟩ is omitted by

mistake. Mr Leigh promised to get it put into a new Nomination, in order to Licence. They are sometimes 30^f, sometimes not 10^f. The Parish contains the Garrison of Sheerness & the adjoyning Ho: ab^t 70. It contains ab^t 70 Ho. besides: of which ab^t 25 are Farm Ho. & a number of these, amounting to 650^f a Year, are rented by out-dwellers, who carry on their Business by Servants. Many Methodists in the Garrison & Houses adjoyning: assemble in a rented Room not licenced. Mr Whitfield[7], Mr Jones[8] & others frequently come to them. But Will Shrubshall, a Shipwright in the Yard generally officiates. Of late Years they have greatly increased; & being united in Interest, proceed as much from temporal as spiritual Views. Seem now at a Stand, & less vehement. They consist chiefly of labouring Men, with two or three inferior Officers. 1760. David Price[9] Chaplain: from Lyminge p. 104. Service once on Sundays. Prayers W. Fr. in Lent, when Cat. is exp. But few Ch^n above 8 Years old are sent, & no Servants. 4 Sacr. Usually betw. 20 & 30 Com. The Offertory money is given by the $Ch W^n$ for schooling Parish Ch^n: & what more is wanting is taken out of the Church Assessment. A Poors Ho. & 3 Acres of Land.

Mr Tysoe, formerly Cur. See above, told Mr Murthwaite[10], his Successor, that Queenborough used to pay to Minster, as the Mother Church 9^d for every Burial: & that the Officers of Minster, fearing, that a renewal of this Demand might tend to bring that of Queenborough & its poor back into Minster, gave him in lieu of it the above-mentioned 3 Acres, called Poors Meadow. But on his Death they resumed them. Abt Burials from the Sailors Hospital see Letters 1763.

A Petiton dated 4 July 1758 & signed by the Patron & Curate was presented to the ABP: setting forth, that they were informed that a new Chapel had been built at Sheerness, & that a Burial Ground was intended to be inclosed contiguous to it, & that the ABP had been petitioned to consecrate them, & praying to be heard against it. The ABP hath not been petitioned to consecrate them.

Mr Delafaye[11] is Chaplain of the {Garrison of} ⟨Ships at⟩ Sheerness. ⟨50^f a year⟩. R. of All Saints, Cant. p. 28 & Cur. of Queenborough p. 222.

Mr David Price, ⟨from Lyminge p. 104. Chaplain to the Garrison⟩ {his Deputy}. See his Letter[12] ab^t Duty & profits. Desires Oct. 1761 to be removed. He was appointed by the Governor of Sheerness, Sr J. Mordaunt[13].

[1] Died in 1768: Hasted VI, p. 228.   [2] This has not been traced.

[3] John Goodyer (16?–1715), m. St Catherine's C 1687, BA 689, MA 1695, V. Bapchild, 1697–1709, V. Newington by Sittingbourne, 1708–15.

[4] (1693–1746), of London, m. Jesus C 1712, scholar 1714, BA 1716, MA 1719, C. Minster, 1719, R. Kenardington, 1721–46, V. Bredgar, 1722–45, R. Luddesdown, 1744–6.

[5] Bought the advowson from the Livesey family: Hasted V, p. 228.

[6] See p. 192, n. 9.

[7] George Whitefield (1714–70), leader of the Calvinistic Methodists.

[8] John Jones (1721–85), of Cardiganshire, m. Trinity O 1736, BA 1739, BA 1742, B. Med 1745, master of Kingswood school, 1748. He was ordained in the 1760s by a bishop of the Greek orthodox church, but was later re-ordained by the bishop of London. He died as vicar of Harwich.

[9] See p. 73, n. 13.   [10] See p. 162, n. 7.   [11] See p. 28, n. 4.

[12] LPL, MS Secker 3, ff. 246–7, Price to Secker, 26 May 1761.

[13] (1697–1780), MP for Pontefract, 1730–4, MP for Whitchurch, 1735–41, MP for Cockermouth, 1741–68. He was the governor of Sheerness from 1752–78.

Page 219

Minster in Shepey continued.

Church & chancel noble & in good Order: North Chancel, belonging to Mr Gore[1], wants some Repair. No Ho. 5 Bells. Mr Randall[2], the richest man in the Island, lives here.

Joseph Murthwaite[3] Cur. here & at Leysdownp. 215. Dead.
Egerton Leigh[4] nom. Cur. by Mr Gore 11 March ⟨lic. 12th⟩ 1759. See p. 218. Resides here. Cur. also of Leysdown p. 215. V. of St Mary Sandwich p. 194 & Tilmanston p. 199.
Wm Ph^p Menzies[5] A.B. 1789.

Lewis Lewis[6], Dep. & Cur of Leysdown p. 215. See p. 370. Gone.
David Martin[7] D. at both 60^f. See 215. Ord Pr. 21 Sept. 1767.
Saml Langley[8] Cur. Sal £30.
Mordaunt Leathes[9] Cur. Sal. £30. lic 1789.

1758 Conf. Minster 11. Sheerness 45. 1762. Minster 67. Sheerness 34.1766 Minster 42. Sheerness 30.

[1] See p. 218, n. 1.
[2] Thomas Randall.
[3] See p. 215, n. 5.
[4] See p. 192, n. 9.
[5] See p. 135, n. 5.
[6] See p. 215, n. 7.
[7] See p. 52, n. 5.
[8] Perhaps (1756–1839), of Checkley, Staffs, m. Worcester, BA 1777, MA 1780, C. Minster, 1785, R. Checkley, 1791–1839.
[9] (17?–1807), C. Minster, 1789, PC Harty, 1796–1807.

Page 220

D. Sittingbourne

Murston. R. All Saints. Sir Tho. Hales Bart & John Hales[1] Esqr. K^s books 10-14-0. ABP Wake 120^f. AD^n Head thinks much more ⟨180^f⟩. 5 Farms, 14 Cottages ⟨See below⟩. Service once on Sundays, & once at Tong. p. { }. [Must be twice, as soon as a Curate can be got for Tong.]. No weekly Prayers. [qu. good Fr. Chr. Day]. Cat. exp. in Lent. 4 Sacr. 6 Com. [very few]. Tenor Bell cracked: will soon be put in Order. 8 Ho. above a mile, & some 5 miles from the Church, saith R. Feb. 25. 1759. Yet he saith in Answers in Inquiries, that the Extent of the Parish is abt 4 miles. Church pretty good, but many things wanting in it. Chancel indifferent, wants white-washing. Ho. out Ho. & Gardens, very handsome & good, by Mr Leigh. Glebe 53 Acres. 2 Bells, 1 cracked. Very unhealthy. AD^n.

Tho. Leigh[2] MA. R 1 Jan 1732. R. of St Margaret Cant. ⟨p. 39⟩ 16 miles off, where he resides. Seq. of St Mary Bredin p. 41. Cur. of Iwade p. 213.
Egerton Leigh[3] Master of Arts R. October 11 1774.
John Hargrave Standen[4] A.M. 1788.

Sir Sam. Bickley[5] Bar^t, ord. Pr by BP Wilcox[6], Cur. 20^f & Surplice Fees. To have more, when he doth the whole Duty. 30^f from Chr. 1759. Serves this twice: & Bapchild p. 204 of which he is V. once. Only 4 or 5 have come, & only 4 or 5 times. AD^n. Mr Leigh will get a Curate to serve Murston solely. AD^n. Mr Gurney[7] Junr to serve this twice & Bapchild once Nov. 1763. Doth, 1764.

Edw. Smith[8] ⟨BA⟩ son to Mr Smith[9] of Borden, {to be} ord. D. Tr. S. 1766. 40^f. To reside at Sittingbourn. Ord. Pr. Dec. 21. 1766. 2. Serves this & Milsted p. 216. Gone.
Rector resides but has a Curate, M^r. Miller[10] Sal £25.

1758 Conf. 25. 1762. 11. 1766. 10

[1] See p. 3, nn. 1, 2.   [2] See p. 39, n. 3.   [3] See p. 192, n. 8.
[4] (17?–1802), of Middlesex, m. Queens' C 1776, scholar 1778, BA 1780, MA 1783, R. Murston, 1788–1802.
[5] See p. 204, n. 4.
[6] John Wilcocks, bishop of Gloucester, 1721–31, bishop of Rochester, 1731–58.
[7] See p. 79, n. 3.   [8] See p. 216, n. 3.   [9] John Smith. See p. 206, n. 7.
[10] Probably Thomas Miller (1737–92), of London, m. Clare 1756, scholar, BA 1760, MA 1763, R. Wormshill, 1767–92.

Page 221
Newington by Sittingbourn V. St Mary. Eton Coll. Propr. & P. K^s books 14^f. Wake 60^f. Certified 72-10-0. Now called 80^f ⟨See below⟩. 27 Ho. in the Street, 12 Farms, 12 Cottages. Service once on Sundays. Prayers W. Fr. in Lent. In that Season Ch^n cat. & sometimes on other Sundays. 4 Sacr. Usually abt 30 Com. at a time. 20 Acres of Land to the Parsonage with its rectorial Tithes, & Tithe in Stockbury Parish let for 20^f a year. To the Vicarage 1 Acre of Land with its vicarial Tithe. To the Repairs of the Church 2 Acres. The Poor have 3 Quarters of Wheat out of the Parsonage, & a small Barn & ½ Acre of Land given by one Tomlin[1]. 1½ Acre of Land called the Play stole, doubtful whether it belongs to Church or Poor. V. Ho. in tolerable Repair. Above 60^f laid out upon it in 1754. V. saith, the Income for several years was but 66^f, & if the Hops be displanted, will be less than ever ⟨Above 100^f Mr Saunders⟩. Church & chancel in good Repair. Ho. good, new fronted & improved by Sir Hugh. Out ho. in good Order. Glebe 1 Acre. 5 Bells.

Sir Hugh Burdett[2] V. 11 Feb. 1741 ⟨dead 5 Sept. 1760⟩. Hath been absent at different time 4½ Years. Resides now at a Shopkeepers: cannot afford to keep House. Complains of a weakness in his Brain.
John Saunders[3] MA Chaplain of Ch. Ch. V. Dec. 1760. Resides See p. 211. 1768 V. of Farningham p. 357. Resides chiefly there. See there abt Curate. Mr Cooper[4] from Marden to be here till Mich. then Dr Benson[5]. Mr Saunders going to Farningham.
Whigmore[6], Cur. was of Queens Coll. Camb. hath been Chaplain to the Ordinary at Chatham near 20 Years. Lives at Brompton near Chatham. Salary { }.
Prat[7] John 1760 V. of Hartlip p. 212.
Henry Friend[8] Cur. of Halstow lic. 1782 Sal. £50. for this & Halstow.

1758. None conf. 1762. 20. 1766. 24

[1] Simon Tomlyn, by his will in 1684, to buy loaves for those present at divine service: Hasted VI, p. 64.
[2] (17?–60), of Fulham, Middlesex, m. Gonville and Caius 1735, BA 1739, C. Wotton Underwood, Bucks, 1740–2, V. Weston Underwood, 1740–2, V. Newington, 1742–60.
[3] See p. 33, n. 3.

4 Samuel Cooper. Perhaps (1736–?), of Postcomb, Oxon, m. Christ Church 1754, BA 1759.
5 John Benson, p. ii n. 29.
6 John Wigmore (17?–74), of Essex, m. Queens' C 1722, BA 1727, C. Caldecot, Herts, 1729, chaplain in Navy, 1738–40, chaplain Chatham, 1738–74.
7 See p. 212, n. 3.   8 See p. 211, n. 5.

Page 222

D. Sittingbourne

Queenborough C. Holy Trinity. Mayor & Jurats of Queenborough P. Belonged to the monastery of Sexburgh. Certified value 20–2–6. ABP Wakes book hath first 25^f, then 50^f. Now 20^f by Assessment. 84 Ho. Most of the Inhabitants Fishermen. No Ho. for the Minister. Whole Service, 2 Sermons on Sundays ⟨See below⟩. Cat. with Lewis's Exp. W. Fr. Sunday in Lent. 4 Sacr. Generally abt 40 Com. A Free School founded by the Corporation, & endowed by the Representatives during pleasure for the Freemens Children. At Easter the whole Offertory Money is the ministers: at other times, ½ is his Property, ½ appropriated to the Poor. There is a Subscription of 8 or 9^f a Year for the Afternoon Sermon. See below. The Church very neat, & Chancel. 5 Bells.
A Lecturer or Cur. elected by Mayor & Jurats lic Apr. 9. 1720 Entry B VI. 326. Cur. VIII. 233.

Theo. Delafaye[1] MA C. ⟨lic⟩ 28 May 1743. Chaplain of ⟨the ships at⟩ Sheerness p. 218 & R. of All Saints Cant. where he resides.
John Bonar[2] M.A. Cur: Licens'd Aug^t: 14 1773.
Joseph Hatherill[3] Licensed June 12 1775. resides.

John Wearg[4], Assistant. Ord. Deacon by BP Wilcox[5]. Brought to Trial for a Forgery, but got off. Hath officiated as a Priest: Drinks with low Company. The Corporation petitioned the ABP to ordain him Priest. The ABP hath required Mr Delafaye over & over to dismiss him. He doth not: pleading, that he can get no other Curate. Died Apr. 1760.
Jones[6], Henry, BA of Ch. Ch. Ox. C. ord. Pr. 21 Sept. 1760. 40^f. Subscription to him for Afternoon Sermon, not above 12^f. Schoolmaster. 1766 wants to omit Afternoon prayers & take a Curacy. Refused. Allowed him to omit Aft. Sermon. Going to Chatham at Mich 1766. The 40^f a year is for both Queenborough & Sheerness.
Wm Lewis[7] AM of Dubl. Coll. P. Apr. 1767. 45^f & 1^f here yearly till 50^f. Gone.
Fox[8] from Boughton Malherb p. 54. 45^f here 15 *** 20^f School.

1758 Conf. 49. 1762. 33. 1766. 31.

1 See p. 28, n. 4.   2 (?–1775), C. Queenborough, 1773–75.
3 Joshua Hatherill (Act Book: xi, 61) 'literate', C. Queenborough, 1775–1811.
4 He has not ben traced.   5 See p. 220, n. 6.   6 See p. 55, n. 13.
7 Probably William Lewis (1725–?), of Limerick, m. Trinity College Dublin 1741, BA 1746, MA 1754.
8 See p. 54, n. 7.

Page 223

Radfield. Libera Capella 2-2-0. Vide Inst. Book old. Ecton. Qu. what this means. On search, nothing hath been found in the Register books concerning Radfield. But the ABP 23 Aug 1492 instituted John Talbot[1] to the free chapel of Rodevild [called in the Margin Rudvyld] in the Parish of Bakchild [probably Bapchild. See here p. 204]. to which he was presented by Rich[d] Lovelas[2] Esq[r]. on the Death of the last Incumbent & made him Custodian in the same. Reg. Morton fol 153a.

[1] Possibly of Bristol, BA Oxford 1463, R. St Mary le Port, Bristol until 1468.
[2] Richard Lovelace, of London, bought Bayford castle between Sittingbourne and Bapchild in the reign of Henry VI: Hasted VI, p. 156.

Page 224

D. Sittingbourne

Rainham V. S[t] Margaret. Belonged to the monastery of Leeds. ABP P. ⟨Adv granted by Qu. Mary⟩. K[s] books 14-4-7. Wake 60[£] & afterwards 140[£] ⟨130[£] clear AD[n]⟩. 88 Ho. besides the principal Street. 4 other Hamlets. The Church very good. Several Absenters both of the poorer sort & others. Whole Service on Sundays. Prayers on all Festivals & Fasts, W. Fr. in Lent & all Passions Week. Cat. exp. in Lent from ABP Wake. 2 Sacr. at each of the great Festivals & at Mich. Number of Com. smaller than might be expected. Religious Tracts distributed. 2 Acres of Land planted with Cherries, 2 with Pears, 2 with Apples, worth 10[£] a Year, given to the Church. Lands in annuities from Lands given to the poor, worth 11-10-0. Rightly applied. Church noble, in good Order: & chancel. Ho & outho. good & in Repair. Glebe 3 Acres. 6 Bells.

Henry Shove[1] MA V. 16 Oct. 1723. V. of Doddington p. 156, where he chiefly resides. Seq. of Newnham p. 168. Cur. of Bredherst p. 236.
Wm Taswell[2] V. 10 Jan[ry]. 1772.
James Richards[3] Vicar, Nov[r] 5: 1777.

Henry Shove[4], son to the V. Priest, Cur. 30[£]. Use of V. Ho. &c. Went to be Cur. of Harrietsham p. 241. at Chr. 1758 was also Cur. of Bredhurst, adjoyning, p. 236.
Will. Polhill[5] to be Cur. when of Age for Deacons orders. Served in the meantime once a Sunday from Chatham. AD[n] May 23. 1759. Ordained before he was of Age, & is a Cur. in Dioc. Roch.
Hen. Thompson[6] BA bapt Jan 1. 1735/6. Ord. Deacon Dec 23. 1759. 3. 35[£]. Son of Tho. Thompson[7] of Petham Esq[r]. He hath also Surpl. Fees, & Use of the House, Furniture & Stable. Gone to Elham p. 99.
Arth. Clark[8] C. & at Upchurch p. 230. Serves Rainham twice Salary as above. See Bobbing p. 206. 1763 R. of Witchling p. 232.
Mr Pow[9], a Scotsman, for some time ⟨Gone. Bad⟩. Now March 1765 Mr Apsley[10] serves this twice & Upchurch once. July 1766 Going to Deal Chapel.
Davis[11] Cur. here & at Upchurch p. 230.
Mr Keefe[12] Cur. Sal. £34.

1758 Conf. 51. 1762. 23. 1766. 6.

[1] See p. 156, n. 7.   [2] See p. 16, n. 13.
[3] (17?-1804), V. Rainham, 1777-1804.   [4] See p. 156, n. 8.
[5] See p. 50, n. 16.   [6] See p. 38, n. 2.
[7] Owned the manor of Kenfield in Petham. He died in 1762, and left Kenfield to Henry, his second son: Hasted IX, p. 312.
[8] See p. 206, n. 6.   [9] He has not been traced.   [10] See p. 6, n. 5.
[11] William Davis. Perhaps of Llanvihangel, Radnorshire, m. Jesus O 1754, or of Rhaydor, Radnorshire, m. Jesus O 1761, BA (Christ Church) 1765.
[12] He has not been traced.

Page 225

Rodmersham V. St Nicolas. Belonged to the Commandery[1] of West-Peckham. Tho. Godfrey Lushington[2] Esqr P. [Sir Edw. Hales[3]. Ecton]. Tenths 16–8. Certified 30$^£$. Wake 35$^£$ ⟨40 clear AD^n see below⟩. 2 small Hamlets. In all 27 Ho. Service once on Sundays. Prayers on good Fr. [qu. Chr. Day]. Cat. exp. in Lent. 4 Sacr. between 20 & 30 Com. An Acre of Woodland given to the Church. A Gift of Sheep to the Poor, lost. See the Answers. 3$^£$ a Year paid to V. out of the Parsonage. V. Ho. is a Cottage, but in good Repair. Church clean & in good Order. Chancel very dirty. Glebe 5½ Acres. 4 Bells. Lic. to take down Spire Entry B. VI. 159.
ABP collated on Lapse 14 Nov. 1722.
1767 Augm. with 400$^£$ by S^r Ph. Boteler & Qus bounty.

John Allet[4] V. 14 Oct. 1751. V. of Teynham p. 177. Lives at Murston, p. 220 a mile off, & serves both from thence. One of the 10 poor vicars. See p. 177. 1767 Gone to Sandwich for health. Dav. Martin[5] Cur. Gone Aug. See 177.
Thomas Edmundson[6] Clerk Vic. Octo^r. 21: 1776.

Mr Dormer[7] R. of Witchling p. 232 allowed to serve this with that for a while. See there
Mr Penry[8] Cur. Sal. £25 & Surplice fees lic. by the Archdeacon.

1758. Conf. 32. 1762. 13. 1766. 10.

[1] i.e. Knights Templar.
[2] Thomas Godfrey Lushington, died in 1757 and was succeeded by James Stephen Lushington (preb of Carlisle).
[3] See p. 33, n. 2.   [4] This should be James Allet. See p. 154, n. 6.
[5] See p. 52, n. 5.
[6] (17?-97), of Middlesex, m. CCCC 1748, V. Rodmersham, 1776-1797.
[7] William Dormer. See p. 212, n. 12.   [8] See p. 204, n. 8.

Page 226

D. Sittingbourne

Sittingbourne V. St Michael. Belonged to the Priory of Clerkenwell. ABP Propr. & P ⟨adv. granted by Qu. Mary⟩. K^s books 10$^£$. Wake 60$^£$. Now called 90$^£$ ⟨100 AD^n⟩. 800 Acres. Abt 130 Ho. all but one within ½ mile of the Church. Service once on Sundays. V. serves Borden the other Part [1759 serves only Sittingbourn, twice]. Prayers W. Fr. in Lent, all Passion Week, & the Holydays at Easter, Whits. Chr. Ch^n cat. at the Schools, not at Church: but V. will do as directed. 4 Sacr. 40 or 50 Com. ⟨see below⟩ [very few]. A small Alms Ho. with

40[s] a Year. 5 Seams of Peas [at 30[s] each] to the Poor from the ABP[s] Lessee: & some small Charities. Part of the Offertory applied to keep Poor Ch[n] at School. 20 or more Com. at Chr. 1758 than ever before. The whole Sunday service was performed in ABP Wakes & ABP Potters time. Church clean & in good Order. Ho. very slight, neat & in good Repair. Stable & chaise Ho. new by Mr Bland. Glebe 1 Acre. 6 Bells. Inside of Ch. & Chancel burnt. 1765 May Church nearly repaired. Chancel going on.

Tho. Bland[1] MA V. 26 Nov. 1742. Cur. of Borden p. 207. [1759 not now.]. Resided in V. Ho. 15 Years: went then for his Health, by a physicians advice to Tunstal, 1½ mile from his Parish church. He hath there an Estate, & {at lease} the Rectory of little Warley in the Hundreds of Essex: but saith, that these with Sittingbourn are but 160[f] a year clear. Yields readily to officiate here twice on Sundays. Desires Tunstall, when vacant. See Letters[2].
Richard Podmore[3] Clerk LLB. Vicar Sept: 7: 1776.
Samuel Evans[4] Clerk, Vicar Mar 27: 1778. resides.

1758 Conf. ⟨here 1285. of this Parish⟩ 99. 1762. Conf. here 570. Of this Parish 48. 1766. May 21 Conf here 521. Of this Parish 51.

[1] See p. 207, n. 5.
[2] LPL, MS Secker 3, f. 250, Secker to Bland, 8 October 1758.
[3] See p. 59, n. 2.   [4] See p. 206, n. 8.

Page 227
Stockbury V. S[t] Mary Magd. Belonged to the Priory of Leeds. DCh. of Rochester P. K[s] books 9–11–0½. Wake first 80[f], then 100[f]. AD[n] Head thinks, 130[f]. V. saith 75 or 80[f] in all. See his Letter. 80 Ho. 260 Inhabitants. Service once on Sundays here & once at Hartlip, 2 miles off. Thus for 11 years, with the Leave of ABP Potter, & Herring. [But ABP Potter had been dead 11 Years, & ABP Herrings book saith twice]. No mention of Cat. At each Sacr. [used to be 4] from 40 to 60 Com. A Donation for teaching 8 Ch[n] to read. Church indifferent & dirty. Chancel tolerable. Ho. mean, but in pretty good Repair. Out Ho. wants Repair. Glebe 9 Acres. 5 Bells.

Caesar Curtis[1] V. 25 July. Min. Can. of Rochester. Served it from thence ⟨8 miles off⟩. No mention of occasional Duty. *** Died June 1759.

Pearce Dixon[2] V. 1 Sept 1759 ⟨Died at the middle of Aug. 1766⟩. Master of Rochester Math. School: was V. of Hartlip. p. 212. *** Serves it from Rochester.
Thomas Frank[3] L.L.B. V. Dec. 11. 1766. does his own duty.
James Jones[4] A.M. Vicar 1795.

James Thurston[5] Cur. Serves it with Bredgarp. 208.

1758 Conf. 21. 1762. 20. 1766. 21.

[1] See p. 212, n. 8.   [2] Ibid., n. 2.   [3] See p. 207, n. 11.
[4] See p. 212, n. 6.   [5] See p. 208, n. 9.

Page 228

D. Sittingbourne

Tong V. S[t] Giles. Belonged to the Abbey of Langden. Dutton Stede[1] Esq[r] presented Nov. 6. 1712 & Jan 18. 1716. ABP. collated on a Lapse Sept. 28. 1723. And Eliz. Holdsworth[2] Patron for that Turn, presented Benj. Longley Dec. 3. 1750 ⟨Mrs Turner[3] of Harriestsham claims the presentation⟩. K[s] books 8-6-8. Certified Value 55-3-0. Now 45[f] or 50[f] clear of Taxes, Tenths &c ⟨See below⟩. 19 Ho. An old Anab. Teacher of low Rank. Service once on Sundays. No Prayers on other Days. [qu. good Fri. Chr Day]. Cat. in Lent, with Lewis's Exp. Few come, sometimes none. 4 Sacr. Abt 10 Com. each time. 10[f] a Year reserved to V. in ABP[s] Lease of the Rectory, by Juxon. Church small, clean. Chancel wants whitewashing. Ho. indifferent, but in Repair, improved by Mr Longley. Stable in good Repair. Glebe 1 Acre. 3 Bells. Very unhealthy. AD[n]. Licence to reside at Sittingbourn for Health Entry B. III.176.

Benj. Longley[4] V. 3 Dec. 1750. V. of Eynesford D. Shoreham, p. 356. Cur. of Ash p. 2 where he resides. Was also Cur. of Woodnesborough p. 203. Rob[t]. Jones Moreton[5] L.L.B. Vicar 1783.

Egerton Leigh[6] Cur of Murston, a mile off p. 220. Gone. 20[f] & Surpl. Fees. Sir Samuel Bickley[7] serves both, till another Cur. can be got here. The People, not liking him, have assessed V. to the poor. He would give more to another. V. of Bapchild p. 204.
Wm Marsh[8] Cur. Nov. 1759 R. of Bicknor p. 205. Going Chr. 1764.
Ch. Allen[9] may be Cur. 1765. V. of Bapchild p. 204. Is Cur. June 1765. Gone.
Edw. Penry[10] V. of Bapchild serves this Mich 1766. Goes to Linstead at LD.
W[m] Marsh[11] again with Bicknor May 1767.

Mr Marsh Cur. Sal £21. & surplice fees lic. by Archdeacon.

1758 Conf. 20. 1762. 5. 1766. 12.

[1] The Stede family had owned the advowson from the time of Elizabeth I, and alienated it in 1735 to William Horsmonden Turner: Hasted VI, p. 142.
[2] Elizabeth, daughter of Jude Holdsworth, see p. 96, n. 6.
[3] Jane, the daughter of Sir William Turner. Her husband, William Horsmonden Turner, owned Harrietsham Place, and died in 1753: Hasted V, p. 450.
[4] See p. 2, n. 3.
[5] (1751-1801), of Navestock, Essex, m. Trinity C 1771, scholar, LLB 1779, V. Great Canfield, Essex, V. Tonge, 1783-1801.
[6] See p. 192, n. 8.   [7] See p. 204, n. 4.   [8] See p. 130, n. 2.
[9] See p. 169, n. 12.   [10] See p. 204, n. 8.   [11] See n. 5

Page 229

Tunstall R. S[t] John Baptist. ABP P. K[s] books 14-8-4. Wake 100[f]. So called now ⟨110[f]⟩. 20 Ho. Service once on Sundays, once at Bredgar, 1½ mile off. Prayers on ⟨Chr. day⟩ S[t] Steph. Ash W. good Fr. Monday in Easter & Mond. Tuesd. in Whits. week. Cat. W. Fr. in Lent, & Exp. on Sunday after. 4 Sacr. Generally betw. 14 & 20 Com. Church & Chancel in good Repair. Ho. new built by last Incumbent: slight, wants Repair. Out Ho. wants Repair. Glebe 10 Acres. 5 Bells.

Certificate for taking down an Outho. 1703 Entry B. V. 91. Leave granted 92. Lic. to Edw. Mores[1] R. to rebuild parsonage VI. 79.

Rob[t] Tyler[2] MA R. 12 May 1740. V. of S[t] Laurence ⟨at Ramsgate⟩ in Thanet p. 263 where he resides 11 months, & one usually here. Died June 12: 1766. Tho. Pennington[3] MA R 14 July 1766. R. of Kingsdown p. 214. Resides here.

Rich[d] Laurence[4] Cur. Salary { }. V. of Bredgar, p. 208. Resides there. Serves both. Quits this.
James Thurston[5] Cur of this & Bredgar p. 208. where see. 22[£].
M[r]. Tucker[6] Cur. of Kingsdowne.
Edw. Porten Benezet[7] A.B. Cur. Sal. £31–10–0 lic. 1790.

1758 Conf. 18. 1762. 7. 1766. 10.

[1] (16?–1740), R. Tunstall, 1711–40.
[2] (1700–66), of Henley, Oxon, m. Jesus O 1715, BA 1718, MA (Gonville and Caius) 1724, V. Sittingbourne, 1723–40, V. Newington, 1726–66, V. St Lawrence Ramsgate, 1740–66, R. Tunstall, 1740–66, chaplain to Lord Lynn.
[3] See p. ii, n. 35.   [4] See p. 2, n. 4.   [5] See p. 208, n. 9.
[6] See p. 129, n. 3.   [7] See p. 214, n. 8.

Page 230
D. Sittingbourne
Upchurch V. S[t] Marys. All Souls Coll. Propr. & P. K[s] books 11[£]. Wake 70[£]. Herring 90[£]. V. saith ⟨it may be rated at⟩ 62 or 63[£], out of which everything is to be deducted: but 90[£] once in 15 years when some Wood is cut. 38 Ho. Service once on Sundays. Prayers on Fr. in Lent. Cat. on Sundays in Lent. 4 Sacr. above 20 Com. each time. No Offertory. Some Bread & Money given to the Poor. No V. Ho. Air unwholesome. Church & Chancel dirty, in pretty good Repair. 5 Bells. By a Constitution of ABP Wake, Benefices of above 8 marks in K[s] books may be held with Fellowships of All Souls, if they exceed not 50[£] a year in present value: otherwise not. Lapsed 1742. Entry B. VIII 211.

Rich[d] Brereton[1] F. of All Souls, V. 3 Feb. 1758. Subwarden of the Coll. Resides there. Void by Cession.
Woolley Leigh Spencer[2] V. 10 Feb. 1766. F. of All Souls.

Robt Wells[3] Cur. of this & Bobbing p. 206. Gone.
Arth. Clark[4] Cur. of both. See p. 206. 1760 Mich. {Gone to} ⟨Serves⟩ Rainham p. 224 with this instead of Bobbing, & resides at Rainham. Salary here £25. See p. 232. Gone.
Mr Pow[5] ⟨bad. Gone.⟩ & now in March 1765 Mr Apsley[6]. See p. 224.
Davis, W[m][7], to be Cur. here & Raynham Aug 1766.
M[r] Keefe[8] Cur. Sal. £25.
Tho[s]. Shorting Cook[9] lic. 1792. Sal. £30.

1758 Conf. 86. 1762. 10.

[1] (1724–), of Gloucester, m. Pembroke O 1741, BA 1744, MA (All Souls) 1748, V. Upchurch, 1758–66.
[2] (1739–97), of Blickling, Norfolk, m. Oriel 1757, BA 1761, V. Upchurch, 1766–97.

³ See p. 206, n. 5.   ⁴ Ibid., n. 6.   ⁵ See p. 224, n. 9.
⁶ See p. 182, n. 4.   ⁷ See p. 224, n. 11.   ⁸ Ibid., n. 12.
⁹ (1770–), of Tenby, co Pembroke, m. Oriel 1789, BA 1793, C. Upchurch, 1792.

Page 231

Warden R. of S[t] John. Godfrey Meynell[1] Esq[r] P ⟨see below⟩. [Mr John Burdus[2] Ecton.]. Tenths 9–9¼. Certified 24[f]. Now called 20[f] ⟨See below⟩. Only 2 Ho. An Alehouse & a Cottage. The Sea is daily washing it away. Service once a month ⟨see below⟩. Sacr. once a Year [must be oftener]. No Offertory. 8[s] a year left for the Poor. Cur. saith it is not worth above 16[f] a year. In ABP Wakes time were 6 Families, & Service once a Fortnight, & 3 Sacr. In ABP Herrings book 5 Families & 4 Sacr. Church & Chancel very mean & dirty. No. Ho. Glebe 4 Acres. 1 Bell.

A presentation by Alderman Meynell[3] of London by a derived Title from the D. of York & his Majesty 1664 Entry B. I. 91. Rejected. Sequestration granted by V. of Leysdown. 20[f] at most, 2 or 3 Ho. No settled minister of a long time Entry B. II. 171. Held by Disp. with Leysdown V. 1674 III. 240. Gilb. Allenson (see below) pres. by Diana Hosier[4], Relict. of Francis Hosier Esq[r] VIII. 43.

Gilbert Allenson[5] BA R. 15 Nov. 1735. Lives in Essex, at Little Parndon.
John Kirby[6] Clerk A.M. Rector June 7: 1776.
John Rice[7] Clerk Rector 1783.

James Allenson [8] Cur. The Rectors Brother. Cur. of East Church 1½ miles off p. 209. where see. No mention of Salary.
M[r] Langley[9] Cur.

1758 None Conf. 1762 None. 1766 None

¹ Hasted notes that in the 1690s the advowson was in the possession of Godfey Meynell; VI, p. 262.
² John Burdus presented John Fetherston, who was rector from 1731 to 1734: ibid., p. 263.
³ Francis Meynell, goldsmith, alderman 1660–66.
⁴ Widow of Francis Hosier, vice-admiral of the White, who died in 1727: Hasted VI, p. 262.
⁵ (1711–76), of Aldenham Herts, m. St John's C 1730, BA 1733, MA 1739, R. Warden, 1735–76, headmaster of Aldenham School, Herts, 1738–57, R. Parndon, Essex, 1742–67.
⁶ (1744–1811), of Isle of Thanet, Kent, m. St John's C 1761, BA 1766, fellow Clare, 1768, MA 1769, R. Warden, 1776–82, V. Mayfield, Sussex, 1780–1810.
⁷ See p. 111, n. 14.   ⁸ See p. 162, n. 8.   ⁹ Samuel Langley, see p. 219, n. 8.

Page 232

D Sittingbourn

Witchling R. S[t] Margaret. Eliz. Conway, widow P. Tenths 8–2. Certified 21[f]. Wake 50[f] ⟨70[f] Mr Clarke see below⟩. 18 scattered Ho. Service once on Sundays [qu. good Fr. Chr. Day]. Cat. every Fortnight. 4 Sacr. A competent number of Communicants. One Papists, Gamekeeper to Lord Teynham[2]. Church & Chancel neat & in good Repair. No Rails. Ho. bad. & much out of Repair. Out Ho. in pretty good Order. Glebe 6 Acres. 3 Bells. 100[f] a year. M[r] Rice. Augm. 1767 with 400[f] by Sir Ph. Boteler & Qus bounty. 1768. Tithe wood from 5[f] to 25[f] a year, suppose 15[f]: augmentation 10[f]: Glebe, tithes &c 75[f]. Mr Dormer.

Tho. Nicholson[3] 13 Nov. 1711. V. of Lenham p. 246. 2½ miles off, where he resides. Died Jan 6. 1763.

Arth. Clarke[4] R. Feb. 1763. See 206, 224, 230. ⟨Pres. by Edw. Baker[5], Patron in full Right of the parish of Bobbing⟩. His Father bought either the next presentation or the Advowson a little before Mr Nicholson's death for 300^f. Presented to a Living ⟨Brentilleth Co. Suff.⟩ Dioc. Norfk. June 1764. Serves this & Lenham, Declared void Apr. 2. 1767.

Wm Dormer[6] R. May 26. 1767 pres, by Richd Springall[7] of St Helens BP^s gate, Linnen Draper. Exchanged a Living in Suffolk for this. Where resides he? May serve this with Rodmersham p. 225 a while, if he will repair his Ho. here.

Morgan Rice[8] Pr. Cur. Lives with R. at Lenham, p. 246. where see.

M^r. Cromp[9] cur. Sal £25.

William Wrighte[10] A.M. Rector 1788
Thos Wm Writhe[11] A.M. Rector 1795.

1758 Conf. 24. 1762. 1. NB. 1766. 7.

[1] The descendant of Thomas Conway, who bought the advowson in 1656: Hasted V, p. 553.
[2] See p. 152, n. 3.
[3] (1676–1763), of Doddington, Kent, m. University 1694, BA 1698, MA 1701, V. Lenham, 1701–63, V. Witchling, 1711–63.
[4] See p. 206, n. 6.
[5] Bought the advowson in 1763: Hasted V, p. 553.
[6] See p. 225, n. 7.
[7] [Springhall]. He bought the advowson for £250: Hasted V. p. 553.
[8] (1722–), of Llandisilio, co Carmathen, m. Jesus O 1743, BA 1747.
[9] Probably Pierrepoint Cromp, see p. 214, n. 6.
[10] (1739–95), of Lincoln, m. St Edmund Hall 1767, BA (St Alban Hall) 1771, MA 1774, R. Witchling, 1788–95.
[11] (1760–1854), of Bridgnorth, m. Wadham 1777, BA?. MA?, R. Witchling, 1795–1854, V. Boughton Blean, 1803–1854.

[Deanery of Sutton]

Page 233
D. Sutton.
Bearsted V. Holy Cross ⟨with the Chapel of Allington Entry B IV. 498⟩. DCh. of Rochester P. Belonged to the Priory of Leeds. Tenths 12–9 Certified 30^f Wake 40^f. Augmented in 1741 with 400^f ⟨by Mr Luke Philips[1] &c⟩. A Purchase made ⟨of 17^f a year⟩. Now 50^f including the Augmentation ⟨55^f AD^n 60 or 70^f Mr Markham⟩. Not 500 Acres: abt 70 Ho. Lewis Cage[2] of Milgate Esqr [7 or 800^f a year]. One Family of Anab. V. Ho. unfit for Residence. Service once on Sundays, as usual. [V. yielded readily to officiate twice, serving no other church, & having a Fortune of his own]. No Prayers on Week-days. Cat. exp. in Lent [now on Sundays afternoon]. 4 Sacr. From 50 to 60 Com. Church & Chancel in very good Order. Ho. mean, but in good repair. No outho. 6 Bells. Mr Packman[3], impropriate Rector refuses to pay procurations. The Rectory paid in 1716.

Henry Rand[4] MA V. 4 July 1733. Resides at Maidstone, 3. miles off. Is here almost every day. Dead abt Nov. 1765.

Samuel Markham[5] LLB. minor Canon of Rochester, V. Dec. 6. 1765. Res. Dec. 1767.

Henry Jones[6], See p. 222. V. 10 Dec. 1767.

Arnold Carter[7], M.A. V. April 2 1773.

Richard Jacob[8], A.M. Vicar 1783.

Charles Cage[9] A.B. Vicar 1795.

Mr Basset[10] serves it from Maidstone, 2 miles off ⟨1766⟩. See p. 250. 22^f & Surpl. Fees. Serves no other Church.

Edw$^{d.}$ Cage[11] Cur. Sal. £25.

1758 Conf. 29. 1762. 32. 1766. 23.

[1] He has not been traced.   [2] The father of Charles Cage (see n. 9).

[3] John Packman: Hasted V, p. 512.

[4] (17?–65), of Kent, m. Queens' C 1724, BA 1728, MA 1731, BD 1740, fellow 1730–57, proctor 1738, V. Bearsted, 1733–65, R. Hickling, Notts, 1756–65.

[5] See p. 16, n. 12.   [6] See p. 55, n. 13.

[7] (1734–?), of Guildford, Surrey, m. Magdalen Hall O 1750, BA (CCCO) 1753, MA 1757, V. Chart Sutton, 1770–73, V. Bearsted, 1773–83.

[8] (1753–95), of Wateringbury, Kent, m. CCCO 1768, BA 1772, MA 1776, BD 1785, V. Bearsted, 1783–95.

[9] See p. 208, n. 7.

[10] Richard Bassett (1730–?), of Laintwit, co. Glamorgan, m. Jesus O 1749, BA 1753.

[11] (1765–1835), m. Emmanuel 1785, BA 1786, MA 1789, C. Bearsted, 1787, C. Lenham, 1790, R. Eastling, 1796–1835, V. Newnham, 1803–35, R. Badlesmere, 1818–35.

Page 234

D. Sutton

Boughton Monchelsea V. St Peter. Belonged to the Priory of Leeds. DCh of Rochester P. K^s books 7–13–4. Wake 60^f. Now called 80^f ⟨AD^n 120^f⟩. 4 miles long, 1 broad. In the middle of the Parish Cocks Heath, betw. 2 & 300 Acres. Near 100 Ho. dispersed all over the Parish. Sir Tho. Rider[1] K^t. [1000^f a year ⟨or 1500. Prudent, worthy, single⟩]. Richd Savage[2] Esqr. Parishioners remarkable for coming to Church. Whole Service. Prayers on publick Days of Fasting & Thanksgiving, as Jan. 30. good Fr. K^s Accession &c. Cat. on Sunday afternoons in Lent. 4 Sacr. at least. Commonly betw. 70 or 80 Com. Land of 3^f a year for poor widows having no Parochial Relief ⟨by Mr Uskins[3]⟩. AD^n. Com. plate, given by one of the Rider Family. Church & Chancel Clean & in good Repair. Ho & outho. want a good deal of Repair. Glebe 19 Acres. 4 Bells. People good.

Peter Wade[4] V. 15 July 1755. Min. Can. of Rochester, where he resides: but comes hither as often as he can. Pres. to Cooling Dioc Roch. 14^f in K^s books. Mr Best[5] the patron desires I wd shew him w^t Favour I can. Returned no answer. Joseph Andrew[6] A.B. Vicar 1783.

Joseph Hardy[7] Pr. Cur. 35^f. Schoolmaster at Sutton Valence p. 254. abt 3 miles off. Hath been Cur. above 8 Years. [Rec. for Prefermt, by Sir Tho. Rider.]. Gone to the C. of Sutton Valence p. 254.

Richard Fletcher[8] BA of Univ. Coll. ord. D. by BP Pearce[9] Lent 1761. To reside in the Parish. Doth so. Hath left the Diocese 1765.

John Howlett[10] Cur 1766. P. 40^f. Resides. Preaches every other Sunday morning at West-Farleigh, 4 miles off. Was a Dissenter.

William Avarne[11] Clerk A.B. Cur. Licensed Sept: 18: 1774. with a Salary of 40^f p ann.

Charles Chawner[12] Clerk Cur Licensed June 12: 1773, with a salary of £40 p ann

Mr Fell[13] Cur. Sal. £40. lic. by Archdeacon.

1758 Conf. 91. 1762. 28. 1766. 24

[1] See p. 65, n. 2.

[2] From 1727 lived at Boughton Mount: Hasted V, p. 343.

[3] Hasted notes that a William Reiffgins gave money and lands for the poor in 1613: V, p. 343.

[4] (17?-83), of Ely, Cambs, m. Kings 1730, BA 1734, MA 1748, minor canon of Rochester, 1737-83, V. Strood, 1747-55, V. Boughton Monchelsea, 1755-83, R. Cowling, 1768-83, V. East Peckham, 1783.

[5] See p. 54, n. 2.

[6] [James] Andrew (Act Book: xi, 362) (1755-1823), of St Michael Penkeuil, Cornwall, m. Exeter 1773, BA 1777, C. Loose, 1777, V. Boughton Monchelsea, 1783-1823.

[7] See p. 65, n. 4.

[8] (1739-?), of Woolwich, m. University 1756, BA 1760.

[9] Zachary Pearce (1690-1774), bishop of Bangor, 1748-56, bishop of Rochester, 1756-74.

[10] (1731-1804), of Bedworth, Warwks, m. St John's O 1749, BA 1755, MA 1795, BD 1796. He taught languages at Maidstone and wrote on political economy before becoming V. Great Dunmow, Essex.

[11] Of Leicestershire, m. Emmanuel 1770, scholar, BA 1773, MA 1776, C. Boughton Monchelsea, 1774.

[12] (1752-1820), of Derbyshire, m. Emmanuel 1772, scholar, LLB 1778, C. Boughton Monchelsea, 1775, R. Church Broughton, Derbs, 1778-1820.

[13] William Fell, C. Boughton Monchelsea, 1790, C. Kingsdown and Milsted, 1804.

Page 235

Boxley V. All Saints. DCh of Rochester Propr. & P. K^s books 12-19-2. Wake first 200^f, then 150^f. So called now. 4 miles long, 3 broad. 94 Ho. Sir Edw. Austen[1] Bar^t. Wm Gore[2] Esqr, Wm Champneys[3] Esqr [Com. of Revenue in Ireland]. James Best[4] Esqr [younger brother of Tho. Best of Chilston Esqr] John Charlton[5] Esqr. 2 Families of Presb. Whole Service, two Sermons. Prayers on all Holydays, & W. Fr. in Lent, when Ch^n are cat. Monthly Sacr. Parishioners very constant in their Attendance. 30^s a Year for the poor, charged on Land, to be distributed by the minister. Offertory money given in Loaves at Chr. Church & chancel very clean & handsome. Ho. neat & handsome, built of Brick by AD^n Sprat[6]. Outhouses purchased by Mr Barrell. 8^f Pension out of the Exchequer. 4 Bells.

Edm. Barrel[7], V. 3 Oct. 1720. 80 Years old, blind. V. of Sutton, near Dartford. Resides 10 months there, 2 months here. Hath resigned Sutton, 1763: in his 88th year. I have excused him from residing here. Dead.

Wm Markham[8] DD. R. 4 May 1765 Dean of Rochester.

Honble Brownlow North[9] LLD. V. March 7. 1771 ⟨Dean of Cant⟩.

William Nance[10] V. May 16 1775.

John Benson[11] D.D. Vicar 1781

Geo. Burvill[12] Cur. 30 Guineas a Year, Easter Offerings, & all Sur-plus Fees. R. of Leybourne Dioc. Roch. Resides constantly at Boxley.

M[r] Parsons[13] Cur.

John Lloyd[14] Cur. Sal. £40. Surplice fees & Easter Offerings £10 lic. by Archdeacon.

1758 Conf. 61. 1762. 17 NB. 1766. 20

[1] (c. 1705–60) 6th Bt. Lived at Boxley Abbey. [2] See p. 218, n. 1.
[3] Tenant of Vinters estate for many years. [4] Died 1782.
[5] Died 1770.
[6] Thomas Sprat (1679–1720), m. Christ Church 1697, BA 1701, MA 1704, student Middle Temple, 1700, preb and archdeacon of Rochester, 1705–20, V. Boxley, 1705–20, R. Stone, 1707–20, canon of Winchester, 1712, canon of Westminster, 1713–20.
[7] (16–1765), of Rochester, Kent, m. Brasenose 1693, BA 1696, MA 1700, R. Kingsdown, 1700– 12, V. Sutton at Hone, 1712–65, R. Fawkenham, 1712, V. Boxley, 1720–65, preb of Norwich, 1702, preb of Rochester, 1705.
[8] (1720–1807), of Kingsale, Ireland, m. Christ Church 1738, BA 1742, MA 1745, BCL & DCL 1752, dean, 1767–76, headmaster of Westminster school, 1753–65, V. Boxley, 1765–71, preb of Durham, 1759, dean of Rochester, 1765–71, bishop of Chester, 1771–6, archbishop of York, 1777–1807, chaplain to King, 1756.
[9] See p. ii, n. 4. [10] See p. 37, n. 8.
[11] See p. ii, n. 29. [12] R. Leyborne, 1758–?.
[13] Robert Parsons (1758–1819), of Oakham, Rutland, m. Lincoln 1775, BA 1778, MA 1782, C. Newington and Halstow, 1780, C. Boxley, 1782, C. Eastwell, 1787, C. Sevenoaks, 1803 (endorsed).
[14] See p. 189, n. 5.

Page 236
D. Sutton
Bredhurst. C. S[t] Peter. Chapel to Hollingbourn 〈See here p. 242〉. R. of Hollingbourn P. Certified 37–17–6. Now called 35£ 〈AD[n] 40£ See below〉. 15 or 16 Ho. Service once on Sundays. Cat. had been neglected. Now to be in Lent. 4 Sacr. 5 or 6 Com. [Very few.]. No Offertory, but 1[s] by Cur. Exempt from AD[n]. Church very mean & dirty: chancel in pretty good Repair. Ho. a mean Cottage, quite out of Repair. A Barn in tolerable Order. Glebe 9 Acres. 2 Bells. No occasional Duty from Mich 1759 to the End of Feb. 1760, except one Burial brought in. It is let, 1760 for 31£ a year AD[n]. No Curacy in the Neighbourhood to be held with it.
Lic. to Cur. 1726 no mention of Nom. Entry B. VII. 117.

Robt Ingram[1] Cur. 24 Jan. 1758. See p. {153, 163,} 99. Exc. at Vis. 1762. Designs to quit at Mich. Resigned Sept. 28. 1762.
Fred. Dodsworth[2] lic. March 23. 1763. See p. 265. To officiate here. A bad story abt him & a woman. Qu.
John Tattersall[3] A.M. 1783.

Henry Shove[4], Jun. officiates here. Lives at Raynham, the next Parish, 3 miles off. Priest 20£ & Surpl. Fees. Gone to Harrietsham p. { }.
Jo. Russell[5], serves it now. V. of Debtling, p. 238 abt 3 miles off. Lives at Maidstone 〈p. 249〉, 5 or 6 miles off. Serves it for Dodsworth May 1763. 1764 Not known how served. D[r] Banson[6] serves it with Thornham. Forbidden.
Shenton[7] serves this & Hartlipp. p. 212 where see.
W[m] Jones[8] of Ch. Ch. ord. Deacon May 1. 1765 to serve both. 20£ here. Ord. Pr. June 2. 1765. Going to Maidstone June 1766.

Mr Prat[9] to serve this & Hartlipp. p. 212.
M[r]. Hudson[10] Cur. Sal. C21. lic. by Archdeacon.

1758 Conf. 13. 1762. 14. 1766. 13

[1] See p. 99, n. 14.   [2] See p. 169, n. 10.
[3] See p. 57, n. 12.   [4] See p. 1, n. 7.
[5] (?-1764). Master of Free School, 1746, V. Leysdown, 1757-7, V. Detling, 1757-64.
[6] John Banson, of Meesden, Herts, m. Trinity Hall 1741, LLB 1745, LLD 1750, fellow 1745-53, R. Swannington, Norfolk, 1751-9, V.Wood Dalling, 1751-9.
[7] See p. 212, n. 10.
[8] (1742-?), of Talley, co. Carmathen, m. Christ Church 1762.
[9] See p. 212, n. 3.   [10] John Hudson, C. Bredhurst, 1790.

Page 237
Bromfield see Leeds

Chart near Sutton V. S[t] Michael. Belonged to the Priory of Leeds. DCh. of Rochester P. K[s] books 8–12–8½. Certified. 47–11–9¼. Wake 50[£] ⟨Near 100[£] 1766⟩. Augm. in 1729 with 400[£] by Mr John Smith[1] & the Governors of the Queens Bounty. A purchase made. Above 40 Ho. One Family of Anab. Service once on Sundays. 4 Sacr. 50 Com. [No mention of Cat. or occasional Duty. June 1759 ⟨the vicar⟩ Had lately performed the Whole Sunday Duty, but not resided. See Letters. *** He saith, that he catechizes in Lent: & that Mr Hardy[2], School master of Town-Sutton just by doth occ. Duty for him. Two small Legacies to the poor. Church large, in good Order: Chancel neat. Ho. mean & much out of Order. Barn wants Repair. Glebe 5 Acres. 6 Bells.

James Hales[3] MA V. 11 Apr. 1733. Lives at Maidstone. See above. Dead before Jan 18. 1766.
Richard Husband[4] ⟨Junr⟩ MA V. 27 June 1766. Min. Can of Rochester.
Arnold Carter[5] M.A. Dec[r]. 15. 1770.
Henry Jones[6] M.A. V. April 2. 1773.
James Williamson[7] B.D. Vicar 1784.
John Smith[8] Vicar 1785.

Fra. Leicester[9] BA of Peterhouse. C. ord D. by BP Thomas[10] of Lincoln. Pr. by me March 15. 1767. 35[£] & Surpl. Fees. & East. Off[s]. Lives in V. Ho. pays 40[s] for it.
M[r]. Hardy[11] Cur.
James Edw. Gambier[12] A.M. cur. Sal. £30. lic.1789.

1758 Conf. 52. 1762. 16 NB. 1766. 25

[1] (1653-1732), of Canterbury, m. St John's C 1669, BA 1673, MA 1676, fellow 1677-83, V. Chart Sutton, 1687-1732, R. Hastingleigh, 1694-1732.
[2] See p. 65, n. 4.
[3] (1699-1766), of Rochester, m. University 1717, BA 1721, MA?, V. Bearsted, 1724-33, V. Chart Sutton, 1733-66.
[4] See p. 112, n. 2.   [5] See p. 233, n. 7.   [6] See p. 55 n. 13.
[7] See p. 203, n. 4.   [8] Ibid., n. 5.
[9] (1735-?), of Herefordshire, m. Peterhouse 1752, scholar 1752, BA 1756.
[10] John Thomas (1691-1766), bishop of Lincoln, 1744-61, bishop of Salisbury, 1761-6.
[11] See n. 2.

[12] (1759–1839), of London, m. Sidney Sussex 1780, scholar, BA 1783, MA 1786, R. Langley, 1789–1839, C. Chart Sutton, 1789, R. St Mary le Strand, Westminster, 1813–39.

Page 238

D. Sutton

Debtling V. St Martin, once a Chapel to ⟨the College of All Saints⟩ Maidstone. ABP P. Exempt from AD^n. Certified 30^f. Now called 70^f. V. saith not 65^f [Doth he mean clear? ⟨Yes. See Letter⟩]. ABP pays 2–13–4 & his Lessee of Maidstone 7–6–8 ⟨clear⟩. Augm. in 1715 with 400^f by ABP {Wake} Tenisons Will & the Queens Bounty ⟨Land purchased 19–10–0 a year. See below⟩. Above 4 miles long. 44 Ho. Service once on Sundays, as in the last V^s time. [In Part of his time at least, & in ABP Wakes time, it was twice]. ⟨V.⟩ Did not cat. Hath begun now, & will continue. 4 Sacr. From 18 to 25 Com. [Too few]. An Annuity of 10^s left to be divided equally between the Minister, Parish Clerk, & Poor. ⟨The⟩ ABP {Juxon} ⟨in 1607 if not earlier⟩ excepted out of his Lease of Maidstone ⟨to the Intent that they shd be enjoyed by⟩ {for} the Vicar ⟨here, the Hay &⟩ all the small Tithes, {but Hops} all having been comprehended in former Leases. Church & Chancel dirty & out of Order. Ho. mean & out of Repair. Out Ho. in pretty good order. 4 Bells. Only the Tithe of Corn & Grain of Debtling being granted to the Lessee of the Rectory of Maidstone, the Vicar hath the Tithe of Hops: I suppose, as small Tithes, which are there reserved to him. Reckoned by Restivo to be 17 Acres. 1767 Augm. with 400^f by Sir. Ph. Boteler & Qu^s bounty.

John Russell[1] V. Feb. 6. 1757 ⟨Deputy⟩ Cur. of Bredherst p. 236. Master of the Grammar School at Maidstone ⟨p. 250⟩, where he resides, & serves both from thence. Saith, the School is 30 Guineas a Year, out of which he pays a large Quit Rent & Repairs, & hath but 10 scholars at a Guinea each; & hath 6 Daughters: that he will quit the Curacy, & do the Whole Duty at this Vicarage, if ever he is able: but hath no prospect of it. See his Letters. 1759 nominated & appointed one of the 10 poor vicars. Died ⟨abt⟩ Jan. 10 1764.

Tho. Baker[2] MA V. Feb. 20. 1764. R of Frinsted p. 239 serves both. So 1767. William Polhill[3] A.B. Vicar. April 30: 1779.

Mr Jordan[4] Cur.

1758. Conf. 31. 1762. 28. 1766. 8

[1] See p. 236, n. 5.
[2] (1717–79), of Wingham, Kent, m. St John's C 1736, BA 1740, R. Frinsted, 1747–79, V. Detling, 1764–79.
[3] See p. 50, n. 16.
[4] Probably John Nesbit Jordan (17?–1818), '10 year man' Emmanuel 1796, MA (Lambeth) 1804, C. Edburton, Sussex, R. Halstead, 1801–3, R. Patching and V. West Tarring, 1803–18.

Page 239

Frinsted ⟨al Frensted⟩ R. St Dunstan. Mr John Bing[1] of Wickhambreux P. Wake sets down no P. A note on Ecton saith, that Strypes Survey book 2. p. 6 makes the Hospital of St Cath. near the Tower P. Kings books 9–11–8. Certified 71–7–4. Now called 70^f ⟨AD^n 80^f. So R. 1763⟩. Abr. Tilghman[2] Esqr. Service once on Sundays, once at Wormshill, a mile off. Prayers & Sermon on good Fr. & Chr. Day. Cat. every other Sunday after 2^d Lesson of Morning Prayer. 4 Sacr. 20 Com. A Free school endowed, with 40^s a Year for 4 Ch^n by { } Wyatt[3]. The minister & Ch W^ns Governors. A Benefaction of 12 Coats: 6 from the Proprietors of Meriams Court to 6 poor men of this Parish. Lost. No Evidence. Parsonage Ho. rebuilt by the present R. Outho. in good Order. Church & chancel in pretty good Repair. Glebe 4½ Acres. 4 Bells.

Tho. Baker[4] R. 4 March 1747. Resides in the Parsonage, which he built. Cur. of Wormshill, p. 257. June 1763 Given him Leave to reside at Canterbury for the Education of his 6 Ch^n, & to take a Curacy near it. See p. 271. Void by Cession Feb. 20. 1764. See p. 238. Inst. again Feb. 28. 1764. Patron John Bing, above. Serves it himself 1765 with his V. of Debtling p. 238.
Edward Smithe[5] A.M. Rector 1779.
$Rich^{d.}$ Cook Tylden[6] A.M. Rect. 1787.

Carver[7] John Cur. of Oriel Coll C. here & at Wormshill. $20^£$ from each born Dec. 15. bapt. Jan. 14. 1740. Ord. D. Sept. 25. 1763. 2. Pr. 3 March 1765. Gone Sept. see. p. 214.

1758 Conf. 20. 1762. 2. NB. 1766. 4

[1] Owner of Yokes-Court manor. Died in 1766: Hasted V, p. 559.
[2] Abraham Tilghman, the owner of Frinsted manor. Died in 1779: Hasted V, p. 559.
[3] John Wyatt of Milsted, in his will of 1722: Hasted V, p. 559.
[4] See p. 238, n. 2.   [5] See p. 216, n. 3.
[6] Ibid., n. 4.   [7] See p. 214, n. 5.

Page 240
D. Sutton
Goudherst. V. St Mary. Belonged to the Mon. of Leeds. DCh. of Rochester P. K^s books 26–19–2. Wake $110^£$. Now $150^£$ ⟨See below⟩. 7 miles by 6. 300 Ho. Edw. Bathurst[1] Esqr. 3 small poor Families on a wild Down, Papists. Go to Mr Darrels[2] of Scotney in Lamberhurst Parish. 11 Families Presb. Teacher, Colvil. Lessened. Whole Service, 2 Sermons on Sundays. A Sermon on good Fr. & Chr. Day. Prayers W. Fr. Holydays. Cat. on W. Fr. from Mids to Mich. Afternoon Sermons sometimes on Cat. Monthly Sacr. & on 3 great Festivals. Com. from 40 to 60. John Horsmonden[3], Esqr endowed a School for Latin & Greek & another for English, with $40^£$ a year, 12 Inhabitants of Goudherst Governors. Well managed. An Alms Ho. for 3 Families. The Vicarage hath been augmented with $400^£$, which is in the 3 per Cent annuities ⟨see below⟩. Worth $130^£$, AD^n ⟨$160^£$, with the House. Mr Polhill⟩. Church & Chancel handsome & in good Order. Ho. & outho. in good Repair. The above $400^£$ to be laid out in Land, by Mr Campion[4], AD^n. Glebe 2 Acres. 6 Bells. Mr Colvill (see above) came to me June 17. 1764 to desire some support towards continuing to officiate there. I refused it mildly.
1765. 8 or 10 elderly Persons, Papists. Whether no younger belonging to them, not said. Dr Denne[5] in a Letter to Mr Herring[6] Sept. 7. 1749 saith that R. Goudhurst hath been in the Maplesden[7] family ever since 1671 & Mr Maplesden in 1749 saith he never p^d any procurations, nor was asked to pay.

John Adey[8] V. 6 Jan. 1757. His voice to week. Serves Loose, p. 248. Resigned July. 2. 1759. exchanging with his Successor.

Robt Polhill[9] V. July 9. 1759. To reside at Mich. Was Cur. of Thornham p. 255. Resides. R. of Shadoxhurst p. 142.

John Banson[10] LLD Cur. 50^f & V. Ho. In Debt. Held two Livings incompatible, calling one a Sine-Cure. Gone.

1758 Conf. 94. 1762. 200. 1766. 97.

---

[1] Resided at Finchcocks, and died in 1772: Hasted VII, p. 72.

[2] The junior branch of the Darell family: see p. 39, n. 5. This is perhaps John Darell: Hasted VII, p. 78.

[3] A clothier, by his will of 1636. He also left money for wood and faggots for poor people: ibid., p. 82.

[4] Henry Campion, who died in 1753: ibid.

[5] John Denne, see p. 406, n. 6.

[6] William Herring, notary public and secretary to archbishop Herring, 1749–54.

[7] The Maplesden family came from Marden. Edward Maplesden died in 1755, unmarried and intestate. He owned the estate of Winchet-hill in Goudhurst: Hasted VII, p. 55.

[8] See p. 75, n. 6.   [9] See p. 142, n. 3.   [10] See p. 236, n. 6.

Page 241

Harrietsham R. S[t] John Baptist. All Souls Coll. P. K[s] books 11-10-0. Wake 110^f. Now 180^f. Between 40 & 50 Ho. Mrs Turner[1], [widow, 1200^f a Jointure, if she marries not again ⟨Lessee of the Rectory of Maidstone⟩. A Tradesmans Daughter of Lenham]. Whole Service on Sundays. No Prayers on Week Days. [Qu. good Fr. Chr. Day]. Cat. in Lent. 4 Sacr. Usually abt 30 Com. One Quested[2] founded 12 Alms Houses for 12 old Persons: of which 6 have abt 10^f a Year each, & 6 of them have 4^f. The Fishmongers Company Governors. Well managed. 3-13-0 yearly from Lands, to the Poor. Sir W[m] Stede[3] gave 10^f a Year in Lands for apprenticing poor Ch[n] of Harrietsham, Milton or Tong. Church & Chancel large & very clean. Ho. & out ho. handsome & in good order. Glebe 54 Acres. 8 Bells.

Petition for rebuilding part of the Ho. 1702 Entry B. V. 77.

Edw. Smith[4] LLD R. 2 Dec. 1743. Gouty, epileptick. Lives at Maidstone 8 miles off, by Leave of ABP Herring, being unable to serve his Church. Will reside, if he recovers his Health. Serves it from Maidstone 1764. Resides here May 1768.

James Robinson Hayward[5] M.A. June 4. 1773. was again instituted 1786.

Straker[6], Cur. 30^f, Easter Offerings, Surpl. Fees, & an Apartmt in the Ho. Dismissed by Order, for his bad character.

Henry Shove[7], Jn[r]. 40^f. Resides in the Parsonage Ho ⟨for wch above 13^f was deducted⟩. Gone to Adisham p. 1. May 1762. Complaint from Parish July 1762. May 1763 D[r] S. is there from Saturday till Monday: is poor, hath 9 Ch[n], hath underlet it for his Life.

Mr Loftie[8] to come from Hothfield p. 66. at Mich 1764 & be in the House 40^f. Resides 1767 May. D[r] Smith saith he will serve it himself at Mich.

Mr Cromp[9]. Cur.

1758. Conf. 70. 1762. 16. 1766. 32.

[1] See p. 228, n. 3.
[2] Marc Quested, citizen and fishmonger of London, in his will of 1642; ibid., p. 458.
[3] He owned Harriestham manor, and was sheriff of Kent in 1614: ibid., p. 449.
[4] (1711-73), of London, m. Queen's O 1728, BCL (All Souls) 1735, DCL 1740, R. Harrietsham, 1743-73.
[5] (1739-1813), m. Trinity O 1756, BA (All Souls) 1763, MA 1756, R. Harriestsham, 1773-1813, R. St Mary le Strand, Westminster, 1781-1813.
[6] Possibly Thomas Straker (1716-), of Cambridge, m. Trinity C 1733, scholar 1734, BA 1738, MA 1741.
[7] See p. 1, n. 7.   [8] See p. 25, n. 5.
[9] Pierrepoint Cromp, see p. 214, n. 6.

Page 242
D. Sutton
Hollingbourne R. All Saints. ABP P. Exempt from AD[n]. K[s] books 28-15-5. Wake 120[£]. Herring 50[£]. There is an Estate of 5 or 600[£] a year leased out. In Chicheleys Register fol. 237 is the Endowment of the Vicarage of Hollingbourn, without Date, & seemingly imperfect. It recites that in the time of his Predecessors, & his own, there had been Vicars, but without a settled Income, & specifies what that Income shall hereafter be. It declares, that the Vicar shall not be bound to officiate in the Chapels of Hokynge & Brodhurste annexed to or depending on that Rectory: but that the Care of finding a Priest to officiate at Hokynge shall belong to the Rector, unless he chuses to officiate personally in the Parish Church & then the vicar shall provide for Hokynge. Collation is to R with chapel Entry B IV. 517.
ib. fol. 238 is the Grant of a Mansion Ho. to the Vicar Leased out on 3 Lives. Reserved rent 39[£] ⟨& 100[£] once in 7 years. So 1663 Entry B. 1. 45⟩. Mr Dodsworth thinks the Estate worth 200[£] a year. One Life old, Mr ⟨Rbt⟩ Fairfax[1] ⟨of Leeds Castle⟩. Other two, Mr Colepepper[2] of the Charterhouse, & Mr Martin[3] Cur. of Leeds.
Lease of R. with Chapel of Hucking annexed conf. 1683 Entry B. IV. 316. Lease 2 Oct. 1698 excepting a Parlor 2 Chambers & a Stable to R. Rent 39[£] at M LD[4], 100[£] once in 7 yrs at LD, ⟨& Insert this clause in every new Lease⟩, R to pay first fruits, Lessee to pay 20[£] a year to V. at M LD & Tenths & Subsidies for the demised premises, & to cause the Cure of Hucking to be served in such manner as the Ordinary shall allow, & repair the mansion Ho. &c IV. 594 &c. Lease 16 Dec. 1725 with covt to rebuild VII. 225. Lease 25 Oct 1731. p. 332. Lease 12 Feb. 1750 now subsisting. An alteration in it or mistake in entring it. In ⟨a⟩ former one, ⟨the⟩ Lessor might use the Rooms reserved, not others: now he loses the 100[l] in 7 years, if he uses any. Also clause of rebuilding (see above) left out. IX. 35 &c. Lease confirmed July 4. 1763. X. 76.

Francis Dodsworth[5] R. 16 Nov. 1757. V. of Minster in Thanet p. 264, 265
John Cautley[6] Master of Arts R. June 28 1774.

[1] (1707-93), MP for Maidstone, 1740-1, 1747-54, and MP for Kent, 1754-68.
[2] John Spencer Colepeper, who sold Greenway-Court to Fairfax: Hasted V, p. 468.
[3] Denny Martin Fairfax (1725-?), of Loose, Kent, m. University 1740, BA 1744, MA 1751, C. Leeds with Bromfield, 1760.

4 Michaelmas and Lady Day: 29 September and 25 March.
5 See p. 156, n. 9.   6 See p. 177, n. 8.

Page 243

Hollingbourne V. All Saints, with the Chapel of Hucking, St Margaret. ABP P. Exempt from AD^n. K^s books 7-6-8. Certified 70$^£$-16-8. So now. ⟨Hucking called 12$^£$ stipend. See below⟩. Hollingbourn near 6 miles long. Contains three Streets, a mile distant from each other, & 104 Families: two of Gentlemen, [not named]. Hucking ⟨2½ miles from Hollingbourn⟩ is two miles long, 17 Ho. near 80 Inhabitants. A few Absenters. One Sunday whole Service at the Church: the next, Service once at each. Between 2 & 3 miles asunder. Prayers at the Church W. Fr. in Lent & all Passion Week: & on certain Holydays with occasional Sermons. Prayers & Sermon Nov. 5. Jan. 30. Cat. in the church in Lent: with printed Exp. repeated to V. at his House, Ch^n sent: not servants, unless before a Confirmation. ⟨Cat. also at the Chapel⟩. 4 Sacr. at each 80 or 90 Com at each time at the Church: about 25 at the Chapel. Lady Nortons[1] Charity, see Tenterden p. 73 ⟨& particulars here. Lost for many years⟩. A Gentleman of the Parish sends several Boys & Girls to two Schools here. The Singers use light & uncommon Tunes here & elsewhere. Shops are needlessly opend on Sundays. Of the Vicarage & Chapel see here p. 242. Church & chancel large, handsome and in good Repair ⟨much improved in pres^t V^s time⟩. Ho. good & in good Repair. Stable new by Mr Waterhouse. ⟨6 Bells⟩. Hucking Chapel & Chancel very mean & shamefully dirty. ⟨Both put into decent Repair in 1762⟩. No Ho. 2 Bells. 20$^£$ a year to Hollingbourn & 12$^£$ to Hucking, pd by Mr Fairfax[2], {AD^n. Qu. whence} ⟨See the Lease in the preceding p. ⟩.
V. collated 1684 Entry B. IV. 427 & 1696 548.
Formerly more Hops, but they suit not the Soil: now 26 Acres, the tithe 10^s each. Hence V. now abt 62$^£$. Hucking 12$^£$ clear stipend, 4$^£$ small tithes. Mr Waterh. Jan. 1763.
Mr Duppa[3], a very worthy & pious Gentleman, lives here, 81. Cieled the Church.
Hops 11$^£$, other small tithes abt 36$^£$, 20$^£$ augmentation from an Estate bought of Mr Colepepper[4] Rec^r of the Charterhouse, by Mr Fairfax, but after ded. Land tax 16$^£$: in all 63$^£$. See Mr Waterhouse Nov & Dec. 1763.

Benj. Waterhouse[5] MA V. 21 Sept. 1741. Resides in V. Ho. & hath always done so. 1766 V. of Westwell p. 75.
Joseph Todd[6] Clerk B.A. V. Decr. 20.1770.
William Hassell[7] Clerk B.A. ⟨Vic⟩ Oct: 11 1773. resides.
Edward Hasted[8] A.B. vicar 1790.
Hucking, wch V. is not obliged to serve, to be served every other Sunday by Mr Marsh[9] of Bicknor p. 205 where see.

1758 Hol. 93. Hucking. 3. 1762. 50. Hucking. 9. 1766 Holl. 41. Hucking 1

1 Dame Frances Norton, gave an estate purchased in 1719: Hasted V, p. 473.
2 See p. 242, n. 1.
3 Baldwin Duppa lived at Hollingbourne-Hill, died 1764: Hasted V, p. 472.
4 See p. 242, n. 2.   5 See p. 75, n. 3.   6 See p. 65, n. 6.
7 See p. 126, n. 7.   8 See p. 17, n. 7.   9 See p. 103, n. 2.

Page 244
D. Sutton
Hucking See Hollingbourn p. 243

Langley R. S[t] Mary. Eliz. Bouverie[1] of Teston in Kent. P. [Sir Edw. Hales[2] P. Ecton]. K[s] books 6–19–9½. Wake 130[£]. So called now⟨150 AD[n]⟩. 600 Acres. 27 Ho. most of them small Cottages. Whole Service, two Sermons, on Sundays. Prayers too seldom on week-Days, because the people cannot attend. Cat. exp. the greatest part of the year. 5 or 6 Sacr. Number of Com. not mentioned. Church small & dirty. Chancel clean & in order. Ho & outho. very bad, & ready to fall. Mr Waterhouse designs to put both in good Order ⟨{Done 1766}⟩. Glebe 20 Acres. 3 Bells. 1767 is building a new House. Coverd in Aug. 19.

David Waterhouse[3] R. 22 March 1710. Learned. Died 28 Oct. 1758. Resided constantly.
David Waterhouse[4] R. 14 Dec. 1758. Resides.
John Kennedy[5] Rector 1780 resides.

1758 Conf. 7. 1762. 14. 1766. 9.

[1] Owner of Langley manor from 1752: Hasted V, p. 350.
[2] See p. 33, n. 2.
[3] (1680–1758), of Wakefield, Yorks, m. Christs 1698, scholar 1699, BA 1702, MA 1705, PC. Tunbridge Wells, 1705–15, R. Langley, 1711–58.
[4] (1718–80), of Langley, Kent, m. Christ Church 1737, BA 1741, MA 1746, R. Langley, 1758–80.
[5] R. Langley, 1780–89.

Page 245
Leeds C. S[t] Nicolas, with Bromfield. S[t] Margaret. Formerly a Priory. ABP Propr. & P ⟨Adv. granted by Qu. Mary⟩. Certified 44-14-4. ABP ⟨Juxon⟩ reserved in his Lease 30[£] to the minister & the Surplice Fees: & ⟨the ABP⟩ pays himself yearly 12-6-8. The 30[£] {ought} ⟨doth⟩ not {to} pay Land tax ⟨See below⟩. 100 Ho. in both. Hon[ble] Rob[t] Fairfax[1] Esq[r] at Leeds Castle: [very fine Park ***]. Walter Hooper[2] Esq[r] at Leeds Abbey, [1500[£] a year, Tenant to ABP]. 10 or 12 negligent incoming to church. They decrease. Service at each church once. Prayers on the Festival Holydays at Leeds. Cat. from Easter to Mich. 7 Sacr. at Leeds: sometimes 100 Com. 5 at Bromfield: abt 30 or 35. Mr Charles Lumsden[3] of Leeds abt 1732 left by Will the Interest of 200[£] to the Minister of Leeds, if resident: if not, to the Poor of the Parish. Through mismanage[mt] of the Trustees, the Paym[t] was stopt & the Interest lost for 5 Years. But ABP Herring procured it to be paid ⟨6[£] a year⟩ at the Bank ever since 1754: & new Trustees appointed, Mr Fairfax & Mr Hooper [see above] & Mr Jumper[4] See below⟩. Offertory partly given for teaching poor Ch[n], partly to poor Communicants. Complaints of the Meredith Family, to whom Mr Hooper succeeds, see in Mr Harrisons Letter, Oct. 24. 1759. Bromfield church very neat, by Mr Fairfax. Chancel new built very handsomely by the late Mr Meredith: very neatly fitted up within by Mr Fairfax. 3 Bells. Leeds Church & Chancel large & noble & clean. Ten Bells. No Ho. Licence to Leeds & Bromfield 1664. Entry B. I. 86. Mr Lumsdens will bears Date 9 Feb. 1728. See it, & a Draught of a Deed by ABP Potter consenting that the money be vested in old S.S. annuities.

1767 augm. with 400$^£$ by S^r Ph. Boteler & Qu^{s}bounty.

Edw. Harrison[5] BA. C. 16 Jan 1725. Hath resided there in an exorbitantly dear hired Ho. near 34 Years, and been absent but 5 weeks. [Lives on Vegetables, gives away good Books. Mr ⟨Denny⟩ Martin[6] a Clergyman who lives with Mr Fairfax,⟨ I think his nephew⟩ officiates often for him gratis]. Hath been sick & in Distress. *** Apr. 1760 Mr Martin hath done the whole Duty for 6 months. Mr Harrison died Oct. 23. 1760, aged 78.

Denny Martin ⟨Fairfax[7] D.D.⟩ M.A C. Nov. 14. 1760 of Univ. Coll. ⟨ord pr. by BP Gilbert[8] of Sarum⟩. See just above. does his own duty.

Charles Cage[9] A.B. 1794.

James Young[10] A.B. 1795.

1758 Conf. 54 1762. 20. Bromfield 6. 1766 Leeds 40. Br. 5.

[1] See p. 242, n. 1. Fairfax also gave four new bells to the church: Hasted V, p. 499.

[2] Inherited Leeds Abbey in 1758. He died in the same year: ibid., p. 497.

[3] Ibid., p. 499.

[4] William Jumper, of Hill-Green house in Stockbury. He inherited Leeds Abbey in 1758, and he served as sheriff in 1761: ibid., p. 497. The Meredith family had owned the Abbey until 1758.

[5] (1686–1760), m. Pembroke Hall 1704, BA 1708, C. Cliffe and Edburton, Sussex, 1716, C. Leeds and Bromfield, 1725–60.

[6] See p. 242, n. 3.   [7] Ibid.

[8] John Gilbert (1693–1761), bishop of LLandaff, 1740–9, bishop of Salisbury, 1749–57, archbishop of York, 1757–61.

[9] See p. 208, n. 7.

[10] (17?–99), m. Christs 1789, BA 1792, C. Stowting and Postling, 1793, C. Leeds with Bromfield, 1795–99.

Page 246

D. Sutton

Lenham V. St Mary ⟨Wake adds, with Royton. A Chapel desolate 1663⟩. Belonged to St Austins, Canterbury. John Styles[1] of Petworth Gent P. See below. Kings books 13–15–2½ Wake 80$^£$. So called Now. 7 miles by 3. One or two Hamlets. 300 Ho. Very few Dissenters. Service once on Sundays. Cat. every Fortnight. Printed Exp. given them. {4} Sacr ⟨twice every Quarter⟩. Abt 40 Com at each. {[very few]}. Mr Honywood[2] founded 6 Alms Houses for 6 poor persons, & endowed them with abt 6$^£$ a Year for each. The Revd Mr Francis Robins[3] gave 3$^£$ a Year to the poor. Mr Laurence[4] of Bredgar p. 208 is to have the next Presentation, & then Mr Best[5] to have the Patronage. In this Parish was the Chapel of Royton. Church & Chancel large, noble & clean. Ho. old, large: Out Ho. small: both in good Repair. Glebe 6 Acres. 8 Bells. 200$^£$ a year. Mr Rice. Mr Nicholson made above 100$^£$.

Tho. Nicholson[6] MA V. 29 {Oct.} ⟨Dec⟩ 1701. R. of Witchling p. 232. Resides here. 85. Died Jan 6. 1763.

Richd Laurence[7] MA V. Feb. 1763. Pres. by – Tilghman & – Fullagar[8] Esq^{r}s, who have been Patrons for the next Turn above 20 Years. Mow Mr Best is patron in full Right. V. also of Bredgar p. 208. To reside here & perform whole Service, if the Living prove worth 100$^£$.⟨March⟩ 1765 will do it now. Doth it 1766.

Thomas Verrier Alkin[9] B.A. V. Oct^r: 22 1772.

Morgan Rice[10] Cur. here & at Wichling p. 232. Salary ⟨above⟩ 34^f a Year, & his Board. Priest. Going Feb. 1763.
Mr Clarke[11] R of Wichling p. 232. Serves this with it. Gone.
Thomas Scott[12] Vicar 1788 resides.
Maurice Lloyd[13] A.M. Vicar 1792.

1758 Conf. 303 ⟨here 816. Of this Parish⟩ 303. 1762 Conf. here 234. Of this Parish 88. 1766 Conf. here 499. Of this Parish 83.

[1] Hasted notes that Richard Styles presented in 1701 and in 1763 Thomas Best of Chilston owned the advowson: V, p. 444.

[2] Anthony Honywood, of Langley, in 1622: ibid., p. 438.

[3] (c.1667-1719), of Chart Sutton, m. St John's C 1685, BA 1689, MA 1692, BD 1700, fellow 1691-8, R. Cockerfield, Suffolk, 1708-19. He left money in his will for the 'most indigent, honest and industrious poor of Lenham': ibid.

[4] See p. 2, n. 4.   [5] See n. 1.   [6] See p. 232, n. 3.

[7] See p. 208, n. 3.   [8] See p. 239, n. 2.

[9] (1726-84), of Canterbury, m. St John's C 1745, C. Acrise and Swingfield, 1769, V. Lenham, 1772-81, V. Eynesford, 1783-84.

[10] See p. 232, n. 8.   [11] Ibid., n. 4.   [12] See p. 56, n. 15.

[13] (1764-1810), of Oswestry, Salop, m. Hertford 1784, BA 1788, MA 1791, V. Lenham, 1791-1810.

Page 247

Linton V. St Nicolas. Belonged to the Hospital of Maidstone. Robt Man[1] Esqr P. K^s books 7-14-4. Certified 61-7-8. Wake 50^f. Now called 80^f. See below. Abt 40 Ho. Mr Manns & Mr Footes[2] Families live in the Parish [Mr Mann is a minor. Mr Foote married his Aunt, & is elder brother to the Vicar.]. Whole Service. Prayers on all Holy Days. Cat. exp. W. Fr. In Lent. 4 Sacr. Generally abt 60 Com. The late Mr Mann built 4 Alms Ho. & left 20^s a Year to each Inhabitant of them, to be nominated by his Heirs. As the value of the Living depends chiefly on Hops, it is decreasing ⟨50 AD^n⟩. The V. Ho. a mere Cottage: but in good Repair. Church & Chancel mean & wants Repair. Out Ho. in pretty good Order. Glebe ½ Acre. 6 Bells.

Francis Hender Foote[3] LLB V. 8 July 1751. R. of Boughton Malherb p. 54. where he resides ⟨10 miles off⟩ & Cur. of Egerton, p. 61.
William Polhill[4] B.A. V. March 12 1773.
Edwd Beckingham Benson[5] A.B. Vicar. Sept: 20: 1779.
Robt. Foote[6] A.M. 1782.

Cha. Locke[7] Pr. Cur. 31-10-0 Surpl. Fees, & voluntary Easter Offerings. Feb. 1763 going to Exeter.
Sam. Weller[8] see p. 248. Cur said to be in Priests Orders. Salary as above. Feb. 1763 Hath my leave to live with his Mother at Maidstone. See my Letter[9].
W. Polhill[10] to be Cur. at LD 1765 to serve it from Maidstone. 3 miles.
M^r. Wood[11]. Cur. Sal. £40.
Wm Winthrop[12] A.B. Cur. Sal. £40 lic. 1793.

1758 Conf. 53. 1762. 33. 1766. 28

[1] [Mann]. Owner of Linton Place from 1727 until his death in 1751. His son Edward Louisa Mann died in 1775: Hasted IV, p. 368.

[2] Benjamin Hatley Foote married Mary, the daughter of Robert Mann.
[3] See p. 54, n. 5.   [4] See p. 50, n. 16.
[5] See p. 54, n. 9.   [6] Ibid., n. 10.
[7] (1733–1802), of Rochester, Kent, m. St John's C 1751, BA 1755, R. North Bovey, Devon, 1775–1802.
[8] (1736–95), of Maidstone, Kent, m. CCCO 1751, BA 1755, MA 1759, DD 1760, R. Steeple Langford, Wilts, and V. St Martin, Oxford.
[9] LPL, MS Secker 3, f. 225, Secker to Weller, 19 April 1763.
[10] See n. 4.   [11] See p. 115, n. 7.
[12] (1770–1845), m. St John's C 1788, scholar, BA 1792, MA 1795, BD 1803, fellow, 1795–1827, C. Linton, 1793, V. Dorking, Surrey, –1845. He left £140,000, making numerous legacies to charities, including £5,000 to St John's C, and the college bought advowsons with the money.

Page 248
D. Sutton

Loose C. All Saints. Was a Chapel {to} ⟨or Cell to the College of All S^{ts}⟩ Maidstone. ABP P. Exempt from AD^n. Wake 80^f. So called now ⟨See below⟩. Depends on Hops. 70 Ho. Denny Martin[1] Esqr. 2 Families of Presb. 2 of Anab. Lessened. 2 Families of Quakers, Husbandmen, who pay Tithes & Dues without Compulsion. A meeting Ho. Lessend. Whole Service. A Sermon on Chr. Day & good Fri. Prayers on Jan 30. Ash W. May 29 Nov. 5. Cat. every other Sunday. Sometimes Sermons on Cat. 4 Sacr. Usually betw. 30 & 40 Com. 500^f given by Mr Beale[2], merchant of Hamburgh to augment the Curacy. It is laid out in Land, & {he} ⟨Cur⟩ hath the Rent. ABP pays him 2-13-4. All the Tithes of Loose had been granted in the Lease of Maidstone: but ⟨the⟩ ABP {Juxon} ⟨in 1607 if not earlier⟩ reserved {to the Curate of Loose} ⟨out of it⟩ the Tithe of Hay, & all small Tithes, {but Hops} to the Intent that the Curate of Loose shd enjoy them. Church in good Repair. North side of Chancel wants Repair. Ho & out Ho. neat & in good Order. 3 Bells. Only the Tithes of Corn & Grain of Loose being granted to the Lessee of the Rectory of Maidstone, & the Tithe of Hay & all small Tithes being there reserved to the Curate of Loose, he enjoys the Tithe of Hops: wch are reckoned in Restivos paper at 80 Acres.

Tho. Franks[3] MA Cur. ⟨licenced⟩ 20 March 1722. Resides: but is in bad State of Health. [mad].
Denny Martin Fairfax[4] D.D. Curate 1782.

John Adey[5] Cur. 30^f & Surpl. Fees. abt 3^f. Resides. Going. Still here, July 4. 1760. Gone. Returned 1762: but going 1763 to Westwell.
Sam. Weller[6]. Deacon, Aug. 1760. Resides at Ld Romneys[7] 1½ mile off. Left it abt Chr. 1761. Mr Hales[8] serves it. See above.
Horne[9] W^m BA of Magd. Ox. Cur. Salary as above. ord. D. 27 Feb. 1763. Will be 24 May 1764. 1. Lives with his father[10], Min of Otham, 2 miles off.
James Andrew[11] Clerk A.B. Curate, Licensed May 26: 1777, with a Salary of £30 p ann.

1758 Conf. 38. 1762. 20. 1766. 24

[1] See p. 242, n. 3.
[2] Richard Beale, formerly of this parish, died in 1702: Hasted IV, p. 365.
[3] He has not been traced.   [4] See p. 242, n. 3.
[5] See p. 240, n. 8.   [6] See p. 247, n. 8.

[7] Robert Marsham (1722–93), 2nd baron Romney. Lived at The Mote, near Maidstone.

[8] James Hales. See p. 237, n. 3.

[9] (1740–1821), of Otham, Kent, m. Magdalen O 1757, demy 1757–68, BA 1761, MA 1764, R. Brede, Sussex, 1769–1821, R. Otham, 1769–1821.

[10] Samuel Horne (1694–1768), of Brede, Sussex, m. Pembroke O 1711, BA 1714, MA 1717, R. Otham, 1727–69, R. Brede, Sussex, 1734–68.

[11] See p. 234, n. 6.

Page 249

Maidstone C. All Saints, with the Chapel of S[t] Faith in Maidstone desecrated, College of ⟨All Saints of⟩ Maidstone was Impr. & P. Now ABP ⟨adv granted by Qu. Mary⟩. Exempt from AD[n]. Not in Charge, nor certified. The Coll and then the ABP, gave 20[£] Salary, which he still gives. And in 1661 he reserved by his Lease 30[£] a year more to be paid by the Lessee, without any Deduction for Taxes. {The} ⟨Mr Lynd,⟩[1] {Curate} had also the ⟨Tithe of Hay & all⟩ small Tithes of the Townships of Week & Stone, ⟨wch were granted to the Curate in 1607, if not earlier⟩ & all Commodities of the Ch. Yard of Maidstone, & all Duties for Oblations, Christenings, Churchings, Marriages & Burials in the Parish, formerly called Alterage, & half the small Tithes of the Town of Maidstone, during his Incumbency, by a Grant from ABP Sheldon[2], 10 July 1677. No prior Grant of this Kind is yet found. ABP Tillotson[3] made the same Grant to Gilbert Innes[4], Curate, 17 May 1692. ABP Tenison[5] 8 Jan 1701 renewed the same Grant to the same person, adding to it a Covenant, that Mr Innes shd not demand Tithe of Hops. And 10 Oct. 1715 he made a like Grant to Samuel Weller[6], whom he had appointed Curate by an Indenture 17 Sept 1712. But in this he both excepts Hops, & the Curate promises not to claim them: & he grants further the Tithe Hay of the College Lands in Stone, & all instead of half the small Tithes of the Town ⟨of⟩ Maidstone except the small Tithes of the Burrough of Westree. ⟨The⟩ ABP {Juxon} ⟨in 1607 if not before⟩ excepted out of his Lease of Maidstone ⟨16 Aug 1661⟩ the Hay & all the small Tithes of Week & Stone {excepting Hops} to the Intent, that the Curate of Maidstone shd enjoy them. And this Clause is continued. Worth in all, 150[£] a Year. AD[n] 110[£] ⟨135[£] Curate pd. See Mr Denne[7] July 10 1765⟩.

Hops are not mentioned in the Lease of ⟨the Rectory⟩ 1607: nor Hops of the College Lands in Stone in 1661. But the latter are mentioned in 1715 & perhaps before: when also the Tithe Hops of Week & Stone are excepted out of the small tithes given to the Curate & allowed to be claimed by the Lessee of the Rectory. But the Tithe Hops of Loose & Debtling were never granted in the Lease of the Rectory, but only of Corn & Grain. Every ABP to make a new Grant of Tithes & Dues to Curate. See Letters Nov. 1759[8]. Abt 19 miles round: betw. 11 & 1200 Ho. Chief Hamlets, Tovel, Shephard & Wilmington Street, Lodington & Harbour Land. L[d]Romney[9] ⟨the moat⟩ abt a mile from the Town. A meeting Ho. of Presb. Teacher, Israel Lewis. Another, who separated from them in 1748: Teacher. W[m] Jenkins. A third of Anab. John Wyche. Rather Lessend. Upper Sort in general religious. Lower corrupted by Elections. Care in licencing Alehouses wd prevent much Evil. Whole Service, 2 Sermons, on Sundays. Sermons on good Fr. Nov. 5: Jan 30 & the Mayors Election. [qu. Chr. Day]. Prayers every morning: & on Holydays, Eves, Saturdays & during Lent, in Afternoons. Cat. exp. W. Fr. in Lent. Sacr. on 1st Sunday of each Month, & on the great Festivals. From 200 to 400 Com. No Ho. for Cur. Church noble & in good Repair. Chancel handsome. Roof wants Repair ⟨Repaired 1760⟩. 8 Bells. Mrs Turner[10] of Harrietsham p. 241 hath a House here & is Tenant of the Rectory.

Lic. to Cur. at length 1692 Entry B. IV. 480 & 1711 VI. 47.

North Gallery erected by S[r] Robert Marsham[11] by Lic. 1713 VI. 121.

Concerning the Right to a vault in the Chancel see Mr Denne Feb. 11 1763.

A parochial Library. Catalogue promised Feb. 4. 1759. Not given.

Of the Gaol see Letters June 1760, 1765.

Of Mr Gunsleys[12] Legacy to the poor See Apr. 1764.

In 1758 there were no Papists. In 1765 there are 2 families come, who do not belong to Maidstone, & can have little Influence. Mr Denne.

[1] Humphrey Lynde, C. Maidstone, 1677–87, V. Boxley, 1679–87.

[2] Gilbert Sheldon (1598–1677), archbishop, 1663–77.

[3] John Tillotson (1630–94), archbishop, 1691–4.

[4] University of Aberdeen, V. Chislet, 1683, V. St John the Baptist, Thanet, 1692, C. Maidstone, 1692.

[5] Thomas Tenison (1636–1715), archbishop, 1694–1715.

[6] (1685–1753), of Reading, Berks, m. St John's O 1700, fellow 1701, BCL 1706, fellow, PC. Maidstone, 1712, R. and V. Newchurch, 1712–31, R. Sundridge, 1731–53.

[7] John Denne (1726–1800), of Bromley, Kent, m. CCCC 1743, BA 1748, MA 1751, fellow, 1749–52, adm. Inner Temple, 1741, PC. Maidstone, 1753–1800 and chaplain of gaol, R. Copford, Essex, 1754. 'For many years insane, the result of being shot by prisoners escaped from gaol': Venn.

[8] LPL, MS Secker 3, ff. 228–9, 26 & 29 November 1759.

[9] See p. 248, n. 7.   [10] See p. 241, n. 1.

[11] Sir Robert Marsham (1685–1724), 5th Bt. MP for Maidstone, 1708–22.

[12] Robert Gunsley, a student at University College, R. Titsey, Surrey, 1581–1618, he left in 1618 lands amounting to £15–5s p. a. for bread every Sunday and clothes.

Page 250
Maidstone continued

A free school founded in Ed. 6[th]s time, & endowed with a Ho. & 20[f] ⟨See below⟩ a Year by the Corporation, who chuse the Master. Present Master, Mr Russell[1] V. of Debtling, p. 238 where See ⟨& below⟩. Two Charity Schools set up by D[r] Woodwards[2] means in 1711. 30 boys, 18 Girls, cloathed & taught in them. Chiefly supported by Subscriptions. Ld Romney[3] & fam. generous benefactors, & in all respects Blessings to this Parish. Sir John Banks[4] built & endowed with 60[f] a year clear, 6 Ho. for 6 poor aged Persons of both Sexes. E. of Aylesford[5] Governor & Trustee. Edw. Hunter[6], twice mayor, built & endowed 6 more on the same Plan. Trustees now, Ld Romney, & Mr Henley[7] of Otham p. 252. Survivor to appoint another, asssited by the Recorder & Minister of other Charities see Newtons Antiquities of Maidstone. The Corporation have found, that ⅓ of the 20[f] a year to the school is given for an Usher, & so pay only ⅔ to the Master. 10[f] a year, given by the County, ever since 1719, to a Clergyman to attend the condemned Criminals. ⟨Assistant⟩ Curate hath it. No Parishioners, who had Small Pox, visited in the last minister time: few now. John Russell (see above) elected by Minister & Inhabs. Corporation, being dissolved, lic 1 Aug 1746 Entry B. VIII. 311. W[m] Polhill[8] Cl. lic. Apr. 12. 1764.

John Denne[9] MA C. 14 Feb 1753. Resides in a hired Ho. R. of Copford, Co. Essex, 4 miles SW from Colchester, 200^f a year. See Mr Dennes Letter 1763.

Richd Bassett[10] of Jes. Coll. Ox. Assistant. Pr. 50^f, Profits of Funeral Sermons, & voluntary Offerings made him at Easter. Hath a Living in Glamorganshire Nov 1763 but stays here. Going 1765.
J⟨ohn⟩ White[11], from Ashford. Febr. 1766 Going to Mr Bell[12] at Ulcome.
Wm Jones[13] from Hartlip.
James Reeve[14] A.B. Cur. Sal. £60.

1758 Conf. ⟨here 1126 of this Parish⟩ 239. 1762 Conf. here 773. Of this Parish 326. 1766 Conf. here June 8. 404. Of this Parish 241.

[1] See p. 236, n. 5.
[2] Josiah Woodward (1656–1712), of Dursley, Glos, m. St Edmund Hall 1673, BA 1676, MA 1679, B & DD 1700, East India Company minister of Poplar, 1689, PC. Maidstone, 1711–12, V. Newchurch, 1712–12.
[3] See p. 248, n. 7.
[4] (1627–99), MP for Maidstone, 1654–68, MP for Winchelsea, 1678, MP for Rochester, 1679–89, MP for Queenborough, 1690–95, MP for Maidstone, 1697–99. In 1657 he purchased the former Carmelite monastery at Aylesford. He left money for the almshouses in 1697 and they were built in 1700: Hasted IV, p. 316.
[5] Heneage Finch (1715–77), earl of Aylesford, MP for Leicester, 1739–41, MP for Maidstone, 1741–7 and 1754–7.
[6] The first mayor after the grant of the new charter, left money in 1748: Hasted IV, p. 316.
[7] See p. 252, n. 1.   [8] See p. 50, n. 16.   [9] See p. 249, n. 7.
[10] See p. 233, n. 10.   [11] See p. 137, n. 7.
[12] William Bell (1711–78), of St Martin's-in-the-Field, Middlesex, m. Trinity O 1728, BA 1731, MA 1734, R. Ulcombe, 1740–78.
[13] See p. 212, n. 11.
[14] (1764–1842), of Lambeth, m. St John's C 1782, scholar 1782, BA 1786, MA 1789, C. Maidstone, 1787–1800, PC. Maidstone, 1800–42, six-preacher, 1819–42.

Page 251
Marden V. ⟨near Goudhurst⟩ St Michael. Belonged to the Priory of Shene in Surrey. ABP Propr. & P. K^s books 7–18–4. Wake 100^f. Now called 120^f ⟨AD^n 200^f. See below⟩. 5 miles long, 5 broad ⟨near⟩ 300 Ho. One Family of Presb. 5 of Anab. Lessend. Whole Service, 2 Sermons on Sundays. Prayers on all Festivals, & twice a week in Lent, w^n Ch^n are cat. Sermons at particular times on some Part of Cat. Monthly Sacr. & on 3 great Festivals. Abt 40 Com. each time. Land of 21^f a Year for the poor: only 1^f given to the Minister for a Charity Sermon on AshW & another on Whit. Tuesday. No Charity School. 20^f a Year reserved to the vicar in the ABPs Lease; by Juxon ⟨No Land Tax deducted⟩. Church & Chancel clean & in good Order: as also Ho & outHo. Glebe 1 Acre. 6 Bells. Rectory worth 300^f a year Mr Monckton ⟨besides 10 Acres. Glebe worth 20^f⟩. 1762 I gave 5 Gs tow^{ds} beautifying the Chancel &c. In the accts of the See for 1643 a pension of 3^f from the ABP to the Vicar is mentioned.
1766 now 150^f clear of Taxes. Depends on Hops, wch are much increased: 7–6 an Acre pd for them: elsewhere 10^s but if raised, they wd charge the vicar to the poor. Dues raised from 140 Persons. House mean, largest Room 14½ square: abt 6½ high: in good Repair. A parlor, Hall, Kitchen, below: 4 or 5 bed chambers.

Jonathan Monckton[1] V. 12 Nov. 1742. Resides constantly in V. Ho. Aged 54 in 1766. Inst. to a Living in Berks or Wilts Apr. 1766.
John Andrews[2] L.L.B. V. Dec. 23. 1766. resides.

Mr ⟨Samuel⟩ Cooper[3] coming to be Cur.3[d] Sunday after LD 1767: cannot board: going into V. House.

1758 Conf. 108. 1762. 24 + 34. 1766. 37

[1] (1712-96), of Cornwall, m. St John's C 1729, BA 1734, MA 1737, V. Sittingbourne, 1740-42, V. Marden, 1742-66, R. Pangbourne, Berks, 1766-96.
[2] (1730-?), of Berkeley, Glos, m. Trinity O 1748, BCL (St Mary Hall) 1759, V. Stinchcombe, Glos, where he was in trouble for permitting a female preacher, LPL, MS Secker 3, fols. 232-3; V. Marden, 1766-?
[3] See p. 221, n.3.

Page 252
D. Sutton
Otham R. S[t] Nicolas. Bowyer Hen{d}ley[1] Esq[r] P. K[s] books 9-17-3½. Wake 115[£]. So called now. 40 Ho. dispersed. M[r] Henley ⟨See below⟩. 3 Families of Anab. Whole Service, 2 Sermons, on Sundays. Prayers on chief Festivals & Fasts. Cat. exp. 3 months in Summer. 5 Sacr. Betw. 60 & 70 Com. on 3 great Festivals: betw. 40 & 50 on the first Sunday in Lent, & at Mich. A small messuage ⟨6[£] a year⟩ given to the Poor by Mr Henley: ⟨who⟩ hath a good Estate: & is a serious man. Used to be Chairman at the Sessions at Maidstone, (being bred to the Law) till he grew old. Church, Chancel, Ho & outHo. in good Order. Glebe 27 Acres. 3 Bells.

Sam. Horne[2] R. 17 May 1727. Good. Resides constantly in the Parsonage Ho.
Will. Horne[3] R. January 19th.1769. resides.

1758 Conf. 28. 1762. 19. 1766. 11.

[1] Owner of Gore-court from c.1712-42, leaving two sons, William and Walter and four daughters, of whom Anne, the youngest, married Samuel Horne (see n. 2.). William died in 1757 and was followed by his son William: Hasted V, p. 517.
[2] See p. 248, n. 9.   [3] Ibid., n. 10.

Page 253
Stapleherst R. All Saints. S[t] Johns Coll. Camb. P. K[s] books 26-5-10. Wake 240[£]. So called now⟨AD[n] 300[£] 325 R⟩. Near 80 Ho. besides the Street [Wake, above 100 in al]. A meeting Ho. of Presb. Teacher, Chapman, their number few: & of Anab. Teacher Austen, increased by Admission into vacant Farms. Whole Service, 2 Sermons, on Sundays. Prayers W. Fr. Holydays. Cat. in Lent. 4 Sacr. Commonly abt 80 Com. A Free School, with Lands of 9[£] a Year, vested in Feoffees. An Exchequer Tallie of 70[£] a Year, after two Lives, one of which is fallen, the other old, said to be given by a Lady, for what purpose is kept a Secret, & to bein a Box in the Church with 3 Locks: but it is feared that one Person hath all the keys: & the ChW[ms] are apprehensive of appointing some Persons, & so the matter remains ⟨See Mr Yorkes[1] opinion abt these⟩. A strong Suspicion of a Mans having children by his Housekeeper. A large Church & Chancel &c clean & handsome. Ho. & out Ho. in good Order, by D[r] Burton. 5 Bells.

Mich. Burton[2] D.D. R. 19 Feb. 1753 ⟨Resided⟩. Dead, March 6 1759.
John Taylor[3] BD R. 16 Aug. 1759. Low voice. Now Aug 1760 DD. Going to
reside. Will do the whole Service, if he can. Resides.
Thomas Thompson[4] B.D. Rector 1785.
Harry Grove[5] Rector 1786.

Jos. Todd[6] Cur. 40^f Ord. Pr. 24 Sept. 1758. 3.
M^r. Barrowdale[7] Cur.
Walter Spenlove[8] A.B. Cur. Sal. £45 & surplice Fees lic. 1790.

1758 Conf. 62. 1762. 84 + 1 1766. 72.

[1] Charles Yorke (1722–70), lawyer, solicitor-general, 1756–61, attorney-general, 1762. MP for
Reigate, 1747–68, MP for Cambridge University, 1768–70, lord chancellor, 1770.
[2] (1701–59), of Wirksworth, Derby, m. St John's C 1718, BA 1722, MA 1726, BD 1734, DD 1749,
fellow, 1727–54, president, 1746–53, V. Hathersage, Derbs, 1728–39, V. St Clement,
Cambridge, 1741, C. Horningsea, Cambs, 1741–53, R. Staplehurst, 1753–9.
[3] (1707–85), of Cockerham, Lancs, m. St John's C 1724, BA 1728, MA 1731, BD 1738, DD 1760,
fellow 1729–61, V. Littlebury, Essex, 1743–59, R. Staplehurst, 1759–85.
[4] (1732–86), of Beverley, Yorkshire, m. St John's C 1749, BA 1755, MA 1758, BD 1766, fellow
1757–86, headmaster Rochester school, 1755–86, V. Darenth, 1758–9, V. Hoo, 1759–86, R.
Staplehurst, 1785–6.
[5] (1747–1808), m. St John's C 1764, scholar, BA 1768, MA 1711, BD 1779, fellow 1769, steward
1783–6, C. Horningsea, Cambs, 1779–83, R. Staplehurst, 1786–1808.
[6] See p. 65, n. 6.   [7] He has not been traced.
[8] (1768–97), of Middlesex, m. Queens' C 1787, BA 1790, MA 1794, C. Staplehurst, 1790.

Page 254
D. Sutton
Sutton Valence al. Town Sutton ⟨V.⟩ St Mary, with the Chapel of East Sutton,
St Peter [Sutton by Dover p. 198 is sometimes called East Sutton]. Belonged to
the Priory of Leeds. DCh of Rochester P. K^s books 7-9-7. Wake 75^f. Now
called 80^f ⟨AD^n 100^f⟩. 3½ miles long, 2 broad. 74 Ho. ⟨In East Sutton. Sir
John Filmer[1] Bart⟩. Two Families of Anab. A few Absenters. Endeavours have
been & shall be used abt them. Service once at Church & Chapel on Sundays. A
Sermon at each. Prayers on the special Festivals and Fasts. Cat. during Lent.
Familiar Expositions procured for them. 4 Sacr. Generally abt 50 Com. ⟨In East
Sutton 40⟩. A free School. ⟨A House, & 12 or 14^f year⟩. Mr Hardy[2] Master,
[Cur. of Boughton Monchelsea p. 234.]. An Alms Ho. containing 6 poor
Persons, chiefly designed for Widows. Founder, Wm Lamb[3] of London Esqr.
Governors, Cloth-workers Company. Revenues, betw. 40 & 50^f a Year. Well
conducted. The Revd Mr Francis Robins[4] left 3^f a Year to the Minister & Ch W^{ns}
for honest poor, not receiving Parochial Relief. In Qu Elizabeths Reign, Geo.
Usmer[5] Esqr & Dame Eliz Filmer[6] left Benefactions of 15^f a Year to the Poor of
East Sutton. So applied. Church ⟨& Chancel⟩ very clean & in good Order. Ho.
very bad, wants Repair in every part. No outho. 4 Bells. Chapel & its Chancel
clean & decent. No Ho. 6 Bells. 10^f a year is vested in Trustees, of w^m Sr John
Filmer is one, for a Curate residing in the Parish House of E. Sutton & diligently
serving the Cure of it, & in default of this, for repairing the Church of E. Sutton.
See Sr Johns Letter. The School endowed with 20^f a yr for the Master, & 10^f for
the Usher. Now both given to the master. Mr Hardy.

Schoolm. licenced 1714 Entry B VI. 158.

Sam. Venner[7] BA V. 17 July 1747. Resides at Cranbrook 10 miles off, where he hath a School [but not Scholars. See p. 58] & serves his Church & Chapel from thence. Mr Hardy, Schoolmaster here, doth occ. Duty. A Tenant in V. Ho. Sequestred Sept. 1760 for a Debt of 500^f ⟨400⟩ to Mr Robinson[8] Banker in the Strand, to wm he is to pay 40^f a Year ⟨for 280^f pd him⟩. He will not serve it ⟨shuts himself up at Cranbrook. 1762 Curacy in Suffolk 30^f⟩. Mr Hardy, Schoolm. here, & Cur. of Boughton Monchelsea p. 234 proposed, at 42^f. Allowed. Died abt Dec 1764.

Nic. Brown[9] M.A. V. 19 March 1765 ord. by me 1760. 1. min. Can. of Rochester. Will reside here wn church consents. Mr Hardy Cur. 1766. Nothing done at the House. May 1768 two new Rooms built: more to be done as soon as can.

1758 Conf. Sutton Valence 57. East Sutton. 43. 1762. Sutton Val. 26 + 3E Sutton 9 1762. S. Val. 31 + 8. E. S. 9.

Mr Prosser[10] Cur.

[1] (1716–97), 4th Bt, MP for Steyning, 1767–74.   [2] See p. 65, n. 4.
[3] William Lamb[e], had been a gentleman of Henry VIII's chapel and was a member of the clothworkers company. In 1578 he also erected a free grammar school: Hasted V, p. 371.
[4] In 1720. He also gave money for two exhibitions to St John's Cambridge for two scholars educated at Lambe's school: ibid.
[5] Gave lands in c. 1567.
[6] Widow of Sir Edward Filmer. She left the money in 1638: Hasted V, p. 382.
[7] See p. 58, n. 13.   [8] He has not been traced.   [9] See p. 66, n. 6.
[10] Probably Samuel Prosser (1773–1825), of Dorstone, Hereford, m. Wadham 1792, C. Sutton Valence, 1796, R. Milton near Canterbury, 1804, R. Southwick, Sussex, 1805–25.

Page 255

Thornham V. St Mary, with ⟨Aldington al⟩ Allington ⟨St Peter⟩ & Cobham. Is there any mention of these elsewhere, as Chapels? ⟨{No} See below⟩. Belonged to the monastery of Combwell ⟨See Reg Warham fol. 142b⟩. William Cage[1] Esq^{r}P. K^s books 8-0-10. Wake 50^f. Said now to be 130^f com. ann. ⟨See below⟩. 5 miles long, 1 broad: incloses at one End almost all Bearsted. Ab^t 50 Ho. Dr Jones[2], a physician. Genl Belford[3] of the Artillery. Whole Service generally on Sundays from 1720 to 1735. But Debtling is but ½ mile off, & Bearsted a mile, & nearer to half the Parish than their own Church. So the Prayers one part of the Day were thinly attended & left off. [Now again 1759 Whole Service]. Prayers at least on one Litany Day in Lent: & then Cat. exp. 4 Sacr. Abt 50 Com. Church Lands, let for 3 Guineas a Year, for the Use & Ornam^t of it. So applied. Other small Benefactions to the Poor. V saith, it is but abt 90^f Cur. & Taxes deducted. It is 150^f. ABP Warham appointed Jan 2. 1525 that Service shd be only a few days in the Year in the Chapel of Allington, wch had been annually annexed to Thornham. Reg. Parker pt 2. fol 91b, 92a. Revd Mr Hodson[4], patron AD^n.

Church very clean & handsome. Great Chancel in good Order: the adjoyning, very bad. Ho. pretty good. out Ho. in good Order: much done to both by Mr Soan. Glebe 30 Acres. 3 Bells.

A Chapel annexed to this Ch. abt 1604, by the Proprietor of an Estate in the Parish called Binbury. No Faculty, or Repair by Proprietors appear. The Present will not repair. ChW^n will. AD^n Oct. 1762.

Jonathan Soan[5] V. 21 {Dec}. ⟨Jan⟩ 1720. Cur. of St Marg. in Rochester. Was Master of K^s School there almost 20 Years; but being in his 70th Year & gouty, hath resigned. 8 miles from Thornham, where he often officiates. V. also of Woodnesborough p. 203. One of the 10 poor vicars. Died abt 13 Jan. 1768.
Hodson[6] Henry V. Feb. 9. 1768, holds it with Sandhurst R 20 miles off. Presented by his Father[7], who had the Advowson from Smallwell[8], who had it from Cage.
John Hodson[9] Vicar 1782 resides.

Mr Robt Polhill[10], Cur. Resides at Boxley 2 miles off. 20$^£$ Easter off & Surpl. Fees. [1759 30$^£$ &c officiating twice. Now V. of Goudherst p. 240. Goes thither at Mich. Dr Banson[11], late Cur. of Goudherst, succeeds. 35$^£$ East. Off. Surpl. Fees. Was offerd V. Ho. but chuses the Ho. at Boxley, wch Mr Polhill left. 1764 Serves it with Bredherst. Forbidden. Doth not 1765.
Dr Banson Cur. 1766. Resides Mich 1767.

1758. Conf. 24. 1762. 11. 1766. 15

[1] William Cage, of Milgate, the son of the MP.
[2] William Jones (died 1780) MD, second husband of the wife of Richard Sheldon, the owner of Aldington manor in the parish: Hasted V, p. 527.
[3] William Belford (1709–1780), artillery officer.
[4] See p. 71, n. 3.   [5] See p. 203, n. 2.
[6] (1719–81), of Headcorn, m. St John's C 1737, BA 1741, MA 1744 R. Sandhurst, 1753–81, V. Thornham, 1768–81, chaplain to the duke of Bolton.
[7] See n. 4.
[8] Joseph Smallwell of Maidstone bought the advowson in 1740. He sold it in 1753 to Henry Hodson: Hasted V, p. 531.
[9] (17–1829), of Sandhurst, 'a literate person', St John's C 1781, V. Thornham, 1782–1829, R. Allingham, 1782–1829, PC. Bredhurst, 1802–29: 'it was probably due to some friendly arrangement with the archbishop of Canterbury that the presentation of the living (which had been held by his grand-father and father, who died in 1781) was allowed to lapse with the understanding that JH should bequickly ordained and succeed to Thornham.' (Venn).
[10] See p. 142, n. 3.   [11] See p. 236, n. 6.

Page 256
D. Sutton
Ulcomb R. All Saints. Gilb. Clarke[1] Esqr P. K^s books 16-5-10. Wake 250$^£$. Now called 300$^£$ ⟨Perhaps more. AD^n 260$^£$⟩. 5 miles long: one Hamlet called Chedworth End: abt 70 Families. Very few Dissenters. Whole Service. Prayers on the principal Festivals, & in Lent, when Ch^n are cat. on week Days, as well as Sundays. Plain Expositions distributed. 4 Sacr. abt 40 Com. each time. 13$^£$ a Year given for the poor. So applied. Parsonage Ho. a very good one, built by Mr Belcher[2] ⟨Lic. 1722 Entry B VI. 415⟩ the last Incumbent. Out ho. in good Order. Church & Chancel, noble & in excellent Order. Glebe 82 Acres. 6 Bells.

Wm Bell[3] MA. R. 7 May 1740. Hath always resided in the Parsonage Ho. Fitzherbert Adams[4] LLB. Rector. June 20: 1778. resides.

J. White[5], going from Maidstone to be Cur. & Tutor to R[s] Son Feb. 1766. Quitting this place March 1767.

John Bell[6] Curate, Licensed May 30: 1774. Salary £40 p. ann.

John Tattersall[7] Curate, Licensed Dec[r]. 21: 1778. Salary £50 p. ann.

Ralph Carr Rider[8] Cur. lic. 1790. Sal. £40.

Henry W[m] Champneys[9] A.B. Cur. 1796. Sal £50 not lic.

1758 Conf. 96. 1762. 38. 1766. 48

[1] Son of Godfrey Clarke, MP for Derbyshire, 1710–34: Hasted V, p. 392.
[2] Stringer Belcher (1691–1739), of Rochester, m. St John's C 1708, BA 1712, MA 1715, R. Ulcombe, 1716–39.
[3] See p. 250, n. 12.
[4] (1745–1805), of Charwelton, Northants, m. Lincoln 1762, BCL 1769, R. Ulcombe, 1778–1805.
[5] See p. 15, n. 12.
[6] (1749–?), of Ulcombe, Kent, m. University 1770, C. Ulcombe, 1774.
[7] See p. 57, n. 12.
[8] (1768–1839), of Ingram, Leeds, m. Merton 1786, BA 1789, C. Ulcombe, 1790, R. Stoke, Kent, 1811–39, C. East Farleigh, 1814.
[9] (1771–1845), of Rochester, m. Christs 1789, BA 1789, BA 1793, MA 1796, C. Ulcombe, 1796, V. Leigh, Lancs, 1798–1800, R. St Margaret's, Canterbury, 1803–6, V. Rainham, 1804–7, V. St Mary Bredin, Canterbury, 1807–21, V. Walton, Yorks, 1807–43, R. Badsworth, Yorks, 1821–45.

Page 257

Wormshill R. S[t] Giles. Governors of Christs Hosp. P. ⟨So 1721 Entry B VI. 389⟩. K[s] books 10[£]. Certified 69-4-0. Wake 80[£]. So called now ⟨73[£] Taxes deducted. Mr Miller⟩. Abt 22 Families. Sober & regular in their Attendance at Church. Service once on Sundays & good Friday [qu Chr. Day]. Cat. every other Sunday. 4 Sacr. 16 or 20 Com. 40[s] a Year, the Rent of 10 Acres of Land, given for the Poor. No Offertory: owing to the mean Condition of the People. Church very dirty & out of Repair. Chancel tolerable. Ho. bad, wants much Repair ⟨amended 1766⟩. Out Ho. in pretty good Repair. Glebe 27 Acres. 4 Bells.

Coll. ⟨of Giles Hinton[1]⟩ by ABP to this R void by Cession of W[m] Paine[2] 11 Jan. 1681 Entry B. IV. 172. Perhaps lapsed. For on Hintons death, Christmas[3] was inst. on Pres. V. 22. Oct. 1767. 70[£] to be laid out on repairs immediately.

Isaac Johnson[4] MA R. 21 Nov. 1741. V. of S[t] Dunstans Cant. p. 33 where he resides. Cur. of little Hardres p. 38. Died Mar. 13. 1767.

Tho. Miller[5] MA R. 17 July. 1767. Will reside. Is at D[rs] Commons Mich. 1767. Cur. of S[t] Dionis Backchurch p. 307.

Josiah Disturnell[6] A.M. Rector 1792.

Tho. Baker[7] Cur. R. of Frinsted p. 239. where he resides. The Churches not a measured mile distant. 20[£]. Gone.

John Carver[8] Cur. See p. 239.

W[m] Marsh[9] R of Bicknor p. 205 C. Chr. 1764. See p. 205. Gone May 1767. Serves it Mich 1767.

1758 Conf. 17. 1762. Wormshill 7. 1766. 6

[1] (16?–1702), m. Merton 1658, BA 1658, MA 1660, B & DD 1670, R. Westbere, 1663, R. Biddenden, 1682–1702, R. Wormshill, 1682–1702, rural dean of Charing, 1683.

2 (1650–97), of Hutton, Essex, m. Magdalene C 1665, BA 1669, MA 1672, DD 1689, fellow 1671, R. Wormshill, 1673–81, R. Frinsted,1674, R. St Mary Whitechapel, London, 1681–97, lecturer Poultry church, 1689, preb of Winchester, till 1689, preb of Westminster, 1694–7, chaplain to king, 1690–7.

3 Edward Christmas (1676–1715), of Southfleet, Kent, m. Hart Hall 1694, BA 1697, MA 1700, R. Wormshill, 1702–15.

4 See p. 33, n. 4.   5 See p. 220, n. 10.

6 (1744–1834), m. Pembroke C 1763, BA 1767, MA 1770, C. Hitcham, Suffolk, 1768, R. Wormshill, 1792–1834.

7 See p. 238, n. 2.   8 See p. 214, n. 5.   9 See p. 130, n. 2.

[Deanery of Westbere]

Page 258

D. Westbere

All Saints Cur. Exempt from the Archdeacon. Not certified. Ecton. Placed between Birchington & Sᵗ Nicolas & marked as desolate, in both Maps of the Diocese. It appears by ABP Winchelseys Register fol. 30 to have been a chapel to Reculver & afterwards to Sᵗ Nicolas p. 267.

Page 259

Birchington See Monkton

Chislet. V. Sᵗ Mary. Belonged to Sᵗ Austins Cant. ABP Propr. & P. ⟨said in the parochial Book 1663 to be given to the ABP in the 3d Exchange⟩. Kˢ books 29-19-9½. Certified 67-19-0¼. Called now 70$^£$ ⟨or 80$^£$. 10$^£$ pd by ABPs Lessee. Called 100 in 1727 Entry B. VII 179⟩. 4 miles long. 90 Ho. ABPs large Woods, E. & W. Blean in this Parish, but separated by the Borough of Hoath [a chapelry belonging to Reculver p. { }. A few poor Ho. amongst these Woods. The Inhabitants have immemorially christend & buried at Hoath, as much nearer than Chislett. V. gives his Dues to the Schoolmaster there, to teach all their Children. Tho. Jones[1] Esqʳ, Justice of Peace, [& ABPˢ Lessee] & some rich Farmers. A few Absenters of low Rank: & 3 Persons of better Fortune & good Morals, who never come to Church. By talking with them on the Subject, their Heads seem disorderd. Service once here on Sundays: once at Hoath by the V. of Reculver. No mention of Cat.]. 5 Sacr. Number of Com. increased. V. being excused from Sesses never meddles in Parish Business. Houses & Land, worth 9-14-0 a Year given to the Church. Petits Gift, 2$^£$ a Year to V. & 2$^£$ to the poor not receiving parish Relief. A Farm of 28$^£$ a Year to such poor by John Taylor[2]. V. laid out 200$^£$ on V. Ho. Chancel was in bad Repair. Mr Jones laid out 100$^£$ upon it 1759. ABP gave 10$^£$ towds cieling it. Church large & handsome. Ho & out Ho. in good Order ⟨Improved by the present V⟩. Glebe 3 Acres. 6 Bells. Inst. 1691 on pres. of Crown by Lapse Entry B. IV. 172.

Nic. Simons[3] V. 17 Oct. 1748. V. of Sᵗ Nicolas in Thanet p. 267. Lived at Chislett 5 years, always ill. Removed to Cant. for his Health & the Education of his 9 Chⁿ. & Served both Parishes once a Sunday: 8 miles from Cant. 3 asunder.

See Letters. Agreed for some time to keep a Resident Cur. Mr Salt[4], to serve one twice, & do the occasional of both, & himself to serve the other twice. But now 1759 he hath Leave to reside on one, & serve both once, as had been usual. Hath an Estate. *** He & his Family have been sickly ascribed to the air 1761. Going to Bath Sept. 1761. Returned Dec. 21. 1762 Hath offerd 50^f ⟨a year⟩ for a Curate.

David Ball[5] Clerk L.L.B. Vicar May 9: 1777.

Sir John Fagg[6]. A.M. Vicar 1785.

Wm Hassell[7] C. of this & St Nicolas p. 267, from Warehorn p. 147. Resides here. 50^f. Pays 8$^£$ for the Vicarage Ho. Resides 1764. Mr Simons lives in Westminster.

John Farnham[8] C. of this & St Nicolas, Licensed May 30: 1774. Salary £50 p. ann.

M^r. Williams[9] Cur Sal £50 for this & St Nicolas.

1758 Conf. 31. 1762. 26. 1766. 41.

[1] Died in 1760.

[2] 'Petits gift' was the £50 left by Thomas Petit of St George's, Canterbury, to be given to young, married poor people. John Taylor left a farm and lands at Marsh-row in this parish in 1582: Hasted IX, p. 105.

[3] (17?-76), of Belgrave, Leics, m. Trinity Hall 1737, LLB 1749, R. Isleham, Cambs, 1743-6, V. Chislet, 1748-76, V. St Nicholas at Wade, 1749-76.

[4] Thomas Salt (17?-1806), of Chesterton, Cambs, m. St John's C 1740, BA 1743, MA 1746, V. Nazing, Essex, 1761-1806, R. Hildersham, Cambs, 1797-1806.

[5] See p. 110, n. 6.

[6] (c.1760-1822), of Kent, m. Clare 1777, BA 1781, MA 1784, fellow 1782-6, V. Chislet, 1785-1803, V. St Nicholas at Wade, 1785-1803, R. Chartham, 1803-22, R. (and patron) Great Hardres and Stelling, 1815-22, 6th Bt, 1791.

[7] See p. 126, n. 7.

[8] (1751-1803), of Cornwall, m. St John's C 1768, scholar 1769, BA 1772, MA 1775, C. Chislet and St Nicholas at Wade, 1774-96, V. Treneglos w. Warbstow, Cornwall, 1796-1803.

[9] Perhaps also p. 267, n. 6.

Page 260

D. Westbere

Herne V. St Martin. [Was a Chapel to Reculver. See ABP Winchelseys Reg. fol. 30.]. ABP Propr. & P. [He lets the great Tithes in the Lease of Reculver]. Exempt from the AD^n. K^s books 20-16-3. Wake 80^f. Herring 100^f ⟨Called in Disp 1751 120^f⟩. V. saith abt 70^f. but thinks Improvements may & shd be made. See the Endowm^t in the Register above, & a Copy of it, & a Certificate of it sent to him. 4 miles long, 2 broad. 140 Ho. Mr Knowler[1], lately removed to London. 5 Absenters. Promise to amend. Whole Service on Sundays. Prayers on Saints Days & W. Fr in Lent, when Cat. is exp. 2 Sacr at each great Festival & at Mich. 30 or 40 Com. A reading & writing School in the Church: sometimes 10 Ch^n, sometimes 40. 12^f a Year given to the Church. V. complains that he hath not Tithe Wood. See Letters & Endowment: by which he is to repair his own Chancel, & pay 40^s a Year to the vicar of Reculver. Church large & handsome, but many things in it out of Order. Chancel in good Repair. Ho. good & convenient. Out ho. in good Repair. Glebe an Acre. 6 Bells.

Will Rogers[2] BA V. 6 July 1756. Resides in V. Ho.
John Duncombe[3] Master of Arts V Nov[r]. 12 1773.
Joseph Price[4] L.L.B. Vicar 1786 resides.
John Wood[5] Vicar 1794.

1758 Conf. 78. 1762. 74. 1766. 54.

[1] Gilbert Knowler, whose family had resided at Herne since Henry VII's reign: Hasted IX, p. 89.
[2] See p. 23, n. 3.   [3] See p. ii, n. 45.
[4] See p. 17, n. 6.   [5] See p. 115, n. 7.

Page 261
Hoath See Reculver

S[t] Johns at Margate in Thanet. V. ABP P. {K[s] books} Tenths 16[s]. Certified
49-12-6. Wake 50[£]. Now called 70[£]. ⟨See below AD[n] 80[£]. 90 Mr Jacob[1], 50[£]
Subscr. in 1762 & as much in 1763⟩. A large Town: 2 or 3 small Villages:
above 400 Ho. A very few Dissenters: who go to Church sometimes. 2 men &
their wives, Quakers. One or two more in an Hospital, founded by one Yoakley
a Quaker for 10 men or women, out of this & 2 or 3 neighbouring Parishes, who
have Coats or Gowns once in two years, some Firing, & abt 6[£] a year in money.
The Trustees are Quakers. Given for Quakers in the first place, but not only.
Pretty well managed. A meeting Ho. in the Hospital. Preaching there 3 or 4
times in a Year: chiefly at Funerals. The Parishioners remarkable for going to
church. Whole Service on Sundays. Prayers on all Holydays, & W. Fr. from the
Beginning of Lent till Mich. Cat. W. Fr. in Lent. Many Ch[n] come. Sacr 1st
Sunday of every month & the 3 great Festivals. From 40 to 90 Com. The ABP
pays 8[£] a year to V. & his Tenant of Salmeston Grange two Bushels of Wheat.
Church large & in good Repair. Chancel very neat. Ho & out Ho. very good. 9[£]
a Year to the poor, AD[n]. Glebe 12 Acres. 5 Bells.
Salmeston & Dean are in this Parish. Philipot p. 386. They belonged to the
Abbey of S[t] Augustin wch H. 8 dissolved & gave the former anno regni 29 to the
See of Cant. ib. Qu. Mary granted the Advowson of Salmeston with Dean to that
See. Wilkins vol. 4. p. 178. The Rectory parsonage & Grange of Salmeston &
Dean were granted to the See 12 July 3 Eliz. & are now leased out on Lives,
excepting the Vicarage, wch is not mentioned in Ecton or Lewis' map.
Lic. to build a Gallery 1714 Entry B. VI. 174.

John Jacob V. 16 Sept. 1749. Resides constantly in V. Ho. V. also of
Tilmanston p. 199. Wd give 40[£] for a Curate. *** Died Dec. 21. 1763.
W[m] Harrison[2] (see below) June 14. 1764.

W[m] Harrison BA C. July 1763 from Chester Dioc. 20[£] & his board. See AD[ns]
Letter Oct. 4. 1763.

M[r]. Williams[3] Cur.
M[r]. Lloyd[4] Cur.

1758 Conf. 77. 1762. Conf. here 424 Of this Parish 158. 1766 Conf. here 386.
Of this Parish 146.

[1] See p. 199, n. 3.

[2] Probably (17?–1809) of Cheshire, m. St Catherine's C 1755, BA 1760, V. St John's Thanet, 1764–1809.

[3] See p. 259, n. 9.   [4] See p. 189, n. 5.

Page 262

D. Westbere

S[t] Laurence at Ramsgate V. Belonged to S[t] Austins Cant. ABP P. K[s] books 7[f]. Wake 100[f] So called now⟨AD[n] 120[f]⟩. Of this, 5[f] reserved in the ABP[s] Lease of Newland Grange in this Parish to the Vicar & 35[f] to the ABP or Vicar ⟨& 2 bushels of wheat in that of Salmeston Grange⟩: & the ABP pays him 6[f]. ⟨The 40[f] was reserved by Juxon. P[d] without any Deduction⟩. The Parish contains 15 Villages & Hamlets. See the Names. Abt 650 Families. Part of the Summer, L[d] Visc. Conyngham[1], [member of Ho. of Commons] W[m] Bookey[2] Esq[r], & Mrs Abbot[3] [widow] all the Year. The Town of Ramsgate hath abt 500 Ho. 1/12 of these Presb. or Anab. Teacher of the former Spence from the Orcades, a modest man: they decline: of the latter, Matthews, a Cooper at Birchington; they keep their Ground. Church too small for the Inhabitants: hence the few Absenters plead want of Room. Whole Service, 2 Sermons, on Sundays. Prayers on all Festivals, & W. Fr. from the beginning of Lent to Mich. Cat. W. Fr. in Lent. 9 Sacr. Above 100 Com. on great Festivals: 70 or more on other Days. A Charity School set up lately for teaching 10 Boys to read & write & 10 Girls to read, knit & sew, supported by Contributors & a Charity Sermon. Not fed, nor cloathed. When they go away, a Bible given them: & some little Tracts by AD[n] Denne[4]. 20[s] for a Sermonon good Fr. 10[s] for one on Asc. Day & sev[l] small Benefactions to the Poor, which see. Church & Chancel very good. Neat Rails since the last Parochial Visitation Ho. & out H pretty good. 19[f] a Year to the poor. AD[n]. Glebe 2 Acres. 5 Bells.

The Rectory was granted by the Crown to the ABP in Exchange 31 Aug. Ed. 6. See Chart Misc. vol. 13. N°. 21.

No part of the Ho. can be repaired: all must be rebuilt. AD[n] Aug. 4. 1766.

Chapel at Ramsgate built by Act of Parliament consecrated July 8. 1791. The vicar of Saint Laurence Patron.

Richard Harvey[5] Sen[r]. A.M. lic. 1791.

[1] Henry Conyngham (c.1705–81), MP for Killybegs, 1727–53, MP for Tiverton, 1747–54, MP for Sandwich, 1756–74, vice-admiral of Ulster 1748–59, created viscount Conyngham in 1756 and baron in 1781.
[2] Member of the East India company.
[3] Dorothy, wife of William Abbot. He died in 1755: Hasted X, p. 410.
[4] John Denne. See p. 240, n. 5. These perhaps included his *The Nature and Design and Benefits of Confirmation* (1726).
[5] See p. 83, n. 10.

Page 263

S[t] Laurence Ramsgate continued

Robt Tyler[1] MA V. 5 May 1740. Resides in V. Ho. 11 months. Usually spends the 12th in or near his R. of Tunstall p. 229 where he then officiates. 1766 M[r] Atkins[2] his Cur. Died June 12. 1766.

Richard Harvey[3] MA V. 18 June 1766. To reside at Mich. resides.
Richard Harvey[4] Jun[r]. L.L.B. Vicar 1793.

1758 Conf. 100. 1762. 99. 1766. 79

[1] See p. 229, n. 2. [2] Probably Francis Atkins, see p. 182, n. 5.
[3] See p. 83, n. 10.
[4] (1769–1836), of Kent, m. CCCC 1784, scholar, LLB 1790, C. St Lawrence in Thanet, 1789 (Venn says 1791), V. St Lawrence, 1793–1836.

Page 264
D. Westbere
Margate See S[t] Johns p. 261

Minster in Thanet V. S[t] Mary. Belonged to S[t] Austins Cant. ABP. P. K[s] books 33-3-4. Wake 250[f]. Now called 200[f] ⟨AD[n] 240⟩. ⟨V. may have 240[f] for his Tithes, asks 270[f] AD[n] June 1767⟩. 3 miles square, besides 100 Acres in Margate Parish. 108 Ho. abt 140 Families. Church well attended. One principal Farmer, an immoral man, & 2 insane women, neglect it. Whole Service, 2 Sermons, on Sundays. Prayers on some principal Festivals & in Lent. Cat. W. Fr. in Lent. Only poor Ch[n] sent. Exp. on most Sunday mornings in parts. 2 Sacr. at each great Festival, one after Harvest. From 50 to above 100 Com. An Alms Ho. for 6 Families belongs to the Parish. Another with a Work Ho. purchased with Money left by D[r] ⟨Richd⟩ Clerke[1]. The Parish give 6[f] a Year for them, which his Feofees lay out in Cloaths for the Poor. The Parish gives 5[f] for teaching poor boys to read & write. D[r] Clerke was vicar of Minster: & by Deed 15 Jan 1625 gave 100[f] to be lent to 4 proper persons natives of Minster for a Term not exceeding 3 Years. Changed now as above. In ABP[s] Lease of Salmeston Grange is a Covenant, that the Lessee shall give to 24 [Answers to Inquiries say, to 6] Inhabitants of Thanet [Answers say, of Minster] nine Loaves of Bread & 18 Herrings [this changed into 3[d]] each, in the first week & middle of Lent, & likewise to 12 [Answers say 3] persons of the same place, 2 Ells of Blanket [changed into 2-6] & every Monday & Friday from the Invention of the holy Cross [May 3] to S[t] John Baptist a Dish of Pease to every Person coming to Salmeston [This last is intirely neglected.]. And to the Vicar of Minster 10[s] [not mentioned in the Answers]. John Cary[2] of Stanwell Co. Mid. Esq[r] gave by will 10 Sept 1685 10[f] a year to be distributed to the poor by ChW[ns] on S[t] Thomas's Day. Done. Ch. & chancel in good Repair, & out Ho. V. is making Ho, very good & handsome. Endowed with part of the gr. Tithes. 15[f] a Year to the poor, AD[n]. Glebe 12 Acres. 5 Bells. V. saith Sept. 30 1760 that V. Ho. adjoyns to & is level with unhealthy Marsh Ground: that no V. hath resided these 100 Years, that he & his Family have been ill all the time: that he hath expended 300[f] on V. Ho. that a modus of 1[s] an Acre for Pasture Ground is falsely pleaded: that Land left by the Sea not 40 Years ago pays 15[s], & the owner calls that a modus.
The Advowson was granted by the Crown to the ABP in Exchange 31 Aug 1 Ed. 6 See Chart Misc. vol 13. N° 21.

[1] Richard Clerke, of London, m. Christs 1579, BA 1583, BD 1593, DD 1598, fellow 1583-98, Lady Margaret Preacher, 1596, V. Minster, 1597-1634, six-preacher, 1602, R. Snargate, 1609-

11, V. Monkton, 1611–34. Left this partly by deed in 1625 and partly by will in 1634: Hasted X, p. 285.

[2] He also left money for the relief of the poor at Stanwell: VCH *Middlesex* III, p. 50.

Page 265
Minster continued

Francis Dodsworth[1] MA V. 28 Nov. 1757. R. of Hollingbourne p. 242. Coming to reside. Came in Oct. 1758. Absent from Apr. to Aug. 1759. Going away for his Health Nov. 1760. 1763 Cur. of Doddington p. 156

Tho. Salt[2] Cur. MA. 45^f & Surpl. Fees. Was Cur to Dr Tunstall[3] 11 Years. Desires a Settlem^t in the Diocese. See Letters. Gone. Got him a Living from Ld Chancellor.
Mr Gill[4] of Monkton serves this till a Cur. can be got.
Fra. Griffin[5] BA of Magd. Hall ord. Deacon Jan 4 & pr. Jan 6. 1761 by BP Thomas[6] of Sarum. C. by Lett. Dim. from me. Not there yet Feb. 14: I believe not ordained. There is a wicked Griffin of Ch. Ch. See Paper. Is this he?
Dodsworth[7] Fred. BA. of Christs Col. brother to V. ord. Deacon Dec. 20. 1761. 3. bapt May 1. 1761. Salary 40^f & Surpl. Fees. lic to Bredhurst p. 236 & going thither March 1763.
Roger Parry[8] BA of Clare Hall ord. by BP Drummond[9]. Cur. 40^f. Easter Offs & Surpl. Fees valued at 10^f ⟨not worth 30^s AD^n⟩. To reside. Apr. 1763. Gone May 1764. Mr Gill[10]. Gone Apr. 1765.
Clarke[11] of Dublin Coll. Pr. C. AD^n hath seen his orders & Test. 1765. Going. Another coming.
Anth. Hinton[12], C. ord. Deacon by BP Terrick[13] Tr. S. 1765. Came before LD 1766. Gone Apr 1767
Wood[14] C. Gone 1767. sd to be returned June.
Gill[15] C Mich 1767.
M^r. Abbot[16] Cur Sal. £50.

1758 Conf. ⟨here 434. of this Parish⟩ 85. 1762. 57.1766. 43.

[1] See p. 156, n. 9.   [2] See p. 259, n. 4.
[3] James Tunstall (1708–62), of Aysgarth, Yorks, m. St John's C 1724, BA 1738, MA 1731, BD 1738, DD 1744, fellow, 1729–48, public orator, 1729–48, R. Sturmer, Essex, 1739–46, treasurer St David's, 1746, V. Minster, 1747–57, R. Great Chart, 1747–57, V. Rochdale, Lancs, 1757–62, chaplain to archbishop Potter.
[4] John Gill (1726–71), of Canterbury, Kent, m. St John's C 1745.
[5] Francis Griffin (1738–?), of Claydon, Oxon, m. Magdalen Hall 1755, BA 1759.
[6] See p. 41, n. 2.   [7] See p. 169, n. 10.
[8] Of Cwm, Flint, m. Clare Hall 1751, BA 1754, chaplain in Navy, 1755–61. Perhaps R. St John's, Clerkenwell, London, 1769–78, V. Guilsfield, co. Montgomery, 1777–86.
[9] Robert Hay Drummond (1711–76), bishop of St Asaph, 1748–61, bishop of Salisbury, 1761, archbishop of York, 1761–76.
[10] See n. 4.
[11] Arthur Clarke (1717–?), of co Limerick, m. Trinty College Dublin 1733, BA 1737.
[12] (1743–1838), of St Andrews, Holborn, London, m. Merton 1764, PC. Norwood, Middlesex, 1775, V. Grandborough, Bucks, 1775–1838.
[13] Richad Terrick (1710–77), bishop of Peterborough, 1757–64, bishop of London, 1764–77.
[14] Possibly John Wood (1719–?), of Keymer, Sussex, m. Brasenose 1738, BA 1742.
[15] See n. 4.

[16] William Abbot (1734–1826), of Ramsgate, m. St John's C 1750, BA 1754, MA 1757, BD 1764, fellow 1755–67, preb of York, 1767, C. Minster, 1790.

Page 266
D. Westbere
Monkton V. St Mary, with Birchington All Saints, & Wode St Mary Magd. [This last is demolished]. DCh. of Cant. Propr. ABP P. Exempt from AD^n. K^s books 13-8-4. Wake 80^f. Now called 100^f. 4 miles long, near 3 broad. Monkton hath 10 Farm Ho. 30 Cottages. Birchington 11 Farms, 71 other Houses: & a Hamlet anciently called Wood Church or the Vill of Wood, but now commonly Acol hath 3 Farm Ho. & 17 Cottages. There were several Families of Anab. But only 2 or 3 remain, of which the Ch^n are baptized & come to Church. An Anab. meeting Ho. at Birchington, little used. There were also Quakers & a meeting Ho. but none now. Service & Sermon at Church & Chapel every Sunday. Prayers in Lent, & cat. 4 Sacr. Abt 40 Com. [Qu. whether meant of Monkton only or both]. Mrs Ann Crisp[1] gave by Will a small Quantity of Land for a School Dame to teach some boys & Girls of Birchington Reading & the Catechism, & give them Bibles &c. Done. 2 Tenemts & Land worth ⟨See below⟩. a Year, given to the Church of Monkton. Justly applied. [See another Benefaction, St Nicolas p. 267]. Church & Chancel indifferent. Ho. good & convenient but wants some Repairs, which are promised ⟨again 1766⟩. Outho. in good Repair. 10^f a Year for beautifying the Church, 5-10-0 for poor widows, to be given by the Vicar, AD^n. 4 Bells. Birchington Church & Chancel ⟨large⟩ in pretty good Repair. No Ho. 5^f a year given for beautifying the Church. Misapplied. 5 Bells.

Peter Vallavine[2] LLB V. 16 Oct. 1729. V. of Preston by Wingham p. 21. where he is bound to reside. Dead Jan 1767.
John Birkett[3] A.B. V. Feb. 4. 1767. House building. Lives at Margate.
Joseph Hardy[4] M.A. V. July 28 1772.
John Prat[5] A.M. Vicar 1786.

John Gill[6], Pr. Cur. 40^f. Lives betw. Monkton & Birchington. [Used to live in V. Ho.]. 1764 Gone to Minster. No Cur. here.
Is. Avarne[7] Cur. ord. D. Tr. S. 1764. P. Chr. 1764. Gone Apr. 1765.
John Gill, returned. Gone
W^m. Williams[8] Cur. Lic. 1792 receives the Tithes by Agreemt. w. the Vicar.

1758 Conf. Monkton 21. Birchington 44. 1762. Monkton 8. Birch. 23. 1766 Monkton 15. Birch. 23

[1] See p. 197, n. 7.   [2] See p. 21, n. 2.
[3] (1743–?), of Stanhope, co Durham, m. Christ Church 1762, BA 1765, C. Monkton, 1767.
[4] See p. 65, n. 4.   [5] See p. 212, n. 3.   [6] See p. 265, n. 4.
[7] Isaac Avarne (1741–1820), of Staffordshire, m. Queens' C 1760, scholar 1761, BA 1764, MA 1767, R. Bassingham, Norfolk, 1772–1820, V. Bourn, Cambs, 1783–8, R. Halesworth, Suffolk and V. Chediston, 1788–1820.
[8] See p. 259, n. 9.

Page 267

St Nicolas At Wade V. ⟨written Atwood Entry B. I. 189. Atwoode III. 94⟩. [Was a Chapel to Reculver, & afterwards had the Chapel of All Saints p. 258 belonging to it.]. ABP P. Exempt from AD^n. K^s books 15–19–7. Wake 60^f. Now called 70^f. Of this, 30^f is reserved in ABP^s Lease. Pension to V. of Reculver 3–3–4. 51 Ho. Some very wealthy Farmers. Service once on Sundays. A Sermon the other Part of the Day at Monkton [2 miles off]. [No mention of Cat. or of Sacr.]. Tho. Paramor[1] by Will 1636 gave 6^f a Year, a Ho. & an Acre of Land for teaching 4 Ch^n of Monkton, & 6 of St Nicolas. So applied John Finch[2] by Will 1605 gave ½ a Farm, the whole ⟨of the Farm⟩ is 75^f a year, to V. ChW^{ns} & Overseers for the Poor of this Parish. So applied. 13 Acres three Roods of Land, rented at 6–17–6 belonging to the Church. Church very handsome, large & in good Repair. Chancel in good Repair. No Ho. Glebe 8 Acres. 5 Bells.

Nic. Simons[3] V: 1 Feb. 1748. V. of Chislet p. 259 ⟨the adjoyning Parish⟩. where see.
Daniel Ball[4] Clerk L.L.B. Vicar, May 13: 1777.
John Fagg[5] A.M. Vicar 1785. Mr Williams[6] Cur. of Chislet.

1758 Conf. 39. 1762. 26. 1766. 37

[1] Hasted X, p. 242.	[2] Hasted says 1705: Ibid.	[3] See p. 259, n. 3.
[4] See p. 110, n. 6.	[5] See p. 259, n. 6.	[6] Ibid., n. 9.

Page 268

D. Westbere

St Peters in Thanet. V. Belonged to St Austins Cant. ABP. K^s books 9^f. Wake first 80^f, then 100^f. So called now. Of this, Wake saith 50^f is an Augmentation. {But by whom?}. D Ch of Canterbury, Impropriators. 17 Hamlets: see the names. 240 Ho. 40 Anab. A meeting Ho. William Copping, Teacher. Some vicious Absenters: chiefly of the lower Rank. Not increased. Whole Service & 2 Sermons, on Sundays. Prayers only on some Particular Fasts, Festivals & State Holydays. A very inconsiderable Part of the Parish lies near the Church. [And V. Ho. far from it]. Abt 40 Ch^n from the School cat. every Saturday morning in the Church, with Exp. by V. Monthly Sacr. abt 50 Com. & at the great Festivals many more. Mrs Eliz. Lovejoy[1] founded a School for teaching 20 poor Ch^n 4 years gratis: 20^f salary to the Master, chosen by the Mayor & Ald. of Canterbury. Trustees, V. ChW^{ns} & Overseer. Lands worth 7–19–0 to the poor: 4–0–6 to the Church. So applied. The Church uncommonly neat: 600^f laid out upon it in the last 12 Years. Lately upwards of 50^f raised by Subscription for Ornamts. The People behave well to their Clergy, & there have been no Quarrels between them for the last Century. Chancel remarkably neat & handsome. Ho. very good, & much improved by Mr Willes. Out Ho. the same. Glebe 1 Acre. 6 Bells. See a Letter May 1 1762 signed Love Church. R^t Honble H. Fox[2] Esqr hath taken a Ho. at Ringsgate in this Par. on the Edge of the Cliff, & is improving it. Mr Dekewer[3] of Hackney hath left 500^f to V. and ChW^{ns} & their Successors to be placed in the Funds & the Interest to be applied for buying Bread & Coals for the Poor of the Parish. Will be p^d in Feb. 1763.

Cornelius Willes[4] V. 26 March 1757 sede vacante. Resides in V. Ho. which is a very pretty, though small one, built 30 Years ago. His absence on his Affairs, a month in a year, supplied by the neighbouring Clergy.
John Piggott[5] Clerk A.B. V. April 3: 1776. resides.

1758 Conf. 68. 1762. 53. 1766. 43

[1] Widow of George Lovejoy, master of Kings school, Canterbury. Her will was proven in 1694: Hasted X, p. 370.
[2] Henry Fox (1705–74), MP for Hindon, 1735–41, MP for New Windsor, 1741–61, MP for Dunwich, 1761–3, secretary of state 1755–6, paymaster-general 1757–65, leader of the house of Commons 1762–3.
[3] John Dekewer (1686–1762). Noted as an 'especial benefactor of this parish': Hasted X, p. 373.
[4] (1724–76), of Birmingham, m. Worcester 1740, BA (Merton) 1745, MA 1747, V. St Peter's Thanet, 1757–76.
[5] Perhaps (1741–?), of Brockley, Somerset, m. Christ Church 1759, V. St Peter's Thanet, 1776–1820.

Page 269
Ramsgate See S[t] Laurence

Reculver V. S[t] Mary, with the Chapel of Hoath, Holy Cross. ABP Impr. & P. [See the Ordination of V. in Winchelseys Reg. fol. 30]. Exempt from AD[n]. K[s] books 9–12–3½. Certified 66–2–3¼. Above 70 ⟨85⟩, of which 20[£] is reserved ⟨by Juxon⟩ in ABPs Lease. ⟨Clear of Taxes by Lease 1760⟩. The Poor Tax is high. In Reculver 31 Ho. in Hoath 54. Ho. in a decayed Condition: a poor Family lives in it. Prayers & Sermon once at Church & Chapel every Sunday. Prayers only on Sundays. [{qu.} good Fr. Chr. Day.]. Cat. will be exp. 3 Sacr at each: [{must be} now 4] & abt 30 Com. [Church hath 2 Spires. Sir Geo. Oxenden[1], saith, it will fall into the Sea in 100 Years]. There hath been no Offertory, but will be. ⟨Is now⟩. 11[£] a year given by 2 Persons to the Poor. See the particulars. And land worth 3[£] a year for repairing the Chapel of Hoath. The last hath not been properly laid out, but will ⟨Is now⟩. Church & Chancel large, pretty good Repair. Chancel floor uneven. Ho. & outHo. very bad. A promise to repair them gradually. Glebe 3 Acres 4 Bells. Chapel of Hoath small, but in Repair. Commandm[ts] new & handsome in the chancel. Pews & Pavem[t] wants some Repair. No Ho. 3 Bells. In 1643 was pd 2[£] from the ⟨A⟩BP to V. See particulars of the income for 1758, 9, 1760. Above 80[£].

Tho. Thompson[2] MA V. 16 Aug. 1757. Had been a Missionary several Years in America & Africa. Resides at Hoath 3 miles from the Church, & one from the Chapel ⟨25[£]⟩. Void by his Inst. to Elham, p. 99. Nov. 24. 1761.
Anth. Lukyn[3] BA V. 22 Feb 1762. Will reside immediately. {I think} made one of the Poor vicars. ⟨March⟩ 1765 hath Leave to reside at Canterbury. See his & the AD[s] Letter. Eyes very bad: 4 ch[n].
Richard Sandys[4] Clerk, Vicar. Febry 12: 1779.
Richard Morgan[5]. Vicar 1782.

Rob[t]. Parry[6] Cur. Sal. £50. Lic. 1790 by Archdeacon.

1758 Conf. 39 1762. Hoath 10. Reculver 18. 1766. Reculver 17. Hoath 17.

[1] See p. 4, n. 5.
[2] See p. ii, n. 46.
[3] See p. 8, n. 9.
[4] (17?–82), of Kent, m. CCCC 1778, C. Westbere, 1777, V. Reculver, 1779–82.
[5] See p. 190, n. 7.
[6] (1757–1814), of Denbigh, m. St John's C 1776, scholar 1779, BA 1780, MA 1783, BD 1790, fellow, 1781–1809, C. Reculver, 1780 (lic endorsed, 1790), R. Staplehurst, 1808–14.

Page 270
D. Westbere.
Sea-Salter V. St Alphage. DCh of Canterbury Propr & P. {Ks books 25-19-18} Tenths 1-2-0. Certified 25-19-8. Wake 30^f, Now called 25^f. But V. saith, the Vicarial Tithes are a little above 30^f ⟨I am told 45^f. AD^n 28^f⟩. He saith not in his Answers, how many Houses ⟨or what Duty⟩: but Wake saith 17 Families, Service once on Sundays, 3 Sacr. [must be 4]. No V. Ho. Very unhealthy. Church indifferent, but in good Repair. Chancel Walls want Repair, & are very green. Service only once a fortnight since V. hath been infirm. 1 Bell, 3^f a year to the poor AD^n. 1762 V. saith he received but 27^f clear. 1764 augmented by DCh ⟨& Governors⟩ with 400^f.

Tho. Patten[1] V. 6 March 1711. Resides in the next Parish. Cur. also of Whitstable p. 273. May 1759 Officiates once a fortnight at each: can do no more. Half-mad, impudent, poor. 1759 10^f; 1760 10^f; 1761 10^f; 1762 10^f; 1763, 10* Died before Oct. 14: 1764.
Tho. Gurney [2] BA V. 15 Jan. 1765. Officiates. Ho. getting ready May 1765. Appointed by me to be one of the poor Vicars, July 8. 1766.
Thomas Gurney[3] July 3 1770.
Thomas Johnson[4] B.A. V. July 5 1774. does his own duty.

Robt Jenkins[5] R. of Westbere p. 272, serves this. ½G a Sunday from DCh.

1758 Conf. See Whitstable 1762. 24. 1766. 19.

[1] (1688–1764), of Cote, Somerset, m. Pembroke O 1705, C. Whitstable, 1712–64, V. Seasalter, 1712–64.
[2] See p. 79, n. 3.			[3] Ibid.				[4] Ibid., n. 4.
[5] (1705–78), of Holme, Norfolk, m. St John's C 1723, BA 1727, MA 1734, R. Westbere, 1734–78, V. Brookland, 1737–43, minor canon of Canterbury.
* This sentence is in a form of shorthand, but the figures presumably represent gifts of money given by Secker to Patten. In his *Autobiography*, p. 51, the archbishop noted that by 1765 he had paid £76 for someone to help out in the living, as well as giving £63 for Patten's support.

Page 271
Stonar See p. 197

Swackliffe, ⟨al. Swalcliffe, al. Swalecliff⟩ R. St John Baptist. Richd Lee[1] Gent P. ⟨R. saith Ld Cowper[2] presented him⟩. K^s books 11-9-4½. Certified 50-4-6¼. Now called 55^f ⟨AD^n 60^f⟩. 10 Ho. Service once on Sundays [qu. good Fr. Chr Day]. No Ch^n fit to be cat. 4 Sacr. from 5 to 7 Com. 1-6-8 given for the Poor. Ch. & Chancel indifferent: much improved since AD^{ns} Visitation 1750. Ho. mean, in tolerable Repair, let to 2 poor Families. Out Ho. in tolerable Repair. Glebe 6 Acres. 1 Bell.

Edw. Squire[3] BA R. 24 Nov. 1733. hath been Cur. above 30 years at Hertford. No man hath resided in the Parsonage here, within memory. Died Aug. 1760. Vincent Warren[4] R. 11 Sept. 1760. Was of Magd. Coll. Oxon 1½ year: then obliged, through Poverty, to go & teach School. Going for 18 months with 2 Sons of the late Mr Wynne of Bedwell Park, Co. Hertf. to Venice, 200^f a year. Returned May 1762. Resides Nov. 1762. July 15. 1763 Gone above 6 weeks: not returning. Sent Mr Quincey[5], who is gone. Mr Rogers[6] of Herne must take Care of it. Mr Warren married in the West.
William Chafy[7] A.M. Rector 1791

Robt Jenkins[8] Cur. 25^f Easter Off. & Surpl. Fees. R. of Westbere p. 272 where see. AD^n will speak to Mr Rogers of Herne to do the occasional Duty here. Now Dec. 1761. See Sea-Salter.
Tho. Baker[9] R. of Frinsted p. 239 where see, Cur. here 21^f. See also p. 273 Going.
Mr Apsley[10] to serve this & Whitstable p. 273 if he may live at Canterbury.
Wm. Warren[11], brother to R. Cur. ord. Deacon Sept. 23. 1764. 2. 30^f here. Gone to N. Church.
Mr Jenkins again 1765.
Thomas Cookes[12] Clerk Cur Licensed Sept[r]. 23: 1776, with a Salary of £25 p. Ann.
M^r. Chafy Cur. Sal. £30.

1758 Conf. 20. 1762. 10. 1766. 11

[1] Richard Lee alienated it c.1727 to the trustees of the infant William, earl Cowper: Hasted VIII, p. 520.
[2] See p. 34, n. 1.
[3] (1698–1760), of Hertford, m. Christs 1715, scholar 1717, BA 1719, R. Swalecliffe, 1733–60.
[4] (1729–91), of Marcham, Berks. m. Magdalen O 1748, chorister 1742–9, clerk 1749–50, R. Swalecliffe, 1760–91. His pupils in Venice were presumably the grand-sons of Richard Wynne, MP for Boston, 1698–1705, who bought Bedwell Park in 1701: VCH *Hertfordshire* III, p. 460.
[5] Quincey, not traced.   [6] William Rogers. See p. 260, n. 2.
[7] See p. 159, n. 2.   [8] See p. 270, n. 5.   [9] See p. 238, n. 2.
[10] William Apsley, m. Merton, C. Rainham 1765.
[11] See p. 133, . 6.
[12] (1734–), of Leytonstone, Essex, m. Worcester 1754, C. Swalecliffe, 1776, R. Notgrove, Glos.

Page 272
D. Westbere
Westbere R. All Saints. The King P. K^s books 7^f. Certified 56–1–0. Wake 60^f. So called now ⟨Is 80^f: was above 100^f. R. imprudent See below⟩. 22. Ho. Prayers & Sermon once a day. Prayers in Lent. Cat. frequently. 4. Sacr. 25 or 26 Com. A schoolmistress. 16^s a Year given for the poor. No Parsonage Ho. It was burnt down. Above 207^f raised by the Rectors, & by Interest, towards rebuilding it. Placed in the Funds by AD^n. The Rector gives 3^f a Year. Church & Chancel in very good Order. Barn in pretty good Order. 12^s towds Communion Wine by Dr Peters[1]. Glebe 2 Acres. 2 Bells.

Robt Jenkins[2] BA R. 29 Nov. 1734. Cur. of Swacliffe p. 271. Lives at Canterbury 4 miles from Westbere, & 10 from Swacliffe: & the two last are at least 7 miles asunder. Preached a Sermon of his Fathers on the Sacramt 22

Sundays together, as he owned: but others say, 14 months: & went on preaching it, notwithstanding the ABPs Admonition, till the Dean of Canterbury got it from him.

Charles Allen[3] A.M. Rector Augs[t]. 6: 1779.

Kay Mawer[4] Rector 1795.

Richard Sandys[5] Clerk Curate, Licensed May 26: 1777, with a Salary of £25 p ann.

M[r]. Naylor[6], Cur.

1758 Conf. 20. 1762. 13. 1766. 14.

---

[1] Charles Peters (1695–1746), of London, m. Christ Church 1710, BA 1713, MA 1724, B & D Med 1732, physician to king, 1733, physician general to the army, 1739, physician to St George's hospital, 1735–46.

[2] See p. 270, n. 5.   [3] See p. 169, n. 12.

[4] (1734–?), of Middleton Tyas, Yorks, m. Trinity C 1753, BA 1757, MA 1760, R. Westbere, 1795.

[5] See p. 269, n. 4.

[6] Christopher Naylor (?1738–1816), of Richmond, Yorks, m. St John's C 1758, BA 1761, MA 1771, R. Llanaber, Merioneth, 1772–7, C. Burnsall, Yorks, 1778–9, R. Roxby, Lincs, 1779–1816, second master Kings School, Canterbury, 1780–2, headmaster, 1782–1816, R. Scremby, Yorks, 1788–1816, C. Westbere, 1790, six-preacher, 1807–16.

Page 273

Whitstable Cur. All Saints Belonged to Plecy Coll. in Essex. ABP. Propr. & P ⟨adv. granted by Qu. Mary⟩. Certified 22–10–0. Wake 40[f]. Now called 25[f]. Of this, ABP pays 10[f] & 10[f] is reserved in the Lease of Whitstable to the ABP or Cur. out of which last 1[f] is deducted for Land-Tax: but should not ⟨See below⟩. 3094 Acres [72 families, Wake: 200 Families, Herring ⟨AD[n]⟩]. Too many Absenters. Service once a Sunday. [Cat. in Summer. Wake]. 3 Sacr. [must be 4]. Sometimes many Com. Some Lands have been given for the Poor. Place unhealthy. The 10[f] a year pd by the ABP hath been pd ever since 3 Eliz. The other 10[f] was charged on the Tenant by ABP Sheldon, 1670. Church indifferent & dirty. Chancel ready to fall: seats, wainscot, paving, scandalous. No Ho. Service, See Sealter. 40[f] a year to the poor, AD[n]. 6 Bells. 1762 Cur. saith he receives but 19[f] clear.

Rich[d] Bate[1] lic to serve the Cure 1710 V. also of Seasalter Entry B. VI. 25. Augmented 1764 with 200[f] given by ABP Wakes will in reversion & 200[f] from Qu[s] Bounty. Again 1767 with 400[f] by Sir Ph. Boteler & Qu[s] bounty.

Tho. Patten[2] Cur. 21 Feb. 1711. V. of Seasalter p. 270 where see. Nov. 1762 Mr Warren[3] will serve it from Swacliff p. 271. Gone June 1763. M[r] Jenkins[4] must serve it every other Sunday, AD[n] July 1763. Mr Baker[5] see p. 271 serves it once a Sunday from Mich 1763. Mr Apsley[6] 1764 see p. 271. Mr Patten died before Oct. 14. 1764.

Tho. Gurney[7] Jan 1765. See here p. 270.

Thomas Johnson[8] Licensed Cur. September 6 1774. resides.

1758 Conf. 82. Probably part from Seasalter. The minister would not give them the Tickets. 1762. 92. 1766. 67.

[1] (1674–1737), of Ashford, Kent, m. All Souls 1691, BA 1692, MA (CCCC), C. Whitstable, 1710–12, V. Seasalter, 1711–12, V. Chilham, 1711–37, R. Warehorne, 1720–37.
[2] See p. 270, n. 1.   [3] Vincent Warren, see p. 271, n. 4.   [4] See p. 270, n. 5.
[5] See p. 238, n. 2.   [6] See p. 271, n. 10.   [7] See p. 79, n. 3.
[8] Ibid., n. 4.

[Diocese of Chichester]

Page 274

Dioc. Chich. D. Pagham
D[r] Bettesworth[1] had a Commission for Eccl Jurisd in Sussex. Now July 2. 1763
D[r] Dennis Clarke[2].

All Saints in Chichester ⟨above 30 miles from Lewes⟩ al. in Palenta al. in Palatin R. ABP P. Tenths 11–9 ⟨Called 10[£] in 1718⟩. Certified 11[£]. 7 Sept 1676 John Holder[3]was instituted to it by the ABP on the Presentation of the King, Patron by Lapse. The ABP always collated to it before. And there is no mention of it in the Books since. Vid Reg. Parker. Par Book 1663. Parish small ⟨45 families in 1717⟩. Inhabitants chiefly of middle Rank. Hon[ble] Coote Molesworth[4] Es[qr]. Some Presbyterians. No Parsonage Ho. Service once a Month by Custom. Rector disposes of Offertory Money.
The Dean of Chichester hath 10 Parishes in & near that City under his peculiar Jurisdiction.
Augmented by Lot. qu when. Land proposed to be purchased 1762.
1762 Neither Church nor Chancel cieled ⟨nor Feb. 1766⟩. Altar & Rails handsome. No Ch. yard or Ho. Wt was Ho. is a Stable: 2 other Stables, wc[h] were messuages 1635.

John Hancock[5] R. Also V. of Barsted p. 275 where see. Died Oct. 23. 1761. Blagden[6] teaches a small School in the Parish, hath another Curacy of abt 40[£] a year, a large & increasing Family. A worthy man. Rec. by BP & Dean. Wrote to Dr Bettesworth. Nov. 29 1761, to grant him the Sequestration, who did it Dec. 1.
Tireman[7], rec. by Mr Clarke, to succeed.
Thomas Durnford[8] Sequestrator 1783.

[1] John Bettesworth, dean and commissary of South Malling, Pagham and Terring, Sussex, 1752–63.
[2] (1717–76), of Barking, London, m. Christ Church 1734, adm. Middle Temple 1735, Gray's Inn 1739, LLB (Trinity Hall C 1741), LLD 1746, adm. Advocate Arches Court 1746, dean and commissary of South Malling, Pagham and Terring, 1763.
[3] (1644–?), of Oxford, m. New College 1663, perhaps 'clero uniy', subscribed 29 Oct 1666.
[4] (1697–1782), 6th son of Robert, 1st viscount Molesworth, adm. Middle Temple 1720.
[5] (1674–1761), of Chester, m. St Johns's C 1691, adm. Inner Temple 1691, V. Barsted, 1732–61. Son of John Hancok, preb of Canterbury, 1719–28.
[6] Bragg Blagden (1715–1781), of Chichester, m. St John's C 1735, BA 1739, MA 1752, R. Mid-Lavant, 1752, R. Brasted, 1764, R. Slindon, 1764–81, perhaps R. Singleton, 1763, acted as C. Pagham, preb of Chichester, 1753, chaplain to the duke of Richmond.

[7] Richard Tireman (1726–92), of London, m. St John's C 1742, fellow, 1742–50, BA 1746, MA 1750, V. St Peter the Great, Chichester, subdean and treasurer Chichester cathedral, V. Henfield, Sussex, 1779, R. Radmell, Sussex.

[8] (1744–1801), of Bramdean, Hampshire, m. Wadham 1761, BA 1765, MA 1769, V. Barsted 1776, sequr, All Saints, 1783.

Page 275

Barsted al. Bergstead V. St Mary Magd. ⟨near Chichester, 6 miles⟩. Belonged to the Priory of Christ Church, Cant. Ecton. ABP P. Kings books 7–18–9. Wake 80$^£$, Herring 90$^£$ ⟨So in 1717⟩. Small Tithes 60$^£$: 20$^£$ p^d by the Revd Mr Gooch[1], ⟨half brother to Sir Thomas[2]⟩ out of the Rectory, which is 200$^£$ a year. Mr Walter[3] ⟨see next line⟩. Extent 7 miles: 5 Tithings, see their Names. Renters of Lands. Come to Church regularly. V. saith, it is but 62$^£$, with the House; & that 10$^£$ is to be deducted out of that for Land Tax & Tenths: & that the Houses may be about 50 or 60 ⟨abt 70 in 1717⟩. Service once on Sundays ⟨So in 1717⟩. Never was any catechizing. 4 Sacr. Seldom less than 40 Com. No Offertory: for they say they maintain their own Poor. Parishioners say, Nov. 1761, that the small Tithes are rented at 60$^£$a year, & 20$^£$ a yr pd out of gr. Tithes: that there are 74 Houses, 700 Inhab. above 6 years old, & 500 above 16. Service once on Sundays & Chr. Day, Fast & Thanksg. Days. Sometimes Omissions. Bodies left in Church unburied sometimes one night, sometimes longer. No catechizing. They desire it, & Sunday Service twice, & if possible, a resident Minister. Ho. not inconvenient: may be fitted up for a Family for 20$^£$.
1762 Nothing wanting to the Church, but a new Carpet for the Altar, wch is orderd & the Wall to be cleared from Shrubs. Ho. in excellent Repair, much improved by present V.

John Hancock[4] V. 4 May 1723. Above 84. R. of All Saints Chichester, p. 274. Resides there, this being a bad Air, & serves both. Died Oct 23. 1761.
Sam. Dugard[5] MA V Nov. 26. 1761. Minister of the Chapel at Gosport, worth above 100$^£$ a year: growing old, & will be sometimes here, as a place of easier Duty, & have a Curate resident to do the whole Service, wn he is not here. 1766 preaches only twice or three in a yr. Curate, Cecil[6], resides at Felpham, officiates once here. Wrote[7]. Mr Dugard hath taken another living, by wch this is voidable. Will get the whole Duty done here. Good.
Thos Durnford[8] Clerk A.M. Vicar May2: 1776.

[1] John Gooch, of Cambridge, m. Caius 1746, scholar, 1746–50, BA 1750, MA 1753, DD (Christs) 1765, fellow Caius 1751, sequrator of Fen Ditton, Cambs, 1753, R. Willingham, 1753, preb of Ely, 1753–1804.
[2] (1721–81), of London, m. Caius 1737, 3rd Bt.
[3] Daniel Walter (–1761), m. Peterhouse: VCH *Sussex* III, p. 126.
[4] See p. 274, n. 5.
[5] (1707–1776), of Gosport, Hampshire, m. Pembroke O 1723, BA 1726, MA 1733. Dugard had been recommended by the duke of Newcastle to Secker for having served the cure of Gosport well: BL, Add MS 39, 930, f. 376, 9 Nov 1761.
[6] Cecil appears not to have been licenced as curate.
[7] LPL, MS Secker 6, ff. 196–99, 20, 27 Feb 1766 & 6 March 1766.
[8] See p. 274, n. 8.

Page 276

Dioc. Chich. D. Pagham

East-Lavant R. St Mary ⟨near Chichester in North⟩. Wake saith, ABP or Earl of Derby[1] is P. John Stanley[2] was inst Dec. 7. 1721 on Ld Derbys pres. & Wm Crooke[3] 2 July 1726 on the same, as Patron in full Right. But {John} ⟨Tho.⟩ Heath[4] Nov. 22. 1752 on the Pres. of Henry Peckham[5] of Chichester Esqr &Wm Milton of the same, Gent. K^s books 20–18–1½. Wake 120$^£$. Herring 200$^£$. The Parish of Lavant is divided into E. & W. Lavant. 34 Ho. Sir John Miller[6] Bar^t. Whole Service on Sundays. Prayers on all Holy Days. Sermons on appointed Fasts. Cat. exp. every Sunday in Lent. 4 Sacr. 18 or 20 Com. This Parish intitled to send 6 boys & 6 Girls to a school in the Parish of Bosgrove, & 4 women, when Vacancies happen, who have an Apartm^t & abt 9$^£$ a Year. See more. A Garden in the Pallant of Chichester, let for 35^s a Year, annexed to this Rectory.

1762 Chancel to be new tiled next year ⟨1766 all that was promised is done⟩. Ho. good, & will be improved by R.

John Betton[7] pres. by the K to it, now void by Lapse, Cession &c prayed Inst. ad. corroborand. titulum. Granted 8 July 1680. The Parochial Book of 1663 refers to Reg. Parker fol. 394 where inst. was given in E. of Dorsets presentation. In Grindals list there it stands as being in the ABPs Gift by the 3^d Exchange.

Tho. Heath[8] R. as above. Resides in the Parsonage Ho. Absent 4 or 5 Sundays in a year: & then officiates at Oakwood Chapel in Surrey, given him by Sir John Evelyn[9] Bart. During this Time, Service is but once a Sunday at his Church. 1766 Resides constantly.

Geo. Owen Cambridge[10] Rector A.M. 1787 again instituted 1791.

[1] James Stanley (1664–1736), 19th earl.

[2] (1693–1781), 2nd son of Sir Thomas Stanley, of Bickerstaffe, Lancashire, m. Sidney Sussex 1710, BA 1714, MA 1717, fellow, 1715, R. East-Lavant, 1721–26, R. Liverpool, 1726–40, R. Winwick, Lancashire, R. Bury, 1743–78, R. Halsall, 1750–7.

[3] (1697–1752), of Southwark, m. Brasenose 1716, R. East Lavant, 1726–52.

[4] (1713–86), of Clandon, Surrey, m. Magdalen O 1739, R. East Lavant, 1752–89.

[5] (1683–1764). Commonly known as 'Lisbon Peckham' because of his connection with the wine trade: VCH *Sussex* III, p. 76. William Milton died in 1783: ibid., p. 21.

[6] (?1772), 5th Bt.

[7] Probably (1641–1721), of Shrewsbury, m. St John's C 1659, BA 1662, MA 1667, preb of Chichester, 1669, R. Stoke, Sussex, 1670, R. Tangmere, Sussex, 1674, R. East-Lavant, 1676 (corrob. 1680)–1721.

[8] See n. 4.

[9] (1706–67), 2nd Bt, MP for Helston, 1727–41 and 1747–67, MP for Penrhyn, 1741–47.

[10] (1756–1841), of Twickenham, m. Queen's O 1774, BA 1778, MA (Merton) 1781, R. East Lavant, 1786–1805, archdeacon of Middlesex and preb of Ely.

Page 277

Horsham is not a Peculiar ⟨But ABP Wake saith, Bishop-ridge in Horsham Parish is⟩. See p. 398.

Pagham V. ⟨near Chichester 5 miles South⟩. St Tho. Becket. Belonged to Canterbury Coll. in Oxford. Ecton ⟨See below⟩ ABP P. K^s books 9–18–9. Wake 80$^£$. V. saith scarce so much: & after paying Cur. & Land Tax, but 43$^£$. 3

miles long, 2 broad: 7 Tithings, 80 Ho. One Presbyterian, Lessee of the great Tithes from St Johns Coll. Camb. who hold them under DCh of Canterbury. Service once on Sundays ⟨twice in 1717⟩. The Church is at one end of the Parish: & others nearer to most of the Parishioners. Service scarce any where twice in Sussex, except Market Towns. No Prayers on Week Days [qu. good. Fri. Chr. Day ⟨Yes⟩]. V. read Prayers on Sunday afternoon & Holydays till none would come. Cat. exp. in Summer. 3 Sacr. as in most of the Country Parishes in Sussex. [will be one at Mich]. Abt 30 Com. Pains have been & will be taken to increase them. The last V. laid aside the Offertory, bec. it kept the Poor from the Communion & the Disuse is general in the Parishes round.
1762. A fine Church in good Repair. A Pewter Tankard for Com. A Flagon orderd for it ⟨Done⟩. Impropriators Tenant will whitewash the Chancel ⟨Done⟩. If all the Tithes were in one Hand they wd be worth between 5 & 600$^£$ a year.

John Carpenter[1] V. 22 July 1729. Resided 25 Years. Hath had great Losses in his Family & bad Health there, & cannot ride safely, nor do the Duty without it. Lives in London to take Care of his only child remaining out of 7. Allowed. aged 56, 1761. R. of Bignor Dioc. Chich. 76$^£$, 15 miles dist.
Robert Charles Blayney[2] A.M. Vicar 1785.
William Stabback[3] A.B. vicar 1792.
William Marler[4] A.M. Vicar 1794.

Sergeant[5], Pr. Cur. 22$^£$, Surpl. fees, Use of Ho. & Garden. Serves Felpham with it, 18$^£$ from thence.
John Rudd[6] ord. pr. by ABP Hutton 19 Sept. 1756. Abt his Allowance, see Letters[7]. Promised an apartmt ⟨in⟩ a Ho. wch is V^s own: shd have an Equivalent, & be pd quarterly. 1765 Gone: dead.
Charles Turner[8] Cur. ord. Pr. Sept 22. 1765 1 or 2. 22$^£$, & an apartm^t serves Siddlesham, a contiguous parish, 18$^£$. Going Mich. 1766.
Tho. Gwatkin[9] Cur. was a Dissenting minister. ord. D. by BP Thomas[10] of Winchester Nov. 23. 1766.

[1] (c.1705-85), of Stoke Rivers, Devon, m. Pembroke C 1716, V. Pagham, 1729, R. Bignor, 1743.
[2] Probably (1758-1824) of Worcester, m. Worcester, BA 1777, MA 1779, V. Pagham, 1785-92.
[3] (1759-1837), of Exeter, m. Balliol 1778, BA 1782, incorp C, MA (Jesus C) 1810, V. Pagham, 1792-94, R. East Anstey, Devon, 1809, PC. Masingleigh, 1809-37, V. St Clether, Cornwall, 1809, R. St Stephen's, Exeter, 1816-37, domestic chaplain to the earl of Harrowby.
[4] ?(1765-1823), of Exeter, m. Balliol 1783, BA 1786, MA 1789, V. Pagham 1794-1823.
[5] See p. 108, n, 8.
[6] (1732-65), of Helperthorpe, Yorks, m. Trinity C 1751, BA 1755, C. Rudston.
[7] LPL, MS Secker 6, f. 261, Secker to Rudd, 31 July 1760, and f. 262, ibid, 19 August 1760.
[8] 'literate'.   [9] He has not been traced.   [10] See p. 41, n. 2.

Page 278
Dioc Chich: D. Pagham
Slindon R. St Mary ⟨6 miles NE of Chichester, near Arundel⟩. May 18. 1708 Tho. Carr[1] of Chichester P. for that Turn by a Grant June 1701 from Arthur Kemp[2] Esqr a Papist, presented Henry Miller[3]. Feb. 23. 1729 Tho. & Cha. Groom[4] Ps for that Turn, presented Wm Groom[5]. Jan 24. 1738 Henry Peckham[6] of Chichester Esqr ⟨P. for that turn⟩ presented Robt Styles Launce[7]. Kings

books 14–13–1½. Wake 80^f. Herring 80^f 〈Called 100 in Disp. for Launce〉. 3 miles from Arundel, 7 from Chichester: 56 Ho. Protestants 185 Papists 85 〈See below〉 Of the last is the Earl of Newburgh[8], a young Man, who married Mr Kemps Daughter & thence hath a large Estate here 〈son of Mr Radcliffe[9] by the Countess of Newburgh[10], a Scotch Title〉. Very charitable to the poor without Distinction. 〈Going to live at Midhurst〉. R. knows not his Priests name 〈Believes it is Clayton〉. No publick Chapel. No Converts to Popery in 20 years, but two domestick Servts of his. They increase chiefly from Intermarriages, & all are dependents on that House. The Protestants are zealous & often admonished. Capt. Burtle[11] wounded at Culloden, & rewarded with 500^f a year, never comes to Church: intimate with the Dean of Chichester[12] 〈Going to Cheshire, his own Country. Dead here, 1761〉. Service once a Sunday here, & once at R^s other Living Binsted 1½ mile off, as usual in this Country. Prayers W. Fr. in Lent, & on holy days, S^{ts} days, at Chr. East. Whits. Cat. on Sundays in Lent, with printed Exp. 3 Sacr 〈will be 4. Are 1761〉. Abt 12 Com. 55^s a Year to the Poor. R. alone gives money at the Offertory. The Hogs Feast given on St Stephens Day by R. to the whole Parish: a Hog of 18 stone, 24 stone of Beef, ½ HHd of Ale, D° of Small Beer, 1½ bushel of Meal in Bread &c See further Description.

See Letter, Aug 1761 abt the Dissoluteness of the people & negligence of Ch W^{ns}.

1762. Church extremely bad: next presentation gen^{ly} sold without minding for whom. 3 Years allowed for Repairs. See particulars. Mr Clarke[13] will visit the Church yearly.

1764, one Side of church hath been new coverd: they will finish it next year. By Indenture 11 July 1745 John Dearling[14] of Chichester merch^t sold to John Pannell[15] of D° merch^t the next presentation to Slindon R & Binsted R. Co. Sussex for 300^f. Dearling bought the Advowson from Kemp. 1766 Feb. Roof secured. Seats bad: 〈mended 1765〉. Com. Table scandalous. Wrote. A new one. 1747/8 65 Fams. Prot^s 199, Papists 109. 1766 65 Fam^s. Prots 240 Papists 86: of wch 21 Ld Ns servts. See Mr Blagdens Letter April 11. 1766.

Robt Styles Launce[16] BA R. as above. Resides in Parsonage Ho. Both the Livings abt 1000^f clear. Ho at Binsted burnt: rebuilt by him. Lost 200^f by a Tenant. See Letters. Writes himself Robt Launce. Above 60. Lame. 1762 lives alone in the parsonage. Sometimes disorderd in his Head. See Mr Clarkes Letters 1762. Shot himself on or before Aug. 10. 1764.

Bragg Blagden[17] M.A. R. Nov. 1764 R. also of Binsted. See above.

John Smelt[18] L.L.B. Rector 1781.

Richd Greene[19] B.A. F. of N. Coll. Cur. £40 & Surpl. fees for this & Binsted D. of age for priests orders. Boards in Slindon.

[1] Captain Thomas Carr: leading Tory: VCH *Sussex* III, p. 99.

[2] This might mean Anthony Kemp, who died in 1715.

[3] (1649–1730), of Chichester, m. St John's C 1667, BA 1670, MA 1683, C. Stondon, Hertfordshire, 1671, C. Kemsing, Kent, 1762, R. Offham, 1675–1708, R. Slindon, 1708–30.

[4] The relations of John Groom of Steyning who had bought the next turn for his son William. He died in 1716: VCH *Sussex* IV, p. 237.

[5] William Groom[e] (1692–1739), m. Peterhouse 1711, of Sussex, BA1714, MA 1724, R. Binsted, Sussex, 1726–39, R. Slindon, 1730–39.

[6] See p. 276, n. 5.

[7] (1698–1764), of Durham, m. St John's C 1717, BA 1720, MA 1739, R. Slindon, 1739–64, R. Binsted, 1739–64.

[8] James Bartholomew (Radcliffe) (1725–86), 4th earl. In 1749 he married Barbara Kemp. She died in 1797 aged 77.

[9] Charles Radcliffe (1693–1746). He was beheaded.

[10] Charlotte Maria (1694–1755), countess of Newburgh.

[11] He has not been traced.

[12] Thomas Ball (1698–1770), of Eccleston, Lancs, m. Brasenose 1716, BA 1719, MA (Caius) 1726, V. Boxgrove, Sussex, 1723–53, schoolmaster in Carolina, 1725–6, V. Eartham, Sussex, 1733–70, preb of Chichester, 1727–70, archdeacon, 1736–70, dean, 1754–70.

[13] William Clarke (1676–1771), of Shrewsbury, m. St John's C 1712, BA 1716, MA 1719, fellow 1717–25, R. Buxted, 1724–68, V. Salehurst, 1743–71, R. Amport, Hampshire, 1770–1, preb of Chichester, 1727, chancellor of Chichester diocese, 1770. Secker commended Clarke for 'the accurate reports concerning the parishes which you have taken the pains to visit at my request': John Nichols, ed, *Literary Anecdotes of the Eighteenth Century*, 9 vols (1812–16), IV, pp. 378–9.

[14] The Dearlings were prominent General Baptists in Chichester: VCH *Sussex* III, p. 164.

[15] He exercised this in 1764: ibid., IV, p. 237.

[16] See n. 7.   [17] See p. 274, n. 6.

[18] (1750–1815), of Donnington and West Wittering, Sussex, m. St John's C 1769, migrated to Sidney Sussex, 1771, LLB 1774, R. Slindon, 1781–1815.

[19] (1739–?), of Stratford-on-Avon, Warwickshire, m. New College 1757, BA 1761, MA 1770.

Page 279

Tangmere R. S[t] Andrew ⟨3 miles E of Chichester⟩. Earl of Derby[1] P. K[s] books 13–5–0. Now called 90[f]. 23 Ho. Service once on Sundays, as for many Years past. 3 Sacr. Abt 12 Com. No publick Cat. of late, because very few Young Persons. Service on Chr. Day, AshW. & good Fr. R. had been exhorted to read afternoon Prayers & cat. & exp. & introduce a Sacr. at Mich. & officiate on the State Holydays & makes general Promises. 1761 Whole service. Catechizing in Summer on Sund. afternoon. 63 or 64 Adults. Directed again 4 Sacr[ts]. 1762 A Parishioner ploughs the Glebe & gathers the Tithes gratis for R. w[ch] makes the Living worth 30[f] a Year more, 120[f] in all. Glebe 25 Acres.

Tho. Wellings[2] R. 15 Jan. 1747. Resides constantly in the Parsonage Ho. Serves no other Cure. Hath nervous Disorders. See above. Hath not been 10 miles fron home in 10 Years. Cannot ride so far. Died Nov. 27. 1767.

Henry Peckham[3] R. Feb. 4. 1768 pres. by D. of Richmond[4], who hath bought the Advowson &sev[f] Estates of L[d] Derby.

Melmoth Skynner[5] A.B. Rector 1795.

[1] Edward Stanley (1689–1776), 20th earl.

[2] (1715–1767), of Sussex, m. Magdalene C 1732, BA 1736, MA 1739, R. Tangmere, 1748–67.

[3] (1712–1795), of Chichester, m. Trinity O 1729, BA 1733, R. Tangmere, 1768–95.

[4] Charles Lennox (1735–1806), 3rd duke of Richmond.

[5] (1736–1822), of London, m. University 1753, BA 1757, R. Tangmere, 1795–98, V. Cocking, Sussex, 1798–1822.

Page 280

Dioc. Chich: D. S. Malling. 1766 Only one Family of Papists in the Deanery. Ab[t] the E. of Dorsets pretention to present see Par. Book 1663

Adburton See Edburton

Buckstead al. Buxted R. S[t] Margaret ⟨9 miles N of Lewes⟩, with the Chapel of Uckfield. Holy Cross. ABP. P. ⟨value see below⟩. 6 miles long, 5 broad.

Buxted hath 149 Ho. & 2 Gentlemens Families ⟨Mr Geo Medley[1] one, 4000£ a year & Wm Nutt[2] Esqr⟩: Uckfield, 103 Ho. & 3 Gentlemens Families: ⟨Sir Tho. Wilson[3], Richd Beard Streatfield[4], Tho. Jackson[5] Esqr⟩. All the 5 exemplary in attending Church. ⟨Miss Fagg[6] at Bucksted⟩. A Deist, who retired from Business in London to Buxted a few Years ago: never comes to Church ⟨i.e. Mr Fulham[7], brother to Preb. of Windsor[8]. Gone⟩. Whole Service. & from Easter to Mich. 2 Sermons in each Church. They are distant 1½ mile. A Sermon on good. Fr. Prayers on all Holydays, W. Fr. in Lent, & all Passion Week. Cat. all Sundays, W & Fr. in Lent. 2 Sacr. at each great Festival, one the I^st Sunday in Lent, one at Mich. Both at Church & Chapel, from 80 to 100 Com. at the great Festivals: & 40 or 50 at the Sundays following. Dr Anth. Saunders[9], Rector here [who died abt the beginning of 1720 ⟨in 1719 aged 76⟩] endowed a School at Uckfield with a good House & 30£ a year, for teaching 6 boys of Buxted & 6 of Uckfield, Reading, Writing & Cat. by a Master & another at Buxted with 9£ a year for Schoolmistresses for 12 Ch^n, and he gave a further Benefaction for putting Ch^n of the Parish apprentices. ⟨See a fuller Account of his Charities here in Mr Clarkes Parochial Visitation articles in 1763 ⟩. 5£ & 1–6–8 besides given to the Poor. And Sir H. Fermours[10] will intitles 15 Boys of this Parish to the Benefit of a Charity School at the adjoining Parish of Rotherfield. But the School is too distant. Kings books 37–5–2½. Herring 280 ⟨190£ clear of all expences, keeping 2 Curates. Mr Clarke 1767⟩. Now above 300£ BP Ashburnham from R. S. Isle wants cieling, mentioned it to Mr Medley, whose Ho. is just by Ch. Parsonage ½ mile off. Moat almost round it. Seems good. Pulpit old. Mr Medley speaks of giving a new one. 6 Bells. Flagon & Plate, Pewter. Everything handsome. Mr Clarke 1763. At Uckfield, Flagon, Pewter: a Chalice & Patten, to be bought out of the offerings. No Ho. A good school Library given by Dr Saunders. ib.

Will. Clarke[11] M.A R 11 Apr. 1724. Resided 20 years. & now part of the Summer, & then preaches every Sunday: but chiefly at Chichester. Hath 2 resident Curates ⟨Priests⟩, who serve no other Cure. One hath 38£, Surpl. Fees & the Use of the Parsonage Ho. the other, 30£, & a Grammar School, which hath been always a very flourishing one. Mr Clarke married the Daughter of Dr Wm Wotton[12], who died here 1726, aged 61. They have one Daughter.

Edward[13] Son of the above Will. Clarke R. Novr. 4th 1766 upon Resignation of his Father.

Mathias D'Oyly[14] A.M. Rector 1787.

Conf. July 14. 1761. 384. Of this Parish 90, & of Uckfield 52.

---

[1] (1720–96), wine merchant from Portugal, MP for Seaford, 1768–80, and MP for East Grinstead, 1783–90. Built Buxted Place: *Sussex* I, p. 366.

[2] Member of the prominent Sussex family, who had a seat at Selmeston: ibid., p. 334.

[3] Thomas Spencer Wilson (1726–98), 6th Bt. He was also a general in the army.

[4] He has not been traced.   [5] He has not been traced.

[6] Margaret Fagg, spinster: VCH *Sussex* IX, p. 202.

[7] He has not been traced.

[8] John Fulham (1699–1777) of Surrey, m. Christ Church 1717, BA 1720, MA (Magdalen) 1736, R. Compton, Surrey, 1722–27, R. Merrow, 1736–52, V. All Saints, Isleworth, 1751–77, preb of Chichester, 1745–73, chaplain of the house of Commons, 1746, archdeacon of Llandaff, 1749–77, canon of Windsor, 1750–77.

[9] (?–1719), m. Wadham 1660, scholar 1661, student of Christ Church 1663, BA 1664, MA 1667,

incorp. Cambridge 1668, DD 1667, DD (Lambeth) 1672?, R. Hollingbourne, 1669–77, R. Buxted, 1674–1719, R. Acton, 1677–1720, chancellor of St Paul's, 1672–1719.

[10] Will of 1732: *Sussex* I, p. 367.   [11] See p. 278, n. 13.

[12] Of Cholsey, Berks, m. New College 1677, BA (St John's O) 1683, MA 1687, DD (Lambeth) 1708, V. Lacock, Wilts, 1690–3, sinecure R. Llandrillo yn Rhos, co Denbigh, 1682–1727, R. Milton Keynes, Bucks, 1693–1727, canon of Salisbury, 1705–27.

[13] (1730–1786), of Buxted, m. St John's C 1748, BA 1752, MA 1755, fellow 1753–64, R. Peper Harow, Surrey, 1758–69, R. Buxted, 1766–86, V. Willingdon, 1768–86, preb of Chichester, 1771, went to Madrid as chaplain to Embassy 1760 and in subsequent years to Minorca.

[14] (1743–1814), of Sussex, m. CCCC 1762, scholar, BA 1765, MA 1768, fellow St John's C 1766, V. Pevensey, Sussex, 1767–1814, R. Buxted, 1787–1814, preb of Ely 1770–87.

Page 281

Buckstead continued

Joseph Wright[1] Cur. at Bucksted. R. of Littlington Co. Sussex. 50$^£$ a year, & pres. to Allfriston V. Co. Sussex 45$^£$ a yr, adjoyning parishes.

Robert Gerison[2] Cur. & Schoolmaster at Uckfield. Sometimes called Margerison. Sometimes writes his Name so.

[1] (1730–84), of Leigh, Lancashire?, m. St John's C 1748, BA 1752, MA 1764, R. Litlington, Sussex, 1763–84, V. Alfriston, 1765–84, chaplain to Mary, Lady Dowager Rollo.

[2] He owned the advowson of East Guildford: VCH *Sussex* IX, p. 152.

Page 282

Dioc. Chich: D. S. Malling

Cliffe near Lewis al. St Thomas the Martyr at Cliff ⟨al. St Cliffe⟩. R. ABP P. Tenths 11–3. Certified 31–7–8. Now called 40$^£$ ⟨See below⟩. Betw. 30 & 40 Acres. 133 Ho. 37 Presb. & Independents: much lessend. 13 Anab. increased by new comers ⟨All These are chiefly at Lewes⟩. 7 Quakers. 6 low Absenters. Service once here & once at the adjoyning Parish of All Saints, Lewes. Also for some years past, Prayers here at 6 in the Evening: a small present made for it by Inhabitants of Lewes. Prayers on Fr. morning: & on { } Holydays alternately with All Saints. Cat. every other Sunday, when the Days are long. Sacr. at the 3 great Festivals, & on the 1st or 2nd Sunday of every other Month alternately with All Saints. From above 30 to above 60 Com. Once a month the neighbouring Clergy preach a Sermon gratis at the 6 O'clock Evening Prayers. John Stansfield[1] abt 130 Years ago gave 20$^£$ to be lent for 2 Years to 3 Parishioners on good Security. So applied still. An Estate of 29$^£$ a Year for the Church & Poor. A Debt contracted upon it for the Church, & a little of it given to the Poor for many years. A House belonging to it, where 4 poor Families live rent-free. Interest of 40$^£$ for the poor. Offertory distributed by Chw^{ns} ⟨men of character⟩. The Income of the Rectory is 34–2–4 from a modus in the Houses & Lands. Marriage fee 5^s Churching 6^d Burying 1^s. Breaking Ground in the Church 6–8, in the Chancel 13–4. To non-parishioners double, & at so 6–8 for Breach of Ch. yard Ground, in wch there will soon be no Room. No Easter Off but ⟨small⟩ voluntary presents from 2 or 3 Persons. Taxed to King & Poor. [The yearly value of All S^{ts} is called in Ecton 9–14–0]. Cliffe Church, small, but neat, esp. altar piece. Not convenient, but tolerable, for a small Cong. Appointmt of a Clerk of the Market at Clive Co. Suss. Entry B. VI. 230. The Com. Table is marble. So no Carpet. The above Estate was left for the Fabrick: was mortgaged for 200$^£$. Mr Baldy, Chwn for sev[l] Years hath advanced 80$^£$ upon it. Mr Clarke from his Parochial Vis. 1763.

Edw. Lund[2] R. 3 June 1725. Was then 34. Lives constantly in All S[ts] Lewis, which he holds by Sequestration. Serves both. Is every day at Cliffe. All S[ts] is abt 16$^£$ a Year. He hath another Parish worth abt 80$^£$. Diligent & good.

Richard Cecil[3] Clerk Rector Febry 24: 1777.

Thomas Aquila Dale[4] A.B. Cur Sal £50 lic. 1790.

Conf. July 15. 1761. 146. Of this Parish 31.

[1] He died in 1627. The grandfather of John Evelyn, the diarist: VCH *Sussex* VII, p. 38.
[2] (1702–77), of Middlesex, m. Peterhouse 1719, R. St Thomas at Cliffe, 1725–77.
[3] (1749–98), of Middlesex, m. Queen's O 1773, BA 1777, R. St Thomas at Cliffe, 1777–98.
[4] (1761–1807), of Salop, m. St John's C 1785, BA 1789, C. Cliffe, 1790–8, R. St Thomas at Cliffe, 1798–1807, R. All Saints', Lewes, 1799–1807.

Page 283

Edburton al Adburton R. S[t] Andrew ⟨9 miles W. of Lewes⟩. ABP P. Kings books 16$^£$. Wake 100$^£$ Herring 120$^£$. R. saith 116$^£$: out of which is p[d] 15$^£$ Land-Tax at 4^s, & a Quit Rent of near 4$^£$. Ecton mentions a Pension of 40^s to the Prior of Lewes. 36 Ho. Prayers & Sermon once on Sundays Chr. Day & good Fr. [Prayers to be twice on Sundays with Exp. on Cat. from LD 1759. See Letters]. Prayers on AshW. Cat once a fortnight in Summer. 8 Sacr. 35 or 40 Com. Offertory given for teaching the Ch[n] of the poor. 2^s a week Church &c in good Order: new cieling. Flagon & Basin pewter ⟨3 Bells⟩. Parsonage Ho. good, & in firm Repair. Mr Clarke par. Vis. 1763.

Charles Baker[1] R. 31 Dec. 1754. Resides & teaches School at Steyning, 4 miles off. The Parishioners certifie, that this is no material Inconvenience to them. He served also Coomb near Steyning, 20$^£$ a Year, which he quits. He pleaded, that before he had Coomb his Neighbours asked him so often to assist them, that he could serve his own Church but once for the most part. He was directed to refuse, when asked too often. 1766 Service twice.

Griffith Griffith[2] A.M. Rector 1784.

John Barnes Backhouse[3] A.M. Rector 1792.

John Yeatman[4] A.M. Rector 1796.

Conf. at Cliffe 12, 15 July 1761

[1] (1720–84), of Radnor, m. Brasenose 1737, BA 1740, MA (St John's C 1774), R. Edburton, 1754–84, V. Leominster, 1776–84, chaplain to George, Baron Cranley.
[2] See p. 189, n. 6.   [3] See p. 80, n. 5.
[4] (1752–?), of Bristol, m. Pembroke O 1770, BA 1773, MA (Oriel) 1777, R. Edburton, 1796–7, V. East Brent, Somerset, 1797, R. Stock Gaylard, Dorset, preb of Wells, 1806.

Page 284

Dioc. of Chich: D. S. Malling

Frampfield ⟨al. Franfield⟩ V. St Tho. Becket ⟨8 miles N E from Lewes⟩. Belonged to the College of Malling. Earl of Thanet[1] P ⟨See below⟩. Tenths 1-6-8. Certified 41-11-0. ⟨Worth 110^f. Mr Wh. had not so much⟩. Above 4 miles over: near 120 Ho. scatterd. There were Presb. abt 30 Years ago, & a Meeting Ho. None now. Whole Service. 2 Sermons, on Sundays. Prayers on Holydays. Cat. was exp. in Lent: but now V. is almost deaf. 2 Sacr. at great Festivals, 1 at Mich. The Number last Chr. both days was 75. Robt Smith[2] in 1719 gave the Interest of 100^f, for teaching poor Ch^n to read: & of another 100^f. 20^s to the minister for a Charity Sermon, & the rest to the Poor.

The Steeple down above 100 Years ago: the Bells all cracked in the Fall, except one, that hangs in the Porch, & is used. ChW^{ns} desire Directions abt the rest. Registers in Parchmt from 31 H. 8. Flagon & Basin Pewter. Church & chancel & Vic. Ho. &c in good Repair. Mr Clarke Par. Vis. 1763.

In Grindals List, copied in Paroch. Book 1663 it stands as in the ABP^s Gift.

Tho. Wharton[3] M.A V. 5 March 1725. Hath constantly resided in the V. Ho. above 32 Years. [seems to have nothing else]. Died towds end of May 1767: was rich.

John Milward[4] BA V. 13 July 1767. ord. Pr by BP Terrick[5] of London July 12.

Joseph Milward[6] V. 27. Decr. 1771.

George Thompson[7] A.M. V. 22^d. July 1776.

Conf. at Bucksted 60, 14 July 1761.

[1] Sackville (Tufton) (1733-86), 8th earl.

[2] Probably alderman Robert Smith, who died in 1721: VCH *Sussex* III, p. 126.

[3] (1698-1767), of Westmoreland, m. Queen's O 1717, BA 1723, MA 1724, V. Framfield, 1726-67.

[4] ?(1728-71), of Sussex, m. Queen's O 1751, BA?, V. Framfield, 1767-71.

[5] Richard Terrick (1710-77), bishop of Peterborough, 1757-64, bishop of London, 1764-77.

[6] ?(1745-), of Westmoreland, m. Queen's O 1764, BA 1769, V. Framfield, 1771-76, ? PC Denby, co. Derby 1799.

[7] ?(1751-1823), of Westmoreland, m. Queen's O 1769, BA 1773, MA 1776, BD 1797, DD (St Edmund Hall) 1800, principal St Edmund Hall, 1800-23, V. Framfield, 1776-1804, V. Bramley, 1800, V. Milford and Hordle, 1800-1823.

Page 285

Glynde V. ⟨Glyn al. Glynde Entry B. II. 146. 2 miles E. from Lewes⟩. Belonged to the College of South Malling. Dean & Canons of Windsor P ⟨See below⟩. Tenths 10-1½. Certified 43-14-6. 23 Ho. BP Trevor[1] lives a Month or two in the Year here. Tho. Hay[2] Esqr Capt. in the Queens Regim^t of Dragoons. Service once on Sundays. Prayers on Chr. day, & in Passion Week. 8 Sacr. of late. Betw. 20 & 30 Com. each time. A Terrier wanted, because V. hath a Portion of Tithes in the adjoyning Parish of Beddingham, concerning the Extent of which, the Terriers of Beddingham are not consistent with each other. BP Trevor augmented it, in Conjunction with the Queens Bounty, in 1759, by taking the Governors 200^f, & setting on it a House & 10 Acres of Land, worth together 17 or 18^f a Year. He is now, 1763, rebuilding the Church on the same Ground, but a new Plan: & the Vicar hath an excellent House. Mr Clarke Par. Vis. 1763.

In Grindals list copied in Paroch. Book 1663 it stands as in ABP[s] Gift.

Tho. Davies[3] BA V. 22 Feb. 1750. Resides constantly in V. Ho. & serves also the Cure of S. Malling, an adjoyning Parish. Serves this twice, & not that, since BP Trevor augmented this.
George Bass Oliver[4] A.B. 1789.

Conf. at Cliffe, July 15. 17.

[1] Richard Trevor (1707–71), bishop of St David's, 1744–52, bishop of Durham, 1752–71. Owner of Glynde Place.
[2] (1733–86). MP for Lewes, 1768–80. Owner of Glyndebourne, 'once a favourite home of the muses': *Sussex* I, p. 346.
[3] ? (1727–89), of Chester, m. Jesus O 1745, BA 1749, V. Glynde,1751–89.
[4] (?–1823), of Leicester, m. Clare 1783, BA 1787, MA 1796, V. Glynde, 1789–1823, V. Belgrave-cum-Birstall, Leics, 1796–1823.

Page 286

Dioc. Chich: D. S. Malling
Isefield R. S[t] Margaret ⟨I believe abt 8 miles N of Lewes⟩. ABP P. K[s] books 9-12-8½. Wake 140[f]. Herring 120[f]. R. saith, ⟨he receives no more than⟩ 105[f]. 38 Ho. besides the Parsonage. Prayers & Sermon once on Sundays [to be twice from LD 1759 ⟨Is so⟩]. & Chr. Day & Nov. 5. Cat. exp. every Sunday in Lent, & before Confirmations. 4 Sacr. Betw. 30 & 40 Com. No Offertory. R. hath laid out near 100[f] on Repairs.
Church, Chancel & Parsonage Ho. in good Repair & Order. 3 Bells. Pewter Flagon & Plate. Mr Clarke Par Vis. 1763.

Geo. Newton[1] BA R. 12 May 1755. Seq. of S[t] John Baptist Southover 6 miles off, where he lives at free-Cost with his Uncle. Had no Dilapidations: is repairing, & will finish in 1759. Not finished 1761. Done 1763.
Griffith Griffith[2] A.M. Rec. 1792.
John Henry Clapham[3] A.B. Rec. 1792.

James Fulthorp[4] Pr. Cur. 20[f] with Surpl. Fees. Serves Horsted, a short mile off: lives in Uckfield, an adjoyning Parish. See above. 1761 Salary 35[f] & Surpl. Fees.

Conf. at Buckstead 15, July 14. 1761

[1] (1730–91), of London, m. Oriel 1748, BA 1752, R. Isfield, 1755–91.
[2] See p. 189 n. 6.   [3] See p. 196, n. 11.   [4] He has not been traced.

Page 287

Lyndfield C. S[t] John Baptist ⟨abt 8 m NW of Lewes near Cuckfield⟩. Belonged to the Coll. of South-Malling. Newton Smithe[1] Esq[r] was Impr. Now, Mr John Neale[2] of Deptford, Gardener, whose Father gave Mr Smithe a Manour for the {great} Tithes, which are worth above 120[f] a Year. Mr Neale gives the Curate 20[f] a Year, who hath also the {Surplice} ⟨Churching⟩ Fees. Mr Bridgen[3], a former Curate, licenced 1712 ⟨with 20[f] a year⟩ applied, it is said, to ABP Wake to procure him an Augmentation: but he got none. ABP Wake saith it is Ecclesia peribus indolata ⟨and so saith the Parochial Book 1663⟩: but afterwds mentions Mr Bridgens Licence.

Extent 4 miles: no Villages: 100 Ho. 3 or 4 Families of note. One Fam. Presb. one Anab. A few of the lowest sort obstinately ignorant & irreligious. Ho. belonging to the Living is in Lay Hands. Prayers & Sermon once. 8 Sacr. Often above 100 Com. Offertory given by minister to poor not receiving Parochial Alms. 4^f a year for the Poor.

The Impr. told the Curate, that he wd not give him 20^f a year, if he cd get the Duty done for less. Th. he thinks no certain sum due.

Of a Dispute betw. Cur & Mr Board[4] abt Ch. yard Fence See Letters, Apr. 1762. Church & Chancel &c in very good Order: 5 good Bells. Flagon Pewter. No House for the Minister. Mr Clarke Par. Vis. 1763

Rowland Lewis[5] Cur. Pr. Resides constantly in the Parish. See above. Serves another Cur ⟨Wivelsfield⟩. Each 20^f.

July 15. 1761 Conf at Cliffe, 42

[1] He has not been traced.　　　　　　　　　　[2] He has not been traced.
[3] William Brigden, (1689–17?), of Salop, m. University 1704, BA 1708, MA 1711, C. Lindfield, 1712, R. Folkington, 1730, R. West Dean, 1731.
[4] William Board (1731–90).
[5] (1727–83), of Kent, m. St John's C 1745, BA 1750, R. Perivale, Middlesex, 1752–83.

Page 288
Dioc. Chich. D. S. Malling
Mayfield V. St Dunstan ⟨12 miles N E from Lewes, a mile from Bucksted⟩. Belonged to Canterbury Coll. in Oxford: Ecton, where ABP is said to be P. But Michael Baker[1] Esqr hath presented the 4 last Times, as P. in full Right ⟨& John Baker[2] Esqr 1663 & 1696⟩. ABP Wake mentions a Rectory, distinct from the Vicarage, & a Presentation of the same Persons to both. But in the book of Entries the vicarage only is mentioned on that occasion ⟨See below⟩. Kings books 17-13-4. Wake 120^f. So called now ⟨It is 200^f at least 1762⟩. 6½ miles long, 3½ broad. 139 Ho. The chief Family, that of the Patron. One woman, a Papist. 6 Anab. 33 Presb. A meeting Ho. Teacher, Mr Downer. Contributions to him but 7^f a year. Declining. Whole Service on Sundays, & 2 Sermons except on Sacr. Days. Sermon on 5 Nov. Chr. Day, Jan 30, good Fr. Prayers every Sts Day. 8 Sacr. At Chr. last 75; & the Sunday after, 65. Cat. with a Lecture in Form of a Sermon, out of the Desk, every Sunday afternoon in Lent & sometimes to Whits. or longer. John Rent[3] gave 150^f, Mich. Baker Esqr 150 Guineas, & a Ho. let for 4^f a year, & others subscribed, to the amount in all of 20^f a Year for a school. 20^f & the Ho. for the Master, 2^f for the 27 Ch^n, who learn Reading, Writing & Accounts. The Minister, & 6 more, Trustees. 20^s a Year to the poor of Mouse-hale Quarter.

In ABP Islips[4] Register fol. 347b is the Ordination of the Vicarage of Maghfield by ABP Boniface in 1262: reciting, that the Pope had given the Rectory to the ABP for ever appointing what the Vicars Income shall be, & the Decanum de Mallyng prout moris est semel in anno procurabit. The Manor, of Mayfield, & Parks of Mayfield & Franckham & the Rectory of M. & advowson of the

Vicarage were granted to the Crown in Exchange 31 Aug. 1. Ed. 6. See Chart Misc. vol. 13. N° 21.
Church ⟨&c⟩ in good order: new seating: floor in some places to be new laid: 6 good Bells Flagon Pewter. Mr Clarke Par. Vis. 1763.

Richd Porter[5] MA V. 8 Jan. 1752. R. of Chailey [or Chayleigh] 14 miles off in his own Gift, & divides his time between them. Hath a temporal patrimony. Studies the Hebrew Metre. Officiates here 1761. Dead Feb. 1762.
Roger Challice[6] MA of Pembroke Hall V. March 30. 1762, hath also Chailey, as his Predecessors had. 1766. Resides here.
John Kirby[7] Vicar 1780.

Farhill[8], Cur. at both Livings. Heir to a considerable Fortune. Was 24 in Feb. 1759 & promised to come for Pr. Orders. Perhaps is ord. Pr. for Chailey. Gone to Bristol sick 1761.

July 14. 1761 Conf. at Bucksted, 120.

[1] Owned the advowson from 1730: VCH *Sussex* IX, p. 92. He was the son of Peter Baker, the vicar, who died in 1729.
[2] He died aged 80 in 1723: ibid., p. 418.   [3] This was in 1749: ibid., p. 420.
[4] Simon Islip, archbishop of Canterbury, 1349–66.
[5] (1716–1762), of Sussex, m. Jesus C 1735, scholar 1735, BA 1738, MA 1743, R. East Hoathly, 1741–52, V. Mayfield, 1752–62, R. Chailey, 1753–62.
[6] (1728–80), of Lapford, Devon, m. Balliol 1746, BA 1749, MA (Pembroke Hall C 1762), C. Ripe, 1759, mentioned in *Turner's diary*, p. 186, R. Chailey 1762–80, V. Mayfield, 1762–80.
[7] See p. 231, n. 6.
[8] George Parker Farhill (1735–90), of Sussex, m. St John's C 1752, scholar, BA 1756, MA 1759, R. Llanvetherine, Monmouth, 1765–9, R. Lurgashall, Sussex, 1778–90, preb of Chichester, 1773–90.

Page 289
Portslade V. S[t] Nicolas. Belonged to the Monastery of S[t] Radegund. The Rectory was granted to the ABP by H. 8 21 July in the 30th year of his Reign. The Vicarage is not mentioned in the Grant. V had always attended the BP of Chichesters Visitation, & is presented by the Crown. And no Presentation or Collation by the ABP appears: but an Institution on the Presentation of the Crown during the vacancy of the See of Chichester Whitg. Reg. part 1. fol. 354 b. Yet in the ABP[s] Lease of the Rectory the Gift or Patronage of the Vicarage is reserved, as also 16[£] a year ⟨by Juxon⟩ to the Vicar, who is now [1759] Ralph Clutton[1], presented by the king as P. pleno jure, & inst. by the BP of Chichester in 1722. See his Letters. He is R. of Horsted-Keynes near E. Grinstead Sussex, & resides there. May 1761 John Clutton[2] Rector of Hangleton, Co Sussex was presented to Portslade valued at 80[£]: to hold them together. Will reside at Portslade, near Shoreham: fears, that taking off the Land-Tax from the pension wd occasion his being charged with Parish Rates, & do him Harm.

[1] (1696–1761), of Newton, Cheshire, m. Brasenose 1712, BA 1717, MA 1725, V. Portslade, 1722–61, R. Horsted Keynes, 1738–61.
[2] (1732–?), of Sussex, m. Magdalene C 1750, BA 1754, MA 1757, fellow 1754, R. Hangleton 1757-, V. Portslade, 1761-.

Page 290

Dioc. Chich: D. S. Malling

Ringmere al Rugmer V. S[t] Mary 〈3 m N E from Lewes〉. Belonged to the Coll. of Malling. ABP. P. K[s] books 13[f]. Wake 100[f]. Now called 140[f]. 3½ miles long. 85 Ho. A Family of Presb. Whole Service. Prayers on S[ts] Days, & W. Fr. in Lent. 8 Sacr. Abt 40 Com. Sibylla Stapley[1] of Broyle Place in this Parish, endowed a free school for 13 Ch[n] with 5[f] a year, & one for 7, with 3[f]. Eliz. Cheyney[2] endowed an Alms Ho. for 2 widows with 3-4-0 a Year. [Mr Henry Snooke[3] hath abt 200[f] a Year here. A very peevish man.

Church in good Repair: 2 Chancels repairing at the Expence of the Impropriator: one, of the Parish. Steeple hath been down 150 years: one Bell in a wooden Tower, within the Ruines of the old Steeple. Flagon Pewter. Commandments to be repaired. Vic. Ho. a thin Shell of Lath & Plaister: in Repair. Built by Mr Snook, wn Rector.

Michael Baynes[4] V. March 26. 1754. V. of Fletching, 8 miles off, where he resides, being domestick Chaplain to L[d] Delawar[5]. A person of bad Fame in V. Ho. Turned Out. See Letters.

George Woodward[6] A.M. V 1786.

Jacob Townshend[7] Cur. 40[f]. Complained of Mr Snookes Behaviour in the Church, & read a Paper against him. See Letter. Gone.

Theodore Fletcher[8]. Absent at Vis. 1761. Exc. Still there 1766.

John Lupton[9] cur lic. 1787. Sal £40.

July 15. 1761 Conf. at Cliffe, 18.

[1] This was in 1699: *Sussex* I, p. 350. [2] By will of 1611: VCH *Sussex* IX, p. 183.
[3] He has not been traced.
[4] (17?-86), Peterhouse, MA 1757, V. Ringmer 1754-86, V. Fletching, 1760-86.
[5] John, baron de la Warr (1693-1766), MP for Grampound, 1715-22.
[6] (1750-1837), of East Hendred, Berkshire, m. Christ Church 1766, BA 1770, MA 1775, V. Fletching, 1786-1837, V. Ringmer, 1786-1812, V. Maresfield, 1812-37.
[7] Possibly [James] Townshend, of Halesowen, Salop, m. University 1741, BA (Merton) 1745.
[8] Theodore Fletcher (1717-?), of Stoke Lyne, Oxon, m. Magdalen O 1734, BA 1737.
[9] (17?-1844), of Leeds, m. Trinity C 1782, BA 1786, MA 1789, C. Ringmer, 1787-1841, R. St Thomas at Cliffe, 1807-41, V. Utling, Essex, 1823-40, R. Ovingdean, 1841-44.

Page 291

South-Malling C. S[t] Michael 〈2 miles N. from Lewes〉. This was a Collegiate Church, consisting of a Dean & Prebendaries, in the Collation & under the immediate Jurisdiction of the ABP till the Surrender 10 March 1545. The College & Deanery were granted 37 H.8 to Sir Thomas Palmer[1] Tanner Not. Mon. p. 549. William Kempe[2] of S. Malling Esq[r] was Impropriator. D[r] Russell[3], a physician, married his only child. The Tithes are worth 150[f] a year. John Stansfield[4] of the Cliffe, near Lewes, Gent. died Feb. 23. 1626, & was buried in the Church of All St[s] in Lewes, & his Monumt sets forth, that at the time of his Death he gave a yearly Pension of 20[f] for ever to a preaching minister to serve the Cure in the Church wch shd be built at S. Malling, where the old was long since decayed. M[r] Kemp, who had the Estate, on wch this 20[f] was charged, used to pay it without deducting Taxes, and sometimes made the Curate a Present, but not in money. Dr Russell lets him have the Surplice Fees, ⟨thinking them due to him⟩ but deducts the full Land-Tax, though other Lands in the Parish are not taxed to the full ⟨but near it⟩. ABP Wake saith, the Curate hath 13^f from the Impropriator & 20^f from the Donation of Mr Smith[5]. Did he not confound this with Lindfield, p. 287? See below. The present Curate is not licenced, nor probably his Predecessor.

Three miles long, one broad. 40 Ho. Luke Spence[6] Esqr, ⟨married Miss Frederick. A son at Eton⟩. Dr Russell, of whom, see above. A Farmer, his 3 Sons & 2 Daughters, Papists. Were so originally. Service once on Sundays, on Chr. Day & good Fr. Cat. only before Conf. 4 Sacr. 30 Com.

No Rails to Com. Table, Sacram^t administered in the Seats. One Bell. Flagon & Plate Pewter. Church in excellent Repair. Built in 1627 by Ch. I & other Benefactors. Ch. Yd large: part walled in for Burials: wall to be repaired. No Ho. for Minister. Mr Clarke par. vis. 1763

The Parochial book 1663 saith it is held by no Institution or Subscription: & hath 20^f a Year from Mr Kemp, who nominates, & 20^f out of the Estate of one Mr Smith, commonly called Dog Smith. It also saith that besides this last 20^f, it hath but 13^f fol. 64.

Tho. Davies[7], Cur. V. of Glynde p. 285. Resides there. It is an adjoyning Parish. Gone.

Wm Hampton[8] signs himself Curate of S. Malling July 3. 1761. A Clergymans son, ignorant, blundering, careless.

Geo. Chilton Lambton Young[9] A.M. lic. 1795. Sal. £20.

July 15. 1761 Conf at Cliffe, 18.

[1] Knighted in 1532.			[2] (1655–1720).
[3] Richard Russell (–1759), exploited new theories of sea-bathing at Brighton. He married William Kemp's daughter Mary in 1719, and bought the manor of Ditchling Garden.
[4] Stansfield also owned land in Shipley: VCH *Sussex* VI, pt II,p. 116. See p. 282, n. 1.
[5] Henry Smith (c.1548–1627), alderman of London. He set up numerous charitable bequests, and was known as 'Dog Smith', because he was always followed by his dog.
[6] JP of South Malling: *Turner's Diary*, p. 329.
[7] See p. 285, n. 3.
[8] Perhaps William Hampton (1728–70), of Rottingdean, Sussex, m. All Souls 1744, BA 1750, R and patron of Plumton.
[9] (1772–1820), of Middlesex, m. Queens' C 1789, BA 1791, MA 1794, PC. South Malling, Sussex, 1795–7, minister Iver, Bucks, 1798–1803.

Page 292

Dioc. Chich: D. S. Malling

Stanmere R. ⟨3 miles W from Lewes⟩. ABP. K^s books, 16^f Wake 70^f. It is 120^f ⟨See below⟩. 9 Ho. & one Farm. All belong to Mr Pelham[1] except a Cottage ⟨[copyhold]⟩ & the Parsonage with 18 Acres of Glebe. Mr Pelham ⟨married Fr. Franklands daughter⟩ & Family reside there several months in the Year. Two Presb. One of them rents the Whole Parish. Whole Service on Sundays. No Prayers on Week days except some Fasts & Thanksgiving Days. [qu. Chr. day, good Fr.]. Cat. some Summer months on Sunday afternoon, with D[r] Singes[2] Abstract. 3 Sacr. at least. Com. from 14 to 26. Pension of 6–8 to the Preb. of Sotheram. Ecton.

Church & Parsonage Ho. in excellent Repair. One Bell. Rectory worth 80[f] a year, besides a neat Ho. & Garden. R. had formerly 9 Acres of Glebe dispersed, & the Right of having 25 Ewes kept in common with the Parish Flock. Instead of these Mr Pelham hath given him 18 Acres together, wch is an equivalent & desires to have this confirmed in the Commons.

Edw. Bland[3] BA R. 1 Nov. 1727. Resides constantly in the Parsonage House.
John Heathfield[4] M.A. R. March 6. 1770.
George Metcalf[5] B.A. R. Feb. 26. 1771.
Ditto May 22. 1771.

July 15. 1761. Conf. at Clife 5.

[1] Thomas Pelham (1728–1805), heir to the duke of Newcastle. He was MP for Rye, 1749–54, and MP for Sussex, 1754–68, became baron Pelham of Stanmer in 1768, and was created earl of Chichester in 1801. In 1754 he married Anne, the daughter of Frederick Meinhart Frankland (the 3rd son of Sir Thomas Frankland, Bt).
[2] Edward Synge, *An Abstract of the Church Catechism* (1744).
[3] (1693–1769), of Westmoreland, m. Christs 1711, scholar 1711, BA 1714, R. Stanmer, 1727–69, R. Pyecombe, 1737–69, chaplain to earl of Ashburnham.
[4] (1735–1810), of Croydon, m. Clare 1754, BA 1756, MA 1759, adm. Middle Temple, 1755, R. Stanmer, 1770–71, V. South Mimms and Northaw, Herts, 1773–90.
[5] (1746–1827), of Skeffington Hall, Yorks, m. Trinity C 1766, BA 1769, MA 1772, C. Stanmer, 1770, R. Stanmer, 1771–1803 (x2), V. Laughton, 1787, R. Birdham, 1790, R. Amport, Hants, 1802–27, canon of Chichester, 1784–1827. Took name of Marwood by act of Parliament in 1809.

Page 293
Wadhurst V. S[t] Peter & S[t] Paul ⟨20 miles N E from Lewes⟩. Wadham Coll. P. K[s] books 15-1-0½. Wake 80[f]. Herring 200[f]. 7 miles, long 4 broad. A market town & 6 Hamlets: near 200 Ho. 3 Anab. A meeting Ho. Teacher, Dobell. 2 Methodists. Whole Service, 2 Sermons, on Sundays. Prayers on all S[ts] Days, & W. Fr. in Lent, when Ch[n] are Cat. 8 Sacr. Abt 140 Com. each time. Mrs Lucy Barham[1] gave 5[f] a Year for teaching 12 poor Ch[n]. 7 Alms Ho. managed by the Parish Officers. John Auberry, or John of Berry, ABP of Canterbury [there never was an ABP or BP of that name] gave 11[f] a year for repairing the Church. Tho. Whitfield[2] of the Middle Temple Esq[r] 10[f] a Year to the Poor. Someother small Gifts.

The Rectory & Advowson of the Vicarage was given by the ABP to the Crown in Exchange 31 Aug 1 Ed. 6 See Chart. Misc. vol. 13 N°21.

Church in good Repair: some of the Seats bad: Timber cut for repairing them. Church & Chancel to be whitewashed next March. 5 good Bells. Extremely fine Communion Plate. Row of Limes darkens the Church, to be cut into a Fan. No Vic. Ho. Glebe, only a small Croft, where the Ho. stood. Lands of 10[f] a Year left for the Fabrick, applied to the poor: might in a few Years seat the Church uniformly. Write to the Commissiary. The Parish have cieled the Chancel over the Com. Table. Mr Short[3] hath abt ½ the gr. Tithes, & wd ciel his, i.e. the N. Side: but near 20 others have the other ½, & some of them will not ciel the S. Side. Mr Clarke Par. Vis. 1763.

Sam. Bush[4] MA V. 11 July 1743. Hath, or fancies he hath, been unable to go to Church for many Years. Hath refused to pay the poors Rate: & his Goods have been distrained. See Letters. Imagines his parishioners & others to be in Conspiracy against him. In the same way 1761, 1763, & 1766.
Alexander Litchfield[5] A.M. 1783.

David Morgan[6] Cur. Resides. 30^f a year ⟨This 30^f alone was the Salary 1750 Entry B VIII. 485⟩. To be made 40^f, if the Surplice Fees fall short. Still there 1766.
Richard Purdy[7] Clerk Cur. Licensed Sept: 18: 1774, with Salary of £50 p. ann.
Edward Rudston Langdale[8] Clerk A.B. Curate. Licensed May 26: 1777 with a Salary of £50 p. ann.

July 14. 1761. Conf. at Bucksted 47.

[1] The wife of John Barham. She left this in 1730: *Sussex* I, p. 415.
[2] In 1623: VCH *Sussex* VII, p. 200.   [3] Probably Peter Short: ibid., p. 158.
[4] ?(1713–83), of Gloucestershire, m. Oriel 1731, BA 1734, V. Wadhurst, 1743–83.
[5] [Lichfield] (1746–1804), of Oxford, m. Wadham 1763, BA 1767, MA 1773, proctor 1780, R. Noke, Oxon, 1773–, V. Wadhurst, 1783–1804.
[6] Possibly of (1729–?), of Llancrwys, co Carmathen, m. Jesus O 1749.
[7] (1753–1808), of Greenwich, Kent, m. Queen's O 1768, BA 1771, MA 1781, BD 1782, DD 1800, lic C. Wadhurst, 1774–77, V. Broad Hinton, Cricklade, R. Ashley, Wiltshire, 1791–1808.
[8] (1755–1838), of London, m. Pembroke C 1773, BA 1777, MA 1780, R. Wadhurst, 1777, R. Chignall-Smealy, Essex, 1790–1838.

Page 294
Dioc. Chich: D. Terring
Patching R. ABP P. K^s books 11–13–4. Wake 160^f ⟨But in another book 100^f⟩. Herring 100^f ⟨See below⟩. 4 miles long, 1¼ broad: Patching hath 13 Ho. Selden, 3. There are 7 more. Most of the Parish belongs to Sir John Shelley[1], who hath a fine Seat called Mechel Green, in the Parish of Clapham, a mile off. One poor old man, with 2 or 3 Ch^n, Papist. R will try to bring him back. The Papists of this Neighbourhood assemble at Ld Montacutes[2], 3 miles off. His priest O'Carroll. Service once on Sundays. When R. resided here, Prayers on all Holydays & W. Fr. in Lent [Why not still?]. Cat. on Sunday Afternoons. Servts sent now. 4 Sacr. Usually abt 17 Com. Were fewer. ChW^n never receives. A person, bred a Papist, always receives: & his brother comes to Church.
See abt the Separation of this from Terring p. 295.
R. Oct 30. 1759 saith it is but 75–10–0 & Land Tax is 11^f. Called in his Disp. 80^f. Ch. Wn^s present, but no Prosecution is carried on. Mr Lewis[3] Apr. 1 1761. 1762. Steeple repairing. Ho. 90 f long, in bad Repair: must be pulled down: 140^f with the old materials wd build a convenient new one. There were 2 Barns: one ruinous wn present R. came, the other well timbered then, dilapidated by him. He cannot rebuild. One Barn best. Will cost 90^f at least. Mr L. will not raise the Tithes by having one. They are sunk by him, & let for 76^f a year.
In 1699 & before held separate from Terring V. wch See. Tho. Blennerhaysett[4] coll to Patching 20 Sept. 1710 Entry B VI. 15. John Rundle[5] 24 July 1725 on Resign of Blennerhaysett VII. 99
Tho. Lewis[6] BA R. 28 Aug. 1746 V. of Terring, p. 296: where he resides & serves both. How far asunder? & on which side of Terring is Patching. There is

a Patching E. Of Steyning. That is a mistake in Cambdens[7] map & shd be
Patcham: & what it calls Patcham W of Terring shd be Patching. BP
Ashburnham[8]. Died Apr. 1766
Rich[d] Rycroft[9] MA R. May. 6. 1766 V. of Terring p. 297.
N.B. This Rectory was united to the Vicarage of Terring July 27: 1767. See
Register book N° 10. Fol. 214.
Edward Phillips[10] Rector 1786.

Cuthbert Whalley[11] Clerk. Cur. Licensed to this Cure and West Terring with a
Salary of £50 p. ann & Surplice Fees, December 28: 1776.

[1] See p. 114, n. 2.
[2] Anthony (Browne) 1686–1767, 6th viscount Montagu.
[3] See n.6.
[4] Perhaps (1679–?), of London MA 1717, R. Patching, 1710–25.
[5] (1693–1740), of Bodmin, Cornwall, m. Queen's O 1713, BA (Exeter) 1717, MA (Kings) 1725,
  R. Clapham, R. Patching, 1725–40. He had perhaps been a chaplain in the Navy, 1719.
[6] ?(1703–1766), of Mothvey, co Carmarthen, m. Jesus O 1719, BA 1723, R. Patching, 1746–66,
  V. Tarring, 1751–66.
[7] William Camden (1551–1623). His *Britannia*, first published in Latin in 1586, contained maps of
  each county.
[8] Sir William Ashburnham, bishop of Chichester, 1754–97.
[9] (17?–86), of London, m. St Catherine's C 1755, BA 1758, MA 1761, DD 1773, R. Patching,
  1766–86, V. Tarring, 1766–86, R. Penshurst, 1773–86. Created a baronet in 1784.
[10] (1726–1803), of Monmouth, m. Pembroke O 1745, BA 1758, MA 1751, V. Meopham, 1786–86,
  R. Patching, 1786–1803, V. Tarring, 1786–1803.
[11] (1751–?), of Lancashire, m. St John's C 1772, scholar 1775, BA 1776, C. Patching and W.
  Tarring, 1776.

Page 295
Terring ⟨al. Tarring⟩ al. West-Terring R. Called a Sine Cure. ABP. P. K[s] books
22–13–4. Wake 170[f]. Herring 200[f]. A Pension of 4[f] a Year to the Vicar. V.
saith he receives 17[f] a Year. See ABP Wakes Peculiars 1717. ABP Peckham[1]
appointed in 1282 that the Chapel of Pasiynges [Patching] which had been
separate from the Rectory of Terring, & then made a Chapel to it, should be
again an intirely separate Rectory Reg. Peckeham fol. 105. In the Rectors
Collation is expressed a Right of presenting to the Vicarage, wch he doth not
enjoy. AD[n] Potter.
D[r] Milles[2] saith, he hath throughly repaired & improved his Ho. here. Lease of
R. for 21 years at 33[f] a yr & 10[f] [instead of 4[f] formerly pd to V. Conf. 1664
Entry B ⟨I⟩. 90. V. then worth 80[f] a yr above the Pension. Lease for 50 at 30[f]
½ yearly to R & 10[f] quarterly to V. excepting to R. Patronage of the 4 Tenemts
&c granted March 26 Conf. March 28. 1667 Entry B. II. 54. Lease for 21 yrs at
30[f] clear ⟨no mention of the 10[f]⟩. Patronage of V. excepted 28 March 1671. III.
116
John Provost[3] inst coll R 4 June 1672 III. 154 grants a lease for 14 yrs conf. 1679
VI. 76
John Strype[4] MA coll. 11 June 1711, that day after Coll. signed a paper, that
whereas there had been abuses by letting collusive Leases to unqualified persons
& other ways, he wd to the best of his skill rectifie them, & not let the Estate or
any Fine to any Tenant more than for 3 yrs to 3 yrs & at a moderate extended
Rent, & wd pay the accustomed due of 17[f] a year to V. VI. 46.

Jeremiah Milles[5] MA [now DD] R 7 Feb. 1746. R. of S[t] Edmunds Lombard Street p. 403 & of Meestham p. 391 and Chanter of Exeter.
Richard Milles[6] A.B. Rector, Jan: 6; 1779.

[1] John Peckham, archbishop of Canterbury, 1279–92.

[2] (1714–1784), of Hampshire, m. CCCO 1729, BA 1733, MA 1735, BA & DD 1747, dean of Exeter 1762, FAS 1741, FRS and pres. Soc. Antiquaries 1765, R. Saltwood. 1744–46, R. Merstham, 1745–, R. St Edmund King, London, 1746, R. West Tarring, 1747–79, treasureship of Lismore, 1735, precentor of Waterford, 1737–44, archbishop's chaplain, 1745, precentor and preb of Exeter, 1747, dean of Exeter, 1762.

[3] Probably John Provote (1648–1711), of Abingdon, Berks, m. Pembroke O 1664, BA 1668, MA 1671, R. West Tarring, 1672–1711.

[4] (1643–1737), of London, m. Jesus C 1662, BA (Catherine Hall) 1666, MA 1669, incorp. Oxford 1671, C. Theydon Bois, V. Low Layton, Essex, 1679–1727, R. West Tarring, 1711–37, dean of Bocking.

[5] See n. 2.

[6] (1754–1823), of London, m. Queen's O 1770, student of Christ Church, BA 1774, MA 1777, preb of Exeter 1778, R. West Tarring, 1779–1823, V. Kenwyn, Cornwall, 1781.

Page 296
Dioc. Chich: D. Terring
Terring V. ⟨A small market Town on the Coast betw. Arundel & New Shoreham half-way betw. Chichester & Lewes. Another SE from Lewes⟩. S[t] Andrew with the Chapel of Durrington, al. Derrington, & Heen al. Hene. ABP. P. K[s] books 8-13-4. Wake, Herring, 80[f]. See below ⟨& p. 295⟩. Terring hath 52 Ho. Salvington, where Selden[1] was born, 20. Derrington 19, Hene 8. Service once on Sundays ⟨twice in 1717⟩. Prayers on W. Fr. & Holydays, till V. was arrested, coming from Church. He will revive the Practice when it is safe. Cat. on a Sunday: & by the Schoolmaster twice a week. Mr Strype[2] the Annalist was R. & gave 5[f] a Year for teaching 12 Ch[n] to read. Dr Milles[3] continues it. 4 Sacr. abt 30 Com. each time. V. Ho a wretched one. V. Oct. 30. 1759 saith it is somewhat above 60[f] ⟨called 60[f] in his Disp⟩ without the Land Tax, & the House. V. complains, that R. takes the Clover Seeds from him, which are small Tithes. So Comyns[4] p. 633 in Gibson[5] p. 678 2[d] Ed. 1762 An organ: Church damp. Parishioners have repaired their own seats & sold them to foreigners. V. Ho. in sufficient repair. V. worth abt 75[f] a year.
John Harrison[6] coll to V. void by death of Edm. Neyns[7] [not named in the former books] 19. July 1676. Entry B. III. 294. John Harison coll to V. void by Cession of Rich[d] { }anly[8] [not mentioned, I believe, before] 22 Apr. 1684 IV. 419. Jerman Dunn[9] V March 16. 1697 on death of Harrison 569. June 13. 1699 he was removed to Patching & June 10 John Gray[10] {inst} coll Terring 604. Edw. Williams[11] coll 1700 p. 618 holds it with Goring V. 135. Fr Conduit[12] coll July 24. 1717 on death of Williams VI. 247. See below. The Chapel of Hene is ½ a mile from Terring Service was performed in it once a Month. It hath lately been converted into a Carpenters shop. The Chapel Warden hath promised to put it into proper Order, which it hath not been for the last 16 years. A late Chapel Warden, who was a smuggler, deposited Rum in it, which was seized there. The present will present it at the next visitation. 1762 Repaired at a considerable Expence, but no Doors. Yard not fenced. Better pull down the Chapel. See above. Dav. Capon[13] coll. to V. 2 Jan 1722 on Resig. of Conduit.

[1] John Selden (1584–1654), jurist. Famous for his *History of Tythes* (1617).
[2] See p. 295, n. 4.   [3] Ibid., n. 2.
[4] John Comyns (c.1667–1740), MP for Maldon, 1701–26. His *Reports of Cases adjudged in the Courts of King's Bench, Common Pleas, and Exchequer* was published posthumously in 1744.
[5] Edmund Gibson, *Codex Juris Ecclesiastici Anglicani: or, the Statutes, Constitutions, Canons, Rubricks and Articles of the Church of England, Methodically Digested under their Proper Heads. With a Commentary, Historical and Judicial* (1713). The second edition appeared in 1761.
[6] (16?–98), of Berkshire, m. New College 1659, BCL 1665, fellow 1659, DCL 1671, advocate of doctor's commons, 1671, V. Tarring, 1676–7, and 1684–98, V. Cromdale, Hampshire, 1679–84, R. Pulborow, 1684–98, preb of Chichester, 1676.
[7] Edmund [Negus], of Northamptonshire, m. Queens' C 1623, BA 1625, MA 1628, R. Albourne, Sussex, 1635, V. Tarring, 1672–6.
[8] Richard [Pauley], (1647–?), of Reading, Berks, m. University 1664, BA 1667, MA 1671, V. Tarring, 1677, V. Cromdale, Hants, 1684.
[9] (16?–1710), of Middlesex, m. St Catharine's C 1673, BA 1674, MA 1677, V. Tarring, 1698–99, R. Patching, 1699–1710.
[10] (16?–1751), of Norwich, m. CCCC 1687, BA 1691, MA 1694, V. Tarring, 1699–1700, R. Southwick, 1700–51.
[11] Of Suffolk, m. CCCC 1684, BA 1688, MA 1702, V. Little Waldingfield, Suffolk, 1690–1700, V. Tarring, 1700–1717, V. Goring, 1704–, chaplain to Earl of Sunderland.
[12] 1753), m. TCD 1700, BA 1704, V. Tarring, 1717–23, lic C. Ash, 1721, R. Snave, 1738–1753.
[13] (1698–1751), of London, m. Trinity C 1719, BA 1720, V. Tarring, 1722–51, V. Patching, 1721–51.

Page 297

Terring V. continued

The Chapel of Derrington is abt a mile from Terring. When it was standing, a Bell belonged to it, sold long ago, & a Silver Chalice, now in the Hands of Mr Bennet, the Chapel Warden, which they speak of selling for the Use of the Poor. A piece of Ground, divided from the Chapel Yard by Hurdles, seems to belong to it: but is now Private Property. The small Tithes of the chapelry are worth 20^f a Year: & the last Terrier but one saith V. is intitled to them in kind. But the last gives him 6–13–4 in lieu of them. This Modus however hath been often broken: but V. is not in Circumstances to contest it.

Tho. Lewis[1] MA V. 8 Nov. 1751. Resides constantly in V. Ho. R. of Patching p. 294. Serves both. Terring near Findon Sussex.
Richd Ryecroft[2] MA. V. May 15. 1766 holds it with Patching p. 294.
Edw. Phillips[3] Vic. 1786.

[1] See p. 294, n. 6.   [2] Ibid., n. 9.   [3] Ibid., n. 10.

Page 298

ABP Wakes Parochial Book, at the End of the Deanery of Terring, puts down these Hamlets, as Peculiars. And so doth the Parochial Book of 1663.

Head-acre in the Parish of St Pancras, Chichester[2)*]

Playstow in the Parish of Kerdford {[or Kesdford. Neither is}. Not in Ecton. But Kirford is, D. Midhurst p. 57[1)*]

Bishopridge in the Parish of Horsham [as mentioned here, p. 277].

[1]* And Mr Wakeford[1] of Chichester, in a Letter 26 Oct 1759 saith that Plaistow is a Chapel of Ease to Kirdford, D. Midhurst, of which Mr Carr[2] is V. who resides at Arundel & Mr James Bayley[3] ⟨Bailley⟩ his Curate, who resides at Kirdford. It is visited amongst the other Peculiars at Chichester. See Mr Wakeford, July 17. 1759.

[2]* There was no Church to this Parish. One is lately built. BP Ashburnham[4].

[3]* Repaired by the Parish. No separate Income belonging to it, or Taxes pd for it. Perhaps built by ABP Kemp[5], who resided at Slindon, 4 miles from Arundel, & had a good Estate at Kirdford, & hence a Peculiar. Chapel chiefly of Wood. No Burial place. Not above 12 poor Houses, not so many Communicants. Shall be 4 Sacramt[s]. No Offertory. Some Dissenters. They diminish. Ch[n] shall be cat. & Service be regularly once a fortnight, wch by ancient Custom was but once a month. Curate in Deacons Orders, will appply for Priests Orders, the first Opportunity. Salary for serving Kirdford & Plaistow, w[ch] are considered as one, abt 40[f], with Surplice Fees. Patron of Kirdford, the Hon[ble] James Lumley[6]. Plaistow is not mentioned in the Institution to Kirdford. It is near Haslemere in Surrey.

[1] Owner of Chidham manor: VCH *Sussex* IV, p. 189.
[2] John Carr (1716–79), of Sussex, m. Christ Church 1726, BA 1730, MA (St Catherine's C 1741), V. Arundel, 1732–79, V. Clapham, 1740–2, V. Kirdford, 1742–79.
[3] He has not been traced.   [4] See p. 294, n. 8.
[5] John Kemp, archbishop of Canterbury, 1452–4.
[6] (c.1709–66) 7th son of Richard, earl of Scarborough. MP for Chichester, 1729–34, MP for Arundel, 1741–7.

Page 299
In the Visitation-book of Mr Mitchel, Register of the Peculiars of S. Malling, I found, ⟨in 1761⟩ the following Names of Places, as making part of those Peculiars

Chilkington, Chapel to West-Meston. Now I find in Ecton p. 58 Chiltington R. And in the new Index Villaris[1], Westmiston near Chiltington: but nothing more. In the Parochial Book of 1663 is enterd Wotton a Hamlet in par. of Chiltington

East-Grinstead. A well known Borough, & a Vicarage. D. of Dorset, P. In 1663 is entred A Hamlet in the parish of Grinsted.

Hartfield. There is a Rectory of that Name in Ecton, p. 66. Earl of Thanet P. & a Vicarage p. 67. The Rector, P.

Wivelsfield. Probably Wilsfield Cur. Priory of Lewes Propr. Ecton p. 65. In the Paroch. Book 1663 is entred A Hamlet in the parish of Wivelsfield.

Wytheham. In the Index Villaris is Withenham, or Withiham near Buckhurst, Sussex. In the Paroch. Book 1663 is entred A Hamlet in the Parish of Withiham In the same Parochial Book 1663 is entred A Hamlet in the Parish of Worth & A Hamlet in the Parish of Lamberhurst. All these fol. 64.

July 15. 1761 I consented, that Francis Wheler[2] & Thomas Farnes[3], Proctors in the BP of Chichesters Court, shd be Proctors also in my Court of Peculiars.

[1] John Adams, *Index Villaris; or, a geographical table of all the cities, market-towns, parishes, villages and private seats in England and Wales, distinguished by symbols* (1680). A new edition appeared in 1700.
[2] An attorney from Lewes: *Turner's Diary*, p. 43. [3] Ibid., p. 223.

Page 300
Dioc. Linc. : D. Risborough
Halton R S[t] Michael. Wake hath put ABP, then Lord Fermannagh[1] P. But Ecton & Herring, Sir Fra. Dashwood[2]. K[s] books 13–6–8. R. saith, 105–10–0. 4 Farm. Ho. abt 15 Cottages. An old Seat of Sir Fra. Dashwood, where his brother, Mr Dashwood King[3], resides sometimes. One Tenant occupies two of the Farms. Service once on Sundays. Cur. will try, if directed to get a Congregation on Week-days: but hath tried in vain to get the Ch[n] to cat. 4 Sacr. Abt 12 Com each time. No Offertory. Service will be twice, as soon as R. can provide for it. Edw. Brown[4] pres. by Sir Fra. Dashwood inst. 24 May 1736 Entry B. VIII. 55. The Advowson was given by the ABP to the Crown 31 Aug 1 Ed. 6. See Chart Misc vol. 13 N° 21. In the Parochial Book of 1663 is a Reference to the Register of Bourchier & Courtenay f. 219.
1767 No Papists.

Will Wroughton[5] MA. R. 5 Aug. 1755. V. of West Wycomb, where he resides, & seldom comes hither, 10 Miles off.
Richard Levett[6] MA of Ch. Ch. R. Dec. 18. 1765 on the Cession of Wroughton.

J. Shaw[7] Cur. 21[£]. V. of Bierton, 2 miles off. Serves it from thence. 1766 R must get one to do the whole Service. Promises.
Thomas[8] Cur. May 1766. Salary { }. Resides in next parish. Gone.
Parry[9] Cur. to come Mich 1767.

Conf. 12 at the BP of Lincolns[10] last Visitation at Aylesbury.

[1] Ralph (Verney), viscount Fermanagh (1683–1752). MP for Amersham, 1717–27, MP for Wendover, 1741–52.
[2] (1708–81), 2nd Bt. MP for Romney, 1741–61, MP for Weymouth, 1761–63. Founder of the Hell Fire club.
[3] John Dashwood King (1716–93), the half-brother of Sir Francis. MP for Bishop's Castle, 1753–61.
[4] (16?–1755), of Middlesex, m. Clare 1708, BA 1712, MA 1715, V. West Wycombe, Bucks, R. Halton, 1736–55.
[5] (1717–1770), of London, m. Trinity C 1735, scholar 1736, BA 1739, MA 755, incorp. at Oxford 1756, R. Halton, 1755–65, V. West Wycombe, 1755–65, R. Welbourn, Lincs, 1765–70.
[6] (1731–1805), of Staffordshire, m. Christ Church 1749, BA 1753, MA 1756, R. Halton, 1765–1805, V. West Wycombe, 1765–1805.
[7] Possibly John Shaw m. Magdalene C 1736.
[8] He has not been traced. [9] He has not been traced. [10] See p. 237, n. 10.

Page 301
Monks Risborough. R. S[t] Dunstan, with the Chapel of Owlswick, S[t] Peter, of which there are now no Remains. ABP P. K[s] books 30[£]. Wake 200[£]. Herring 220 ⟨So Disp 1738⟩. 6 miles long, 1 broad. Contains Risborough. Whiteleaf, Ascott, Meadle & Owlswick: each hath abt 20 Families. 30 scatterd Ho. & Cottages. In all 129 Ho. One Presb. 3 Anab. Families. One Man & 2 Women

Quakers. The Man & his Ancestors have long occupied 80^f a Year; & ever since the Restoration they have let their Tithes be taken quietly. He is going. They were once numerous, & had a meeting Ho. & Burial Place here. Some come seldom to Church: 5 or 6 scarce ever. Of low Rank. Admonished. Whole Service, 2 Sermons every Sunday. Prayers on Holydays, W. Fr. in Lent, & all Passion Week. Many Ch^n cat. in Lent. Lewis's Exp. given them. Some persuaded to get Portions of it by Heart. 8 or 10 Sacr. At great Festivals 50, at other times 20 Com. Dr Quarles[1], formerly R. gave a Close of 40^s a year for teaching 4 or more Boys Reading & Cat. R. pays for as many Girls. Dr Hody[2] & Dr Quarles, formerly Rectors, gave money, now vested in Lands of 9–10–0 a year for putting out poor Boys Apprentices by R &Ch Wns. R. hath as many Loads of Beech out of certain Woods, as will supply his Ho. with Feuel. Benefactor unknown. Persons guilty of Fornication are regularly presented, but seldom punished.

Held by Mr Tomkins[3] with Lambeth, but by a royal Disp. 1671 Entry B. III. 138.

* The parson of Risborough habibit decimas equisorium et pullanorum Regis et ajistament in parco Regis. Claus [Close Rolls in the Tower] 6 Ed. 3. membr. 39. 1767 No Papists.

*This is a mistake. The Parson of Monks Risborough has no such Claims. Such as they are, they belong to the Perpetual Curacy of Princes Risborough – when there was a Palace & a Park.

[1] William Quarles (1666–1727), of Northamptonshire, m. Emmanuel 1686, BA 1689, MA 1692, DD 1712, R. Monks Risborough, 1708–27.
[2] Humphrey Hody (1660–1707), of Odcombe, Somerset, m. Wadham 1676, scholar 1677, BA 1679, MA 1682, fellow 1685, BD 1689, DD 1693, regius professor of Greek, 1698–1705, R. St Michael Royal and St Martin's Vintry, London, 1695–1702, R. Monks Risborough, 1702–7, archdeacon of Oxford, 1704–7, chaplain to Tenison, 1695.
[3] Thomas Tompkins (16?–75), of London, m. Balliol 1651, BA 1655, fellow (All Souls') 1657, MA 1658, proctor 1663, BD 1665, DD 1673, R. St Mary Aldermary, 1665–9, R. Great Chart, 1667, R. Lambeth, 1669–75, R. Monks Risborough, 1672–75, canon of Exeter 1669, chaplain to archbishop Sheldon.

Page 302
Dioc. Linc. D. Risborough

Monks Risborough continued

Jos. Gerard[1] MA R. 13 Jan. 1738. Resides constantly in the Parsonage Ho. except when he goes for a few Days to Steukley Co. Bucks of which he is Vicar.
James Gerrard[2] D.D. Rector 1783.
George Heath[3] D.D. Rector 1789.

Gerard[4], son to R. BA of Wadh. Coll. to be ordained, by ⟨BP Hume⟩[5] Deacon Tr. S. 1763 for Cur. Salary 30^f & Board.

[1] Joseph (1700–83), of Staffordshire, m. Oriel 1718, BA (Merton) 1722, MA 1728, V. Banbury, V. Stewkley, 1734, R. Monks Risborough, 1739–83, archbishop's chaplain, 1739.
[2] (1741–89), of Monks Risborough, m. Wadham 1757, BA 1761, MA 1765, B & DD 1777, warden, 1777–89, C. Monks Risborough, 1763, R. Monks Risborough, 1783–89.
[3] (1747–1822), of Exeter, m. Kings 1764, BA 1768, MA 1771, DD (Lambeth) 1791, fellow 1767–

76, assistant master Eton, 1775–91, headmaster, 1792–1801, R. Monks Risborough,1789–1801, R. Brasted, 1800–1805, V. Sturminster Marshall, V. Piddletown, Dorset, 1805, canon of Windsor, 1800–22, archbishop's chaplain, 1785.

[4] See n. 2.

[5] John Hume, bishop of Bristol, 1758, bishop of Oxford, 1758–65, bishop of Salisbury, 1765–82.

Page 303

Sutton & Buckingham Preb. with Horley & Hornton 110-3-6. This is an Entry in A Parochial Book made in Jan. 1715/6[1]. But on what Authority, is not there said. It was a Prebend in the Church of Lincoln. The same Entry is transcribed into ABP Herrings Book. It stands as a Peculiar in the Parochial Book of 1663 fol 65.

[1] i.e. Haynes' Book: LPL, VG 2/1. Survey by John Haynes, 1716.

Page 304

Dioc. Linc. D. Risborough
Wotton Underwood. See p. 400.

[Diocese of London]

Page 305

Dioc. London. D. Arches
All Hallows Bread Street. R. ⟨K^s B. 17–13–9⟩ with St John Watling Street ⟨R⟩. K^s B. 15-19-7. ABP DCh. Cant. P. Now 140$^£$. 172$^£$ ⟨Dr Hall⟩. See the Limits. 110 Ho. Chiefly eminent Tradesmen. 5 or 6 keep Coaches. Two Papists of common Rank. A few Presbyterians. Lessend. Too many Absenters, rather of the lower sort. Not increasing. Whole Service, 2 Sermons, on Sundays. Prayers on Holydays, W. Fr in Lent, when Ch^n & Servants are examined for Confirmation. Sacr. on 3 great Festivals & first Sunday in every Month. From 30 to 80 Com. ⅓ of Offertory money distributed by the Minister, ⅔ by the Ch W^{ns}: generally to the Poor after Church, esp. poor Communicants. A Charity School for Bread Street & Cordwainers Ward, for 50 Boys & 30 Girls, ⟨not lodged or fed, but⟩ cloathed, taught, put out. Lands, Houses & money, given to Church & Poor: some now under Question by the Rector. The Church is All-Hallows. Lease of Ground for 40 years conf.
⟨Entry B.⟩ III. 185. VIII. 21.
Lecturer admitted 1683 IV. 416 VI. 210, 398.
1766 only 1 family of 5 persons acknowledge themselves Papists.

Will Warnford[1] LLB. R. 18 July 1730. Pres. by DCh Cant. Lives in St Johns Clerkenwell: assisted occasionally by his Son. Hath no licenced Cur. But is not James Adams[2] Cur. Died March 29. 1760.
Charles Hall[3] DD. R. Apr. 23. 1760. Void by Cession Oct. 10. 1761. See p. 318.

John Lynch[4] MA R. Dec. 29. 1761 ⟨now D.D.⟩ pr. by DCh Cant. Officiates himself.
William Maurice[5] M.A. Septr. 20. 1771.

Richd Stainsby ⟨Jnr⟩ Cur. Gone. 1761 Wm Rider[6], Master of St Pauls School.
Edm. Warneford[7] Lecturer. Cur. of Cripplegate. R. of Firwicke Co. ⟨East⟩ Sussex 46^f, 30^f clear to him. This Lecture 8^f Rent charge on Houses, 30^f subscription. To be licenced.
Owen Perrott Edwardes[8] A.M. Lecturer, Licensed Decr. 30 1773.
Robert Watts[9] Thursday Evening Lecturer lic. 1794.

1759 Conf. 8. 1760. 11. 1761. 1762, 2.
1763. 3. 1764. 10. 1765. 1. 1766. 1.
1767 Conf. 99. Of this Parish, 16. 1768 none

[1] (1701–1760), of Somerset, m. New College 1718, BCL (St Mary Hall) 1725, R. All Hallows, 1730–60.
[2] He has not been traced.
[3] See p. 163, n. 3.
[4] See p. 1, n. 5.
[5] (1733–1819), of Westminster, m. Hertford 1750, BA 1754, MA 1757, DD (Lambeth??), lecturer united parishes St Swithin and St Mary Bothaw, 1762, Tuesday lecturer St Dunstan's in the East, R. All Hallows, 1771–1819, ?R. Wennington, Essex, royal chaplain.
[6] (1723–85), of London, m. St Mary Hall 1739, scholar Jesus 1744–9, BA 1743, master of St Paul's, C. All Hallows, 1761, lecturer St Vedast and St Michael Quern, 1768, chaplain to Mercer's company.
[7] (1723–), of Gloucestershire, m. Oriel 1739, BA (Corpus) 1744, MA 1745, lecturer All Hallows, 1767.
[8] Of Pembrokeshire, m. Trinity College Dublin 1748, BA 1752, MA 1755, incorporated at Cambridge, 1777.
[9] (1754–1842), of Middlesex, m. St John's C 1778: a ten year man, MA (Lambeth) 1797, assistant to librarian of Sion College, 1785–9, librarian, 1799, evening lecturer, All Hallows, 1794, V. St Helen's Bishopsgate, 1795, preb of St Paul's, 1797–42, R. St Alphage, 1799–1842, Sunday evening lecturer All Hallows, 1813.

Page 306
Dioc. Lond. D. Arches
All Hallows Lombard Street. R. DCh. Cant P. K^s books 22-6-8. Wake 110^f. Herring 200^f. Abt 100 Ho. One Family of Papists, of middle Rank. Sev^l Presb. Anab. & Quakers. Two of the last pay their legal Dues without Compulsion: the rest by Distress. Whole Service, 2 Sermons. Prayers W. Fr. & Holydays. R. expounds the Catechism to the Charity Ch^n of Langborn Ward, near, not in his Parish, & to others that will attend. Sacr. monthly & at 3 great Festivals. Between 40 & 50 Com. Gifts to Church & poor near 200^f a year. See the Accounts signed by ChW^{ns}. 1^f for a Sermon on good Friday. 3-2-8 from Mercers Company, not paid since 1744. No Ho. fit for R. to live in. Lease of a Shop for 31 yrs Conf. by ABP Entry Book 1. 20. Another for 40 yrs 1670 II. 20. Lease of the Parsonage Ho. for 40 yrs 1692 IV. 491. Lecturer Licenced 1695. 535.

1766 No Papists.

Tho. Broughton[1] R. also of Wotton in Surrey, 12–18–9 in K^s Books ⟨150$^£$⟩, where he resides the Summer Months, & in Hatton Garden the Winter.
William Barford[2] DD. Rector, March 7: 1778.
Edward Walsby[3] D.D Rector 1793.

Cur. some reputable Clergyman, Priest. Salary, after the Rate of 40 Guineas a year. 1765 Mr Reeve[4]. 1766. Mr Millar[5]. 1767 Mr Reid[6].

John Parfect[7], of Oriel, Lecturer. Cited to Vis. 1760 ⟨Not cited⟩. Absent. Wm. Jarvis Abdy[8] Lecturer Lic. 1781.

1759 Conf. 9 1760. 22. 1761, 15. 1762, 4. 1763. 6 1764. 18. 1765. 10. 1766. 2. 1767. 9 1768. 18

[1] (1712–77), of Oxford, m. University 1731, BA (Exeter) 1737, fellow, 1734–41, MA (Pembroke C) 1749, R. Wotton, Surrey, 1752–77, lecturer All Hallows, 1753, R. All Hallows, 1755–77.
[2] See p. ii, n. 32.
[3] (1751–1815), of Norwich, m. CCCC 1769, scholar, BA 1773, MA 1776, fellow, 1774, proctor 1779, DD (Trinity) 1790, V. Sawston and Whittlesford, Cambs, 1777–8, R. Lambourn, Essex, 1780–90, returned to Cambridge as preceptor to Prince William Frederick, 1790, R. All Hallows, 1793–1801, V. Milton by Sittingbourne, Kent, 1801–4, R. St Dionis Backchurch, 1804–15, preb of Canterbury, 1793–1815.
[4] Perhaps William Reeve (1736–?), of Harlexton, Norfolk, m. Emmanuel 1753, scholar, BA 1758, MA 1761, PC. Raydon, Suffolk, 1758, V. Dersingham, Norfolk, 1769–75.
[5] Thomas Miller (1737–92), of London, m. Clare 1756, BA 1760, MA 1763, R. Wormshill, Kent, 1767–92.
[6] Perhaps William Reid, of London, m. Queen's O 1747, BA 1751, MA 1754.
[7] (1725–), of Stroud, Kent, m. Oriel 1742, BA 1745, MA 1748, DD 1764, lecturer All Hallows, 1753.
[8] Lecturer All Hallows, 1781, lecturer St Mary le Bow, London, 1800.

Page 307
St Dionis Backchurch, Limestreet R. DCh. Cant P. K^s books 25$^£$, Wake 120$^£$ Herring 250$^£$ ⟨So Disp. 1756. 275 Dr Curteis 1763⟩. See the Limits. 130 Ho. Sir James Creed[1] K^t Repr. for Canterbury. Sir Jospeh Hankey[2] K^t & Alderman, Sir Tho. Hankey[3] K^t. 2 Papists, Victuallers: & a reputed Papist, Clerk to Sir Jos. Hankey[4]. 11 Presb. 4 Indep. Families, Mercht^s & Shopkeepers. 20 Anabaptists. 9 Quakers. Increased. It is near their grand Meeting Ho. in White Hart Court Lombard Street. Only one refuses to pay his legal Dues: and they are recoverd by applying to the Ld Mayor. Abt 30 Absenters. Not increased. Some are understood to go to Church in the country. Some plead, that on Sundays only they can ride for their Healths. Whole Service, 2 Sermons on Sundays. Prayers twice a Day. Cat. once a week in Lent. Only 2 Ch^n sent last Lent. Sacr. on 3 great Festivals & Ist Sunday of every Month. 25 Com each time on an Average. A Charity School in the Ward for 50 Boys, clothed, taught, put out. Lands & Houses worth above 120$^£$ a year belong to the Parish, besides smaller Gifts. All applied to their proper Uses. No. Ho. fit to receive R^s Family.
Lease of Shops, Rent 21$^£$, for 40 yrs conf. Entry B III V. 340. VIII. 395. 1766 Two families of Papists & 3 lodgers & 4 servts.

Tho. Curteis[5] MA [now D.D] R. 22 Dec. 1756. R. & V. of Sevenoake p. 374 ⟨375⟩ & Preb. of Cant. Resides chiefly at the two last.

D[r]. Tatton[6] DD R. Sep[r]. 8th 1775.
John Lynch[7] L.L.D. 1782.

Durand Rhudde[8] Cur. Pr. 50[£] a year ⟨& extra Fees⟩ & Lect. {to be} lic. R. of S[t] Thomas, Southwark
Sam. Freeman[9] ⟨civilian⟩ of Tr. Hall, Cur. Feb. 1764. { } Same salary.
Thomas Miller[10] C. Apr. 1767. Lic. ord. Pr by BP Osbaldiston[11] in 1762.

Dixon[12] DD. of Queens Coll. Oxon Lecturer. Gone ⟨see above⟩.
John Moir[13] Lecturer Lic. 1785.

1759 Conf. 14. 1760. 4. 1761. 5. 1762. 7. 1763. 10. 1764. 1. 1765. 1. M[r] Freeman preached on Conf. See his Letter. 1766 none. 1767. 8. 1768. 9

[1] (c. 1695–1762), MP for Canterbury, 1754–61.
[2] Haberdasher, knighted in 1737. He died in 1769.
[3] Banker, commissioner of the lieutenancy for the city of London. Knighted in 1745.
[4] See n. 2.   [5] See p. ii, n. 17.   [6] Ibid., n. 16.
[7] See p. 1, n. 4.   [8] See p. 196, n. 6.
[9] m. Trinity Hall C 1754, scholar 1756, C. St Dionis Backchurch, 1764.
[10] See p. 306, n. 5.
[11] Richard Osbaldeston (1690–1764), bishop of Carlisle, 1747–62, bishop of London, 1762–64.
[12] (1710–87), of Cumberland, m. Queen's O 1729, BA 1734, MA 1737, BD 1757, DD 1758, principal St Edmund Hall, 1760–87, lecturer St Dionis Backchurch, 1755, V. Chedworth, Glos, 1759, V. Bramley, Hants, 1759.
[13] 'literate', C. St Dionis Backchurch, 1784, lecturer St Dionis Backchurch, 1785.

Page 308
Dioc Lond. D. Arches
St. Dunstans in the East. R. ABP P. K[s] books 60–7–11. Wake, Herring, 200[£]. See the Limits. 270 Ho. 2 publick Halls & the Trinity House. A few Families of Dissenters. 3 of Quakers: 2 do not refuse their Dues. From the 3[d] they are got by a Lord Mayors Warrant. Whole Service, 2 Sermons, on Sundays. Prayers W. Fr. & Holydays in the Morning. Offers made to cat. in Lent, but none come. Sacr 1st Sunday in the Month: ab[t] 60 Com. & on the 3 great Festivals many more. Offertory money, (after a small Allowance to the Clerk & Sexton) divided, by old Custom, betw. R and Sen[r] ChW[n] to distribute. R. distributes his Share openly, at the Vestry, thrice a Year. A work Ho. Well managed. Sir John Moore[1], 50 or 60 Years ago, endowed with 10[£] a year a Reading & Grammar School for 12 boys: the Master, whom R. nominates, to be paid for as many more as he can get. The Parish gives him a School Room. A Charity School, belonging to Tower Ward for teaching, clothing & putting out 60 Boys & 60 Girls: the Girls only to Service. In abt 50 Years, 1393 have been put out. 700[£] for it in the Orphans Fund at 4 per Cent. See printed Rules. No Parsonage Ho. Lease for 40 yrs conf 1671 Entry B. III. 144. Another 1716 VI 221 See IX. 307. Lecturer for 1 yr chosen & lic. VI. 238.
1766 no Papists.
John Jortin[2] MA [now DD] R. 7 May 1751. Lives in Town.
Thomas Winstanley[3] M.A. R. Jan[ry] 28. 1771.
Martin Benson[4] A.M. 1789.
John Lloyd[5]. LLB. 1791.

Spark Canham[6], Pr. Cur. 40^f, part of Surpl. Fees &c lives near to the Parish & is very punctual. Gone into the Country 1763.

Vicesimus Knock[7] Cur. See p. 313 Salary 40^f & Fees of Baptisms.

Edward Davis[8]- Curate.

Thomas Waters[9] A.M. Cur. Sal £50. lic. 1791

James Townley[10], Sunday Lecturer 〈lic〉 24 Jan 1738. R. of St Leonard East-Cheap p. 309.

Will. Berriman[11] T{hur}〈ue〉sday Afternoon Lecturer. It is for 9 Months in the Year, & in the Gift of the Mercers Company.

Wm Morice[12] -Tuesday Lecturer 1759

Conf. 18. 1760. 24. 1761, 3. 1762. 28. 1763, 11. 1764. 11. 1765. Conf. here 66 Of this Parish 28. 1766. 8. 1767. 11. 1768. 12

[1] (1620-1702). Lord mayor of London, 1681. MP for London, 1685.

[2] (1693-1770), of London, m. Jesus C 1715, scholar, BA 1719, MA 1722, DD (Lambeth) 1755, V. Swavesey, Cambs, 1727-31, reader at New Street Chapel, Bloomsbury, 1731, R. Eastwell, Kent, 1737-42, R. St Dunstan's in the East, 1751-70, V. Kensington, 1762÷70, preb of St Paul's, 1762-70, archdeacon of London, 1764-70.

[3] (1716-89), of Wigan, Lancashire, m. Brasenose 1734, BA 1737, MA (Trinity C) 1766, R. St Dunstan's in the East, 1771-89, preb of Peterborough, 1781-89.

[4] See p. 134, n. 2.   [5] See p. 189, n. 5.   [6] C. St Dunstan's, 1754-63.

[7] [Knox] (1739-79), of All Hallows, London, m. St John's O 1745, BCL 1753, C. St Dunstan's in the East, 1763, lecturer St Michael's Crooked Lane, assistant to Merchant Taylors' School, headmaster Tunbridge School, 1772-8.

[8] Perhaps (1747-?), of Ruthen, co. Denbigh, m. Christ Church 1767, BA 1771.

[9] (1760-1831), of Chelsea, Middlesex, m. Magdalen Hall 1783, BA 1787, MA 1790, B & DD 1808, C. St Dunstan's in East, 1791, master of Emmanuel Hosp. Westminster at his death.

[10] (1714-78), of London, m. St John's O 1732, BA 1735, MA 1738, Sunday lecturer St Dunstan's in the East, 1739, R. St Benet's, Gracechurch and St Leonard's, Eastcheap, 1749-60. Perhaps also V. Hendon, 1775-78, master Merchant Taylors' School, 1760s.

[11] (1750-1814), of Beverley, Yorks, m. St John's C 1768, scholar 1768, BA 1773, C. Messingham with Butterwick, Lincs, 1773, R. South Ferriby, 1776-83, R. Saxby, 1776-83, chaplain to the earl of Harrington.

[12] See p. 305, n. 5.

Page 309

St Leonards Eastcheap R. 〈K^s books, 25-10-0〉 united with St Benets Grace-Church 〈R. K^s books 18-1-3〉. This last not a peculiar. DCh. Cant & DCh St Pauls, Patrons alternately. Both together 140^f, Wake, Herring. 50 Ho. 4 or 5 Quakers, some pay their Dues without Compulsion, others not. The only Church is that of St Bennet, 3^f a year given to the minister, equally divided betw. R. & Lecturer. These Answers must relate only to St Leonards. It is said, that there are no week-day Prayers. The Rector of St Michaels Crooked Lane saith, that the R. of St Leonards & St Bennets told the BP of London it was for want of a Congregation, & he acquiesced. R. saith, there are Prayers on Festivals, & he tried on W. Fr. in vain. See a Letter of Complaint, July 1760. R. will try again. The omission before his time. Lease of parsonage Ho. of St L. for 40 yrs at 5^f Conf 1671 Entry B. III. 70.

James Townley[1] Lecturer of St Dunstans in the East p. 308. Lives in Christs

Hospital Newgate Street. Now Aug 1760 Master of Mercht Taylors School.
Heneage Asley[2] Rector.
Robert Wyatt[3] 1789.
George Gaskin[4] D.D. 1791.

Arch. Brakenridge[5] to be Cur. 40^f. Aug. 1760, 1765 vis 30^f. Dead. No C. in his stead Dec 1766.
Thomas Miller[6] MA C. 50^f May 1767 P.
Joshua Winter[7] Cur.

Tho. Green[8], M.A. Lecturer, lic. by BP of London.
Erasmus Middleton[9] Clerk Lecturer, Licensed Jan 27: 1775.

1759 None Conf. 1760. 1. 1761, 12. 1762, None. 1763, 3. 1764, 4. 1765. 11. 1766. 1. 1767. 10. 1768. 1

[1] See p. 308, n. 10.
[2] R. St Leonard's, Eastcheap, 1760–89.   [3] R. St Leonard's, Eastcheap, 1789–91.
[4] (1752–1829), of Islington, Middlesex, m. Trinity O 1771, BA 1775, MA 1778, B & DD 1788, C. Hayes, Middlesex, 1774, C. St Vedast Foster Lane, 1774, lecturer Islington, 1776, C. Stoke Newington, 1778–97, R. Sutton and Mepal, Isle of Ely, till 1791, R. S Benet's Gracechurch w St Leonard's Eastcheap, 1791, R. Stoke Newington, 1797, preb of Ely, 1823, secretary to SPCK, 1786–1823.
[5] (1736–), of Westminster, m. St John's O 1754, BCL 1761, C. St Leonard's Eastcheap, 1760–65.
[6] See p. 306, n. 5.
[7] (1745–1816), of Bishops Stortford, Herts, m. St John's C 1762, BA 1766, MA 1770, BD 1775, R. Codford St Mary, Wilts, 1790–1816.
[8] (1731–1783), of Kent, m. Peterhouse, 1749, scholar 1749, BA 1753, MA 1756, assistant master of Merchant Taylors' School, 1753, headmaster, 1778–83, lecturer St Leonard's, Eastcheap, chaplain St Thomas' Hospital, Southwark.
[9] (1739–1805), of Lincolnshire, m. St Edmund Hall 1767, 'one of six young men expelled for being a methodist' in 1768, lecturer St Leonard's, Eastcheap, 1775, R. Turvey, Beds., 1804–5, editor of *Biographica Evangelica* (1779–86).

Page 310
Dioc. Lond. D. Arches
St Mary Aldermary R. K^s books 41^f, united with St Tho. Apostle, R. K^s books 12^f. Not a Peculiar. ABP & DCh. St Pauls. Patrons alternately. Wake, Herring 240^f together. Tithes 150^f. Ground Rent 26-13-4 & 10^s. Houses 22^f, 16^f, 16^f. A Gift Sermon 1^f. Surplice Fees 8 or 10^f ⟨Dr Taylor saith 170^f clear⟩. 89 Ho. A Grocer, Papist: 12 Presb. One Indep. One Anab. One Moravian, 3 Quakers. They pay their dues without Compulsion. Too many Absenters. Whole Service, 2 Sermons on Sundays ⟨Morn. Prayers on W. Fr. & Holydays⟩. No Cat. ever. Sacr on 1st Sunday of every Month, abt 30 Com. & on the 3 great Festivals, many more. Poor Ch^n are sent to the Charity School of Breadstreet & Cordwainers Ward, & there lodged, fed &c [not lodged or fed, p. 305]. Land of 40^f a year at Bromley in Kent, & Houses of 62^f a year in the Parish, given to the Church & Poor. So applied. The above Gift Sermon is by the Cooks Company, with 20^s to Cur. Clerk, Sexton, & 1^f to the Poor. Lease of a Tenem^t for 40 yrs Conf by ABP Entry B. I. 67. See VII. 349.
1766 1 family of Papists in one of the parishes.

John Taylor[1] MA [now DD] R 11 May 1747. Pres. by the King, on the promotion of Dr Lavington[2], pres by DCh St Pauls. Lives in Pickadilly & serves it 10 months in 12. AD^n of { }.
George Wollaston[3] Collated R March 28 1774. & again 1790.
John Hyde[4] A.M. Collated Rector 1790.

John Brown[5] Cur. 35$^£$ Had but 30$^£$ from Dr Lav. Lives in the Old Jewry. Pr. Serves no other Cure.
John Frith[6] Cur. Sal. £40. Lic 1785.

Henry Foulkes[7] Lecturer ⟨Lic. 29 March 1753⟩. Cited to Vis. 1760. Absent. Watts Wilkinson[8]. Lect^r. 1780.

1759 Conf. ⟨100, of this Parish⟩ 26. 1760. 12. 1761, 4. 1762, 7. 1763, 1. 1764, 5. 1765 None. 1766 None. 1767. 3. 1768. 12

[1] (1712–74), of Kidlington, Oxon m. Christ Church 1730, MA 1743, B & DD 1752, R. St Mary Aldermary, 1747–74, archdeacon of Bedford, 1745–56, archdeacon of Leicester, 1756–72, preb of Lincoln, 1750, preb of Salisbury, 1762–74.
[2] See p. 55, n. 9.
[3] (1739–1826), of London, m. Sidney Sussex 1754, BA 1758, MA 1761, fellow, 1758, DD (Queens') 1774, R. Dengie, Essex, 1762–?74, R. Stratford, Suffolk, 1763–74, R. St Mary Aldermary, 1774–90, FRHS 1763.
[4] (1740–1805), of Yorkshire, m. Christ's 1757, scholar 1757, BA 1761, MA 176, C. East Dereham, Norfolk, R. Stoke Talmage, Oxon, 1785–1805, V. Sunbury, Middlesex, 1785–1805, R. St Mary Aldermary, 1790–1805, chaplain to George, prince of Wales.
[5] Perhaps (1732–?), of London, m. St John's O 1750.
[6] Perhaps (1723–?), of Thurlow, Suffolk, m. Trinity C 1740, scholar 1743.
[7] Perhaps (1718–79), of Berrw, co. Montgomery, m. Jesus O 1738. He died having been the curate of St Margaret Pattens, London.
[8] (1760–1840), of London, m. Worcester 1776, BA 1780, afternoon lecturer St Mary Aldermary, 1780–1840, and Tuesday lecturer St Bartholomew-by-the-Exchange.

Page 311
St Mary Bothaw R. K^s books 10–10–0 with St Swithin R. K^s books 15–17–11. Not a Peculiar. DCh Cant. & Salters Company Patrons alternately. Wake, Herring 140$^£$. 40 Ho. The Church is St Swithins. ⟨No Dissenters, but⟩ A Barber, Moravian ⟨See below⟩. Whole Service, 2 Sermons, on Sundays. Prayers every Day. Cat. exp. every Week in Lent. Few Ch^n come. Sacr every Month 40 or 50 Com. each time. Sev^l Foreigners, who go to Fr. & Dutch churches: sev^l Ho. inhabited by Dissenters. Mr Wells March 31. 1761. But see his Account above.
Lease {conf} entred, not sd to be conf. 1674 Entry B III 242 &c Conf p. 246. The Salters Company have sold their Turn, to wch I believe the BP of London institutes.
1766 No Papists in St Mary Bothaw.

Will. Ayerst[1] DD R. Preb. of Cant. where he resides being old & infirm. R. of North-Cray & Rokesley Dioc. Roch. died May 9 1765.
Beachcroft[2] R. May 1765 pres, I believe by his Father. Speaks not loud enough to be heard Dec. 1766.
Richd Palmer[3] D.D. 1776. Inst: by BP London.

Tho. Wells[4] Cur. Pr. 40^f. Resides in St Swithins. Serves no other Cure. In the Country for his Health at Vis. 1760. Bad Health 1766.

Joseph Fox[5], MA. Lecturer. Lic. 27 Sept 1753.
Wm Morice[6] Licensed Feb. 1. 1762. Crown Co. Breadstr.
Mr Layton[7] Lecturer.

1759 None. Conf. ⟨but some at St Pauls⟩ 1760. 1. 1761, 2. 1762, 5. 1763, 3. 1764, 6. 1765, 2. 1766, 1. 1767, 12. 1768 none.

[1] See p. ii, n. 8.
[2] Robert Beachcroft (1708–?), son of Samuel of All Hallows Barking, m. Balliol 1724, BA 1728, MA 1733.
[3] See p. ii, n. 30.
[4] (1714–85), of Cutton, Northants, m. Clare 1735, BA (Sidney Sussex) 1738, V. Warden, Beds, 1739, clerk St Swithin's, London.
[5] Perhaps of Totnes, Devon, m. Exeter 1712, BA (Trinity) 1715, MA 1722, V. Berry Pomeroy, Devon, 1723.
[6] See p. 305, n. 5.
[7] Either Nicholas Layton (1747–?), of Fenchurch Street, London, m. Balliol 1765, BA 1768, MA 1772, or Thomas Layton (1765–1833), of London, m. Trinity C 1783, BA 1788, MA 1791, R. East Hatley, Cambs, 1798–9, V. Chigwell, Essex, and V. Theydon Bois, 1803–33.

Page 312
St Mary le Bow K^s books 33–12–3½ with
St Pancras Soper Lane K^s books 13–6–3 &
All Hallows Honey Lane K^s books 9–3–9. Not a peculiar.
ABP. twice, Grocers Comp. once. Wake, Herring, 200^f. In all 3,160 Ho. 20 Families of Presb. 3 of Quakers. They pay without Compulsion the Money charged by Act of Parl. on Houses. Two Sermons on Sundays & many occasional ones. Prayers twice every Day. Ch^n & Servts cat. every year before the Conf. Sacr. on All Saints Days & Holy days & Ist Sunday of every Month. Monthly Com. a^{bt} 70. On great Festivals abt 100. ChW^{n}s account for the Offertory money. Poor Ch^n go to the same ward School with those, p. 305, 310. Several Donations for Sermons & for poor, which see. R. hath two Houses, but none fit to reside in. A Lease by R. of some Ground in Ch. y^d conf. 1665 Entry B. 1. 128. Again for 56 yrs from 1 May 1670 III. 37. Lease of site of late parsonage Ho. of Soper Lane for 40 yrs conf. p. 58. A Lease conf. p. 283.
Dr Benj. Calamy[1] admitted preacher 5 Sept. 1684. IV. 42b
Dr Tho. Hutchinson[2] preacher or Lecturer 9 Jan 1684 433. Sam Bradford[3] MA coll 21 Nov. 1693. 495. Sam Lisle[4] pres by the Crown on Bradfords promotion inst 8 July 1721. Tho. Newton[5] by Crown on Lisles promotion Inst 14 Apr. 1744.
1766 No Papist in Bow, 1 in Pancras.
Tho. Newton MA [now DD] R 14 Apr. 1744. Pres by the King on Dr Lisles promotion. Absent 3 or 4 months in Summer BP of Bristol.
Wm Sclater[6] D.D. R. 26 June 1771. presented by Grocers Comp.
East Apthorp[7]. D.D. Rector Mar 7: 1778. Collated by the Archbishop.
Griffith Griffith[8] A.M. Rector 1792 D°.
Brook Heckstall[9] LLB, Pr. Cur. 50^f at least. Having some Fortune of his own, serves no other Cure.

Downes[10], Lecturer. {Hath a Ch} R. of S[t] Michael in Woodstreet. Good. Died. Nov. 23. 1759.

Brook Heckstall. See above. Doth he continue Cur. Yes. Signed the Fiat for his Licence as Lecturer, Dec. 12. 1760.

M[r] Salt[11]. Curate & Lecturer.

1759 Conf 4. 1760. 28. Conf. in all here, 120. 1761. 6 1762. Conf. here 90. Of this parish, 14, 1763, 2. 1764. Conf. here 111, of this Parish 24. 1765. 2. 1766. Conf. here 44. Of this Parish 18. 1767. 6. 1768 Conf. here 102. Of this Parish 20.

[1] (1642-86), of London, m. Sidney Sussex 1661, migrated to St Catherine's 1664, BA 1665, MA 1668, DD 1680, fellow till 1681, V. St Mary Aldermary, 1677-84, V. St Lawrence Jewry, 1683, preacher St Mary le Bow, 1684, preb of St Paul's, 1685.

[2] Perhaps (1658-?), of Durham, m. Peterhouse 1676, scholar, BA 1679, BA 1680, MA (St John's) 1683, lecturer St Mary le Bow, 1685.

[3] (1652-1731), of London, m. CCCC 1672, MA 1680, DD 1705, master 1716-24, minister of St Thomas', Southwark, 1691, R. St Mary le Bow, 1693-1720, lecturer All Hallows, Bread Street, -1716, preb of Westminster, 1708-23, bishop of Carlisle, 1718-23, dean of Westminster, 1723-31, bishop of Rochester, 1723-31, royal chaplain.

[4] See p. 27, n. 3.

[5] (1704-1782), of Lichfield, Staffordshire, m. Trinity C 1723, scholar 1724, BA 1727, MA 1730, DD 1745, fellow 1729, incorp Oxford 1733, R. St Mary le Bow, 1744-69, lecturer St George's Hanover Square, 1747, preb of Westminster, 1757-61, precentor of York, 1759-61, president of Sion College, 1760 preb of St Paul's, 1761-82, bishop of Bristol, 1761-82, dean of St Paul's, 1768-82, royal chaplain, 1755-61, Boyle lecturer, 1754.

[6] (1710-78), of Loughton, Essex, m. CCCO 1727, BA (Trinity) 1731, MA (New College) 1734, B & DD, 1769, R. Loughton, Essex, ?-78, R. St Mary Le Bow, 1771-78.

[7] (17?-1816), of Boston, America, m. Jesus C 1751, BA 1755, MA 1758, chancellor's medal 1755, fellow, 1758-61, DD (Lambeth) 1778, SPG missionary at Cambridge, New England, 1759-64, V. Croydon, 1765-93, R. St Mary le Bow, 1778-92, lecturer St Michael Royal, 1784, preb of St Paul's, 1792-1816, chancellor of St Paul's, 1791-2.

[8] See p. 283, n. 2.

[9] C. St Mary le Bow, 1758- , lecturer St Mary le Bow, 1760.

[10] Lecturer St Mary le Bow, 1744-59, R. St Michael in Wood Street.

[11] Perhaps Thomas Salt, (1721-1806), of Cambridgeshire, m. St John's C 1740, BA 1743, MA 1746, C. and lecturer St Mary Le Bow, V. Nazeing, Essex, 1761-1806, R. Hildersham, 1797-1806, archbishop's chaplain, 1797.

Page 313

S[t] Michaels Crooked Lane R. ABP P. K[s] books 26-8-4. Wake 100[£] Herring 160[£]. 118 Ho. Several turned into Warehouses. Number of Dissenters unknown. They decrease. But the Methodists increase: & their Teachers ⟨Whitfield[1] & Ch. Wesley[2]⟩ baptize Ch[n] & visit the Sick, without the Rectors Leave. 3 Families of Quakers. Pay their Dues without much Trouble. Very many Absenters, & increasing. Two Sermons on Sundays. Lecturer reads Prayers in the Afternoon. On W. Fr. & Holydays, Prayers, if 2 or 3 meet to make a Congregation, which rarely happens. No Ch[n] or Serv[ts] sent to be cat. There is now no such Custom in London. Charity Schools supply the Defect. Sacr. 1st Sunday of every Month. Com. abt 20. [Not said how many of the great Festivals.]. A preparation Sermon {every} ⟨on the⟩ Friday before. A religious Society meets here: have Prayers every Week-day Evening at 8, & an early Sacr. every Sunday morning, except the 1st in the Month. Encouraged by R. No Methodists amongst them. Money

left for Bread to the poor. Not given in Bread. See papers & the ABP[s] Direction abt it[3]. R. saith, at Vis. in 1760, that the poor will not take the Bread.
Lease of site of parsonage Ho. 1681 for 40 yrs Entry B I. 183 &c. Arbitration given by ABP concerning part of the premises VII. 287. comp. 157.
1766 3 papists, lodgers, of low Degree. Frequent changes of Lodgers.

Tho. Kemp[4] DD R. 1 Dec. 1747. Resided in Parsonage Ho for 7 or 8 years: the last at Camberwell, not 3 miles off, & keeps no Curate. Pleads, that he is chaplain to his wife, Lady Bamff. See Letters[5]. Also, that his Health is declining.
Walter Earle[6] M.A. R. Aug[st] 10. 1769.
Theophilus Lane[7] MA. R.
Sam. Ward[8], Cur. Feb. 1766. D. 40[£] Gone Dec. Required May 1767 another to be got.
Weeden Butler[9] A.B. Cur. Sal. £40 lic. 1796.

Vicesimus Knock[10] Lecturer. Assistant to Merch[t] Taylors School: Doth occ. Duty sometimes. Jan. 1763 Gone a yr & half ago.
Richd Dodd[11], chosen 5 Aug. 1761. Ord. pr. by BP Keene[12] 6 Dec. 1762. Lic. March 1 1763. Resigned.
Peter James[13], chosen June 29 1763. Licensed Oct. 14. 1763.
Tilney[14] elected, R. will not sign Certificate 1765. He doth not officiate. Appointed 1766.
John Dyer[15] Lecturer Lic. 1771.
M[r] Harrison[16] Thursday Lecturer.

1759 None Conf. 1760. 3. 1761. 11. Conf. here in all 103. 1762, 4. 1763, 1. 1764. 7. 1765. 1. 1766. 3. 1767. 6. 1768. 8.

Turn over

---

[1] See p. 218, n. 7.

[2] Charles Wesley (1707–88), Methodist and hymn writer.

[3] LPL, MS Secker 6, f. 253, Secker to churchwardens, 1 February 1759.

[4] (1701–69), of London, m. St John's O 1719, BA 1723, MA 1727, BD 1732, DD 1736, R. West Cheam, Surrey, 1738–47, R. St Michael Crooked Lane, 1747–69.

[5] LPL, MS Secker 6, ff. 255–8, Kemp to Secker, 8 December 1759.

[6] (1726–72), of Malmesbury, Wiltshire, m. Oriel 1741, BA 1745, MA 1748, V. Hendon, R. St Michael Crooked Lane, 1769–72.

[7] (1741–1816), of Fanhope, Herefordshire, m. Brasenose 1756, BA 1759, MA 1763, R. St Michael Crooked Lane, 1772–1816.

[8] (17?–90), adm, as '10 year man' Trinity C, 1773, C. St Michael Crooked Lane, 1766–7, R. Cotterstock and Glapthorn, Northants, 1773–90.

[9] (17?–1831), of Chelsea, Middlesex, m. Sidney Sussex 1790, BA 1794, MA 1797, C. St Michael Crooked Lane, 1796, evening lecturer Brompton, 1811, minister of Charlotte Street chapel, Pimlico, 1814, R. Great Woolston, Bucks, 1816–31.

[10] See p. 308, n. 7.

[11] Richard Dodd (1738–?), of Bourne, Lincs, m. Lincoln, BA 1760, lecturer St Michael Crooked Lane, 1761–63.

[12] Edmund Keene (1714–81), bishop of Chester, 1752–71, bishop of Ely, 1771–81.

[13] (1738–91), m. Peterhouse 1756, scholar 1755, chapel clerk 1756, BA 1759, MA 1766, R. Ightham, Kent, 1781–91.

[14] Lecturer St Michael Crooked Lane, 1766.

[15] Lecturer St Michael Crooked Lane, 1771.

[16] Richard Harrison (1763–1824), of St Giles, Middlesex, m. Queen's O 1782, BA 1786, minister of Brompton chapel and joint lecturer at St Martin's-in-the-Fields, 1793–1824, joint lecturer of St Botolph, Bishopsgate.

Page 314
Dioc. Lond. D. Arches
S[t] Michaels Crooked Lane continued

Mr Shackleford[1], Cur. & Lecturer of S[t] Peters Cornhill, is minister of the religious Society, lives but a little way from this Parish, & assists R. in Burials & all sudden Cases: for which he hath an allowance from R. Also the Lecturer is ready to assist. And he hath immediate notice for the Clerk, when he is wanted. In summer only one Family came to week-Day Prayers, & desired him to leave off. This winter he hath begun again & will try.

[1] Richard Dickson Shackleford (1744–1829), of London, m. St John's O 1761, scholar 1761–4, fellow 1764, BA 1765, MA 1769, BD 1774, DD 1785, proctor 1773, FRSA 1792, C. St Peter's Cornhill, lecturer St Michael Queenhithe, Perhaps 3rd and 2nd undermaster Merchant Taylors' School, 1778, V. St Sepulchre, Snow Hill, 1784–1829.

Page 315
S[t] Michael Royal or Riol R ⟨al. College Hill⟩. K[s] books 7[£] with S[t] Martins Vintry R. K[s] books 18–13–4. Not a peculiar. DCh Cant. & BP of Worcester alternate P. Wake, Herring, 140[£]. 58 Ho. Warehouses &c. 3 Presb. Families. 2 Sermons on Sundays. Prayers 10. Sat. Saints Days & Holydays in the morning, & on Fr. afternoons, with a Sermon. For this Sermon the Clothworkers Company pay 10[£] a year, & the Mercers Company paid 13–6–8 till their Bankrupcy. Sacr. on 1st Sunday of each Month, & 3 great Festivals. Abt 40 Com. Whittingtons Coll. under the Direction of the Mercers Company. An Estate in Essex of 15[£] a Year, of which the Minister hath ⅓. Some other Benefactions, in which he is not concerned. This Acct relates only to the first of the united Parishes. The Church is S[t] Michaels. No Glebe or Ho. for the R. The Friday Lecture was revived by the commissioners for charitable Uses, & the Master of Whittington Coll, the R of All-hallows Honey Lane, R. of S[t] Stephen Wallbrook, & R. of S[t] Peters Cornhill appointed to nominate a Lecturer to the ABP 1702. Entry B. V. 42 ⟨See VII, 9 & 173. VIII, 303, 350⟩. Sunday Lect. lic. 23 Aug 1721 VI 377. See VII. 115.
1766 No Papists

John Young[1] BA R. 5 March 1753. Resided till called away by the Illness of his Father, D[r]. Arthur Young[2], now dead. Resides, 1760, near the Temple. Hath no Cur. In Berkeley Square.
John Fenton[3] Clerk, Rector Nov[r]: 27: 1775, on the Presentation of the Lord Bp of Worcester[4] p. h.v.
John Benson[5] D.D Rector 1780.
Geo. Fred[k]. Louisa Nicolay[6] A.M. R. 1790.
Lewis Steward[7] Pr. Cur. Lives near. 36–8–0. R. will augment it, if desired. Dead.
Cokayne[8] W[m]. Cur. See below, & Letters. Salary 37–16–0. Why?

Richard Dickson Shackleford[9] BA ⟨& F⟩ of St Johns Oxon. D. 40$^£$. Lect. of St Mich. Queen Hythe 25$^£$. ⟨June 1767, to be P. in Dec. Done⟩. Martin Benson[10] Cur. Sal £50.

Sunday Lecturer, D^r ⟨W^m⟩ Cokayne, Prof. Astr. Gresh. Coll. F. of St Johns, Oxon. *** Abs. Vis. 1760 because engaged to preach elsewhere. Chosen Lecturer in 1753. Not licenced. Chosen Lect. of St Geo. Martyr, Southw. June 1761.
Mr Day[11], late of Shoreditch
Friday Lecturer ⟨see above⟩ Mr ⟨Tho⟩ Franc{klyn}⟨klin⟩[12], F. of Trin. Coll. Camb. &c. Not cited to vis. 1761.
Thomas Walker[13]. Friday Lecturer.

Sunday Lecturer, after Mr Day { } Smith[14], {who never applied to me} lic 1762. John LLoyd[15], of Jes. Oxf. Chosen 29 June 1765 lic. Febr.

1759 None conf. 5. 1760. In 1761, none. 1762.10. 1763. 1. 1764. 3. 1765 None. 1766. 8. 1767. 2. 1768 None

[1] (?-1786), m. King's 1747, BA 1751, MA 1754, DD 1777, fellow 1750, fellow of Eton 1776, R. St Michael Royal, 1753-75, preb of Worcester, 1768-86.
[2] See p. ii, n. 15.
[3] (1747-1780), of Newcastle, Staffordshire, m. Hertford 1764, R. St Michael Royal, 1775-1780.
[4] Brownlow North. See p. ii, n. 4.   [5] Ibid., n. 29.
[6] (1764-1847), m. Christ Church 1781, BA 1784, student 1787, R. St Michael Royal, 1790, V. Little Marlow, Bucks, 1821-.
[7] He has not been traced.
[8] (1718-98), of Doveridge, co. Derbs, m. St John's O 1736, BA 1740, MA 1744, BD 1751, DD 1754, proctor 1750, Gresham professor of astronomy, 1752-95, lecturer St Michael Crooked Lane 1753, lecturer St George the Martyr, Southwark, 1761, R. Kilkhampton, 1763-98.
[9] See p. 314, n. 1.   [10] See p. 134, n. 2.
[11] Probably Edmund Day (1698-1762), of Kimbolton, Huntingdonshire, m. St John's O 1716, BA 1720, lecturer All Hallows Bread St, 1722-62.
[12] (1721-85), of London, m. Trinity C 1739, scholar 1740, BA 1743, MA 1746, DD 1770, fellow, 1745-58, regius professor of Greek, 1750-9, lecturer St Michael Royal, 1748, V. Ware and Thundridge, Herts, 1759-77, V. Brasted, 1777-84, preacher St Paul's Covent Garden.
[13] Perhaps, of Surrey, m. Queens' C 1760, lecturer St Michael Royal, 1784.
[14] Richard Smith, lecturer St Michael Royal, 1762. Perhaps R. Islington, 1768-72.
[15] Possibly (1742-1803), of Llanstephan, Carmarthenshire, m. Jesus O 1758, BA 1762, MA 1765, BD 1772, V. Holywell, Flints.

Page 316
Dioc. Lond. D. Arches.
St Vedast, Foster Lane R. K^s books 33-5-10 with St Michael Querne R. K^s books 21-10-5. Not a Peculiar. ABP & DCh. of St Pauls alternate P. Wake, Herring 160$^£$. Pens of 1-6-8 to DCh. See the Limits. Both Parishes have 180 Ho. A Servt maid converted from Popery. 7 or 8 Presb. Families: some often come to Church, all subscribe to the Morning Prayers & treat the minister with Respect. One Methodist Family: a sort of meeting in the House. One of Quakers, who pay their Tithes regularly. Some few Absenters on slight Pretences: one or two from Irreligion & Immorality. The Church is St Vedasts. 2 Sermons on Sundays. Morning Prayers W. Fr. Holydays: Evening Prayers at 6 every day, but Sunday, by Subscription. Cat. was exp. on Fr. Evenings in Lent: but none, though

admonished, have come for the last 2 or 3 years. Sacr. 1st Sunday of each Month, abt 50 Com. & on 3 great Festivals, abt 90. Minister distributes ⅓ of Offertory, & keeps an account: ChW[ns] ⅔. Sir John Johnson[1] K[t] in 1690 founded a School for teaching 12 Ch[n] writing & Accounts gratis. None have offerd lately. He also left a Legacy for apprenticing a Boy once in 2 Years. Poor Ch[n] have the Benefit of the Ward Charity School, which hath a Fund of near 1000[f] and in which 60 Boys & 40 Girls are taught, clothed & put out. Gifts of abt 20[f] a year for the poor: Bread, Coal, &c. 5 or 6 Tenemts belong to the Parish: Rent 70[f] including Taxes &c. Trustees of the School sometimes get Methodist, & antinomian Preachers. Cur. afraid to offend them: but hath signified by Disapprobation. Lecturer appointed 1702 Entry B. V. 77.

Nath. Marshall[2] pres. by DCh S[t] Pauls Apr. 19. 1716. Is. Maddox[3] 1729 on his Death by BP John Thomas[4] by K. on Maddoxes promotion 22 Nov. 1736. T. L. Barbauld[5] by K. on Thomas's promotion.

1766 One housekeeper a papist.

[1] Alderman and goldsmith. He was knighted in 1696.
[2] (16?-1730), of Middlesex, m. Emmanuel 1696, LLB 1702, DD 1717, V. St Pancras, London, 1706-16, R. Finchley, 1707-30, R. St Vedast's, Foster Lane, 1716-30, canon of Windsor, 1722-30, lecturer St Lawrence Jewry, lecturer at St Mary, Aldermary, 1714, royal chaplain, 1715-30.
[3] Isaac Maddox (1697-1759), of London, educated at Aberdeen, MA (Edinburgh) 1723, incorp. Queen's O 1724, BA 1724, MA Queens' C 1728, DD 1731, V. Whiteparish, Wiltshire, 1724, R. St Vedast's, 1730-36, preb of Chichester, 1725-44, dean of Wells, 1734, bishop of St Asaph, 1736-43, bishop of Worcester, 1743-59, chaplain to bishop of Chichester.
[4] See 237, n. 10.
[5] Theophilus Lewis Barbauld (1709-79), of London, m. Trinity C 1724, scholar 1725, BA 1728, MA 1731, R. St Vedast's, 1744-79.

Page 317
S[t] Vedast continued

Theoph. Lewis Barbauld[1] MA R. 13 Aug. 1744 Presented by the Crown on the Promotion of D[r] Thomas[2] to the See of Lincoln. Chaplain to the Princess of Hesse[3], resides at Cassel.
Francis Wollaston[4] LLB. Rector. April 13: 1779, presented by the Dean & Chapter of S[t] Pauls London. Patrons p. h.v.

Rich[d] Wynne[5] MA of All Souls Coll. Pr. Cur ⟨lic. 23 Sept. 1752⟩. Hath kept Ho. in the Parish the last 6 Years, & serves no where else. Salary 30[f]. Fees abt 20[f]. Subscr. for reading Prayers 15 or 20[f]. See below. Resigned the Curacy Mids. 1762.
John Prince[6] Curate.

Norman Mead[7], Lecturer ⟨lic. 25 May 1737⟩. Chapl. to the BP of Lincoln[8]. Lives in Albermarle Row. He hath resigned, March 1762.
Wynne Rich[d], see above. Chosen March 25: 1762, unanimously. Licenced Apr. 1762. Made R. of S[t] Alphage.
{Wm Rider[9] Cur March 1766 Head Master of St Pauls School.}.
Fra. Cherondell[10]. In his Absence R officiates.
John Hewlett[11] Lect Lic. 1786.

1759 Conf. 21. 1760. 9. 1761. 9. 1762, 5. 1763 Conf here 111, of this Parish 60. 1764. 8. 1765. 4. 1766. 2. 1767. 9. 1768. 11.

1 See p. 316, n. 5.   2. Ibid., n. 4.
3 Mary (1723-72), princess of Hesse, 4th daughter of George II. In 1740 she married Frederic, landgrave of Hesse-Cassel.
4 (731-1815), of London, m. Sidney Sussex 1749, LLB 1754, adm. Lincoln's Inn 1750, R. Dengie, Norfolk, 1758, R & V. West Dereham, Norfolk, 1761-9, R. Chislehurst, 1769-1815, R. St Vedast's, 1779-1815, precentor of St David's, 1777, FRS 1769.
5 (1719-?), of Whitford, co. Flint, m. Jesus O 1739, BA (All Souls) 1742, MA 1748, C. St Vedast's, 1752, lecturer St Vedast's, 1762, R. Ayot, Herts, R. St Alphege, London, 1762.
6 Perhaps (1754-1833), of Lambeth, m. Oriel 1772, BA 1775, chaplain to the Magdalen charity in London for 40 years, V. Enford, Wilts, 1793-1833.
7 (1699-1766), m. King's C 1719, BA 1723, MA 1729, lecturer of St Vedast's, 1737, preb of Lincoln, 1745-66, R. Wapperham, Norfolk, 1747-66, preb of Salisbury, 1765-6.
8 See n. 2.
9 (1723-85), of London, m. St Mary's Hall 1739, scholar Jesus O 1744-9, BA 1745, lecturer St Vedasts, 1768, chaplain to Mercers' company.
10 He has not been traced.
11 Perhaps (1762-1844), of Chetnole, Dorset, adm '10 year man' 1786, BD 1796, lecturer St Vedast's, 1786, morning preacher at the Foundling Hospital, 1797. He kept a school at Shackleford, Surrrey, and was R. Hilgay, Norfolk, 1819-44.

Page 318
Dioc. Lond. D. Bocking

Bocking R. St Mary. ABP P. K^s books 35-10-0. Wake, Herring 300^f. Cur saith, 450^f. The Parish goes betw. 3 & 4 miles along the Road from London to Sudbury, & is above 30 miles round. No Villages or Hamlets: betw. 3 & 4000 Inhabitants. Manufacture of Bays. A Few Presb. & Anab. Perhaps 4 or 500 Independents. A large Meeting Ho. Teacher Tho. Davidson, who hath an Assistant. Some of them have Considerable Fortunes. They increase only by Births. A few Methodists & Moravians, who have strolling Teachers in private Houses. One poor Family of Quakers: a meeting Ho. used once in 5 or 6 weeks. Very many Absenters, from the common motives. It is hoped they do not increase. 2 Sermons on Sundays. Prayers on all Festivals, & Twice a Week in Lent. Ch^n & Servts cat. on Sunday afternoons in Summer. Monthly Sacr. 100 Com. BP Gauden[1], when Dean of Bocking [for so R. is called] endowed a free School with a Farm of 15^f a year & a School House for teaching 30 poor Boys to write & read for 3 years betw. 7 & 12. Electors & Governors, Dean of ⟨the parish of⟩ Bocking, Rector of Stisted, V. of Braintree. Serj. Bendlow[2] endowed an Alms Ho. See more of it. Several Lands & Tenemts given to the poor, for money, Linnen, Bread. Duly applied. A meeting House of Independents. Tho. Mitchel Teacher, registred at the Commons Apr. 28. 1760 ⟨Cur. knows nothing of it 1761⟩. In what Repair is the ⟨Parsonage⟩ House? Chancel pews bad. Palis before Ho. quite decayed. Floors of back Front wch is of Timber, sunk. 1762 House well repaired & much improved.

I was told at Bocking July 24. 1761, that sev^l persons then living remembered a Visitation there by ABP Tenison, abt 58 Years before. One person specified the year 1704. They mentioned a Sermon preached, which is a further Evidence that it was not merely a Confirmation $^{1)*}$

The Profits of the Jurisdiction are a^{bt} 5^f a year. Income of the Rectory ab^t 440^f. Curate 50^f. Repairs 10^f. Land & Window Tax near 45^f. Tithe feast near 7^f.

Other things abt 6$^£$.

Of the neglect of baptizing their Ch^n for some years, & the Methods taken to cure it, See Dr Hall June 17 & Sept 28. 1763.

[1]* Articles of Visitation for the deanery of Bocking to be answered at the Visitation of the ABP of Canterbury Apr. 27. 1704. Amongst the 4° pamphlets in MS Lambeth Library N° 877[3]

Geo. Sayer[4], D.D. See next p.

Charles Hall[5] DD. R. 10 Oct. 1761. See p. 305. 1764 R. of S. Church p. 321.

Nicholas Wakenham[6] Master of Arts, R. November 5 1774.

July 24. 1761. Conf. of this Parish 160, of Stisted 51, of Braintree 3

[1] John Gauden (1605–62), dean of Bocking, 1641, bishop of Exeter, 1660–2, bishop of Worcester, 1662.

[2] William Bendlowe, who owned Brent Hall and was 'distinguished by his piety and munificence to the poor'. He was a Roman Catholic, becoming serjeant at law under Queen Mary. He died in 1584: *Essex* I, p. 662.

[3] *Articles of Visitation and Enquiry Concerning Matters Ecclesiastical; Exhibited to the Minister, Church-wardens, and Sidesmen, of every Parish within the Deanery of Bocking* (1704): LPL, H5133.234/24.

[4] (1696–1761), of London, m. Oriel 1714, BA 1717, MA 1719, B & DD 1733, V. Witham, Essex, 1722–61, canon of Durham, 1725, archdeacon of Durham, 1730–61, R. Bocking, 1741–61.

[5] See p. 163, n. 6.

[6] (17?–1802), of Modbury, Devon, m. King's 1741, BA 1745, MA 1748, DD (Lambeth) 1775, fellow 1744, R. Brome with Oakley, Suffolk, 1750–74, R. Ingham and Timworth, 1755–90, R. Bocking, 1774–1802, joint commissary deanery of Bocking, 1774–1802.

Page 319

Bocking continued

Geo. Sayer[1] DD. R. 20 Nov. 1741. Resides at Brussels ⟨Died there July 26 1761⟩. AD^n of Durham. V. of Witham, Essex. {Three lines crossed out}

Robt Clavering[2] was made R. & Commissary of Bocking 31 July 1714 as Sir W. Dawes[3] had been ⟨whose Instrumnt see Entry B IV. p. 589⟩. Wm Beauvoir[4] was made R. & Com. 25 July 1719. David Wilkins[5] made R. of Hadleigh Nov. 17. 1719 & Com. of Bocking jointly with Beauvoir Nov. 25. Robt Wake[6] made R. of Bocking 17 March 1723 & Com. of Bocking[1]*

John Cutler[7] Cur. 50$^£$ Hath resided constantly almost 22 Years.

Henry Wakenham[8] Cur.

Mr Cutler is also Surrogate. No Clergyman hath attended the Visitation in 22 Years, excepting the Rector of Stisted: & he only once.

Mr Rushworth[9], Register of the Arches, is Register of all the Peculiars. Mr Cheslyn[10] is his Deputy ⟨Vis. in Whits week⟩. Now 1761, Mr Cheslyn Junr[11].

[1]* jointly with Wilkins March 25. 1724. These Commissions were during the ABP^s pleasure, & the two that follow here ⟨Rich. Ibbetson[12] insti R. of Hadleigh 9 Sept 1714 & Wm Birch[13] 17 Dec 1717 were not Commissaries⟩. 14 Apr. 1737 John Walker[14] DD. inst. R. of Bocking. 11 Nov. 1725 & David Wilkins DD. inst. R. of Hadleigh 17 Nov. 1719 were constituted by a Commission joyntly & severally Deans & Commissaries throughout the Deanery of Bocking: assuming

John Haynes[15], the ABP[s] principal Register, or his Deputy, for actuary or
Scribe. And for 500 years past as many joint commissions appear, as single see
Newcourt vol. 2.
28 Jan 1741 Geo. Sayer DD & David Wilkins DD. were constituted &c.
D. Wilkins died in 1745. Geo Sayer ⟨made commissary March 29. 1748⟩. 1761
D[r] Sayer & Tho. Tanner[16] DD. R. of Hadleigh, made joint Deans or
Commissaries: & on D[r] Sayers Death D[r] Tanner & D[r] Hall Rector of Bocking
were made Nov. 2. 1761.
Nic. Wakeham[17] Clerk A.M. & Tho[s]. Tanner D.D. were appointed Commissar-
ies Nov[r.] 5: 1774.

[1] See p. 318, n. 4.
[2] (1671–1747), of Tillmouth, Devon, educated at Edinburgh (MA 1693), m. Lincoln 1693, BA
1693, MA 1696, B & DD 1716, fellow and tutor University, 1701, canon Christ Church 1715,
regius professor of Hebrew, 1715–47, dean of Hereford, 1706–29, R. Hadleigh, 1712–14,
treasurer of St David's, 1713, R. Bocking, 1714–19, R. Marsh Gibbon, Bucks, 1719, bishop of
Llandaff, 1725–9, bishop of Peterborough, 1729–47, archbishop's chaplain.
[3] Sir William Dawes (1671–24), 3rd Bt. R. Bocking, 1698–14, bishop of Chester, 1708–14,
archbishop of York, 1713–24.
[4] (1669–1723), of Guernsey, m. Pembroke O 1687, BA (All Souls) 1691, MA (CCCC) 1704, R. St
Saviour's Guernsey, 1692, R. Bocking, 1719–23.
[5] (1655–1745), of Prussia, MA (Oxford) 1712, DD (Cambridge) 1717, professor of Arabic, 1724,
R. Little Mongeham, 1716–9, R. Great Chart, 1719, R. Hadleigh, Suffolk, 1719–45, R. Monks
Eleigh, 1719–45, Lambeth librarian, 1715–8, joint commissary deanery of Bocking, 1719, preb
of Canterbury, 1720–45, archdeacon of Suffolk, 1724–45.
[6] (16?–1725), of Northamptonshire, m. Brasenose 1684, scholar Trinity 1685, BA 1687, MA 1690,
fellow, 1693, V. Fritwell, Oxon, 1690–1703, R. Farthingstone, Northants, 1714–20, V.
Ogbourne, Wilts, R. Buxted, 1720–4, R. Bocking, 1724–5.
[7] He has not been traced.
[8] (1762–1839), of Suffolk, m. Pembroke C 1782, BA 1786, MA 1789, C. Bocking, 1786, R.
Culford and Timworth, Suffolk, 1790–1829, R. West Stow, 1801–20.
[9] Edward Rushworth, Joint Register of Arches, 1734.
[10] Richard Cheslyn, Proctor, 1728.   [11] Edward Cheslyn, Proctor, 1752.
[12] (1679–1731), of Ledstone, Yorks, m. University 1695, BA 1699, fellow (Oriel) 1700, MA 1701,
R. Lambeth, Surrey, 1701–, R. Hadleigh, 1714–17, preb of Exeter 1716, precentor of Exeter,
1723, archdeacon of Exeter, 1726–31, archbishop's chaplain, 1716.
[13] (1688–1742), of Leacroft, Staffordshire, m. Trinity C 1709, BA 1710, MA 1713, LLD (Lambeth)
1720, R. Monks Eleigh, Suffolk, 1717–9, R. Hadleigh, 1717–9, chancellor diocese of Worcester,
1717, R. Fladbury, Worcs, 1719, R. All Saints', Evesham, 1724, V. Blockley, 1727, preb of
Worcester, 1727, archbishop's chaplain.
[14] Of Huddersfield, m. Trinity C 1710, scholar 1711, BA 1714, MA 1717, BD (Lambeth) 1725, DD
1728, Dean and R. Bocking, 1725, R. Great Easton, Essex, 1726–30, chancellor of St David's,
1727–41, archdeacon of Hereford, 1729, R. St Mary Aldermary, London, 1730–41, V. St
Thomas the Apostle, 1730–41.
[15] John Haynes, notary public 1714, secretary to archbishop Tenison, 1715.
[16] See p. ii, n. 14.   [17] See p. 318, n. 6.

Page 320
Dioc. Lond. D. Bocking
Lachingdon with Lalling al. Lawling R. ⟨near 20 miles from Bocking S & a little
to E. of Dingey Head⟩. S[t] Michael. ABP P. K[s] books 37[£]. Now for 170[£]. 19 Ho.
2 Families of Methodists, who go to a Meeting Ho. at Malden: the younger part
come often to church. Prayers & Sermon once. All the Houses near ½ mile from
Church: only 4 within a mile: several nearer to other churches. R. endeavoured

to have the whole service, but could not have a Congregation. And the Inhabitants certifie, that they cannot attend twice, & are satisfied with a non-resident Curate. Cat. in Lent [Is to be exp. in Summer]. 3 Sacr. [will be 4]. 12 or 14 Com. Land, worth 50ˢ a Year, given for the repair of the Church. So applied. There was a Chapel at Lalling: but scarce the memory of it remains. R. hath given good Books, & set up a School in Summer.

Jos. Cuthbert[1] MA R. 17 March 1746. R. of Bulvan ⟨al. Bulfann al. Bulpham⟩ in Essex, 25 miles off, ⟨val. in Disp. at 120ᶠ⟩ & as far to the South from Bocking E. of Hornden.
[1765 Lives at Hornden, joining Bulvan for Health. See a complaint agst him, & his Defence 1765.

Richards[2], Cur. R. of Fambridge, the next parish. Resides for the Benefit of his Children, at Maldon, 4 miles from Lachingdon. 26ᶠ. A resident Cur. till the last 2 or 3 years. See above.

[1] Joseph Cuthbert (1715–99), of Wiltshire, m. St John's C 1733, BA 1737, MA 1747, R. Bulphan, Essex, 1739–99, R. Latchingdon, 1747–99, chaplain to the earl of Levens.
[2] Frederick Richards (1707–61), of Middlesex, m. Queens' C 1724, BA 1728, MA 1743, R. Little Wigborough, 1734–61, R. North Fambridge, 1742–61.

Page 321
South Church R. ⟨Vulgo, Sea-Church, 25 m. from Bocking in the S. near Carnvey Isle, near Rochford⟩. ABP P. Kˢ books 27–0–10. Wake 100ᶠ. Herring 180ᶠ ⟨or 200ᶠ⟩. 27 Ho. & cottages. Prayers & Sermon once a Sunday. R. endeavoured for many Years to introduce afternoon Prayers: read a Lecture on the Cat. but often could not get 3 Persons. They would go to Sermons. Advised him to try Lectures in the Form of Sermons. Prayers & Sermon on Chr. Day, Jan 30. good Fr and Prayers on May 29 & other State Festivals, if there be a Congregation. Chⁿ are cat. in Lent. It will be continued longer, with an Exp. R. will endeavour to have a Sacr. at Mich. Hitherto only on the 3 Festivals. 12 or 15 Com. They were much fewer. Disp to R for non-res 3 yrs bec. unwholesome 1666 Entry B. II. 9. The Parish is on a Gravel, with good water. The Country abt it, bad.

Tho. Pickering[1] MA R 10 July 1734. V. of North-Weald near Epping Essex ⟨150ᶠ⟩. Hath resided at S. Church 4 months, every year but the last. Dead, Jan. 1764.
Charles Hall[2] DD R March 13. 1764. R. of Bocking ⟨p.⟩ 318.
Walter Wynn Driffield[3] Master of Arts R. November 18 1774.

John Nixon[4] BA of Cath. Hall, Pr. Cur. Resides in Parsonage Ho. when R. is absent. 40ᶠ. Dead. Nov. 1759. Served once by a neighbour 1761. R. will get the whole Service done, if he can.
Adey[5] Cur. 1761
Henry Ellis[6] BA of Sᵗ Johns, Oxf. Resides in the Parsonage Ho. To perform the Whole Service at 10 & 2. 40ᶠ. Serves Wakering 2 miles off at 3. 20ᶠ
James Bennet[7] A.B. of Sᵗ Johns College Cam. C. Chr. 1766. Resides. Serves this only. dead.
David Lloyd[8] BA. of Jes. Oxford March 1768. Resides.

Thomas Archer[9] A.B. Cur. Sal. £45 lic. 1794.

[1] (1707–64), of London, m. Trinity C 1725, scholar 1726, BA 1729, MA 1732, R. Southchurch, 1734–64, V. North-Weald, Essex, 1755–64.
[2] See p. 163, n. 6.
[3] Walter [Wren] Driffield (1744–1828), of Chelsworth, Suffolk, m. Trinity C 1763, scholar 1764, BA 1767, MA 1770, V. Erwarton, Suffolk, 1767–1801, V. Tolleshunt D'Arcy, 1770–, R. Southchurch, 1774–1828.
[4] (17?–59), of Wharles, Lancashire, m. St Catherine's C 1752, BA 1757.
[5] Perhaps John Adey. See p. 75, n. 6.
[6] (1735–?), of Rhode, Somerset, m. Brasenose 1752, BA (St John's) 1755.
[7] (1735–?), m. St John's C 1754, scholar, BA 1761, C. Simpson, Bucks, 1761.
[8] Possibly (1740–94), of Hay, co. Brecon, m. Jesus O 1759, BA 1763.
[9] (1750–?1832), of Finchley, Middlesex, m. Trinity C 1767, scholar 1771, perhaps R. Foulness, Essex, 1815–32.

Page 322
Dioc. Lond. D. Bocking
Stisted R. All Saints ⟨near Bocking⟩. ABP P. K[s] books 22[£] ⟨Called 260 in 1663⟩. Wake 260[£] Herring 225[£]. One Village: Farm Ho. & Cottages scattered over the Parish. In all 125. Inhabitants in 1743, 557: in 1755, 618. Sam. Savill[1] Esq[r] Lord of the Manor: lives 6 months here, 6 at Colchester. Several wealthy occupiers of their own Estates. 14 Families of Dissenters: ⟨&⟩ 9 in wch only one Party dissents. The Boys follow the Father, the Girls the Mother. The Presb. go to Coggeshall: the Indep. who are the most, to Bocking. All come occasionally to Church: except the Communicants in the Meeting Houses: & of late some of these let their Ch[n] come in bad weather. Absenters, as elsewhere. 3 Anab. their wives not: their Ch[n] bapt. 2 Sermons on Sundays. Prayers on all Holydays & Fr. or W. in Lent, & Sat. Evening before the Sacr. days, wch are the 3 great Festivals, & the 1st Sunday in each Month. At most not 40 Com. The pres[t] R. introduced the Offertory. It is ab[t] 9[s] a time, which he distributes in 3[d] Loaves: & fears these Loaves have reconciled some Dissenters to the Church. Ch[n] cat. Saturdays before Sacr. Exp. occasionally in Sermons. A few Ch[n] taught to read, chiefly at Mr Savills Charge.
Held with Hadleigh 24 miles dist. Entry B. IV. 88
BP Gibson[2] had it ⟨1700⟩, but it bec⟨a⟩me void in 1703 by his Cession [I believe by taking Lambeth] & John Dowsing[3] was coll. V. 116

Sam. Jackson[4] R. 4 Oct. 1742. Resides constantly in the Parsonage Ho. & doth ½ the Sundays Duty.
John Barlow Seale[5] D.D. 1792.

John Hodgkin[6] Fr. of Brazen-Nose Cur. Ord Pr at Oxford 1753, Resides, 35[£] & in Fees & E. Offerings abt 5[£] more.
W[m] Hughes[7] BA of Trin. Coll. Camb. bapt 16 Feb. 1744/5. Ord D. 20 Sept. 1767. 2. 40[£].
George Pearce[8] AB. Cur, Sal. £50. Lic 1794.

July 24. 1761. Conf. at Bocking 51.

[1] [Saville] (c.1700–63). Inherited the lordship in 1735. MP for Colchester, 1742–7: *Essex* II, p. 13.
[2] Edmund Gibson (1669–1748), bishop of Lincoln, 1716–20, bishop of London, 1720–48.

[3] (1655–1722), of Cottenham, Cambs, m. St John's C 1670, BA 1673, MA 1677, R. Ampthill, Beds, 1680, R. Isleham, Cams, 1684, minor canon of St Paul's, 1688, R. Stisted, 1704–6, R. Monks Eleigh, 1706–15, R. Cottenham, Cambs, 1715–22.

[4] (1709–92), of Nantwich, Cheshire, m. Brasenose 1726, BA 1729, MA 1732, R. Stisted, 1742–92.

[5] (1753–1838), of Derby, m. Emmanuel 1769, Christs 1773, scholar, 1774, BA 1774, MA 1777, DD 1789, PC. of Stow cum Quy, Cambs, 1774, R. Stisted, 1792–1838, R. Anstey, Herts, 1805–38.

[6] (1726–?), of Tattenhall, Cheshire, m. Brasenose 1747, BA 1751, MA 1753.

[7] Of Pembrokeshire, m. Trinity C 1763, BA 1767, MA 1770, C. Stanstead, Suffolk, 1767. He was ordained priest in 1769. Perhaps V. Ware, Herts, 1781–91.

[8] Of Essex, m. Christs 1789, CCCC 1790, scholar, BA 1794, MA (Trinity Hall) 1835.

Page 323

Boreley R. Within the Jurisdiction of the AD[n] of Colchester. The Rector attends the BP of Londons Visitation: but the ChW[ns] that of the Dean of Bocking. The new Rector 1761 promised to attend the ABP[s] Visitation.

Robert Morton[1] R. Dead 1761

[1] Perhaps (1714–61), of Shropshire, m. St John's C 1733, BA 1737, MA 1748, R. Borley, 1758–61.

Page 324

Dioc. Lond. D. Bocking

Coxhall al. Coggeshall. A Hamlet, belonging to the Parish of great Coggeshall. No Chapel. The ChW[n] is subject to the ABP[s] Jurisdiction. Mr Gullifer[1], the Vicar, was cited to the ABP[s] visitation 1761.

Runsell is mentioned in the Register List, as a Hamlett, of which the Church Wardens have for many Years omitted to attend the ABP[s] Visitation, & denied his Jurisdiction. I cannot find the name any where. But see here p. 330.
* The Manor of Harrow on the Hil was given by the ABP to the Crown in Exchange 31 Aug. 1 Ed. 6 See Chart Misc Vol 13 N° 21

[1] Joseph Gullifer (17?–67), of Suffolk, m. CCCC 1730, BA 1735, MA 1750, C. Coggeshall, 1739, V. Coggeshall, 1746–67, V. Burnham, 1750–67, chaplain to Lord Fitzwalter.

Page 325

Dioc. Lond. D. Croydon
Harrow R. Granted to Ch. Ch Oxon by H. 8, 11 Dec. 1546.

Harrow V. S[t] Mary, with the Chapel of Pinnour, S[t] John Bapt. Sir John Rushout[1] Bart, P. [qu. if as Lessee to Ch. Ch.]. Kings books 33–4–2. Now abt 140[f]. 9 miles long, 4 or 5 broad. Contains no Hamlets. See the Names. Harrow excl. of Pinnor 300 Ho. Pinnor 105. Sir John Rushout, Lord of the Manor, M[rs] Stapylton[2], Lady Caroline Egerton[3], Francis Herne[4], Tho. Matthews[5], Rich[d] Page[6], { } Bridges[7], Ja. Greenville[8], Cha. Palmers[9] Esq[r]. Many Presb. A few Indep. Anab. & Methodists. A meeting Ho. in Pinnor, Teacher ⟨James⟩ Medgewick. Lessened. A meeting in a Barn at Weald. Teacher unknown. Col.

Gumley did, & Mrs Edwards doth, attend there. Many Absenters who own they do ill, without amending. Whole Service on Sundays. Prayers on W. Fr. & Holydays. There was cat. & Exp. in Lent: but only the poorest Ch[n] came, & that by Compulsion: so it was laid aside, to avoid Contempt ⟨Promise 1760 to revive it⟩. Sacr. twice at each great Festival, once at Mich. From 40 to 60 Com. ⟨2 Sermons every Sunday at Pinnour. No cat. 4 Sacr. 40 or 50 or more Com⟩. A free Grammar School, founded by John Lyon[10]. Revenue for its Support, for Exhibitions in the Universities & many other charitable Purposes, abt 400[f] a Year. Tho. Thackeray[11] DD Master, ⟨Resigned 1760. Mr Sumner[12], master. Mr Heath[13] master, 1774⟩. Will. Prior[14] MA under-master, with each an Assistant. 6 Governors. See their Names. Well managed. Several other Schools: one by the above Dissenting minister. Several Charities in Bread & money, which see. 4 Acres of Land, left ⟨by F. Tyndal[15] of this place⟩ to the preaching minister of Pinnor. The chief Dissenters put one another into the Feofment, as Trustees, & let it out under half the Value.[1]* Some Land bought for him with Timber sold off the 4 Acres. 4[f] a Year left him by the late Lady Franklyn. Also a House is left to him.

16 Dec. 1511. ABP Warham[16] collated pleno jure Cuthbert Tunstall[17] to the Rectory of Harowe al. Herghes in the Deanery of Croydon vacant by the Death of the last Incumbent. And May 23. 1512 he granted to him an Exemplification of Letters of ABP William [Courteney][18] 13 Apr. 1396, which were an Exemplification of Letters of ABP S[t] Edmund[19] without date ⟨He died in 1242⟩, notifying his Institution of a Vicar of Herghes (called likewise by ABP Courtenay Hamvehulle & by ABP Warham Harowe at Hill) presented by the Rector, & appointing in what things the Income of the Vicarage & the Chapels of Pinnore & Thokyntone shd consist ⟨Reg. Courtney fol. 179a. And⟩ Reg. Warham fol. 344 a. See also Reg. Courteney fol 179a. See * in p. 324

[1]* They say this was abt 1742 ⟨in 1744⟩ when it {is} was impoverished & in 1765 a new Lease will be let at a higher Rent. See a paper abt it.

1761 Stone work of the Tower & rough Cast of the Church want mending & the Commanm[ts] cleaning. Speak to Sir John Rushout & Mr Jennings[20] abt beautifying the Chancel. Pinnor: Roof of side Isles to be repaired: walls, windows, floors of Pews, porch, altar piece, Frames & Wheels of Bells, mansion Ho. in bad Condition. Necessary Ho. in Ch. yd to be removed. Evidences of Benefactions not well kept.

---

[1] (1685-1775), 5th Bt. MP for Malmesbury, 1713-22, MP for Evesham, 1722-68.

[2] Elizabeth Gerrard, who married Miles Stapledon in 1716, the owner of Flambards manor. She died in 1766: VCH *Middlesex* IV, p. 209.

[3] Lived in a large house along the east edge of Weald Common: ibid., p. 185.

[4] He bought Flambards manor in 1767: ibid., p. 209.

[5] Lived near Sudbury Common: ibid., p. 194.

[6] Lived at Wembley House: ibid., p. 208.

[7] Lady Jane Brydges, who lived at Pinner Hall: ibid., p. 179.

[8] Possibly a member of the Grenville family, a leading local family: VCH *Middlesex* IV, p. 198.

[9] [Palmer], lived at Paines Place. He died in 1777: ibid., p. 179.

[10] John Lyon founded Harrow school in 1592: VCH *Middlesex* IV, p. 170.

[11] (1693-1760), of Hampsthwaite, Yorks, m. King's 1712, BA 1716, MA 1719, BD 1728, fellow 1715, assistant master Eton, R. Little Chishill, Essex, 1728-60, R. Heydon, 1728, head-master of Harrow, 1746-60, chaplain to the prince of Wales, 1748, archdeacon of Surrey, 1753-60.

[12] Robert Carey Sumner (1729-?71), m. King's 1748, BA 1752, MA 1755, DD 1768, fellow 1750, assistant master Eton, 1751-60, head-master of Harrow, 1760-71.

[13] Benjamin Heath (1739–1817), of Exeter, m. King's 1759, BA 1763, MA 1766, DD 1783, fellow 1762–8, assistant master Eton, 1763–71, head-master of Harrow, 1771–85, R. Walkern, Herts, 1781–1817, R. Farnham-Royal, Bucks, 1802–17.

[14] (1721–?), of Eton, m. Pembroke O 1740, BA 1743, MA (King's) 1752, DD 1775, C. Pinner, 1750–60, head-master Repton, 1767–79.

[15] Francis Tyndal[e], left 3 acres of land in 1630: VCH *Middlesex* IV, p. 256. Lady Franklyn was Mary, widow of Christopher Clitherow of Pinner, and widow of Sir Thomas Franklyn, 3rd Bt (1656–1728). She died in 1737.

[16] William Warham (?1450–1532), bishop of London, 1502–4, archbishop of Canterbury, 1504–32.

[17] (1474–1559), R. Harrow, 1511, bishop of London, 1522–30, bishop of Durham, 1530–53 (deprived). Restored on Mary's accession.

[18] William Courten[a]y (1342?–96), archbishop of Canterbury, 1381–96.

[19] St Edmund (1170?–1240), archbishop of Canterbury, 1234–40.

[20] Perhaps Edward Jennings, who owned the advowson of Hayes in 1759: VCH *Middlesex* IV, p. 33.

Page 326
Dioc. Lond. D. Croydon
Harrow V. continued

Fra. Saunders[1] MA V. 3 May 1727. Resides constantly in the Ho. belonging to him. Infirm of late. Wife, no Ch[n]. Estate in Wales. D[r] Saunders[2] of S[t] Martins a kin to him.
Walter Williams[3] Clerk A.B. Vicar Dec[r]. 19: 1776. vacated by Cession and reinstituted April 9: 1779.

Sam. Glasse[4] Cur. Ord. Pr. 24 Sept. 1758. 1. 40[f]. Resides in the parish. Quitted.
William Williams[5] P. 1764. 40[f].

Will Prior[6], Cur. at Pinnor lic. {Apr} ⟨May⟩ 1. 1750. No salary mentioned. Lives at Harrow. 2 miles off. See p. 326. Going Chr. 1760 to a Living in Bedfordshire.
James Willes[7], was a Painter, ord. Pr. by BP Thomas[8] of Lincoln Cur. Jan 2 ⟨6.⟩ 1761. V. promises in his Title to allow him 40[f] a year, but allows only 8[f], with some Surpl. Fees, wch with w[t] is mentioned p. 325 & voluntary Contributions made 40[f] to Mr Prior, & may make 60[f] to a Cur. residing, wch Mr Willis intends. Makes Complaints abt the House, wch see
Walter Williams Cur. lic. Apr. 26. 1764.
Rich[d] Roderick[10] Nov[r]. 1767. Ordained Priest Decr. 18th. 1768. Salary 40[f] Queens Col. Oxford.
Nom & Lic. to Pinnour Salary 50[f] & upwards Entry B. VI. 204.

1760 ⟨Sent 500 Tickets⟩ Aug 17. Conf. of Pinnor 54, of Hayes 4, of Harrow 220. 1762 at Killingdon of Harrow 8 of Pinnor 1. See the Letters. 1765, at D°. 21.

[1] Francis Saunders (1700–76), of Llandaveglog, co. Carmarthen, m. Jesus O 1716, BA 1720, MA 1723, V. Harrow, 1727–76.

[2] Erasmus Saunders, of Blockley, Worcs, m. Merton 1734, BA 1737, MA 1740, BD 1751, DD 1753, V. Wantage, 1755, Oxon, V. St Martin's-in-the-Fields, London, 1756, R. Kingsdown, 1757, canon of Windsor, 1756, preb of Rochester, 1756.

[3] See p. 178, n. 5.

4 (1753–1812), of Puriton, Wilts, m. Christ Church 1752, BA 1756, MA 1759, B & DD 1769, C. Harrow, 1758, R. Hanwell, Middlesex, –85, V. Epsom, Surrey, 1782–5, V. Wanstead, Essex, 1786, preb of Wells, 1790, preb of St Paul's, 1798–1812.

5 (1737–?), of Pembrokeshire, m. St John's C 1754, BA 1758, C. Harrow, 1764, R. Hayes, 1788–.

6 See p. 325, n. 14.   7 C. Pinner, 1761.   8 See p. 237, n. 10.

9 Perhaps David Roderick (1745–1830), of Langathen, co. Carmarthen, m. Queen's O 1763, BA 1767, MA 1769, a junior master at Harrow school, V. Sherbourne and Windrush, Glos, PC. Cholesbury, Bucks, 1784–1830.

Page 327

Hayes R. S[t] Mary with the Chapel of Norwood. Edw. Jennings[1] Esq[r] P [in trust for Geo. Cooke[2] Esq[r]]. K[s] Books 40[£]. A Lease from Will Keith[3] R. ⟨inst 29 Aug. 1739⟩ to Geo. Cooke Esq[r] for his own Life & his two Sons confirmed by the ABP 17 Jan. 1750. Lessee to pay the Rector 66[£] a year Rent, & 100[£] a year to the Vicar, & the Subsidies due for the Vicarage & to repair the Mansion Ho. & save harmless the Rector from Dilapidations, Subsidies, Synodals & Proxies. The Rector to pay the Tenths for the Rectory & Vicarage. The Lease is, of the Rectory of Hayes with the Chapel of Norwood annexed, & the Manor of the Rectory &c. In the Book of Augmentation Leases[4] from 12 to 28 Car. 2. the 36th Lease is one of the Rectory 28 June 1680 confirmed by ABP Sancroft 10 Sept 1680. ⟨See it in Entry Book IV. 112&c⟩. Another Lease 3 Oct. 1700 is entred at length in Reg. Tenison pt 2. fol 308, 309. ⟨See another 23 Oct. 1713 in wch a Fine is mentioned Entry B. VI. 134 & at large in Register. Another VII. II. Again 258. IX. 30⟩. Concerning the Endowm[t] of a Vicarage here, which made the Rectory what is commonly called a sine Cure, though the contrary Intention appears in the Instrument, see here p. 328. Of late only 20[£] a Year hath been paid by the Lessee to the Rector, & no Fine upon a Renewal.

The Rectory is thought to be worth 800[£] a Year.

Will. Jennings[5] BD R. 27 Apr. 1759 on the Death of Will. Keith the last Incumbent. He was fully informed, before his Institution, of the Rent to which he is intitled, & his Right to a Fine on Renewal, & warned against all Simoniacal Agreements. And he is a man of good character.

William Williams[6] Rector 1788.

1 Jennings was a lawyer.

2 George John Cooke, son of Sir George Cooke of Harefield. The Cooke family were lords of the manor of Hayes from 1729 until 1777: VCH *Middlesex* IV, pp. 22, 33.

3 (?–1759), Aberdeen, MA, C. Norwood, 1734, R. Hayes, 1739–59.

4 LPL, VG 7, pp. 55–7.

5 (1725–88), of Westminster, m. Oriel 1741, BA 1745, MA (Merton) 1748, BD 1758, R. Hayes, 1759–88.

6 See p. 326, n. 5.

Page 328

Dioc Lond. D. Croydon

Hayes V. S[t] Mary with the Chapel of Norwood K[s] books 20[£]. Edw. Jennings[1] Esq[r] P. [in trust for Geo. Cooke[2] Esq[r]]. The ordination of this V. was made by ABP Warham[3] 25 May 1520 & is in his Register fol. 388. 1. It expresses, that the Rectory is in the Gift of the ABP & reserves to him the Collation of the

Vicarage, & endows it with 20^f a year to be paid by the Rector, & orders a Ho. to be built for the Vicar & obliges the Vicar to find a Chaplain to serve Norwood Chapel, & have the whole Cure of Souls in that part of the Parish; & throughout the Parish when the Vicarage is vacant, or his Help is otherwise wanted. See more Particulars. Now the Lessee of the Rectory pays the Vicar 100^f a Year: who pays 40^f a Year to the Curate of the Chapel: which was augmented with 400^f, I think in 1725, & Land of abt 16^f a Year purchased with the money. 1761 Bottom of Chancel to be cleaned, & wainscot behind the Altar to be repaired, & windows glazed, & a Seat allotted to the vicar. No Ho. [See above]. Benefaction Deeds. to be procured & preserved.

{Pinnor} ⟨Norwood⟩ 1761 Almost every thing bad. See particulars. Speak to Mrs Cook.

Rob. Keith[4] nom. by V. lic to Norwood Entry B. VII. 6. Cha. Manning[5] inst 25 Sept. 1739 pres. by Geo. Cooke on death of James Baker[6]. VIII. 144. Resigned Sept. 9. 1756 IX. 265.

It contains the Hamlets of Hayes, Yeading & Botwell abt 140 Ho. Mr Blencowe[7], Mr^s Barnardiston[8]. Few or no Methodists, being much lessened since the last Incumbents time. Some few Absenters. [Doth this account include Norwood, which is not named, even as a Hamlet?]. Whole Service on Sundays: but afternoon Prayers were not always usual. Prayers on all Holydays, in the Ember weeks, & W. Fr. in Lent. V. will cat. as soon as he hath finished a Course of Cat. Sermons. Monthly Sacr. 20 or more Com. each time. The Chapel of Norwood a mile & half from Hayes. Prayers & Sermon there once on Sundays. To be twice. Is so, 1765.

V. hath no House. ABP Warham orderd one to be built for him. See here p. 327. The manor of Heese al. Hayes, & the Advowsons of the Rectory & Vicarage were given by the ABP to the Crown in Exchange 31 Aug 1 Ed. 6. See Chart Misc vol. 13. N° 21. And Pinner Park at the same time. Vid. ib.

[1] See p. 327, n. 1. [2] Ibid., n. 2.
[3] See p. 325, n. 6. [4] C. Norwood, 1723–30.
[5] (1715–?), m. Caius 1732, scholar 1736, BA 1736, V. Hayes, 1739–56.
[6] (1689–1739), of Stapleford, Wilts, m. Merton 1704, BA 1707, V. Hayes, 1730–39.
[7] A prominent family in the parish: VCH *Middlesex* IV, p. 22.
[8] A descendant of Sir Thomas Barnardiston, Bt, whose family lived at Eltham.

Page 329
Hayes V. continued.

Anth. Hinton[1] V. 14 Feb. 1757 ⟨on Res. of Manning[2]⟩. Resides constantly in a hired Ho. Desired to be admitted to the Curacy of the Chapel, of which he is Patron. But the Ordination directs them to be different Persons: & no Vicar hath had the chapel. And it being augmented, by 1 Geo. I Stat 2. c. 10. $ 4 the vicar can have no Profit from it. But is he bound to nominate a Curate for the Chapel with so large a Salary as 40^f a year? Mr Hinton gives also 20^f ⟨He calls it 10^f 1761⟩ a Year to the Family of his Predecessor, which he saith he did not previously promise. Yet he complains of Poverty. He teaches a School. He had Busbys[3] Lecture in 1758. Applied for it 1761 Qu. 1767 Resides: but having the

Stone, nominates ⟨Tho⟩ Thompson[4] of Harrow School, 6 miles off, for his Assistant. Ord D. June 14. 1767. Above 24. 30$^£$ 2 or 3.
John Nevill Freeman[5] A.M. vicar 1792.

John Will Hopkins[6] BA of New Coll. licenced Cur. ⟨of Norwood⟩ 10 June 1759. Salary, see before. To reside from Mich. Resides, whole Service, 1760. Resigned, on an Exchange. Jul. 1762.
Geo. Charles Black[7], nominated by Mr Hinton Jul or Aug 1762. Hath a Living in {Northamptonshire} ⟨Bedfordshire Battlesden R.⟩ but will reside here. Licensed Aug. 4. 1762. Here 1765.
George Gaskin[8] Curate, Licensed with a Salary of £35 p. ann Feb: 28: 1774.
George Henry Glasse[9] Cur. Hayes Sal. £40. Lic. 1784.
John Crofts[10] A.B. Cur D°. Sal. £30. Lic 1790.
David Bird Allen[11] A.B. Cur D^0. Sal £40 lic. 1793.
Anthony Hinton[12] Junr. Clerk, licensed to the perpetual Curacy of the Chapel of Norwood, by Trial from his Grace, June 29: 1775.

1760. Conf. at Harrow, of Hayes 4, of Norwood none

[1] (1717–92), m. Magdalene C 1747, V. Hayes, 1757–92.
[2] See p. 328, n. 5.
[3] Founded by Richard Busby (1606–95), head-master of Westminster school.
[4] 'literate', C. Hayes, 1767.
[5] (1764–1843), of Uxbridge, Middlesex, m. Exeter 1782, BA 1786, fellow, 1787–92, MA 1791, V. Hayes, 1792–1843.
[6] (1734–?), of Hayes, Middlesex, m. New College 1752, BA 1756, MA 1766, C. Norwood, 1759–62, R. Upminster, Essex, 1762–, R. St Mary le Strand, 1777–.
[7] Probably (1723–75), of Cadiz, Spain, m. Worcester 1737, BA 1740, C. Norwood, 1762–75.
[8] See p. 309, n. 4.
[9] (1761–?), of Harrow, Middlesex, m. Christ Church 1775, BA 1779, MA 1782, C. Hayes, 1784, R. Hanwell, Middlesex, 1785.
[10] (1767–?), of Bristol, m. Christ Church 1785, BA 1789, MA 1792, C. Hayes, 1790–3, R. Great Berkhamsted, Berks, 1793–.
[11] (1770–1831), of Pembroke, m. Trinity O 1787, BA 1791, MA 1794, C. Hayes, 1793, R. Manerdyvy, Pembroke, –1831, R. Burton, 1814–31.
[12] (1743–1838), of St Andrews, Holborn, London, m. Merton 1764, C. Norwood, 1775, V. Granborough, Bucks, 1775–1838.

Page 330
Dioc Lond. D. Croydon
Throckington, free Chapel, destr. K^s books 4–13–4. Ecton. The three first Words are in Wake. Thokyntone was a Chapel to Harrow: See here p. 325.

In ABP Wakes Parochial Book p. 102 the 3 following Hamlets are mentioned as peculiars in the County of Suffolk & Deanery of Bocking. They are mentioned in the Parochial Book of 1663, as in that Deanery.

Milton-Shore in the Parish of Prittlewell. But this Parish is in Essex D. Rochford Ecton p. 271.

Runsel in the Parish of Danbury: which is also in Essex D. Chelmsford Ecton p. 268. See here p. 324.

Callow-Green in the Parish of Purleigh: which is also in Essex. D. Dengey Ecton p. 269.

[Diocese of Norwich]

Page 331

Dioc. Norw. Co. Norfolk

Denton R. S[t] Mary ⟨Not a peculiar. Entred rightly p. 404⟩. M[r] Postlethwayt[1], by his Will dated 5 Sept. 1713. gave the Advowson to the ABP of Canterbury for the Time being, in trust that he should collate [present] a Fellow, or one who had been Fellow of Merton Coll. K[s] books 24[£]. Now called 250[£] ⟨See below⟩. Postlethwayte was Master of S[t] Pauls School, & said to be so by ABP Tenisons Recommendation. Knights Life of Colet[2], p. 385. Mr Sandby saith 1750, that it is but 150[£] a year exclusive of the Taxes.

Geo. Sandby[3] MA R. 30 May 1750. DD. & Master of Magd. Coll. Camb. 1760.

[1] John Postlethwayte (1650–1713), of Millom, Cumberland, m. Merton 1671, BA 1675, MA 1778, master of Tenison's school, St Martin's-in-the-Fields, 1680, high-master of St Paul's School, 1696–1713.
[2] Samuel Knight, *The Life of Dr John Colet* (1724).
[3] (1717–1807), m. Merton 1734, BA 1737, MA 1741, DD (Magdalene C) 1760, master 1760, vice-chancellor 1760, chancellor of diocese of Norwich, 1768, R. Denton, 1750–1807.

Page 332

Dioc. Norw. Co. Norfolk

Castle Rising al East Rising R. in the Deanery of Lynn. In D[r] Tanners Book of the Diocese of Norwich it is said, I think from Domesday Book, to be locus exemptus ab omni Jurisdictione episcopali & archidiaconi, exceptis inductis, quae pertinent ad archidiaconum. It stands as a Peculiar in the Parochial Book of 1663 fol 65.

Page 333

North Wotton R [V. Ecton ⟨who calls it V⟩]. in the Deanery of Lynn. 24 Nov. 1605 Adam Furnes[1] MA was instituted by Sir Edw. Stanhope[2] Vicar General to the Vicarage of Northwotton in the County of Norfolk under the immediate Jurisdiction of the See of Canterbury, lawfully vacant, to which he was presented by the King, the true & undoubted Patron. Reg. Bancroft fol. 271. It stands as a Peculiar in the Parochial Book 1663 fol 65.

[1] (1574–?), m. St John's C 1573, BA (Clare) 1577, MA 1580, schoolmaster at Depden, Suffolk.
[2] (c.1546–1608), m. Trinity C, BA 1563, MA 1566, LLD 1575, vicar-general of the diocese of Canterbury, c. 1583, MP for Marlborough, 1584–86, chancellor of the diocese of London, 1591–1608.

Page 334

Dioc. Norw. C. Norfolk

Royden al. Rydon R. in the Deanery of Lynn. It is said in D[r] Tanners Book I think from Domesday Book to be within the Liberty of Rysing [see here p. 332] & to have the same Exemption. It stands as a Peculiar in the Parochial Book of 1663 fol 65.

Page 335

South Wotton R in the Deanery of Lynn.

26 June 1613. Tho. Ridley[1] LLD Vicar General instituted Richd Goldinge[2] MA to the Rectory of Southwotton in the Diocese of Norwich & immediate Jurisdiction of the See of Canterbury, vacant by the Death of the last Incumbent, to which he was presented by the King, the true & undoubted Patron Reg. Abbot part 1 fol. 396b.

In D[r] Tanners book, are these words, I think from Domesday Book: non visitabur ab Archidiacono. The Institutions to it are carried there no further to them to 1404. It stands as a Peculiar in the Parochial Book 1663 fol 65.

[1] (c.1548–1629) of Ely, BA Trinity C 1571, MA 574, DD 1583, DCL 1598, MP for Chipping Wycombe, 1586–7, MP for Lymington, 1601, chancellor of the diocese of Winchester, 1596–c. 1611, vicar-general to the archbishop of Canterbury, c. 1611–29.
[2] m. St John's C 1606, BA 1610, MA 1613.

Page 336

Dioc. Norw. Co. Norfolk

Mintling C. in the Deanery of Lynn.

In BP Tanners Book is this Entry, as from Domesday Book. Appropriatur Priori & Conv. de Norvico – non visitatur ab Archidiacono quia est de Maneriis Prioris Norvici. And afterwards in another Hand: Donata fuit haec Ecclesia monachis Ecclesiae Cath. Norv. apud Linnam commorantibus ab Herberto[1] Ep. Norv. – appropriata eisdem per Joannem de Grey[2] Ep. Norvic. circa AD 1205. It stands as a Peculiar in the Parochial Book 1663 fol 65.

[1] Herbert, first bishop of Norwich, 1119.
[2] John de Grey (died in 1214), bishop of Norwich, 1200–1214.

Page 337

Dioc. Norw. Co. Norfolk.

Thurforth al Thursford in the Deanery of Wallsingham R. I find it not in BP Tanners Book. It stands as a Peculiar in the Parochial Book 1663 fol 65 by the Name of Thursford by Fakenham.

Page 338

Dio. Norw. Co. Suffolk. D. Bocking

Ash near Campsey al. Campsey Ash R. Said in a marginal Note in Parochial Book written 1715/6 to have been passed away by ABP Cranmer[1] in the time of Ed. 6. See Ect. It doth not appear by D[r] Tanners Book of the Diocese of Norwich that either the Patronage or the Jurisdiction of this Living was ever in the ABP. It is mentioned as a Peculiar in the Parochial Book of 1663 fol. 61.

[1] Thomas Cranmer (1489–1556), archbishop of Canterbury, 1533–56.

Page 339

Hadleigh R. S[t] Mary ⟨7 miles W. of Ipswich⟩. ABP P. K[s] books 45-2-1. Now called 300[£]. 5 miles long, 2½ broad. A market Town, of 407 Ho. & a Hamlet of 34 Ho. 8 poor persons, Papists. Abt 100 Presb. A meeting Ho. Isaac Toms, Teacher. 5 Anab. In 1754, Inhabitants of the Town 2092: of the Hamlet, 168. Many that seldom attend Church, reproved & discouraged. 2 Sermons on Sundays. Prayers twice every day. [Now 1759 once only, the Congregation being very small. & the Curate infirm. See Letters ⟨see below⟩]. Cur. reads Prayers at the Chapel of an Alms Ho. W. Fr. Cat. exp. W. Fr. in Lent. Ch[n] & Servts duly sent. Monthly Sacr. 100 Com. & at 3 great Festivals, at least 200. A small part of Offertory money given to the poor Com. of that Day: the rest by R. & ChW[ns] to bind out Apprentices. Some Donations to Schools & many to Poor. Prayers to be twice daily from Mich 1759, Parishioners promising to attend better.

Rich. Smalbroke[1] D.D. coll. 8 Feb. 1708. Robt Clavering[2] MA 2 Feb. 1711 on cess. of Smalbroke.

Rich. Ibbetson[3] 9 Sept 1714 on Cession of Clavering.

Lease of Tenemt[s] for 40 yrs 1721 Entry B VI. 388. Again 8 June 1761 Entry B. X. 2.

The ABP collated to Hadleigh in 1325. Dr Tanners book p. 1368.

1767 4 women of low Rank, & 2 daughters of one of them, Papists.

Tho. Tanner[4] MA [now DD] R. 19 Oct. 1745. Resides constantly in the Parsonage Ho. unless when required at Canterbury, where he is Prebendary. R. also of Monks Eleigh p. { }. A very good & useful Justice of Peace.

Thomas Drake[5] D.D. Rector 1786.

George Watson[6] D.D. Rector 1790.

Edw. Auriol Hay Drummond[7] D.D. Rector 1796.

Tho. Ottey[8] MA, Pr. Cur. 55[£] & Easter Offerings. Going.

Will. Hewett[9]. Caius Coll. Cambr.

Thomas Wallace[10] A.B. Cur Sal £50. lic 1790.

George Matthew[11] A.B. Cur. Sal £60. lic 1791.

1754 BP of Norwich, by ABP[s] Appointmt confirmed here the Parishioners of Hadleigh, Monks Eleigh, & Moulton [certainly the last is too far off. July 26. 1761 I confirmed here, of Hadleigh 353, Monks Ely 59, Parishes not peculiars 23.

1770. BP of Norwich confirmed here, by Abp[s] desire.

[1] [Smalbrooke] (1673–1749), of Rowington, Warks, m. Trinity O 1688, demy Magdalen 1689–98, BA 1692, MA 1695, fellow 1698–1709, BD 1707, DD 1708, R. Withington, Glos, 1716, V. Liugwardine, Herefordshire, 1711, R. Hadleigh, 1709–12, preb of Hereford, 1709, treasurer of Llandaff, 1712, bishop of St David's, 1724–31, bishop of Lichfield and Coventry, 1731–49, chaplain to Tenison.

[2] See p. 319, n. 2.   [3] Ibid., n. 12.

[4] See p. ii, n. 14.   [5] See 131, n. 6.

[6] (1749–1813), of Bury St Edmunds, m. Trinity C 1766, scholar 1769, BA 1770, MA 1774, DD 1782, R. Hadleigh, 1790–6.

[7] (1758–1829), of Westminster, m. Christ Church 1774, BA 1778, MA 1780, B & DD 1794, R. Hadleigh, 1796–1829, dean of Bocking, R. Dalham, Suffolk, 1823–9, preb of York and Southwell, chaplain to king.

[8] (1721–?), of Chester, m. Brasenose 1737, BA 1740, R. Stoke, Suffolk, 1754–.

[9] (1723–88), of Norfolk, m. Caius 1741, scholar, 1740–7, BA 1745, MA 1750, fellow, 1747–67, C. Hadleigh, R. Bodham, Norfolk, 1767–80, R. Baconsthorpe, 1767–88.

[10] (1764–1855), of Essex, m. CCCC 1783, scholar, BA 1787, MA 1790, C. Hadleigh, 1790, R. Liston, Essex, 1800–55.

[11] (1769–1833), of Bury St Edmunds, m. Trinity C 1786, scholar 1788, BA 1790, MA 1793, fellow, 1792, C. Hadleigh, 1791, V. St James', Bury St Edmunds, 1793–9, preacher at St James', Westminster, V. Greenwich, 1812–33, chaplain to duchess of Brunswick, chaplain to the earl of Bristol.

Page 340

Dioc. Norw. Co. Suffolk.

Monks Ely, al. Monks Illeigh, al. Munsellith R. ⟨5 miles NW of Hadleigh⟩. ABP P. K^s books 13–18–11½. Wake, Herring 160^f. One Village of 109 Ho. Two Papists. One Family of Presb. 4 Absenters. 2 Sermons on Sundays. A Sermon Jan. 30. good Fr. Nov. 5. Prayers on all Holidays. Cat. exp all Lent. Ch^n & Servants duly sent. 4 Sacr. abt 60 Com. The Rents of some Cottages given for Bread for the Poor.

The King presented in 1271 the ABP^{rick} of Cant. being vacant Dr Tanners book p. 1378.

1767 A Taylor, his wife & ch^n papists.

Tho. Tanner[1] MA [now DD] R. 24 Oct. 1745. R. of Hadleigh p. 339 where he resides: but ususally preaches here once a fortnight from LD to Mich.
Charles Cotes[2] A.M. rector 1786.

Giles Emley[3] Pr. Cur. 40^f, use of Parsonage Ho. and Garden & two orchards & Ch. Yard, Surpl. Fees. & Easter Offerings.

Conf. See Hadleigh: p. 339.
July 26 1761 I conf. at Hadleigh. 59 of this Parish.

[1] See p. ii, n. 14.

[2] (1751–1800), of Woodcote, Salop, m. University 1768, BA (All Souls) 1773, MA 1777, R. Monks Eleigh, 1786–1800.

[3] (1713–?). of Crudwell, Wilts, m. St Edmund Hall 1732, BA 1736.

Page 341

Moulton R. St Peter K^s books 13–6–8 ⟨a little E of Newmarket 25 miles W of Hadleigh⟩.

Moulton V. St Peter K^s books 4–7–8½.

V. of Multone ordained by ABP Peckham[1], lest the Cure shd be neglected, the R. having other business Reg. Peckham fol 55a.

The Rectory was passed away by ABP Cranmer[2] under Ed. 6. [Haynes's book: & granted by Qu. Eliz to Edw. Stafford[3] Esqr. See Chart Misc. vol. 12 N° 48.

See D[r] Tanners Book p. 1241. Was in ABP[s] Patronage, but passed away by Cranmer under Ed. 6. Parochial Book 1663.

John Gee[4] of Cambridge Gent. Presented John Gee[5] Clerk to the Vicarage. ⟨(He writes himself Rector) & afterwds, sold the Advowson to Chr. Coll. Cambr⟩. Fiat for Inst. dated May 27. 1734. Herring 140[£]. Extent 12 miles: 30 Ho. Whole Service on Sundays, unless w[n] R hath no Curate at his other Parish. Prayers on Fasts & Thanksgivings, & W. Fr. in Lent, w[n] also Cat. is exp. 4 Sacr. 30 Com. R. by a voluntary Contribution of his own hath settled a Schoolmaster. Lands of 5[£] a Year given to the Church, & of 15[£] a year to the Poor. 12[£] at Interest for the Poor. All well applied. It were to be wished that Visitations were sometimes held in this Parish.

W[m] Huxley[6] coll. 4 Jan 1676/7 to the Rectory of Muleton al. Moulton Co. Suffolk void by death of Fra. Seyliard[7] Entry B. III. 305. { } Dudley Bradbury[8] coll. to R & V. of Mouton void by death of Fra. Syliard p. 311. On Bradburys Death, John Gee as above. Entry Book VIII. 2 [what is become of R. {Line crossed out}

John Gee V. See above. Hath always resided in the Parsonage Ho. V. also of Burwelll, Co. Suffolk ⟨a few miles off⟩. Designs to divide his Time between them. See his Letter, amongst Ord. Papers. Returned hither Nov. 1760.

Thos. Murhall[9] R & V 6 July 1772.

Edward Wilson[10] A.M. Vicar 1784.

John Strachey[11] BA of Tr. Coll. Camb. C. Ord. Deacon Aug. 24. 1760. 1. 30[£] or Guineas a Year, & his Board. Gone to Westm. Sch.

[1] John Peckham, archbishop of Canterbury, 1279–92.
[2] Thomas Cranmer (1489–1556), archbishop of Canterbury, 1533–56.
[3] He has not been traced.   [4] He has not been traced.
[5] (1702–72), of Cambridgeshire, m. Peterhouse 1719, scholar 1719, BA 1724, MA 1727, fellow 1728, V. Stapleford, Cambs, 1726–9, V. Burwell, 1729–72, V. Moulton, 1734–72.
[6] (1707), m. Christs, BA, V. Moulton, 1677–. Probably C. Dullingham, Cambs, 1696–1707.
[7] (1628–76), of Kent, m. Sidney Sussex 1644, BA 1648, MA (Caius) 1651, fellow Sidney 1650, intruded fellow Caius 1654, V. Mayfield, Sussex, 1660–4, R. Moulton, 1663–76.
[8] m. Trinity C 1663, BA 1667, MA 1675, V. Moulton, 1676–1734.
[9] V. Moulton, 1772–84.
[10] (1748–1823), of Lockington, Yorks, m. Christs 1763, scholar 1765, BA 1767, MA 1770, fellow 1771–85, R. Fen Drayton, Cambs, 1772, V. Moulton, 1784–1823, R. Dalham, Cambs, 1811–23.
[11] (1738–1818), of Edinburgh, m. Trinity C 1756, BA 1760, MA 1763, LLD 1770, fellow 1761, C. Moulton, R. Epringham, Norfolk, 1769–1818, R. Thwaite, 1773–1818, archdeacon of Suffolk, 1781, preb of Llandaff, 1786, preacher at the Rolls chapel, 1783–1817, chaplain to the bishop of Norwich, royal chaplain, 1774–1818.

Page 342

Dioc. Oxon. D. Monks-Risborough. Entry B. V. 292.

Newington R. S[t] Giles, with the Chapel of Britwell Prior. ABP P. K[s] book 18-13-4. Wake 250. Herring 300[£]. 3 miles long, 2 broad: exclusive of Britwell Prior, which is 4 miles from the rest of the Parish. 4 Hamlets. Holcomb, Brockhampton, Berrick Prior, Britwell-Prior. In all 55 Ho. M[rs] Bayly[1], widow, rich, religious, charitable. Sir Edw. Simeon[2] Bart, Papist. A Priest in his Ho. called Richardson ⟨none lately perverted⟩. Whole Service, excepting the 1st Sunday in the Month, when Evening Prayers are read, & a Sermon preached at

Britwell. Prayers on the Holydays following the great Festivals: & on Ash W. good Fr. Jan 30, May 29 June 22. Nov 5. Cat. Sunday afternoons in Lent ⟨will be in Summer too⟩, with Wakes Exp. 4. Sacr. Abt 30 Com.
1767 Sir Edw. Simeon, aged 84, Mr Browning his Priest, 6 men & 5 women his Servants, a widow Gentlewoman & her daughter, Papists: in all, 15.

Philip Billingsley[3] R. 30 Apr. 1754. Resides constantly in the Parsonage Ho. R. also of Swincomb. Co. Oxon.
George Stinton[4] DD. R. 10 July. 1771.
James Cornwallis[5] BP. of Lich & Cov. 1781.
Charles Moss[6] A.M. Rector 1794.

William Palmer[7] A.M. Cur. Sal. £55. lic. 1795.

[1] She has not been traced.
[2] (1682–1768) 2nd Bt. He became a Catholic non-juror in 1715.
[3] (1730–71), of Dover, Kent, m. Queen's O 1749, BCL 1756, R. Newington, 1754–71, R. Swincomb, Oxon, 1754–71.
[4] See p. 149, n. 4.   [5] See p. ii, n. 6.
[6] (1763–1811), m. Christ Church 1780, BA 1783,MA 1786, B & DD 1797, chaplain of the house of Commons, 1789, R. Sherfield, Herts and preb of Salisbury, 1786, R. Newington, 1794, preb of Westminster, 1792, preb of St Paul's, 1797, chancellor of Bath and Wells, bishop of Oxford, 1807–11.
[7] Perhaps (1771–1853), of Chardstock, Dorset, m. Worcester 1788, BA (Balliol) 1791, MA 1794, B & DD 1812, V. Yarcombe, Dorset, 1800–53.

Page 343

In the Book mentioned here p. 303 were the following Entries.

Prebend of Cropredy & Tame in Com. Oxon 46$^£$. This Entry is also in the Parochial Book of 1663 fol 65.

Ecclesia de Milton.
In the Parochial Book 1663 is this Entry V. Milton. K^s books 15$^£$

In a folio MS in the Lambeth Library, which is called Registrum album[1] fol. 1.b. is the following Entry. Archiepus Cant. habet Juridictionem in Collegio de Merton Oxon. & approbationem Testamentorum inibi monentium. Vid. Regist Bowcher fol 45. Reynolds fol 57. See a paper drawn up by Dr Astry[2], containing, amongst other things, a Transcript of an Instrumt of Sutton[3] BP of Lincoln. dated 4 Non. Nov. 1294 in wch it is recited, that his predecessor Gravesend[4] did, Id. Sept. 1266 appropriate the Church of St John Baptist to Merton College, salva rationabili Vicaria aut alia sustentatione ministrorum ejuisdem per nos vel successoribus nostris vue Scholarum & Fratrum ipsorum ministros idoneos praesentabit: & that his said predecessor did also appropriate to the College the Church of St Peters in the East, Oxon. salva rationabli Vicaria ad quam custos idoneos Vicarios nobis & successonbus nostris praesentabit. And these two appropriations BP Sutton confirms: & gives a mandate to the AD^n of Oxford to induct the Scholars & Brethren of Merton.

[1] 'Registrum Album Collecteana ex Registris Archiepiscorum Cantuar(ensium)', made by Thomas Yale, chancellor of Archbishop Parker, dated 1570. It is at Lambeth Palace Library.
[2] Richard Astry (1632–1714) antiquary.

[3] Oliver Sutton (died 1299), bishop of London, 1280–99.
[4] Richard Gravesend (died 1279), bishop of London, 1258–79.

[Diocese of Rochester]

Page 344

Dioc. Roch. D. Shoreham

{30} ⟨31⟩ in all, at least.

Aynesford. See Eynesford

Bexley V. St Mary ⟨3 miles SW of Dartford. Impr. Mrs Dare[1] of Kensington⟩. Belonged to the Priory of Canterbury. Tho. Coote[2] ⟨He presented Piers⟩ of Coote Hall in Ireland P. [Mr Selwyn[3] P. Ecton]. ⟨Mr Townshend[4], Member for Cambr. AD^n Potter⟩. K^s books 13-4-7. Herring, Wake 80$^£$ V. saith, the Profits are let for 84$^£$ a Year, the Glebe is 3 Acres. 5 miles long, 2½ broad: 7 villages: abt 230 Ho. 700 Inhabitants. Richd Calvert[5] Esqr of Hall Place. Some Mercht^s &c See their Names. Mr Goddard[6], a Papist, lived here. His Ho. in which is a Chapel, now empty. At Wellend, an unlicenced Conventicle of abt 20 Methodists, have met every Sunday for 3 Years under some of Mr Wesleys[7] Teachers: do not increase. One Quaker occupies Land, not an Inhabitant: refuses to pay Tithes. Prayers twice on Sundays, Sermon once, excepting when Homilies are appointed by Authority. Homilies read, Articles explained, Scripture expounded in afternoon, if no Cat. wch there generally is 6 months. Prayers on Holydays & Litany Days, & 2 Evenings in the Week, esp. 4 Winter months. Sacr. every first Sunday of the Month & the great Festivals. From 30 to 60 Com. Offertory money given in Bread. Mr John Styleman[8] left 100$^£$ a Year for building Alms ho. for & maintaining 12 Poor Persons: with 2 Guineas for a yearly Sermon, & 3 for a Dinner for V. Ch W^{ns} &c. Several considerable charities besides, which see. BP of Rochester confirms at Dartford, 3 miles off. 1761 AD^n Potter Paroch. vis. Sev^l little things, wch see, to be amended in the Ch. Ho & outHo. in good Order. 3^d in pound at whole Rents raises 38$^£$.

Henry Piers[9] MA V. 30 July 1737. Resides in V. Ho.
Wm Green[10] M.A. April 10. 1770.

1760 Conf. at Dartford by BP Pearce[11] 25. 1764. 20. 1767. 32

[1] Eleanor Dare, married to Thomas Dare of Taunton, and daughter of Thomas St George: Hasted II, p. 182.
[2] Hon. Thomas Coote, of Cootehill, co. Cavan, Ireland. He died in 1741.
[3] John Selwyn, lessee of the manor of Danson Hill: Hasted II, p. 172.
[4] Hon. Thomas Townshend (1701–80), MP for Winchelsea, 1722–27, MP for Cambridge, 1727–74. He spoke on 18 March 1765 on a bill to facilitate the exchange of Church lands and 23 February 1773 against the motion to abolish subscription to the 39 articles at Cambridge.
[5] Tenant to Edward Austen of Boxley Abbey.
[6] Austin Parke Goddard, owner of Brampton Hall: Hasted II, p. 173.
[7] John Wesley (1703–91), evangelist and founder of Methodism.
[8] In his will of 1732: Hasted II, p. 178. He died in 1734.
[9] (1695–1770), of Chichester, m. Dublin 1713, BA 1718, MA 1722, V. Bexley, 1737–70.

[10] (1716–?), of Lighthorne, Warwks, m. All Souls 1734, BA 1737, MA 1751, B & DD 1766, V. Bexley, 1770–.

[11] Zachary Pearce (1690–1774), bishop of Bangor, 1748, bishop of Rochester, 1756.

Page 345

Brasted R. S[t] Martin ⟨3 miles W of Sevenoak⟩. ABP P. K[s] books 22–6–3. Wake 160[£]. Herring 200. Mr W. Herring[1] saith, 250[£]. 8 miles long, 1 broad. One village. Ab[t] 100 Ho. ⟨50 in town, 20 in Fields⟩. Hon[ble] Mrs Verney[2] ⟨dead⟩. 10 Anab. A few Absenters, plead their Distance. Whole Service on Sundays, 2 Sermons in Summer. Prayers on very few Days else. Cat. every Sunday after 2[d] Lesson of Evening Service ⟨Ch[n] well invited, backwd to come⟩. 8 Sacr. 35 or 40 Com. each time ⟨20⟩. An Alms Ho. for 3 Persons, founded by { } Crow[3] Esq[r]. No Revenue. W[m] Newman[4] left a Farm of 15[£] a year to R. & ChW[ns] for cloathing the Poor. BP of Rochester confirms at Westerham, 2 miles off. 1761 Cur. gives 200[£], lets it, to every one their own Tithe, at 220[£]: worth 260[£] ⟨See below⟩. Glebe 44 Acres, meadow & arable: 20 Acres woodland, called Parsons Marsh, very poor, 12[d] in pound, ½ Rents, raises 47[£]. Many little things, which see, much amiss in the Church: the Parsonage Ho. needs a thorough Repair. 1764. Let for 280[£], besides 30[£] Glebe in Hand. Lic. to pull down part of the Buildings on condition to make the rest better 1694 Entry B. IV. 504.

Michael Bull[5] R. July. 27. 1708. Made one of the 6 Preachers 16 Feb. 1701. Resides in the Parsonage Ho. Died 26 Aug. 1763.
Geo. Secker[6] DD. R. Oct. 12. 1763. R. of All Hallows the great p. 402 died March 21 1768.
James Parker[7] MA R Apr. 6. 1768. Will reside.
William Vyse[8] Batchelor of Law. R. December 30 1772.
Thomas Francklin[9] D.D. Rector April 1: 1777.
William Skinner[10] A.M. Rector 1784.
George Moore[11] A.M. Rector. 1795.

Geo. Harris[12] Pr. Cur. 20[£] a Year & his Board. Resides. Gone.
Marmaduke Lewis[13]. Resides at Westerham 1½ mile off.
Richard Hinckley[14] Clerk A.B. Cur. Lic Sept: 23: 1776, with a Salary of £50 p. an.
William Moreton Moreton[15] A.M. Cur. Sal. £50 Lic. 1787.
Thomas Dickes[16] A.B. Cur. Sal. £50. lic. 1794.

July 11. 1760. Conf. at Sevenoak 21. 1764. 40. 1767. 15

[1] Of Kensington, notary public and secretary to archbishop Herring, 1749–54.
[2] Owner of Brasted-Place: Hasted III, p. 154.
[3] William Crow in 1618: ibid, p. 155.   [4] In 1736: ibid.
[5] See p. ii, n. 33.   [6] Ibid., n. 21.
[7] (1724–72), of Portugal, m. Balliol 1740, BA 1743, MA (Kings) 1749, DD 1768, R. Brasted, 1768–72, preb of Lichfield, 1762–72.
[8] (1742–1816), m. Brasenose 1758, BCL (All Souls) 1772, DCL 1774, R. Newington and Brasted, 1772–7, R. St Mary Lambeth, 1777–1816, R. Sundridge, 1777–1816, archdeacon of Coventry, 1793, canon residentiary of Lichfield, 1798–1816.
[9] See p. 315, n. 12.
[10] (1728–95), of Sherston, Wilts, m. Pembroke O 1744, BA 1747, MA 1750, R. Brasted, 1784–95, preb of Hereford.

11 (1771–1845), son of archbishop Moore, m. Christ Church 1788, BA 1792, MA 1795, R. Brasted, 1795–1800, R. Wrotham, 1800–45, preb of Canterbury, 1795–1845, archbishop's chaplain.
12 Perhaps of London, m. CCCC 1736, BA 1739.
13 (1730–1806), of Westerham, Kent, m. Christ Church 1748, BA 1752, MA 1755, R. East Garston, Berks, 1761, R. Lullingstone, Kent, 1772–1806.
14 (1753–?), of Lichfield, Staffs, m. Merton 1771, BA 1775, C. Brasted, 1776.
15 William Moreton [Taylor] (1759–?), of Westfield, Sussex, m. Magdalen O 1775, BA 1779, MA 1782, R. Brasted, 1787–94.
16 (1770–1845), of Middlesex, m. Jesus C 1789, BA 1793, MA 1796, fellow and president, C. Brasted, 1794, V. Comberton, Cambs, 1810–, V. Whittlesford, 1830–45, joint registrar of the archiepiscopal and commissary court of Canterbury, 1802–45.

Page 346
Dioc. Roch. D. Shoreham.
Chevening R. St Botolph. ⟨4 miles NW of Sevenoak⟩. ABP P. K^s books 21-6-8. Wake 150$^£$. Herring 260$^£$ ⟨R. saith 250$^£$⟩. Pension to R. of Shoreham 20^s Ecton. 7 miles long, scarce a mile broad. A Hamlet called Chipsted. 134 Ho. 496 Inhabitants. Ld Stanhope[1] at Chevening: Mr Polhill[2] at Chipsted. 4 Families of Methodists of low Rank. Their Teacher here was Bligh, a Labourer. They now go to Sevenoake. 20 Anab. of ordinary Rank. A meeting Ho. Teacher Snow, & sometimes Benge. Increase only by Children. Whole Service on Sundays. Prayers on Chr. Day, good Fr. Easter Monday & all occasional Fasts. Cat. in Lent ⟨abt 15 come⟩. 7 Sacr. Not often 20 Com. Offertory distributed by Ch. W^{ns}. Mrs Wyndham[3] left 100$^£$ in 1714 for putting out Ch^n by R & Ch W^{ns}. Mrs Stroude[4] gave 100$^£$ in 1718 for setting up ⟨by the same⟩ Girls put out with Mrs Wyndhams money. The 200[1] is now increased to 300$^£$, Lucy Countess Stanhope[5] gave 1000$^£$ in 1724 now increased to 1300$^£$ to Trustees for putting out yearly 3 or 4 Ch^n. The present Lady Stanhope[6] directs it with the strictest attention. BP. of Rochester confirms at { } Westerham, 4 miles off.
1761 some little things amiss at the Church. Rubbish & material laid at the bottom behind the pews. Parsonage Ho. &c elegant & in good Repair. 6^d in pound at a Rents raises 26$^£$
Lic. for rebuiding Ho. 1707 Entry B. V p. 251.
Exch. of ⟨some⟩ Glebe for Lands of E Stanhope VI. 274.

Tho. Herring[7] MA R. 8 May 1751. Resides & serves the Cure. R. also of Cullesden p. 405 & Preb. of York.
Samuel Preston[8] Master of Arts September 13 1774.

John Stonard[9] A.B. Cur Sal £40. Lic 1794.

July 11. 1760. Conf. at Sevenoak 12. 1764. 14. 1767. 12.

1 Philip (1714–86), 2nd earl Stanhope.
2 Charles Polhill, owner of Chipstead House from 1754: Hasted III, p. 120.
3 Rebecca Wyndham in 1714: ibid., p. 123.   4 Catherine Stroud: ibid.
5 (c.1694–1723), wife of James (1673–1721), 1st earl Stanhope.
6 Grisel (1718–1811). The *Gentleman's Magazine* vol LXXXI, p. 661 noted that she was 'remarkable for acuteness of understanding, and exquisite sensibility of heart' and for her charity and religion.
7 (17?–74), of Cambridgeshire, m. CCCC 1737, BA 1741, MA 1744, fellow, 1743–6, R. St Mary Stoke, Ipswich, R. Harbledown, 1749–50, R. Cullesden, Surrey, 1749, R. St Anne's Soho, R.

Chevening, 1751–74, preb of York, 1747–74, preb of Southwell, 1747–74, preb of Chichester, 1761–74, joint registrar Prerogative Court of Canterbury, 1753–74.

8 (1719–1803), of Oxford, m. Magdalen Hall 1736, BA 1740, MA (Queens' C) 1774, R. Chevening, 1774–1803.

9 (1769–1849), of Lambeth, m. Brasenose 1789, BA 1793, MA 1796, B & DD 1817, C. Chevening, 1794, C. Sundridge, 1801, C. East Malling, 1810, R. Aldingham, Lancs, 1814–49.

Page 347

Chiddingstone R. St Mary. ABP P ⟨8 miles S. of Sevenoak⟩. K^s books 28–9–4½. Wake 150$^£$. Herring 250$^£$ ⟨286$^£$ Mr Bale: to each his own Tithe⟩. The Parish is rather small, and hath not above 10 Ho. together in the most populous part ⟨109 families in 1717⟩. Henry Streatfield[1] Esqr. Whole Service on Sundays. Prayers W. Fr. in Lent {only [qu.} Chr. Day good Fr. &c]. Cat. frequently, esp. in Lent. A very decent & R. believes numerous Appearance of Com. 8 times in the Year. 8 Boys & 8 Girls taught to read & write: Dr Tenison[2] gave 4$^£$ a year, which R. continues. BP of Rochester confirms at Tunbridge, 5 miles off. Dr Potter saith it is worth above 300$^£$. 1761 6^d at full Rents raises 61–10–0. Parsonage Ho. &c neat & in good Order. Lic. to appropiate a Seat in the Chancel to High Street Ho. 1731 Entry B. VII 321.
Lic. to Dr Tenison to alter & improve Ho. 391.
Abt Charities here See Answers to ABP Wake in 1717.

Sackvile Spencer Bale[3] MA R. 29 Apr. 1755. R. of Westhyham [Dioc. Chich. Ecton p. 66] 7 miles off ⟨180$^£$⟩. Resides there: but frequently officiates here, & wd oftener, if he did not attend the D. of Dorsets[4] Family, as Chaplain, in the Summer. Very deaf, but his speaking not hurt by it.
Sackville Stephens Bale[5] L.L.B. Rector 1783.

Henry Austin[6] Pr. Cur. 50$^£$ serves this Cure only.
Tho. Baker[7] coming from Burstow p. 384 March 1763. 45$^£$ & Surpl. Fees 1765.

1760 Conf. at Tunbridge by BP Pearce 31. 1764. 36. 1767. 23.

1 Owner of Chiddingstone Burghersh manor and died in 1762: Hasted III, p. 221.
2 Thomas Tenison (1701–42), of Sundridge, Kent, m CCCC 1711, m. Clare 1716, LLB 1721, LLD (Trinity Hall) 1726, fellow, 1725–8, archdeacon of Carmarthen, 1727–42, V. Lydd, 1727–42, R. Chiddingstone, 1727–42, chancellor of the diocese of Oxford, 1734–42, preb of Canterbury, 1739–42.
3 (1724–83), of London, m. Christ Church 1742, BA 1746, MA 1749, R. Withyham, Sussex, V. Rottingdean, Sussex, 1751, R. Chiddingstone, 1755–83.
4 See p. 201, n. 1.
5 (1754–1836), of London, m. Christ Church 1771, BCL 1778. R. Chiddingstone, 1783–1836.
6 Of Kent, m. Queens' C 1743, BA 1747, MA (Clare) 1750, fellow Queens', fellow Clare, 1748–69, PC. Shipbourne, Kent, R. West Wickham, 1761.
7 See p. 384, n. 8.

Page 348

Dioc. Roch. D. Shoreham
Clive al. Cliffe at Hoo. R. St Helen ⟨6 miles N. of Rochester⟩. ABP P. K^s books 50$^£$. Wake 200$^£$. Herring 300$^£$ ⟨See below⟩. 80 Ho. most of them near the Church. 2 Anab. Whole Service on Sundays. Prayers at the great Festivals, & on the State Holydays. Cat. at the usual Times. 4 Sacr. betw. 20 & 30 Com. 5$^£$ a

Year & a Ho. left for teaching poor Ch[n] to read. Donations of 13–15–0 to the Poor. Rightly applied. A very unhealthy Place. Parsonage Ho. a mile from the Church. The R[s] Tenant pays him 200[f] a Year, & pays the Land Tax, & 35[f] a Year to the Curate, & 15[f] for Mutton Pyes, & Bread & Beer to every parishioner on S[t] James's day.

The Rector is not cited to the Commissarys Visitation. He grants Licences & Administrations within his own parish: & so did his Predecessors: having a Seal for that purpose. Johnson[1], in his addenda to vol. 1. of his Collection of Eccl. Laws, A.D. 803 observes, that this is a Parish most singularly exempt: for the Incumbent is the ABP[s] immediate Surrogate. And he adds, that by a Rescript of ABP Reynolds dated 1317 in Somners Ant. of Cant p. 354 [It is, in the Edition of 1703, in the Appendix p. 79 N° 75] it appears, that the Rectors of 18 Churches, there named, had the Exercise of all Spiritual Jurisdiction within their several Parishes, till he extinguished their Privileges, & subjected them to his Commissary. Johnson endeavours to shew in the same place, that this is not Cloves ho, where the Council was held. The English Topographer 8[vo] Lond. 1720 [by R. Rawlinson[2] LLD] saith p. 93 'At Cliff in this County [Kent] was a spiritual Court, held annually for the probate of Wills in that Parish: to wch I am apt to believe, belonged an old brass seal, not long since found on Black-heath in this County, wch is exactly delineated from the Original, & seems to have this Inscription round it. S. Officielit + Jurisdictiois de liba poch de Clyff. [I doubt of elit +. The seal is a Hand holding a Cross.].

James Harwood[3] R. Nov. 13. 1755. V. of Dartford, 5 miles off, where he resides. Was Chaplain to BP Wilcox[4]. Appeared at the ABP[s] Personal Visitation at Sevenoak, with the other Clergy of the Deanery July 11. 1760.
John Simpkinson[5] A.M. Rector Aug[t] 12: 1778.

Lewis Jones[6] MA Cur. 40[f] Surpl. Fees, East. Off wch R. makes up 5[f], if below it. Pr. Resides. Hath served Higham since the last Incumbents Death, but doth the same duty at Cliff. Gone.
Will. Chester[7], Cur. Pr. 1760. Gone.
Walter Owen[8] BA of Ch. Ch. 50[f]. Ord. D. by BP Ellis[9]. 22 Aug. 1756. Pr. by BP Cornwallis[10] 20 Dec. 1761. 3.
John Prat[11] V. of Hartlipp p. 212. Resides 1764. Going June 1767.
Vincent Green[12] BA of S[t] Johns Camb. bapt. 9 Dec 1743. Ord D. 20 Sept. 1767. ⟨Pr Dec 20⟩, 40[f]. Surpl Fees & East Off.
Matthew Weddel[13]. Cur. Sal £50 1789.

1760 ⟨16⟩ 13 Conf. at Rochester 1764. 21. 1767. 15

---

[1] John Johnson, *A Collection of all the Ecclesiastical Laws, Canons, Answers, or Rescripts, with other memorials concerning the government, discipline and worship of the Church of Emgland* (1720).

[2] Richard Rawlinson, *The English Topographer* (1720).

[3] (1714–78), of London, m. Christ Church 1732, BA 1736, MA (Merton) 1739, R. Ibstock, Leics, R. Uppingham, Rutland, V. Dartford, 1755–78, R. Cliffe, 1755–78.

[4] Joshua Wilcocks, bishop of Gloucester, 1721–31, bishop of Rochester, 1731–58.

[5] (1735–1815), of Kingsland, Herefordshire, m. Wadham 1753, BA (All Souls) 1757, MA (New College) 1759, R. Cliffe, 1778–1815, V. Cobham, Surrey, 1797–1815.

[6] Probably (1710–?), of Tallyllyn, co. Merioneth, m. Jesus O 1727, BA 1730, MA 1733.

[7] (1735–?), of Cheltenham, Glos, m. Queen's O 1753, BA 1757, C. Cliffe, 1760.

8 (1735–?), of Landibie, co. Carmarthen, m. Christ Church 1752, BA 1756.
9 Anthony Ellys (1690–1761), bishop of St David's, 1752.
10 Frederick Cornwallis (1713–83), bishop of Lichfield and Coventry, 1750, archbishop of Canterbury, 1768.
11 See p. 212, n. 3.
12 (1742–?), of Shoreham, Kent, m. St John's C 1762, scholar 1765, BA 1766, C. Cliffe, 1767, C. Amberley, Sussex.
13 C. Cliffe, 1789.

Page 349

Crayford al. Eard R. St Paulinus ⟨Eareth al. Eard Lambard p. 268. He names not Crayford. 2 miles W. of Dartford⟩. May 12. 1711. Ri. Collins[1] inst. Presented by Ld Westmorland[2] P. pleno jure on the Death of Gilb. Crockat[3]. May 9. 1738 Phil Twisden[4] inst. Presented by Tho. Tenison[5] DD & Cha. Worsley[6] Esqr Executors & Trustees of Sir Hen. Farmer[7] Bart, on the Death of Collins. Nov. 10. 1744 John Fermor[8] inst. by Tho[9]. son of Dr Tenison P. pleno jure, on Twisdens Resig. May 14. 1753 James Pipe[10] inst. Presented by Fra. Austen[11] of Sevenoake, Esqr P. for that Turn on Fermors Cession [who had probably sold the Presentation]. K^s books 35–13–4 Wake 120$^£$. Herring 350$^£$ ⟨AD^n Potter 300$^£$⟩. 112 Ho. ⟨150 Fam. AD^n Potter⟩. 2 Quakers: pay their Dues without Compulsion. Whole Service on Sundays Prayers on every Holyday ⟨W. Fr. in Lent⟩. 4 Sacr. betw. 20 & 30 Com. each time [very few]. BP of Rochester confirms at Dartford, 2 miles off. 1761 sev^l things amiss at Ch. Mr Blackwoods[12] Chap. & Mr Barnes's[13] Chap. mentioned. Parsonage Ho. &c extremely good, & in excellent order. 1^s in pound raises 40$^£$.

James Pipe R. as above. In Summer 1758 had not been at his Living for 2 Years. See other Complaints against him. He died June 1. 1759.
Philip Walter[14] BA 26 Nov. 1759. I deferred his Institution to the last Day, suspecting Simony: but could not obtain Proof of it. Resides, 1760. ChW^{ns} find no Fault with him. Officiates himself 1765.

Lovett[15], Cur. 40$^£$. Lives in the Parish. Gone, 1760.
Abt one Hornby[16], who desired this Curacy, see BP Pearce Sept. 1760.
Alfred William Roberts[17] A.B. Cur. Sal. £40. Lic. 1787.

1760 Conf. by BP Pearce at Dartford 17. 1764. 27. 1767. 30

1 (1679–1738), m. Brasenose 1695, BA 1699, V. Burham, Kent, 1701, V. Meopham, Kent, 1707–11, R. Crayford, 1711–38, naval chaplain at Chatham.
2 Thomas Fane (1683–1736), 12th earl of Westmoreland.
3 (16–1711), MA St Andrews, R. Langdon, 1695–1711, R. Crayford, 1702–11.
4 (1678–17?), of London, m. Christ Church 1696, BA (University), R. Crayford, 1738–44, R. Eastling, Kent, 1744, bishop of Raphoe, 1747.
5 See p. 347, n. 2. He was the executor of Sir Henry Fermor, the patron.
6 He has not been traced.   7 Fermor, 1st Bt. Died in 1734.
8 (1720–?), of Sevenoaks, m. Queen's O 1737, R. Crayford, 1744–53.
9 Thomas Tenison, gent.
10 (1722–59), of Stafford, m. Pembroke O 1739, BA 1742, MA 1745, R. Crayford, 1753–9.
11 Francis Austen (1698–1791), a solicitor who lived at The Red House in Sevenoaks. The great-uncle of Jane Austen.
12 John Blackwood, owner of Old Place House, died 1777: Hasted II, p. 277.
13 Miles Barne, owner of Crayford manor from 1750: ibid., p. 275.

[14] (1728–1806), of Moreton Hampstead, Devon, m. Clare, 1749, BA 1753, R. Crayford, 1759–1806.

[15] Perhaps Dale Lovatt (1719–?), of Penkhull, Staffs, m. Magdalen Hall 1738, BA 1742.

[16] Possibly James Hornby (1714–?), of St Andrew's Holborn, m. Brasenose 1730.

[17] (1763–1843), m. Trinity C 1783, BA 1787, MA 1792, V. St Peter's, St Albans, Herts, 1801–20, R. Little Burstead, Essex, 1820–43, PC. Billericay, 1821–43.

Page 350

Dioc. Roch. D. Shoreham

Darenth al. Daruth V. S[t] Margaret ⟨2 miles S. of Dartford⟩. Belonged to the Priory of Rochester. DCh of Rochester P. Tenths 19–10¾. Certified 45[£]. Now 80[£]. 50 Ho. Service once, as usual ⟨twice in Summer 1717⟩. The Church of Sutton at Hone is abt half a mile off. Prayers & Sermon on the greater Festivals. A ruined Chapel [not named]. Cat. in Lent. 4 Sacr. Abt 20 Com. 4–6–8 & 1–4–0 given to the Poor annually in Bread. ChW[ns] distribute the Offertory money. BP of Rochester confirms at Dartford, 2 miles off. 1761. Mr Farrant[1], Lessee of Rectory, shd ciel the Chancel, it wd cost but 3 or 4[£]. Sev[l] things at Church want mending. And a few at V. Ho. wch is an ordinary one. A mile from Darenth are the Ruines of S[t] Margarets Chapel, in this Parish. Near it 2 or 3 Acres, wch is the chief part of the Glebe.

Tho. Thompson[2] MA V. Sept. 1758. Master of the Kings School at Rochester. 33–6–8 from the Church. Only 2 Scholars besides the Kings Scholars. Resigned July 5. 1759.
Tho. Frank[3] LLB. V. Aug. 22. 1759. Cur. of Chatham, said to be worth 150[£] a Year. BP Pearce. Min Can. of Roch. Resides there. Resigned Dec. 5. 1766. V. of Stockbury p. 227.
Samuel Denne[4] V. May. 18. 1767 holds it with { }.

Rich. Bathurst[5] Cur. Licenced for Sutton at Hone ⟨¾ of a mile off⟩, in Dioc. ⟨Roch⟩ which he serves. Resides at Darenth in V. Ho. 20[£] & Surpl. Fees. Pr. James White[6] Cur. Vis. 1765 20 G[s].

1760. Conf. by BP Pearce at Dartford 9. 1764. 14. 1767. 10

[1] William Farrant: Hasted II, p. 372.
[2] (1732–86), of Beverley, Yorkshire, m. St John's C 1749, BA 1755, MA 1758, BD 1766, headmaster Rochester School, 1755–86, V. Darenth, 1758–9, V. Hoo, 1759–86, R. Staplehurst, 1785–6.
[3] See p. 207, n. 11.
[4] (1730–99), of Westminster, m. CCCC 1748, BA 1753, MA 1756, V. Lamberhurst, 1754–67, V. Darenth, 1767–99, V. Wilmington, 1767–99.
[5] (1728–?), of Goudhurst, Kent, m. St Edmund Hall 1744, BA (Brasenose) 1748.
[6] (1739–?), of Wilmington, Kent m. Brasenose 1757, BA 1761.

Page 351

Downe. Said to have been a Chapel to Orpington. Now a Licence is granted to it, as to a separate Curacy. {V.} ⟨R.⟩ of Orpington p. 372 ⟨See below⟩. 40[£] ⟨of wch 13–6–8 from the Lessee of the Rectory of Orpington. See Orpington V. p. 372⟩. 45 Ho. Many Absenters, obstinate from Custom. Service once a Sunday, & once at Hayes p. 362. No Prayers on Week-Days, but in Lent. [{qu.} good Fr.

Chr. day &c]. Cat. on Sundays in Lent. 4 Sacr. 7 or 8 Com. [Extremely few]. The minister complains of the low State of Religion, & desires the assistance of the civil Magistrate or the spiritual Court. 1761 much wanting to be done at the Church. A Ho. left by Will to the Repairs of it, let for 3^f a year, wch is added to the Church Rate. 1^s in pound at ½ Rents raises 28^f. Cur. hath 13-6-8 as above, 15^f from Small Tithe, 4-15-0 from a Ho. with a Garden & Acre of Land, in all 33-1-8, besides Surplice Fees.

Cur. chosen by R. of Orpington, licensed to receive Orders to serve Downe a chapel annexed to the Rectory Entry B IV. 311.

1763 May. Nothing done of wt was orderd 1761. Promise now to begin immediately. Curates Ho. see above, much out of Repair. Pales of ½ Ch. Y^d belong to one Mr Glover[1] of London.

1765 Vis. Cur. believes every thing orderd is done.

Will. Farquhar[2] MA Cur. licenced 31 March 1755. Resides in the Parish of Hayes ⟨p. 362⟩, & serves both, 4 miles asunder.

Francis Fawkes[3] Master of Arts Licensed April 19 1774.

Thomas Browne[4] A.B. Licensed Octr 4: 1777.

Henry Fly[5] A.M. Licensed 1788.

Thos Pennington[6] A.M. Cur. Sal. £25 lic. 1791.

Conf. See Hayes 362

[1] Richard Glover, merchant, owner of Downe-court: Hasted II, p. 56.
[2] Aberdeen MA 1761, R. Hayes, 1755-74, C. Downe, 1755-74.
[3] (1720-77), m. Jesus C 1738, scholar, BA 1742, MA 1743, C. Bramham, Yorks, C. Croydon, Surrey, PC. Orpington, 1755-74, V. St Mary Cray, 1755, V. Knockholt, 1755, R. Hayes, 1774-7, R. Downe, 1774-7, chaplain to Princess dowager of Wales.
[4] (1721-88), m. Trinity C 1741, BA (St John's C) 1741, C. Hadlow, 1747, C. Knockholt, 1777, C. Downe, 1777-88.
[5] (1744-1833), of Cripplegate, London, m. Brasenose 1762, BA 1766, fellow, MA 1773, B & DD 1797, minor canon St Paul's, 1783, PC. Knockholt, 1788-1820, PC. Downe, 1788-1817, V. Willesden, 1821, PC. Kingsbury with Twyford.
[6] See p. 199, n. 7.

Page 352
Dioc. Roch. D. Shoreham
Eard See Crayford p. 349

East-Farley V. ⟨3 miles S. of Maidstone⟩. Was appropriated by ABP Reynolds[1] to the Hospital at Maidstone. Ecton. ⟨Improp. Ld Westmoreland[2]⟩. The King, P. K^s books 6-16-8. Wake, Herring 35^f ⟨See below[1)]*⟩. Between 60 & 70 Ho. ⟨75 or 80 Fam AD^n Potter⟩. 2 Families of Dissenters. Some Absenters of low Rank, notwithstanding much Admonition: but greatly lessend. Whole Service on Sundays & Chr. Day. Prayers once & Sermon on good Fr. Prayers the day after the 3 great Festivals. Prayers, if a Congregation, on W. Th. Sat. in Passion Week &c. Cat. from Easter to the End of Oct. Will be Exp. 4 Sacr. abt 40 Com. generally each time. John Francklin[3], Citizen of London gave 100^f in 1609, with which 6 Ho. for poor were built, 2 Schools for Reading, Sewing &c to which the minister & Parishioners send Ch^n. Mr Harris[4], late V. gave 50^s a Year to buy

Linnen for the Poor. V. Ho. was ruinous, now repaired. BP of Rochester confirms at West-Malling, 5 miles off.

[1]* In ABP Wakes Book 35$^£$ is struck out, & 80$^£$ put. AD^n Potter saith, it is now 130$^£$. Qu. if not from Hops, or something uncertain. 2/3 From the Hops. 1761. A Chapel adjoyning to the Chancel belongs to Mr Brown[5] of Essex who hath a Farm here, called Pimps Farm. Sev^l Repairs wanting at Church. 6^d in pound at full Rents raises 30$^£$. Vic Ho & Gard. made extremely neat by pres^t V. at considerable Expence. Garden small. Glebe very little.

Ezekiel Paul De la Douespe[6] BA V. 28 Feb. 1752. Was obliged to board 2 miles from his Church. Now for 3 Years hath resided in V. Ho. excepting a visit of 5 or 6 weeks to his Father & Mother in London.
Henry Friend[7] A.M. Vicar 1795.

Edward Hasted[8] Junr Lic. 1784 Sal. £40.

1760. Conf. by BP Pearce at W. Malling, 25. 1762 at Maidstone 12. 1764 by BP Pearce 4. 1767. 13

[1] Walter Reynolds, archbishop of Canterbury, 1313–27.
[2] See p. 349, n. 2. [3] John Franckelden: Hasted IV, p. 380.
[4] Arthur Harris (1656–1727), of Maidstone, m, Trinity O 1671, BA (New Inn Hall) 1674, MA 1677, C. Aldington, 1678, V. East Farleigh, 1685–1727: 'A man of exemplary life and conversation, and of extensive charity': Hasted IV, p. 383.
[5] Thomas Browne: ibid.
[6] (1727–94), m. Clare 1746, BA 1749, MA 1752, V. East Farleigh, 1752–94.
[7] See p. 211, n. 5. [8] See p. 17, n. 7.

Page 353

East-Malling V. St James ⟨4 miles W. of Maidstone⟩. Belonged to the Monastery of Malling. Sir Roger Twisden[1] Bart P. ⟨& Impropr.⟩. K^s books 10-8-4. Wake Herring 130$^£$ ⟨See below. Abt 130$^£$, 1762⟩. 4 miles long, 2 broad. 2 Hamlets, Larkfield & New Head. Abt 150 Ho. & 800 Inhabitants. The Patron lives here. One Family of 5 Persons, Papists. Go to Mass at their Fathers Ho. at Ditton. Whole Service on Sundays. Prayers W. Fr. & Festivals. Cat. in Lent, with Lewis's Exp. Sacr. on the great Festivals, & 5 other Times, Abt 70 Com. Offertory given chiefly by the minister to the sick & needy, & for teaching 16 Ch^n to read. 8$^£$ a Year given for this to a Master & Mistress. Tithe of Hay & Seeds given to the Vicarage by Judge Twisden[2]. Eleven Acres of Land by Sir Tho. Twisden[3]. 10$^£$ ⟨1762 12$^£$⟩ a Year out of Lands called Severnham, in Tewkesbury Parish, to augment the Vicarage, by Sir Rob. Brett[4] of West-Malling. [{Was this in Conjunction with the Qus Bounty?}]. ⟨It is paid the V. as one of the four Lecturers of West-Malling⟩. 5$^£$ a Year for putting a Child Apprentice, by Judge Twisdens Lady[5]. BP of Rochester confirms at West-Malling 2 miles off.
1761. V. Ho. let with Garden & Ch. yd & an Acre of Glebe to Mrs Bartholomew, for 20$^£$ a year. A Building with mud walls in Ch. Yd, added to the Stable, wch Mr Jacobs thinks he need not repair. Very perverse: owned V. was said to be worth much above 130$^£$, but wd not answer questions ⟨Called in Mr Jacobs Disp. 180$^£$⟩. Sev^l Repairs wanting, Sir R. Twysden sd BP Sherlock[6] told him BP^s had no power to order them. 6^d in pound at full Rents raises 25$^£$.

Rich[d] Jacob[7], V. 21 Oct. 1757. V. of New Romney p. 137. Resides here in a Ho. as convenient for himself & the Parish as V. Ho. [Qu. in what Condition is V. Ho. He saith, very good. {Dead Oct.} Died Sept. 1762.

Hill[8] Dan. AB V. Oct. 20. 1762 was C. of Ospring p. 170 & Schoolm. of Faversham. Quits both, & will reside here.

Hugh Frazer[9] Cur. Sal £50. lic. 1788.

1760 Conf. at West-Malling, by BP Pearce, 27. or 30. 1762 At Maidstone 17. 1764. By BP Pearce 45. 1767. 56.

[1] (1705–772) 5th Bt, MP for Kent, 1741–54.
[2] Thomas Twisden (1602–83) 1st Bt, MP for Maidstone, 1646–8, 1660, judge in court of king's bench 1660.
[3] (1668–1728) 3rd Bt, MP for Kent, 1722–7.
[4] By will in 1620: Hasted IV, p. 528.
[5] Lady Jane Twisden in 1702: ibid., p. 514. Mrs Bartholomew was probably Elizabeth, from Addington, who died in 1775: p. 547.
[6] Thomas Sherlock (1678–1761), bishop of London, 1748–61.
[7] See p. 137, n. 1.   [8] See p. 158, n. 6.
[9] (1764–1805), of Aberdeen, m. Balliol 1782, BA 1786, MA 1798, C. East Malling, 1788, R. Woolwich, 1805–37.

Page 354
Dioc. Roch. D. Shoreham
East-Peckham R. An Impropriation, held by Sir {Roger} ⟨{qu if not} Will⟩ Twisden[1], as Lessee to DCh Cant. K[s] books 23[£].

East-Peckham V. S[t] Michael ⟨8 miles from Maidstone, 10 miles SE of Sevenoak⟩. DCh Cant. P. K[s] books 14[£] ⟨Now 190[l.] Depends on Hops. 140 in Disp IX. 80. 200[£] ib. V. 258⟩. Above 3 miles long, abt 3 broad. 200 Ho. & Cottages. Sir Will Twisden. A widow & her Daughter Papists. They live on a Farm. All her Sons Protestants. Roads bad, & ¾ of the people more than 2 miles from the Church. Yet there is a large Congregation, & all the People of Substance come as often as they can. Whole Service on Sundays. Prayers Ash. W. good Fr. Chr. Day & S[t] Stephens. Cat. once a week in Lent with D[r] Stebbings[2] Exp. 2 Sacr at each of the great Festivals & Mich. Abt 50 Com. BP of Rochester confirms at W. Malling 4 miles off.
1761 Many Repairs wanting in Church & Sir W[m] Twysdens Chap. wch shd be laid to the Chancel. 6[d] in the pound at ½ Rents raises 30[£]. V. Ho. mean & small: but intended to be much improved.

Henry Hall[3] MA V. 6 July 1756. R. of Harbledown p. 37. Resides there. R. also of Orpington sine Cure p. 371. Died Nov. 1. 1763.
John Davis[4] DD. V. Apr. 21. 1764. R. of Hamsey Co. Suss. 170[£] & Preb of Cant. Licence of non residence granted him during pleasure 12 May 1764. Lives at his own House near. Dead.
William Tatton[5] DD. V. Aug. 29. 1766.
George Berkeley[6] LLD. V. Sept: 16: 1775.
Richard Lucas[7] D.D. Vicar 1787.
Austen Gamman[8], Deacon, [now Pr. 2]. Cur. 40[£] ⟨& Surpl. Fees⟩. Resides in V. Ho.

Thomas Vyner[9] L.L.D. Rector 1789.

Geo. St John Mitchell[10] Cur. Sal £50. lic. 1787.

1760 Conf. by BP Pearce at Malling 65. 1764. 38. 1767. 47

[1] William Twisden (1706–67) 6th Bt, of Roydon Hall in East Peckham. The confusion here is understandable. The Twisden family had two branches, both of which held a baronetcy. To add to the confusion, there was much inter-marriage between the two branches.
[2] Henry Stebbing (1687–1763), *A Collection of Papers written in defence of the doctrine and discipline of the Church of England. To which are added a short exposition of the Church Catechism, and a sermon concerning the excellency of the Knowledge of Christ Jesus* (Cambridge, 1727).
[3] See p. 37, n. 4.   [4] See p. ii, n. 19.   [5] Ibid., n. 16.
[6] Ibid., n. 31.   [7] Ibid., n. 18.
[8] (1734–?), of Wrotham, Kent, m. University 1751, BA 1755, MA, 1758.
[9] (1753–1804), of Frankton, Warwks. m. University 1771, BCL 1782, V. East Peckham, 1789–1804, preb of Canterbury, 1782–1805.
[10] Probably (1761–1814), of Ireland, m. TCD 1778, BA 1783, C. East Peckham, 1787, PC. Leeds w. Broomfield, 1801–14.

Page 355

Eynesford al. Aynesford R. St Martin ⟨6 miles N of Sevenoak⟩. ABP P. Kings books 12–16–8. Wake, Herring 250^f. Lady Dyke[1] is Lessee of the great Tithes & pays 40^f a year to R & 20^f to V. which last was reserved ⟨in 1681⟩ by Francis Potter ⟨Porter[2]⟩, Rector, Kennet of Impr. p. 306. ABP Sancroft is said to have induced him to it. ⟨Reserved in a Lease by Francis Porter conf. in 1667 Entry B. II. 112 not mentioned in 1675 III. 254⟩. The present Lease is for 21 Years from 17 July 1758: & doth not oblige the Lessee to pay the Land Tax. The Fine for 7 Years is said to be 100^f. BP of Rochester confirms at Dartford, 6 miles off. The Estate was 190^f or 200^f a Year in 1758, & 130^f fine taken ⟨150 Mr Hall[3]⟩. The Rectors 40^f a year is taxed at 24^f, & the vicars 20^f at 12^f.
1761. Parsonage Ho. lett in 3 or 4 Tenem^{ts}: in good Repair.
Lease 14 Nov. 1681 for 21 years. Vicar made a party Entry B. IV. 175. 1663.
Estate worth 190^f a year besides the Rent & Augmentation.

John Lynch[4] DD. R 27 Oct. 1731. See here p. 4.
George Secker[5] MA R June 27. 1760. Resigned Oct. 13. ⟨11⟩ 1763
John Fowell[6] D.D. R Oct. 14. 1763 R. of Hunton p. 364

[1] Lady Ann Dyke, wife of Sir Thomas Dyke. She died in 1763.
[2] Francis Porter (1620–74), of Nether Langwith, Notts, m. Oriel 1637, BA 1641, MA 1644, R. Eynesford, 1666–74.
[3] See p. 37, n. 4.   [4] See p. ii, n. 1.
[5] Ibid., n. 21.   [6] See p. 4, n. 9.

Page 356

Dioc. Roch. D. Shoreham
Eynsford al Aynesford V. St Martin ⟨6 miles N. of Sevenoak & Wrotham⟩. {ABP} ⟨R. of Eynesford⟩. P. Kings books 12^f. Wake, Herring 70^f ⟨See below⟩. The Lessee of the Rectory pays 20^f ⟨liable to Land Tax⟩. 5½ miles long, 3 broad; 2 Villages, 105 Ho. The Inhabitants of one Village, 2 miles from the

Church, go to Cray Church, which is nearer. Usually whole Service. Was otherwise formerly. See Answers[1]. Leave desired to assist a Neighbour, or take another Curacy, if offerd. Prayers on Ash W. good Fr. Easter Monday [& surely Chr. Day]. Scarce a Congregation then. Cat. in Lent, with APB Wakes Exp. Servts not sent. 5 Sacr. 35 or 40 Com ⟨above 20 AD^n Potter⟩ [very few]. Sir Percival Hart[2] gave in 1622, 13-4 to the Vicar for a Sermon in January on repentance, & 2$^£$ to the Poor pd by Lady Dyke[3], descended from him, living chiefly at Lullingston ⟨Castle⟩ a mile off, an Example, of Piety & Charity, Lessee of the great Tithes. Mr Roper[4] gave 2$^£$ a year to the Poor, out of Lands at Greenwich. Bp of Rochester confirms at Dartford, 6 miles off. Curate saith, the Tithes are let for 70$^£$, & the Sermon & Surplice Fees make abt 6$^£$, besides the Pension of 20$^£$. Church & Chancel good. V. Ho. old, but in Repair.
1761 A Chapel on S. side of Church ⟨& open to it⟩, belonging to Mr Collins[5] of Nockholt to be repaired or pulled down. He promises to take Care abt it. Some little things wanting at Church. 6^d in pound at ½ Rents raises 10$^£$. V. Ho. in good order. 1763 Mr Collins cannot be expected to repair his Chapel, having but little of the Estate, to wch it belonged. he shd take it down, or give it to ChW^{ns} to take down, & build up that Side of the Ch, & make a window in it, for wch the materials will pay, & may have a pew there. Notice of this given to him. 1765 Vis. Tiling in Repair: never was cieled: materials, being chiefly Flints, will not pay for taking it down.

Benj. Longley[6] BL V. 23 June 1750. V. of Tong p. 228 & Cur. of Ash p. 2. where he resides
Thomas Verrier Alkin[7] Vicar 1783.
James Andrew[8] D.D. 1784.
Henry Montague Davis[9] A.M. 1791.

Robert Wilkin[10], Pr. Cur. Resides in V. Ho. 30$^£$ a year, Surpl. Fees. & Easter Offerings, abt 6$^£$. Accused by one Prior of ommitting prayer for Parlt $^{&c}$, at least in afternoons. Promises, 20 Apr 1762. Allowed to officiate at Lullingstone (see above) the only Ho in that Parish, w^n Lady Dyke is there, & Mr Lamb[11] the minister absent ⟨at Bristol⟩ but desired to do the whole Service at his own Church besides. 1765 accused by one Mr Floyd[12] of not reading Prayers decently. Ch W^{ns} were told it, & sd there was no Cause of Complaint.

John Hay Dalmatry[13] Cur. Sal. £40. lic. 1792.

July 13. 1760. Conf. at Wrotham 32. 1764 By BP Pearce at Dartford 44. 1767. 21.

[1] LPL, Original returns: MS 1134/5, ff. 127-30.
[2] Resided at Lullingstone house: Hasted II, p. 535.
[3] See p. 355, n. 1.   [4] Sir Anthony Roper, knighted in 1603.
[5] Probably Thomas Collins, owner of the mansion of Kirkby-court: Hasted II, p. 499.
[6] See p. 2, n. 3.
[7] (1746-84), of Canterbury, m. St John's C 1765, BA 1769, MA 1772, C. Acrise and Swingfield, 1769, V. Lenham, 1772-81, V. Eynesford, 1783-4
[8] See p. 50, n. 14.   [9] See p. 4, n. 5.
[10] Perhaps (1722-?), of Brough Sowerby, Westmoreland, m. Queen's O 1740, BA 1745, MA 1748.
[11] Davies Lambe (1716-71), of Southwell, Notts, m. St John's 1735, BA 1738, MA 1741, fellow, 1739-49, R. Ridley, Kent, 1740-71, R. Lullingstone, 1748-71.

[12] See LPL, MS Secker 6, f. 210: 'Copy of a Letter lately sent to the revd. Mr Wilkins at Eynesford [1 January, 1763].

[13] (1768–?), of Walthamstow, Essex, m. Hertford, 1789, BA 1794.

Page 357

Farningham ⟨near Dartford⟩ V. St Peter & St Paul ⟨6 miles NW of Wrotham⟩. Belonged to the Priory of Canterbury ⟨DCh. Impropr.⟩. ABP P. K^s books 9–5–10. Wake 60. Herring 90$^£$ ⟨or more, not 100$^£$. Not taxed⟩. 3 miles long, ¼ of a mile broad. 50 Ho. ⟨60 AD^n Potter⟩. Service once on Sundays ⟨See below⟩. Prayers Ash W. good Fr. & all Fast Days [{qu} & Chr. Day]. Cat. every Sunday in Lent. 4 Sacr. From 30 to 40 Com. A large Private School for Reading, Writing & Arithmetick. 14–13–4 a Year to the Poor. 20^s a Year given by a former V. lost. Service was twice, till the Parishioners consented, that Mr Thomas, the late Curate, shd take another Curacy: & will now be twice again ⟨Is so 1760⟩. Abt 17 miles from London. Direct near Dartford, 5 miles off: where BP of Rochester confirms, at Dartford 5 miles off.

1761. Repairs wanting chiefly to the Chancel. Parsonage Ho. a mean little Brick Building, in repair. V. Ho. old, too large: in as good order as can be expected. 6^d in the pound at full Rents raises 33$^£$.

9 Acres of Glebe abt the House, whch is near the Church: a pretty Garden: good Country.

John Pery[1] MA ⟨now DD⟩ V. 8 Feb. 1754. ⟨Was before that, & is,⟩ R of Ash, Dioc. Rochester, 4 miles off. Resides there. {qu} Value, 250$^£$ a Year. Died 24 Oct 1767.

John Saunders[2] MA V 13 Apr. 1768 V. of Newington p. 221 ⟨22 miles off⟩. Will reside chiefly here, & offer the Curacy of Newington to Mr Heathfield.

Thomas[3] BA of Jes. Coll Oxon. Pr Cur. 30$^£$ & Surpl. Fees & Use of Ho. & Gardens ⟨worth 40$^£$ in all⟩. Serves the Cure of Fawkham, 4 miles off. Died abt Whits. 1759.

John Heathfield[4] coming Feb. 1760 from Hartlip p. 212. Same Allowance. Ord. Pr. Sept. 23. 1759. 2. 40$^£$ & Surpl. Fees, with Ho. & Ground. Vis. 1765.

July 13. 1760 Conf. at Wrotham 28. 1764. By BP Pearce at Dartford 21. 1767. 16

[1] [Perry] (1713–67), of Pattingham, Staffs, m. Pembroke O 1731, BA 1736, MA, DD (Christ Church), V. Clent, Staffs, 1736, R. Ash, –67, V. Farmingham, 1754–67.

[2] See p. 33, n. 3.

[3] Probably John Thomas, of Llanllooney, co. Carmarthen, m. Jesus O 1747, BA 1751.

[4] See p. 212, n. 9.

Page 358

Dioc. Roch. D. Shoreham

Gillingham V. St Mary with the Chapel of Lydging al. Lidsing ⟨ABP Wakes Book adds Upbury. Upberry Entry B. III. 295. 2 miles E of Rochester⟩, St Mary Magd. ⟨5 miles S from Gillingham⟩. Belonged to the Monastery of Sexburgh. Brazen Nose Coll. [& the Trustees of Middleton School, Ecton] P. ⟨Mrs Proby[1] of Rochester, Lessee⟩. K^s books 15–13–11½. Wake 100$^£$. Herring, ⟨AD^n

Potter⟩. 200^f. It comprehends part of the village of Brumpton, & abt 290 Ho. with 7 in Lydging. A few Methodists: lessened. Many Absenters, mostly Shipwrights, of whom the Parish chiefly consists. Not increased. Whole Service at the Church, excepting once a Month in the Afternoon, when the Service is at Lydging. 4 miles off. Prayers on the Holydays of the great Festivals, W. Fr. in Lent, Passion Week 30 Jan. 29 May, 5 Nov. [{qu} Directed 22 June]. Cat. on Sundays in Lent. Some Ch^n come, no Servants. 5 Sacr. abt 60 Com. Lands, Tenements & Pensions, in all abt 10^f a Year, given to the Poor. So applied. BP of Rochester confirms at Rochester, 2 miles off. Brumpton, lately built, the most populous part of the parish 1½ mile from Gillingham. Not ½ mile from Chatham. So they go thither to Church. Few Ch^n in proportion: few of these taught. Great part of the People belong to the Dock Yard & are profane.
1761. NE wall of Middle Chancel, belongs to Coll. must be rebuilt, & the Roof repair'd. N. Isle, belongs to Mr Lambert[2], in a shameful Condition. Mr Lamberts chapel, & an opposite one mentioned. Ch yd fenced by a dead Hedge. V. Ho. &c almost new & put in good Order by V. at a great Expence. Lydging, mean, ruinous, no Bell, shd be sufferd to fall. Only 4 or 8 Ho^s. & within ½ mile of Bredhurst. 1^s in pound at ½ Rents raises 3^f. A thatched V. Ho. let for 30^s, seldom pd. Notoriously unwholesome Entry B IV 538.

John Jenkinson[3] MA V. 10 Jan. 1753. Resides in his proper House. 1765 hath thoroughly repaired the Chancel of the Chapel: the Ho there fallen. R. of Ruckinge p. 139.
Houstonne Radcliffe[4] D.D. Vicar. 1780.

William Bagshaw Harrison[5] Cur. Sal £50 lic. 1795.

1760 Conf. by BP Pearce at Rochester 20. 1764. 22. 1767. 34.

[1] Widow of John Proby of Wouldham who died in 1758. She died in 1771: Hasted IV, p. 241.
[2] Thomas Lambard, owner of Gillingham manor: ibid, p. 231.
[3] See p. 139, n. 6.   [4] See p. 15, n. 8.
[5] (1769-1849), of Daventry, Northants, m. Merton 1786, BA 1790, MA 1809, C. Gillingham, 1795, V. Darenth, 1801-1801, V. Goudhurst, 1801-1849.

Page 359
Donativa in Gillingham 6-13-4

This is transcribed from Mr Haynes's & ABP Wakes Parochial Books. It stands in the Book 1663.

Page 360
Dioc Roch. D. Shoreham.
Grayne, al St James in the Isle of Greane V. ⟨13 miles N. of Rochester⟩. Belonged to the Prioress & Nuns of St Mary & St Sexburgh in Shepey. ABP P. Ecton. No Evidence of that. July 5. 1716 Wm Reeves[1] Gent P. for that Turn. Feb. 5 1753 Tho. Best[2] of Chilston Esqr P. in full Right. Jan 17. 1756 Rich. Peck[3] of Milton near Gravesend Ironmonger. P. in full Right ⟨See below⟩. Kings books 9-11-8. Herring 60^f ⟨Right. Clear of Taxes &c⟩. 3 miles long, 2 broad. 23 Ho. Many Absenters. Motive unknown. No V. Ho. Service once on

Sundays. Most of the Parishioners far from the Church. Seldom 40 come: often not 20, in bad weather none. Will be Cat. in Lent. No Com. at Chr. 1758. Dr Plume[4] left 5^f a Year towds a School. None for many Years. One will be set up to teach the Ch^n the Cat. at least, if not to read also it is hoped the Arrears will be pd to it ⟨See Mr Hancorn[5] Dec. 8. 1759⟩. From Rochester to Grayne very unhealthy. Mr Hancorn saith, Mr Nynn[6] ⟨[a Baker]⟩ of Gravesend hath been for 20 years & is now Patron. See his Letters Nov. 26, Dec. 5. 1759 ⟨& see below⟩. BP of Rochester confirms at Rochester 13 miles off. It is near Queenborough: but the water between. 1761 Mr Page[7] of Rochester Impropr. He takes in Kind. No Building of any kind belonging to V. Much Repair wanting at Ch. 1^s in pound raises 27^f. Sr Edw. Hales[8] Patron in full Right 1664 Entry B. I. 91. Mr Jones[9] Cur. calls the sequestrator, Mr Hide, June. 9. 1765.

Francis Ireland[10] ⟨BA⟩ V. Jan. 17. 1756. Absconds for Debt. R. of Longfield, 10 miles W. of Rochester, worth 50^f a Year, under 5^f in K^s books.
John Dolman[11] Clerk V. April 22. 1771.
Luke Phillips[12] V December 6 1774.
Richd Hancorn[13] Cur. 30^f from Sequestrator. V. of Stoke the next Parish. Resides at Rochester, 13 miles from Grayne & saith no Clergyman is nearer. Serves only these two.

J. Jones desires to serve it with Woldham Dioc. Roch, Apr. 1764. See Letter ⟨Allowed⟩. Gone. Scarce any Service, Vis. 1765. [Dec. 1765 No Service for 11 weeks. BP Pearce writes to the Minister of Stoke, I think Higgins, 3 miles off, to serve it. Mr Hancorn, Sequestrator. 30^f. Oct 1767 Mr Whaite[14] from Rochester, the last 18 months.

---

[1] He has not been traced.   [2] See p. 54, n. 2.   [3] He has not been traced.
[4] Thomas Plume (1630–1704), of Maldon, Essex, m. Christ 1646, BA 1650, BD 1661, DD 1673, V. East Greenwich, 1658–1704, R. Merston, 1662–1704, R. Little Easton, 1665, archdeacon and preb of Rochester, 1679–1704.
[5] See n. 13.   [6] Walter Nynn: Hasted IV, p. 257.   [7] John Page: ibid.
[8] (c.1626–84) 2nd Bt, MP for Maidstone, 1660, MP for Queenborough, 1661–79.
[9] Probably John Jones (1718–?), of South Cerney, Glos, m. Brasenose 1736.
[10] (1715–?), of Westminster, m. Christ Church 1733, BA 1737, V. Grain, 1756–71, R. Longfield.
[11] Perhaps (1740–74), of Bristol, m. Wadham 1757, BA 1761, V. Grain, 1771–4, PC. Little Brickhill, V. Chalke.
[12] Perhaps (1752–1828), of Llannynis, co Brecon, m. St Edmunds Hall 1792, V. Grain, 1774–1813, C. Ifield, 1810, R. Ifield, 1812–28.
[13] (1728–89), of Herefordshire, m. St John's C 1746, BA 1750, MA 1753, V. Stoke, 1753–65. He quitted the clerical profession after inheriting the seat of Hollingbourne-Hill in 1765; Hasted V, p. 472.
[14] Possibly Thomas Whaites, of Norfolk, m. CCCC 1756, BA 1760.

Page 361
Halstead R. St Margaret. ABP P. K^s books 5–17–11. ⟨18 miles form London. 5 miles NW of Sevenoak⟩. Wake 70^f. Herring 90^f. ⟨R. saith not 80^f⟩. 14 Ho. Mr Bagshaw[1], who resides in London, but is here occasionally: 3 Farm Ho. the rest Cottages. Service once on Sundays [Chr. Day, good Fr. & all occasional Fasts & Thanksgivings {[No mention of Prayers on other Days]}. Few Ch^n: no Cat. R. exhorts Parents to bring their Ch^n to Church, that they may early distinguish the Lords Day from others. 4 Sacr. 5 or 6 Com. or w^n Mr Bagshaw is there, 7 or 8.

An Alms Ho. for 2 or 3 Families, built in 1720 by { } Lansden[2] Esq[r]. No Endowmt. Church new built, well pewed, decent. Parsonage Ho. large enough for the Living: repaired abt 5 years ago, & ever since ⟨justly⟩ looked on by the Parish Officers as in good Repair. Glebe Land abt 3 Acres. Edw. Ashe[3] of London Merch[t] gave by Will 26 Apr. 1657 to the Church & poor, out of the Cock, & the Bell on the Hoop in Philpot Lane, a Rent Charge of 5[£]. Applied so by the Parish Officers. R. will encourage a Woman to teach the Ch[n] to read ⟨Hath done it, 1760⟩: he hath endeavoured in vain to get more Communicants. The BP of Rochester confirms at Westerham 5 miles off. John Hoadley[4] coll. 21 Nov. 1678. Walter Foot[5] coll. July 10. 1725 on the death of Hoadley. Carswell Winder[6] inst. as below on pres. of the Crown by lapse on the Death of Foot. 1761. Mr Bagshaw, see above, an Ironmonger, who hath bought the great Ho. late Ld Veres[7], will put in order wt wants it. 1[s] in pound at ½ or ⅔ Rents raises 9 or 10[£]. Pars. Ho. small, brick. That & out Ho[s] in good Condition.

Carswell Winder MA R. 23 June 1742. ⟨Pres. by Crown on Lapse⟩. Resides on the Cure of Kempsing & Seale, ⟨2 Parishes⟩, 5 miles off. Here almost every Week. Only Curate: false. See above. Promised on a vacancy to Ld Vere for Mr Hunter. Paralytick: amended by a thunderstroke.
George Stinton[8] D.D. Aug[st]. 25. 1770.
{Richard} ⟨Edward⟩ Hardy[9] B.A. R. Oct[r] 8th 1771.

Will. Winder[10], Cur. Pr. Brother to R. Resides in the Parsonage Ho. 20[£] ⟨& Surpl. Fees⟩. Cur. also of Otford, abt 3 miles off, p. 377. Quitting Otford for Knockholt p. 369.
Thomas Sackville Curteis[11] Clerk, Curate Licensed May 26. 1777 with a Salary of £40 p. ann.

July 11. 1760 Conf. at Sevenoak 6. 1764 by BP Pearce 9. 1767. 3

---

[1] Robert Bagshaw, owner of Halstead Place from 1755: Hasted III, p. 17.
[2] Probably John Lansdell, the owner of Halstead Place until 1738: ibid.
[3] Originally from Wiltshire. Owned Halstead Place in the seventeenth century: ibid., p. 13.
[4] 'Of St John's C', when ordained. R. Halstead, 1678–1725.
[5] (1689–1750), of Madley, Herts, m. Brasenose 1707, BA 1711, MA (King's) 1719, V. Chalgrave, Beds, 1712–43, V. Harlington, 1718–50, R. Halstead, 1725–42, R. Hockliffe, Beds, 1743–50.
[6] (1706–70), of Bray, Berks, m. Trinity O 1723, BA 1727, MA 1731, R. Halstead, 1742–70.
[7] Lord Vere Beauclerk, 3rd son of the duke of St Albans.
[8] See p. 149, n. 4.
[9] (1715–97), of Tunstall, Lancs, m. Christs 1733, scholar 1735, BA 1737, R. Halstead, 1771–97, R. Sevenoaks, 1775–7, master of Sevenoaks school.
[10] (1721–91), of Berks, m. Pembroke O 1739, BA 1743.
[11] (17?–1831), of Kent, m. Jesus C 1771, scholar 1772, LLB 1778, C. Halstead, 1777, R. Sevenoaks, 1777–1831.

Page 362
Dioc. Roch. D. Shoreham
Hayes al. Heese R. S[t] Mary ⟨3 miles E of Croydon⟩. Rector of Orpington P. Tenths 13–9¼. Certified 49[£]. Wake 60[£]. Herring 70[£] ⟨Right⟩. One small village, & abt 48 Ho. R[t] Hon[ble] Wm Pitt[1] Esq[r]. He & Lady Esther[2] constant at Church & Sacramt. Sev[l] Absenters of mean Rank: go to Alehouses, instead of Church. Not used to be rebuked by their Ministers. Private exhortation hath

prevailed on some. Service once on Sundays. No Prayers on Week Days, but in Lent ⟨See next line⟩, wⁿ Chⁿ are cat. twice a week. 4 Sacr. 6 or 7 Com. each time [Incredibly few]. {Qu.} Chr. Day, Good Fr. State Fasts & Festivals. A Lady in 1693 left a few Acres of Land, rented at 3ᶠ a year, for educating poor Chⁿ. So applied. Offertory was distributed by the Clerk. Now by R. to such as come oftenest to Church. The same Complaints, as at Downe, p. 351 which see. Parsonage Ho. rebuilding ⟨Going on 1760⟩. See answers. A Pension of 16–8 to the Rector of Orpington. Ecton.
1761. The whole Church much out of Repair. 6ᵈ in pound at ½ Rent raises 18ᶠ. Yet whole Rents sd not to be 400ᶠ. Which is the mistake? Parsonage Ho. almost finished, but at a Stand. Barn wants Repairs. Coach house, ruinous, needless. 1764 Tithe was let for 70ᶠ, Glebe for 11–15–0. R. hath now both in his own Hands. There is also a Coppice with { } a year: & R. now lets pews in the Chancel for 6–6–0. He must now pay 7ᶠ for the poors Rate of the Tithe & 1–2–0 further of the Glebe, & 5–4–0 for Land Tax & 1–2–6 for Window Tax. He lives in the House.

Wᵐ Farquhar³ MA R. 31 March 1755. Cur. of Downe, p. 351. Lodges at a Farm Ho. in the Parish, till the Parsonage is rebuilt.
Oct. 13. 1761. Promised the next nomination to Mr Pitt.
Francis Fawkes⁴ Master of Arts R. April 11 1774.
John Scott⁵ L.L.B. Instit Oct; 2ᵈ 1777. on the presentation of Chaˢ Plumptre⁶. D.D. Rector of Orpington Pat. p. j.

1760 June 8. Conf. at Croydon 6 at Bromley by BP Pearce⁷ 2. 1765 June 11. Conf. at Croydon 9. 1767 by BP Pearce at Bromley 13. 1767. 21

¹ (1708–78), MP for Old Sarum, 1735–47, MP for Seaford, 1747–54, MP for Aldborough, 1754–6, MP for Buckingham, 1756, MP for Okehampton 1756–7, MP for Bath, 1757–66, earl of Chatham, 1766.
² (1720–1803), Hester, created baroness Chatham in 1761.
³ See p. 351, n. 2.   ⁴ Ibid., n. 3.
⁵ (1707–?), of Snape, Yorks. m. St John's C 1727, LLB (Sidney) 1735, R. Hayes, 1777–.
⁶ (17?–79), of Nottingham, m. Clare, 1731, BA 1734, MA (Queens' C) 1738, BD 1746, DD 1752, fellow Queens', 1737–48, V. Harston, Cambs, 1737–45, R. Wimpole, 1745–52, V. Whaddon, 1745, R. St Mary Woolnoth, London, 1752–79, R. Orpington, 1763–79, preb of Norwich, 1749–51, archdeacon of Ely, 1751–79.
⁷ Zachary Pearce (1690–1774), bishop of Bangor, 1748, bishop of Rochester, 1761.

Page 363
Heavor al Hever ⟨al Heber⟩ R. Sᵗ Peter ⟨8 miles S of Sevenoak. Mr Lewis¹ P. Ecton⟩. Maurice & Mary Smalt, Wᵐ & Eliz Braban² P. at the last Presentation: 3 different Persons at the preceding. Kˢ books 15–17–3½. Wake, Herring 80ᶠ or 100ᶠ ⟨150, 160ᶠ or 170ᶠ a year Mr Newe⟩. Part of the Hamlet of Linkhill belongs to this Parish. 62 Ho. Some vicious Absenters. Whole Service on Sundays. Prayers Jan. 30. Ash W. good Fr Easter Mond. Tuesd. 5 Nov. Chr. Day & 3 next Days. Cat. in Lent ⟨& part of Summer ADⁿ Potter⟩. Parents backward to send Chⁿ. 4 Sacr. 18 or 20 Com. ⟨30 ADⁿ Potter⟩. 8 or 10ˢ a Year to the Poor. Fences of Ch. Yd were neglected: will be better kept up. The little Alehouses require the notice of the magistrate, or some worthy Prelate. See

Letter to R. A pension of 13–4 to the Prior of Combwell. Ecton. BP of Rochester confirms at Westerham, 7 miles off.

1761 Much repairing & cleaning needed. Mr Waldos[3] chancel mentioned. R. lets the Singers have a Seat in the Chancel. Parish shd repair it 6^d in pound at ½ Rents raises 15$^£$. Mr Hamlin P.

The Advowson was sold ⟨for 1800$^£$⟩ {in} ⟨18 Dec⟩ 1753 by the Patrons abovementioned (the women being Sisters & Coheirs of Jonathan Steevens[4] the younger) to Mr Hamlin the Rector, & by him granted in 1754 to Richd Stone[5], whose sister he was abt to marry, in trust to be sold for her benefit, if a pension of 60$^£$ a year was not duly paid her.

Tho. Hamlin[6] BA. R. 30 Oct. 1753. Resides in the Parsonage Ho. Preached Vis. Serm. at Sevenoak, July 11. 1760 *** Died July 1762.

Stafford Newe[7] R Dec. 20. 1762 presented by Tho. Frederick Hamlin[8], an infant, eldest son of the above Tho. Hamlin. See Mr Wilbrahams[9] Opinion. Resides.

July 11. 1760 Conf at Sevenoak 7. 1764 by BP Pearce 6. 1767. 4

[1] George Lewis (1676–1748), of Abergwilly, Carmarthen, m. Jesus C 1694, migrated to St John's C, BA 1698, MA 1707, chaplain to Lord Henry Scott's regiment in Ireland, 1706, V. Westerham, 1706–48, R. Hever, 1721–48.
[2] Mary and Elizabeth were the daughters of the earl of Sussex. He died in 1715 and they later alienated the advowson: Hasted III, p. 201.
[3] Timothy Waldo, the son of a prosperous London merchant, bought Hever castle in 1745 and died in 1786: ibid.
[4] He has not been traced.   [5] He has not been traced.
[6] (17?–62), of Sussex, m. Clare 1742, BA 1746, R. Hever, 1753–62.
[7] (1727–96), of Sandford, m. Balliol 1743, BA 1746, R. Hever, 1762–96.
[8] See n. 6.
[9] See p. 176, n. 3. LPL, MS Secker 6, f. 249: Wilbraham's opinion, 13 December 1763.

Page 364

Dioc. Roch. D. Shoreham

Hunton al. Huntingdon R. St Mary ⟨5 miles S. of Maidstone⟩. ABP P. K^s books 16–13–1½. Wake 140$^£$ Herring 160$^£$ ⟨near 200$^£$ AD^n Potter. See below⟩. 64 Ho. dispersed. D^s of St Albans[1] hath a Ho. & Land & resides here part of the Year. Whole Service on Sundays. Prayers on all Holyday morning & Fasts. Cat ⟨W. Fr⟩ in Lent ⟨15 or 20 Ch^n⟩. Sacr. 1st Sunday in each Month & on the 3 great Festivals From 30 to 40 Com ⟨40 or 50 AD^n Potter⟩. BP of Rochester confirms at W. Malling 6 miles off. Glebe 22 Acres, worth 20^s an Acre: see other Particulars in BP Gibsons Memorandum[2] 1701. 1761. Pews bad: they talk of making new: encourage it: other things out of Repair. 6^d in pound at ½ Rents raises 21$^£$. Parsonage Ho. &c in good Repair. A Cottage called the Vicarage Ho. with a Garden. Lets for 50^s by R. Chw^{ns} not regularly chosen. Soon after 1701, a good 140$^£$. Dr Gibson

1763: worth 185 or 190. Of this, 160 Acres Hop Ground. If displanted it wd be 25$^£$ less. Mr Denne. Worth 220$^£$ at least. Dr Fowell.

Herbert Taylor[3] MA R. 8 Feb. 1748. V. of Patricksbourn p. 20 where he resides. Desired by AD^n Potter to resign it to his Son[4]. Died Sept. 29. 1763.

John Fowell[5] D.D. R. Oct. 14. 1763. R. of Eynesford p. 335 vacant by cession July 3 1764.
Beilby Porteus[6] MA R. Aug 19. 1765. R. of Ruckinge p. 139.
Lord George Murray[7] 1788.

Edw. Taylor[8] MA Cur. Son to R. Ord. Pr. March 11. 1759. 2. 40^f. Chaplain to a Regiment. Gone to Bellisle May 1767.
John Harbin[9] See p. 55. Indiscreet, in Debt. 40^f & Surpl. Fees.

1760 Conf. by BP Pearce[10] at Malling 21. 1762 at Maidstone 15. 1764. by BP Pearce 17. 1767. 21

[1] See p. 58, n. 10. [2] LPL, Archbishops Papers, Tenison, f. 129.
[3] See p. ii, n. 36. NB Secker seems to have mistranscribed 1728 as 1748.
[4] Edward Taylor. See p. 20, n. 5.
[5] See p. 4, n. 9. [6] See p. 139, n. 1.
[7] (1761–1803), m. New College 1779, BA 1782, DD 1800, dean of Bocking, R. Hunton, 1788–1801, bishop of St David's, 1802–3.
[8] See p. 20, n. 5. [9] See p. 55, n. 8.
[10] See p. 362, n. 7.

Page 365
Ifield R. St Margaret ⟨5 miles W. of Rochester⟩. Tho. Chiffinch[1] ⟨of Northfleet⟩ Esqr P. Tenths 8–8½. Certified 26–10–0. Now 30^f: taxed at 23^f. The Parish is between 3 & 400 Acres ⟨2 & 300 AD^n Potter⟩: Rent of it abt 160^f a Year. The Houses are 9, & stand at Singlewell, ½ mile from the Church. Philip Brandon[2] Esqr. One Farm Ho. The rest, labourers. No Parsonage Ho. from time immemorial. Service every other Sunday Morning. No Ch^n capable of saying their Catechism. R will endeavour to get them taught at his own Expence ⟨He doth⟩. 3 Sacr. 4 or 5 Com. ⟨He will endeavour to have 4 Sacr. & more Com⟩. No Offertory. R. will introduce a 4th, & endeavour to increase the number, & have an Offertory. Sermon every other Chr. Day, if a Congregation: & every Fast or Publick Thanksgiving. The Parishioners are much nearer to the Rectors other church of {Ifield} ⟨Nursted⟩, than many Parishioners are to their own Church. BP of Rochester confirms at {Gravesend} ⟨Rochester⟩, 4 miles off. Notice given of Conf. None likely to come. 1761 Ch. small: ⟨much⟩ out of Repair: better rebuilt at Shinglewell (see above) only no Room for Ch. yd there. Mr Chiffinch & Mr Hugeson[3] Patron of Nutsted or Nursted agree to present alternatively to both: 7 Acres of Glebe, in Northfleet, for wch 7 Groats pd to the Church of Rochester. Of the Patronage of this R in 1704 see Entry B. V. 146.

John Landon[4] BA R. 12 Apr. 1744. R. also of Nursted ⟨He writes it, Nustead⟩ Dioc. Roch. worth betw. 30 & 40^f a Year; where likewise he officiates every other Sunday Morning; and Cur. of Southfleet, where he resides, & officiates twice every Sunday. Hindred by the Gout from coming to my Visitation July 11. 1760. 1767 Sept. Disabled from Duty by a stroke of the palsy, going to a Relation in Herefordshire. Mr Howell[5] of Northfleet to serve this & Nursted, as Mr Landon served them with Southfleet.
William Crakelt[6] Clerk, Instituted Octo^r. 30: 1777.

1760 Conf. by BP Pearce at Rochester 3. 1764 at Gravesend 6.

[1] Inherited the advowson in 1727 and died in 1775: Hasted III, p. 313.

[2] The owner of Hever-Court: Hasted III, p. 347.

[3] John Hugessen, the owner of the manor and advowson of Nutsted from 1731: ibid.

[4] (1699-1777), of Credenhill, Herefordshire m. Brasenose 1721, BA (Christ Church) 1735, R. Ifield, 1744-77, R. Nutsted, 1754-77.

[5] John Howell. Perhaps (1732-?), of Llangunllo, co. Cardigan, m. Jesus C 1749, BA 1753, MA 1756.

[6] (17?-1812), C. Northfleet, 1769, V. Chalk, 1774, R. Ifield, 1777-1812.

Page 366

Dioc. Roch. D. Shoreham

Ightham R. St Peter ⟨a mile or two S. of Wrotham⟩. Wm James[1] Esqr P. in full Right {1718} ⟨1724⟩. {Tho. Chiffinch[2] Esqr P. Ecton}. K^s books 15-16-8. Wake, Herring 80$^£$ or 100$^£$ ⟨See below 166⟩. 2 miles long, very narrow: 8 small Hamlets in it, & sixty odd small Farm Ho. & Cottages. Sandys part Heath not inclosed. In the Skirts of it are, Wm Glanville[3] of St Clere Esqr Member for Hyth ⟨see below⟩, Wm James of Ightham Court Esqr, P. Wm Selby[4] of the Mote Esqr. Two Anab. One, of the Quakers, Principles abt Tithes, who brought their Bill into the House of Commons[5], & pays himself, as he advises others, when & what he pleases. Whole Service on Sundays. A Sermon on Chr. Day, good Fr. Nov. 5 &c. There were 2 private Chapels, at St Clere & the Mote. Cat. in Lent every Sunday. Was Exp. [qu.] 4 Sacr. 40 or 50 Com. ⟨10 or 12 AD^n Potter⟩. One Farm pays 1$^£$ a year to the poor: another 1^s a week in Bread, a third six 4^d Loaves: distributed by R, & ChW^{ns}. The last distribute the Offertory. The Lords day being neglected. R. preached twice a Day, till he was struck with a Palsy 3 years ago. BP of Rochester confirms at W. Malling. 5 miles off.

1761, 186$^£$ besides Ho. & Gard. Glebe 6 Acres. Mr Selbys[6] burial place mentioned. 3^d in pound as ⅔ sd to raise only 10$^£$. Many Repairs wanting at Ch. Parsonage Ho &c good & putting in good Order. Some out Ho. bad & needless.

Ralph Leigh[7], MA. R. 3 Feb. 1724. Resided till 3 years ago. See above. Now at Mr Joynes's at Gravesend. 70. Dead, May, 1760.

Will Halford[8] MA R. 2 July 1760. Curate of St Thomas, Southwood {said to} holds it for a minor, the Patrons 2^d son, abt 13. Dead May 1763. Mr Hardy[9] p. 381 to succeed.

Samuel Dawson[10] R. Sept. 1. 1763. Resides 1765.

Henry Croker[11] R. July 26th 1769.

E. Weller[12] Cur. Son to the Minister of Maidstone. R. of Allington Dioc. Roch. wch the neighbouring Clergy supply for him once a month. Resides at Ightham, 40$^£$. Continued on the same Terms by Mr Halford. Gone.

James[13], Peter BA Cur 40$^£$. born June 9 1738, ord. Deacon March 7. 1762. 1. Gone Feb. 1763 to Dulwich Coll.

Demetrius James[14] B.A. R. June 7. 1773.

Peter James[15] A.M. Rector, 1781.

George Bythesea[16] A.M. Rector 1791.

July 13 1760 Conf. at Wrotham 65. 1764 By BP Pearce at Malling 24. 1767. 35.

[1] The owner of Ightham Court. He died in 1780: Hasted V, p. 37.

[2] Lived at Northfleet: ibid., p. 17.

[3] (c.1686-1766), MP for Hythe, 1728-66. St Clere was a manor in the parish.

[4] Resided at Ightham Mote and died in 1773: Hasted V, p. 43.

[5] Presumably the 1736 bill. See S.J.C. Taylor, 'Sir Robert Walpole, the Church of England and the Quakers' Tithe Bill of 1736' *Historical Journal* XXXVII (1985), 51–77.

[6] See n. 4.

[7] (1691–1760), of Blackrod, Lancs, m. Brasenose 1710, BA 1714, MA (Kings) 1722, R. Ightham, 1725–60.

[8] R. Ightham, 1760–3.   [9] See p. 361, n. 9.   [10] R. Ightham, 1763–69.

[11] Temple Henry Croker (1730–c.90), of Ireland, m. Trinity C 1746, m. Christ Church 1746, BA 1750, MA 1760, R. Ightham, 1769–73, R. St John's, Capisterre, St Christopher, West Indies, chaplain to earl of Hillsborough.

[12] Edward Weller (1732–?), of Maidstone, Kent, m. CCCO 1748, BA 1752, MA 1756, BD 1763.

[13] See p. 313, n. 13.

[14] (1749–81), of Ightham, m. Wadham 1767, R. Ightham, 1773–81.

[15] See n. 13.

[16] (1765–1800), of Upper Hardres, Kent, m. Oriel 1782 BA 1786, MA 1789, R. Ightham, 1791–1800.

Page 367

Keston al Keyston R. ABP P. ⟨5 miles SE of Croydon⟩. Tenths 13^s. Certified 40^f. Now 70^f or more ⟨1762 Tithe 70^f. Glebe once let for 6^f⟩. 900 or 1000 Acres. 30 Ho. most of them Cottages. Mr Calcraft[1] [with Mrs Bellamy[2]. They go to Church] & Mr Nesbit[3]. Full half the Parish, esp. of the common people, never go to Church in their Lives. Owing to their Ignorance & Vices & the Libertinism of the Age ⟨More come now, 1760⟩. Service once on Sundays: was twice, & Ch^n examined in Cat. whilst R. was able. Disused for want of Attendance. No week day Prayers, {qu.} but on Chr. day, good Fr. &c]. 4 Sacr. Very few come. ChW^{ns} never. 10 Easter 1759. R. will complain at the Visitation. He contributes to a Charity school for the poor Ch^n. It is in the neighbourhood, ⟨& increases⟩. Scarce 6^d given at the Offertory, but what R. gives. Fornication, Drunkeness, Profaneness, increase every day. The Parsonage Ho. is rather a Cottage ⟨very neat & in good order AD^n Potter⟩: 14 miles from London. R. hath laid out 200^f Charity money on the Church & Chancel. BP of Rochester confirms at Bromley, 4 miles off. 1761 Casemts shd be made in Windows & sev^l other things done. 1^s in pound at full Rents raises 21^f.

Wm Best[4] DD R. 5 June 1742. Minister of St Laurence, London. Resides here. Paralytick &c. Cannot officiate. Died Aug. 23. 1761
John Taylor Lamb[5] ⟨AB⟩ R. Nov. 21. 1761, from Leysdown, p. 215. Serves it from Croydon.
James Hodgson[6] Master of Arts. Collated R. June 14 1774.

Brown[7] Pr. Cur. Also Cur. of Cudham, where he resides. 20^f, made up 30^f. A deserving object of Charity. *** Going to Knockholt Dec. 1761.
Charles Henry Laprimaudaye[8] A.B. Cur Sal. £30. Lic. 1786.

1760 June 8. Conf. at Croydon 8. 1763. Sept. 11 one was to have come, but did not. 1761. by BP Pearce at Bromley 1. 1766. Aug. 31. 3.

[1] John Calcraft (1726–72), MP for Calne, 1766–8, MP for Rochester, 1768–72.

[2] George Anne Bellamy (1731–88), actress. The mistress of John Calcraft.

[3] John Nesbit: Hasted II, p. 37.

[4] (1695–1761), of Kenilworth, Warwks, m. Balliol 1712, BA 1716, MA 1719, BD 1726, DD 1730, V. St Lawrence Jewry, London, 1729–61, R. Keston, 1742–61.

[5] See p. 215, n. 1.
[6] (1750–1811), of Leominster, Herefordshire, m. Christ Church 1766, BA 1770, MA 1773, R. Keston, 1774–99, schoolmaster Croydon hospital, 1774–1801.
[7] See p. 351, n. 4.
[8] (1765–1848), of London, m. Christ Church 1782, BA 1785, C. Keston, 1786, V. Leyton, Essex, 1800–48.

Page 368
Dioc. Roch. D. Shoreham
Knockholt See Nockholt

Lydging See Gillingham p. 358

Meopham V. St John Baptist ⟨6 miles N of Wrotham⟩. Belonged to the Priory of Canterbury ⟨now to Ch. Mr Markett[1] Lessee⟩. ABP P. K^s books 16–3–4. Wake, Herring, 120$^£$ ⟨besides taxes⟩. Above 4 miles long, near 4 miles broad. Two Divisions, West-borough & East-borough: Hamlets in each. See the names. 113 Ho. Whole Service from beginning of Lent to Nov. Afterwards, only once ⟨See below⟩. Cat. every Sunday in Lent. Ch^n sent. 4 Sacr. 50 Com. 1$^£$ a year, for a Sermon on New Years Day, 2$^£$ for 20 poor persons at Church that Day & not receiving Alms. BP of Rochester confirms at Gravesend, 6 miles off. Cur. wd read Prayers twice in Winter, but the people will not come. Exhorted them to try again, Vis. 1760. He promised. 1761 Whole Chancel shd be cieled, as Church, & over Com. table is: & sev^l things done. 6^d improved at full Rents raises 45$^£$, Parsonage being excused: else it wd be 60$^£$. V. Ho neat & small, in pretty good Order: but some Repairs wanting.

Tho. Wright[2] V. 31 Oct. 1718. Hath been 33 Years absent, on verbal Leave from ABP Wake to assist his Father, who hath long been dead. Is now 67, pleads Infirmities, Badness of the Air here, the Illness of a brother. Excused, while his brother is ill. Lives at Henstridge near Shaftesbury Dorset. Served a Cure in Dorsetshire: not now. Incapable of doing anything. Died abt Mich. 1762.
Samuel Sandys[3] LLB V. 19 Feb. 1763. Was of Queens Coll. Oxon & Chaplain of Morden Coll. He is to reside.
John Tatham[4] M.A. V. March 6. 1770.
Edw. Phillips[5] A.M. Vicar 1786.
Cha. Whitehead[6] Pr. Cur. 35$^£$ serves no other Cure. Lives ⟨at Ash⟩ 3 miles off. Married a Farmers widow & keeps a Farm there.
Edward Smedley[7] A.M. Vicar 1786.

Gervase Whitehead[8] A.B. Cur. Sal £42. Lic. 1787.
Timothy Mangles[9] A.B. Cur. Sal. £40 Lic. 1791.

July 13. 1760 Conf. at Wrotham 28. 1764 by BP Pearce at Gravesend 25. 1767. 27

[1] John Market, lessee of Meopham manor: Hasted III, p. 361.
[2] (169?–1763), of London, m. CCCC 1711, BA 1715, V. Meopham, 1718–62, chaplain to earl of Warwick.
[3] (1727–1804), of Graythwaite, Lancs, m. Queen's O 1746, BCL 1752, R. Lexden, Essex, 1769–1804.
[4] (1733–86), of Wiston, Suffolk, m. Christs 1752, scholar 1752, BA 1756, MA 1760, C. Wiston, 1756–7, C. St Paul's Cray, Kent, 1757–70, V. Meopham, 1770–86, V. Lexden, Essex, 1770–86.

[5] See p. 294, n. 10.
[6] Of Kent, m. CCCC 1738, BA 1742, MA (Clare) 1745, fellow Clare 1748, V. Cudham, Kent, 1746–80, V. Downe, 1753–64, R. Ash, 1779–82.
[7] (1750–1825), m. Trinity C 1770, BA 1783, MA 1776, fellow 1775, usher at Westminster school, 1774–1820, sometime reader at Rolls chapel, V. Little Coates, Lincs, 1782–1816, V. Meopham, 1786–1816, R. Bradford Abbas, Dorset, 1812–25, R. Clifton Maybank, 1812–16, R. Powderham, Devon, 1816–25.
[8] (1763–1838), of Kent, m. Jesus C scholar 1783, BA 1785, MA 1788, fellow 1790, C. Meopham, 1787, master Sevenoaks School, till 1813, V. All Saints', Cambs, V. Kemsing, Kent, 1817–38.
[9] m. Trinity C 1787, scholar 1787, BA 1791, MA 1794, C. Meopham, 1791–5, R. Aisthorpe, Lincs, 1795–1803.

Page 369

Nockholt al. Knockholt C. ⟨5 miles NW of Sevenoak⟩. R. of Orpington P. 2 miles long, one broad: 22 or 23 Ho. Wake 60^f or 40^f ⟨30^f reserved in Lease of R of Orpington, besides his Ho. & Glebe Entry B. VI. 250, 252. But this 30^f I think is left out in next Lease p. 344 w^n it a grant to Cur. p. 352 &c See VIII. 288⟩. Herring 60^f. Prayers & Sermon once on Sundays & other extraordinary Days. Cat in Lent. 4 Sacr. Abt 10 Com. Complaint of Cur. & Parishioners of Nockholt agst the Lessee of Orpington for Substraction of Tithes, usually pd to the Cur. of Nockholt. Also of the V. of Orpington. The Lessees State of the Case &c. In ABP Wakes Papers at Ch. Ch. vol. 2. No Ho. where Cur. can decently reside. BP of Rochester confirms at Westerham, 5 miles off. Cur. hath all the small Tithes & ⅔ of great Tithes, excepting wood, by a different Lease from that wch is granted to the R. of Orpington. Mr Hall to Dr Ducarel 22 Dec. 1761[1].

1761 sev^l Repairs wanting. 6^d in pound at full Rents raises 9^f. 12 Acres of Freehold Land, left to the will of one Stephens[2] for the use, not sd what use, of the Parishioners, called Church Lands, let to Mr James Collins[3] at 6^f a year wch is added to the Church Rate. He is the only Substantial man in the Parish, seems well disposed, & promises to influence the people rightly. A small Ho. near the Church belonging to the Cur. with 2½ Acres of Land, let to the clerk at 6–10–0. Licence to serve it Entry B. III. 37.

1763 Ch & Chancel put into good order.

Fra. Fawkes[4] MA Cur. ⟨licenced⟩ 31 March 1755. V. Orpington p. 372. where he resides.
Thos. Browne[5] A.B. Cur. licenced Oct^r.: 4: 1777.
Henry Fly[6] A.M. Cur. licensed 1788.

Geo. Davis[7] MA Pr. Deputy. Master of Sevenoak School. Hath quitted.
John Horne[8] BA of St Johns Coll Camb. ord. Deacon Sept. 23 1759. 2. 30^f. Assists in the School at Sevenoak ⟨5 miles off⟩. To officiate here twice when he can. Mr Browne[9], see p. 367, doth occasional Duty. Gone. Mr Davis hath resumed the Curacy. May 1760 Gone.
Winder[10] Will. Cur. See p. 361. Gone 1761.
Cowper[11] John BA of CCCC. born 7 Nov. 1737 ord. Deacon May 1761. 1. 30^f
Brown[12] Tho. was Curate of Keston ⟨& Cudham⟩ going to serve this instead of Keston, Chr. 1761. Called John Brown Vis. 1765 P. 26^f & Surpl. fees.
Thomas Pennington[13] A.M. Cur. Sal £21. lic. 1791.

1760 None conf. 1764 by BP Pearce at Bromley 1. 1767. 23

[1] LPL, MS 1163, f. 150.
[2] Richard Stevens in 1647: Hasted II, p. 82.
[3] He has not been traced.
[4] See p. 351, n. 3.
[5] Ibid., n. 4.
[6] Ibid., n. 6.
[7] (1748–?), of Carmarthenshire, adm. 'ten year man' St Johns C 1791, BD 1791. In holy orders when admitted in 1780.
[8] [Horne Tooke] (1736–1812), m. St John's C 1754, BA 1758, MA 1771 [opposed in Senate, but formally carried], adm. Inner Temple 1756, C. Knockholt, 1759–60, PC. St Lawrence, New Brentford, 1760–73. Took up John Wilkes' cause in the Middlesex election of 1768, and formed the Constitutional Society in 1771. Championed the cause of parliamentary reform. Was elected MP for Old Sarum, 1801–2, after which an act was passsed making clergy ineligible for seats in the house of Commons.
[9] See p. 367, n. 7.
[10] See p. 361, n. 10.
[11] (1737–70), of Herts, m. CCCC 1755, scholar 1759, BA 1759, MA 1762, fellow 1763, bursar 1767–70, C. Knockholt, 1761, R. of Foxton, Cambs, 1765–70. Brother of the poet William Cowper.
[12] See p. 351, n. 4.
[13] See p. 199, n. 7.

Page 370

Dioc. Roch. D. Shoreham

Northfleet V. S[t] Botolph ⟨8 miles from Dartford. 2 miles SW of Gravesend, where BP of Rochester confirms⟩. Belonged to S[t] Gregorys Priory Cant. ⟨Impror. Mr Tho. Swift[1] lives here⟩. The King, P. K[s] books 21[£]. Wake, Herring 100[£] ⟨90[£]. Ho. &c make up 100. AD[n] Potter⟩. 4 miles long, 2 broad. Church at one End. See the Boundaries & names of the several parts, in the Answers. Tho. Chiffinch[2] Esq[r]. Geo. Eliot[3] Esq[r]. See below. 162 Ho. One person, suspected to be a Papist. A few Families of Dissenters. Some of them come frequently to Church. The Farmers & Tradesmen come to Church in the Morning: not so often in the Afternoon, it being distant & most of them not inclined. The Chalk-Cliff men direct themselves on Sundays like the Colliers in the North. Two Gentlemen Absenters ⟨See below⟩. One holds little Correspondence with any in the Parish. The other either is a Papist, or a Jacobite, or is unwilling to appear in so publick a Place. Whole Service on Sundays & good Fr. Prayers W. Fr. Holydays & throughout Passion Week. 8 Sacr. at the 4 usual Times. 15 Com on Chr. Day last: & 12 next Sunday, of whom 3 came both Days. A good School master, who catechizes the Ch[n]. The Vicarage is endowed with a Portion of the great Tithes. 1761. Sev[l] small Repairs wanting. Mr Morrice[4], late High Bailiff of Westm. lives here, by the name of Thomson on acct. of Debt. He & a real Thomson never come to Ch. Vic Ho. Barn, Stable, Coach Ho. Gardens in great Order.

Tho. Harris[5] MA V. 14 Nov. 1726. ⟨Good ***⟩. Hath resided ever since in the V. Ho. adjoyning to the Ch. Yard. Doth all the Duty, except when he changes with his Curate ⟨John Locker[6]⟩ at Gravesend, ½ mile off, of which he is Rector. Died Dec. 27. 1762.

S[t] George Molesworth[7] MA of Wadham Coll. V. 3 Feb. 1763. Wife hath a large fortune: will reside 8 mo[s] & have a resident Cur. for the rest: thinks it 160[£] a yr. 1765 Vis. Resides sometimes a month together. Cur. doth the Duty.

Lewis Lewis[8] Cur. ord. Pr. by BP Beauclerk[9] 1754 40[£] & Surpl. Fees. Gone.

Richd Bathurst[10] of Brazen N. Pr. He hath a Living in Essex: to bring orders &c
Nov. 1763. Resides 1765.
John Howell[11] ord. D & P by me. C. LD 1767 40^f & Surpl. Fees. See Ifield p.
365.
Wm Crakelt[12] CharterHouse ordain'd Deacon 18 Decr 1766. Salary £40.

1760 Conf. by BP Pearce at Dartford 13. 1764. at Gravesend 12. 1767. 5 at
Dartf.

[1] He has not been traced.   [2] See p. 365, n. 1.
[3] Owner of Wombwell Hall in the parish: Hasted III, p. 310.
[4] He has not been traced.
[5] (169?–1762), of Oxon, m. Brasenose 1712, BA 1716, MA 1722, C. Bishopsbourne, 1719, V.
Frindsbury, 1725, R. Stourmouth, 1726, R. Gravesend, 1726–62, V. Northfleet, 1726–62.
[6] He has not been traced.
[7] (1731–96), of London, m. Wadham 1752, BA 1757, MA 1760, student of Lincoln's Inn, 1748,
V. Northfleet, 1763–96. Died in Hamburgh.
[8] (1700–?), of Cilycwm, Carmarthen m. Jesus O 1716.
[9] Lord James Beauclerk, bishop of Hereford, 1746–81.
[10] (1728–), of Goudhurst, m. St Edmund Hall 1744, BA (Brasenose) 1748.
[11] See p. 365, n. 5.   [12] Ibid., n. 6.

Page 371
Orpington R. All S^{ts} ⟨7 miles E of Croydon⟩ qu. with the Chapel of St Mary
Cray. ABP. P. K^s books 30–14–4½. Wake, Herring 40^f {[Surely more.]} ⟨That
is the reserved Rent in the Rectors Lease, besides 26–13–4 for the V. of
Orpington & 13–6–8 to Cur. of Down & 30^f to C. of Nockholt⟩. Leased out for
three Lives to {Mr Gee} ⟨Richd Gee[1] of Orpington Esqr⟩ whose Life is one: the
other is a Person above 61, but healthy. Dr Ward[2] had 540^f for putting in a Life,
which is very near a year & ⟨a⟩ quarters improved Rent. Mr Gee wd now give
540^f to exchange this Persons Life & his own ⟨for his two Sons Lives, who are
minors. His wifes Life is the 3^d⟩. Mr Hall: see his Letter 14 Dec. 1761. But an
act of Parlt {is} ⟨was thought⟩ necessary, the Trustees being empowerd to renew
only when a Life falls. Co. of Chancery hath given them Leave to exchange.
When R. will come to preach, or instruct the people, Lessee covenants to
entertain him & 2 attendants & 3 Horses 4 times in a year 8 Days at a time.
Robt Uvedale[3] coll. dd R. cum capellis annexis 9 Jan 1691 Entry B IV. 474.
Lease of R by him to Mr Gee 30 Sept 1699 p. 670 Lease of R. from him VI. 250.
Joseph Barton[4] inst. 14 Sept 1722 on death of Uvedale p. 410.

Lease of R. confirmed 28. Sept. 1762.

Henry Hall[5] MA R. 26 March 1755. R. of Harbledown p. 37 where he resides,
& V. of East Peckham p. 354. Died Nov. 1. 1763.
Charles Plumptre[6] DD R Nov. 1763.
William Clarke[7] A.M. Rector 1782.

[1] (1706–91).   [2] See p. 168, n. 2.
[3] (1642–1722), of Warwickshire, m. Trinity C 1660, BA 1663, MA 1666, LLD 1682, R.
Orpington, 1692–1722, R. Barking, Suffolk, 1700.
[4] Perhaps (1660–1742), of Haxton, Wilts, m. New Inn Hall O 1679, BA 1682, V. Sellinge, 1680, R.
Orpington, 1722–42.
[5] See p. 37, n. 4.   [6] See p. 362, n. 6.

[7] (1738–1820), of Newnham Courtenay, m. Magdalene C 1756, BA 1760, R. Orpington, 1782–1820, V. Willesden, Middlesex, 1795, V. Wyrandisbury, Bucks, 1803.

Page 372

Dioc Roch. D. Shorham

Orpington V. ⟨7 ⟨10⟩ miles E of Croydon⟩ All Saints qu. with the Chapel of St Mary Cray. R. of Orpington P. Tenths 1–3–0¼. Certified 45$^£$. Wake 50$^£$ Herring 100$^£$ ⟨120$^£$ AD^n Potter. 26–13–4 from the Lessee of the Rectory⟩. 4½ miles long 1½ broad. 2 small Hamlets: 100 Ho in all. Tho. Westbrook[1], who rents a small Farm, & his Family, Papists. A Priest comes thither abt once a month, said to be called Elston, & to belong to the Sardinian Ministers Chapel. One Family of Quakers, who pay Dues without Compulsion. A few profligate Persons of low Rank Absenters. Service once on Sundays at Orpington, once at St Mary Cray, a mile off. Mostly the same Congregation. Sermon on Chr. day & good Fr. Prayers on Holydays alternatively at each. Cat. every Sunday in Lent. Exp. in Sermons. 4 Sacr. abt 20 Com ⟨12 AD^n Potter at Orp 25 at St M. Cray⟩. BP of Rochester confirms at Bromley, 5 miles off. 1761 ⟨Orpington⟩. Many things amiss in Ch. & Chancel ⟨all well repaired 1763⟩. Vic Ho. &c made very neat & good by Mr Fawkes at great Expence. 6^d in pound at ½ Rents raises 21$^£$. St Mary Cray many things amiss at the Chapel. Mr Hyde[2], a merch^t near Smithfield, who lately bought an Estate of abt 15$^£$ a year belonging to the Chapel & hath 40$^£$ a year more in the Parish, will have nothing to do with the Chapel. No Ho. belonging to the Chapel. 1^s in pound at full Rents raises 50$^£$. Mr Gee, the Lessee of the Rectory lives in the Parish. The above 26–13–4 & the 13–6–8 for Down were settled by Robt Say[3] DD R. of Orpington & Prov. of Oriel Coll. by Lease dated 23 Aug 1687 & entred in the Registry of DCh of Canterbury: for wch he abated 400$^£$ in his Fine. 1763. Parishioners have effectually repaired the Chancel. The whole Building wants a new Coat of rough Cast wch wd cost dear: it hath been hinted to them.

Fra. Fawkes[4] MA V. 31 March 1755. Resides in V. Ho.
Cur. of Nockholt p. 369
John Till[5] clerk LLB. Vicar. June 23: 1774.
Henry Pratt[6] A.M. Vicar. Janry 1778.

1760. Conf. by BP Pearce at Bromley, Orpington 29, St Marys Cray 38. St Pauls Cray 7 qu. 1764 St Mary Cray 37 Orpington 24. 1767. 33

---

[1] He has not been traced.   [2] He has not been traced.
[3] (16?–1691), of Slinfold, Sussex, m. Hart Hall 1632, BA 1623, fellow Oriel, 1638, DD 1660, provost, 1653–91, R. Orpington, 1639–, R. Marsh Gibbon, Bucks, 1661–91.
[4] See p. 351, n. 3.
[5] (17?–1820), of London, m. Queens' C 1761, LLB (Caius) 1768, V. Orpington, 1774–7, R. Hayes, 1777–1827, R. Orpington, 1820–27.
[6] (1730–1802), of Tughill, Staffs, m. University 1747, BA 1751, MA 1754, V. Orpington, 1778–1802.

Page 373
Otford See Shoreham R. p. 377

Penshurst R. S[t] Johns Baptist ⟨8 miles S of Sevenoak⟩ Earl of Leicesters[1] Heirs P. K[s] books 30–6–0½. Wake, Herring 300[f] ⟨Charged with a heavy poor sess 350[f] Entry B VII. 364⟩. Worth more. 7 miles long. Shaped like the Figure 8. Church towds the middle. See the Names of the Divisions. 159 Ho. Chiefly straggling. Hon[ble] Mrs Perry[2] of Penshurst Place: 3 Daughters, one Son a Minor. Abt 40 Farmers. Few Absenters, considering the Distance & bad Roads, esp. in Afternoon. 2 Sermons on Sundays: 35 of the Afternoon Sermons catechetical. Prayers W. Fr. in Lent & the Holydays of Chr. Easter, Whits. Cat. W. Fr. in Lent. Few Ch[n] sent, & no Servants. Sacr. 1st Sunday of each month, Chr. good Fr. Easter, Whits. Seldom many above 20 Com. at once: but above 100 in all. 30[s] a year for ringing the great Bell twice a Day: 50[s] to the Poor. Offertory money distributed by the minister on S[t] Thomas's Day, by a List, settled with ChW[n]s &c and an acct of it kept. A poor man & his wife go to the new Chapel at Tunbridge Wells, of Persons called Methodists, but by themselves Independents. See Sevenoak p. 375. BP of Rochester confirms at Tunbridge, 5 miles off. 1761 sev[l] Repairs wanting. Mr Harveys[3] Ch. yd Gate & Mr W[m] Saxbys[4] Chapel mentioned. Parsonage Ho & outho. &c in good Order. 10 bad old Ho[s] belonging to the Rectory, shd be lett on Building Lease. 6[d] in pound at ½ Rents raises 28–14–2½.

Hopton Williams[5] R. 14 May 1743. Resides in Parsonage Ho. Hath been absent but 2 Sundays in the last 8 Years. Above 30 Years an Incumbent in Kent.
Henry Beauclerk[6] M.A. R. March 26. 1770.
Richard Rycroft[7] D.D. R. January 19 1773.
Matthew Nicholas[8] D.D. Rector 1786.

William Metcalfe[9] Clerk A.B. Curate, Licensed Febry 24: 1777. with a Salary of £50 p. ann & Surplice Fees.

1760. Conf. at Tunbridge by BP Pearce 28, or 26. 1764 50. 1767. 43.

[1] Jocelyn (16?–1743), 7th earl of Leicester, viscount l'Isle and baron Sidney of Penshurst.
[2] Elizabeth, wife of William Perry, the owner of Penshurst Place. He died in 1757 and she died in 1783: Hasted III, p. 247.
[3] Thomas Harvey, of Tunbridge, inherited Red Lease House in 1740 and died in 1779: ibid., p. 253.
[4] He bought Chafford Place in 1743 and died in 1783: ibid., p. 252.
[5] (1704–70), of Dingestow, co. Monmouth, m. St Edmund Hall 1721, BA (Trinity O) 1725, MA 1728, R. Stourmouth, 1729–43, V. Preston by Wingham, 1729–43, R. Penshurst, 1743–70.
[6] (1746–1817), of Westminster, m. Christ Church 1763, BA 1767, MA 1769, R. St Mary's, Somerset, London, 1770–, R. Penshurst, 1770–2, R. Greens Norton and R. Leckhampstead, Bucks, 1781–.
[7] See p. 294, n. 9.
[8] (1707–96), of Shalford, Surrey, m. CCCO 1723, BA 1727, MA 1730, fellow 1731–45, BD 1738, DD 1743, dean of divinity, 1744, V. Willoughby, Lincs, 1740, R. Swaby, Lincs, 1743, V. Breeding, Sussex, 1744–86, R. Penshurst, 1786–96.
[9] (1752–1827), of Ingleton, Yorks, m. Sidney Sussex 1772, BA 1775, MA 1778, minor canon Ely, 1778–1827, PC. Stuntney and V. Witcham, Cambs, till 1827, JP Isle of Ely.

Page 374

Dioc. Roch. D. Shoreham

Sevenoake R. S[t] Nicolas. Sir Cha. Farnaby[1] P. Wake adds, sed fiducarius pro Rectore. K[s] books 13-6-8. Wake, Herring 200[f]. The Rector & Vicar were different Persons, before the present. Hugh Owen[2] V. inst. to R. 10 Nov. 1703 Entry B. V. 103. Resigns ⟨V⟩ to his Son. Hugh Owen[3] 21 May 1706 p. 221, 227. Tho. Curteis[4] inst. Sept. 12. 1716 on death of Owen. Tho. Curteis[5] the son inst as below on the Death of his Father, pres. by Sackvile[6] Bale Esq[r] Tho. Clare[7] & Wm Mackett[8] Gentlemen VIII. 328.

Tho. Curteis R. 28 Apr. 1747 ⟨V. also see p. 375⟩. R. of S[t] Dionis Backchurch p. 307. Preb. of Cant.

Edward Hardy[9] R June 19 1775. L.B. See V. Sevenoake.

Tho[s]. Sackville Curteis[10] LLB. Instituted to the Rectory (sine cure) Dec[r]. 22. 1777.

---

[1] (1674-1741), 1st Bt. In 1758 his son Thomas (c.1708-60) 2nd Bt, was the patron.

[2] m. Trinity C 1667, BA 1671, MA (Peterhouse) 1674, fellow 1672-9, V. Sevenoaks, 1678-1703, R. Sevenoaks, 1703-6.

[3] m. Jesus C 1699, BA 1704, R. Sevenoaks, 1706-16.

[4] (16?-1747), of Derbyshire, m. CCCC 1676, R. Wrotham, 1715-47, R. Sevenoaks, 1716-47.

[5] See p. ii, n. 17.

[6] Of St Martin's, London. The joint patron of Sevenoaks in 1747 and 1750.

[7] A gentleman from Hythe.   [8] Ibid.

[9] See p. 361, n. 9.   [10] Ibid., n. 11.

Page 375

Sevenoake V. S[t] Nicolas. R. of Sevenoake P. K[s] books 15-3-1½. Haynes 60[f], 200[f]. Wake 200[f], 70[f]. Herring 200[f] ⟨See below⟩. 6 miles long, 2 broad. Above 300 Ho. Many Families of Note [not named] in & ab[t] the Town & the 2 Hamlets or Liberties of Riverhead & the Weald. A Congregation of Anab. in a licenced Room: Teacher Michael Bligh, a labouring man. Another, called Methodists, but by themselves Independents: See Penshurst p. 373. They have only Itinerant Teachers: one of them Cha. Perronet[1], in whose name their Meeting Room is licenced. A Quaker, came a few weeks ago. A few low Persons seldom come to Church: motives unknown. [shd be asked]. Whole Service. Prayers on W. Fr. Holydays. Cat. disused for some years. V. distributes Lewis's Exp. & finds the Youth well prepared for Confirmation ⟨Dr Curteis[2] will endeavour to revive it⟩. Sacr. monthly. Number of Com. large. A free School, & Almshouse of 32 Apartmts, with 16 out-Pensioners, who have 2-6 a week. It is one very ancient Foundation, incorporated by Q. Eliz. Two wardens, appointed by 4 Assistants or Governors, who are now, Duke of Dorset[3], Sir Tho. Farnaby[4] Bar[t], Henry Bosville[5] Esq[r], Tho. Lambard[6] Esq[r], & are chosen annually by the Parishioners on Mich. Day. Revenues above 500[f] a year. Every thing well managed. A Donation of Bread from Lands: another Donation of 5[f] a year from Lands, abt which Doubts have lately arisen. Offertory money considerable: chiefly laid out by V & Chw[n]s in Beef & Bread for the Poor in Winter. A Pension of 3-6-8 to the Rector of Shoreham. Ecton. The Names of the Schoolmaster & Usher see p. 369. BP of Rochester confirms at Westerham, 5 miles off. A pretty Parsonage

Ho. A V. Ho. just built, not quite finished. Good Church bad: small vestry, with brick floor. Earth heaped up. Cupola with a Ball.

1761. Sev^l Repairs wanting. R & V. owned to be worth 400^f. Qu. if not more. V. is called in Disp. 1756 200^f Entry B IX. p. 275.

Schoolm. pres. by Guardians & Overseers of School, admitted & licenced by ABP 1696 Entry B IV. 549, 565. V. 222 VI. 64 by the Wardens & Assistants VII. 422.

See a List of Goods belonging to the Church.

[1] Charles Perronet (1723–76). One of John Wesley's itinerant preachers. He later fell out with Wesley over the issue of separation from the Church.
[2] See p. ii, n. 17.   [3] See p. 201, n. 1.
[4] See p. 374, n. 1. The owner of Kippington manor. He died in 1760: Hasted III, p. 88.
[5] The owner of Bradbourne manor. He died in 1761: ibid., p. 84.
[6] In 1711 he inherited Rumpshot estate. He died in 1769: ibid., p. 90.

Page 376
Dioc. Roch. D. Shoreham
Sevenoake V. continued

Tho. Curteis[1] ⟨pres. by Sackvile Bale[2] & Wm Mackett[3]⟩ MA [now DD] ⟨{R. &}⟩ V. 19 Dec. 1750. ⟨R. before⟩ See here p. 373. Resides the greater part of the Year in the Parsonage Ho.
Edward Hardy[4] Clerk V. June 30: 1775 on the presentation of David Papillon[5] Esq & Hester his wife.
Thos. Sackville Curteis[6] LLB. Inst. to the Vicarage Decr 22: 1777.

John Hughes[7] Pr. Cur. 40^f. Resides. Serves no other Cure. So 1765, 1767
Robert Parsons[8] Cur. not licensed. Sal. C { }.

July 11. 1760 ⟨sent 750 Tickets⟩ Conf. here ⟨351⟩ of the Peculiars 319: of Dioc. Roch. 32. Of Sevenoak 191. BP Pearce confirmed of my Peculiars in Shoreham Deanery this year 373. 1764 he confirmed of this parish here 164. 1767 He confirmed of my Peculiars here 225 of this Parish 83.

[1] See p. ii, n. 17.   [2] See p. 374, n. 6.
[3] Ibid., n. 8.   [4] See p. 361, n. 9.
[5] Hester Papillon was the daughter of Thomas Curteis. She married David Papillon from Acrise.
[6] See p. 361, n. 11.
[7] Possibly (1726–?), of Cirencester, Glos. m. Balliol 1744, BA 1747.
[8] See p. 235, n. 13.

Page 377
Shoreham R. ⟨4 miles NW of Sevenoak⟩ St Peter & St Paul, with the Chapel of Otford, St Bartholomew. DCh of Westm. P. K^s books 34-9-9½. Chapel now 45^f. 64 Ho. Service alternately [qu]. Cat. every Sunday in Lent. 4 Sacr. Generally betw. 30 & 40 Com. ⟨24 AD^n Potter⟩. 5^f & 1^f a year to the poor in Bread. [Note, all this relates to the Chapel]. No Ho. for the minister of the Chapel. This R. is an Impropriation of DCh of Westm. Ld Willoughby[1] of Brooke is their Lessee. Ecton. See below.

ABP {Morton} ⟨Warham⟩[2] 3 July 1531 because sev[l] persons can more easily bear a burthen than one, ordained a vicarage in the Church of Shoreham with the Chapel of Otford annexed to it, the Rectory being, & the Vicarage to be in the ABP[s] Gift. R. to pay V. 20[£] a year quarterly. V. is to have a House built him & to provide a Chaplain for Otford R. to bear all the burthens belonging to Ch. & Chapel. See other provisions. Reg. Warham fol. 412, 413. 1761 value 20[£] from DCh of Westm. Queens Bounty 8[£] & Surpl. Fees. Mr Golding[3], a good man, under-tenant to Ld W. Gr. & small Tithes 200[£] a year. Sev[l] Repairs wanting. 6[d] in pound at ½ Rents raises 20[£]. No Ho. for Cur. DCh have a Ho. in wch Mr Golding lives; & the vicarage Ho. let as a Cottage at 3[£] a year.

Tho. Manningham[4] admitted ⟨& lic. on nom. of DCh.⟩ to the Chapel of Otford 9 March 1743 ⟨Dead⟩. No Admission to the Rectory of Shoreham can be found. Resides at Eartham, near Arundel. Hath quitted this, 1760.
Will. Winder[5]. See below.

Will. Winder Pr. Cur. 20[£] ⟨& Surp. Fees from DCh of Westm⟩. Resides on his other Curacy, [of Halsted, p. 361] 3 miles off. {Gone.} So at Vis. 1765. The living under Sequestration.

Otford Chapel. D. & CH. Westminster Patrons.

Nath[l]. George Woodrooffe[6] A.B. Cur. lic. 1791.

July 11. 1760 Conf. at Sevenoak, of Otford 30. 1764 by BP Pearce 12. 1767 Shoreham 23 Otford 10

[1] John Verney (1738–1816), 14th lord Willoughby de Broke.
[2] William Warham (1450?–1532), archbishop of Canterbury, 1504–32.
[3] The Golding family owned the manor of Wainscot in Frindsbury, and lived in Upper Halling: Hasted III, p. 539.
[4] (1717–?61), m. St John's C 1735, BA 1739. Perhaps also V. Wisborough Green, Sussex, 1748–61.
[5] PC. Otford. Died in 1791.
[6] (1765–1851), of London, m. St Edmund Hall 1786, BA 1790, MA 1793, C. Knockholt and Downe, 1789, C. Shoreham, 1790, PC. Otford, 1791–1802, V. Somerford Keynes, Wilts, 1803–51.

Page 378
Dioc. Roch. D. Shoreham
Shoreham V. S[t] Peter & S[t] Paul ⟨See Shoreham R. p. 377⟩. DCh. of Westm. P ⟨Geo. Ballard[1] of Leatherhead Esq[r]⟩. Tenths 1–8–8 Certified 45[£]. 60[£], tenths paid: augm. by DCh, 17–6–8 Wake ⟨See below⟩. 12 or 14 miles in Circuit: abt 150 Ho. Widow of Tho. Borrett[2] Esq[r], Protonotary of Common Pleas. 5 or 6 Persons, & V[s] Family, called Methodists. They meet at his Ho. have daily Prayers & Singing: the Scriptures are read, & 4 Days in the week expounded. All Parishioners invited. Others welcome. Thus for many years. One Gentleman comes to his Ho. in the sporting Seasons, seldom comes to Church. Exhorted in vain. Whole Service on Sundays. Prayers on all Holydays: twice a week in Lent: every day in Passion week: a Sermon on good Fr. Cat exp. in Summer. Ch[n] only come, & duly. 12 Sacr. Abt 40 Com. each time. Alms Houses for 3 persons, with 1[s] a week & Firing to each. Charged on Mr Borretts Estates. 5 or 6 little

Schools. John Borrett Esq[r] Father of Tho. left 5[£] a year to the Master of a Free School, whilst there was one. None now. But it is given for teaching poor Ch[n] to read & work. An Estate, now 13[£] a year, given to the Poor by Tho. Terry, Yeoman, in 1628.[3] The above John Borrett left them 3[£] a Year.

There was a Confirmation at Shoreham in 1719, & at Sevenoake 2 or 3 years afterwards. But for near 40 Years no ABP hath come to the Peculiars. BP of Rochester confirms 9 miles off, at Westerham. 1761. V. makes but 80[£]: believes it worth much more. All vicarial Tithes: 9 Acres Glebe: 10[£] a yr from Westm. Mrs Borretts chap mentioned. Sev[l] small Repairs wanting. 6[d] in pound at ½ Rents raises 27[£]. V. Ho. old & awkard but that & outho. in good Repair. 1765 Mr Polhill[4] the Impropriator hath given Orders for repairing the Chancel.

Vincent Perronet[5]. V. 17 Feb. 1727. Resides in V. Ho. & serves the Parish. Charles Wake[6] B.D. Vicar 1785.

Thomas Sampson[7] Cur. Sal. £40. Lic. 1786.
Nath[l]. Geo. Woodrooffe[8] A.B. Cur. Sal. £42 surplice fees & Vic. House. Lic. 1790.

July 11. 1760 Conf. in Sevenoak 35. 1764. 31. by BP Pearce 1767 see last p.

[1] He has not been traced.
[2] (1657–1739). Master of the Inner Temple and protonotary.
[3] Hasted says in 1728: II, p. 10.
[4] Charles Polhill of Chipstead near Chevening. Owned estates in Shoreham: ibid., p. 9.
[5] (1693–1785), m. Queen's O 1714, BA 1718, MA (CCCC) 1724, C. Sundridge, 1718, V. Shoreham, 1728–85.
[6] (1748–?), of East Knoyle, Wilts, m. CCCO 1764, BA 1768, MA 1772, BD 1781, R. Fenny Compton, 1796–.
[7] 'literate', C. Shoreham, 1786.   [8] See p. 377, n. 6.

Page 379

Sundridge al Sundrich R. ⟨2 miles W. of Sevenoak⟩. ABP P. K[s] books 22–13–4. Wake 250 Herring 300[£]. 7 miles long. 100 Ho. ⟨112 in 1717⟩. Lieut. Gen. Campbel[1]. Mr Mompesson[2]. One Farmer Anab. No professed Infidels. Whole Service on Sundays ⟨2 Sermons from Whits. to Mich⟩. Prayers on few Festivals ⟨Chr. good Friday, &c⟩ besides. Cat. in Lent. 8 Sacr. 10 or 12 or more Com. ⟨60 in 1717⟩. A small free School, endowed with 10[£] a Year by Humph. Hyde[3] Esq[r] in 1719. Under the Direction chiefly of R. 50[s] a year left by Mr Lewis[4] for 4 Sermons, for Bread & for Bibles ⟨see more abt charities in 1717⟩. BP of Rochester confirms at Westerham, 3 miles off. Afternoon Sermons in Summer: desired they might be cat. ones, & ch[n] cat. before them. 1761 sev[l] Repairs wanting. 1[s] in pound at ½ Rents raises 50[£]. Mr John Whitakers[5] needs repairing: very rich & covetous: lives at Wrotham comes not to Ch. Mr Hydes Chapel mentioned. Parsonage Ho. outho. & Gardens very neat & good & in great Order. 1765 Chancel belongs to Mr Whitaker, who saith he wd repair it. ABP Tenison confirmed here abt 1703.

John Frankland[6] MA ⟨R⟩ 19 Jan 1753. Residentary of Chichester ⟨3 months⟩. Times of being here uncertain. More now, 1760. ***
William Vyse[7] LLD. Rector Dec[r]. 17: 1777.

James Meadlow[8]. Pr. Cur. 40$^£$ & Surpl. Fees. Resides in R. Ho.
Edmund Roberston[9] Pr. Cur. 1765
Thomas White[10] A.B. Cur. Sal. £50. lic. 1794.

July 11. 1760 Conf. at Sevenoak 16. 1764 by BP Pearce 30. 1767. 20.

[1] Colonel John Campbell, the owner of Combebank in the parish: Hasted III, p. 140. He became the duke of Argyle in 1761.
[2] Thomas Mompesson: ibid., p. 127.
[3] The Hyde family owned Sundridge manor: ibid., p. 131.
[4] This should be Ellen Lewis, by her will in 1646: ibid., p. 143.
[5] The son of Thomas Whitaker, the sheriff of Kent in 1743: ibid., p. 373.
[6] (1716–77), of Bristol, m. Sidney Sussex 1730, BA 1733, MA (St John's C) 1737, fellow 1736–42, V. Eastbourne, Sussex, R. Sundridge, 1753–77, preb of Chichester, 1742–77.
[7] See p. 345, n. 8.　　　　　　　　　　　　　[8] He has not been traced.
[9] Probably of Chichester, m. Clare 1740.
[10] (1772–?), of Lambeth, Surrey, m. Trinity C 1790, BA (Pembroke) 1794, adm Inner Temple 1786, C. Sundridge, 1794.

Page 380
Dioc. Roch. D. Shoreham
Wrotham al. Wroteham R. St George with Chapel of Stansted, St Mary. ABP P.
K^s books 50–8–½. Haynes 200$^£$, 500$^£$. Wake 200$^£$, & with V. 500$^£$. Herring. R. 500.
ABP Simon Islip[1] ordained a Vicarage in the Church of Wroteham, which had then the Chapel of Stanstede annexed, in 1314. See Reg. Islip fol. 205. This Ordination ABP Arundel[2], first reciting it, explains & corrects 7 Jan 1402. See Reg. Arund. pt. 1. fol. 357 b, 358 a
Tho. Curteis[3] inst. V. void by death of Philip Sandford[4] 18 Oct. 1714. Was inst R. 25 May 1715.
A Lease of Wrotham R with Stansted Church or Chap. annexed & of the Parsonage Ho. & Ch. Yds of Wrotham & Stansted, made by R. to his son for 21 years, Rent 60$^£$. Conf. 1665 Entry B. 1. 133. Another 1674 III. 249.
Cha. Layfield[5] coll. to R. 27 Jan 1676/7 on Res. of his Father Dr Edw. Layfield[6] Entry B. III. 307. Grants a Lease of it 5 Oct 1680 wch see Entry B. IV. 125. Lic. to alter & add to R. Ho. VI. 215.

John Potter[7] DD R. 6 Feb. 1746. See p. 128.
Honble James Cornwallis[8] M.A. R. Octr. 2. 1770.
George Stinton[9] D.D. Rector 1781.
Charles Tarrant[10] D.D. Rector 1783. Richard Levett[11] A.M. Rector 1791.

Francis Meeke[12] Clerk Licensed to the Curacy of Stansted May 30. 1774 with a Salary of 40 p. ann.

[1] Archbishop of Canterbury, 1349–66.
[2] Thomas Arundel (1353–1414), archbishop of Canterbury, 1396–1414.
[3] See p. 374, n. 4.
[4] (1659–1714), of Shrewsbury, m. Christ Church 1665, BA 1668, MA (Jesus C) 1680, V. Wrotham, 1680–1714.
[5] (1649–1715), of Hertfordshire, m. St John's C 1666, BA 1670, MA 1674, BD 1679, DD 1692, R. Wrotham, 1677–1715, R. Chilbolton, Hants, 1699–1715, canon of Winchester, 1687.

[6] (1605–80), of London, m. St John's O 1620, BA 1624, MA 1628, DD (Cambridge) 1633, R. Ibstock, Leics, 1632, archdeacon of Essex, 1634, V. All Hallows, Barking, 1635, R. East Horsley, Surrey, 1637, R. Wrotham, 1638 and 1665–76, R. Colne Wakes, 1640–66, R. Barnes, Surrey, 1663–80.

[7] See p. ii, n. 3.   [8] Ibid., n. 6.   [9] See p. 149, n. 4.

[10] (1724–91), of Fordingbridge, Hants, m. Balliol 1741, BA 1744, MA 1747, B & DD 1760, R. North Tidworth, Wilts, 1757–60, R. St Mary le Strand, London, 1759–61, V. Staines, Middlesex, 1760–3, prebendary of Bristol, 1751–76, sub-dean of Salisbury, 1755, R. St George's Bloomsbury, 1761, dean of Carlisle, 1763–4, dean of Peterborough, 1764, preb of Rochester, 1776, V. Lamberhurst, Sussex, 1776, R. Wrotham, 1783–91, chaplain to King.

[11] (1727–1800), of Lichfield, Staffs, m. Christ Church 1746, BA (Pembroke) 1749, MA 1752, R. Little Berkhamsted, 1753, R. Wrotham, 1791–1800.

[12] (1750–1801), of Yorks, m. Christs 1769, BA 1773, MA 1776, C. Stansted, 1774, V. Towcester, Northants, 1782–4, V. Eccleshall, Staffs, 1793–1801, preb of Ripon, 1782, preb of Lichfield, 1794–1801.

Page 381

Wrotham ⟨al Rootham⟩ V. S[t] George, with the Chapels of Stansted S[t] Mary, & Plaxtol, & the Rectory of Woodland, of which see below, annexed. ABP. P. K[s] books 22–5–10. Haynes 60, 300. Wake R. & V. 500[£] Herring V. 300[£] ⟨800[£] D[r] Potter. V. called 200[£] in his Disp Entry B. VIII. 329⟩. 7 miles long, 3 broad. Contains Plaxtol, Couch, Neppucar, Stansted & Woodlands. Abt 200 Farmers, 50 Tradesmen, Publications &c 190 Poor. M[r] Haddock[1], Justice of Peace & Member for Rochester, lives at Wrotham ⟨Batchelor, good natured⟩. Ld Vane[2] hath a Ho. & Gardens & Park in Plaxtol, now let to Ld Falkland[3], but generally empty. See Names of Persons who have Land, but not Houses in the Parish. Many Absenters from Ignorance & bad Habits. John Whitaker[4] a wealthy Farmer, from a Quarrel with a former Curate: Farmer Kettles widow & her Relations, because disobliged abt a Pew. Few poor Families come to church: & this Evil increases. Whole Service, 2 Sermons on Sundays. Prayers on all Holydays, & W. Fr. in Lent, w[n] Cat. is exp. Gratuities given, & many Ch[n] sent. Sacr. 1st Sunday of every month: 10 or 12 Com. Whits. Chr. abt 20: Easter abt 40. This at Wrotham. At Stansted, 2 miles off, Service once on Sundays. Cat. in Lent: few attend. 4 Sacr. abt 20 Com. At Plaxtol, 4 miles off, Service once on Sundays. Cat. exp. W. Fr. in Lent, with Gratuities: well attended. 4 Sacr. 20 Com. A considerable School at Wrotham for reading, writing & accounts: to which V & others send many Ch[n]. Some Benefactions in money to the poor, well applied by Ch. W[ns] & Overseers. The Parish Church of Woodland had long been ruinous, & no mark of it remained. The Income was but 3–14–6 [This is the Value in the K[s] books, besides that of Wroxham.]. There were but 4 small Houses. The Churches were but 2 or 3 miles asunder. The Parishioners, & particularly 5 Land holders, petitioned ABP parker to unite the two Parishes. He did so 20 July 1571 by the name of the Vicarage of Wrotham with the Church of Woodland annexed: saving to the Queen the first Fruits & tenths, & himself & successors the Inst. Fees & Procurations & to the Dean of Shoreham the Procurations, of both, as if they had never been united. Conf. by DCh of Cant 25 Nov. 1571. Reg. Parker pt 1, fol 405, 406.

BP of Rochester confirms at W. Malling, 5 miles off. There is a Parsonage & a V. Ho.

1761. at Plaxtol, some small things wanting. 6[d] in pound at ½ Rents raises 23[£].

At Stansted many things wanting, wch shall be done. Vic. Ho. Barnes &c good & in thorough Repair.

Phil. Sandford[5] coll. to V. void by death of John Williams[6] June 25. 1680 Entry B. 108. I think there is a coll. in a former book.

Lic. to administer the Sacramt in the Chapel of Plaxtol 1711 VI. 65. It had been anciently used for religious Offices.

Ab[t] Taxations to the Church & Walls of the Ch. Yard here & elsewhere, see Godolphins Abridgmt[7] App. p. 10.

---

[1] Nicholas Haddock (1723–81), MP for Rochester 1754–61.
[2] William Holles Vane (1714–89), 2nd viscount.
[3] Lucius Charles (Cary) (c. 1707–85), 7th viscount Falkland.
[4] See p. 379. n. 5. [5] See p. 380. n. 4.
[6] Venn suggests this is John Williams, (c. 1636–1709), of Northamptonshire, m. Magdalen Hall O 1653, BA 1655, MA 1658, DD 1690, V. Wrotham, 1662–80, R. St Mildred Poultry, 1673–96, R. St Mary Colechurch, 1673–96, canon of St Paul's, 1683, preb of Canterbury, 1692–96, bishop of Chichester, 1696–1709.
[7] John Godolphin, *Repertorium Canonicum; or, An Abridgment of the Ecclesiastical Laws of this realm, consisting with the temporal* (2nd ed. corrected, 1680).

Page 382
Dioc. Roch. D. Shoreham
Wrotham V. continued

John Potter[1] DD V. 6 Feb. 1746. Resides usually in the Parsonage Ho. See p. 128.
Hon[ble] James Cornwallis[2] M.A. V. Oct[r]. 2[d]. 1770.
George Stinton[3] D.D. Vicar. 1781.
Charles Tarrant[4] D.D. Vicar 1783.
Richard Levett[5] A.M. Vicar. 1791.

Tho. Barnett[6], F. of Queens Coll. Ox. Pr. Cur. of Wrotham: Lives there. 50[f] & all Surpl. fees.

Edw. Hardy[7]. Pr. Cur. of Stansted, & Assistant at Wrotham in V[s] absence. 40[f] & all Surplice Fees. Serves no other Cure. refused to preach a Vis. Sermon, with D[r] Potters Approbation, bec. only Cur. Going to be R. of Ightham at Mich 1763.

John Saunders[8], Pr. Cur. of Plaxtol: lives there. 25[f] & all Surplice Fees: & 8[f] a year from a Ho. & Land, formerly given to the Cur. of Plaxtol for ever. Cur. also of Kingsdown Dioc. Roch of w[ch] D[r] Saunders[9] of S[t] Martins is minister.
Thomas Dalison[10] B.A. Cur. Licens'd April 7 1773.
John Henry Powell[11] lic. 1792.

⟨1760 sent 780 Tickets and 2000 Tracts⟩. July 13. 1760 Conf. here ⟨546. i.e.⟩ 292 of the peculiars, 254 of Dioc. Roch. Of this Parish 140. 1764 Conf. by BP Pearce 91. 1761. 97

---

[1] See p. ii, n. 3. [2] Ibid., n. 6. [3] See p. 149, n.4.
[4] (1724–91), of Fordingbridge, Hants, m. Balliol, BA 1744, MA 1747, B & DD 1760, preb of Bristol, 1751–76, R. North Tidworth, Wilts, 1757–60, preb of Salisbury, 1759, R. St Mary le Strand, 1759–61, V. Staines, Middlesex, 1763, R. St George's, Bloomsbury, 1761, dean of Calisle, 1763–4, preb of Rochester, 1776, V. Lamberhurst, 1776, R. Wrotham 1783–91.

5 (1727–?), of Lichfield, Staffs, m. Christ Church 1746, BA (Pembroke) 1749, MA 1752. Perhaps R. Little Berkhamsted, 1753.
6 (1721–), of Kirkby Stephen, Westmoreland, m. Queen's O 1739, BA 1744, MA 1748.
7 See p. 361, n. 9.　　　　　8 See p. 33, n. 3.　　　　　9 See p. 326, n.2.
10 [Dalyson], (1733–92), of Middlesex, m. St John's C 1750, BA 1755, R. Manton, Leics, 1757–92, PC. Plaxtol, 1773–92.
11 (1757–?), of Westminster, m. Exeter 1781, PC. Plaxtol, 1792–1802.

[Diocese of Winchester]

Page 383
Dioc. Winch. D. Croydon
Barnes R. St Mary. DCh. of St Pauls P. K^s books 9–3–4. Wake 150$^£$. Herring 200$^£$. Pension of 6–8 to the Lord, Ecton. 150 Ho. A mile long, ½ mile broad. Mr Hoare[1] the Banker. 2 or 3 Presb. from London in the Summer, but go to Church. Mr Whitaker[2], Counsellor & Mr Tonson[3] Bookseller, Absenters, on a misunderstanding with the last R. The first leaving the Parish. The last intends to come to Church. Whole Service on Sundays Two Sermons in Summer. Prayers always on Holydays: & 8 months in the Year, W. Fr. R. will exp. Cat. every Sunday in the Summer. Monthly Sacr. in Summer: only on Chr. Day in Winter. Abt 20 Com. ordinarily. Offertory money given by R. usually to the Clerk, Beadle & other Poor. 1761 Gates wanting to the Church Yard, & Commandm^{ts} to be made legible & clean. Church old: outside much damaged by the Weather: something shd be done to it. One Rose[4], a Citizen of London, buried here, hath left 20^s a Year to the parish, to keep a Rose Tree planted on his Grave. 1767. Sept. outside decently repaired. Ornamts at Mr Hoares Expence. Stone Corners of the Tower decayed. Only 3 Bells in it: frames rotten: no peal rung. Leave desired to sell two towds Repairs.

Ferdinando Warner[5] LLD R. 10 July 1758. Resides constantly in the Parsonage Ho. Hath no Curate. Going Sept. 21. 1761 to Ireland for 3 months. His Son[6], resident, to do the weekly Duty & Dr Morel[7], from Chiswick, the Sunday.
Christopher Wilson[8] D.D. R Novr. 2^d. 1768.
John Jeffreys[9] D.D. Rector 1792 resigned
John Jeffreys[10] A.M. Rector 1795.

Lewis Lewis[11] BA of Ch. Ch. 20$^£$ ord Deacon 1 July 1760. 2. Hath a school at Roehampton. Ord Pr. Ssept. 21. 1760. Gone to Cronslot.
Robert Strong[12] L.L.B. Cur. Sal. £60. lic. 1793.

1760 Conf. at Putney 31. 1763 None. 1766, 18. See Rectors Letters[13]

1 Henry Hoare (1705–85). Resided also at Stourhead, Wilts.
2 Possibly a relation of alderman William Whitaker, who died in 1754.
3 Jacob Tonson (died 1767), publisher, admired by Samuel Johnson.
4 Edward Rose, who died in 1653: *Surrey* III, p. 321.
5 (1703–68), of Tewkesbury, Glos, m. Clare 1742, LLD (Lambeth) 1754, V. Ronde, Wilts, 1730, R. St Michael Queenhithe, 1747, R. Barnes, 1758–68.

[6] John Warner (1736–1800), of London, M. Magdalene C 1754, migrated to Trinity C, BA 1758, MA 1761, DD 1773, R. Hockliffe and Chalgrove, Beds, 1771, R. Stourton, Wilts, 1790–1800, chaplain to the English embassy in Paris, 1790–5, taken prisoner in France, 1795.

[7] Thomas Morrell (1703–84), classical scholar, of Eton, m. King's C 1722, BA 1727, MA 1730, fellow 1725, DD 1743, PC, Kew, 1731, R. Buckland, Herts, 1737. He resided chiefly at Turnham Green.

[8] (17?–92), of Leeds, St Catherine's C 1733, BA 1737, MA 1740, DD 1753, fellow 1737–45, proctor 1742–3, V. Coton, Cambs, 1742, R. Barnes, 1768–92, preb of St Paul's, 1777, bishop of Bristol, 1783–92.

[9] (1719–98), of London, m. Christ Church 1737, BA 1741, MA 1746, B & DD 1769, R. Berkhamsted, Herts, 1756–98, R. Barnes, 1792–5, canon of St Pauls, 1779.

[10] (1771–1840), of Berkhamsted, Herts, m. Christ Church 1788, BA 1792, MA 1795, R. Barnes, 1795–1839, R. Friern Barnet, Middlesex, 1798–1840.

[11] See p. 215, n. 7.

[12] (1766–1849), of Wandsworth, Surrey, m. Trinity O 1783, BCL 1792, C. Barnes, 1793, R. Brampton Abbots, Heref, 17990, and of first portion of Bromyard until his death in 1849.

[13] LPL, MS Secker 6, ff. 194–5, Warner to Secker, 24 September 1763.

Page 384

Dioc. Winch. D. Croydon

Burstow R. St Bartholomew ⟨20 miles S. of Croydon⟩. The King P. ⟨Abt. the Advowson see Book of 1663⟩. K^s books 15-13-4. Wake 150$^£$. Herring 250$^£$. Called 200$^£$ in the Certificates for a Dispensation. 16½ miles round. 55 Ho. Walter Harris[1] Esqr. 6 or 7 Anab. meet in a private Ho. Teacher, { } English, officiates once a month here: & on other Sundays elsewhere. Whole Service on Sundays. Sermon on Chr. Day & good Fr. There was no Cat. but will be on Sundays in Lent. 4 Sacr. From 20 to 30 Com usually. 4$^£$ a Year of Smiths Charity given to this Parish: & 75$^£$ for clothing 6 poor persons annually ⟨[left by Dr Cook[2] & Dr Flamsteed[3]] who was Rector here⟩. R. hath given Bread & pays 5 per cent for it. 1761 Bellfrey & Ch. porch in a very bad Condition. Commandmts & sentences to be made more legible. Trees in Ch. yd. to be dressed.

Edm. Latter[4] MA R. 3 May 1757. Resides usually at his other Living of Bidborough Dioc. Roch. 20 miles off, ⟨near Tunbridge⟩ called in the Certificates 100$^£$. Often come & officiates here.
Arthur Edwd. Howman[5] A.M. 1790.

Joseph Edwards[6] Pr. Cur. Resides in Parsonage Ho. 40$^£$ & surpl. Fees. Doubtful if the Cur will suit him. Gone LD. 1760.
{Owen Evans[7] BA Ord Deacon June 1. 1760 40$^£$}
Tho. Baker[8], 1760. {ord} BA of Clare Hall C. ord. Pr. by BP Cornwallis[9]. Dec. 30 1761. 1. Going at Lady Day to Chiddingstone.
Pollock[10] Tho. LLD of Aberdeen C. ord. D. by me Feb 27 1763. 40$^£$ & Surpl. fees. but to pay 6$^£$ for the whole Ho. & Garden. 2 or 3.
Jackson[11] Edw. 40$^£$. May 1764. In prison Sept 1764. Only a few Days. Resides. 1765 serves another parish with this, & this sometimes but once. Is there Mich. 1767.
John Bulman[12] P. by BP Terrick[13] Tr. S. 1768. See his Papers. 40$^£$ & Surpl Fees.

[1] Owner of Burstow Park from 1743–65: VCH *Surrey* III, p. 179.
[2] Ralph Cooke (1606–84), R. St Gabriels, Fenchurch St, R. Burstow, 1637–84, preb of Rochester.

[3] John Flamsteed (1646-1719), of Derby, m. Jesus C, appointed astronomer royal, 1675, R. Burstow, 1695-1719.

[4] (1708-89), of Kent, m. St John's C 1724, BA 1728, MA 1733, R. Bidborough, 1732-89, R. Ashurst, 1746-57, R. Burstow, 1757-89.

[5] (17?-1848), of Norfolk, m. Queens' C 1782, scholar 1786, BA 1786, MA 1789, C. Gissing, Norfolk, 1787, R. Burstow, 1790-1848, V. Shiplake, Oxon, 1799-1848, master St Nicholas hospital, Salisbury, 1819, minor canon of Windsor, 1823-7, preb. of Salisbury, 1842-8.

[6] Perhaps (1707-?) of Stoke, Staffs, m. Madgalen Hall 1724, BA 1728, MA 1731.

[7] (1737-?), of Cardigan, m. Trinity C 1755, scholar 1759, BA 1760, MA 1773, R. Ford, Sussex, 1783, R. Slaugham, 1783.

[8] Of Tonbridge, m. Clare 1756, BA 1760, fellow 1764.

[9] Frederick Cornwallis (1713-83), bishop of Lichfield and Coventry, 1750-68, archbishop of Canterbury, 1768-83.

[10] Aberdeen LLD (Marischal College) C. Burstow, 1763.

[11] Perhaps (1724-?), of Surrey, m. CCCC 1743, BA 1747.

[12] Perhaps John Bulman, adm. '10 year man' Christs 1778.

[13] Richard Terrick (1710-77), bishop of Peterborough, 1757, bishop of London, 1764.

Page 385

Charlewood R. S[t] Nicholas ⟨20 miles S. of Croydon⟩. Matth. Wise[1] of Warwick Esq[r] P. K[s] books 19-6-8. Wake, Hering, 200[£]. Extent 30 miles. One Village. No Hamlets. Houses 110. One Gentleman. Yeoman 40. Farmers 60. Anab. 12 or 13. No meeting Ho. Meet once a month. Many of them come frequently to Church. Many Quakers. No meeting Ho. Pay their Dues without Compulsion: decrease, Some come to Church. The Congregation increases. Whole Service, 2 Sermons, on Sundays. Prayers every Saints day & twice a Week in Lent. Cur. hath exp. Cat almost every Sunday. 3 Sacr. 30 Com. at Chr. 70 at Easter. A Free School for 5 Ch[n], whom the Clerk hath taught for 40 Years. 7[£] a year to the poor, given by the minister & ChW[ns]. Not commonly reckoned unwholesome. 1762 Parsonage Ho. large, in good Condition. Out-houses large, repairing, almost finished. Rectors chancel repairing. Church & other chancels to be plaisterd & white washed & Roofs well coverd. 3[£] a Year Smith Benefaction, 40[s] by Mrs Earl[2], charged on Lands for Persons who do not receive Charity. Mentioned in Grindals Register fol 571 as being in the ABPs Gift.

Henry Blackett[3] R. March 20. 1749. Generally resides in Parsonage Ho. Absent one acct of his Mothers Illness. Returned. Went away Oct 1759 on acct of Health not returned July 1760. See his Letter. Resides ½ the year.
Norman Fothringham[4] R. Sept[r]. 11. 1770.
Joseph Davie[5] B.D. Rector 1784.
William Ellis[6] A.M. Rector 1792.

Tho. Williams[7] Cur. 50[£]. Resides in Parsonage Ho. Educated in Oxford, Priest. Probably not ordained. Gone. See a Paper abt him & Caution agst him. The above Account is written by him.
Owen Evans[8] BA ord. Deacon June 1. 1760. 2. 45[£] Pr. 17 May 1761.
Tho. Atkins Cur. P. 1765. Vis.
Mich. Baynes[9] BA. Cur. Ord. Pr. Dec. 20. 1767 ⟨3⟩. 45[£] & Surpl. Fees in R[s] absence abt 2[£]. Lives in Parsonage Ho.

[1] The son of Henry Wise who brought Charlwood Place in 1716. Matthew died in 1776: *Surrey* II, p. 191.

[2] 'Earl's gift': ibid., p. 186.

[3] (1727-70), of Hampton Court, Middlesex, m. Trinity O 1743, BA 1746, MA 1749, R. Charlwood, 1750-70.

[4] (1745-?), of Inverarity, co Angus, m. Balliol 1762, BA 1766, MA 1769, B & DD 1780, R. Charlwood, 1770-84.

[5] (1747-92), of Haseley, co Warwick, m. Trinity O, BA 1767, BA 1770, BD 1778, DD 1788, R. Charlwood, 1784-92, V. Navestock, Essex, 1788-92.

[6] (17?-1834), of London, m. Trinity C 1779, LLD (Trinity Hall) 1787, R. Thames Ditton, 1791-1834, R. Charlwood, 1792-92, PC. East Molesey, 1797-1834.

[7] Possibly (1717-?), of Lowes, co Radnorshire, m. Jesus O 1739. See LPL, Caution Book, 1758-85, pp. 5-6.

[8] (1737-?), of Cardigan, m. Trinity C 1755, scholar 1759, BA 1760, MA 1773, R. Ford, 1765-?, R. Slaugham, Sussex, 1783-.

[9] (1742-?), of Oxford, m. University 1760, BA (St Mary Hall) 1764.

Page 386

Dioc. Winch. D. Croydon

Cheam al Chaihame ⟨Direct near Croydon⟩ R. S[t] Dunstan ⟨7 miles W. of Croydon⟩ S[t] Johns Coll. Ox. P. K[s] books 17-5-5. Wake, 160[£], 200[£]. 70 Ho. many of them Cottages. Lady Dowager Stourton[1], Papist. Tho. Sergison[2] Esq[r], member for Lewes. Mrs Wyatt. Mr Edm. Sanxay[3], Surgeon. Rev[d] Mr Gilpin[4], teaches a private school. A Chapel in Lady Stourtons Ho. Priest, called Healley. 2 Families ⟨of low Rank⟩ perverted in 11 Years. See Papers abt this matter. Many Perverted in the Neighbourhood ⟨July 1766 Papists have been quiet for some time⟩. A few Presb. come to Church, but not to Sacr. Too many Absenters from Negligence or Wordliness. It is hoped they do not increase. Chiefly of low Rank. Whole service on Sunday {[No mention of other days]}. Cat. throughout Lent, with Lewis's Exp. 4 Sacr. A pretty many Com. for the size of the parish. Prayers on all Holy days 6[£] a year charged on Land by one Mr Pierson[5] for the Poor who come constantly to Church: distributed by R. Abt 6[£] of Mr Smiths Charity by R & ChW[ns], who give a yearly acct of it. 1761 Chancel behind the altar wants to be repaired & cleaned & the Windows & Tiling mended & Lady Stourtons Chancel to be cleaned, where a monument for one of the Family was set up without acquainting the R. & a large Crucifix put {on} ⟨over⟩ it. Roof of Church & Frames of Bells want repairing, & Rails & Pales of Ch. yd. Trees in Ch. yd. inconvenient to Persons going to Church. Ld of Manor [qu. who] saith they are without the old Fence, & will let nothing be done to them. Ch. Yd. Fence said to belong to private Persons: but ordinary will oblige the Parish, & leave it to its Remedy agst those Persons. And if private Persons will not repair their Chancels & Chapels, the Parish may, & rate them. Dr Simpson[6]

Right of Pres. disp. with S[t] Johns Coll 1703 Entry B V. 78. Purchased by Coll. for 380[£] in 1638.

James King[7] DD R. 1 Dec. 1747. Resides constantly in the Parsonage Ho. & doth the Whole Duty.

Henry Peach[8] B.D. Rector 1780.

Ja[s]. Wat Wilbraham[9] Cur. Sal. £50. lic. 1789.

1760 June 8. Conf. at Croydon 35. 1763. Sept 11. 15. 1766 Aug. 31. 29.

[1] Catharine (1697-1785), owner of manor of East Cheam. In 1712 she married Lord Petre, and in 1743 she married Charles Stourton, who died in 1753.

2 (1701–66), MP for Lewes, 1747–66.   3 Edmund Sanxay (1714–87).
4 William Gilpin (1724–1804), of Carlisle, m. Queen's O 1740, BA 1744, MA 1748, master of
  Cheam school, V. Boldre, Hants, 1777–1804, preb of Salisbury, 1783–1804. Writer on the
  picturesque.
5 By his will of 1719: *Surrey* II, p. 480.
6 Sir Edward Simpson (c.1699—1764), advocate Doctors' Commons, 1738, chancellor of the
  diocese of Bath & Wells, 1738, and of London, 1747–58, dean of Arches, 1758, MP for Dover,
  1759–64.
7 (1706–80), of London, m.. Christ Church 1722, BA 1726, MA 1729, B & DD 1740, R. St Michael
  Crooked Lane, 1733–47, R. West Cheam, 1747–80.
8 See p. 179, n. 3.
9 (1758–?), of Chester, m. Brasenose 1777, C. Cheam, 1789.

Page 387

Croydon V. St John Baptist. Belonged to the monastery of Bermondsey. A
Pension to the Abbot of 5-6-8. ABP P. Tenths 2-3-10½. Certified 45$^£$. Wake,
Herring, 150$^£$ ⟨& with voluntary Benefactions, 200$^£$. 246 Mr Greenhill[1]⟩. 5
miles or more in Diameter. About 1000 Ho. The principal Street near a mile
long. 3 Hamlets, Waddon, Shirley, Adscombe. The chief Families are London
merchants & Traders. Presb. meeting Ho. Teacher, Stockford. Anab. meeting
Ho. Principal Teacher, Harrison. Not numerous, except in Summer, by Lodgers
from London. So the Quakers, who have also a meeting Ho. V. hath no great
Reason to complain of them abt Dues. Many Absenters: but not increased, or
more than elsewhere. Whole Service, 2 Sermons on Sundays. Prayers on
Festivals, & W. Fr. morning, & Sat. Afternoon. 20 Charity Ch^n & some from
the work-house cat. in Lent. The former repeat Synges Exposition[2], Sacr. on
good Fr. 3 great Festivals & 1st Sunday of each month: From 40 to 60 Com. &
on gr. Festivals many more. ABP Tenison founded a School for 10 Boys to learn
Reading Writing & Arithm. & 10 Girls Reading, Writing & Needle &
Household-work. 5 Governors, who fill up Vacancies. 53$^£$ a year besides the
School House. David Ellis[3] founded an Hosp. for 7 Poor People: endowed with
40$^£$ a Year V. & ChW^{ns} & 4 Inhabitants Governors, who fill up Vacancies. ABP
Whitgifts[4] School & Hosp. under ABP^s Direction. Charities to the Poor, of 100$^£$
a Year or more: managed by the Parish Officers & Vestry, under the Inspection
of 2 Justices in the Parish. Church large & handsome, & clean within: wants
outside Repairs. V. Ho. built by ABP Wake, cost 600$^£$, raised by Arches, not
damp. Adjoins to Ch. yd. The great Tithes belonged to the ABP: & are sd to
have been exchanged with Secretary Walsingham[5] for Waddon Manor: & to
belong now, one half to Ld ⟨Visc.⟩ Montacute[6], & others to {Ld} ⟨the Earl of⟩
Shannon[7]. 1761 Frames of Bells & Lost bad, & the Pales on the N. Side. No
Table of Benefactions. Register of Burials & Bapt kept by the Clerk: to be alterd
wn the present dies. Money, given for marrying young women, said to be
employed in putting out Apprentices.
Lic. to teach the free School 1675 Entry B. III. 253.
Gift of a Corrody to Hen. Mills[8] intending him to be Schoolm. 11 Apr. 1712.
VI. 72. Made Schoolm. 26 June 1712 p. 78. John Taylor Lamb[9] the present
Master of Whitgifts School lic. 31 Oct 1751.

1 John Russell Greenhill (1730–?), of the East Indies, m. Trinity O 1746, BCL 1754, DCL 1759, R.
  Cottisford, 1762–, R. Fringford, Oxon, R. Marsh Gibbon, Bucks, 1779–.
2 See p. 292, n. 2.   3 In 1443: *Surrey* II, p. 556.

4 John Whitgift (c. 1530–1604), archbishop of Canterbury, 1583–1604.
5 Francis Walsingham (c. 1530–90), chief of the secret service under Queen Elizabeth.
6 Anthony (1686–1767), 6th viscount Montagu.
7 Henry Boyle (1686–1764), speaker of the House of Commons (Ireland), 1733–56, created earl of Shannon in 1756.
8 (1675–1742), of Wells, Somerset, m. Trinity O 1691, BA 1694, MA 1698, master of the Free school, Wells, 1699, master Free school, Croydon, 1712–22, R. Merstham, Surrey, 1724–42, canon of Wells, 1702.
9 See p. 215, n. 1.

Page 388

Dioc. Winch. D. Croydon
Croydon V. continued.

John Vade[1] MA V. 3 Jan. 1755. Generally resides in V. Ho. ⟨Was before that & is still⟩ V. {also} of S[t] Nicolas in Rochester ⟨100[£] a year⟩, which he visits as often as he conveniently can. Died June 9. 1765.
East Apthorpe[2] MA. V. July 11. 1765. Resides.
John Ireland[3] A.M. Vicar 1793.

John Russel Greenhill[4] LLD Cur. 45[£]. Resides. Going 1762.
John Smith[5] C. He is V. of Warlingham, wch he quits for his Health.

Sent 2000 Tracts 600 Tickets for Croydon, 200 blank for Cheam, Hayes, Keston, Mestham.
1760. June 8. Conf. 285. Of this Parish 212. 1763 Sept 11. Conf. 136. Of this Parish, 101. 1766. Aug. 31. Conf. 134. Of this Parish 90.

1 (1723–65), of Bromley, Kent, m. Clare 1740, BA 1744, MA 1747, R. Isleham, 1746–51, V. St Nicholas, Rochester, 1751–65, V. Croydon, 1755–65, chaplain to bishop of Rochester.
2 See p. 312, n. 7.
3 (1761–1843), of Ashburton, Devon, m. Oriel 1779, BA 1783, MA 1810, B & DD 1810, V. Croydon, 1793, V. Shoreham, 1806–16, preb of Westminster, 1802, dean of Westminster, 1816–42, founded the professorship of exegesis of Holy Scripture at Oxford.
4 See p. 387, n. 1.
5 Probably (1704–94), of London, m. Trinity C 1720, BA 1725, MA 1728, chaplain, 1727–58, R. St Saviour's Southwark, Surrey, 1730–53.

Page 389

Cullesden R. Not a peculiar. See p. 405.

East Horseley R. S[t] Martin ⟨20 miles SW of Croydon⟩. ABP P. K[s] books 12–16–5½ ⟨Called in Disp. Entry B. VII. 376. 110[£]⟩. Wake 80[£], 120[£]. Herring 80[£] ⟨See below⟩. 3½ miles long, 1 broad. The Houses not far distant from each other except 3. The 2 principal Farm Ho. uninhabited. Geo. Lane[1] Esq[r], of Bramham, Yorkshire. Abt 25 Absenters of low Rank. Service once on Sunday & Chr. day: bec. the Living is fallen from 110[£] to 48–10–0 ⟨See below⟩. Prayers Dec. 26. Jan 30. Ash W. good Fr. Easter Monday, Ascension Day. Cat. on Sunday afternoons in Lent. Ch[n] & servts not sent, but agst a Confirmation. [Perhaps only Charity Ch[n] cat. at other times. 4 Sacr. 14 or 15 Com. [not said how many Houses ⟨30⟩]. Mrs Lane maintains a School of 6 boys & 4 Girls, who are lodged, fed, clothed, taught to read, knit, sew & spin Linnen, & designed for

Servants. None put out yet ⟨She hath dropt it⟩. 2^f of Mr Smiths Charity, taxes & Repairs deducted, for Poor not receiving Alms. 50^f in money, reduced long ago to 25^f applied to Pay a Poors Rate. 2½ Acres of Land let at 12-6: no Rent paid for 10 Years. Bishop Mead 4^f a year: none for 10 years ⟨Mr Lane of Bramham hath the Land⟩. Complaint of Drinking on Sunday, & other Profanations of it. May 1759, the Farms are lett, & R. hopes the Income will rise in a Year or two. 1762 It is not improved. 1764. Now near 100^f. Ld Bingley[2] kept Estates in his own Hands, & paid R. just what he wd. BP Newton[3].

[1] George Fox, who by act of parliament in 1751 took the surname of Lane, according to the will of his uncle, James viscount Lanesborough. He became Lord Bingley in 1762, and died in 1773: *Surrey* III, p. 32.
[2] See n. 1.
[3] Thomas Newton (1704–82), bishop of Bristol, 1761–82, dean of St Paul's, 1768.

Page 390
Dioc. Winch. D. Croydon
East Horseley R. continued

Jos. Greenhill[1] BA R. 20 March 1727. R. also of E. Clandon ⟨near Guilford⟩, 2 miles off, 10-6-10½ in K^s books, now 87-10-0. Hath always resided at one of the Parsonage Houses, now at the latter, but reserves ⟨the best⟩ part of the former. Lately at London & Bath, [& May 1759 at Bristol] for his Health. Mr Pearsal[2], Master of Guilford School supplied his Absence, for a Guinea a Sunday: [6 or 8 miles off]. Hopes to be able to keep a settled Curate soon. Hath something of his own. Anonymous Complaint agst him, Jan 11–1760 for not residing, not having a resident Curate, & for total Failure of Service sometimes in his Churches. He answers, that no such Failure hath been above 3 or 4 times in above 30 Years, when he was ill. Resides at E. Clandon constantly 1760. A good man, & esteemed, & careful: but hath an hereditary oddness. BP Newton[3].

Richard Blackett Dechair[4] L.L.B. Rector 1788.
Edward Lambert[5] Rector 1792.
William Love[6] Cur. Sal. £50. Lic. 1786.

1762. May. 30 conf. at Guilford by BP of Winchester[7].

[1] (1704–88), of Abbots Langley, Herts, m. Sidney Sussex 1723, BA 1727, MA 1728, R. East Horsley, 1728–88, R. East Clandon, 1733–88.
[2] See p. 146, n. 1.   [3] See p. 389, n. 3.   [4] See p. 105, n. 3.
[5] (1749–1818), of Langford, Wilts, m. Magdalen O 1767, demy 1767–70, R. East Horsley, 1792–1818.
[6] C. East Horsley, 1786.
[7] John Thomas (1691–1766), bishop of Peterborough, 1747–57, bishop of Salisbury, 1757–61. bishop of Winchester, 1761–81.

Page 391
Mestham al. Meestham ⟨al. Merstham. Entry B. IV. 59⟩. R. St Catharine ⟨10 miles S. of Croydon⟩. ABP P. Kings books 22-1-8. Wake, Herring 160^f ⟨called 200 Entry B. VIII 203⟩. 70 Ho. 18 miles from London. A poor old man & his wife, lodgers, Papists. Molineux, a Priest, lives at Ryegate, supposed to

be titular BP of Winchester: but they have no Connexion with him. A Quaker, who died lately, pd his tithes without Scrupple. Some ragged Poor, absenters. Whole Service on Sundays. Prayers on Easter Mondays, good Fr. Holy Thursd. & S[t] Stephens. No Congregation on State Holydays, much less on others. Cat. on Sunday Afternoons from Mids to Mich. with Rewards in Books & money. Abt 30 Ch[n] attend, & are examined in The Cat. broke into Short Questions[1]. 4 Sacr. Sermon on the preceding Saturdays. Abt 40 Com. at gr. Festivals, 30 at Mich. Mr Henry Mills[2] R. [from 1725 to 1742] gave 5[f], & Mr Doc{k}minique[3] Lord of the Manor 10[f], for teaching poor Ch[n] to read & work. The Revd Mr Tattersall[4], who married Dockminiques Heiress, now Lady of the Manor, discontinues the 10[f] & threatens to take away ⟨[the School &]⟩ an Alms Ho. bult by Dockminique ⟨[as being on the Waste, & Ground not granted by the Lord.]⟩. R. pays for teaching 15 boys 7 girls to read & work. 3 or 4[f] of Mr Smiths Charity, according to Taxes, given to poor not having Parochial Relief. parsonage Ho. not large enough for R[s] Family. Cur. saith, 1760, that it is in very bad Repair. R. promises to repair it. See his Letter. 1761 Ho. to be rebuilt. Altar piece to be new, or mended. N. & middle Chancels to be repaired. Ch. yd. to be cleaned & Bushes grubbed up.

Jer. Milles[5] MA [DD] R 24 Oct 1745. See p. 295 ⟨403⟩, Served this, w[n] he cd hire a Ho. near. Now serves his Parish of S[t] Edm. Lombard Str. or resides on his chantorship of Exeter [or elsewhere]. 1762 Dean of Exeter.
Richard Richardson[6] A.M. Rector 1784.
Martin Benson[7] A.M. Rector 1791.

Rice [2]. Evan[1]. BA of Jes. Coll. Ox.[8] Pr. Cur. Lives in Parsonage Ho. 40[f] & Surpl. fees. Careful & good.

1760 June 8 Conf. at Croydon 22. 1763 Sept. 11. 11. 1766. Aug. 31. 5.

[1] *The Church Catechism broke into Short Questions. To which are added Prayers for the Charity Schools* (1709).
[2] See p. 387, n. 8.
[3] Paul Docminique (1639–1735), merchant and MP for Gatton, 1705.
[4] Probably James Tattersall (1712–84), of Chipstead, Surrey, m. Trinity C 1731, scholar 1733, BA 1736, MA 1742, V. Charing, Kent, 1746–55, R. St Paul's, Covent Garden, 1754–5 and 1758–84, R. Streatham, 1755.
[5] (1714–84), of Highclere, Hants, m. CCCC 1729, BA 1733, MA 1735, B & DD 1747, R. Saltwood, 1744–5, R. Merstham, 1745–84, R. St Edmund King, R. West Terring, 1747–79, treasurer of Lismore Cathedral 1735, precentor of Waterford, 1737–44, preb of Exeter, 1747, dean of Exeter, 1762.
[6] (1753–1839), of Worcester, Brasenose 1774, BA 1778, MA 1782, B & DD 1810, PC. Witton Gilbert, co. Durham, 1780, R. Merstham, 1784–91, R. Brancepeth, 1806, minor canon of Durham, chancellor of St Paul's.
[7] See p. 134, n. 2.
[8] (1712–?), of Llanlluwlhoy, co. Carmarthen, m. Jesus O 1732, BA 1735.

Page 392
Dioc. Winch. D. Croydon
Mortlake. Chapel to Wimbledon. DCh. of Worcester P. Contains East-Sheene. Abt 300 Ho. Near 40 Families of Distinction. See the names of above 20. Many Presb. some of Note. No meeting Ho. used or likely to be used. They all come

constantly to Church. Many Absenters: none of note: decrease. Whole Service, 2 Sermons on Sundays. Prayers W. Fr. & Holy days. Charity Ch[n] Cat in Lent. Monthly Sacr. 70 or 80 Com. at each. Alms Ho. for 4 Women who have 15[d] a week & Cloaths yearly. 10 boys & 10 Girls taught by voluntary Contributions to read & work. Some put out Apprentices, w[n] there is money. Interest of 650[f] given in Coals at Chr. The settled Income of the Minister is 40[f] a year. 1761. Pavemt in S. Isle sunk. One of the 3 Urns over the Com. Table Lost. Stiles of Ch. yd. want Repair. Chancel to be white washed & Sentences made more legible. L[ds] Prayer &c placed too high to be read, on making a new Altar piece. Mr, now Ld, Spencer[1], Lessee. His Ten[t] lives in Parsonage Ho. Out of Repair. Cupola in the church wants repairing & ornamenting: weather - Cock blown down, to be put up, or a Ball, wch the Parish have. Garter Inn, above 20[f] a year, given to the Repair & ornamt of the Church, 1717.
Cur. licensed. Fiat directed to Vic. Gen. 20 June 1672 Entry B. III. 156.
Lic. to serve this & Putney see p. 394. lic. to serve this VIII. 59
Tho. Cornthwaite[2] MA Cur ⟨nominated by DCh Worc. lic⟩ 16 Dec. 1751. V. of Hackney, where he resides. Hath the above settled Income.

J. Marsden[3] Pr. Deputy. Chapl. to BP Drummond[4]. Resides in the Parish. Paid by voluntary Contributions [120[f] a Year].
Richard James[5] Cur. 1763, 1765, 1766.

1760 Conf. at Putney 91. 1763. 19. 1766. 39

[1] John Spencer (17?-83), viscount Spencer 1761, earl Spencer 1765.
[2] (1721-99), of London, m. Trinity C 1739, scholar 1740, BA 1743, MA 1746, fellow 1743, adm. Gray's Inn, 1741, C. Mortlake, 1751-99, V. Hackney, 1753-99.
[3] John Marsden (1731-96), of Barnsley, Yorks. m. Christ Church 1749, BA 1753, MA 1756, B & DD 1777, V. Felixkirk, Yorks, 1765-93, R. Bolton Percy, 1774?, precentor of St Asaph, 1760, preb of Southwell, 1762-96, preb of York, 1785.
[4] Robert Hay Drummond (1711-66), bishop of St Asaph, 1748-61, bishop of Salisbury, 1761, archbishop of York, 1761-66.
[5] (1730-81), of London, m. Christ Church 1748, V. Broad Hinton, Wilts, -81.

Page 393
Newington Butts R. S[t] Mary. BP of Worcester P. K[s] books 16[f]. Now betw. 170 & 200[f]. A mile Square. Contains Wallworth, Blackman Street, Kent Street, Newington. Betw. 8 & 900 Ho. Not many, or considerable Sectaries of any Sort. No Papists or Moravians. R. hath heard of no Quakers, that refuse to pay his Dues. Whole Service on Sundays: 2 Sermons, one by the Lecturer. Prayers W. Fr. Holydays. Cat. W. Fr. in Lent. Monthly Sacr. betw. 30 & 40. Com. & on gr. Festivals. [Not said how many then]. Drapers Alms-houses for 8: founded by John Walter[1] in 1650. The Company Governors: 6 to be of this Parish. Fishmongers Alms Ho. & Lock-Hospital partly in this Parish. A voluntary Charity School for 20 boys. See the particulars. Sev[l] Benefactions to the poor, which See.
Lease of pt of Glebe conf 1739 VIII. 140.
An Act of Parlt abt part of the Glebe 176. Lease of it X. 66.
In the Parochial Book of 1663 is an Entry that the ABP was patron, till Cranmer granted it away & it came to the See of Worcester 1546.

Sam. Horsley[2] LLB R. 17 Jan. 1759. Resides in the Parsonage Ho. Hath no Curate. Lodges in St Martins, to assist his Father[3]. Clerk in orders there Charles de Guiffardiere[4] B.D. Rector 1794.

Hugh Pugh[5] BA of Ch. Ch. Pr. by BP Thomas[6] of Lincoln Chr. 1759. C. 40^f. Resides. Afterwads Bisset[7]
James Ozanne[8] Nov. 19. 1763. Ord. by BP Harris[9] of Landaff. Hath a small Living in Wales, 40$_f$. Going LD 1766.
Wm Sayle[10] A.B. C. Mich 1767. 80 Guineas Salary.
William Crawford[11] Cur. Sal. £50. lic. 1785. resigned.
Mr. Dickinson[12] Cur. not licensed. Sal £ { }.
John Free[13] DD. Lecturer, licenced by ABP Herring ⟨14 Jan. 1748⟩. Abt 40^f a Year by voluntary Subscription. Thursday Lecturer of St Mary at Hill & V. of East-Coker, Som.
William Crawford. Lecturer Lic. 1785.

23 March 1760 Conf. 100. 1761, at St Michaels Cr. Lane 12. 1762, None. 1763. 6. 1764. 6. 1765. 6. 1766. None 1767. 7. 1765 11.

[1] Clerk to the draper's company: *Surrey* III, p. 460.
[2] (1733–1806), of St Martin's Westminster, m. Trinity Hall 1751, scholar 1753, LLB 1758, R. Newington Butts, 1759–93, R. Albury, Surrey, 1774–79, R. Thorley, Wilts, 1779, V. South Weald, Essex, 1782–93, archdeacon of St Albans, 1781–8, preb of St Pauls, 1784–94, preb of Gloucester, 1787–93, bishop of St David's, 1788–93, bishop of Rochester, 1793–1802, bishop of St Asaph, 1802–6.
[3] John Horsley (17?–77), was a nonconformist, graduated Edinburgh 1724, R. Newington Butts, 1754–58, R. Thorley, Herts, 1745–77, lecturer St Martin's, Westminster.
[4] 1810), R. Newington Butts, 1794–1810, R. Berkhamstead, 1798–1810, preb of Salisbury, 1798.
[5] (1735–1809), of Dolgelly, co Merioneth, m. Christ Church 1754, BA 1758, MA 1762. Died as R. Brithdie, near Dolgelly.
[6] John Thomas (1691–1766), bishop of Lincoln, 1744–61, bishop of Salisbury, 1761–6.
[7] Possibly Alexander Bissett (1714–?), of Westminster, m. Christ Church 1734, BA 1736, MA 1741, BD 1753.
[8] Chaplain in Royal Navy, 1734, V. Caerwent, 1736–79.
[9] John Harris, bishop of LLandaff, 1728–38.
[10] (17£–99), of Notts, m. St John's C 1751, BA 1755, C. Great Barton, Beds, R. Chelworth, Soms, 1744–99.
[11] (1751–1827), of Newington Butts, m. Trinity C 1769, scholar, BA 1772, MA 1775, DD 1801, fellow, 1773, C. Newington, 1775, lecturer Newington, 1785, R. Bleddfa, Radnor, 1788–93, archdeacon of Carmathen, 1793–1827, R. Trottiscliffe, 1794–1827, R. Milton, 1797–1827.
[12] Robert Dickinson (1770–1847), of Heversham, Westmoreland m. Queen's O 1786, BA 1791, MA 1795, C. Newington Butts, lecturer, 1797, R. Headley, Hants, 1818–48.
[13] (1712–85), of Oxford, m. Christ Church 1727, BA 1730, MA 1733, B & DD (Hertford) 1744, headmaster St Olave's Grammar School, Southwark, lecturer Newington, 1749–85.

Page 394
Dioc. Winch. D. Croydon
Putney. St Mary. Chapel to Wimbledon, DCh of Worcester P. ⟨John Spencer[1] Esqr their Tenant⟩. Near 3 miles long & two broad. 289 Ho. & 49 at Roehampton. In Putney Sir Jacob Downing[2] Bart, Sir Josh. Van Neck[3] Bart. Sir Richd Adams[4] Baron of the Exch. Revd Dr Pettiward[6] ⟨near 4000^f a year⟩ &c. In Roehampton 4 or 5 Families of Fortune. No whole Family of Dissenters, but one of Quakers lately settled. The poor do not come duly to Church. Whole

Service, 2 Sermons, on Sundays. Prayers W. Fr. Sat. & Holydays. Great Numbers of Ch[n] cat. 3 times a Week in Lent. No Servts. Sacr. 1st Sund. in each month, good Fr. Chr. Easter, Whits. Large Number of Com. A free School founded by Mr Tho. Martin[6] for 20 Watermens Sons of Putney, or if wanting, of the Neighbourhood, who are clothed & educated. 11 Gentlemen of the Town Governors. Income above 100[f] a Year. School House very handsome. An Alms Ho. founded by Sir Abr. Dawes[7] in 1648 for 12 single Persons of Putney. Income 40[f] a year. His Descendants Governors: now D[r] Pettiward. Sev[l] Gifts to the poor, which see. No Ho. belonging to the minister. Church small: Chancel fitted up with Pews. New Burial Ground wanted.

A private Chapel at Roehampton 1½ ⟨mile⟩ from the Church, adjoyning to Mr Birds[8] Ho. who opens & shuts it at pleasure, being his property. Prayers & sermon every Sunday, 3 Sacr. The minister appointed & paid by the Inhabitants of Roehampton: from whom the minister of Putney receives no Gratuity, though he is obliged to perform the Parochial Duty.

Curate licenced to Putney 1663 Entry B. I. 36. No no. mentioned. W[m] Hopkins[9] nom. by Ch. of Worc. lic. to serve the Cure of Putney & Mortlake 1678. IV. 48. ⟨Lic. on nom. from DCh Worcester VI. 256, 338⟩.

Schoolm. licenced VI. 244.

The Stipend of the minister of Putney is 40[f] a Year.

[1] See p. 392, n. 1.

[2] Jacob Garrard Downing (c. 1717–64), 4th Bt. MP for Dunwich, 1749–61 and 1763–4.

[3] (?–1777). Son of the paymaster of the land forces of the United Provinces. He came to England in 1722 and made a large fortune out of commerce. He was created a baronet in 1751.

[4] Recorder of the City fo London, knighted in 1752.

[5] Roger Pettiward. See p. 196, n. 8. The family had owned a large estate in the parish since the Restoration.

[6] By will of 1684.

[7] 'an eminent loyalist in the time of Charles I, and one of the richest commoners of the time': *Surrey* III, p. 301.

[8] The chapel was built in 1632. It was pulled down in 1777 by Thomas Parker, who built a new one: ibid., p. 260.

[9] (1647–1700), of Evesham, m. Trinity O 1661, BA 1665, MA (St Mary Hall) 1675, DD (Trinity) 1692, canon of Worcester, 1675, C. Putney, 1678–1700, lecturer St Lawrence Jewry, 1680, V. Wolverely, Worcs, 1681, R. Harvington, 1682.

Page 395

Putney continued

Sam. Holcomb[1] MA lic. 7 May 1744. Now 1760 DD. & R. of Stoke. Resigned by the Surrender of his Licence Jan. 28. 1762.

Benj. Newcombe[2] D.D. nominated & licenced Jan 28. 1762. R. also of S[t] Mildreds Poultry & Preb. of Worcester.

Thomas Fountaine[3] Clerk A.M. Licensed Dec[r]. 16: 1775, on the Nomination of the Dean & Chapter of Worcester.

Thomas Hughes[4] A.M. lic. 1788.

John Fludger[5] Deputy. Pr. Resides in the town. Serves no other Cure. Hath the Easter Offerings ⟨abt 12[f]⟩: & a generous Subscription from the Inhabitants. Rents the Parsonage Ho. at 16[f]: too dear. Neither DCh nor Mr Spencer will repair it. His Steward promised in 1761.

Henry Whitfield[6] D.D. Deputy.

Minister of Roehampton Chapel

May 18. 1760 Conf. here 371. Of this Parish 187. Sept. 18 ⟨1763⟩ Conf. here 189. Of this Parish 125. Sept. 14. 1766. Conf. here 284: of this Parish 154

[1] (1704–?), of St Clement's, London, m. Trinity O 1722, BA 1728, MA 1729, C. Putney, 1744–62.
[2] (17?–75), of Middlesex, m. Queens' C 1734, BA 1738, MA 1741, DD 1757, C. Putney, 1762, R. St Mildred's Poultry, 1762–75, V. Walehurst, 1768–75, preb of Worcester, president Sion College, 1767, dean of Rochester, 1767–75.
[3] (1737–1815), of London, m. Trinity C 1757, scholar, BA 1760, MA 1763, fellow 1762, V. Old Windsor, Berks, 1771, preb of Worcester, 1774, PC. Putney, 1775–8, R. North Tidworth, Wilts, 1780–8, V. Bromsgrove, Worcs, 1788–1815, V. Tarrington, Heref. 1789–1815.
[4] (1757–1833), of co. Denbigh, m. St John's C 1773, scholar, BA 1777, MA 1780, DD (Lambeth) 1817, PC. Putney, 1788–1803, R. Peasemore, Berks, 1801–7, R. Turweston, Bucks, 1802–4, V. Chiswick, 1808–9, V. Kilken, Flint, 1809–33, V. Uffington, Berks, 1811–33, clerk of closet, tutor in royal family, chaplain duke of Cumberland, 1802, preb of Westminster, 1793–1807, preb of St Paul's, 1807–33.
[5] ? John Fludyer (1712–?), of Abingdon, Berks, m. Pembroke O 1728, BA 1732, MA 1735.
[6] (1741–1813), of Plymouth, m. Pembroke C 1758, BA 1762, MA 1765, DD 1777, fellow 1763, V. Alveley, Essex, R. St Margaret Lothbury, London, 1768–1813, R. Wexham, Bucks, 1771–, C. Putney, 1779.

Page 396
Dioc. Winch. D. Croydon
Wimbledon R [rather Cur] S[t] Mary. DCh. of Worcester Impr. & P. It was impropriated, with many other of the greatest Benefices, since 1534. Ecton. Putney & Mortlake are [or were] Chapels to it. 130 Ho. John Spencer[1] Esq[r] Lord of the Manor, Mr Baron Smythe[2], Sir Abraham Janssen[3], Dr Peter Shaw[4], Mr Hays[5], Mr Banks[6], Mr Rush[7], Several eminent Merchants & Lawyers. A woman, who keeps a Chandlers Shop, Papist. Mr Spencer is Lessee of the Rectory. The Surplice Fees, & Fees from Burials are excepted, out of his Lease, to the Minister. And these, with a Stipend from the Church [I believe, 40[£] a year] & the Easter Offerings, are his Income. Church well attended. Mr Spencers Family exemplary. Whole Service from LD to Mich. Once from Mich to LD. Morning Service not over, till one. A long & dirty Walk from the Houses to the Church. They who keep Coaches, generally then in London. [Service might begin earlier]. Cat. in Lent, Sacr. on gr. Festivals: & generally twice betw. Whits & Chr. [Number of Com. not mentioned.] Mr Spencer hath given 2 Acres of Ground & 50 Guineas for a Charity School: near 300[£] subscribed, & the Building almost finished. 25[£] a year charged by Lady Dorothy Cecil[8], Da. of Ld Visc. Wimbledon, on Lands now belonging to Jacob Tonson[9] Esq[r], to keep up her Fathers Monumt, teach poor Ch[n] to read, put out Apprentices, buy materials for Poor People to manufacture, and Produce to be given to the old & impotent. No. Ho. for the Minister. Church repairing & beautifying. 1761.
Licence to serve the Cure Entry B. I. 155. II. 84 by fiat on his Present by DCh See VI. 340.

John Cooksey[10] MA Cur. ⟨lic⟩ July 1739. Resides from Easter day to Advent: then attends his Church in London: but is generally here some Days in each week.

Herbert Randolph[11] B.D. Licensed July 3: 1777, on the Nomination of the Dean and Chapter of Worcester.

Jackson[12] Pr. Schoolmaster of Streatham supplies the Curates absence.
William Hussey[13] Clerk. Assistant Curate. licensed MA R. 13: 1775. Salary 50 p. ann.

1760 Conf. at Putney 62. 1763 45. 1766, 73: 27 of them but 13 years old.

[1] See p. 392, n. 1.
[2] Sidney Stafford Smythe (1705–78), MP for East Grinstead, 1747–50, baron of the Exchequer, 1750, chief baron, 1772–7.
[3] Died in 1765. The son of South-sea director. [4] (1694–1763), physician to George II and III.
[5] Adam Hayes, who died in 1785. He accompanied Lord Anson on his voyage round the world.
[6] Henry Bankes (1710–74), alderman of London: *Surrey* III, p. 279.
[7] Samuel Rush (1715–83), owner of vinegar factory in Southwark, which was in the Rush family from 1641–1790: ibid., p. 590.
[8] Left in 1651. The daughter of Sir Edward Cecil (1581–1638): ibid., p. 283.
[9] See p. 383, n. 3.
[10] (1706–77), of Worcs, m. Merton 1722, BGA 1726, MA 1729, C. Wimbledon, 1739–77.
[11] (1748–1819), of Petham, Kent, m. CCCO 1762, BA 1765, MA (Magdalen) 1768, BD 1777, precentor St Pauls 1812, V. Canewdon, Essex, R. Hanwell, PC Wimbledon, 1777–1819.
[12] Could be William Jackson, of St Martin-in-the-Fields, m. Pembroke C 1715, BA 1720.
[13] (17?–1831), of Burwash, Sussex, m. CCCC 1772, CA 1775, MA 1778, fellow 1776–81, C. Wimbledon, 1775, V. Sandhurst, 1781–1831.

Page 397
ABP P. not Ordinary.

[Diocese of Chichester]

Page 398
Dioc. Chic. ABP P. not Ordinary
Horsham V. St Mary. Belonged to the Priory of Rasper. Ecton. K[s] books 25[f].
Now Tithes 156 Glebe 12[f] Offerings 8[f] Surpl. Fees 12[f]. Somewhat more.
Troublesome in collecting. Taxed at 70[f], & pays nothing to the poor. A Corporation Town. Much reformed by the present V. A Cur. must be always kept. L[d] Irwin[1] lives here. ABP Wake saith, Bishopridge in this Parish is a peculiar.
ABP collated in Vacancy of the See of Chichester 1696 Entry B. IV. 546 pres. VI. 419. 407. VII. 214.
The parochial Book of 1663 refers for the Right of presentation to Reg. Abbot fol. 159 b & saith it was given by the king in Exchange.

Tho. Hutchinson[2] DD V. 25 Sept 1742. Resides V. of Cocking, Co. Sussex 100[f] a yr.
Francis Atkins[3] V. April 18th 1769.

Portslade see here p. 289

[1] Henry (Ingram), Viscount Irwin (Irvine) (1691–1766), MP for Horsham, 1721–36.

[2] (1699–1760), of Cornforth, Durham, m. Lincoln 1715, BA 1718, MA 1721, BD (Hart Hall) 1733, DD 1738, V. Cocking, V. Horsham, 1742–69.

[3] (1720–96) of Renwick, Cumberland, m. Queen's O 1738, BA 1742, MA (Emmanuel) 1770, V. Horsham, 1769–96, V. Stymping, Sussex, 1772–86, V. Poynings, 1786–96, preb of Chichester, 1781–96.

[Diocese of Lincoln]

Page 399

Dioc Linc.

ABP P. not Ordinary

Little Brickhill C. Sr Mary. Belonged to the Priory of Combwell in Kent. ⟨Said in Paroch. Book 1663 to come from Sr John Gage[1] Kt⟩. ABP Impropriator. R. in K^s books 9$^£$. Certified 27–14–10 ⟨29–10–0 Ecton⟩. Another acct ⟨in Ecton⟩ Certified 29–10–0. 14$^£$ reserved to it by Juxon in the ABP^s Lease. Near 40$^£$ a year with the Tythe wood

70 Houses inhabited. 2 noted Shopkeepers, called Muggletonians, go to no place of Worship. Not above 9 or 10 come to Church in a Morning, besides Ch^n. More, in afternoon, wn the Sermon is now. Many Alehouses. Ch. W^{ns} will not present. Court takes no notice of the ministers Complaints. Minister hath well repaired the Parsonage Ho. Church is much out of Repair, & the Parish will not be able to keep it {in Repair} ⟨up⟩ many years longer. Whole ⟨Sunday⟩ Serviced, except wn called to assist a Neighbour: then once. Prayers on Holydays &in Lent, till there was no Congregation. Cat. on Sundays in Lent: but few Ch^n sent, & no Servts. 4 or 5 Sacramts in a year, if a Congregation. No Ch W^n hath rec^d in 13 Years.

John Moseley[2] MA collated by ABP to this V. being in {the} his peculiar Jurisdiction 22 Dec. 1664. Void by Cession. ⟨But a note in the margin of the Entry Book, that the ABP is not to collate but present to BP of Lincoln⟩. Tho. Harwood[3] cl. presented by ABP to this V. 3 July 1671 void by Cession. John Smyth[4] pres. to BP of Linc. March 6. 1665 on Moseleys Death Entry Book I. 164. Geo Badeley[5] pres. 23 Dec 1673 on Harwoods Death. Robt Woodward[6] licenced to serve the Cure 29 Feb. 1703/4. V. 112. Wm Cawne[7] lic. on the Cession of John Harrison[9], called a pre. 11 Apr. 1711 VI. 40.

Wyat[1] Francis[2] [9] Cur. Licenced 7 March 1747 ⟨on death of Mr Martin[10]⟩. Resides.

V. also of Bromeham Co. Bedf. Certified 57$^£$.

Michael Woodward[11] Licensed Cur. September 6 1774.

John Burton Watkin[12] A.M. 1779.

This Curacy was augmented in 1768 with £200 from the late AB^P & £200 from the Governors of Queen Annes Bounty. Laid out in the purchase of Land 1776.

[1] See p. 77, n. 1.

[2] Perhaps (1616–?), of Godshill, Isle of Wight, m. New Inn Hall 1634, BA 1636, MA 1639, V. Little Brickhill, 1664–66.

3 Perhaps [Harward], m. Caius 1633, BA 1637, C Ilkeshall, 1662, R. Dickleburgh, Norfolk, C. Sampford, Essex, V. Little Brickhill, 1671-3.

4 V. Little Brickhill, 1666-71.

5 (1648-), of Great Ness, Salop, m. Jesus O 1667, BA 1671, V. Little Brickhill, 1673.

6 (1664-1737), of Salford, Beds, m. All Souls 1680, BA 1683, MA 1687, perhaps V. Stantonbury, Bucks, 1685-1706, R. St Helen's Abington, Berks, 1689-92, V. West Ilsley, Berks, 1689-1737, C. Little Brickhill, 1703-4, V. Burton Dassett, Warwks, 1704-5, V. Astwood, Bucks, 1705-6.

7 (1675-1716), of Beds. m. Peterhouse 1694, R. Wavendon, Bucks, 1702-16, C. Little Brickhill, 1711-16.

8 (1668-), of Ireland, m. Trinity College Dublin 1685, Trinity C 1690, CCCC 1690, C. Little Brickhill, 1704-11, R. South Stoke, Lincs, R. East Torrington, Lincs, 1735.

9 m. Emmanuel 1725, BA 1729, V. Heckington, Lincs. 1741-?, C. Little Brickhill, 1748.

10 Died in 1748. Perhaps Charles Martyn, m. Balliol BA.

11 (1737-79), of Salford, Beds, m. Brasenose 1763, PC. Little Brickhill, 1774-9.

12 (1747-1822), of Yelvertoft, Northants, m. New College 1764, BA 1767, MA 1778, C. Little Brickhill, 1779, R. Crux-Easton, Hants, 1781-, V. Marshfield, Glos, 1781-1822.

Page 400
{ABP P. not Ordinary}

Dioc. Linc. D. Monks Risborough
Wotton Underwood C. All Saints. Belonged to the Priory of St Gregorys near Canterbury. Not in K^s books. Certified 43$^£$. Present value, see below. 2000 acres. 36 Houses. The Family seat of the Grenvilles, now inhabited by the Rt Honble Geo. Grenville[1], next Brother to Earl Temple[2]. The Rectory was exchanged with that Family by Act of Parliam^t in 1742 for Borestall Farm, {or} ⟨alias⟩ Mussel Farm: which Farm is now leased by the ABP reserving 11$^£$ a Year Rent & 45$^£$ a Year Pension to Him or the Curate. He resides in the House belonging to his Cure. Whole Service on Sundays.
Cat. exp. in Lent. 4 Sacr. 30 Com. 3$^£$ a Year, payable from Land for apprenticing a poor godly Boy. Offertory distributed by the minister. ChW^{ns} have for many Years attended the BP of Lincolns Visitation: the Curate not, except now & then: the present Curate never. He never was cited to the Visitation at Risborough or Halton. Income, the above 45$^£$ a year, without Deduction. Surplice fees abt 10^s. The Ch. Yard & a little Bit of Ground worth 40^s a year.
40^s a year was reserved to this Curacy by ABP Juxon.
Licence to ⟨Rob. Vicaris[3] to⟩ serve the Cure 1672. Entry B. III. 188. To Tho. Richards[4] 1675 on resign. of Vicaris III. 268. To Owen Jones[5] 1678/9. Form at Length IV. 66. V. 106. VIII. 182.
1767 No Papists.

Lilly Butler[6] BA. Cur. Lic by ABP March 16. 1756 ⟨ord. pr. by BP Beauclerk[7]⟩. Resides. Presented, Sept. 1761, to the Vicarage of Witham: designs to continue here some time.
Thomas à Beckett[8] A.M. 1782.

1 (1712-70), MP for Buckingham, 1741-70, secretary of state, 1762.

2 Richard Grenville (1711-79), MP for Buckingham, 1734-41 and 1747-52, MP for Buckinghamshire, 1741-47, lord Cobham, 1749-52, when he succeeded his brother as earl Temple.

3 m. Trinity O 1658, BA (St Alban Hall) 1662, MA 1664, C. Wotton Underwood, 1673-75, R. Heythrop, Oxon, 1675.

4 (1644–), of Helmdon, Northants, m. Caius 1661, BA (Trinity) 1665, R. Helmdon, 1668–75, C. Wotton Underwood, 1675–.

5 (1649–), of Aberfrau, co. Angelsey, m. Jesus O 1668, C. Wotton Underwood, 1679, R. Cosheston, Pemb, 1700–.

6 (17?–92), of Bletchingley, Surrey, m. Clare 1750, BA 1754, MA 1757, C. Wotton Underwood, 1756–82, V. Battersea, Surrey, 1757–8, V. Witham, Essex, 1761, dean of Ardagh, Ireland, 1785–90.

7 Lord James Beauclerk, bishop of Hereford, 1746–81.

8 (1751–?), of West Lavington, Wilts, m. Brasenose 1768, BA 1772, MA 1778, PC. Wotton Underwood, 1782.

[Diocese of London]

Page 401

Dioc. Lond ABP P. not Ordinary

All Hallows Barking V. Belonged to the Abbess & Nuns of Barking in Essex. Granted 37 H.8 to ABP in Exchange. Kings books 36–13–4. Haynes 170$^£$, 276$^£$. V. pays a Pension of 10$^£$ to the King. See below.

Lease of V. Ho. for 40 yrs at 4$^£$ Conf. by ABP 1671 Entry B. III. 68. The Advowson was granted by the Crown to the ABP in Exchange 31 Aug. 1 Ed. 6. See Chart Misc. vol 13. N° 21. This must have been in part a Confirmation of the former Grant. See above here.

Income 1749 Yearly Tithe of Houses 250–13–4. Rent of Glebe Houses 60$^£$ Surplice Fees 40$^£$ In all 350–13–4. Deduct Curates fixed Stipend. 30$^£$ to Curate for 50 sermons at 10–6. 26–5–0 Taxes, Repairs, Short paym^{ts} 80$^£$. In all 136–5–0. Remains 244–8–4. Dr Geekie will deduct more for the last Articles 14–8–4 & take 230$^£$.

AD^n Heads Acct 1767. Tithes of Houses, if full 273–10–0. Three Glebe Houses 61–16–0. Surplices Fees abt 40$^£$. In all 375–6–0. Also 4$^£$ for 6 yearly Sermons. Deduct fee Farm Rent to Ld Harcourt[1] 13–13–4. & Kings Tax for the 3 Houses. The Curate is Lecturer & saith his Income as above & from Lecture is 80$^£$.

Wil. Geekie[2] DD. V. 10 Jan 1732. Archd. of Gloucester, R. of Southfleet Dioc. Roch. & Preb. of Cant. where he resides. Died July 22. 1767
George Stinton[3] DD. V. Inst. 17 Sept. 1767
M^r. Johnes[4] Vicar 1783.

Murden[5], Cur.
Pugh[6] Cur 1767.

1 Simon Harcourt (1714–77), 2nd viscount and created earl in 1749.
2 See p. ii, n. 9.   3 See p. 149, n. 4.
4 Samuel Johnes (1756–1852), of Ludlow, Salop, m. Christ Church 1774, BA 1778, fellow All Souls, MA 1782, V. All Hallows, 1783–1852, R. Welwyn, Herts, 1797–1852. Took additional name of Knight in 1813 by royal licence.
5 Cornelius Murdin (1714–68), of London, m. Sidney Sussex 1733, BA 1735, MA 1738, fellow 1738, V. Ixning, Suffolk, 1759–68.
6 C. All Hallows, 1767.

Page 402

Dioc. London. ABP P. not Ordinary

All Hallows the great, or the more, or ad Faenum ⟨Fenne 1663⟩ R. united with All Hallows the less, C. The Site & Ch. Yard of which last is now a Burial place. The former granted by Exchange to ABP 37 H.8. K[s] books 41–18–1½. Now 260[f]. Vid. Rot 474 Term Mich II Banc. Reg [This Reference is transcribed from Mr Haynes's Book].

Lease for 40 yrs, 10[f] Quit Rent, Conf. 1672 Entry B III. 150.

The Advowson was granted by the Crown to the ABP in Exchange 31 Aug. 1 Ed. 6. See Chart. Misc. vol. 13. N° 21.

Chr. Hussey[1] DD R. 27 July 1731. Dead

Geo. Secker[2] MA R 1761. 1763 R. of Brasted p. 345 ⟨died March 21. 1768⟩.

Will. Talbot[3] MA R March 28. 1768.

Hon[ble] James York[4] M.A. R. July 22[d]. 1769.

Robert Richardson[5] D.D. Rec Octo[r]. 26: 1776.

William Vincent[6] D.D. Rector 1778.

[1] (1684–61), of London, m. Trinity C 1703, scholar 1704, BA 1707, MA 1710, DD 1731, fellow, 1709, R. All Hallows, 1731–61, R. West Wickham, 1732–61, chaplain duke of Dorset, master Free School, Sevenoaks.

[2] See p. ii, n. 21.

[3] (1719–74), of London, m. Exeter 1737, BA 1743, MA 1744, V. Kineton, Warwks, 1768, R. St Giles, Reading, 1768–74. He was at one time drawn to the Moravians, but remained an Anglican. Talbot was present at Secker's death-bed. He himself died of a fever contracted during the course of his parochial visiting.

[4] [Yorke] (1730–1808), son of Philip, Lord Chancellor Hardwicke, m. CCCC 1748, MA 1752, DD 1770, R. Great Horkesley, Essex, 1754–6, V. St Giles, Reading, 1765–8, R. All Hallows, 1768–76, preb of Rochester, 1754–6, canon of Windsor, 1756–62, dean of Lincoln, 1762, bishop of St David's, 1774–9, bishop of Gloucester, 1779–81, bishop of Ely, 1781–1808.

[5] (1731–81), of Middlesex, m. Emmanuel 1745, BA 1750, MA 1753, DD 1766, fellow 1755, R. Wallington, Herts, 1759–81, preb of Lincoln, 1762–81, R. All Hallows, 1776–8, R. St Anne's, Westminster, 1778–81, royal chaplain.

[6] (1739–1815), of London, m. Trinity C 1758, scholar, BA 1761, MA 1764, DD 1766, fellow 1763, usher Westminster school, 1762–71, under master 1771–8, head master, 1788–1802, V. Langdon, Worcs, 1778, R. All Hallows, 1778–1803, R. St John's Westminster, 1803–7, R. Islip, Oxon, 1807–15, president of Sion College, 1798, preb of Westminster, 1801, dean of Westminster, 1802–15, royal chaplain.

Page 403

Dioc. Lond ABP P. not Ordinary

S[t] Edmund the King or Lombard Street, or Grass Church R. with S[t] Nicolas Acons R. {ABP P.} ⟨ABP & King Patrons alternately⟩. Kings books 21–14–2. United with S[t] Nicolas Acon R of which the Site is now a Burial place. The King P. K[s] books 13[f]. The Patronage now alternate. Both 180[f] & a Ho. 40[f]. R. saith, he will rebuild his Parsonage Ho. in 1761. See his Letter in Mestham. Done.

Jer. Milles[1] MA [DD] R. Oct. 1745 presented by the King. See p. 295, 391.

Henry Dimock[2] A.M. Rector. presented by the ABP. 1784

Bulkley[3], Lecturer.

[1] See p. 295, n. 5.   [2] See p. 113, n. 6.

[3] Probably either Robert [Bulkeley] (1737–?), of Llanbaboe, Angelesey, m. Jesus O 1754, BA 1758, or Samuel (17?–1809), of London, m. Clare 1748, BA 1753, MA 1736, DD (Oxford) 1800, R. Hinton, Northants, 1771–1809, preb of Bristol, 1794.

[Diocese of Norwich]

Page 404

Dioc Norw. ABP P. not Ordinary

Denton R. Co Norf. St Mary ⟨Entred before, p. 331. Stands properly here. But see there⟩. Mr Postlethwayt[1] by his will; Sept. 1713 gave the Advowson to the ABP on Condition to present a Fellow or one who had been Fellow of Merton Coll. K^s books 24$^£$. Now 250$^£$.

Geo. Sandby[2] MA R. ⟨pres.⟩ 30 May 1750.

[1] See p. 331, n. 1.   [2] Ibid., n. 3.

[Diocese of Winchester]

Page 405

Dioc. Winch Co. Surrey ABP P. not Ordinary

Cullesden R. al. Coulsdon. St John Evangelist. K^s books 21–16–5½. Herring 172$^£$ ⟨So in Disp 1751⟩. 210$^£$. Now 230$^£$.

A retired Place. Only Farmers: not numerous. 5 miles from Croydon, 7 from Ewel. Ho. stands on much Ground. Great part of it ruinous: but might be made comfortable, by lessening the old part, & adding to the new, which a Lady, who farmed the Rectory, is said to have built lately. Glebe, 80 Acres, inclosed, near the House, let at 45$^£$ a Year, & the rest of the parsonage at 185$^£$, all to one man. Probably both might be raised. No chapel. Two Sermons on Sundays. This in writing from Dr Halifax[1], vicar of Ewell, June 1761.

The Advowson was granted by the Crown to the ABP in Exchange 31 Aug 1 Ed. 6. See Chart. Misc. vol 13, N° 21. Concerning Presentations by others, & the Judgmt in favour of the ABP, see there N° 66.

Ld Folkestone[2] saith the Chancel is in a very bad Condition. Mr Herring saith the Church & that are in good Repair 1764. 1765 He hath orderd Repairs, wch two Days will complete, & whitewashing. Ch W^{ns} have promised to keep the Church walls dry.

Tho. Herring[3] MA R. 6 Dec. 1749. R. of Chevening p. 346 where he resides, & Preb. of York.

Henry Godricke[4] Clerk, presented June 22. 1774.

[1] James Hallifax (1719–?), of Rugby, m. Balliol 1736, BA 1740, MA 1743, B & DD 1758, V. Ewell, Surrey, R. Cheddington, Bucks, 1765–.

[2] Jacob des Bouverie, Lord Folkestone (1694–1761), MP for New Sarum, 1741–47. Created viscount Folkestone in 1747. Owner of Coulsdon manor: *Surrey* II, p. 450.

[3] See p. 346, n. 7.

[4] (1722–1807), of London, m. St John's C 1741, BA 1745, V. Lingfield, Surrey, 1749–1807, R. Coulsdon, 1774–1807. Perhaps also V. of Godmerham, 1772–2.

Page 406

Dioc. Winch. Co. Surrey ABP P. not Ordinary

Lambeth R. St Mary. K^s books 32–15–7½. Dr Robt Porey[1] was R. died in 1669.

Tho. Tomkins[2]. BD domestick chapl. to ABP {inst.} ⟨pres.⟩ Nov. 29. 1669.

Geo. Hooper[3] BD dom. chapl. pres. 9 Sept. 1675 on Tomkins's death.

Edm. Gibson[4] { } on Rich. Ibbetson[5] DD on { }.

John Denne[6] 24. Nov. 1731 on Ibbetsons death. Called in Disp. 300$^£$ Entry book VII. 399, 340. Died 5 Aug 1767.

Beilby Porteus[7] D.D. R. inst. Aug 19. 1767 R. of Hunton, p. 364.

W^m. Vyse[8]. D.D. 1777. presented by the Crown (jure prerogativa) on Promotion of B. Porteus.

On a Petition of the Inhabitants in 1711 to the Commissioners for building 50 New Churches, representing that the parish of Lambeth was 7 miles long, & contained 1800 Houses, & that the people in general were poor, & that Stockwell or Lambeth Dean wd be a proper place for a church; & that Sr John Thornicroft[9] Lord of the Manor of Stockwell, had offerd 2 Acres of Land on the waste there ⟨called Common Green⟩ for a Church, a Burial Ground & a Ministers House: the Commissioners approved this Plan: & the Principal Persons having Right of Herbage there consented to give it up. And March 23. 1714 the Ground there was orderd to be staked out. But it seems not to have been done. Also in 1711 the Commissioners voted, that there shd be a 2^d new church in Lambeth Parish: I believe in that part which lies near Camberwell. In the same year, whilst only one was intended Dr Gibson then Rector, & many of the parishioners proposed that a piece of Ground adjoyning to Caroon House in South Lambeth was the fittest place, as appears by this Certificate. But this was opposed strenuously by others, because South Lambeth was near enough to the Parish Church, & Stockwell had 102 Houses, & Lambeth Dean 133 Houses, more distant. Another place proposed in 1711 was a Field called Ladder-stile Field by the wash-wayside in Lambeth Dean but Stockwell was then preferred. March 31. 1720 On a Petition from the minister & Inhabitants, the Commissioners orderd a more convenient Place to be sought between South Lambeth & Fox Hall. In a Petition without Date, but signed by Dr Ibbeston, Rector, by Mr Angell[10] & many Inhabitants, a Church at Stockwell or Lambeth Dean is requested. But after all, nothing was done. Extracted from the Minutes of the Commissioners, & the Papers laid before them. The ABP does not appear to have taken any part in the whole Affair.

[1] [Pory], (16–69), of London, m. Christs 1625, BA 1629, MA 1632, BD 1639, DD 1666, R. St Margaret's, New Fish Street, London, 1640–3 and 1660–, R. Thorley, Herts, 1640–3 and 1660–2, R. Hollingbourne, Kent, 1661, R. Much Hadham, Herts, 1662, R. Lambeth, 1662–69, archdeacon of Middlesex, 1660, canon of St Paul's and Chichester, 1660, archbishop's chaplain.

[2] See p. 301, n. 3.

[3] (1640–1727), of Grinsley, Worcs. m. Christ Church 1657, BA 1661, MA 1663, BD 1673, DD 1677, R. Havant and East Woodhay, Hants, 1672, R. Lambeth, 1675–1703, dean of Canterbury,

1691–1704, precentor of Exeter, 1677, bishop of St Asaph, 1703–4, bishop of Bath and Wells, 1704–27. Wells, 1704–27.

[4] (1669–1748), of Knipe, Westmoreland, m. Queen's O 1686, BA 1691, MA 1695, fellow 1695, DD 1702, Lambeth librarian, R. Stisted, Essex, 1700–4, R. Lambeth, 1703–7, precentor of Chichester, 1703, archdeacon of Surrey, 1710, bishop of Lincoln, 1716–23, bishop of London, 1723–48.

[5] See p. 339, n. 3.

[6] (1693–1767), of Littlebourne, Kent (son of the woodreeve to the see of Canterbury), m. CCCC 1709, BA 1713, MA 1716, DD 1728, fellow 1716–21, PC. St Benet's, Cambridge, 1720, R. Greens Norton, Northants, 1721–6, V. St Leonard, Shoreditch, London, 1723–67, V. St Margaret's, Rochester, 1729–31, R. Lambeth, 1731–67, preb and archdeacon of Rochester, 1728, Boyle lecturer, 1725–8.

[7] See p. 139, n. 1.   [8] See p. 345, n. 8.

[9] (1659–1725), 1st Bt.   [10] William Angell: *Surrey* III, p. 531.

Page 407

{Blank page}

Page 408

Dioc. Winch. Co. Surrey ABP P. not Ordinary

Warlingham V. All Saints, with Chelsham Chapel S[t] Leonard. Belonged to the Monastery of Bermondsey. Kings books 11–12–11. Now { }. The ABP doth not enjoy a Right of presentation here. On what Grounds he may claim it, see separate papers.

John Smith[1] Vic. see. pa. 388.

[1] See p. 388, n. 5.

[Diocese of Chester]

Page 409

Dioc. Chester. Co. Lanc. ABP P. not Ordinary

Blackbourn V. S[t] Mary. Belonged to the Monastery of Whalley. K[s] books 8–1–8. By the Parl. Survey 1647 it hath 50 Acres of old Inclosure & 20 of new, with 2 Ho. & a Barn, 35[f]: Pension from ABP, 26–13–4: Surpl. fees 10[f]. Sev[l] Ho. on the Glebe 14–16–8 others at 10[s] each 9–10–0. In all 96[f]. Wake p. 114 for the first Article hath 50 Acres of old Incl. 20[f]. 20 of new 5[f] uncultivated Land 10[f]. And he omits the two last Articles: which brings it to 71–13–4. Then he adds Juxons Augm. 70[f] & a Farm bought by Sancroft 33[f]. In all 174–13–4. The Endowm[t] of the V. of Blackbourn is not in the BP[s] Registry

Fra. Price[1] presented 25 Oct. 1677 on death of Leonard Clayton[2] Entry B III. 323. John Holmes[3] on Prices death 12 Apr. 1706. V. 212.

The Rectories of Rachdale, Blackeborne & Whalley & the Manor of Littlebourne with their chapels &c and other appurtenances were given by the Crown to the ABP in Exchange 31 Aug 1 Ed 6. See Chart Misc. vol. 13 N° 21.

The Lease of the Rectory grants it with the Chapels of Law & Salmesbury, but reserves the patronage of the Vicarage, & the nomination to the several Chapels. The Income of the Vicarage was 140$^£$ in 1683 out of wch the Vicar pd 4$^£$ a year to Law Chapel, 4$^£$ to Samlesbury, 2-8-0 for Tenths, Pension, Procurations & Synodals, & 30$^£$ to a Curate to preach in the Afternoon at Blackburn. Mr Prices Letter to ABP March 29. 1683[4].
See a valuation of the Income at 169$^£$.

John Woollin[5] V. 266 July 1742.
John White[6] Clerk V. July 29 1772.
Thomas Starkie[7] A.M. Vicar. 1780.

[1] (16?-1706), m. University 1658, BA 1662, V. Blackburn, 1677-1706.
[2] (1616-77), of Little Harwood, Lancs, m. St Mary Hall 1636, BA 1639, MA 1642, V. Blackburn, 1647 and 1662-77, R. Stockport, 1674-77.
[3] [Holme] (16?-1738), V. Blackburn, 1706-38.
[4] LPL, TR 10, f. 15.
[5] (1700-72), of Wakefield, Yorks, m. Merton 1716, BA 1720, MA (Oriel) 1722, BD 1735, V. Blackburn, 1742-72, R. Elmley, 1742-72.
[6] (1730-80), of Essex, m. Trinity C 1759, BA 1764, MA 1767, fellow 1765, V. Blackburn, 1772-80.
[7] (1750-1818), of Downham, Lancs, m. St John's C 1767, scholar, BA 1771, MA 1774, fellow 1771-82, V. Blackburn, 1780-1818.

Page 410
Dioc. Chester. Co. Lanc. Chapels in Blackbourn Parish.
They are 7. and 14$^£$ a Year is paid to the ministers of them by the Lessee, pursuant to the {Will} ⟨Gift in 1688/9⟩ of Mrs Cordelia Fleetwood[1], then Lessee. The Nomination to them is reserved to the ABP in the Lease. But it appears not ⟨upon search⟩, that he ever hath nominated. ABP Sancroft[2] purchased an Estate ⟨for himself & for his successors⟩ for the Augmentation of these 7 Chapels, which he leased. May 26. 1688 to the then Vicar for 21 Years, if he shd so long continue Vicar at a Pepper-Corn Rent, as his Successors also are to do: the Vicar to let the Estate & receive the Rents, & distribute them amongst the Curates of the Chapels, or some of them, in such shares as the ABP for the time being shall appoint under his Archiepiscopal Seal, & in default of such Appointmt, as the vicar shall think their merits & necessities require. And the Vicar may deduct his necessary Expences, & 40^s a year for his Trouble. And before Chr. in every year, & within 6 months after the Expiration of the Term, the Vicar, his Executors or Administrators, shall give a true & full acct under their Hands to the ABP of all Receipts, Pay^{mts} & Transactions relating to this Trust. This Lease hath been renewed from time to time. The Estate is said to have been purchased with a Fine wch Sancroft recd in 1685. And he did receive then 830$^£$.[1]* Abt the Patronage, see Law Chapel, p. 412. The Vicar is presented to the Vicarage only: but if he hath been used to nominate to the Chapels, perhaps the Endowment was like that of Whalley which see p. 419. Concerning the Chapels & Parish church see a Letter of Mr Price[3] the vicar to ABP Sancroft March 29. 1683[4].
[1]* See an excellent Letter of his, July 5. 1684[5], relative to this Benefaction, then intended. V. saith 1765 that the Estate is worth 48$^£$ a year. Qu. how he distributes. It is said that he gives only 14$^£$.

See a Paper[6] copied from the Church Book of Blackburn, where it was entred in 1617 concerning the paym[t] of 5[£] a year to the poor on the Inclosure of the ABPs waste there.

Balderston S[t] Leonard. Certified to be of no value. Augm. 7 Feb. 1742 with 400[£] by John Potter[7] BD then V. of Blackbourn & the Queens Bounty. Purchase made Nov. 15. 1743. Certified again, 14[£]. Aug 3 May 1756 by James Collinson[8], Executor of D[r] Stratford[9] & Q[s] bounty, with 400[£]. The Vicar nominates.

[1] Principal householder in Blackburn in the late seventeenth century: VCH *Lancashire* VI, p. 237.
[2] William Sancroft (1617–93), archbishop of Canterbury, 1678–90.
[3] See p. 409, n. 1.   [4] LPL, TR 10, ff. 15–16.
[5] LPL, TR 10, f. 57, Sancroft to 'Mr Controller'.
[6] LPL, TR 10, ff.1–2, 12 Jan 1617/18.   [7] See p. ii, n. 3.
[8] He has not been traced.   [9] William Stratford, see p. 64, n. 5.

Page 411
Chapels in Blackbourn Parish

Darwen S[t] James. Certified 6–16–8. Augm in 1719 with 40[£] by Mr Nath. Symonds[1] Sen. & Qu[s] bounty. Purchase made 27 March 1722. Certified again, 1733, 25–166–8. Augm. with 400[£] by Rev Mr John Holme[2] & Rev. Mr John Folds[3]. Purchase 7 Dec. 1734. The Vicar nominates.

Harwood S[t] Bartholomew. Built 1505. Cert. 14–15–4 Augm. 1735 with 400[£] by Mr James Whalley[4] & Qu[s] Bounty. Purchase made 10 Nov. 1740. The Vicar nominates. 4–6–8 given to it yearly by Qu. Eliz. out of Charity Rents in Lancashire

[1] 'Augmented in 1719 by Mr Eccles and others': *Notitia Cestriensis. Or Historical Notices of the Diocese of Chester, by the Right Rev. Francis Gastrell, D.D.*, ed. F.R. Raine, Chetham Society, VIII, IXX, XXI, XXII (1845–1850) 2 vols. II, part 2, p. 284.
[2] See p. 409, n. 3.
[3] (c.1697–1772), of Blackburn, m. Brasenose 1716, BA 1720. He was the incumbent of Darwen chapel from 1722–72. He was also licensed to Balderstone.
[4] Probably the James Whalley who purchased Clerk Hill in 1715: VCH *Lancashire* VI, p. 387.

Page 412
Chapels in Blackbourn Parish

Lango. Certified 7–6–8. Augm. ⟨with 200[£]⟩ by Lot 1746. Purchase made 11 May 1753. Certified again, 1750, 14–6–8. Augm. with 400[£] by John Woollin[1] V. of Blackbourn & Q[s] bounty. Purchase made for both augmentations 11 May 1753. The Vicar nominates.

Law or Lowchurch al. Walton. S[t] Leonard. Certified 15–18–8. Abt 1754 Sir Henry Hoghton[2] Bar[t], a Dissenter, wd have augmented this Chapel, provided the Patronage were vested in him for ever. Mr Montague[3], Secretary to the Q[s] Bounty, judged from the ABP[s] Leases, that it ⟨& that of the other chapels⟩ was vested in the See: & heard that some eminent Civilians in ABP Wakes time, thought so on more general Reasons. Nothing was done. See D[r] Chicheleys[4] Letters in 1733. As in the Lease of the Rectory only the Patronage of the Vicarage is reserved ⟨mistake⟩, the Lessee seems intitled to the Patronage of the

Chapels. But see here p. 410 〈409〉. The Nomination to the Chapels is also reserved in the Lease of the Rectory. It hath been augmented: but the Vicar still nominates.

1 See p. 409, n. 5.
2 (1679–1768), 5th Bt. MP for Preston, 1710–13 and 1715–22 and 1727–41, MP for East Looe, 1724–27.
3 Henry Montague, secretary to Queen Anne's Bounty, 1737–66.
4 Richard Chicheley (1686–17?), of London, m. Christ Church 1701, fellow All Souls', BA 1704, MA 1708.

Page 413

Chapels in Blackbourn Parish

Samlesbury St Leonard. Certified 14–16–8. 1765 Hath been hitherto served by the same Person with Low als Walton p. 412. Now they are augmented & abt to be separated: for wch ABP^s consent is necessary. BP Keene[1]. The Vicar still nominates.

Tockholes St Michael. Certified 15–1–8 Augm. 1725 with 400^f by Ralph Livesay[2] Esqr & Q^s Bounty. Purchase made 8 Apr. 1736. The vicar still nominates.

Walton see Law
Besides these Chapels a 4° MS at Lambeth mentions Healy as a Chapel under Blackburne.

1 Edmund Keene (1714–81), bishop of Chester, 1752–71, bishop of Ely, 1771–81.
2 [Livesey]. Owner of the manor of Livesey. He died in 1725: VCH *Lancashire* VI, p. 286.

Page 414

Dioc. Chester. Co. Lanc. ABP P. not Ordinary

Rachdale V. St Chadd. Belonged to the Monastery of Whalley. K^s books 11–4–9¼. Now 500^f. The last Incumbent said 700^f. The Present, 500^f. ABP Impr. His Lessee pays 15^f to the Schoolm. 2^f to the Usher, 8^f to V. 5^f to Cur. of Saddleworth, 2^f to Cur. of Butterworth. He also pays 6–13–4 to V. 2^f to Cur. of Saddleworth & 1–6–8 to Cur. of Butterworth, till the first mentioned 15^f & 2^f also paid from Blackbourn [for which I see no provision made] & then out of this 15^f & 2^f V is to have 10^f Cur. of Saddleworth 4^f, & Cur of Butterworth 3^f. It seems intended, that the 6–13–4, 2^f, & 1–6–8 are to cease then. If so, the Lessee will pay 10^f less than before. Saddleworth, once a separate Parish, now a Chapelry, is in Yorkshire. Ecton saith, from Kennet of Impr. p. 308 that ABP Sancroft settled a pension on this Parish. The above Paymts were in 1661. Dr Tunstall[1] thinks Kennet was misinformed. The Curate hath the 8^f & 6–13–4 mentioned above, as pd to the Vicar, & 10^f a year more from the Vicar, wch with Surplice Fees makes above 50^f a Year.
Lic. to a schoolmaster at Rachdale as being in ABP^s peculiar Jurisd. 1697. Entry B. IV. 569 [By mistake].
Dr Sam. Dunster[2] pr. 2 Apr. 1722 on death of Hen. Pigott[3] VI. 403.
Nathaniel Foster[4] pres. July 25 1754 on death of Dunster.

John Shaw[5], clerk, nom. by ABP to be schoolm. Nov. 27. 1755 on Res. of{ } Sutcliffe[6] Clerk ⟨See below⟩.

How Rachdale came to be the ABP see here p. 409. His Lease of the Rectory excepts the Patronage of the Vicarage.

The Parochial Book of 1663 mentions the Schoolmasters place, value 15$^£$ & the Ushers, val. 2$^£$ as in the ABPS Gift.

The only Income of the Vicarage is from the Glebe.

James Tunstall[7] DD V. 12 Nov. 1757. Died March 28. 1762.
Tho. Wray[8] DD inst. Apr. 10. 1762. See p. 56, 149.
Richard Hind[9] D.D. Vicar 1778.

[1] See p. 265, n. 3.

[2] (1675-1754), of Westminster, m. Trinity C 1693, scholar 1694, BA 1697, MA 1700, DD 1713, R. Chinnor, Oxon, 1716, V. Paddington, V. Rochdale, 1722-54, preb of Salisbury, 1717-48, preb of Lincoln, 1720, chaplain to earl of Shrewsbury and duke of Marlborough.

[3] (1628-1722), of Forton, Staffs, m. Lincoln 1642, BD 1660, R. Brindle, Lancs, 1651-1722, V. Rochdale, 1662-1722.

[4] (1718-57), of Plymouth, m. Pembroke O 1732, fellow CCCO, BA 1735, MA 1739, BD 1746, DD 1750, preb of Bristol, V. Rochdale, 1754-7, archbishop's chaplain.

[5] Master Grammar School, 1755.   [6] [Joseph] Sutcliff, V. Rochdale, 1730-45.

[7] See n. 1.   [8] See p. 56, n. 3.

[9] (1716-90), of Lillingstone Lovel, Oxon, m. Christ Church 1730, BA 1733, MA 1736, proctor 1744, BD 1745, DD 1750, V. Shering, Essex, 1754, R. St Anne's Soho, London, V. Rochdale, 1778-90, V. Skipton, 1778-90.

Page 415

Chapels in Rachdale Parish.

The Patronage of them is not reserved to the ABP in the Lease, which mentions only two, Saddleworth & Butterworth ⟨& grants them with their Endowmts & along with the Rectory⟩. The Income of all depends greatly on Contributions.

Butterworth. Not mentioned in ABP Herrings book ⟨or Ecton⟩. See p. 414. There is now no such Chapel. The Chapel of Miln Row is in Butterworth Township.

Littleborough. St James. Certified 10$^£$. Herring, all 50$^£$. Augm. by Lot, 1745, with 200$^£$. Purchase made July 10. 1750. Certified 17$^£$ Augm. 1748 with 400$^£$ by Joseph Keighly[1] Clerk & Q^s bounty. Purchase made July 10. 1750. The Vicar still nominates.

[1] [John] Keighley, incumbent from 1745-69. The previous incumbent had been Joseph Sutcliff from 1730-45: VCH *Lancashire* V, p. 234.

Page 416

Chapels in Rachdale Parish

Milnrow. Certified 13-13-6. Herring, abt 50$^£$. Augm. 1717 with 400$^£$ by Sam. Chetham[1] Esqr & Q^s bounty. Purchase made 4 Dec. 1721. The Vicar still nominates.

Rachdale. A Chapel in the Town, abt 60$^£$ Herring. Not mentioned in Ecton.

Saddleworth. S[t] Chadd. In Yorkshire. Certified 16–10–0. Abt 60[£], Herring. See p. 414. Augm. 1737, with 400[£] by Sam. Dunster[2] DD. Vicar of Rachdale & Q[s] bounty. Purchase made in 14 March 1743. 7[£] yearly from the Lessee. See p. 414. Mr Higginbottom[3] hath been Cur. near 40 years. Worth in all near 100[£] a year. The vicar still nominates.

[1] Owner of Castleton Hall. He died in 1744; VCH *Lancashire* V, p. 224.
[2] See p. 414, n. 2.   [3] John H[e]gginbottom, C. Saddleworth, 1721–71.

Page 417
Chapels & School in Rachdale Parish

Todmerdine, S[t] Mary. Certified 2[£], including 1[£] for the Ho. Ecton. 16[£], Herring. Augm. 1721 with 400[£] by Mr John Starkey[1] ⟨& Q[s] bounty⟩. Purchase made 1 Dec. 1736. The vicar still nominates. 1767 Complaint from Mr Hargrave[2] the Curate there, sent to the BP of Chester.

Whitworth. S[t] Bartholomew. Certified 6–6–8. In the Gift of {Mr} ⟨John⟩ Starkey ⟨Esq[r]⟩, abt 50[£], Herring. Augm. 1720 with 400[£] by Mr John Starkey & Q[s] bounty. Purchase made 12 July 1723. It is presumed, that he is intitled to nominate.

The Schoolmaster is nominated by the ABP. Wake. The Usher also. Herring. See p. 414.

[1] According to VCH *Lancashire* VI, p. 500, John Starkie died in 1697. He was succeeded by his son Piers.
[2] Robert [Hargreaves] (c.1694–1770), of Skipton, Yorks, m. St John's C 1710, BA 1715, PC Todmorden, 1742–70. In 1750 he was engaged in a severe contest with his parishioners as to the right of appointing churchwardens: Venn.

Page 418
Dioc. Chester. Co. Lanc. ABP P. not Ordinary Whalley

V. All Saints. Belonged to the Monastery of Whalley. K[s] books 6–3–9. ABP Impr. whose Lease reserves to V. the Easter Book, consisting of sev[l] Tithes & Paymts, which see, excepting for the Tithery of Bowland, & the Surplice Fees, for wch he is to find Communion Bread & Wine in the Church & chapels, except for the Tithery of Bowland. The Lessee also pays out of the reserved Rent[1]*, ⟨50[£] wch the ABP used to pay⟩ {& 70[£] besides it, to the V. & Curates, of wch V. hath 38[£]. 10[£] of the 70[£] may be given by the ABP to any other preacher at Whalley: & out of the 50[£] are to be paid all dues to the BP & AD[n]}. Wake states the ⟨vicars⟩ income thus: pd by ABP (as above) 38[£]: by the Curates for East Dues. & Surpl Fees as by a Decree 42[£] ⟨of Exchequer 1679, wch see. There were then 10 chapels: Acrington, Castle, Goodshaw, Holm, Marsden, Whitwell, not named⟩. Perquisites 3[£]. But in Parl. Survey, East Dues are 70[£]. {The rest of the 50[£] & 70[£] is divided amongst the Curates in a Schedule annexed to the Lease ⟨Sir Ralph Ashton[1] reckoned the Easter dues &c in ABP Juxons time at 120[£], which was too much⟩. 120 Ho. Wake. 16 miles over. 5 of the chapelries are market Towns: ⟨were⟩ 16 in all. One demolished. The Lease grants the Chapels of Padiham, Clitherow, Downham, Colne, Burnley, Church, Altham, Haslingden, Bowland, Pendle [probably now called New-church in Pendle] Trawden, Rosendal [probably now called New-church in Rossendale] & of the Castle of Clithero, with all chapels &c of these, Bowland & Trawden are not by those names in the present List: & Acrington, Holme, Marsden, Whitwell & Goodshaw, which are in the present List, are not by those names in the Lease.

[1]* to the BP & AD^n of Chester, ⟨under whose Jurisd. the parsonages be for procurations⟩ & to the Vicar & Chaplains, {wch the ABP used to pay them}: of which ⟨nothing is now pd to the BP & AD^n, but⟩ {according to ABP Wake, the Vicar hath 18$^£$ ⟨& 8 chapels, 14$^£$⟩. And besides the reserved Rent, he pays 10$^£$ to the Vicar or some preacher at Whalley as ABP shall direct: [it is now p^d the Vicar] & 60$^£$ to the Vicar, & Chaplains, as ABP directs, by a Schedule; wch gives 10$^£$ of it to the Vicar. This ⟨last⟩ 60$^£$ by Juxon. So the Vicar hath thus 38$^£$ & hath also 42$^£$ from the Easter Roll.
Pres. to Whalley 30 Nov. 1703 Entry B. V. 105.
How Whalley came to the See of Cant. See here p. 409.
In the Endowmnt 1330 66 marks with some other Profits are given to the Vicar: but he is bound to find Curates & Bread & Wine for the Chapels. In the Lease of 1620 wch is the earliest, 50$^£$ a yr is reserved to the BP, AD^n, vicar & Curates, & 10$^£$ Increase: wch 60$^£$ Vicar & Curates receive. After the Restoration, the Easter book, & 60$^£$ a year more is given to him & them. Mr Johnson in 1767 demands the 66 marks &c.

Will Johnson[2] MA V. 31 Aug. 1738.
William Baldwin[3] LLB. V. 19 June 1776.

[1] Sir Ralph Assheton (c.1605–80), 2nd Bt, MP for Clitheroe, 1625–80.
[2] (1712–92), of Ellingham, Norfolk, m. Magdalene C 1731, BA 1734, MA 1737, V. Whalley, 1738–76: 'he was engaged in many disputes with his parishioners and with the Archbishop of Canterbury as patron, but succeeded in all. He retired to Prescott, where he died in 1792': Venn.
[3] [Thomas] Baldwin (1744–1809), of Essex, m. Peterhouse 1762, scholar 1763, LLB 1763, V. Whalley, 1776–1809. He became non-resident on succeeding his father as V. Leyland, 1802–9.

Page 419
Chapels in Whalley Parish.
In the Endowment of the Vicarage, dated 1330, & extant ⟨in the Lichfield Registry, and from thence⟩ registred in BP Bridgmans[1] Leiger book [who was made BP of Chester in 1619] is this Clause: Insuper idem Vicarius in qualibet Capella unum sacerdotem, Vinum & panem, senagia [synodals] & procurationes consuet' singulis annis, sumptibus propriis inveniet. The ABP reserves to himself in his Lease the Nomination of the Chaplains & Curates. But since the year 1690, before which the BP^s Secretaries did not transmit their Papers to the Office, there is no Instance of such a Nomination. It is generally by the vicar, except where under the Bounty Act he hath conveyed it to Sir Nath. Curzon[2], Mr Townley[3] of Royle, or Mr Starkie[4] of Huntroyd: who now nominate to most of the Chapels. No mention is made of any such Conveyance in the Books of the Governors of the Queens Bounty. The Chapels were 16, now 15. See more concerning them in the last p. & in what follows here.

Acrington. Certified 15^s. ABP Wake, saith, this was left to it by a Will, & that voluntary Contributions were abt 8-12-0, & Service once a fortnight, & the Number of Families 105, & the Distance from Whalley 5 miles. Augm. in 1732 with Q^s bounty & 200^f by Mr Roger Kay^5 & Mr John Hopkinson. Purchase made 1735. 1762, I gave 25^f towrds enlarging the Chapel. The vicar still nominates.

1 John Bridgeman (1577–1652), bishop of Chester, 1619–52.
2 Sir Nathaniel Curzon (c.1676–1758), 4th Bt. MP for Derby, 1713–5, MP for Clitheroe, 1722–27, MP for Derbyshire, 1727–54. Curzon was a staunch Tory and in the 1730s was chairman of a committee appointed to enquire into the proceedings of the ecclesiastical courts.
3 Thomas Townley, died 1770: VCH *Lancashire* VI, p. 446.
4 Piers Starkie, who died in 1760: VCH *Lancashire* VI, p. 495.
5 The Revd. Roger Kay died in 1729. He left £100 on condition that the people raised another £100. This was done by 1731: VCH *Lancashire* VI, p. 426.

Page 420

Chapels in Whalley Parish

Altham, St James. Certified 11-15-8: of which {is} ⟨the old stipend is 4^f &⟩ reserved in the ABP^s Lease ⟨by the Schedule⟩ 6^f. ABP Wake saith {10^f &} that the Perquisites are 1-15-0, the Service every other Sunday, the Families 79, the Distance from Whalley, 3 miles. Augm. 1722 by Q^s Bounty & Sir Nath. Curzon^1, who is now Patron. Purchase 1746.

Burnley, St Peter. A market Town. Certified 23-16-9 and augm in 1716 by Q^s Bounty & Edm. Townley^2 Esqr, & purchase made in 1719. Then certified 37-16-9 in 1726 & augm. again as before, & purchase made in 1732. ABP Wake saith, that it hath 300 Families, is 5 miles from Whalley, & is abt 50^f: 4^f old stipend out of the 50^f, & 7-16-0 by the schedule, both from ABP, 3^f the Gift of Mr Townley^3 the father, 5^f of the Son, 3-18-4 from Dutchy Lands, 1-3-0. Interest of 23^f, 1^f Legacy of Mr Hastley^4 [or Hartley] 7^f Perquisites, 16^f Augmentation. [In all 48-11-4. Then he adds, a Reversion given by Mr Townley before the 2^d Augmentation, which he doth not name, or part of it? Mr Townley nominates to it.

Castle, i.e. Clithero Castle. Had ⟨4^f⟩ Stipend out of the 50^f, & 2^f by the Schedule. But being demolished the 4^f is given to Whitewell & the 2^f to Clithero Town chapel.

1 See p. 419, n. 2.
2 Revd Edmund Townley, who died in 1729. R. of Slaidburn: VCH *Lancashire* VI, p. 450.
3 One of these is probably Nicholas Townley, who died in 1699: ibid., p. 446.
4 Robert Hartley, incumbent from c.1674 to 1688. He left the money to the curate of Burnley, 'if he shall read Morning Prayer in the church of Burnley every morning except he be hindered upon urgent occasions or sick or impotent; the occasion to be judged of and allowed by two of the neighbouring ministers if any dispute arise': ibid., p. 452.

Page 421
Chapels in Whalley Parish
Church or Church-Kirk, St James. Certified 12–17–8 i.e. 4$^£$ Stipend out of the 50$^£$, 6$^£$ by the Schedule, a Legacy of 16^s, Perquisites 2–1–8. Augm. 1722. by Q^s Bounty & Nath. Curzon[1] Esqr, who thus became Patron. Purchase, 1725. 140 Families. 4 miles from Whalley. Wake reckons the Augm. 20$^£$.

Clithero, St Michael. A market Town, 107 Families, 7 miles from Whalley. Certified 22–12–6. 4$^£$ Stipend out of the 50$^£$, 7–10–0 by the Schedule, 2$^£$ ⟨by⟩ D° which had belonged to the Castle Chapel; from Lands in Clithero 5$^£$, from Dutchy Lands 3–1–0½, Perquisites 2–12–4½. These make 24–3–5. Augm. 1722 by Q^s Bounty & Nath. Curzon Esqr, who thus became Patron. Purchase 1725, 16$^£$ a year.

Colne, St Bartholomew: A market Town, 470 Families, 7 miles from Whalley. Certified 30–16–2. Wake reckons it 37–10–0. 4$^£$ stipend out of the 50$^£$, 7–10–0 by the Schedule, & abt 26$^£$ other Payments.

[1] See p. 419, n. 2.

Page 422
Chapels in Whalley Parish
Downham, St Peter. 86 Families. Certified 10–15–4. i.e. 4$^£$ Stipend out of the 50$^£$, 6$^£$ by the Schedule, abt 15^s Perquisites. Wake mentions besides, 6$^£$ to the Schoolmaster. Augm. 1722 by Q^s Bounty & Nath. Curzon[1] Esqr, who thus became Patron. Purchase 1725, which Wake calls 17$^£$, & so values the whole at 33–15–0. It was certified again 30–15–4 & augm. again 1726 by Q^s Bounty & the Rev^d Mr James Cowgill[2] & a purchase made 1727.

Goodshaw. 7 miles from Whalley, 120 Families. No Endowment. Augm. 1741 by Lot, Purchase 1743. Certified 7$^£$ & augm. by Lot 1750, Purchase 1752. Service every other Sunday by Contributions before the Augmentations.

Haslingden, St James. A market Town, 7 miles from Whalley, 257 Families. Certified 17–18–9 i.e. 4$^£$ Stipend out of the 50$^£$, 7–10–0 by the Schedule, 12^s p^d from Lands, 5–16–7 Perquisites. Augm 1719 by Q^s Bounty, & Mr Geo. Hargrave[3] & others. Purchase 1722, wch Wake calls 17$^£$, & so values the whole at 34–18–7. The Vicar still nominates.

[1] See p. 419, n. 1.
[2] Of Yorkshire, m. Trinity Hall 1703, BA 1704, V. Downham. Lancs, 1724, V. Clitheroe, 1739–43, R. Bentham, Yorks, 1743–8.
[3] [Hargreaves]: VCH *Lancashire* VI, p. 432. He gave £200.

Page 423
Chapels in Whalley Parish
Holme. Within the Chapelry of Burnley, 8 miles from Whalley. 92 Families. No Endowm^t. Service every other Sunday. Augm. by Lot 1741, Purchase 1746. Again by Lot 1749. No Purchase yet, 1759. Tho. Whitaker[1] of Holme Esqr

nominated to it in 1742, wch was the last nomination, & is supposed to have been usurped on the Vicar. He formally gave up his Claim in 1764.

Marsden. In the Chapelry of Colne. 7 miles from Whalley, 74 Families. The Cur. of Colne officiates there the first Sunday in every month. Certified 16^s-8^d. A Lot drawn for it 1743, but set aside, as it belongs to Colne.

New Church in Pendle, St Mary. I suppose called Penden in the Lease. 5 miles from Whalley. 230 Families. Certified 1-12-0. 12^s the Gift of Mr or Sir Edm. Ashton[2]. Perquisites small. Augm. 1722. by Q^s Bounty & Nath. Curzon[3] Esqr, who thus became Patron. Purchase 1725 which Wake calls 16$^£$, & reckoning the voluntary Contributions 13$^£$ values the whole at 29$^£$.

[1] Holme had been the property of the Whitaker family since the fifteenth century. One Thomas Whitaker died in 1752, and his son, also Thomas, died in 1760: VCH *Lancashire* VI, p. 482. The nomination of 1742 went to Anthony Weatherhead, of Giggleswick, Yorks. m. Christs 1699, BA 1703, V. Holme, 1742-60.

[2] [Assheton] (1620-95), 3rd Bt. Brother to Sir Ralph, see p. 418, n. 1.

[3] See p. 419, n. 2.

Page 424
Chapels in Whalley Parish
New-Church in Rossendale, Holy Trinity. 9 miles from Whalley, 237 Families. Certified 23-10-0, Ecton. A Law-suit depending concerning the Value, which it is to be hoped will be 60$^£$, Wake. The Inhabitants in 1762 say it is worth 120$^£$.

Padiam, Padiham, or Padisham, St Leonard. 3 miles from Walley, 150 Families. Certified 15-9-9. Wake reckons it 5-16-8 thus: From Dutchy Lands 6-6-8, A Gift of Mr Starkey[1] 3$^£$, from a House & Land of his 2-10-0, A Gift of another Mr Starkey[2] 1$^£$, a Gift of Mr Ashton[3] 10^s, Perquisites 2-10-0. Augm. 1750 by Q^s Bounty & Peirce Starkey[4] Esqr. Purchase 1732. Mr Starkey claims the Nomination, & is {said} ⟨thought⟩ to be intitled to it.

Whitewell ⟨formerly called Bowland⟩, 7 miles from Whalley, 107 Families. Certified 6$^£$, ⟨of⟩ which 4$^£$ was transferred from Clithero Castle Chapel hither. Augm. 1717 with Land worth 400$^£$ by Robert Parker[5] Gent. & with 200$^£$ from Q^s Bounty. Purchase made with the last 1755. So Wake reckons it 34$^£$. The vicar still nominates.

[1] John Starkie, who died in 1697: VCH *Lancashire* VI, p. 500.
[2] William Starkie, who died in 1703: *Notitia Cestriesnsis*, II part 2, p. 343.
[3] See p. 423, n. 2.   [4] Piers Starkie, see p. 419, n. 4.
[5] Robert Parker was the sheriff of the county in 1710. He died in 1718: VCH *Lancashire* VI, p. 25.

INDEX OF PEOPLE, INSTITUTIONS
AND PRINCIPAL SOURCES

Sources which appear on nearly every page, such as the surveys instigated by archbishops Wake and Herring and archdeacon Head, Ecton's *Thesaurus*, and the King's Book (full references for which can be found in the list of ABBREVIATIONS) and the very frequent references to the archbishops' registers have not been indexed. All references are to the original pagination, and modern spelling has been adopted. References to the INTRODUCTION are in italics.

INDEX OF PARISHES, CHAPELS AND PLACES

This is an index of the principal places mentioned in the text, and does not include those mentioned in the footnotes. Places have not been indexed when they only refer to another living held by the incumbent which is also a principal parish in the *Speculum* (these can be traced through the INDEX OF PEOPLE). All references are to the original pagination, and modern spelling has been adopted. References to the INTRODUCTION are in italics.

Church of England Record Society

COUNCIL AND OFFICERS FOR THE YEAR 1995

Patron
The Right Rev. and Right Hon., the LORD RUNCIE

President
Professor P. COLLINSON, C.B.E., M.A., Ph.D., D.Litt., D.Univ., F.B.A.,
F.A.H.A., F.R.Hist.S., Trinity College, Cambridge CB2 1TQ

Honorary Vice Presidents
E.G.W. BILL, O.B.E., M.A., D.Litt., F.S.A., F.R.Hist.S.
Professor D.S. BREWER, M.A., Ph.D., Litt.D., F.S.A.

Honorary Secretary
The Rev. G.L. CARTER, M.A., D.Phil., Brasenose College, Oxford OX1 4AJ

Honorary Treasurer
R.A. BURNS, M.A., D.Phil., Department of History, King's College London,
The Strand, London WC2R 2LS

Honorary General Editor
S.J.C. TAYLOR, M.A., Ph.D., F.R.Hist.S., Department of History, University
of Reading, Whiteknights, Reading RG6 2AA

Other Members of Council
K.C. FINCHAM, B.A., Ph.D., F.R.Hist.S.
C.M. HAYDON, M.A., D.Phil., F.R.Hist.S.
Mrs F.M. HEAL, M.A., Ph.D., F.R.Hist.S.
The Rev. Professor P.B. HINCHLIFF, B.A., Ph.D., M.A., B.D., D.D.
C.J. KITCHING, B.A., Ph.D., F.S.A., F.R.Hist.S.
The Rev. J.D. MALTBY, B.A., Ph.D.
W.J. SHEILS, B.A., Ph.D., F.R.Hist.S.
J.R. WOLFFE, M.A., D.Phil., F.R.Hist.S.

Executive Secretary
Miss M. BARBER, M.A., F.S.A., c/o Lambeth Palace Library, London SE1 7JU

'The object of the Society shall be to advance knowledge of the history of the Church in England, and in particular of the Church of England, from the sixteenth century onwards, by the publication of editions or calendars of primary sources of information.'

Membership of the Church of England Record Society is open to all who are interested in the history of the Church of England. Enquiries should be addressed to the executive Secretary, Miss Melanie Barber, at the above address.

PUBLICATIONS

1. VISITATION ARTICLES AND INJUNCTIONS OF THE EARLY STUART CHURCH. VOLUME I. Ed. Kenneth Fincham (1994)
2. THE SPECULUM OF ARCHBISHOP THOMAS SECKER: THE DIOCESE OF CANTERBURY 1758–1768. Ed. Jeremy Gregory (1995)
3. THE EARLY LETTERS OF BISHOP RICHARD HURD 1739–1762. Ed. Sarah Brewer (1995)

Forthcoming Publications

THE BRITISH DELEGATION AND THE SYNOD OF DORT. Ed. Anthony Milton

GERMAN CONVERSATIONS, BISHOP GEORGE BELL, THE CHURCH OF ENGLAND AND GERMAN PROTESTANTISM, 1928–1957. Ed. Andrew Chandler

VISITATION ARTICLES AND INJUNCTIONS OF THE EARLY STUART CHURCH. VOLUME II. Ed. Kenneth Fincham

THE DIARY OF AN OXFORD PARSON: THE REVEREND JOHN HILL, VICE-PRINCIPAL OF ST EDMUND HALL, OXFORD, 1805–1808, 1820–1855. Ed. Grayson Carter

THE 1669 RETURN OF NONCONFORMIST CONVENTICLES. Ed. David Wykes

ANGLO-CATHOLIC COMMUNICANTS' GUILDS AND SOCIETIES IN THE LATE NINETEENTH CENTURY. Ed. Jeremy Morris

THE DIARIES OF BISHOP BEILBY PORTEUS. Ed. Andrew Robinson

Suggestions for publications should be addressed to Dr Stephen Taylor, General Editor, Church of England Record Society, Department of History, University of Reading, Whiteknights, Reading RG6 2AA.